Journalizing and Posting

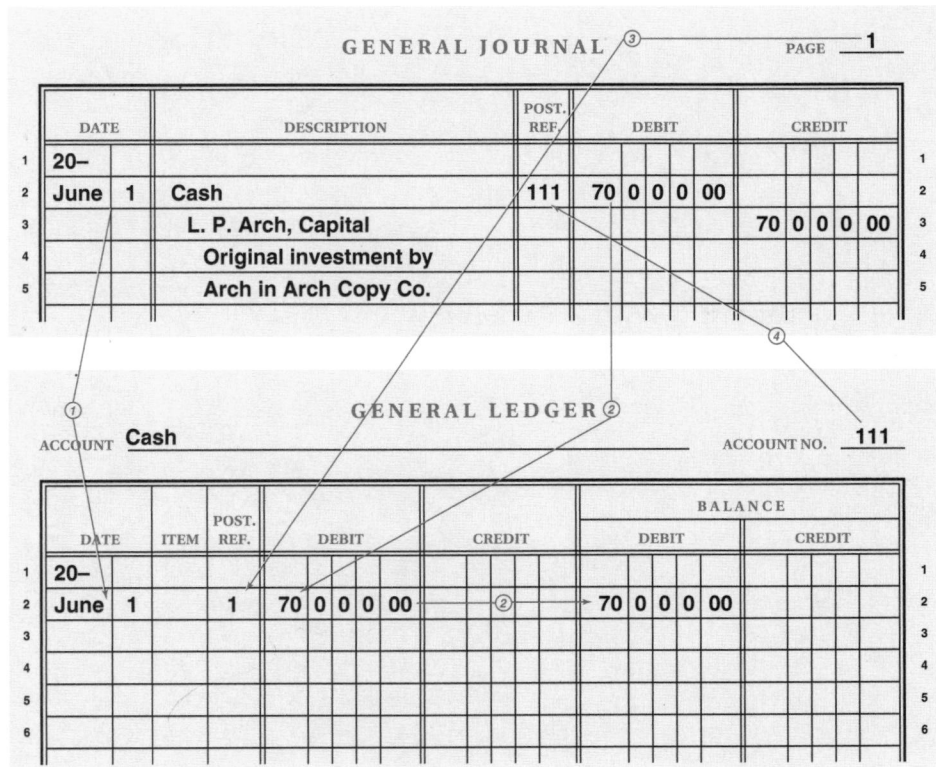

GENERAL JOURNAL ③　　　PAGE 1

DATE		DESCRIPTION	POST. REF.	DEBIT	CREDIT	
1	20–					1
2	June 1	Cash	111	70 0 0 0 00		2
3		L. P. Arch, Capital			70 0 0 0 00	3
4		Original investment by				4
5		Arch in Arch Copy Co.				5

① Date of transaction
② Amount of transaction
③ Page number of the journal
④ Ledger account number

GENERAL LEDGER ②

ACCOUNT Cash　　　　ACCOUNT NO. 111

	DATE	ITEM	POST. REF.	DEBIT	CREDIT	BALANCE DEBIT	BALANCE CREDIT	
1	20–							1
2	June 1		1	70 0 0 0 00	②	70 0 0 0 00		2
3								3
4								4
5								5
6								6

The Work Sheet

Account Name	Trial Balance		Adjustments		Adjusted Trial Balance		Income Statement		Balance Sheet	
	Debit	Credit	Debit	Credit	Debit	Credit	Debit	Credit	Debit	Credit
	Assets				Assets				Assets	
		Liabilities				Liabilities				Liabilities
		Capital				Capital				Capital
	Drawing				Drawing				Drawing	
		Revenue				Revenue		Revenue		
	Expenses				Expenses		Expenses			

Steps in the Closing Process

R Close the Revenue accounts into Income Summary.
E Close the Expenses accounts into Income Summary.
I Close the Income Summary Account into the Capital Account, transferring the net income or net loss to the Capital Account.
D Close the Drawing account into the Capital Account.

College Accounting

College Accounting

EIGHTH EDITION

1–13

Douglas J. McQuaig
Wenatchee Valley College

Patricia A. Bille
Highline Community College

HOUGHTON MIFFLIN COMPANY   BOSTON   NEW YORK

Senior Sponsoring Editor: Bonnie Binkert
Senior Development Editor: Chere Bemelmans
Associate Editor: Jessica Carlisle
Editorial Associate: James R. Dimock
Senior Project Editor: Cecilia Molinari
Editorial Assistant: Celeste Ng, Sean McGann
Senior Production/Design Coordinator: Carol Merrigan
Manufacturing Manager: Florence Cadran
Senior Marketing Manager: Steven W. Mikels

This book is written to provide accurate and authoritative information concerning the covered topics. It is not meant to take the place of professional advice. The companies and financial information in this book have been created for instructional purposes. No reference to any specific company or person is intended or should be inferred. Any similarity with an existing company is purely coincidental.

Cover image: © John Still/Photonica.

Credits

Introduction
p. 2, Tony Freeman/Photo Edit; p. 4, Michael Newman/PhotoEdit; p. 5, © Syracuse Newspaper/The Image Works.

Chapter 1
p. 8, © Lee Snider/Corbis; p. 10, Tony Freeman/PhotoEdit, Inc.; p. 16, Bob Daemmrich/Stock Boston.

Chapter 2
p. 39, S. Dooley/Getty Images; p. 49, Terry Huseby/Getty Images; p. 52, Myrleen Ferguson/PhotoEdit, Inc.

(Credits continued on page C-1.)

Printed in the U.S.A.

Library of Congress Control Number: 2003109888

ISBN: 0-618-381627

123456789-DOW-08 07 06 05 04

This text is sincerely dedicated to the students who will use it.

Every possible effort has been made to produce an understandable, up-to-date, and accurate presentation of the fundamentals of accounting.

This text is intended to be an important element in your course, as well as an invaluable future reference for you in the preparation of your career in business.

Best wishes for your success.

Douglas J. McQuaig

Patricia A. Bille

Contents

PART TWO

ACCOUNTING FOR CASH AND PAYROLL

PART THREE

THE ACCOUNTING CYCLE FOR A MERCHANDISING BUSINESS: USING SPECIAL JOURNALS

Preface

ollege accounting students have diverse goals: to train for a job in accounting, to train for other careers, or to prepare for advanced studies in accounting and business. With these goals in mind, we designed *College Accounting* as an up-to-date, understandable, and teachable basic accounting text—one that has earned a reputation for developing students' practical accounting skills. But today's students need more than just basic accounting skills; students need to feel comfortable with rapidly changing technology, understand how to make sound ethical and business decisions, and become successful problem solvers and communicators. Our Eighth Edition has therefore been revised with these important goals in mind:

- Introducing new technology supplements for both students and instructors.
- Thoroughly updating our end-of-chapter pedagogy to emphasize ethics, problem solving, and communications.
- Updating our text to increase its relevance in today's world.

NEW INSTRUCTIONAL TECHNOLOGIES

Because students are increasingly expected to know how to use spreadsheets and commercial general ledger software, we have added or updated a number of electronic ancillaries, giving instructors a range of options in integrating technology into the College Accounting course.

For Students

NEW! College Accounting Resources for Students CD-ROM New to the Eighth Edition, this student CD-ROM includes the thoroughly updated Houghton Mifflin General Ledger Software for Selected Problems and Spreadsheet Applications for Selected Problems; Excel Working Paper templates; links to ACE quizzes and SMARTHINKING™, and many other study resources. *College Accounting Resources for Students* CD-ROM is packaged with every *College Accounting* textbook.

NEW! Electronic Working Papers with Study Guide For the first time, we are offering the complete contents of the print *Working Papers with Study Guide* in electronic format. These Word and Excel files contain all of the spreadsheets students need to complete the end-of-chapter problems in the textbook as well as all of the study guide material in the print *Working Papers with Study Guide*.

NEW! SMARTHINKING In partnership with SMARTHINKING, we offer personalized, online tutoring during typical homework hours. Students can interact live online with an experienced SMARTHINKING "e-structor" (online tutor), submit questions and spreadsheets anytime for response by an e-structor within 24 hours, and review independent study resources—including interactive web sites and Frequently Asked Questions posed to SMARTHINKING e-structors—around the clock.

Interactive Learning Center   The student web site at **http://college. hmco.com/accounting/students/**, updated for the Eighth Edition, expands the concepts and ideas presented in the text. The site offers interactive chapter quizzes—ACE quizzes—that consist of 10 multiple choice and 10 true/false questions for each chapter, enabling students to test what they've learned and to find out why their answer is correct or incorrect. Excel working paper templates, suggested Internet research activities, business readings, performance objectives, key terms on electronic flash cards, and company links are also offered on the student web site.

NEWLY UPDATED! **Houghton Mifflin Windows General Ledger Software**   Completely updated for the Eighth Edition of *College Accounting*, Houghton Mifflin Windows General Ledger Software offers complete coverage of accounting concepts and procedures in an extremely simple and user-friendly, computerized environment. Selected problems from *College Accounting*, Eighth Edition, can be solved using this program. The new GLS has an updated interface and expanded features—such as the ability to export files to Peachtree. GLS software is included on the new *College Accounting Resources for Students* CD-ROM.

Peachtree Educator's Edition   This popular accounting software tool is now available to students. The educational version is the same as the professional version used by most businesses. At the option of the instructor, students can use this commercial package or the Houghton Mifflin Windows General Ledger Software to work selected problems in the text and accompanying practice sets. Instructors who prefer to use QuickBooks, another popular commercial software package, can do so by obtaining a site license or offering the option of QuickBooks on the web; all text problems can be worked using either the current version of Peachtree or QuickBooks.

Spreadsheet Applications for *College Accounting*   These spreadsheet files let students solve end-of-chapter problems using Excel spreadsheet software. Students can select from prepared templates or use them to solve end-of-chapter problems accompanied by the spreadsheet icon. Instructions explaining how to convert Excel templates to Lotus and solve the problems are a feature of this program. Spreadsheet applications are included on the new *College Accounting Resources for Students* CD-ROM.

Practice Sets   A wealth of manual and computerized practice sets is available for use with *College Accounting*, Eighth Edition. A complete listing and description of each practice set and its support package can be found in the *Instructor's Resource Manual with Solutions*. New to the Eighth Edition is the *Balloon Adventure* practice set, a sole proprietorship service business. Also new to the Eighth Edition is the *Spa Magic* practice set, based on a sole proprietorship merchandising business. Both practice sets cover a one-month accounting period, enabling the student to acquire experience in dealing with the entire accounting cycle, and can be worked manually or used with a CD-ROM. The CD-ROM gives the student the option of completing either practice set electronically using Peachtree 8.0, QuickBooks 2004, or Houghton Mifflin Windows General Ledger Software.

For Instructors

Interactive Learning Center   The instructor web site at **http://college. hmco.com/accounting/instructors/index.html**, updated for the Eighth Edition, offers additional instructor resource material. The site offers complete electronic solutions to all end-of-chapter exercises and problems in the textbook. In Excel, these solutions are completely formatted so instructors can do what-if analyses. Teaching ideas and techniques, instructor outlines, performance objectives, and key terms are also offered on this site.

NEW! PowerPoint Slides   These slides, available on the instructor web site, include accounting forms, tables, and art from the textbook as well as supplementary teaching examples and demonstration problems.

NEW! HMClassPrep with HMTesting Instructor CD-ROM   This new CD-ROM includes the complete electronic solutions in Excel to all exercises and problems in the textbook as well as additional resources to enhance teaching of accounting. This CD-ROM also includes our powerful computerized testing resource, HMTesting.

NEW! Blackboard Course Cartridges and WebCT e-Packs   These cartridges provide flexible, efficient, and creative ways to present learning materials and manage distance-learning courses. Specific resources include chapter overviews, check figures for in-text problems, practice quizzes, PowerPoint slides, and Excel Solutions. In addition to course management benefits, instructors may make use of an electronic gradebook and receive completed assignments from students enrolled in the course via the Internet.

EMPHASIS ON ETHICS, PROBLEM SOLVING, AND COMMUNICATIONS

Because today's business environment is increasingly complex, we have thoroughly updated our end-of-chapter pedagogy to emphasize ethics, problem solving, and communications. *College Accounting,* Eighth Edition, provides a wealth of exercise and problem material that is supported by the *Working Papers with Study Guide* (offered in print or on CD-ROM), offering instructors a wide choice of classroom illustrations and assignments. Each chapter ends with comprehensive review and study material consisting of a review of performance objectives; a glossary; discussion questions; exercises; several components—Reflections on the World Wide Web, Consider and Communicate, What's Wrong with This Picture?, Critical Thinking, and A Matter of Ethics—that foster problem solving and communication skills; and two sets of comparable A and B problems, progressing from simple to complex in difficulty.

- **Discussion Questions**   Questions based on the main points in the text and appropriate for either class discussion or for homework are included at the end of each chapter.
- **Exercises**   For practice in applying concepts, exercises are provided with each chapter. Each exercise is described briefly in the margin with a reference to the appropriate performance objective.

- **NEW!** **Reflections on the World Wide Web**   This new feature follows through from Windows on the World Wide Web (our new chapter-opening feature) to provide students with meaningful web experience and activities. These exercises provide opportunities for students to do hands-on web browsing and sharpen their oral and written communication skills as well as their critical thinking skills.
- **Consider and Communicate**   Each Consider and Communicate question requires that students first think about the concepts presented in the chapter. Then they are asked to explain the concepts by applying what they have learned.
- **NEW!** **What's Wrong with This Picture?**   New to the Eighth Edition, each What's Wrong with This Picture? assignment describes a set of accounting circumstances and asks students to use their knowledge of accounting, their experiences, and their common sense to form a response.
- **Critical Thinking**   Critical Thinking exercises provide an opportunity for students to develop their problem-solving skills and employ their knowledge of accounting to complete a task. The Critical Thinking feature is appropriate for individual or team responses and requires yet a higher level of thinking than the What's Wrong with This Picture? feature.
- **A Matter of Ethics**   This exercise presents a situation and asks students to decide whether the action is ethical. Students are also asked to suggest what implications the described behavior might have. These exercises are particularly valuable in fostering discussion by the class or in small groups.
- **Problems**   Each chapter contains four A problems and four B problems. The A and B problems are parallel in content and level of difficulty. They are arranged in order of difficulty, with Problems 1A and 1B in each chapter being the simplest and the last problem in each series being the most comprehensive. A Check Figure accompanies each problem so students can compare their total and correct errors in computation.

THOROUGHLY REVISED AND RELEVANT TEXT

We have completely revised and updated the Eighth Edition to increase its relevance for today's complex and challenging world.

Major Content Changes

A complete list of content changes from the Seventh to the Eighth editions is available in the Transition Guide (located on the instructor web site or in the *Instructor's Resource Manual with Solutions*), but here is a brief listing of the most important content changes:

- **Chapter 1: Asset, Liability, Owner's Equity, Revenue, and Expense Accounts**   Owing to a change in accounting rules regarding the recording of purchases of supplies, we now debit Supplies Expense for small- to medium-sized service businesses.
- **Chapter 4: Adjusting Entries and the Work Sheet**   We eliminated the adjusting entry for Supplies because of the rule change.

- **Chapter 8: Employee Earnings and Deductions** We have updated the tax percentages while adding a section describing laws that affect payroll activities.
- **Chapter 10: The Sales Journal and the Purchases Journal** We have condensed the three chapters on special journals into two chapters. Chapter 10 now includes the sales and purchases journals as a result of adopter input. Chapter 11 still contains the cash receipts and cash payments journals.

Special Text Features and Enhancements in the Eighth Edition

- **Complete Revision and Review** The text and the end-of-chapter assignment materials have been thoroughly revised, updated, and reviewed.
- **Full-Color Design with Photographs** The Eighth Edition maintains its exciting full-color design complete with two or three color photographs and accompanying captions in each chapter. These photographs help students visualize the concepts discussed in the chapter and glimpse them in practice.
- **NEW!** **Mentor Profiles** Prominent business people whose professional lives began with accounting are featured throughout the text. Our hope is that their stories and words will encourage and inspire our students and provide good role models as they advance in their careers.
- **Drawings of Concepts** Many chapters contain pictorial images to appeal to students' varied learning styles and enhance the text, color-coded forms, and rich illustrations.
- **Transparent Acetate Pages** In Chapter 4, Adjusting Entries and the Work Sheet, we have created transparency overlays that allow students to build a work sheet in stages, better visualizing the steps involved in the process.
- **Windows on the World Wide Web** These chapter openers provide a hands-on look at many of today's most well-known businesses that are active on the Web. Each window first introduces students to the company, then asks a series of questions about the company that relate directly to the chapter topics. We provide web addresses for further investigation of the company. These questions and addresses are designed to prompt discussion, written responses, or additional questions surrounding the chapter.
- **NEW!** **Reflections on the World Wide Web** This end-of-chapter feature follows through from Windows on the World Wide Web to provide students with meaningful web activities. Students are exposed not only to web exploration but also critical thinking, problem solving, and communication activities.
- **Extended Examples** Arch Copy Co. is integrated throughout Chapters 1 to 5 to illustrate the completion of the accounting cycle for a sole-proprietorship service business using a general journal.

Dodson Plumbing is featured throughout Chapters 10–13 to illustrate the completion of the accounting cycle for a sole-proprietorship merchandising business using special journals.

- **Student Annotations** Additional Remembers and FYIs have been added to this edition. Remembers summarize key concepts for students, and FYIs are brief, interesting pieces of information about current business practice.
- **NEW!** **The Computer Lab** Designed to give students experience in using computers to manage accounting transactions, this continuous general ledger problem featuring Jeep Jockeys, a sole proprietorship service

business, begins in Chapter 3 by opening the accounting books for Jeep Jockeys. Students are required to enter into general ledger software (Peachtree, QuickBooks, or Houghton Mifflin's Windows General Ledger) the company name, company type, as well as the chart of accounts before journalizing and posting the first month's transactions and printing a trial balance. After Chapter 4 (Adjusting Entries and the Work Sheet), students continue with Jeep Jockeys by completing the end-of-the-month adjustments and printing the financial statements. After Chapter 5 (Closing Entries and the Post-Closing Trial Balance), students again work with Jeep Jockeys to close the books for the month and print a post-closing trial balance.

● **Icons** The following four icons accompany end-of-chapter assignments and highlight a variety of skill-development exercises:

The first icon on the left indicates exercises designed to enhance students' verbal and written communication skills as well as their group skills.

The second icon on the left indicates assignments that involve critical thinking, to emphasize the importance of understanding how specific accounting procedures relate to accounting as a whole.

Problems that can be solved using the Houghton Mifflin Windows General Ledger program are designated by the third icon on the left.

Problems that can be worked using Spreadsheet Applications for College Accounting are identified by the fourth icon on the left.

● **Check Figures** Check Figures appear alongside every A and B problem's instructions in the text.

● **NEW!** **Before a Test Checks** New to this edition, this feature provides questions (true/false, multiple choice, matching, and completion) and brief application problems after every two to four chapters. These pretest checks let students check their understanding of what they have read and practiced in the preceding chapters prior to taking a test.

● **NEWLY UPDATED!** **Accounting Cycle Review and Comprehensive Review Problem** These features give students the opportunity to apply accounting procedures to help them understand the process they have just studied in a series of chapters (1–5) and (7–13). Both Problems A and B involve the full accounting cycle, one for Wind Chasers and the other for Water Wings, both sole-proprietorship service businesses.

The Comprehensive Review Problem following Chapter 13 involves the full accounting cycle for Fine Fabrics, a sole-proprietorship merchandising business.

ACCESSIBLE AND USER FRIENDLY CONTENT

Although the Eighth Edition of *College Accounting* has been updated and revised, some things have not changed—and will never change. Drawing from more than 64 years of combined teaching experience, we continue to provide students with a strong basic knowledge of accounting terms, concepts, and procedures. The text is logically organized, liberally illustrated, and paced in a manner that is easy for students to read and understand. Generous use of white space provides an uncluttered reading environment with ample area for student or instructor notes.

Focus on the Fundamentals

College Accounting, Eighth Edition, presents the fundamentals of accounting in a practical, easy-to-comprehend manner. Great emphasis is placed on developing a firm foundation of fundamental procedures. Appropriate repetition enables students to develop self-confidence and to make progress in gradual stages. This repetition is accomplished through extensive use of examples and color-coded illustrations. Color photographs round out the text, which is designed to serve the wide range of student experiences. Recording business transactions is directly related to the fundamental accounting equation. Each newly introduced transaction is fully illustrated and is supported with T account examples. Comprehensive reviews of T accounts, organized in relation to the fundamental accounting equation, appear in the *Working Papers with Study Guide,* student web site, and *College Accounting Resources for Students* CD-ROM to assist as students review material and complete assignments.

Reading Comprehension

College Accounting, Eighth Edition, is a very readable text. We write in short sentences and use many illustrations to help students relate the words to the procedures. Each chapter of *College Accounting* has been reviewed by business instructors who teach English as a Second Language courses and English for Special Purposes courses, as well as by students enrolled in these classes. With their assistance and advice, we have taken steps to ensure that the text is accessible to all readers.

Each chapter is limited to the presentation of one major concept, which is amply illustrated with business documents and report forms. As terms are introduced in color, they are defined thoroughly and are used in subsequent examples. Comprehension is also enhanced through the use of "Remember" and "FYI" statements. These short, marginal notes present a learning hint or a practical tip or information about the topic. End-of-chapter summaries review each performance objective presented in the chapter using text and illustrations.

Emphasis on Accounting Terminology

We firmly believe that accounting is the language of business and that learning new terminology is an essential part of a first course. Each key term is printed in green and is explained when it is first introduced. The end-of-chapter glossary repeats the definitions of the terms presented in the chapter. In addition, page numbers are included for each glossary term, making it easy for students to refer to a term in the chapter. The glossary terms are included on electronic flash cards on the student web site providing yet another interactive opportunity for learning.

Proven Color-Coded Pedagogy

The Eighth Edition of *College Accounting* continues to implement a color-coded pedagogy that helps students recognize and remember key points. The pedagogical use of color also helps students understand the flow of accounting data and identify different types of documents and reports used in accounting. Finally, the use of color in this text helps students identify the performance objectives for each chapter, recognize the performance objectives called for in each exercise, and review material efficiently and effectively.

- **Performance objectives** are highlighted in the margin with green headings. They are listed at the beginning of each chapter and restated alongside the related text discussion. A performance objective number serves as reference to the objectives in the chapter summary, exercises, and problems.
- **Key terms** are printed in green. They are defined in the text and repeated in a glossary at the end of the chapter.
- **Remembers**, also in the margin, have maroon headings. They are learning hints or summaries. These marginal notes often alert students to common procedural pitfalls and help them complete their work successfully.
- **FYIs**, in the margin with orange headings, are practical tips or information about accounting and business.
- **Tables**, outlined in purple, help students quickly identify material that must be examined as a unit and is not part of the running text.

The Eighth Edition's consistent use of color extends to the treatment of accounting forms, financial statements, and documents in the text and end-of-chapter assignments.

- **Source documents**, such as invoices, bank statements, facsimiles, and other material that originates with outside sources, are shown in yellow.
- **Working papers, journals, ledgers, trial balances, and other forms and schedules** used as part of the internal accounting process are shown in green.
- **Financial statements**, including balances sheets, income statements, statements of owners' equity, and statements of cash flows, are shown in blue.

This distinctive treatment differentiates these elements and helps students see where each element belongs in the accounting cycle. Seeing these relationships helps students understand how accountants transform data into useful information.

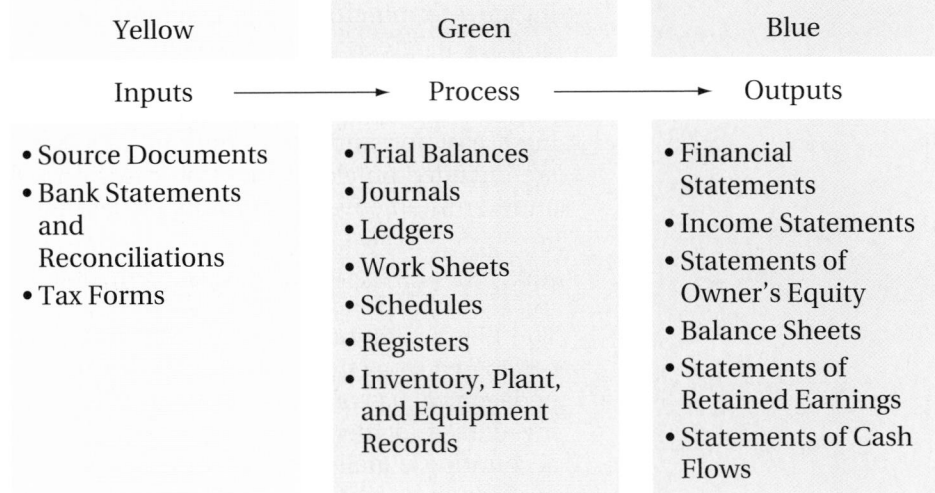

Yellow	Green	Blue
Inputs ⟶	Process ⟶	Outputs
• Source Documents • Bank Statements and Reconciliations • Tax Forms	• Trial Balances • Journals • Ledgers • Work Sheets • Schedules • Registers • Inventory, Plant, and Equipment Records	• Financial Statements • Income Statements • Statements of Owner's Equity • Balance Sheets • Statements of Retained Earnings • Statements of Cash Flows

GUARANTEE OF QUALITY MATERIAL

Successful use of an accounting text depends on more than the interesting and memorable presentation of material by the instructor and the text. The overall quality of the opening windows, examples, illustrations, color photographs, end-of-chapter questions, exercises, and problems, as well as ancillary materials are critical to learning and retaining the facts and concepts to cover in the course. Instructors and students must be assured that these materials are complete, consistent, and accurate.

Together with our publisher, we have taken a multistep approach to ensure quality materials for classroom use. The quality control system begins with in-depth reviews of the original manuscript and concludes with accuracy reviews of page proof by instructors who are actively teaching the course.

FLEXIBLE CHAPTER COVERAGE

College Accounting, Eighth Edition, is designed primarily for use in a course extending two or three quarters or two semesters. The text is divided into parts: Chapters 1 through 5 cover the full accounting cycle for a sole proprietorship service business. Chapters 6 through 9 cover the combined journal, bank accounts, and payroll accounting. Chapters 10 through 13 cover special journals and the full accounting cycle for a merchandising firm.

The following appendices expand content coverage and increase the instructor's options for structuring the course:

- **Appendix A: Methods of Depreciation (after Chapter 4)**   This appendix describes methods of depreciation, including the Modified Accelerated Cost Recovery System.
- **Appendix B: Bad Debts (after Chapter 7)**   This appendix covers the allowance and specific charge-off methods.
- **Appendix C: Inventory Methods (after Chapter 13)**   This appendix discusses methods used to determine the amount of the ending inventory for a merchandising business.
- **Appendix D: Financial Statement Analysis (after Chapter 13)**   This appendix describes percentages and ratios used to interpret information in financial statements.
- **Appendix E: The Statement of Cash Flows (after Chapter 13)**   This appendix discusses the indirect method of determining cash flows.

Because many students take only one quarter or one semester of accounting, Appendices A through E offer a brief exposure to the basics of depreciation, the valuation of receivables and inventory, the statement of cash flows, and financial statement analysis.

SUPPLEMENTARY LEARNING AIDS FOR STUDENTS AND SUPPORT MATERIALS FOR INSTRUCTORS

For the Eighth Edition, we have assembled the most comprehensive package of student and instructor aids—both print and electronic—to complement a wide variety of teaching styles and course emphases. The complete *College Accounting* teaching and learning package is listed below. The components of our expanded technology package is described in detail earlier in the preface, and detailed descriptions of each element of the support package are available in the *Instructor's Resource Manual with Solutions* and instructor web site.

For Students

NEW! **College Accounting Resources for Students CD-ROM**

NEW! **Electronic Working Papers with Study Guide (CD-ROM)**

NEW! **SMARTHINKING (Internet)**

Interactive Learning Center (Internet)

Houghton Mifflin Windows General Ledger Software (CD-ROM)

Peachtree Educator's Edition (CD-ROM)

Spreadsheet Applications for *College Accounting* (CD-ROM)

Practice Sets (Print and CD-ROM)

Working Papers with Study Guide The *Working Papers with Study Guide* contains rich discussions of the following topics to assist students in their study of accounting:

- Review of T Account Placement and Representative Transactions
- How to Study Accounting
- How to Solve Accounting Problems
- Ten-Key Skills Review
- Introduction to Spreadsheets
- Review of Business Mathematics
- How to Work a Practice Set
- Suggested Abbreviations for Account Titles

The *Working Papers with Study Guide* also includes forms for student use in completing all of the problems in the textbook. The *Working Papers with Study Guide* is available in the following volumes:

- Working Papers with Study Guide 1–9
- Working Papers with Study Guide 1–13
- Working Papers with Study Guide 14–26
- Electronic Working Papers with Study Guide 1–26

Suggested Homework Check Questions Appearing in the *Instructor's Resource Manual with Solutions*, these questions, keyed to end-of-chapter assignments, provide students with the opportunity to practice the interpretive portion of the accounting process.

Accounting Video Workshop A professionally prepared and thoroughly revised VHS videotape is available that presents important accounting topics and allows students to review material which they may find difficult to master. An Accounting Video Guide with teaching tips is included.

Small Business Video This exciting video examines Specialized Bike Components, a California-based company that has established a reputation as the innovator of higher-quality mountain bikes. The video provides a brief background on the company and its president and then focuses on major accounting issues such as inventory handling and control, the collection of receivables, and financial statements used for decision making.

Practice Sets A complete selection of manual and computerized practice sets is available for use with *College Accounting*, Eighth Edition. A complete listing and description of each practice set and its support package can be found in the *Instructor's Resource Manual with Solutions*.

- *Divesports* is a unique source document simulation that requires students to work through seven months of continuous business activity for a sole proprietorship service business; *Divesports* adds merchandising in Chapter 10. *Divesports* can be assigned between Chapters 3 and 13.

- *Sounds Abound*, Second Edition, is a computerized practice set that covers a month in the life of a sole proprietorship. Assigned after Chapter 5, *Sounds Abound* can be used with Houghton Mifflin's General Ledger Software program.

- **NEW!** *Balloon Adventures* is a source document simulation. *Balloon Adventures* is a sole proprietorship service business using a general journal and can be assigned after Chapter 9. (It replaces *Crystal Clean*.)

- *Oak Creek Canyon Jewelers* gives students experience in recording fourth-quarter payroll and preparing end-of-quarter and end-of-year reports for sole proprietorship. Assigned after Chapter 9, *Oak Creek Canyon* can be worked with Peachtree.

- *Rug Bug* gives students experience with a wholesale business. Assigned after Chapter 13, *Rug Bug* can be worked with Peachtree.

- **NEW!** *Spa Magic* is a source document simulation. It is a sole proprietorship merchandising business featuring special journals and payroll, and can be assigned after Chapter 13; it can be worked with Peachtree, Quick-Books, or Houghton Mifflin's General Ledger Software program. (It replaces *Whitewater Kayaks*).

- *The Wax Works: A Cumulative Shoebox Practice Set with Business Papers* is a realistic exercise in which the student/bookkeeper is "hired" by a sole proprietorship retail candle shop. It can be assigned after Chapter 13.

For Instructors

Interactive Learning Center

NEW! **PowerPoint Slides**

NEW! **HMClassPrep with HMTesting Instructor CD-ROM**

NEW! **Blackboard Course Cartridges and WebCT e-Packs**

Instructor's Resource Manual with Solutions The *Instructor's Resource Manual with Solutions* contains valuable resources to assist instructors in teaching accounting:

- The Transition Guide contains a list of content changes from the Seventh to the Eighth editions. This information will aid you in making a smooth transition from the former to the new edition.
- Review of T Account Placement and Representative Transactions.
- Suggested Homework Check Questions with Solutions, keyed to end-of-chapter assignments, provide students with the opportunity to practice the interpretive portion of the accounting process. Suggested answers are included as well.
- Difficulty and Time Chart
- Suggested Abbreviations for Account Titles
- For each chapter, Teaching Objectives, Key Points, and Lecture Outline.
- Solutions for all questions, exercises, and problems in the textbook.

The *Instructor's Resource Manual with Solutions* is available in the following volumes:

- Instructor's Resource Manual with Solutions 1–13
- Instructor's Resource Manual with Solutions 14–26

Test Bank with Achievement Tests (A and B)

Teaching and Solutions Transparencies

Instructor's Guide to Accounting Video Workshop

Instructor's Solutions Manual for all Practice Sets

ACKNOWLEDGMENTS

We sincerely thank the editorial staff of Houghton Mifflin for their continuous support. Also, we thank our many students at Highline Community College for their observations and evaluations.

During the writing of the Eighth Edition, we consulted many users of the text throughout the country. Their constructive suggestions are reflected in the changes that we have made. Unfortunately, space does not permit mention of all those who have contributed to this volume. Those reviewers and advisors who have contributed to *College Accounting* through their reviews, class testing, and accuracy checking are as follows:

Joe Adamo, *Cazenovia College;* Teresa Anderson, *Eastern New Mexico University;* Gregory D. Barnes, *Clarion University;* Charles M. Betts, *Delaware Technical and Community College;* Lee Cannell, *El Paso Community College;* Jean Condon, *Mid-Plains Community College Area (Nebraska);* Mark Dawson, *Duquesne University;* Patricia A. Doherty, *Boston University School of Management;* Talaat Elshazly, *College of Charleston;* Michael Girvin, *Highline Community College;* Christine Uber Grosse, *Thunderbird, The American Graduate School of International Management;* Dennis A. Gutting, *Orange County Community College;* David Hall; Scott Hays, *Central Oregon Community College;* Thea Hosselrode, *Allegany College of Maryland;* Susan D. Looney, *Mohave Community College;* Gail A. Mestas; Wanda Metzgar, *Selland College of Applied Technology;* George J. McGowan; Michael

Monahan; Howard Mount, *Highline Community College;* Jenine Muscove, *Bradford Hall Career Institute;* Therese H. Palacios, *San Antonio College;* Cathy Pekarek; Robin Shurtz; Alice Sineath, Forsyth *Technical Community College;* Marion Taube, *University of Pittsburgh;* Josephine Vondras, *Orange County Community College;* and Kay Westerfield, University of Oregon.

We would also like to specially thank the following people for their contributions as members of the McQuaig Advisory Board:

Marjorie Ashton, *Truckee Meadows Community College;* Richard Dugger, *Kilgore College;* Donna Eakman, *Montana State University, Great Falls;* David Groom, *University of Hawaii—Maui Community College;* Ray Ingram, *Southwest Georgia Technical College;* Lori Jacobson, *North Idaho College;* Ernie Keller, *Montana State University, Great Falls;* Paul Muller, *Western Nevada Community College;* Jon Nitschke, *Montana State University, Great Falls;* Janet Pasterkamp, *Montana State University, Great Falls;* Joel Peralto, *University of Hawaii—Hawaii Community College;* Bob Sanner, *Central Community College;* and Jack Wiehler, *San Joaquin Delta College.*

As always, we would like to thank our families for their understanding and cooperation. Without their support, this text would never have been written. Heartfelt appreciation is extended to Beverlie McQuaig for her detailed proofreading and good humor. Pertinent suggestions for updating the material were given by Judith McQuaig Britton, C.P.A., of Smith, Bunday, Berman, Britton; John McQuaig, C.P.A., of McQuaig and Welk; and Laurie McQuaig Ramaley, D.C. We also express continued gratitude to Bruce Bille, Tracy Bille-Newkirk, and James Newkirk, C.P.A., for their encouragement and assistance, and to the memory of Ryan Bille and Wesley and Adeline Harris for their courage and inspiration.

Douglas J. McQuaig
Patricia A. Bille

Introduction to Accounting

Performance Objectives

After you have completed this introduction to accounting, you will be able to do the following:

1. Define *accounting*.

2. Explain the importance of accounting information.

3. Describe the various career opportunities in accounting.

Accounting is often called the language of business because, when confronted with events of a business nature, all people in society—owners, managers, creditors, employees, attorneys, engineers, and so forth—must use accounting terms and concepts to describe these events. Examples of accounting terms are *net, gross, yield, valuation, accrued, deferred*—the list could go on and on. So it is logical that anyone entering the business world should know enough of its "language" to communicate with others and to understand their communications.

As you acquire a knowledge of accounting, you will gain an understanding of the way businesses operate and the reasoning involved in making business decisions. Even if you are not involved directly in accounting activities, you will certainly need to be sufficiently acquainted with the "language" to be able to understand the meaning of accounting information, how it is compiled, how it can be used, and its limitations.

You may be surprised to find that you are already familiar with many accounting terms. Recalling your personal business activities and relating them to your study of accounting will be very helpful to you. For example, when you purchased this textbook, you exchanged cash or a promise to pay cash for the book. As you will see, this exchange is an accounting event. You are going to recognize many activities and terms as you begin your study of accounting.

DEFINITION OF ACCOUNTING

OBJECTIVE 1
Define accounting.

Accounting is the process of analyzing, classifying, recording, summarizing, and interpreting business transactions in financial or monetary terms. A business transaction is an event that has a direct effect on the operation of an economic unit, is expressed in terms of money, and is recorded. Examples of business transactions are buying or selling goods, renting a building, paying employees, and buying insurance.

The primary purpose of accounting is to provide the financial information needed for the efficient operation of an economic unit. The term **economic unit** includes not only business enterprises but also not-for-profit entities,

1

Accounting is an important part of all types of businesses. These cruise ships require the same extensive recordkeeping as any large destination resort. The ship is a large floating hotel with guests, employees, management, recreational activities, restaurants, and shops.

such as government bodies, churches and synagogues, clubs, and fraternal organizations. Business enterprises or organizations may be called firms or companies. All of these entities require some type of accounting records. An **accountant** is a person who keeps the financial history of the transactions of an economic unit in written form.

Because it is important that all those who receive accounting reports be able to interpret them, a set of rules or guidelines for the accounting process has been developed. These guidelines or rules are known as **generally accepted accounting principles (GAAP)**.

Bookkeeping and Accounting

There are distinctions between bookkeeping and accounting. The two processes are closely related, but there is no universally accepted line of separation. Generally, bookkeeping involves the systematic recording of business transactions in financial terms. Accounting functions at a higher level. An accountant sets up the system that a bookkeeper uses to record business transactions. An accountant may supervise the work of the bookkeeper and prepare financial statements and tax reports. Although the bookkeeper's work is more routine, it is hard to draw a line where the bookkeeper's work ends and the accountant's begins.

IMPORTANCE OF ACCOUNTING INFORMATION

OBJECTIVE 2
Explain the importance of accounting information.

Anyone who aspires to a position of leadership in business or government needs a knowledge of accounting. A study of accounting gives a person the necessary background and also gives him or her an understanding of the scope, functions, and policies of an organization. A person may not be doing the accounting work, but he or she will be continually dealing with accounting forms, language, and reports.

Users of Accounting Information

Owners Owners have invested their money or goods in a business organization. They desire information regarding the company's earnings, its prospects for future earnings, and its ability to pay its debts.

Managers Managers and supervisors have to prepare financial reports, understand accounting data contained in reports and budgets, and express future plans in financial terms. People who have management jobs must know how accounting information can be developed in order to evaluate performance in meeting goals.

Creditors Creditors lend money or extend credit to the company for the purchase of goods and services. The company's creditors include suppliers, banks, and other lending institutions, such as loan companies. Creditors are interested in the firm's ability to pay its debts.

Government agencies Taxing authorities verify information submitted by companies concerning a variety of taxes, such as income taxes, sales taxes, and employment taxes. Public utilities, such as electric and gas companies, must provide financial information to regulatory agencies.

Accounting and Technology

Before the invention of calculators and computers, all business transactions were recorded by hand. Now computers perform routine recordkeeping operations and prepare financial reports. Computers are used today in all types of businesses, both large and small. One question often arises: "Is the computer taking over accountants' jobs?" Actually, with the introduction of computers, more jobs have been created to fulfill management's need for more information.

Regardless of whether a business uses a computer, the nature of accounting is the same. The computer is a powerful tool of the accountant. However, as a tool, the computer is only as useful as the ability of the operator. The operator must be skilled to key the correct information into the computer program. Otherwise, as the saying goes, "garbage in, garbage out."

CAREER OPPORTUNITIES IN ACCOUNTING

OBJECTIVE 3
Describe the various career opportunities in accounting.

To find job opportunities in accounting, all you need to do is read the newspapers' classified advertisements or browse the Internet. Although the jobs listed in these ads require varying amounts of education and experience, most of them are for positions as accounting clerks, general bookkeepers, or accountants. Let's take a look at the requirements and duties of these positions.

Accounting Clerk/Technician

An accounting clerk/technician does routine recording of financial information. The duties of accounting clerks vary with the size of the company. In small businesses, accounting clerks handle most of the recordkeeping functions. In large companies, clerks specialize in one part of the accounting system, such as payroll, accounts receivable, accounts payable, cash, inventory, or purchases. The minimum requirement for most accounting clerk positions is one term or semester of an accounting course.

General Bookkeeper

Many small- and medium-sized companies employ one person to oversee their bookkeeping operations. This person is called a general or full-charge bookkeeper. The general bookkeeper supervises the work of accounting clerks. Requirements for this job vary with the size of the company and the complexity of the accounting system. The minimum requirement for most general bookkeeper jobs is one or two years of accounting as well as experience as an accounting clerk.

Paraprofessional Accountant

To bridge a gap between the general bookkeeper and the professional accountant many firms are hiring **paraprofessional accountants**. They are able to manage the duties of the general bookkeeper as well as many of the duties of a professional accountant under that accountant's supervision. Qualifications generally include a two-year degree or certificate in accounting as well as appropriate prior experience.

Accountant

The term *accountant* describes a fairly broad range of jobs. The accountant may design and manage the entire accounting system for a business. The accountant may also prepare the financial statements and tax returns and perform audits. Many accountants enter the field with a four-year college degree in accounting; however, it is not unusual for accountants to start at entry-level positions and work their way up to management positions. Although accountants are employed in every kind of economic unit, they are classified into one of three categories: public accounting, managerial or private accounting, and not-for-profit accounting. We'll briefly look at these categories.

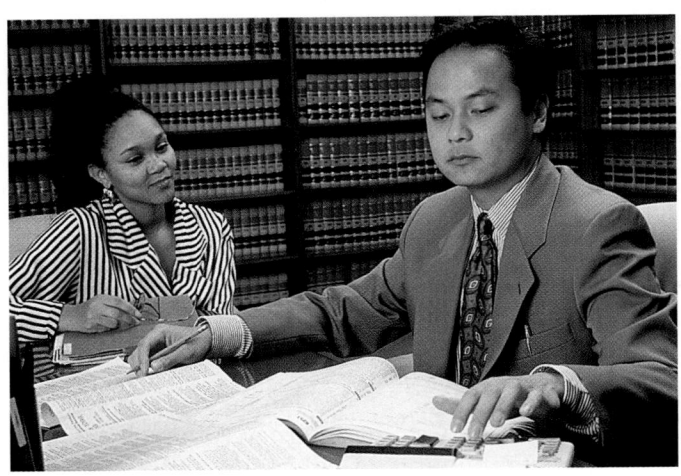

Accountants are employed in every kind of economic unit. Many start in entry level positions and work their way up to management.

Public Accounting Certified public accountants (CPAs) are independent professionals who provide services to clients for a fee. To become a CPA, a person must have a college degree, pass a rigorous examination, and generally complete a work-experience requirement. Public accountants design accounting systems, prepare tax returns, provide financial advice about business operations, and audit financial statements.

Managerial or Private Accounting Most people who are accountants are employed by private business organizations. These accountants (not necessarily CPAs) manage the accounting system, prepare budgets, determine costs of products, and provide financial information for managers and own-

Charitable organizations must be closely attuned to their cash situation as funds are donated and in turn shared with those in need. Those who manage charities must be able to report to the public and various government agencies where the money comes from, where it has gone, and how much was kept to run the charity.

ers. Accountants have many opportunities to advance into top management positions. The Certified Management Accountant (CMA) exam has become an important partner to the CPA credentials.

Not-for-Profit Accounting Not-for-profit accounting is used for government agencies, hospitals, churches and synagogues, and schools. Accountants for these organizations prepare budgets and maintain records of revenues and expenses. It should be noted that some not-for-profit organizations do in fact make a profit; however, the profit is kept in the organization and not distributed. For example, a hospital makes a profit and then reinvests the profit in modern equipment. Local, state, and federal government bodies employ vast numbers of people in accounting positions.

CHAPTER REVIEW

Check out ACE for a Review Quiz at

http://college.hmco.com/ accounting/students/.

ACE self-test

Review of Performance Objectives

1. Define *accounting*.

   Accounting is the process of analyzing, classifying, recording, summarizing, and interpreting business transactions in financial or monetary terms. It is also an information system and the language of business.

2. Explain the importance of accounting information.

   A study of accounting gives a person the necessary background to understand the scope, functions, and policies of an organization.

3. Describe the various career opportunities in accounting.

   Accountants, paraprofessional accountants, bookkeepers, and accounting clerks will find employment opportunities in several areas—in the public sector, the private sector, or not-for-profit organizations.

Glossary

Accountant A person who keeps the financial history of the transactions of an economic unit in written form; sometimes mistakenly called a bookkeeper. (2)

Accounting The process of analyzing, classifying, recording, summarizing, and interpreting business transactions in financial or monetary terms; sometimes mistakenly called bookkeeping. (1)

Economic unit Includes both business enterprises and not-for-profit entities, such as government bodies, churches and synagogues, clubs, and fraternal organizations. (1)

Generally accepted accounting principles (GAAP) The rules or guidelines used for carrying out the accounting process. (2)

Paraprofessional accountant A person who is qualified in accounting to assume the duties of a general bookkeeper as well as some of those of a professional accountant under that accountant's supervision. (4)

Transaction An event directly affecting an economic entity that can be expressed in terms of money and that must be recorded in the accounting records. (1)

1

Asset, Liability, Owner's Equity, Revenue, and Expense Accounts

Performance Objectives

After you have completed this chapter, you will be able to do the following:

1. Define and identify *asset, liability,* and *owner's equity* accounts.

2. Record a group of business transactions, in column form, involving changes in assets, liabilities, and owner's equity.

3. Define and identify *revenue* and *expense* accounts.

4. Record a group of business transactions, in column form, involving all five elements of the fundamental accounting equation.

As we stated in the Introduction, accounting is the process of analyzing, classifying, recording, and summarizing business transactions. We now introduce the analyzing, classifying, and recording steps in the accounting process.

ASSETS, LIABILITIES, AND OWNER'S EQUITY

OBJECTIVE 1
Define and identify *asset, liability,* and *owner's equity* accounts.

The Fundamental Accounting Equation

Assets are properties or things of value, such as cash, equipment, copyrights, buildings, and land, owned and controlled by an economic unit or

business entity. By the term **business entity**, we mean that the business is an economic unit in itself, and the assets or properties of the business are completely separate from the owner's personal assets. However, the owner has a claim on the assets of the business and a responsibility for its debts. **The owner's right, claim, or financial interest is expressed by the word equity in the business.** Another term that could be used is **capital**. Whenever you see the term **owner's equity**, it means the owner's right to or investment in the business.

Assets	=	Owner's Equity
Properties or things of value owned by the business		Owner's *right* to or investment in the business

Suppose the total value of the assets is $26,000 and the business entity does not owe any amount against the assets. Then,

Assets	=	Owner's Equity
$26,000 =		$26,000

Or suppose the assets consist of a truck that costs $23,000. The owner has invested $11,000 for the truck, and the business entity has borrowed the remainder from the bank, which is a **creditor** (one to whom money is owed). This business transaction or event can be shown as follows:

Assets	=	Liabilities	+	Owner's Equity
Items owned		Amounts owed to creditors		Owner's investment
$23,000	=	$12,000	+	$11,000

We have now introduced a new classification, **liabilities**, which represent debts. They are the amounts that the business entity owes its creditors. The debts may originate because the business bought goods or services on credit,

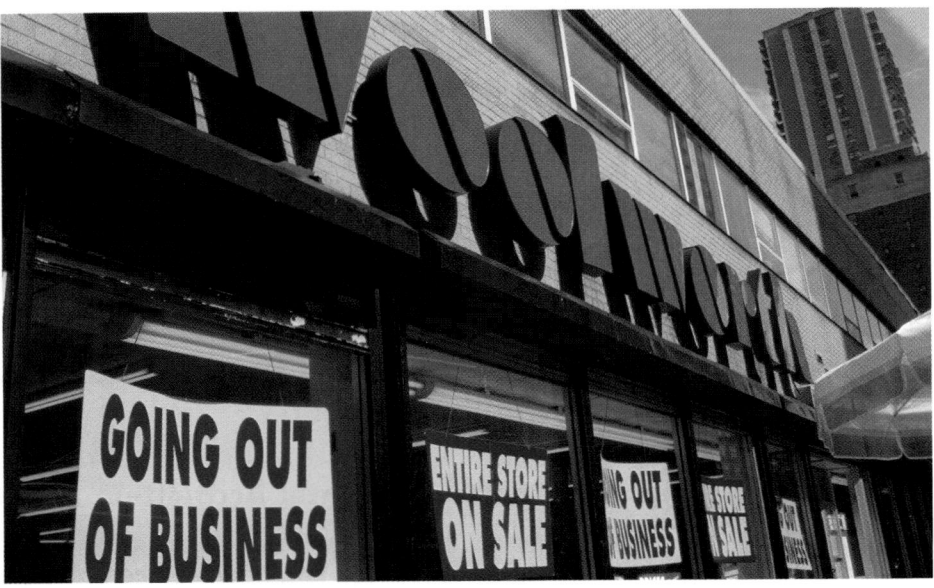

borrowed money, or otherwise created an obligation to pay. The creditors' claims to the assets have priority over the claims of the owner.

An equation expressing the relationship of assets, liabilities, and owner's equity is called the **fundamental accounting equation (Assets = Liabilities + Owner's Equity).** We'll deal with this equation constantly from now on. If we know two parts of this equation, we can determine the third. Let's look at some examples.

Determine Assets Ms. Burns has $9,000 invested in her travel agency, and the agency owes creditors $2,000; that is, the agency has liabilities of $2,000. Then,

<u>Assets</u>	=	<u>Liabilities</u>	+	<u>Owner's Equity</u>
?	=	$2,000	+	$9,000

We can find the amount of the business's assets by adding the liabilities and the owner's equity:

$ 2,000 Liabilities
+   9,000 Owner's Equity
$11,000 Assets

The completed equation now reads

<u>Assets</u>	=	<u>Liabilities</u>	+	<u>Owner's Equity</u>
$11,000	=	$2,000	+	$9,000

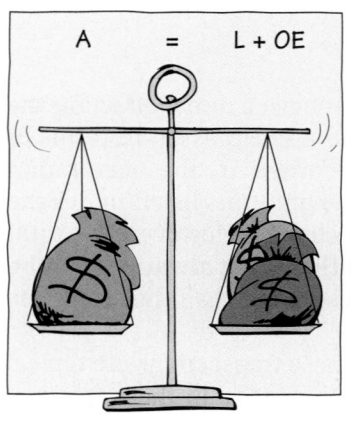

Like a balancing scale, the equation stays in balance by making equal or offsetting increases and decreases to one side or both sides.

Determine Owner's Equity Mr. Shea owns an auto lube shop. His business has assets of $36,000, and it owes creditors $5,000; that is, it has liabilities of $5,000. Then,

<u>Assets</u>	=	<u>Liabilities</u>	+	<u>Owner's Equity</u>
$36,000	=	$5,000	+	?

We find the owner's equity by subtracting the liabilities from the assets:

$36,000 Assets
−   5,000 Liabilities
$31,000 Owner's Equity

The completed equation now reads

<u>Assets</u>	=	<u>Liabilities</u>	+	<u>Owner's Equity</u>
$36,000	=	$5,000	+	$31,000

Determine Liabilities Mr. Stan's insurance agency has assets of $32,000; his investment (his equity) amounts to $20,000. Then,

<u>Assets</u>	=	<u>Liabilities</u>	+	<u>Owner's Equity</u>
$32,000	=	?	+	$20,000

Assets owned by a business may be as small as its office supplies or as large as its delivery van or building.

To find the firm's total liabilities, we subtract the equity from the assets:

$32,000 Assets
−   20,000 Owner's Equity

$12,000 Liabilities

The completed equation reads

Assets   =   **Liabilities**   +   **Owner's Equity**

$32,000 = $12,000   + $20,000

Recording Business Transactions

OBJECTIVE 2

Record a group of business transactions, in column form, involving changes in assets, liabilities, and owner's equity.

As you know, business transactions are events that have a direct effect on the operations of an economic unit or enterprise and are expressed in terms of money. Each business transaction must be recorded in the accounting records. As business transactions are recorded, the amounts listed under the headings Assets, Liabilities, and Owner's Equity change. However, **the total of one side of the fundamental accounting equation must always equal the total of the other side.** The categories under these three main headings are called **accounts.**

Let's look at a group of business transactions. These transactions are typical of those seen in a service or professional type of business. In these transactions, let's assume that L. P. Arch establishes her own business and calls it Arch Copy Co. Arch Copy Co. is a **sole proprietorship,** or a one-owner business.

Transaction (a) Arch deposited $70,000 in a bank account in the name of the business. Arch deposits $70,000 cash in a separate bank account in the name of Arch Copy Co. This separate bank account will help Arch keep her business investment separate from her personal funds. This is an example of the **separate entity concept,** according to which a business is treated as a separate economic or accounting entity. The business is independent or stands by itself; it is separate from its owners, creditors, and customers.

The Cash account consists of bank deposits and money on hand. The business now has $70,000 more in cash than before, and Arch's investment has also increased by $70,000. The account denoted by the owner's name followed by the word *Capital* records the amount of the owner's investment, or equity, in the business. The effect of this transaction on the fundamental accounting equation is as follows:

Assets	=	**Liabilities**	+	**Owner's Equity**
Items owned		Amounts owed to creditors		Owner's investment
Cash	=			L. P. Arch, Capital
(a) +70,000	=			+70,000

Besides cash, an investment may be in the form of goods, such as equipment. The word *Capital* used under Owner's Equity therefore does not always mean that cash was invested.

Transaction (b) **Bought equipment, paying cash, $33,000.** Arch's first task is to get her company ready for business; to do that, she needs the proper equipment. Accordingly, Arch Copy Co. buys equipment whose cost is $33,000 and pays cash. **It is important to note at this point that Arch does not invest any new money. She simply exchanges part of the business's cash for equipment.** Because equipment is a new type of property for the firm, a new account, Equipment, is created. Equipment is included under Assets. As a result of this transaction, the accounting equation changes:

	Assets		=	**Liabilities**	+	**Owner's Equity**
	Items owned			Amounts owed to creditors		Owner's investment
	Cash	+ Equipment	=			L. P. Arch, Capital
Initial Investment	70,000		=			70,000
(b)	−33,000	+33,000				
New balances	37,000 +	33,000	=			70,000
	70,000				70,000	

Transaction (c) **Bought equipment on account from Melton Office Supply, $7,000.** Arch Copy Co. buys equipment costing $7,000 on credit from Melton Office Supply.

The Equipment account shows an increase because the business owns $7,000 more in equipment. There is also an increase in liabilities because the business now owes $7,000. The liability account **Accounts Payable** is used for short-term liabilities or charge accounts, usually due within thirty days. (The company to which we owe money is called a creditor.) There is now a total of $77,000 on each side of the equals sign. Because Arch Copy Co. owes money to Melton Office Supply, Melton Office Supply is called a creditor of Arch Copy Co.

	Assets		=	**Liabilities**	+	**Owner's Equity**
	Items owned			Amounts owed to creditors		Owner's investment
	Cash +	Equipment	=	Accounts Payable +		L. P. Arch, Capital
Previous balances	37,000 +	33,000	=			70,000
(c)		+ 7,000		+7,000		
New balances	37,000 +	40,000	=	7,000	+	70,000
	77,000			77,000		

Observe that the recording of each transaction must yield an equation that is in balance. For example, transaction (b) resulted in a minus $33,000 and a plus $33,000 *on the same side*, with nothing recorded on the other side, and transaction (c) resulted in a $7,000 increase to both sides of the equation. It does not matter whether you change one side or both sides. **The important point is that whenever a transaction is properly recorded, the accounting equation remains in balance.**

Transaction (d) Paid Melton Office Supply, a creditor, on account, $2,000. Arch Copy Co. pays $2,000 to Melton Office Supply, to be applied against the firm's liability of $7,000.

With this payment, cash is being reduced. At the same time, the firm *owes* less than before, so the transaction should be recorded as a reduction in liabilities.

	Assets	=	Liabilities	+	Owner's Equity
	Items owned		Amounts owed to creditors		Owner's investment
	Cash + Equipment =		Accounts Payable +		L. P. Arch, Capital
Previous balances	37,000 + 40,000 =		7,000	+	70,000
(d)	−2,000		−2,000		
New balances	35,000 + 40,000 =		5,000	+	70,000
	75,000			75,000	

Transaction (e) Owner invested equipment in the business. Arch invested her own personal data processing equipment in Arch Copy Co. having a **fair market value** of $6,200. **Fair market value is the present worth of an asset.** It is the amount that would be received if the asset were sold on the open market. Additional investments may be in the form of equipment, cash, tools or real estate.

	Assets	=	Liabilities	+	Owner's Equity
	Items owned		Amounts owed to creditors		Owner's investment
	Cash + Equipment =		Accounts Payable +		L. P. Arch, Capital
Previous balances	35,000 + 40,000 =		5,000	+	70,000
(e)	+6,200				+6,200
New balances	35,000 + 46,200 =		5,000	+	76,200
	81,200			81,200	

Accounting, as we said before, is the process of analyzing, classifying, recording, summarizing, and interpreting business transactions in terms of money. Look at the transactions thus far for Arch Copy Co. and see if you recognize that we have gone through certain steps (in the form of questions). Let's illustrate these steps using transaction **(e),** owner invests equipment in the business.

1. **What accounts are involved?** Equipment and L. P. Arch, Capital are involved.
2. **What are the classifications of the accounts involved?** Equipment is an asset and L. P. Arch, Capital is an owner's equity account.

3. **Are the accounts increased or decreased?** Equipment is increased because Arch Copy Co. has more equipment than before. L. P. Arch, Capital is increased because Arch has a greater investment than before.
4. **Is the equation in balance after the transaction has been recorded?** Yes.

Next, we record the transaction. We will stress this step-by-step process throughout the text. This example serves as an introduction to **double-entry accounting**. The "double" element is demonstrated by the fact that each transaction must be recorded in at least two accounts, keeping the accounting equation in balance.

Summary of Transactions

Let's summarize the business transactions of Arch Copy Co. in column form, identifying each transaction by a letter of the alphabet. To test your understanding of the recording procedure, describe the nature of the transactions that have taken place.

	Assets		=	Liabilities	+	Owner's Equity
	Cash +	Equip.	=	Accounts + Payable		L. P. Arch, Capital
Transaction (a)	+70,000					+70,000
Transaction (b)	−33,000	+33,000				
Balance	37,000 +	33,000	=			70,000
Transaction (c)		+7,000		+7,000		
Balance	37,000 +	40,000	=	7,000 +		70,000
Transaction (d)	−2,000			−2,000		
Balance	35,000 +	40,000	=	5,000 +		70,000
Transaction (e)		+6,200				+6,200
Balance	35,000 +	46,200	=	5,000 +		76,200
	81,200			81,200		

The following observations apply to all types of business transactions:

1. Every transaction is recorded as an increase and/or decrease in two or more accounts.
2. One side of the equation is always equal to the other side of the equation.

   In this chapter we are using a column arrangement as a practical device to show how transactions are recorded. This arrangement is useful for showing increases and decreases in various accounts as a result of the transactions. We also showed new balances after recording each transaction.

REVENUE AND EXPENSE ACCOUNTS

OBJECTIVE 3
Define and identify *revenue* and *expense* accounts.

Revenues are the amounts earned by a business. Examples of revenues are fees earned for performing services, income from selling merchandise, rent income for the use of property, and interest income for lending money. Revenues may be in the form of cash or credit card receipts. Revenues may also result from credit sales to charge customers, in which case cash will be received at a later time.

Expenses are the costs that relate to earning revenue (or the costs of doing business). Examples of expenses are wages expense for labor performed, rent expense for the use of property, interest expense for the use of money, and advertising expense for the use of various media (for example, newspapers, radio, and direct mail). Another example is supplies expense to include supplies used in the completion of a task performed by a service business, such as cleaning fluids used by a carpet cleaner company. Expenses may be paid in cash when incurred (that is, immediately) or at a later time. Expenses to be paid at a later time involve Accounts Payable.

Revenues and expenses directly affect owner's equity. **If a business earns revenue, an increase in owner's equity occurs. When a business incurs or pays expenses, owner's equity decreases.** For the present, think of it this way: If the company makes money, the owner's equity is increased. If the company has to pay out money for the costs of doing business, then the owner's equity is decreased. Revenues and expenses fall under the umbrella of owner's equity: Revenue increases owner's equity; expenses decrease owner's equity.

Chart of Accounts

The **chart of accounts** is the official list of accounts *tailor-made* for the business. All the company's transactions must be recorded using the official account titles.

We now present the chart of accounts for Arch Copy Co. Some of the accounts are new to you, but they will be explained as we move along. When numbering account titles, the 100s are used for assets, the 200s are used for liabilities, the 300s are used for owner's equity accounts, the 400s are used for revenue accounts, and the 500s are used for expense accounts. You will encounter longer account numbers, but the first digit will usually be the same for any service business. In any case, use the exact account titles listed in the company's chart of accounts. Any changes must be approved by management.

FYI

When setting up and maintaining the chart of accounts on a computer, you may find that you must reserve the 500 accounts for cost accounts (used in a merchandising business). You may need to number expenses as 600s. Read the setup instructions in your software package.

Chart of Accounts

Assets

111 Cash
113 Accounts Receivable
117 Prepaid Insurance
124 Equipment

Liabilities

221 Accounts Payable

Owner's Equity

311 L. P. Arch, Capital
312 L. P. Arch, Drawing

Revenue (increase in Owner's Equity)

411 Income from Services

Expenses (decrease in Owner's Equity)

511 Wages Expense
512 Rent Expense
513 Supplies Expense
514 Advertising Expense
515 Utilities Expense

OBJECTIVE 4
Record a group of business transactions, in column form, involving all five elements of the fundamental accounting equation.

Recording Business Transactions

Soon after the opening of Arch Copy Co., the first customers arrive, beginning a flow of revenue for the business. Let's examine more transactions of Arch Copy Co. for the first month of operations.

Transaction (f) Sold services for cash, $2,520. Arch Copy Co. receives cash revenue of $2,520 in return for services performed for customers over two weeks. In other words, the company earns $2,520 for services performed for cash customers. Revenue has the effect of increasing owner's equity, but because the company wants to know how much revenue is earned, we set up a special column for revenue. The revenue account for Arch Copy Co. is called Income from Services. The accounting equation is affected as follows (PB stands for previous balance, and NB stands for new balance).

	Assets		= Liabilities +		Owner's Equity		
	Cash	+ Equipment	Accounts Payable	L. P. Arch, Capital	+ Revenue		
PB	35,000 +	46,200	= 5,000	+ 76,200			
(f)	+2,520				+2,520 (Income from Services)		
NB	37,520 +	46,200	= 5,000	+ 76,200	+	2,520	
		83,720			83,720		

Transaction (g) Paid rent for the month, $700. Shortly after opening the business, Arch Copy Co. pays the month's rent of $700. Rent is payment for the privilege of occupying a building.

It seems logical that, if revenue is added to owner's equity, then expenses (the opposite of revenue) must be subtracted from owner's equity. To be consistent, a separate column is set up for expenses.

We want to have a running total of the amount of expenses to be subtracted from owner's equity. To keep up this running total, as each new expense is incurred (or comes into being), it must be added to the previous total.

	Assets		= Liabilities +		Owner's Equity		
	Cash	+ Equip.	Accounts Payable	L. P. Arch, Capital	+ Revenue	− Expenses	
PB	37,520 +	46,200 =	5,000	+ 76,200	+ 2,520		
(g)	−700					+700 (Rent Expense)	
NB	36,820 +	46,200 =	5,000	+ 76,200	+ 2,520	− 700	
		83,020			83,020		

Because the time period represented by the rent payment is one month or less, we record the $700 as an expense. If the payment covered a period longer than one month, we would record the amount under an asset called Prepaid Rent.

Let's review the mental process for formulating the entry by asking:

1. **What are the accounts involved?** In this transaction, they are Cash and Rent Expense.

2. **What are the classifications of the accounts involved?** Cash is an asset, and Rent Expense is an expense.

3. **Are the accounts increased or decreased?** Cash is decreased because after the payment we have less cash than we had before. Rent Expense is

Banks and other financial institutions sell their services to other businesses as well as to individuals.

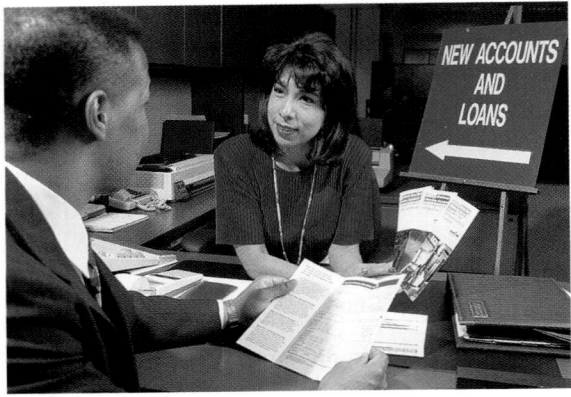

increased. Thus there is a $700 reduction in total owner's equity as a result of the expense.

4. **Is the equation in balance after the transaction has been recorded?** Yes.

Transaction (h) Arch Copy Co. bought supplies on credit. Arch Copy Co. buys paper and toner costing $600 on credit from Nebel Computers, Etc. Paper and toner are considered to be supplies to be used up by Arch Copy Co. in the performance of printing services and are recorded as an expense. For a service business, for tax purposes (IRS Notice 2001-76) supplies may now be originally recorded as an expense rather than being added to an inventory account.

	Assets	=	Liabilities +	Owner's Equity		
	Cash + Equip.		Accounts Payable	L. P. Arch, + Revenue − Expenses Capital		
PB (h)	36,820 + 46,200 =		5,000 +600	76,200 + 2,520 − 700 +600 (Supplies Expense)		
NB	36,820 + 46,200 =		5,600 +	76,200 + 2,520 − 1,300		
	83,020			83,020		

Transaction (i) Arch Copy Co. paid for insurance. Arch Copy Co. paid $360 for a one-year liability insurance policy. At the time of payment, the company has not used up the insurance, and so it is not yet an expense. As the insurance expires (is used), it will become an expense. **However, because it is paid in advance for a period longer than one month, it has value and is therefore recorded as an asset.**

	Assets	= Liabilities +	Owner's Equity	
	Cash + Equip. + Ppd. Ins.	Accounts Payable	L. P. Arch, + Revenue − Expenses Capital	
PB (i)	36,820 + 46,200 + −360 +360	= 5,600 +	76,200 + 2,520 − 1,300	
NB	36,460 + 46,200 + 360 =	5,600 +	76,200 + 2,520 − 1,300	
	83,020		83,020	

At the end of the year or accounting period, an adjustment will have to be made to take out the expired portion (that is, coverage for the months that have been used up) and record it as an expense. We discuss this adjustment in a later chapter.

Observe that each time a transaction is recorded, the total amount on one side of the equation **remains equal** to the total amount on the other side. As proof of this equality, look at the following computation:

Cash	$36,460	**Accounts Payable**	$ 5,600
Equipment	46,200	**L. P. Arch, Capital**	76,200
Prepaid Insurance	360	**Revenue**	2,520
			$84,320
		Expenses	−1,300
	$83,020		$83,020

Steps in Analyzing Transactions

Now that we have recorded transactions in all five classifications of accounts, let's pause to go through the steps we have followed:

Step 1 Read the transaction to understand what is happening and how it affects the business. For example, the business has more revenue, or has more expenses, or has more cash, or owes less to creditors.

Step 2 Identify the accounts involved and decide whether the accounts are increased or decreased. Look for Cash first; you will quickly recognize if cash is coming in or going out.

Step 3 Decide on the classifications of the accounts involved. For example, Equipment is something the business owns, and it's an asset; Accounts Payable is an amount the business owes, and it's a liability; Rent is an expense.

Step 4 After recording the transaction, make sure the accounting equation is in balance.

Transaction (j) Arch Copy Co. received a bill for an expense. Arch Copy Co. receives a bill from the *City News* for newspaper advertising, $200. Arch Copy Co. has simply received the bill for advertising; it has not paid any cash. Previously, we described an expense as money to be paid for the cost of doing business. An expense of $200 has now been incurred (or has taken place), and it should be recorded as an increase in expenses (Advertising Expense). Also, since the company owes $200 more than before and intends to pay at a later time, this amount should be recorded as an increase in Accounts Payable.

	Assets			= Liabilities +		Owner's Equity		
	Cash +	Equip. +	Ppd. Ins.	Accounts Payable	L. P. Arch, Capital	+ Revenue −	Expenses	
PB	36,460 +	46,200 +	360 =	5,600 **+200**	+ 76,200	+ 2,520 −	1,300 **+200** (Advertising Expense)	
NB	36,460 +	46,200 +	360 =	5,800	+ 76,200	+ 2,520 −	1,500	
		83,020				83,020		

Transaction (k) Arch Copy Co. sold services on account. Arch Copy Co. signs a contract with Walker Company to do their printing on a credit basis. Arch Copy Co. completes a printing job and bills Walker Company $1,050 for services performed.

A company uses the Accounts Receivable account to record the amounts due from charge customers (legal claims against charge customers). Since Arch Copy Co.'s claim against Walker Company is $1,050 more than before the transaction took place, it seems logical to add $1,050 to Accounts Receivable. Revenue is earned or recognized when the service is performed, even though the $1,050 has not been received in cash. So we count the $1,050 as an increase in revenue and an increase in Accounts Receivable. Keep in mind that Accounts Receivable is an asset. An asset is something that is owned, and Arch Copy Co. owns a claim of $1,050 against Walker Company.

	Assets				=	Liabilities	+		Owner's Equity		
	Cash	+ Equip.	+ Ppd. Ins.	+ Accts. Rec.		Accounts Payable		L. P. Arch, Capital	+ Revenue	− Expenses	
PB (k)	36,460	+ 46,200	+ 360	+1,050	=	5,800	+	76,200	+ 2,520 +1,050 (Income from Services)	− 1,500	
NB	36,460	+ 46,200	+ 360	+ 1,050	=	5,800	+	76,200	+ 3,570	− 1,500	
			84,070						84,070		

When Walker Company pays the $1,050 bill in cash, Arch Copy Co. will record this transaction as an increase in Cash and a decrease in Accounts Receivable. At that time, Arch Copy Co. will not have to make an entry for the revenue account, because the revenue was earned and recorded when the service was performed.

Transaction (l) **Arch Copy Co. paid creditor on account.** Arch Copy Co. pays $1,800 to Melton Office Supply, its creditor (the party to whom it owes money), as part payment on account.

	Assets				=	Liabilities	+		Owner's Equity		
	Cash	+ Equip.	+ Ppd. Ins.	+ Accts. Rec.		Accounts Payable		L. P. Arch, Capital	+ Revenue	− Expenses	
PB (l)	36,460 −1,800	+ 46,200	+ 360	+ 1,050	=	5,800 −1,800	+	76,200	+ 3,570	− 1,500	
NB	34,660	+ 46,200	+ 360	+ 1,050	=	4,000	+	76,200	+ 3,570	− 1,500	
			82,270						82,270		

Transaction (m) **Arch Copy Co. paid an expense in cash.** Arch Copy Co. receives a bill from Regional Power, Inc. for $160. Because the bill was not previously recorded as a liability and is to be paid immediately, we record the amount directly as an expense. The accounting equation is affected as follows:

	Assets				=	Liabilities	+		Owner's Equity		
	Cash	+ Equip.	+ Ppd. Ins.	+ Accts. Rec.		Accounts Payable		L. P. Arch, Capital	+ Revenue	− Expenses	
PB (m)	34,660 −160	+ 46,200	+ 360	+ 1,050	=	4,000	+	76,200	+ 3,570	− 1,500 +160 (Utilities Expense)	
NB	34,500	+ 46,200	+ 360	+ 1,050	=	4,000	+	76,200	+ 3,570	− 1,660	
			82,110						82,110		

Transaction (n) Arch Copy Co. paid creditor on account. Arch Copy Co. pays $200 to the *City News* for advertising. Recall that this bill had previously been recorded as a liability in transaction (j). The equation is as follows:

	Assets				=	Liabilities +		Owner's Equity		
	Cash	+ Equip.	+ Ppd. Ins.	+ Accts. Rec.	=	Accounts Payable	+	L. P. Arch, Capital	+ Revenue	− Expenses
PB	34,500	+ 46,200	+ 360	+ 1,050	=	4,000	+	76,200	+ 3,570	− 1,660
(n)	−200					−200				
NB	34,300	+ 46,200	+ 360	+ 1,050	=	3,800	+	76,200	+ 3,570	− 1,660
		81,910						81,910		

Transaction (o) Arch Copy Co. paid an expense in cash. Arch Copy Co. pays wages of a part-time employee, $2,130.

	Assets				=	Liabilities +		Owner's Equity		
	Cash	+ Equip.	+ Ppd. Ins.	+ Accts. Rec.	=	Accounts Payable	+	L. P. Arch, Capital	+ Revenue	− Expenses
PB	34,300	+ 46,200	+ 360	+ 1,050	=	3,800	+	76,200	+ 3,570	− 1,660
(o)	−2,130									+2,130
										(Wages Expense)
NB	32,170	+ 46,200	+ 360	+ 1,050	=	3,800	+	76,200	+ 3,570	− 3,790
		79,780						79,780		

Transaction (p) Arch Copy Co. buys equipment on account and makes a cash down payment. Arch Copy Co. buys additional equipment from Melton Office Supply for $3,520, paying $620 down, with the remaining $2,900 on account. Because buying an item on account is the same as buying it on credit, both *on account* and *on credit* are used to describe such transactions.

	Assets				=	Liabilities +		Owner's Equity		
	Cash	+ Equip.	+ Ppd. Ins.	+ Accts. Rec.	=	Accounts Payable	+	L. P. Arch, Capital	+ Revenue	− Expenses
PB	32,170	+ 46,200	+ 360	+ 1,050	=	3,800	+	76,200	+ 3,570	− 3,790
(p)	−620	+ 3,520				+2,900				
NB	31,550	+ 49,720	+ 360	+ 1,050	=	6,700	+	76,200	+ 3,570	− 3,790
		82,680						82,680		

Again, because the equipment is expected to last for years, Arch Copy Co. lists this $3,520 as an increase in the assets. Note that three accounts are involved in this transaction: Cash, because cash was paid out; Equipment, because the company has more equipment than before; and Accounts Payable, because the company owes more than before.

Transaction (q) Arch Copy Co. receives cash on account from credit customer. Arch Copy Co. receives $850 from Walker Company to apply against the amount billed in transaction (k). Walker Company now owes Arch Copy Co. less than it did, and so Arch Copy Co. deducts the $850 from Accounts Receivable. An exchange of assets has no effect on the total of the equation.

		Assets				= Liabilities +			Owner's Equity		
	Cash	+ Equip.	+ Ppd. Ins.	+ Accts. Rec.		Accounts Payable	+	L. P. Arch, Capital	+ Revenue	− Expenses	
PB (q)	31,550 +850	+ 49,720	+ 360	+ 1,050 −850	=	6,700	+	76,200	+ 3,570	− 3,790	
NB	32,400	+ 49,720	+ 360	+ 200	=	6,700	+	76,200	+ 3,570	− 3,790	
		82,680						82,680			

Arch Copy Co. previously listed the amount as revenue, so it should definitely not be recorded as revenue again. Think of paying income tax twice on the $850—once is enough.

Transaction (r) Arch Copy Co. sells services for cash. Arch Copy Co. receives revenue from cash customers for the rest of the month, $4,220.

		Assets				= Liabilities +			Owner's Equity		
	Cash	+ Equip.	+ Ppd. Ins.	+ Accts. Rec.		Accounts Payable	+	L. P. Arch, Capital	+ Revenue	− Expenses	
PB (r)	32,400 +4,220	+ 49,720	+ 360	+ 200	=	6,700	+	76,200	+ 3,570 +4,220 (Income from Services)	− 3,790	
NB	36,620	+ 49,720	+ 360	+ 200	=	6,700	+	76,200	+ 7,790	− 3,790	
		86,900						86,900			

Transaction (s) Owner makes a cash withdrawal. At the end of the month, Arch withdraws $2,500 in cash from the business for her personal living costs. A **withdrawal** may be considered the opposite of an investment in cash by the owner and is treated as a temporary decrease in owner's equity because it is made in anticipation of profits. Withdrawals are different from expenses. Expenses are paid to someone else for the cost of goods or services used in the business, whereas withdrawals are paid directly to the owner. A withdrawal may consist of cash or other assets.

Because the owner takes cash out of the business, there is a decrease of $2,500 in Cash. This also decreases Capital, because Arch has reduced her equity. We record $2,500 as a minus under Capital and label it as Drawing.

		Assets				= Liabilities +			Owner's Equity		
	Cash	+ Equip.	+ Ppd. Ins.	+ Accts. Rec.		Accounts Payable	+	L. P. Arch, Capital	+ Revenue	− Expenses	
PB (s)	36,620 −2,500	+ 49,720	+ 360	+ 200	=	6,700	+	76,200 −2,500 (Drawing)	+ 7,790	− 3,790	
NB	34,120	+ 49,720	+ 360	+ 200	=	6,700	+	73,700	+ 7,790	− 3,790	
		84,400						84,400			

Summary of Transactions f Through s

Figure 1 on the opposite page summarizes business transactions (f) through (s) of Arch Copy Co. with the transactions identified by letter. To test your understanding of the recording procedure, describe the nature of the transactions.

	Assets				=	Liabilities	+	Owner's Equity		
	Cash	+ Equip.	+ Ppd. Ins.	+ Accts. Rec.	=	Accounts Payable	+	L. P. Arch, Capital	+ Revenue	− Expenses
Bal.	35,000	46,200			=	5,000		76,200		
(f)	+2,520								+2,520 (Income from Services)	
Bal.	37,520	+ 46,200			=	5,000	+	76,200	+ 2,520	
(g)	−700									+700 (Rent Expense)
Bal.	36,820	+ 46,200			=	5,000	+	76,200	+ 2,520	− 700
(h)						+600				+600 (Supplies Expense)
Bal.	36,820	+ 46,200			=	5,600	+	76,200	+ 2,520	− 1,300
(i)	−360		+360							
Bal.	36,460	+ 46,200	+ 360		=	5,600	+	76,200	+ 2,520	− 1,300
(j)						+200				+200 (Advertising Expense)
Bal.	36,460	+ 46,200	+ 360		=	5,800	+	76,200	+ 2,520	− 1,500
(k)				+1,050					+1,050 (Income from Services)	
Bal.	36,460	+ 46,200	+ 360	+ 1,050	=	5,800	+	76,200	+ 3,570	− 1,500
(l)	−1,800					−1,800				
Bal.	34,660	+ 46,200	+ 360	+ 1,050	=	4,000	+	76,200	+ 3,570	− 1,500
(m)	−160									+160 (Utilities Expense)
Bal.	34,500	+ 46,200	+ 360	+ 1,050	=	4,000	+	76,200	+ 3,570	− 1,660
(n)	−200					−200				
Bal.	34,300	+ 46,200	+ 360	+ 1,050	=	3,800	+	76,200	+ 3,570	− 1,660
(o)	−2,130									+2,130 (Wages Expense)
Bal.	32,170	+ 46,200	+ 360	+ 1,050	=	3,800	+	76,200	+ 3,570	− 3,790
(p)	−620	+3,520				+2,900				
Bal.	31,550	+ 49,720	+ 360	+ 1,050	=	6,700	+	76,200	+ 3,570	− 3,790
(q)	+850			−850						
Bal.	32,400	+ 49,720	+ 360	+ 200	=	6,700	+	76,200	+ 3,570	− 3,790
(r)	+4,220								+4,220 (Income from Services)	
Bal.	36,620	+ 49,720	+ 360	+ 200	=	6,700	+	76,200	+ 7,790	− 3,790
(s)	−2,500							−2,500 (Drawing)		
	34,120	+ 49,720	+ 360	+ 200	=	6,700	+	73,700	+ 7,790	− 3,790

Left Side of Equals Sign		Right Side of Equals Sign	
Cash	$34,120	**Accounts Payable**	$ 6,700
Equipment	49,720	**L. P. Arch, Capital**	73,700
Prepaid Insurance	360	**Revenue**	7,790
Accounts Receivable	200		$88,190
	$84,400	**Expenses**	−3,790
			$84,400

FIGURE 1

CHAPTER REVIEW

Check out ACE for
a Review Quiz at

http://college.hmco.com/
accounting/students/.

Review of Performance Objectives

1. Define and identify *asset, liability*, and *owner's equity* accounts.

   Assets are cash, properties, or things of value owned by the business. *Liabilities* are amounts the business owes to creditors. *Owner's equity* is the owner's investment or net worth.

2. Record a group of business transactions, in column form, involving changes in assets, liabilities, and owner's equity.

   The accounting equation is stated as assets equals liabilities plus owner's equity. Under the appropriate classification, a separate column is set up for each account. Transactions are recorded by listing amounts as either additions to or deductions from the various accounts. The equation must always remain in balance.

3. Define and identify *revenue* and *expense* accounts.

   Revenue consists of amounts earned by a business, such as fees earned for performing services, income from selling merchandise, rent income for the use of property, or interest earned for lending money. *Expenses* are the costs of earning revenue—that is, of doing business—such as wages expense, rent expense, interest expense, and advertising expense.

4. Record a group of business transactions, in column form, involving all five elements of the fundamental accounting equation.

   The accounting equation has been expanded and appears as follows:

   Assets = Liabilities + Owner's Equity (Capital) + Revenue − Expenses

   Accounts are classified and listed under each heading. Transactions are recorded by listing amounts as either additions to or deductions from the various accounts. The equation must always remain in balance.

Glossary

Accounts The categories under the Assets, Liabilities, and Owner's Equity headings. (10)

Accounts Payable A liability account used for short-term liabilities or charge accounts, usually due within thirty days. (11)

Accounts Receivable An account used to record the amounts owed by charge customers (legal claims against charge customers). (18)

Assets Cash, properties, and other things of value owned by an economic unit or business entity. (7)

Business entity A business enterprise, separate and distinct from the persons who supply the assets it uses. Property acquired by a business is an asset of the business. The owner is separate from the business and in fact has claims on it and a responsibility for its debts. (8)

Capital The owner's investment, or equity, in an enterprise. (8)

Chart of accounts The official list of account titles to be used to record the transactions of a business. (14)

Creditor One to whom money is owed. (8)

Double-entry accounting The system by which each business transaction is recorded in at least two accounts and the accounting equation is kept in balance. (13)

Equity The value of a right or claim to or financial interest in an asset or group of assets. (8)

Expenses The costs that relate to earning revenue (the costs of doing business); examples are wages, rent, interest, and advertising. They may be paid in cash immediately, or at a future time (accounts payable). (14)

Fair market value The present worth of an asset or the amount that would be received if the asset were sold to an outsider on the open market. (12)

Fundamental accounting equation (Assets = Liabilities + Owner's Equity) An equation expressing the relationship of assets, liabilities, and owner's equity. (9)

Liabilities Debts or amounts owed to creditors. (8)

Owner's equity The owner's right to or investment in the business. (8)

Revenues The amounts a business earns; examples are fees earned for performing services, sales of merchandise, rent income, and interest income. They may be in the form of cash, credit card receipts, or accounts receivable (charge accounts). (13)

Separate entity concept The concept by which a business is treated as a separate economic or accounting entity. The business stands by itself, separate from its owners, creditors, and customers. (10)

Sole proprietorship A one-owner business. (10)

Withdrawal The taking of cash or other assets out of a business by the owner for his or her own use. (This is also referred to as *drawing*.) A withdrawal is treated as a temporary decrease in owner's equity. (20)

QUESTIONS, EXERCISES, AND PROBLEMS

Discussion Questions

1. Define assets, liabilities, owner's equity, revenues, and expenses.
2. Explain the separate entity concept.
3. How do Accounts Receivable and Accounts Payable differ?
4. Describe two ways to increase owner's equity and two ways to decrease owner's equity.
5. How will the fundamental accounting equation change if supplies are purchased on account? Explain how this purchase will or will not change the owner's equity.
6. When an owner withdraws cash or goods from the business, why is this considered an increase to the Drawing account and not an increase to the wages account?
7. Define *chart of accounts*, and identify the categories of accounts.
8. What account titles would you suggest for the chart of accounts for a jeep touring company owned by J. Dern? List the accounts by account category and include an appropriate account number for each.

Exercises

Exercise 1-1 Complete the following equations:

a. Assets of $20,000 = Liabilities of $7,300 + Owner's Equity of $_____
b. Assets of $_____ − Liabilities of $18,000 = Owner's Equity of $27,000
c. Assets of $27,000 − Owner's Equity of $13,300 = Liabilities of $_____

Exercise 1-2 Determine the following amounts:

a. The amount of the liabilities of a business that has $59,300 in assets and in which the owner has $35,200 equity.
b. The equity of the owner of a van that cost $32,000 who owes $8,400 on an installment loan payable to the bank.
c. The amount of the assets of a business that has $9,240 in liabilities and in which the owner has $23,480 equity.

Exercise 1-3 Dr. H. H. Ryley is an ophthalmologist. As of December 31, Dr. Ryley owned the following property that related to his professional practice, Ryley Eye Clinic:

Cash, $2,380
Professional Equipment, $60,000
Office Equipment, $12,460

On the same date, he owed the following business creditors:

Milton Supply Company, $3,120
Javez Equipment Sales, $2,970

Compute the following amounts in the accounting equation:

Assets $_____ = Liabilities $_____ + Owner's Equity $_____

Exercise 1-4 Describe a business transaction that will do the following:

a. Increase an asset and increase a liability
b. Decrease an asset and decrease a liability
c. Decrease an asset and increase an expense
d. Increase an asset and increase owner's equity
e. Increase an asset and decrease an asset
f. Increase an asset and increase revenue

Exercise 1-5 Describe a transaction that resulted in the following entries:

	Assets			= Liabilities +	Owner's Equity
	Cash +	Office Equipment	+ Professional Equipment	Accounts Payable	B. Loren, Capital
(a)	+14,300				+14,300
(b)	−1,650		+1,650		
Bal.	12,650		+ 1,650 =		14,300
(c)		+550		+550	
Bal.	12,650 +	550	+ 1,650 =	550 +	14,300
(d)	−1,200		+6,000	+4,800	
Bal.	11,450 +	550	+ 7,650 =	5,350 +	14,300
(e)	−1,000			−1,000	
Bal.	10,450 +	550	+ 7,650 =	4,350 +	14,300

P.O. 1,3

Classify accounts.

Exercise 1-6 Label the following accounts as asset (A), liability (L), owner's equity (OE), revenue (R), or expense (E):

a. Office Supplies Expense
b. Professional Fees
c. Prepaid Insurance
d. T. Domzal, Drawing
e. Accounts Payable
f. Service Income
g. T. Domzal, Capital
h. Rent Expense
i. Accounts Receivable
j. Wages Expense

P.O. 4

Describe various transactions.

Exercise 1-7 Describe a transaction that resulted in the following changes in accounts:

a. Rent Expense is increased by $850, and Cash is decreased by $850.
b. Advertising Expense is increased by $741, and Accounts Payable is increased by $741.
c. Accounts Receivable is increased by $185, and Service Income is increased by $185.
d. Cash is decreased by $420, and C. Taylor, Drawing, is increased by $420.
e. Equipment is increased by $750, Cash is decreased by $250, and Accounts Payable is increased by $500.
f. Cash is increased by $530, and Accounts Receivable is decreased by $530.

P.O. 2,4

Describe various transactions.

Exercise 1-8 Describe the transactions that are recorded in the following equation.

	Cash +	Accounts Receivable	+Equipment	=	Accounts Payable	+	J. Ohno, Capital	+	Revenue	−	Expenses
	Assets			**= Liabilities +**			**Owner's Equity**				
(a)	+22,000		+5,000				+27,000				
(b)	−1,050										+1,050 (Rent Expense)
Bal.	20,950	+	5,000	=			27,000			−	1,050
(c)		+1,800							+1,800 (Service Income)		
Bal.	20,950 +	1,800	+ 5,000	=			27,000		1,800	−	1,050
(d)	−4,000		+15,000		+11,000						
Bal.	16,950 +	1,800	+ 20,000	=	11,000	+	27,000 +		1,800	−	1,050
(e)	−2,000						−2,000 (Drawing)				
Bal.	14,950 +	1,800	+ 20,000	=	11,000	+	25,000 +		1,800	−	1,050
	Total	36,750			Total		36,750				

REFLECTING ON
THE WORLD WIDE WEB

Recall from Performance Objective 1 in the chapter that the fundamental accounting equation expresses the relationship of assets, liabilities, and owner's equity. This is what the balance sheet reports. Using information from Gap Inc.'s balance sheet, found on page 24 of the 2000 annual report, create a completed accounting equation (Assets = Liabilities + Stockholders' Equity). The term Stockholders' Equity is used for Gap Inc. because the company sells shares of its stock to the public. Gap Inc.'s total assets equal $7,012,908,000; total liabilities equal $4,084,669,000 (current liabilities of $2,799,144,000 plus long-term liabilities of $1,285,525,000); and total stockholders' equity equals $2,928,239,000. As you can see, when we place these amounts into the fundamental accounting equation, the total of one side of the equation equals the total of the other side of the equation.

Assets	=	Liabilities	+ Stockholders' Equity
$7,012,908,000	=	$4,084,669,000 +	$2,928,239,000

1. If you purchase a pair of jeans from the Gap for $40 cash, how will the store record this transaction? (Ignore sales taxes.)
2. How would Gap record a $3,000 payment for its monthly rent for one of its stores?

CONSIDER AND COMMUNICATE

A friend of yours wants to start her own pet sitting business. She already has a business license that is required in her city. She has had a personal checking account for years. You have told her that she also needs to open a separate account for her business needs, but she does not understand why. Explain to her why she should have a business account separate from her personal account. Use some of the language of business you have learned in your text's introduction and in this chapter.

WHAT'S WRONG WITH THIS PICTURE?

Alan Walter has just opened Walter's Computer Service. He has calculated the following amounts and then placed them in the fundamental accounting equation as he remembers it from his accounting class five years ago. He asks that you review his figures and give your opinion because he wants to start out on a correct footing.

Money in the drawer	$1,395
What I owe people	284
What people owe me	895

	Assets	=	Liabilities	+	Owner's Equity
	1,395		895		
	284				
Totals	1,679	=	895	+	?

Alan's Proof: A − L = OE

1,679 − 895 = 784 OE

1. Do you agree with Alan's calculations?
2. If not, show how you would explain it to Alan using the classifications of the fundamental accounting equation.

CRITICAL THINKING

Please read the following memorandum and follow the instructions set forth.

MEMORANDUM

TO: Your Name   DATE: July 31, 20—
FROM: J. Robbins,   SUBJECT: Calculations for Barrow Co.
            Supervisor

Please provide the following ASAP (as soon as possible).

1. The balance of cash in Barrow Company's checkbook shows $9,960. I need to know if this ties to or matches the Cash account balance. I do know that total assets amount to $43,650. Office Equipment amounts to $3,550. Other noncash assets are Warehouse Equipment, $27,340 and Prepaid Insurance, $2,800.
2. A. Barrow, the owner, wants to know the amount of his owner's equity. I pulled the outstanding bills, which amount to $7,394.
3. Please put the information in a memo addressed to me.
4. Thank you for your prompt response.

PROBLEM SET A

For additional help, see the demonstration problem at the beginning of each chapter in your Working Papers.

P.O. 1,2,3,4   **Problem 1-1A** In July of this year, R. P. Jones established a business called Jones Realty. The account headings are presented below. Transactions completed during the month follow.

Assets	= Liabilities +	Owner's Equity	
Cash + Office Equipment	Accounts Payable	Capital	, + Revenue − Expenses

a. Jones deposited $12,000 in a bank account in the name of the business.
b. Paid the office rent for the current month, $700, Ck. No. 1000 (Rent Expense).
c. Bought office supplies, paying cash, $364, Ck. No. 1001 (Supplies Expense).
d. Bought office equipment on account from Baxter Computers, $6,200.
e. Received a bill from the *Weekly Journal* for advertising, $382 (Advertising Expense).
f. Paid on account to Baxter Computers, a creditor, $900, Ck. No. 1002.
g. Sold services for cash, $3,160 (Service Income).
h. Received and paid the bill for utilities, $148, Ck. No. 1003 (Utilities Expense).
i. Paid on account to the *Weekly Journal,* a creditor, $382, Ck. No. 1004.
j. Paid van expenses, $256, Ck. No. 1005 (Van Expense).
k. Jones withdrew cash for personal use, $1,030, Ck. No. 1006 (R. P. Jones, Drawing).

Check Figure

Left side of equals sign total, $17,580

Instructions

1. In the equation, write the owner's name above the term *Capital.*
2. Record the transactions and the balance after each transaction. Identify the account affected when the transaction involves revenue, expenses, or a withdrawal.
3. Write the account totals from the left side of the equals sign and add them. Write the account totals from the right side of the equals sign and add them. If the two totals are not equal, first check the addition and subtraction. If you still cannot find the error, reanalyze each transaction.

P.O. 1,2,3,4

Problem 1-2A In March, M. Haas, M.D., established the Haas Sports Medical Clinic. The clinic's account headings are presented below. Transactions completed during the month of March follow.

Assets		= Liabilities +	Owner's Equity	
Cash + Office Equipment	+ Professional Equipment	Accounts Payable	Capital	, + Revenue − Expenses

a. Haas deposited $20,000 in a bank account in the name of the business.
b. Paid the rent for the month, $950, Ck. No. 1000 (Rent Expense).
c. Bought supplies on account from Hernandez Co., $1,470 (Supplies Expense).
d. Bought professional equipment on account from Terrel Company, $6,800.
e. Bought office equipment on account from Daily Co., $364.
f. Sold professional services for cash, $4,610 (Professional Fees).
g. Paid on account to Terrel Company, a creditor, $1,950, Ck. No. 1001.
h. Received and paid the bill for utilities, $172, Ck. No. 1002 (Utilities Expense).
i. Paid the salary of the assistant, $1,200, Ck. No. 1003 (Salary Expense).
j. Sold professional services for cash, $3,200 (Professional Fees).
k. Haas withdrew cash for personal use, $1,560, Ck. No. 1004 (M. Haas, Drawing).

Check Figure

Cash, $21,978

Instructions

1. In the equation, write the owner's name above the term *Capital*.
2. Record the transactions and the balance after each transaction. Identify the account affected when the transaction involves revenue, expenses, or a withdrawal.
3. Write the account totals from the left side of the equals sign and add them. Write the account totals from the right side of the equals sign and add them. If the two totals are not equal, first check the addition and subtraction. If you still cannot find the error, reanalyze each transaction.

P.O. 1,2,3,4

Problem 1-3A B. Levitt, Attorney at Law, opened his office on October 1. The account headings are presented below. Transactions completed during the month follow.

Assets				= Liabilities +		Owner's Equity		
Cash +	Prepaid + Insurance	Office + Equipment	Library	Accounts Payable	Capital	, + Revenue − Expenses		

a. Levitt deposited $21,000 in a bank account in the name of the business.
b. Bought office equipment on account from Morgan Company, $14,700.
c. Levitt invested his personal law library, which cost $5,700. (Increase the account Library and increase the account B. Levitt, Capital.)
d. Paid the office rent for the month, $760, Ck. No. 2000 (Rent Expense).
e. Bought office supplies for cash, $885, Ck. No. 2001 (Supplies Expense).
f. Bought insurance for two years, $186, Ck. No. 2002.
g. Sold legal services for cash, $2,460 (Professional Fees).
h. Received and paid the telephone bill, $228, Ck. No. 2003 (Telephone Expense).
i. Paid the salary of the part-time receptionist, $960, Ck. No. 2004 (Salary Expense).
j. Bought gas and oil for the van, paying cash, $288, Ck. No. 2005 (Van Expense).
k. Sold legal services for cash, $2,120 (Professional Fees).
l. Paid on account to Morgan Company, a creditor, $1,500, Ck. No. 2006.
m. Levitt withdrew cash for personal use, $2,075, Ck. No. 2007 (B. Levitt, Drawing).

Check Figure

Right side of equals sign total, $39,284

Instructions

1. In the equation, write the owner's name above the term *Capital*.
2. Record the transactions and the balance after each transaction. Identify the account affected when the transaction involves revenue, expenses, or a withdrawal.
3. Write the account totals from the left side of the equals sign and add them. Write the account totals from the right side of the equals sign and add them. If the two totals are not equal, first check the addition and subtraction. If you still cannot find the error, reanalyze each transaction.

P.O. 1,2,3,4

Problem 1-4A N. R. Nolan started Nolan Pest Service on May 1 of this year. The account headings are presented below. During May, Nolan completed the transactions that follow.

Assets					= Liabilities +		Owner's Equity		
Cash +	Accounts + Receivable	Prepaid + Insurance	Truck +	Equipment	Accounts Payable	Capital	, + Revenue − Expenses		

a. Nolan deposited $6,000 in a bank account in the name of the business.
b. Bought a used truck from Domke Motors for $11,250, paying $1,200 in cash, and placing the remainder on account.
c. Bought equipment on account from Fancher Company, $1,800.
d. Paid the rent for the month, $260, Ck. No. 3001 (Rent Expense).
e. Bought insurance for the truck for the year, $576, Ck. No. 3002, Policy No. 311D.
f. Sold services for cash for the first half of the month, $2,175 (Service Income).
g. Bought supplies for cash, $573, Ck. No. 3003 (Supplies Expense).
h. Sold services on account, $444 (Service Income).
i. Received and paid the bill for utilities, $96, Ck. No. 3004 (Utilities Expense).
j. Received a bill for gas and oil for the truck, $327 (Truck Expense).
k. Sold services for cash for the remainder of the month, $3,642 (Service Income).
l. Nolan withdrew cash for personal use, $1,050, Ck. No. 3005.
m. Paid wages to the employees, $2,040, Ck. Nos. 3006–3008 (Wages Expense).

Check Figure

Cash, $6,022

Instructions

1. In the equation, write the owner's name above the term *Capital.*
2. Record the transactions and the balance after each transaction. Identify the account affected when the transaction involves revenue, expenses, or a withdrawal.
3. Write the account totals from the left side of the equals sign and add them. Write the account totals from the right side of the equals sign and add them. If the two totals are not equal, first check the addition and subtraction. If you still cannot find the error, reanalyze each transaction.

PROBLEM SET B

For additional help, see the demonstration problem at the beginning of each chapter in your Working Papers.

P.O. 1,2,3,4

Problem 1-1B On June 1 of this year, E. Roe, Optometrist, established the Roe Eye Clinic. The clinic's account names are presented below. Transactions completed during the month follow.

Assets		= Liabilities +		Owner's Equity	
Cash +	Office Equipment	Accounts Payable	Capital	, + Revenue	− Expenses

a. Roe deposited $10,500 in a bank account in the name of the business.
b. Paid the office rent for the month, $640, Ck. No. 1001 (Rent Expense).
c. Bought supplies for cash, $1,216, Ck. No. 1002 (Supplies Expense).
d. Bought office equipment on account from Jason Equipment, $15,290.
e. Bought a computer from Ryan Office Outfitters, $3,840, paying $800 in cash and placing the balance on account, Ck. No. 1003.
f. Sold professional services for cash, $1,421 (Professional Fees).

g. Paid on account to Ryan Office Outfitters, a creditor, $800, Ck. No. 1004.
h. Received and paid the bill for utilities, $153, Ck. No. 1005 (Utilities Expense).
i. Paid the salary of the assistant, $950, Ck. No. 1006 (Salary Expense).
j. Sold professional services for cash, $2,414 (Professional Fees).
k. Roe withdrew cash for personal use, $1,250, Ck. No. 1007 (E. Roe, Drawing).

Check Figure

Left side of equals sign total, $27,656

Instructions

1. In the equation, write the owner's name above the term *Capital.*
2. Record the transactions and the balance after each transaction. Identify the account affected when the transaction involves revenue, expenses, or a withdrawal.
3. Write the account totals from the left side of the equals sign and add them. Write the account totals from the right side of the equals sign and add them. If the two totals are not equal, first check the addition and subtraction. If you still cannot find the error, reanalyze each transaction.

P.O. 1,2,3,4

Problem 1-2B On July 1 of this year, J. Vance, established the Vance Rehab Clinic. The organization's account headings are presented below. Transactions completed during the month of July follow.

Assets			= Liabilities +		Owner's Equity		
Cash +	Office Equipment	+ Professional Equipment	Accounts Payable	Capital	,	+ Revenue	− Expenses

a. Vance deposited $12,300 in a bank account in the name of the business.
b. Paid the office rent for the month, $955, Ck. No. 2001 (Rent Expense).
c. Bought supplies for cash, $375, Ck. No. 2002 (Supplies Expense).
d. Bought professional equipment on account from Rehab Equipment Company, $15,300 (Professional Equipment).
e. Bought office equipment from A-Tech Computers, $3,870, paying $850 in cash and placing the balance on account, Ck. No. 2003.
f. Sold professional services for cash, $4,280 (Professional Fees).
g. Paid on account to A-Tech Computers, a creditor, $800, Ck. No. 2004.
h. Received and paid the bill for utilities, $273, Ck. No. 2005 (Utilities Expense).
i. Paid the salary of the assistant, $1,450, Ck. No. 2006 (Salary Expense).
j. Sold professional services for cash, $3,622 (Professional Fees).
k. Vance withdrew cash for personal use, $1,800, Ck. No. 2007 (J. Vance, Drawing).

Check Figure

Cash, $13,699

Instructions

1. In the equation, write the owner's name above the term *Capital.*
2. Record the transactions and the balance after each transaction. Identify the account affected when the transaction involves revenue, expenses, or a withdrawal.
3. Write the account totals from the left side of the equals sign and add them. Write the account totals from the right side of the equals sign and add them. If the two totals are not equal, first check the addition and subtraction. If you still cannot find the error, reanalyze each transaction.

P.O. 1,2,3,4

Problem 1-3B M. A. Pitts, a graphic artist, opened a studio for her professional practice on August 1. The account headings are presented below. Transactions completed during the month follow.

	Assets			= Liabilities +	Owner's Equity	
Cash +	Prepaid + Insurance	Office + Equipment	Photo Equipment	Accounts Payable	, + Revenue − Expenses Capital	

a. Pitts deposited $14,620 in a bank account in the name of the business.
b. Bought office equipment on account from Superior Equipment Company, $7,120.
c. Pitts invested her personal photographic equipment, $5,162. (Increase the account Photo Equipment and increase the account M. A. Pitts, Capital.)
d. Paid the rent for the month, $550, Ck. No. 1000 (Rent Expense).
e. Bought supplies for cash, $796, Ck. No. 1001 (Supplies Expense).
f. Bought insurance for two years, $924, Ck. No. 1002.
g. Sold graphic services for cash, $2,896 (Professional Fees).
h. Paid the salary of the part-time assistant, $600, Ck. No. 1003 (Salary Expense).
i. Received and paid the bill for telephone service, $64, Ck. No. 1004 (Telephone Expense).
j. Paid cash for minor repairs to graphics equipment, $76, Ck. No. 1005 (Repair Expense).
k. Sold graphic services for cash, $2,848 (Professional Fees).
l. Paid on account to Superior Equipment Company, a creditor, $420, Ck. No. 1006.
m. Pitts withdrew cash for personal use, $960, Ck. No. 1007 (M. A. Pitts, Drawing).

Check Figure

Right side of equals sign total, $29,180

Instructions

1. In the equation, write the owner's name above the term *Capital*.
2. Record the transactions and the balance after each transaction. Identify the account affected when the transaction involves revenue, expenses, or a withdrawal.
3. Write the account totals from the left side of the equals sign and add them. Write the account totals from the right side of the equals sign and add them. If the two totals are not equal, first check the addition and subtraction. If you still cannot find the error, reanalyze each transaction.

P.O. 1,2,3,4

Problem 1-4B On March 1 of this year, D. L. Porter established Porter Catering Service. The account headings are presented below. Transactions completed during the month follow.

	Assets				= Liabilities +	Owner's Equity	
Cash +	Accounts + Receivable	Prepaid + Insurance	Truck +	Equipment	Accounts Payable	, + Revenue − Expenses Capital	

a. Porter deposited $14,500 in a bank account in the name of the business.
b. Bought a truck from Compton Motors for $12,490, paying $3,500 in cash and placing the balance on account, Ck. No. 500.

c. Bought catering equipment on account from Gallo Company, $2,236.
d. Paid the rent for the month, $520, Ck. No. 501 (Rent Expense).
e. Sold catering services for cash for the first half of the month, $1,920 (Catering Income).
f. Bought supplies for cash, $172, Ck. No. 502 (Supplies Expense).
g. Bought insurance for the truck for one year, $454, Ck. No. 503.
h. Received and paid the heating bill, $54, Ck. No. 504 (Utilities Expense).
i. Received a bill from Quick Gas and Lube for gas and oil for the truck, $98 (Gas and Oil Expense).
j. Sold catering services on account, $1,927 (Catering Income).
k. Sold catering services for cash for the remainder of the month, $2,412 (Catering Income).
l. Paid the salary of the assistant, $1,240, Ck. No. 505 (Salary Expense).
m. Porter withdrew cash for personal use, $1,950, Ck. No. 506 (D. L. Porter, Drawing).

Check Figure

Cash, $10,942

Instructions

1. In the equation, write the owner's name above the term *Capital*.
2. Record the transactions and the balance after each transaction. Identify the account affected when the transaction involves revenue, expenses, or a withdrawal.
3. Write the account totals from the left side of the equals sign and add them. Write the account totals from the right side of the equals sign and add them. If the two totals are not equal, first check the addition and subtraction. If you still cannot find the error, reanalyze each transaction.

2

T Accounts, Debits and Credits, Trial Balance, and Financial Statements

Performance Objectives

After you have completed this chapter, you will be able to do the following:

1. Determine balances of T accounts having entries recorded on both sides of the accounts.

2. Present the fundamental accounting equation with the T account form, and label the plus and minus sides.

3. Present the fundamental accounting equation with the T account form, and label the debit and credit sides.

4. Record directly in T accounts a group of business transactions involving changes in asset, liability, owner's equity, revenue, and expense accounts for a service business.

5. Prepare a trial balance.

6. Prepare (a) an income statement, (b) a statement of owner's equity, and (c) a balance sheet.

7. Recognize the effect of transpositions and slides on account balances.

We introduced the fundamental accounting equation as *Assets = Liabilities + Owner's Equity*. We also discussed the recording of transactions involving two other classifications of accounts: *Revenue* and *Expenses*. With the addition of Revenue and Expenses, the fundamental accounting equation was brought up to its full size of five account classifications. There are only five classifications; so, as far as you go in accounting—whether you are dealing with a small, one-owner business or a large corporation—there will be these five major classifications of accounts.

In this chapter, we will record the same transactions in T account form, and we will prove the equality of both sides of the fundamental accounting equation. We will do this by means of a trial balance, which we will discuss later in this chapter.

THE T ACCOUNT FORM

So far, we have recorded business transactions in a column arrangement. For example, the Cash account column in the books of Arch Copy Co. is shown below.

Cash Account Column

Transaction	**(a)**	70,000
Transaction	**(b)**	−33,000
Balance		37,000
Transaction	**(d)**	−2,000
Balance		35,000
Transaction	**(f)**	+2,520
Balance		37,520
Transaction	**(g)**	−700
Balance		36,820
Transaction	**(i)**	−360
Balance		36,460
Transaction	**(l)**	−1,800
Balance		34,660
Transaction	**(m)**	−160
Balance		34,500
Transaction	**(n)**	−200
Balance		34,300
Transaction	**(o)**	−2,130
Balance		32,170
Transaction	**(p)**	−620
Balance		31,550
Transaction	**(q)**	+850
Balance		32,400
Transaction	**(r)**	+4,220
Balance		36,620
Transaction	**(s)**	−2,500
		34,120

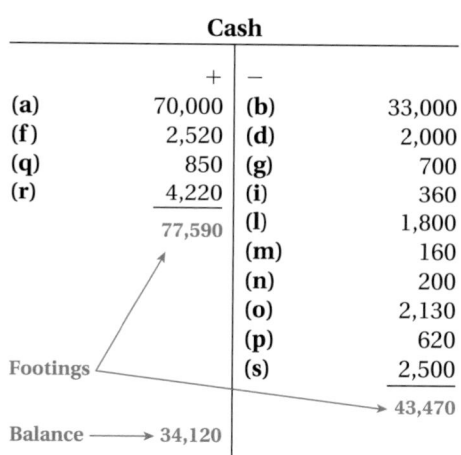

Cash

	+		−
(a)	70,000	**(b)**	33,000
(f)	2,520	**(d)**	2,000
(q)	850	**(g)**	700
(r)	4,220	**(i)**	360
	77,590	**(l)**	1,800
		(m)	160
		(n)	200
		(o)	2,130
		(p)	620
Footings		**(s)**	2,500
			43,470
Balance	34,120		

As an introduction to the recording of transactions, the column arrangement had the following advantages:

1. **In the process of analyzing the transaction, you**
   a. Recognized the need to determine which accounts are involved.
   b. Determined the classification of the accounts involved.
   c. Decided whether the transaction resulted in an increase or a decrease in each of these accounts.

2. **You further realized that, after each transaction had been recorded, the two sides of the fundamental accounting equation were in balance. In other words, the total of one side of the accounting equation equaled the total of the other side.**

Now, instead of recording transactions in a column for each account, we will use a **T account form** for each account. *The T account form has the advantage of providing two sides for each account; one side is used to record increases in the account, and the other side is used to record decreases.*

After we record a group of transactions in a T account, we add both sides and record the totals in small, pencil-written figures called **footings**. Next, we subtract one footing from the other to determine the balance of the account. For the Cash account, shown previously, the balance is $34,120($77,590 − $43,470).

We now record the balance on the side of the account having the larger footing, which, with a few minor exceptions, is the plus (+) side. The plus side of a T account is the side that represents the **normal balance** of that account. The normal balance may, however, fall on either the left or the right side of an account, depending on what type of account it is. To review, we presented the T account for Cash; Cash is classified as an asset, and all assets look like the following T account:

OBJECTIVE 1
Determine balances of T accounts having entries recorded on both sides of the accounts.

Assets

+	−
Left	Right

However, **not all classifications of accounts have the increase side on the left.**

Recall that we placed revenue and expenses under the "umbrella" of owner's equity. Revenue increases owner's equity, and expenses decrease owner's equity. The T accounts for this situation are as follows:

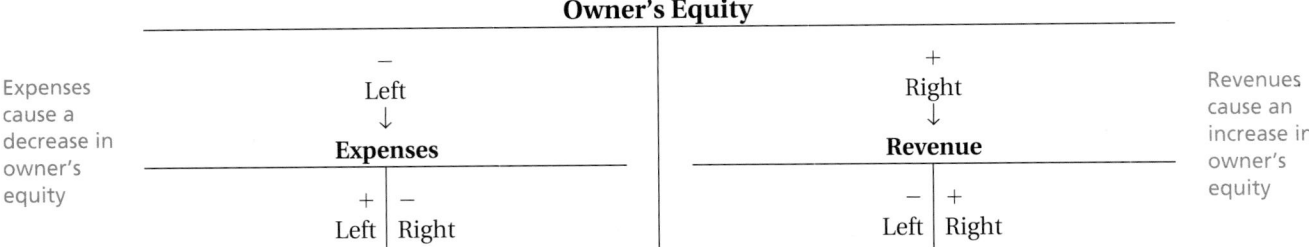

Expenses cause a decrease in owner's equity

Owner's Equity

−   +
Left   Right
↓   ↓
Expenses   **Revenue**

+	−		−	+
Left	Right		Left	Right

Revenues cause an increase in owner's equity

Increases in owner's equity are recorded on the right side of the account. Because revenue increases owner's equity, additions to revenue are also recorded on the right side.

Decreases in owner's equity are recorded on the left side of the account. Because expenses decrease owner's equity, additions to expenses are also recorded on the left side.

Using the five classifications of accounts, the fundamental accounting equation looks like this:

$$\text{Assets} = \text{Liabilities} + \underbrace{\qquad\qquad \text{Owner's Equity} \qquad\qquad}_{\text{Capital} + \text{Revenue} - \text{Expenses}}$$

REMEMBER!
The entry for a business transaction may include any combination of pluses and minuses: pluses and pluses, pluses and minuses, or minuses and minuses.

Because revenue and expenses appear separately in the income statement, we will stretch out the equation to include them as separate headings, as shown here:

$$\text{Assets} = \text{Liabilities} + \text{Capital} + \text{Revenue} - \text{Expenses}$$

We can now restate the equation with the T account forms and plus and minus signs for each account classification:

Assets	=	Liabilities	+	Owner's Equity	+	Revenue	−	Expenses
+ | −		− | +		− | +		− | +		+ | −
Left | Right		Left | Right		Left | Right		Left | Right		Left | Right

OBJECTIVE 2
Present the fundamental accounting equation with the T account form, and label the plus and minus sides.

Before we go on, let us point out the increase, or plus, side of each account classification. You can recognize these in the accounting equation using T accounts.

Assets	The *left* side is the *increase* side.
Liabilities	The *right* side is the *increase* side.
Owner's Equity	The *right* side is the *increase* side
Revenue	The *right* side is the *increase* side.
Expenses	The *left* side is the *increase* side.

Because revenue is an addition to owner's equity, the placement of the plus and minus signs is the same as for owner's equity. On the other hand, because expenses are treated as deductions from owner's equity, the placement of the plus and minus signs is reversed. We will use this form of the fundamental accounting equation throughout the remainder of the text.

Your accounting background up to this point has taught you to analyze business transactions to determine which accounts are involved and to recognize that each amount should be recorded as either an increase or a decrease in these accounts. Now the recording process becomes a simple matter of knowing which side of the T accounts should be used to record increases and which should be used to record decreases. **Generally, you will not be using the minus side of the revenue and expense accounts, since transactions involving revenue and expense accounts usually result in increases in these accounts.** An exception to this statement is where errors have been made and require correction. Let's now add the last element to the T account before we record the familiar Arch Copy Co. transactions.

THE T ACCOUNT FORM WITH DEBITS AND CREDITS

OBJECTIVE 3
Present the fundamental accounting equation with the T account form, and label the debit and credit sides.

The left side of a T account is called the **debit** side; the right side is called the **credit** side. The T accounts representing the accounting equation now contain both the signs and the words *Debit* and *Credit*. There are only five classifications of accounts. These classifications are contained in the fundamental accounting equation:

Assets	=	Liabilities	+	Owner's Equity	+	Revenue	−	Expenses
+ | −		− | +		− | +		− | +		+ | −
Debit | Credit		Debit | Credit		Debit | Credit		Debit | Credit		Debit | Credit

The following table summarizes debits and credits and how they are affected by increases and decreases. **The critical rule to remember is that the amount placed on the debit side of one or more accounts MUST equal the amount placed on the credit side of another account or accounts.**

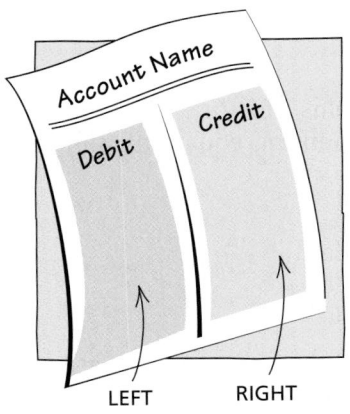

Debit is always the left side of the account, and credit is always the right side of an account. The + or − however, changes with the type of account.

Debits Signify		**Credits Signify**	
Increases in {	Assets Drawing Expenses	Decreases in {	Assets Drawing Expenses
Decreases in {	Liabilities Capital Revenue	Increases in {	Liabilities Capital Revenue

Before we begin recording, notice the new T account below the Capital account, L. P. Arch, Drawing. Recall that the Capital account is increased when amounts are invested and decreased when amounts are taken out.

Capital

−	+
Debit	Credit
	Amounts invested

Drawing

+	−
Debit	Credit
Amounts withdrawn	

We reserve the minus or debit side of the Capital account for permanent withdrawals, those made when the owner decides to reduce the size of the business permanently or when a net loss forces such a reduction. This concept is best illustrated by showing the Drawing T account under the umbrella of the Capital account.

Capital

−	+
Debit	Credit

Drawing

+	−
Debit	Credit

RECORDING BUSINESS TRANSACTIONS IN T ACCOUNTS

OBJECTIVE 4
Record directly in T accounts a group of business transactions involving changes in asset, liability, owner's equity, revenue, and expense accounts for a service business.

Our task now is to learn how to record business transactions in the T account form. First, let's review the steps in analyzing a business transaction.

1. **Decide which accounts are involved.**
2. **Classify the accounts involved** (asset, liability, capital, revenue, expense).
3. **Decide if the accounts involved are increased or decreased.**
4. **Decide which accounts are debited and which accounts are credited.**
5. **Check to see if the equation is in balance after the transaction has been recorded.**

For example, let's analyze the first transaction of the Arch Copy Co. transactions using this five-step process. To formulate the entry, you must be able to visualize the fundamental accounting equation in the form of T accounts. With that in mind, the first transaction is as follows:

In transaction (a), Arch deposited $70,000 in a bank account in the name of the business. This transaction results in an increase to Cash with a debit and an increase in the Capital account with a credit.

1. **Decide which accounts are involved.** The two accounts involved are Cash and L. P. Arch, Capital.
2. **Classify the accounts involved (asset, liability, capital, revenue, expense).** Cash is an asset and L. P. Arch, Capital, is an owner's equity account.
3. **Decide if the accounts involved are increased or decreased.** Cash is being deposited in the bank account, an increase to Cash. The owner has invested that cash in the business and has increased L. P. Arch, Capital.
4. **Write the transaction as a debit to one account (or accounts) and a credit to another account (or accounts).** Since Cash is an asset and Cash is increased, Cash is debited. We now need an offsetting credit. L. P. Arch, Capital, is an owner's equity account and is increased. L. P. Arch, Capital, is credited. You now have a debit equal to a credit.
5. **Check:** There is at least one account debited and at least one account credited, *and* the total amount(s) debited equal the total amount(s) credited. **You now have a debit equal to a credit, a $70,000 debit to Cash and a $70,000 credit to L. P. Arch, Capital.**

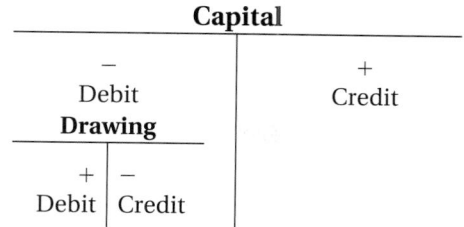

Stores such as this bike shop classify revenue accounts for each service activity—sales, repairs, and rentals. They may also classify expense accounts separately.

The resulting transaction in T account form follows:

Cash

	+	−
	Debit	Credit
(a)	70,000	

L. P. Arch, Capital

	−	+
	Debit	Credit
		(a) 70,000

In transaction (b), Arch Copy Co. bought equipment, paying cash, $33,000. This transaction results in an increase to Equipment with a debit and a decrease to Cash with a credit.

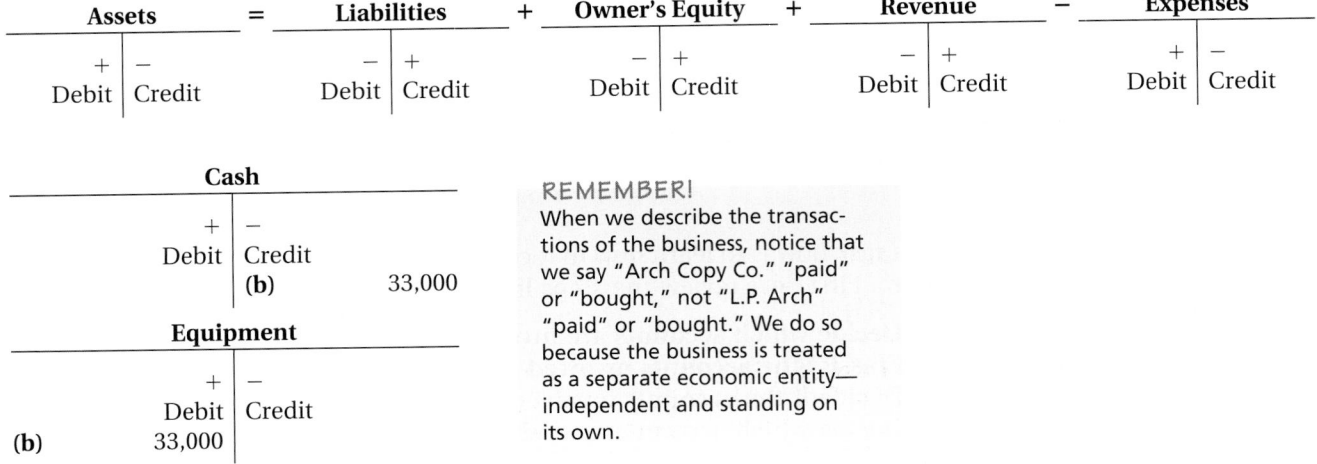

REMEMBER!
When we describe the transactions of the business, notice that we say "Arch Copy Co." "paid" or "bought," not "L.P. Arch" "paid" or "bought." We do so because the business is treated as a separate economic entity—independent and standing on its own.

In transaction (c), Arch Copy Co. bought equipment on account from Melton Office Supply, $7,000. This transaction results in an increase to Equipment with a debit and an increase to Accounts Payable with a credit and is shown in T accounts as follows:

Assets	=	Liabilities	+	Owner's Equity	+	Revenue	−	Expenses
+ / −		− / +		− / +		− / +		+ / −
Debit / Credit		Debit / Credit		Debit / Credit		Debit / Credit		Debit / Credit

Equipment	Accounts Payable
+ / −	− / +
Debit / Credit	Debit / Credit
(c) 7,000	(c) 7,000

In transaction (d), Arch Copy Co. paid Melton Office Supply, a creditor, $2,000. This transaction results in a decrease to Cash with a credit and a decrease to Accounts Payable with a debit.

Assets	=	Liabilities	+	Owner's Equity	+	Revenue	−	Expenses
+ / −		− / +		− / +		− / +		+ / −
Debit / Credit		Debit / Credit		Debit / Credit		Debit / Credit		Debit / Credit

Cash	Accounts Payable
+ / −	− / +
Debit / Credit	Debit / Credit
(d) 2,000	(d) 2,000

In transaction (e), L. P. Arch invests her personal computer in the business with a fair market value of $6,200.

Assets	=	Liabilities	+	Owner's Equity	+	Revenue	−	Expenses
+ | −		− | +		− | +		− | +		+ | −
Debit | Credit		Debit | Credit		Debit | Credit		Debit | Credit		Debit | Credit

Equipment

+	−
Debit	Credit
(e) 6,200	

L. P. Arch, Capital

−	+
Debit	Credit
	(e) 6,200

Here is a restatement of the accounts after recording transactions (a) through (e). To test your understanding of the process, trace through the recording of each transaction and describe what happened in the transaction. Footings or subtotals (remember, always write the footings smaller than the entries and in pencil) are required to compute the balances of the accounts. The balances are written in the accounts on the side with the larger total.

Assets	=	Liabilities	+	Owner's Equity	+	Revenue	−	Expenses
+ | −		− | +		− | +		− | +		+ | −
Debit | Credit		Debit | Credit		Debit | Credit		Debit | Credit		Debit | Credit

Cash

+	−
Debit	Credit
(a) 70,000	(b) 33,000
	(d) 2,000
	35,000
Bal. 35,000	

Accounts Receivable

+	−
Debit	Credit

Prepaid Insurance

+	−
Debit	Credit

Equipment

+	−
Debit	Credit
(b) 33,000	
(c) 7,000	
(e) 6,200	
Bal. 46,200	

Accounts Payable

−	+
Debit	Credit
(d) 2,000	(c) 7,000
	Bal. 5,000

L. P. Arch, Capital

−	+
Debit	Credit
	(a) 70,000
	(e) 6,200
	Bal. 76,200

L. P. Arch, Drawing

+	−
Debit	Credit

Income from Services

−	+
Debit	Credit

Wages Expense

+	−
Debit	Credit

Rent Expense

+	−
Debit	Credit

Supplies Expense

+	−
Debit	Credit

Advertising Expense

+	−
Debit	Credit

Utilities Expense

+	−
Debit	Credit

REMEMBER!
The normal balance of an account classification is on the plus side.

FYI
The T account is not only a learning tool, but will serve you well as a problem-solving device when you need to analyze a transaction prior to recording it—manually or on a computer.

Let's pause to see if the two sides of the equation are equal by listing the balances of the accounts:

Account Name	Accounts with Normal Balances on the Left or Debit Side	Accounts with Normal Balances on the Right or Credit Side
	Assets Drawing Expenses	Liabilities Capital Revenue
Cash	$35,000	
Equipment	46,200	
Accounts Payable		$ 5,000
L. P. Arch, Capital		76,200
	$81,200	$81,200

In transaction (f), Arch Copy Co. sold services for cash, $2,520. This transaction results in an increase to Cash with a debit and an increase to Income from Services with a credit.

Assets	=	Liabilities	+	Owner's Equity	+	Revenue	−	Expenses
+ | −		− | +		− | +		− | +		+ | −
Debit | Credit		Debit | Credit		Debit | Credit		Debit | Credit		Debit | Credit

Cash

+	−
Debit	Credit
(f) 2,520	

Income from Services

−	+
Debit	Credit
	(f) 2,520

In transaction (g), Arch Copy Co. paid rent for the month, $700. This transaction results in an increase to Rent Expense with a debit and a decrease to Cash with a credit.

Assets	=	Liabilities	+	Owner's Equity	+	Revenue	−	Expenses
+ | −		− | +		− | +		− | +		+ | −
Debit | Credit		Debit | Credit		Debit | Credit		Debit | Credit		Debit | Credit

Cash

+	−
Debit	Credit
	(g) 700

Rent Expense

+	−
Debit	Credit
(g) 700	

In transaction (h), Arch Copy Co. bought paper and toner for $600 on account from Nebel Computers, Etc. This transaction results in an increase to Supplies Expense with a debit and an increase to Accounts Payable with a credit.

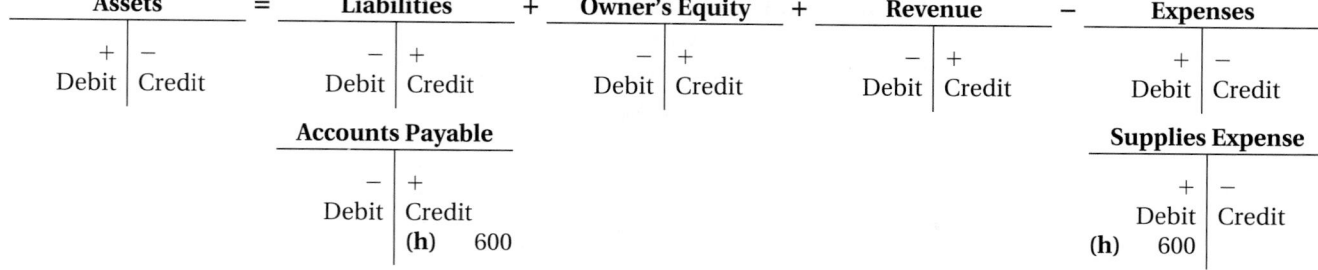

Assets	=	Liabilities	+	Owner's Equity	+	Revenue	−	Expenses
+ | −		− | +		− | +		− | +		+ | −
Debit | Credit		Debit | Credit		Debit | Credit		Debit | Credit		Debit | Credit

Accounts Payable

− | +
Debit | Credit
(h)   600

Supplies Expense

+ | −
Debit | Credit
(h)   600

In transaction (i), Arch Copy Co. bought a one-year liability insurance policy, $360. This transaction results in an increase to Prepaid Insurance with a debit and a decrease to Cash with a credit.

Assets	=	Liabilities	+	Owner's Equity	+	Revenue	−	Expenses
+ | −		− | +		− | +		− | +		+ | −
Debit | Credit		Debit | Credit		Debit | Credit		Debit | Credit		Debit | Credit

Cash

+ | −
Debit | Credit
| **(i)**   360

Prepaid Insurance

+ | −
Debit | Credit
(i)   360

In transaction (j), Arch Copy Co. received a bill for newspaper advertising from *City News*, $200. This transaction results in an increase to Advertising Expense with a debit and an increase to Accounts Payable with a credit.

Assets	=	Liabilities	+	Owner's Equity	+	Revenue	−	Expenses
+ | −		− | +		− | +		− | +		+ | −
Debit | Credit		Debit | Credit		Debit | Credit		Debit | Credit		Debit | Credit

Accounts Payable

− | +
Debit | Credit
(j)   200

Advertising Expense

+ | −
Debit | Credit
(j)   200

In transaction (k), Arch Copy Co. sold printing services on account to Walker Company, $1,050. This transaction results in an increase to Accounts Receivable with a debit and an increase to Income from Services with a credit.

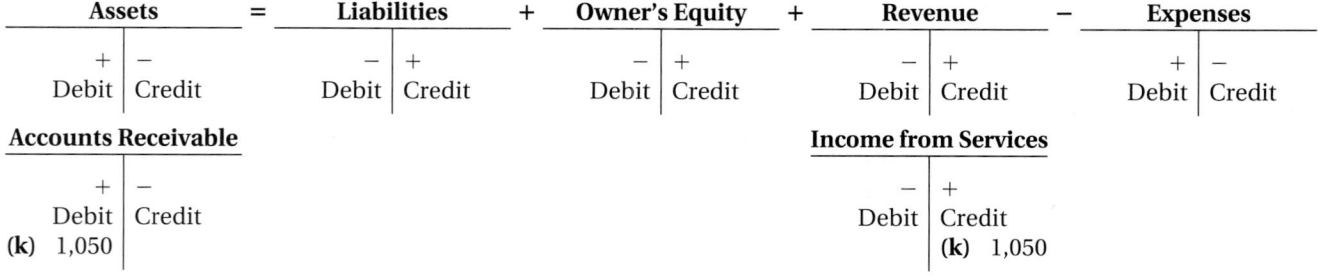

Assets	=	Liabilities	+	Owner's Equity	+	Revenue	−	Expenses
+ | −		− | +		− | +		− | +		+ | −
Debit | Credit		Debit | Credit		Debit | Credit		Debit | Credit		Debit | Credit

Accounts Receivable

+ | −
Debit | Credit
(k)   1,050

Income from Services

− | +
Debit | Credit
| **(k)**   1,050

In transaction (l), Arch Copy Co. paid on account to Melton Office Supply, $1,800. This transaction results in a decrease to Accounts Payable with a debit and a decrease to Cash with a credit.

Assets	=	Liabilities	+	Owner's Equity	+	Revenue	−	Expenses
+ | −		− | +		− | +		− | +		+ | −
Debit | Credit		Debit | Credit		Debit | Credit		Debit | Credit		Debit | Credit

Cash		Accounts Payable
+ | −		− | +
Debit | Credit		Debit | Credit
(l) 1,800		(l) 1,800

In transaction (m), Arch Copy Co. received and paid the electric bill, $160. The result of this transaction is an increase to Utilities Expense with a debit and a decrease to Cash with a credit.

Assets	=	Liabilities	+	Owner's Equity	+	Revenue	−	Expenses
+ | −		− | +		− | +		− | +		+ | −
Debit | Credit		Debit | Credit		Debit | Credit		Debit | Credit		Debit | Credit

Cash								Utilities Expense
+ | −								+ | −
Debit | Credit								Debit | Credit
(m) 160								(m) 160

In transaction (n), Arch Copy Co. paid on account to *City News*, $200. This transaction results in a decrease to Accounts Payable with a debit and a decrease to Cash with a credit.

Assets	=	Liabilities	+	Owner's Equity	+	Revenue	−	Expenses
+ | −		− | +		− | +		− | +		+ | −
Debit | Credit		Debit | Credit		Debit | Credit		Debit | Credit		Debit | Credit

Cash		Accounts Payable
+ | −		− | +
Debit | Credit		Debit | Credit
(n) 200		(n) 200

In transaction (o), Arch Copy Co. paid the wages of the part-time employee, $2,130. This transaction results in an increase to Wages Expense with a debit and a decrease to Cash with a credit.

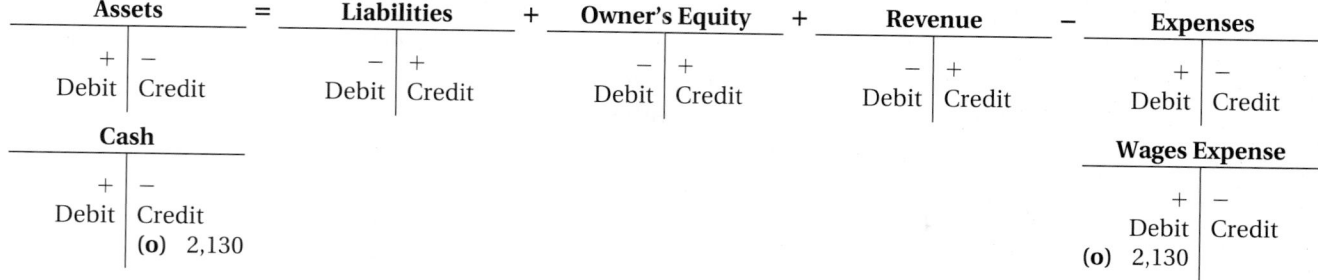

In transaction (p), Arch Copy Co. bought additional equipment from Melton Office Supply, $3,520, paying $620 in cash and placing the balance on account. This transaction results in an increase to Equipment with a debit, an increase to Accounts Payable with a credit, and a decrease to Cash with a credit. This is called a **compound entry**; that is, more than one debit or more than one credit is recorded.

In transaction (q), Arch Copy Co. received cash from Walker Company on account, $850. This transaction results in an increase to Cash with a debit and a decrease to Accounts Receivable with a credit.

In transaction (r), Arch Copy Co. sold services for cash, $4,220. This transaction results in an increase to Cash with a debit and an increase to Income from Services with a credit.

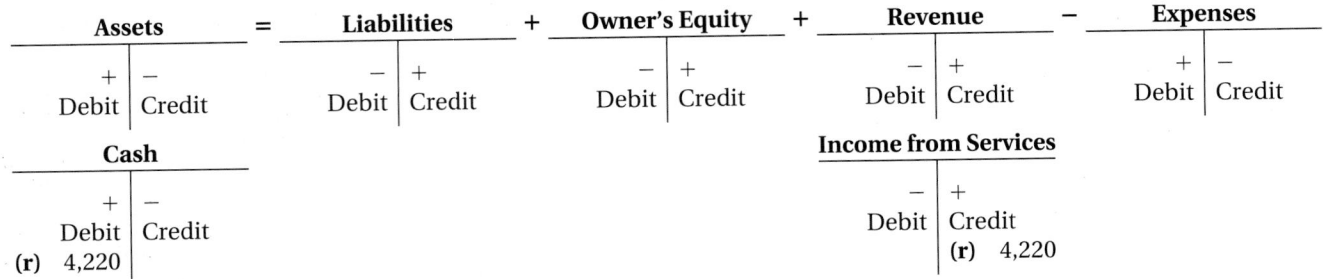

In transaction (s), L. P. Arch withdrew cash for her personal use, $2,500. This transaction increases L. P. Arch, Drawing with a debit and decreases Cash with a credit.

Assets	=	Liabilities	+	Owner's Equity	+	Revenue	−	Expenses
+ | −		− | +		− | +		− | +		+ | −
Debit | Credit		Debit | Credit		Debit | Credit		Debit | Credit		Debit | Credit

Cash	L. P. Arch, Drawing
+ | −	+ | −
Debit | Credit	Debit | Credit
(s) 2,500	(s) 2,500

The Drawing account is used to record temporary decreases in Owner's Equity. The owner takes money out of the business for his or her living expenses hoping that the withdrawals will be offset by net income. If, instead, the owner permanently reduces his or her investment in the business, the Capital account is debited.

Summary of Transactions

FYI

Traditionally, accountants use the abbreviations Dr. for Debit and Cr. for Credit.

The following T accounts show the transactions as they are ordinarily recorded. Footings are shown in color. You will notice that the balance of each account is normally on the plus side. Note that, in recording expenses, you place the entries only on the plus, or debit, side. Also, in recording revenue, you place the entries only on the plus, or credit, side.

Assets	=	Liabilities	+	Owner's Equity	+	Revenue	−	Expenses
+ | −		− | +		− | +		− | +		+ | −
Debit | Credit		Debit | Credit		Debit | Credit		Debit | Credit		Debit | Credit

Cash

+	−
(a) 70,000	(b) 33,000
(f) 2,520	(d) 2,000
(q) 850	(g) 700
(r) 4,220	(i) 360
77,590	(l) 1,800
	(m) 160
	(n) 200
	(o) 2,130
	(p) 620
	(s) 2,500
	43,470

Bal. 34,120

Accounts Receivable

+	−
(k) 1,050	(q) 850

Bal. 200

Prepaid Insurance

+	−
(i) 360	

Equipment

+	−
(b) 33,000	
(c) 7,000	
(e) 6,200	
(p) 3,520	

Bal. 49,720

Accounts Payable

−	+
(d) 2,000	(c) 7,000
(l) 1,800	(h) 600
(n) 200	(j) 200
4,000	(p) 2,900
	10,700

Bal. 6,700

L. P. Arch, Capital

−	+
	(a) 70,000
	(e) 6,200
	Bal. 76,200

L. P. Arch, Drawing

+	−
(s) 2,500	

Income from Services

−	+
	(f) 2,520
	(k) 1,050
	(r) 4,220
	Bal. 7,790

Wages Expense

+	−
(o) 2,130	

Rent Expense

+	−
(g) 700	

Supplies Expense

+	−
(h) 600	

Advertising Expense

+	−
(j) 200	

Utilities Expense

+	−
(m) 160	

FYI

A memory tool that helps some students to memorize debits and credits in T accounts is the trial balance equation $A + D + E = L + C + R$.

THE TRIAL BALANCE

OBJECTIVE 5
Prepare a trial balance.

You can now prepare a trial balance by simply recording the balances of the T accounts in two columns. The **trial balance** is a listing of account balances in two columns—one labeled Debit and one labeled Credit—to prove that the total of all the debit balances equals the total of all the credit balances. A trial balance is not considered a financial statement; it is, as the name implies, a trial run by the accountant to prove that the total of the debit balances equal the total of the credit balances. This is evidence of the equality of the two sides of the fundamental accounting equation. The accountant must prove that the accounts are in balance before preparing the company's financial statements.

Arch Copy Co.
Trial Balance
June 30, 20—

Column headings identify
information in each column

ACCOUNT NAME	DEBIT	CREDIT
Cash —————— *Accounts listed*	34 1 2 0 00	
Accounts Receivable *in order of the*	2 0 0 00	
Prepaid Insurance *chart of accounts*	3 6 0 00	
Equipment	49 7 2 0 00	
Accounts Payable		6 7 0 0 00
L. P. Arch, Capital		76 2 0 0 00
L. P. Arch, Drawing	2 5 0 0 00	
Income from Services		7 7 9 0 00
Wages Expense	2 1 3 0 00	
Rent Expense	7 0 0 00	
Supplies Expense	6 0 0 00	
Advertising Expense	2 0 0 00	
Utilities Expense *Single underline beneath*	1 6 0 00	
figures to be added	90 6 9 0 00	90 6 9 0 00

Dollar signs are
not used on a
trial balance.

Double underline beneath
column totals

FIGURE 1

In preparing a trial balance, shown in Figure 1, record the accounts with balances in the same order as they are listed in the chart of accounts.

- Assets
- Liabilities
- Owner's Equity
- Revenue
- Expenses

The normal balance of each account is on its plus side. Remember that when there is more than one entry in an account, we record the totals in footings and subtract one footing from the other to determine the balance. **Record this balance on the side of the account with the larger footing.** (Here we record the Drawing account balance in the debit column because it has a debit balance. We do not deduct Drawing from the Capital account when we prepare the trial balance.) The following table indicates where each of the account balances would normally be shown in a trial balance.

	Trial Balance	
Account Titles	**Left or Debit Balances**	**Right or Credit Balances**
Assets	Assets	
Liabilities		Liabilities
Capital		Capital
Drawing	Drawing	
Revenue		Revenue
Expenses	Expenses	
Totals	XXXX XX	XXXX XX

MAJOR FINANCIAL STATEMENTS

Earlier we listed summarizing as one of the five basic tasks of the accounting process. To accomplish this task, accountants use financial statements. A **financial statement** is a report prepared by accountants to summarize the financial affairs of a business for managers and others, both inside and outside the business.

Note that the headings of all financial statements require three lines:

1. Name of the company (or owner, if there is no company name)
2. Title of the financial statement
3. Period of time covered by the financial statement, or its date

Also, note that dollar signs are placed at the head of each column and with each total. Single lines (drawn with a ruler) are used to show that the figures above are being added or subtracted. Lines should be drawn across the entire column. A double line is drawn under the final total in a column.

The financial statements are all interconnected. The income statement must be prepared first, followed by the statement of owner's equity, and then the balance sheet.

The Income Statement

The **income statement** shows total revenue minus total expenses, which yields the net income or net loss. The income statement shows the results of business transactions involving revenue and expense accounts—in other words, how the business has performed—over a period of time, usually a month or a year. When total revenue exceeds total expenses over the period, the result is **net income**, or profit. If the total revenue is less than the total expenses, the result is a **net loss**.

The income statement in Figure 2 shows the results of the first month of operations for Arch Copy Co.

For convenience, the individual expense amounts are recorded in the first amount column. Thus, the total expenses ($3,790) may be subtracted directly from the total revenue ($7,790).

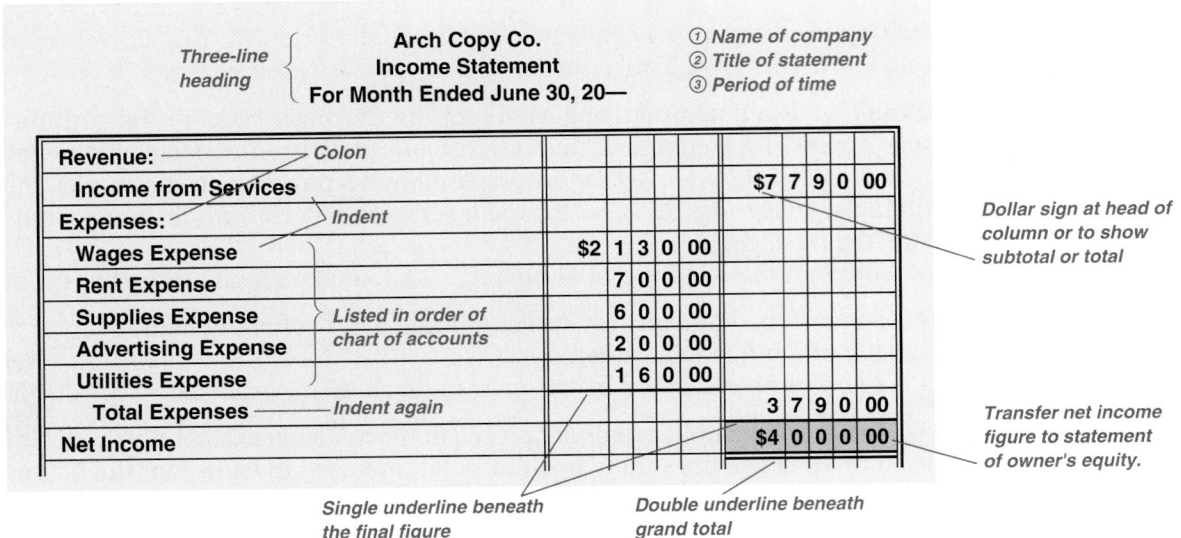

FIGURE 2

FYI
Compare the third line of the income statement heading with the third line of the balance sheet heading shown in Figure 4.

The income statement covers a period of time, whereas the balance sheet has only one date: the end of the financial period. On the income statement, the revenue for June, less the expenses for June, shows the results of operations—a net income of $4,000. To the accountant, the term *net income* means "clear" income, or profit after all expenses have been deducted. Expenses are usually listed in the same order as in the chart of accounts. Revenue and expense amounts are taken directly from the trial balance. If total expenses were greater than the revenue, then a Net Loss would be recorded.

The Statement of Owner's Equity

O B J E C T I V E   6b
Prepare a statement of owner's equity.

We said that revenue and expenses are connected with owner's equity through the financial statements. Now let's demonstrate this by a statement of owner's equity, shown in Figure 3, which the accountant prepares after he or she has determined the net income or net loss on the income statement.

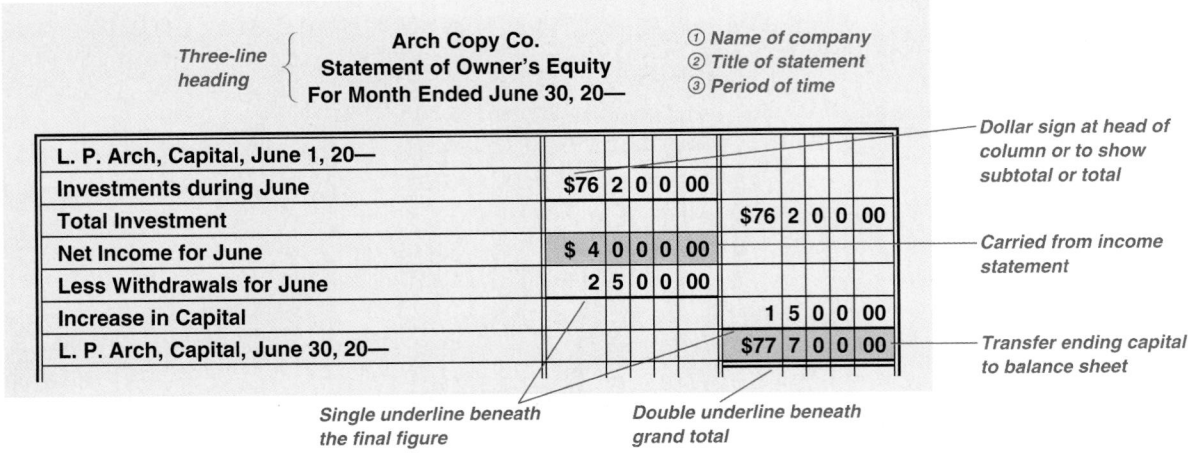

FIGURE 3

The **statement of owner's equity** shows how—and why—the owner's equity, or Capital account, has changed over a stated period of time (in this case, the month of June). Notice the third line in the heading of Figure 3. It shows that the statement of owner's equity covers the same period of time as the income statement.

Now look at the body of the statement. The first line shows the zero balance in the Capital account at the beginning of the month. An investment of $76,200 was made by L. P. Arch: total investment $76,200. Two items have affected owner's equity during the month: A net income of $4,000 was earned, and the owner withdrew $2,500. To perform the calculations smoothly, move to the left-hand column and list these two items, subtracting withdrawals from net income ($4,000 − $2,500 = $1,500). The difference ($1,500) represents an increase in capital. This difference is placed in the right-hand column to be added directly to the total capital. The final figure is the ending amount in the owner's Capital account.

The Balance Sheet

OBJECTIVE 6c
Prepare a balance sheet.

After preparing the statement of owner's equity, we prepare a balance sheet. The **balance sheet** shows the **financial position**, or the condition of a business's assets offset by claims against them as of one particular date. It summarizes the balances of the asset, liability, and owner's equity accounts on a given date (usually the end of a month or year). The balance sheet is, thus, like a snapshot—a picture of the financial condition of the business at that particular date.

The ending capital balance in the balance sheet is taken from the statement of owner's equity. Note that the accounts appear in the same order as in the chart of accounts.

In the **report form** of the balance sheet, the elements in the accounting equation are presented one on top of the other. A balance sheet prepared on June 30 for Arch Copy Co. in report form would look like Figure 4.

Arch Copy Co.
Balance Sheet
June 30, 20—

Assets											
Cash	$34	1	2	0	00						
Accounts Receivable		2	0	0	00						
Prepaid Insurance		3	6	0	00						
Equipment	49	7	2	0	00						
Total Assets						$84	4	0	0	00	
Liabilities											
Accounts Payable						$ 6	7	0	0	00	
Owner's Equity											
L. P. Arch, Capital						77	7	0	0	00	
Total Liabilities and Owner's Equity						$84	4	0	0	00	

——— Carried from statement of owner's equity

FIGURE 4

ERRORS EXPOSED BY THE TRIAL BALANCE

If the debit and credit columns in a trial balance are not equal, then it is evident that we have made an error. Possible mistakes include the following:

- Making errors in arithmetic, such as errors in adding the trial balance columns or in finding the balances of the accounts.
- Recording only half an entry, such as a debit without a corresponding credit, or vice versa.
- Recording both halves of the entry on the same side, such as two debits rather than a debit and a credit.
- Recording one or more amounts incorrectly.

Procedure for Locating Errors

Suppose that you are in a business situation where you have recorded transactions for a month in the account books, and the accounts do not balance. To save yourself time, you need to have a definite procedure for tracking down the errors. The best method is to do everything in reverse, as follows:

- Look at the pattern of balances to see if a normal balance was placed in the wrong column on the trial balance.
- Re-add the trial balance columns.
- Check the transferring of the figures from the accounts to the trial balance.
- Verify the footings and balances of the accounts.

As an added precaution, form the habit of verifying all addition and subtraction as you go along. You can thus correct many mistakes *before* the time comes to prepare a trial balance.

FYI

Even if debits equal credits, this does not necessarily mean that there were no errors in the recording of the transactions. For example, a transaction may have been forgotten, it may have been included twice, or it may have been written for an incorrect amount.

Although using a computer greatly reduces the occurrence of addition and subtraction errors, it does not prevent the occurrence of other kinds of errors, such as recording transactions incorrectly.

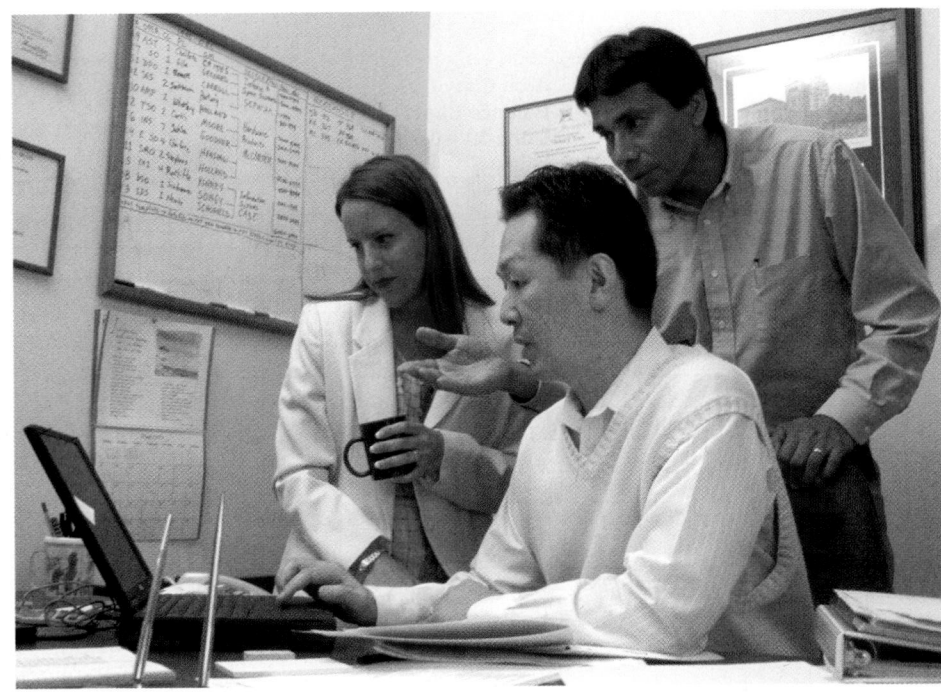

When the trial balance totals do not balance, the difference might indicate that you forgot to record half of an entry in the accounts. For example, if the difference in the trial balance totals is $20, you may have recorded $20 on the debit side of one account without recording $20 on the credit side of another account.

Another possibility is to divide the difference by 2; this may provide a clue that you accidentally recorded half an entry twice. For example, if the difference in the trial balance is $600, you may have recorded $300 on the debit side of one account and an additional $300 on the debit side of another account. Look for a transaction that involved $300 and then see if you have recorded both a debit and a credit. By knowing which transactions to check, you can save a lot of time.

Transpositions and Slides

OBJECTIVE 7
Recognize the effect of transpositions and slides on account balances.

If the difference is evenly divisible by 9, the discrepancy may be either a transposition or a slide. A **transposition** means that the digits have been transposed, or switched around, when the numbers were copied from one place to another. For example, one transposition of digits in 916 can be written as 619.

Correct Number	Number Copied	Difference	Difference Divided by 9
916	619	297	297 ÷ 9 = 33

A **slide** is an error in placing the decimal point; in other words, a slide in the decimal point. For example, $27,000 could be inadvertently written as $2,700:

Correct Number	Number Copied	Difference	Difference Divided by 9
27,000	2,700	24,300	24,300 ÷ 9 = 2,700
64,000	6,400	57,600	57,600 ÷ 9 = 6,400

Or the error may be a combination of a transposition and a slide, as when $450 is written as $54:

Correct Number	Number Copied	Difference	Difference Divided by 9
450	54	396	396 ÷ 9 = 44

Again, the difference is evenly divisible by 9 (with no remainder).

CHAPTER REVIEW

Check out ACE for a Review Quiz at

http://college.hmco.com/ accounting/students/.

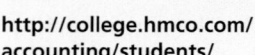

Review of Performance Objectives

1. Determine balances of T accounts having entries recorded on both sides of the accounts.

   Add the amounts listed on each side of the T account. The totals are called footings. To get the account balance, subtract the total of the smaller side from the total of the larger side. Record the account balance on the larger side.

2. Present the fundamental accounting equation with the T account form, and label the plus and minus sides.

Assets	=	Liabilities	+	Owner's Equity	+	Revenue	−	Expenses
+ | −		− | +		− | +		− | +		+ | −
Left | Right		Left | Right		Left | Right		Left | Right		Left | Right

3. Present the fundamental accounting equation with the T account form, and label the debit and credit sides.

Assets	=	Liabilities	+	Owner's Equity	+	Revenue	−	Expenses
+ | −		− | +		− | +		− | +		+ | −
Left | Right		Left | Right		Left | Right		Left | Right		Left | Right
Debit | Credit		Debit | Credit		Debit | Credit		Debit | Credit		Debit | Credit

4. Record directly in T accounts a group of business transactions involving changes in asset, liability, owner's equity, revenue, and expense accounts for a service business.

   The transactions are recorded by first recognizing and classifying the accounts involved. Next, decide whether the accounts involved are increased or decreased, and record the amounts as additions or subtractions in the accounts. The equation must always remain in balance.

5. Prepare a trial balance.

   A trial balance is a list of all account balances in two columns—one labeled Debit and one labeled Credit. The trial balance shows that both sides of the accounting equation are equal. The heading consists of the company name, Trial Balance, and the date.

6. Prepare (a) an income statement, (b) a statement of owner's equity, and (c) a balance sheet.

   (a) An income statement shows the results of operations of a business for a period of time. It includes revenue and expense accounts and reports either a net income or a net loss. (b) A statement of owner's equity shows the activity in the owner's equity, or Capital account, for a period of time. It includes the balance in the Capital account at the beginning of the period plus any additional investments and any increase or decrease in capital as the result of a net income (or a net loss) minus any withdrawals. (c) A balance sheet shows the financial condition of a business at a particular date in time. It summarizes the balances of the asset, liability, and owner's equity accounts on a given date.

7. Recognize the effect of transpositions and slides on account balances.

   An error in a trial balance may be a transposition or a slide. The clue is whether the difference in account balances or trial balance totals is evenly divisible by 9. With a transposition, some digits have been switched around. With a slide, the decimal point has been recorded in the wrong place.

Glossary

Balance sheet A financial statement showing the financial position of an organization on a given date, such as June 30 or December 31. The balance sheet lists the balances in the asset, liability, and owner's equity accounts. (51)

Compound entry A transaction that requires more than one debit or more than one credit to be recorded. (45)

Credit The right side of a T account; to credit is to record an amount on the right side of a T account. Credits represent increases in liability, capital, or revenue accounts and decreases in asset, drawing, or expense accounts. (38)

Debit The left side of a T account; to debit is to record an amount on the left side of a T account. Debits represent increases in asset, drawing, or expense accounts and decreases in liability, capital, or revenue accounts. (38)

Financial position The resources or assets owned by an organization at a point in time, offset by the claims against those resources and owner's equity; shown on a balance sheet. (51)

Financial statement A report prepared by accountants that summarizes the financial affairs of a business. (49)

Footings The totals of each side of a T account, recorded in small, pencil-written figures. (36)

Income statement A financial statement showing the results of business transactions involving revenue and expense accounts over a period of time. (49)

Net income The result when total revenue exceeds total expenses over a period of time. (49)

Net loss The result when total expenses exceed total revenue over a period of time. (49)

Normal balance The plus side of a T account. (36)

Report form The form of the balance sheet in which assets are placed at the top and liabilities and owner's equity are placed below. (51)

Slide An error in placing the decimal point in a number. (53)

Statement of owner's equity A financial statement showing the activity in the owner's equity Capital account, over the financial period. (51)

T account form A form of account shaped like the letter T in which increases and decreases in the account may be recorded. One side of the T is for entries on the debit or left side. The other side of the T is for entries on the credit or right side. (36)

Transposition An error that involves interchanging, or switching around, digits during the recording of a number. (53)

Trial balance A list of all account balances to prove that the total of all the debit balances equals the total of all the credit balances. (47)

QUESTIONS, EXERCISES, AND PROBLEMS

Discussion Questions

1. Explain how a trial balance and a balance sheet differ.
2. Explain why the term *debit* doesn't always mean "increase" and why the term *credit* doesn't always mean "decrease"?
3. What are footings in accounting?
4. How are the three financial statements shown in this chapter connected?
5. What is a compound entry?
6. List two reasons why the debits and credits in the trial balance might not balance?
7. Give an example of a slide and an example of a transposition. Explain how you might decide whether an error is a slide or a transposition.
8. What do we mean when we say that revenue and expense accounts are under the "umbrella" of owner's equity?

Exercises

P.O. 4

Describe transactions.

Exercise 2-1 During the first month of operation, Hale's Auto Supply recorded the following transactions. Describe what has happened in each of the transactions (a) through (k).

Cash		
(a) 3,200	(b)	435
(k) 1,025	(c)	98
	(e)	75
	(g)	900
	(i)	92
	(j)	325

Accounts Receivable	
(h) 615	

Equipment	
(f) 3,720	
(g) 1,835	

Accounts Payable	
(d) 280	
(g) 935	

C. S. Hale, Capital	
	(a) 3,200
	(f) 3,720

C. S. Hale, Drawing	
(j) 325	

Income from Services	
	(h) 615
	(k) 1,025

Rent Expense	
(b) 435	

Utilities Expense	
(i) 92	

Advertising Expense	
(c) 98	

Supplies Expense	
(d) 280	

Miscellaneous Expense	
(e) 75	

P.O. 2,3

Draw T accounts and record the plus and minus signs.

Exercise 2-2 On a sheet of paper, set up the fundamental accounting equation with T accounts under each of the five account classifications, noting plus and minus signs on the appropriate sides of each account. Under each of the five classifications, set up T accounts, again with the correct plus and minus signs and debit and credit, for each of the following accounts of Bevin Engine Repair.

Cash	Income from Services
Accounts Receivable	Rent Expense
Equipment	Wages Expense
Accounts Payable	Utilities Expense
A. Bevin, Capital	Supplies Expense
A. Bevin, Drawing	Miscellaneous Expense

P.O. 2,3,4

Record transactions in T accounts.

Exercise 2-3 R. Carter operates Carter's Cleaners. The company has the following chart of accounts:

Assets

Cash
Accounts Receivable
Prepaid Insurance
Cleaning Equipment
Truck
Office Equipment

Liabilities

Accounts Payable

Owner's Equity

R. Carter, Capital
R. Carter, Drawing

Revenue

Income from Services

Expenses

Wages Expense
Truck Expense
Utilities Expense
Supplies Expense
Advertising Expense

Using the chart of accounts above, record the following transactions in pairs of T accounts. Give the T account to be debited first and the account to be credited to the right. Show debit and credit and plus and minus signs. (Example: Received and paid the bill for the month's rent, $480.)

Rent Expense			**Cash**	
Dr.	Cr.		Dr.	Cr.
+	−		+	−
480				480

a. Received and paid the electric bill, $81.
b. Bought supplies on account, $234.
c. Paid for insurance for one year, $420.
d. Made a payment on account to a creditor, $537.
e. Received and paid the telephone bill, $86.
f. Sold services on account, $875.
g. Received and paid the gasoline bill for the truck, $129.
h. Received cash on account from customers, $936.
i. Carter withdrew cash for personal use, $400.

P.O. 4

Classify accounts.

Exercise 2-4 List the classification of each of the following accounts as A (asset), L (liability), OE (owner's equity), R (revenue), or E (expense). Write Debit or Credit to indicate the increase side, the decrease side, and the normal balance side.

Account	Classification	Increase Side	Decrease Side	Normal Balance Side
0. Cash	A	Debit	Credit	Debit
1. Wages Expense				
2. Equipment				
3. J. Roe, Capital				
4. Service Revenue				
5. J. Roe, Drawing				
6. Accounts Receivable				
7. Rent Expense				
8. Fees Earned				
9. Accounts Payable				

P.O. 5

Prepare a corrected trial balance.

Exercise 2-5 At Your Service owned by L. Mas, hired a new bookkeeper who is not entirely familiar with the process of preparing a trial balance. All the accounts have normal balances. Find the errors, and prepare a corrected trial balance for December 31 of this year.

At Your Service
Trial Balance
December 31, 20—

ACCOUNT NAME	DEBIT	CREDIT
Accounts Receivable		9 5 0 0 00
Cash	3 3 0 0 00	
Accounts Payable		8 6 0 0 00
Equipment	26 0 0 0 00	
L. Mas, Capital		26 6 0 0 00
L. Mas, Drawing		1 8 0 0 00
Prepaid Insurance		1 4 0 0 00
Income from Services		33 0 0 0 00
Rent Expense		3 6 0 0 00
Supplies Expense	1 7 0 0 00	
Utilities Expense	3 5 0 0 00	
Wages Expense	17 4 0 0 00	
	51 9 0 0 00	84 5 0 0 00

P.O. 5,6

Prepare trial balance and financial statements.

Exercise 2-6 During the first month of operations, Ace Modeling Agency recorded transactions in T account form. Prepare a trial balance dated March 31 of this year. Prepare an income statement, statement of owner's equity, and balance sheet.

Cash				Accounts Payable		Salary Expense	

Cash

Bal.	8,100	(b)	350
(d)	8,500	(e)	1,600
(j)	7,580	(g)	175
		(h)	3,400
		(i)	2,200

Accounts Receivable

(f)	2,600

Office Furniture

(b)	350

Office Equipment

(a)	2,800

Accounts Payable

		(a)	2,800
		(k)	82

R. Ralston, Capital

		Bal.	8,100

R. Ralston, Drawing

(i)	2,200

Modeling Fees

		(d)	8,500
		(f)	2,600
		(j)	7,580

Salary Expense

(h)	3,400

Rent Expense

(e)	1,600

Utilities Expense

(g)	175

Supplies Expense

(k)	82

P.O. 7

Determine the effects of errors.

Exercise 2-7 The following errors were made in journalizing transactions. In each case, calculate the amount of the error and indicate whether the debit or the credit column of the trial balance will be understated or overstated.

	Amount of Difference	Debit or Credit Column of Trial Balance Understated or Overstated
0. Example: A $149 debit to Accounts Receivable was not recorded.	$149	Debit column understated
a. A $32 debit to Supplies Expense was recorded as $320.		
b. A $255 debit to Accounts Payable was recorded twice.		
c. A $79 debit to Prepaid Insurance was not recorded.		
d. A $63 credit to Cash was not recorded.		
e. A $180 debit to Equipment was recorded twice.		
f. A $54 debit to Utilities Expense was recorded as $45.		

P.O. 7

Determine the effects of errors.

Exercise 2-8 Which of the following errors would cause a trial balance to have unequal totals? As a result of the errors, which accounts are overstated (by how much) or understated (by how much)?

a. A purchase of office equipment for $280 was recorded as a debit to Office Equipment for $28 and a credit to Cash for $28.
b. A payment of $160 to a creditor was debited to Accounts Receivable and credited to Cash for $160 each.
c. A purchase of supplies for $105 was recorded as a debit to Equipment for $105 and a credit to Cash for $105.
d. A payment of $96 to a creditor was recorded as a debit to Accounts Payable for $96 and a credit to Cash for $69.

REFLECTING ON
THE WORLD WIDE WEB

Let's review what you've learned in this chapter and apply it to Fox Entertainment Group, Inc. as you look at the SEC report, you'll see how Fox recorded the sale of THN. Recall the steps in analyzing a business transaction in Performance Objective 4. Fox's sale of THN affected only asset accounts, which included a $155 million credit (decrease) to Ownership Interest in THN, a $100 million debit (increase) to Cash, and a $55 million debit (increase) to Notes Receivable. Notice that the total amount of debits and the total amount of credits in this transaction are equal.

Interest in THN			Cash			Notes Rec.	
+	−		+	−		+	−
Debit	Credit		Debit	Credit		Debit	Credit
	155		100			55	

Also recall the fundamental accounting equation: Assets = Liabilities + Capital + Revenue − Expenses. The accounting equation has remained unchanged by the transaction above. Only asset accounts were affected, and because total debits and total credits to assets were equal, the equation remained unchanged.

1. Is a trial balance included here? Why or why not?
2. What was Fox Entertainment's Cash balance for the years ending in June 30, 2000, and June 30, 2001? Place these amounts as the beginning and ending balances in a T account for Cash, and then record the sale of THN in this account. If only one other cash transaction took place during the year, what might it have been and for how much?

CONSIDER AND COMMUNICATE

Another accounting student is having difficulty understanding how the fundamental accounting equation stays in balance in a compound entry with one debit and two credits. Consider, for example, that a business bought equipment for $6,000, paid $2,000 in cash, and placed the remainder on account.

This means that there are two credits and one debit—one debit and one credit on the left side of the equation and the other credit on the right side of the equation. How does the equation stay in balance?

WHAT'S WRONG WITH THIS PICTURE?

An accounting tutor has drawn the following T accounts for two of her students who are having trouble understanding where the plus and minus signs are placed as well as where debit and credit go. What would you do to assist these students and their tutor?

Assets		=	Liabilities		+	Owner's Equity		+	Expenses		–	Revenue	
+	–		–	+		–	+		–	+		+	–
Debit	Credit		Credit	Debit		Credit	Debit		Credit	Debit		Debit	Credit

A MATTER OF ETHICS

A new bookkeeper can't find the errors that are causing the month-end trial balance for his firm to be out of balance. The bookkeeper is too shy to ask for help at the office, so he takes the financial records home and asks his mother, a retired bookkeeper, to help him locate the errors. Discuss the ethics of the situation in which he has placed himself.

PROBLEM SET A

For additional help, see the demonstration problems at the beginning of each chapter in your Working Papers.

P.O. 1,2,3,4

Problem 2-1A During February of this year, R. Bullard established Bullard Shoe Repair. The following asset, liability, and owner's equity accounts are included in the chart of accounts:

Cash	Accounts Payable
Shop Equipment	R. Bullard, Capital
Store Equipment	Supplies Expense
Office Equipment	

The following transactions occurred during the month of February:

a. Bullard deposited $25,000 cash in a bank account in the name of the business.
b. Bought shop equipment for cash, $1,835, Ck. No. 1000.
c. Bought supplies on account from Miller Company, $325.
d. Bought store shelving from Kelley Hardware on account, $749.
e. Bought office equipment from Steven's Office Supply, $425, paying $125 in cash and placing the balance on account, Ck. No. 1001.
f. Paid on account to Kelley Hardware, a creditor, $150, Ck. No. 1002.
g. Bullard invested his personal leather working tools in the business with a fair market value of $500.

Check Figure

Cash balance, $22,890

Instructions

1. Write the account classifications (Assets, Liabilities, Owner's Equity, Revenue, Expense) in the fundamental accounting equation, as well as the plus and minus signs and Debit and Credit.
2. Write the account names on the T accounts under the classifications, place the plus and minus signs for each T account, and label the debit and credit sides of the T accounts.
3. Record the amounts in the proper positions in the T accounts. Write the letter next to each entry to identify the transaction.
4. Foot and balance accounts.

P.O. 1,2,3,4,5

Problem 2-2A J. Cox established Cox Photo Service during June of this year. The accountant prepared the following chart of accounts:

Assets

Cash
Computer Software
Office Equipment
Neon Sign

Liabilities

Accounts Payable

Owner's Equity

J. Cox, Capital
J. Cox, Drawing

Revenue

Income from Services

Expenses

Advertising Expense
Supplies Expense
Rent Expense
Utilities Expense
Wages Expense
Miscellaneous Expense

The following transactions occurred during the month of June:

a. Cox deposited $18,000 cash in a bank account in the name of the business.
b. Bought office equipment for cash, $950, Ck. No. 1001.
c. Bought computer software from Moss Computer Center, $740, paying $240 in cash and placing the balance on account, Ck. No. 1002.
d. Paid current month's rent, $750, Ck. No. 1003 (Rent Expense).
e. Sold services for cash, $1,272 (Income from Services).
f. Bought a neon sign from Quick Sign Company, $1,535, paying $535 in cash and placing the balance on account, Ck. No. 1004.
g. Received bill from *The Daily* for advertising, $845 (Advertising Expense).
h. Bought supplies on account from Central Supply, $960.
i. Received and paid the electric bill, $220, Ck. No. 1005.
j. Paid on account to *The Daily*, a creditor, $845, Ck. No. 1006.
k. Sold services for cash, $2,334.
l. Paid wages to an employee, $720, Ck. No. 1007.
m. Cox invested his personal computer (Office Equipment) in the business with a fair market value of $1,400.
n. Cox withdrew cash for personal use, $800, Ck. No. 1008.
o. Received and paid the bill for city business license, $45, Ck. No. 1009 (Miscellaneous Expense).

Check Figure

Trial balance total, $25,466

Instructions

1. Record the owner's name in the Capital and Drawing T accounts.
2. Correctly place the plus and minus signs for each T account, and label the debit and credit sides of the accounts.
3. Record the transactions in the T accounts. Write the letter of each entry to identify the transaction.
4. Foot the T accounts and show the balances.
5. Prepare a trial balance, with a three-line heading, dated June 30, 20—.

P.O. 1,2,3,4,5,6

Problem 2-3A Dr. D. Brill, a physical therapist, opened Brill Physical Therapy Clinic. His accountant provided the following chart of accounts:

Assets

Cash
Accounts Receivable
Office Equipment
Office Furniture

Liabilities

Accounts Payable

Owner's Equity

D. Brill, Capital
D. Brill, Drawing

Revenue

Professional Fees

Expenses

Rent Expense
Salary Expense
Utilities Expense
Miscellaneous Expense

The following transactions occurred during July of this year:

a. Brill deposited $20,000 in a bank account in the name of the business.
b. Bought filing cabinets on account from Morris Office Supply (Office Equipment), $380.
c. Paid cash for chairs and carpets (Office Furniture) for the waiting room, $1,015, Ck. No. 1000.
d. Bought a photocopier from BJ's Office Equipment, $700, paying $200 in cash, placing the balance on account, Ck. No. 1001.
e. Received and paid the telephone bill, which included installation charges, $225, Ck. No. 1002.
f. Sold professional services on account, $2,136.
g. Received and paid the bill for the state physical therapy convention, $470, Ck. No. 1003 (Miscellaneous Expense).
h. Received and paid the electric bill, $104, Ck. No. 1004.
i. Received cash on account from credit customers, $818.
j. Paid on account to Morris Office Supply, a creditor, $210, Ck. No. 1005.
k. Paid the office rent for the current month, $725, Ck. No. 1006.
l. Sold consulting services for cash, $1,850.
m. Paid the salary of the receptionist, $735, Ck. No. 1007.
n. Brill withdrew cash for personal use, $1,200, Ck. No. 1008.

Check Figure

Net Income, $1,727

Instructions

1. Record the owner's name in the Capital and Drawing T accounts.
2. Correctly place the plus and minus signs for each T account, and label the debit and credit sides of the accounts.
3. Record the transactions in the T accounts. Write the letter of each entry to identify the transaction.
4. Foot the T accounts and show the balances.
5. Prepare a trial balance as of July 31, 20—.
6. Prepare an income statement for July 31, 20—.
7. Prepare a statement of owner's equity for July 31, 20—.
8. Prepare a balance sheet as of July 31, 20—.

P.O. 1,2,3,4,5,6

Problem 2-4A On July 1, K. Rosa opened Rosa's Quick Clean. Rosa's accountant listed the following chart of accounts:

Cash
Prepaid Insurance
Equipment
Furniture and Fixtures
Accounts Payable
K. Rosa, Capital
K. Rosa, Drawing
Laundry Revenue
Wages Expense

Supplies Expense
Rent Expense
Utilities Expense
Miscellaneous Expense

During July, the following transactions were completed:

a. Rosa deposited $15,000 in a bank account in the name of the business.
b. Bought tables and chairs for cash, $525, Ck. No. 1200.
c. Paid the rent for the current month, $650, Ck. No. 1201.
d. Bought washers and dryers from Forbis Equipment, $15,500, paying $5,000 in cash and placing the balance on account, Ck. No. 1202.
e. Bought laundry supplies on account from Wendel Distributors, $615.
f. Sold services for cash, $972.
g. Bought insurance for one year, $394, Ck. No. 1203.
h. Paid on account to Forbis Equipment, a creditor, $525, Ck. No. 1204.
i. Received and paid the electric bill, $138, Ck. No. 1205.
j. Paid on account to Wendel Distributors, a creditor, $125, Ck. No. 1206.
k. Sold services to customers for cash for the second half of the month, $927.
l. Received and paid the bill for the business license, $35, Ck. No. 1207, (Miscellaneous Expense).
m. Paid wages to an employee, $935, Ck. No. 1208.
n. Rosa withdrew cash for personal use, $500, Ck. No. 1209.

Check Figure

Net Loss, ($474)

Instructions

1. Record the owner's name in the Capital and Drawing T accounts.
2. Correctly place the plus and minus signs for each T account, and label the debit and credit sides of the accounts.
3. Record the transactions in the T accounts. Write the letter of each entry to identify the transaction.
4. Foot the T accounts and show the balances in each account.
5. Prepare a trial balance as of July 31, 20—.
6. Prepare an income statement for July 31, 20—.
7. Prepare a statement of owner's equity for July 31, 20—.
8. Prepare a balance sheet as of July 31, 20—.

PROBLEM SET B

For additional help, see the demonstration problem at the beginning of each chapter in your Working Papers.

P.O. 1,2,3,4

Problem 2-1B During December of this year, G. Edburg established Gerta's Gym. The following asset, liability, and owner's equity accounts are included in the chart of accounts:

Cash
Exercise Equipment
Office Equipment
Video Equipment
Accounts Payable
G. Edburg, Capital
Supplies Expense

During December, the following transactions occurred:

a. Edburg deposited $27,000 in a bank account in the name of the business.
b. Bought exercise equipment for cash, $7,015, Ck. No. 1001.
c. Bought a scanner on account from Hernandez Company, $189.
d. Bought a printer (Office Equipment) on account from Cyber Warehouse, $789.
e. Bought supplies on account from Desk Mates, $275.
f. Edburg invested her video equipment with a fair market value of $3,500 in the business.
g. Made a payment to Hernandez Company, a creditor, $95, Ck. No. 1002.

Check Figure

Balance of Cash, $19,890

Instructions

1. Write the account classifications (Assets, Liabilities, Owner's Equity, Revenue, Expense) in the fundamental accounting equation, as well as the plus and minus signs and Debit and Credit.
2. Write the account names on the T accounts under the classifications, place the plus and minus signs for each T account, and label the debit and credit sides of the T accounts.
3. Record the amounts in the proper positions in the T accounts. Write the letter of each entry to identify the transaction.
4. Foot and balance accounts.

P.O. 1,2,3,4,5

Problem 2-2B B. Wylie established Computer Nerds during November of this year. The accountant prepared the following chart of accounts:

Assets	**Revenue**
Cash	Income from Services
Computer Software	
Office Equipment	**Expenses**
Neon Sign	Advertising Expense
	Supplies Expense
Liabilities	Rent Expense
Accounts Payable	Utilities Expense
	Wages Expense
Owner's Equity	Miscellaneous Expense
B. Wylie, Capital	
B. Wylie, Drawing	

The following transactions occurred during the month:

a. Wylie deposited $20,000 in a bank account in the name of the business.
b. Paid the rent for the current month, $600, Ck. No. 2001.
c. Bought office desks and filing cabinets for cash, $850, Ck. No. 2002.
d. Bought a computer and printer (Office Equipment) from Vega Computer Center for use in the business, $3,500, paying $1,500 in cash and placing the balance on account, Ck. No. 2003.
e. Bought a neon sign on account from Sign Co., $1,600.
f. Wylie invested her personal computer software with a fair market value of $1,000 in the business.
g. Received a bill from *Retailer News* for newspaper advertising, $185.
h. Sold services for cash, $988.
i. Received and paid the electric bill, $188, Ck. No. 2004.
j. Paid on account to *Retailer News*, a creditor, $185, Ck. No. 2005.
k. Sold services for cash, $1,245.
l. Paid the wages to the employee, $810, Ck. No. 2006.

m. Received and paid the bill for the city business license, $65, Ck. No. 2007 (Miscellaneous Expense).

n. Wylie withdrew cash for personal use, $650, Ck. No. 2008.

o. Bought printer paper and letterhead stationery on account from Office Suppliers, $118.

Check Figure

Trial balance total, $26,951

Instructions

1. Record the owner's name in the Capital and Drawing T accounts.
2. Correctly place the plus and minus signs for each T account, and label the debit and credit sides of the accounts.
3. Foot the T accounts and show the balances.
4. Prepare a trial balance with a three-line heading, dated November 30.

P.O. 1,2,3,4,5,6

Problem 2-3B R. Moore, a dentist, opened a clinic in the name of Moore Clinic. Her accountant prepared the following chart of accounts:

Assets

Cash
Accounts Receivable
Office Equipment
Office Furniture

Liabilities

Accounts Payable

Owner's Equity

R. Moore, Capital
R. Moore, Drawing

Revenue

Professional Fees

Expenses

Rent Expense
Salary Expense
Utilities Expense
Miscellaneous Expense

The following transactions occurred during June of this year:

a. Moore deposited $28,000 in a bank account in the name of the business.

b. Bought a facsimile machine from Mason's Equipment for $295, paying $100 in cash, and placing the balance on account, Ck. No. 1001.

c. Bought waiting room chairs and tables (Office Furniture), paying cash, $1,218, Ck. No. 1002.

d. Bought an intercom system on account from Royal Office Supply (Office Equipment), $255.

e. Received and paid the telephone bill, $92, Ck. No. 1003.

f. Sold professional services on account, $1,384.

g. Received and paid the electric bill, $95, Ck. No. 1004.

h. Received and paid the bill for the State Dental Convention, $250, Ck. No. 1005 (Miscellaneous Expense).

i. Sold professional services for cash, $1,885.

j. Paid on account to Royal Office Supply, a creditor, $105, Ck. No. 1006.

k. Paid the rent for the current month, $540, Ck. No. 1007.

l. Paid salary of the receptionist, $725, Ck. No. 1008.

m. R. Moore withdrew cash for personal use, $750, Ck. No. 1009.

n. Received $450 on account from patients who were previously billed.

Check Figure

Net Income, $1,567

Instructions

1. Record the owner's name in the Capital and Drawing T accounts.
2. Correctly place the plus and minus signs for each T account, and label the debit and credit sides of the accounts.
3. Record the transactions in the T accounts. Write the letter of each entry to identify the transaction.

4. Foot the T accounts and show the balances.
5. Prepare a trial balance as of June 30, 20—.
6. Prepare an income statement for June 30, 20—.
7. Prepare a statement of owner's equity for June 30, 20—.
8. Prepare a balance sheet as of June 30, 20—.

P.O. 1,2,3,4,5,6

Problem 2-4B On May 1, B. Brenon opened Self-Service Laundry. His accountant listed the following chart of accounts:

Cash
Prepaid Insurance
Equipment
Furniture and Fixtures
Accounts Payable
B. Brenon, Capital
B. Brenon, Drawing
Laundry Revenue
Wages Expense
Supplies Expense
Rent Expense
Utilities Expense
Miscellaneous Expense

During May the following transactions were completed:

a. Brenon deposited $20,000 in a bank account in the name of the business.
b. Bought chairs and tables (Furniture and Fixtures) paying cash, $880, Ck. No. 1000.
c. Bought laundry supplies on account from Fess Supply Company, $225.
d. Paid the rent for the current month, $485, Ck. No. 1001.
e. Bought washing machines and dryers from Bell Equipment Company, $12,500; paying $2,500 in cash, and placing the balance on account, Ck. No. 1002.
f. Sold services for cash for the first half of the month, $815.
g. Bought insurance for one year, $460, Ck. No. 1003.
h. Paid on account to Bell Equipment Company, a creditor, $800, Ck. No. 1004.
i. Received and paid electric bill, $108, Ck. No. 1005.
j. Sold services for cash for the second half of the month, $635.
k. Paid the wages to the employee, $840, Ck. No. 1006.
l. Brenon withdrew cash for his personal use, $800, Ck. No. 1007.
m. Paid on account to Fess Supply Company, a creditor, $175, Ck. No. 1008.
n. Received and paid bill from the county for sidewalk repair assessment, $220 (Miscellaneous Expense), Ck. No. 1009.

Check Figure

Net Loss, ($428)

Instructions

1. Record the owner's name in the Capital and Drawing T accounts.
2. Correctly place the plus and minus signs for each T account, and label the debit and credit sides of the accounts.
3. Record the transactions in the T accounts. Write the letter of each entry to identify the transaction.
4. Foot the T accounts and show the balances.
5. Prepare a trial balance as of May 31, 20—.
6. Prepare an income statement for May 31, 20—.
7. Prepare a statement of owner's equity for May 31, 20—.
8. Prepare a balance sheet as of May 31, 20—.

3

The General Journal and the General Ledger

Performance Objectives

After you have completed this chapter, you will be able to do the following:

1. Record a group of transactions pertaining to a service enterprise in a two-column general journal.

2. Post entries from a two-column general journal to general ledger accounts.

3. Prepare a trial balance from the ledger accounts.

4. Correct entries using the ruling method.

5. Correct entries using the correcting entry method.

Recall that *recording* is a step in the definition of accounting. Here we introduce the *journal* as the official record of business transactions. We have recorded business transactions as debits and credits to T accounts. We introduced T accounts because, in the process of formulating debits and credits for business transactions, it's easier to visualize these debits and credits as the plus and minus sides of the T accounts involved. **Formulating the appropriate transaction debits and credits is the most**

important element in the accounting process. It represents the very basic foundation of accounting, and all the structure represented by financial statements and other reports is entirely dependent upon it. After determining the debits and credits, the accountant records the transaction in a journal and a ledger.

The initial steps in the accounting process are

1. Record business transactions in a journal.
2. Post entries to accounts in the ledger.
3. Prepare a trial balance.

In this chapter, we present the general journal and the posting procedure.

THE GENERAL JOURNAL

We have seen that an accountant must keep a written record of each transaction. You could record the transactions directly in T accounts; however, only part of the transaction would be listed in each T account. A **journal** is a book in which business transactions are recorded as they happen. In the journal, both the debits and the credits of the entire transaction are recorded in one place. Actually, the journal is a diary for the business, in which you record in day-by-day order all the events involving financial affairs. A journal is called a *book of original entry*. In other words, a transaction is always recorded first in the journal. The process of recording a business transaction in the journal is called **journalizing**. The information about transactions comes from business papers, such as checks, invoices, receipts, letters, and memos. These **source documents** furnish proof (objective evidence) that a transaction has taken place, and they should be identified in the journal entry whenever possible. The basic form of journal is the **two-column general journal**. The term *two-column* refers to the two columns used for debit and credit amounts.

As an example of journalizing business transactions, let's use the transactions for Arch Copy Co. The pages of the journal are numbered in consecutive order. This is the first page, and so we write a 1 in the space for the page number. Also, we must write the date of each transaction. Let's begin with the first entry.

OBJECTIVE 1
Record a group of transactions pertaining to a service enterprise in a two-column general journal.

Transaction (a) June 1: L. P. Arch deposited $70,000 in a bank account in the name of Arch Copy Co.

First, we will show the complete journal entry.

GENERAL JOURNAL   PAGE ___1___

	DATE		DESCRIPTION	POST. REF.	DEBIT	CREDIT	
1	20–						1
2	June	1	Cash		70 0 0 0 00		2
3			L. P. Arch, Capital			70 0 0 0 00	3
4			Original investment by Arch				4
5			in Arch Copy Co.				5

To explain the entry, we break it down line by line. On the first line at the top of the page, we record the page number where indicated. On line one, we record the year in the left part of the Date column. On the second line, we record the month in the left part of the Date column and the day of the month in the right part of the Date column. We don't have to repeat the year and month until we start a new page, or until the year or month changes. (Because our illustrations are separated, however, the month may be repeated to eliminate confusion.)

| | GENERAL JOURNAL | | Page number | PAGE →1 |

	DATE		DESCRIPTION	POST. REF.	DEBIT	CREDIT	
1	20–						1
2	June	1	} Date				2
3							3

Decide which accounts should be debited and credited. We do this by first deciding which accounts are involved and whether they are increased or decreased. We then visualize the accounts and their plus and minus sides.

Cash is involved in our example. Cash is an asset because it falls within the definition of "things owned." Cash is increased, and the increase side of Cash is the left or debit side. So we debit Cash $70,000.

L. P. Arch, Capital, is involved. L. P. Arch, Capital, is an owner's equity account because it represents the owner's investment. L. P. Arch, Capital, is increased, and the increase side of Capital is the right or credit side. So we credit L. P. Arch, Capital $70,000. Let's show these entries by referring to our reliable fundamental accounting equation with the accompanying T accounts:

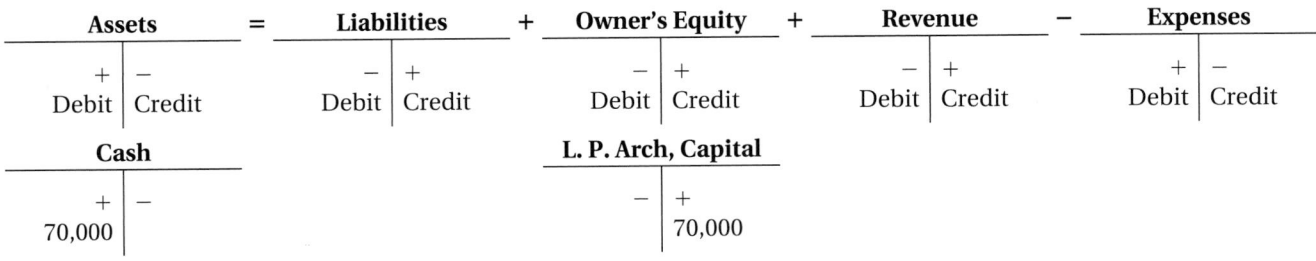

You perform this process mentally. If the transaction is more complicated, draw the T accounts on scratch paper. Using T accounts is the accountant's way of drawing a picture of the transaction. You must get into the T account habit; it will be a great help to you in the future.

Always record the debit part of the entry first. Enter the account title—in this case, Cash—in the Description column. Record the amount—$70,000—in the Debit amount column.

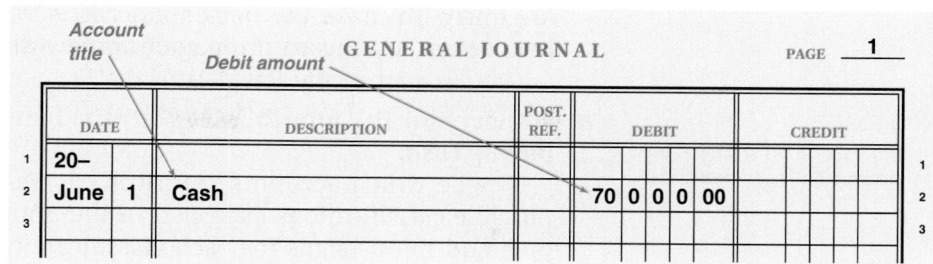

GENERAL JOURNAL   PAGE ___1___

	DATE		DESCRIPTION	POST. REF.	DEBIT	CREDIT	
1	20–						1
2	June	1	Cash		70 0 0 0 00		2
3							3

Account title → *Debit amount* →

Next, record the credit part of the entry. Enter the account title—in this case, L. P. Arch, Capital—on the line below the debit in the Description column, indented about one-half inch. On the same line, write the amount in the Credit column.

GENERAL JOURNAL   PAGE ___1___

	DATE		DESCRIPTION	POST. REF.	DEBIT	CREDIT	
1	20–						1
2	June	1	Cash		70 0 0 0 00		2
3			L. P. Arch, Capital			70 0 0 0 00	3
4							4
5							5
6							6

Indent the account title that is credited

You should now write a brief explanation, in which you should refer to business papers, giving such information as check numbers, receipt numbers, or invoice numbers. You may also list names of charge customers or creditors, or terms of payment. Enter the explanation below the credit entry, indented an additional one-half inch.

GENERAL JOURNAL   PAGE ___1___

	DATE		DESCRIPTION	POST. REF.	DEBIT	CREDIT	
1	20–						1
2	June	1	Cash		70 0 0 0 00		2
3			L. P. Arch, Capital			70 0 0 0 00	3
4			Original investment by				4
5			Arch in Arch Copy Co.				5
6							6

Indent again for the explanation

For an entry in the general journal to be complete, it must contain (1) the date, (2) a debit entry, (3) a credit entry, and (4) an explanation. To anyone thoroughly familiar with the accounts, the explanation may seem quite obvious. Nevertheless, record the explanation as a required, integral part of the entry. To make the journal entries easier to read, leave one blank line between each transaction in your homework.

Transaction (b) June 2: Arch Copy Co. bought equipment costing $33,000 paying cash.

Decide which accounts are involved. Next, determine which of the five possible classifications each part of the transaction applies to. Visualize the plus and minus signs for each classification. Decide whether the accounts are increased or decreased. When you use T accounts to analyze the transaction, the results are as follows:

Equipment			Cash	
+	−		+	−
Debit	Credit		Debit	Credit
33,000				33,000

Now journalize this analysis below the first transaction. Record the day of the month in the Date column. Remember, you do not have to record the month and year again until the month or year changes or you use a new journal page.

GENERAL JOURNAL   PAGE __1__

	DATE		DESCRIPTION	POST. REF.	DEBIT	CREDIT	
1	20–						1
2	June	1	Cash		70 0 0 0 00		2
3			L. P. Arch, Capital			70 0 0 0 00	3
4			Original investment by				4
5			Arch in Arch Copy Co.				5
6							6
7		2	Equipment		33 0 0 0 00		7
8			Cash			33 0 0 0 00	8
9			Bought equipment for cash.				9

Skip a line between entries in homework

Transaction (c) June 3: Arch Copy Co. bought equipment costing $7,000 on credit (on account) from Melton Office Supply. Again start with the T accounts.

Equipment			Accounts Payable	
+	−		−	+
Debit	Credit		Debit	Credit
7,000				7,000

After skipping a line in the journal, record the day of the month and then the entry. In journalizing a transaction involving Accounts Payable, always state the name of the creditor in the explanation. Similarly, in journalizing a transaction involving Accounts Receivable, always state the name of the customer who charged the amount in the explanation.

GENERAL JOURNAL PAGE ___1___

	DATE	DESCRIPTION	POST. REF.	DEBIT	CREDIT	
10						10
11	3	Equipment		7 0 0 0 00		11
12		Accounts Payable			7 0 0 0 00	12
13		Bought equipment on				13
14		account from Melton				14
15		Office Supply.				15

When a business buys an asset, the asset should be recorded at the actual cost (the agreed amount of a transaction). This is called the **cost principle**. For example, suppose that the $7,000 that Arch Copy Co. paid for the equipment from Melton Office Supply was a bargain price, as Melton Office Supply had been asking $8,500 for the equipment. The day after Arch Copy Co. took possession of the equipment, it received an offer of $8,100 from another party, but the offer was declined. Arch Copy Co. *should record the cost of the equipment as the actual amount paid in the transaction that occurred*, which is $7,000. This is true even though the fair market value may indeed be $8,100.

Transaction (d) June 4: Arch Copy Co. pays $2,000 to Melton Office Supply as partial payment to be applied against the firm's liability of $7,000. Picture the T accounts like this:

Cash		Accounts Payable	
+	−	−	+
Debit	Credit	Debit	Credit
	2,000	2,000	

In this case, we see that cash is going out, so we record it on the minus side. We now have a credit to Cash and have completed half of the entry. Next, we recognize that Accounts Payable is involved. We ask ourselves, "Do we owe more or less as a result of this transaction?" The answer is "less," so we record it on the minus, or debit, side of the account.

GENERAL JOURNAL PAGE ___1___

	DATE	DESCRIPTION	POST. REF.	DEBIT	CREDIT	
16						16
17	4	Accounts Payable		2 0 0 0 00		17
18		Cash			2 0 0 0 00	18
19		Paid Melton Office Supply				19
20		on account.				20
21						21
22						22
23						23
24						24

ACCOUNTING MENTOR PROFILE

ERICA KENNEDY
Global Accounting Support Supervisor for a Global Logistics Company

What do Italy, South Korea, China, Greece, Ireland, and Great Britain have to do with accounting? For Erica Kennedy, the global accounting support supervisor for a global logistics company, they are among the countries she has traveled to as she supervises and trains staff on accounting software. In fact, her international company has hundreds of offices in over fifty countries—each using the same accounting software, unique to the industry, that is programmed in-house and tailored for the different fiscal and legal requirements of each country.

Without her solid theoretical foundation in accounting fundamentals, she would not be where she is now. Erica believes that journal entries are the best foundation for understanding accounting. And she in turn considers accounting an essential success factor in the business world, one that has provided endless combinations and possibilities for her career.

Before traveling to a country, she first researches its fiscal and legal requirements. She tailors the software to comply with local regulations, then writes the requirements for the software development team. After testing any changes, she writes the user documentation.

The last, and most rewarding, part of her job is training users to implement the accounting system. She has found this combination of accounting and travel to be rewarding and fascinating.

Erica has also taught accounting students at a community college. She urges her students to complete all homework, develop good habits, and learn to write well—writing is essential in business. And once again, she stresses the importance of understanding and making journal entries. She finds that knowing about financial statement preparation and financial statement analysis are two other extremely valuable skills. Where in the world will these skills take her next?

"I loved geology, but only liked accounting. On the other hand, I felt accounting would provide a better opportunity... to start working professionally. And because of accounting, I get to do what I love to do—teach people how to use accounting systems around the world."

Now let's list the transactions for June for Arch Copy Co. with the date of each transaction. The journal entries are illustrated in Figures 1, 2, and 3.

June
1. Arch invests $70,000 cash in her new business.
2. Buys equipment costing $33,000, paying cash.
3. Buys equipment costing $7,000 on credit from Melton Office Supply.
4. Pays $2,000 to Melton Office Supply to be applied against the firm's liability of $7,000.
4. Arch invests her personal equipment in her new business valued at $6,200.
7. Receives cash revenue, $2,520.
8. Pays rent for the month, $700.
10. Buys paper and toner on account from Nebel Computers, Etc., $600.
10. Pays for one-year liability insurance policy, $360.

FIGURE 1

GENERAL JOURNAL   PAGE ___1___

	DATE		DESCRIPTION	POST. REF.	DEBIT	CREDIT	
1	20–						1
2	June	1	Cash		70 0 0 0 00		2
3			L. P. Arch, Capital			70 0 0 0 00	3
4			Original investment by				4
5			Arch in Arch Copy Co.				5
6							6
7		2	Equipment		33 0 0 0 00		7
8			Cash			33 0 0 0 00	8
9			Bought equipment for cash.				9
10							10
11		3	Equipment		7 0 0 0 00		11
12			Accounts Payable			7 0 0 0 00	12
13			Bought equipment on				13
14			account from Melton Office				14
15			Supply.				15
16							16
17		4	Accounts Payable		2 0 0 0 00		17
18			Cash			2 0 0 0 00	18
19			Paid Melton Office Supply				19
20			on account.				20
21							21
22		4	Equipment		6 2 0 0 00		22
23			L. P. Arch, Capital			6 2 0 0 00	23
24			Investment by				24
25			Arch in Arch Copy Co.				25
26							26
27		7	Cash		2 5 2 0 00		27
28			Income from Services			2 5 2 0 00	28
29			Cash revenue.				29
30							30
31		8	Rent Expense		7 0 0 00		31
32			Cash			7 0 0 00	32
33			For month ended June 30.				33
34							34
35		10	Supplies Expense		6 0 0 00		35
36			Accounts Payable			6 0 0 00	36
37			Bought paper and toner				37
38			on account from Nebel				38
39			Computers, Etc.				39

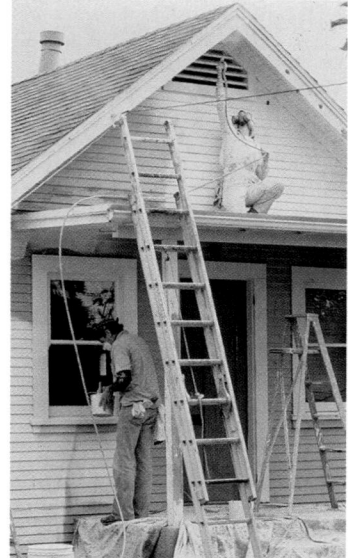

Heavy-duty ladders, spray painting machines, and a truck to carry it all in are part of the equipment used by these house painters.

June   14   Receives bill for newspaper advertising from *City News*, $200.
15   Arch Copy Co. signs a contract with Walker Company to perform printing work and then bills Walker Company $1,050 for services performed.
15   Pays $1,800 to Melton Office Supply as a partial payment on account.

GENERAL JOURNAL   PAGE __2__

	DATE		DESCRIPTION	POST. REF.	DEBIT	CREDIT	
1	20–						1
2	June	10	Prepaid Insurance		3 6 0 00		2
3			Cash			3 6 0 00	3
4			Premium for one-year liability				4
5			insurance policy.				5
6							6
7		14	Advertising Expense		2 0 0 00		7
8			Accounts Payable			2 0 0 00	8
9			Received bill for advertising				9
10			from City News.				10
11							11
12		15	Accounts Receivable		1 0 5 0 00		12
13			Income from Services			1 0 5 0 00	13
14			Billed Walker Company for				14
15			services performed.				15
16							16
17		15	Accounts Payable		1 8 0 0 00		17
18			Cash			1 8 0 0 00	18
19			Paid Melton Office Supply				19
20			on account.				20
21							21
22		18	Utilities Expense		1 6 0 00		22
23			Cash			1 6 0 00	23
24			Paid bill for utilities, Regional				24
25			Power, Inc.				25
26							26
27		20	Accounts Payable		2 0 0 00		27
28			Cash			2 0 0 00	28
29			Paid City News in full.				29
30							30
31		24	Wages Expense		2 1 3 0 00		31
32			Cash			2 1 3 0 00	32
33			Paid wages of part-time				33
34			employee.				34

FIGURE 2

June 18 Receives and pays bill for utilities from Regional Power, Inc., $160.

20 Pays *City News* for advertising, $200 in full. (This bill has been previously recorded.)

24 Pays wages of part-time employee, $2,130.

26 Buys additional equipment costing $3,520 from Melton Office Supply, paying $620 down with the remaining $2,900 on account.

GENERAL JOURNAL   PAGE ___3___

	DATE		DESCRIPTION	POST. REF.	DEBIT	CREDIT	
1	20–						1
2	June	26	Equipment		3 5 2 0 00		2
3			Cash			6 2 0 00	3
4			Accounts Payable			2 9 0 0 00	4
5			Bought equipment on				5
6			account from Melton Office				6
7			Supply.				7
8							8
9		30	Cash		8 5 0 00		9
10			Accounts Receivable			8 5 0 00	10
11			Received from Walker				11
12			Company to apply on account.				12
13							13
14		30	Cash		4 2 2 0 00		14
15			Income from Services			4 2 2 0 00	15
16			Cash revenue.				16
17							17
18		30	L. P. Arch, Drawing		2 5 0 0 00		18
19			Cash			2 5 0 0 00	19
20			Withdrawal for personal use.				20

FIGURE 3

REMEMBER!
Every business transaction requires at least one debit and at least one credit. In a general journal, the debit part of the entry is recorded first. The credit part of the entry is recorded next, followed by a brief explanation of the transaction.

June 30 Receives $850 from Walker Company to apply on amount previously billed.
30 Receives cash revenue, $4,220.
30 Arch withdraws cash for personal use, $2,500.

POSTING TO THE GENERAL LEDGER

You can see that the journal is the *book of original entry*. Each transaction must first be recorded in the journal in full. However, it is difficult to determine the balance of any one account, such as Cash, from the general journal entries. So the **ledger account** has been devised to give us a complete record of the transactions recorded in each individual account. The **general ledger** contains all the accounts. It may be a loose-leaf binder so that you can add or remove pages. The process of transferring information from the journal to the ledger accounts is called **posting**.

The Chart of Accounts

FYI
While charts of accounts vary from business to business, the beginning numbers for assets, liabilities, owner's equity, revenues, and expenses are standard for a service business. Some account numbers are much longer than three digits.

The accounts in the ledger are arranged according to the chart of accounts, which **is the official list of the ledger accounts in which transactions of a business are recorded**. Assets are listed first, liabilities second, owner's equity

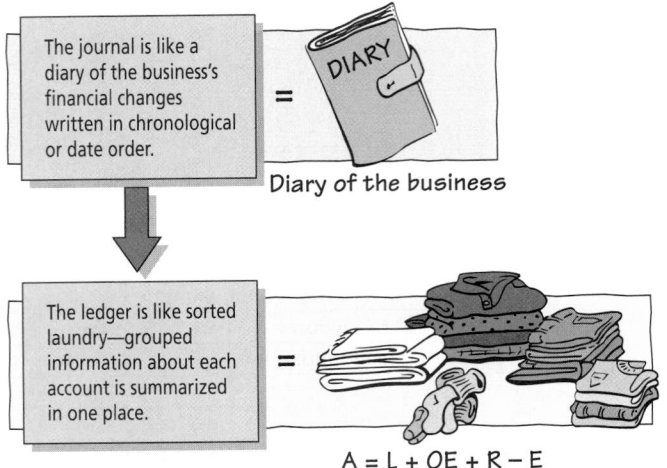

The journal is like a diary of the business's financial changes written in chronological or date order. = Diary of the business

The ledger is like sorted laundry—grouped information about each account is summarized in one place. = A = L + OE + R − E

third, revenue fourth, and expenses fifth. The chart of accounts for Arch Copy Co. is as follows:

Chart of Accounts

Assets (100–199)

111 Cash
113 Accounts Receivable
117 Prepaid Insurance
124 Equipment

Liabilities (200–299)

221 Accounts Payable

Owner's Equity (300–399)

311 L. P. Arch, Capital
312 L. P. Arch, Drawing

Revenue (400–499)

411 Income from Services

Expenses (500–599)

511 Wages Expense
512 Rent Expense
513 Supplies Expense
514 Advertising Expense
515 Utilities Expense

Notice that the arrangement of the chart of accounts consists of the balance sheet accounts followed by the income statement accounts. The numbers preceding the account titles are the **account numbers**. Accounts in the ledger are kept by numbers rather than by pages because it is hard to tell in advance how many pages to reserve for a particular account. When you use the number system, you can add sheets easily. The digits in the account numbers also indicate account *classifications*. For most companies, assets start with 1, liabilities with 2, owner's equity with 3, revenue with 4, and expenses with 5. The second and third digits indicate the positions of the individual accounts within their respective classifications.

The Ledger Account Form (Running Balance Format)

We have been looking at accounts in the simple T account form primarily because T accounts illustrate situations so well. The debit and credit sides are specifically labeled. The T account form is used to solve problems because it is such a good way to picture account activity. However, determining the balance of an account using the T account form is difficult. You must add both columns and subtract the smaller total from the larger. To overcome this disadvantage, accountants generally use the four-column account form with Balance columns in the general ledger. Let's look at the Cash account of Arch Copy Co. in four-column form (Figure 4) compared with the T account form. *Leave the Post. Ref. column blank for now.*

REMEMBER!
To analyze transactions, accountants use T accounts to draw pictures of the transactions. As transactions become more complicated, this is a "must."

Cash

	+		−	
(a)	70,000	(b)	33,000
(f)	2,520	(d)	2,000
(q)	850	(g)	700
(r)	4,220	(i)	360
	77,590	(l)	1,800
		(m)	160
		(n)	200
		(o)	2,130
		(p)	620
		(s)	2,500
			43,470

| **Bal.** | **34,120** | |

GENERAL LEDGER

ACCOUNT **Cash**   ACCOUNT NO. **111**

	DATE	ITEM	POST. REF.	DEBIT	CREDIT	BALANCE DEBIT	BALANCE CREDIT	
1	20–							1
2	June 1			70 0 0 0 00		70 0 0 0 00		2
3	2				33 0 0 0 00	37 0 0 0 00		3
4	4				2 0 0 0 00	35 0 0 0 00		4
5	7			2 5 2 0 00		37 5 2 0 00		5
6	8				7 0 0 00	36 8 2 0 00		6
7	10				3 6 0 00	36 4 6 0 00		7
8	15				1 8 0 0 00	34 6 6 0 00		8
9	18				1 6 0 00	34 5 0 0 00		9
10	20				2 0 0 00	34 3 0 0 00		10
11	24				2 1 3 0 00	32 1 7 0 00		11
12	26				6 2 0 00	31 5 5 0 00		12
13	30			8 5 0 00		32 4 0 0 00		13
14	30			4 2 2 0 00		36 6 2 0 00		14
15	30				2 5 0 0 00	34 1 2 0 00		15

Transaction Amount   Running Balance

FIGURE 4

Note the calculation of the running balance. In the abbreviated form, it looks like this:

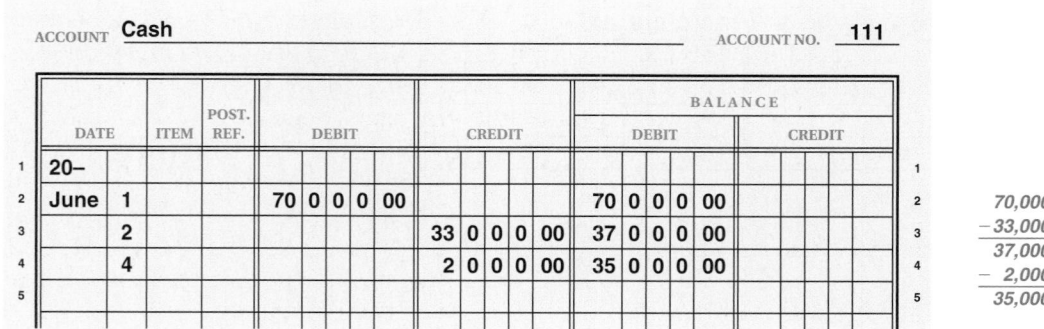

ACCOUNT **Cash**   ACCOUNT NO. **111**

	DATE	ITEM	POST. REF.	DEBIT	CREDIT	BALANCE DEBIT	BALANCE CREDIT	
1	20–							1
2	June 1			70 0 0 0 00		70 0 0 0 00		2
3	2				33 0 0 0 00	37 0 0 0 00		3
4	4				2 0 0 0 00	35 0 0 0 00		4
5								5

70,000
−33,000
37,000
− 2,000
35,000

The Posting Process

OBJECTIVE 2
Post entries from a two-column general journal to general ledger accounts.

In the posting process, you must transfer the following information from the journal to the ledger accounts: the *date of the transaction, the debit and credit amounts,* and the *page number* of the journal. Post each account separately, using the following steps. Post the debit part of the entry first. After locating the account in the ledger, you need to do the following steps.

1. Write the date of the transaction in the account's Date column.
2. Write the amount of the transaction in the Debit or Credit column and enter the new balance in the Balance columns under Debit or Credit.

3. Write the page number of the journal in the Post. Ref. column of the ledger account. (This is a **cross-reference**; it tells where the amount came from.)
4. Record the ledger account number in the Post. Ref. column of the journal. (This is also a cross-reference; it tells where the amount was posted.)

Entering the account number in the Post. Ref. column of the journal should be the last step. It acts as a verification of the three preceding steps.

The first transaction for Arch Copy Co. is illustrated in Figure 5. Let's look first at the debit part of the entry.

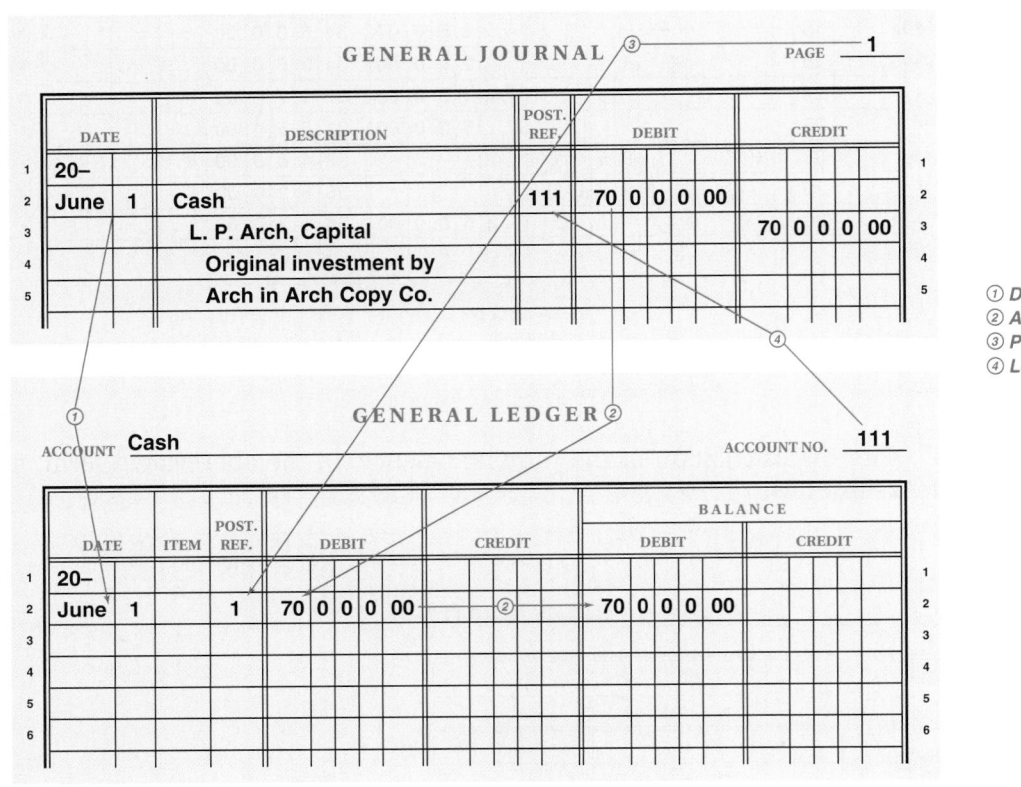

① Date of transaction
② Amount of transaction
③ Page number of the journal
④ Ledger account number

FIGURE 5

Next we post the credit part of the entry, as shown in Figure 6.

The accountant usually uses the Item column only at the end of a financial period. The words that may appear in this column are *balance, closing, adjusting,* and *reversing.* We will explain the use of these terms later.

Incidentally, some accountants use running balance–type ledger account forms that have only one balance column. However, we have used the two-balance-column arrangement to show clearly the appropriate balance of an account. For example, in Figure 5, Cash has a $70,000 balance recorded in the Debit column (normal balance). In Figure 6, L. P. Arch, Capital, has a $70,000 balance recorded in the Credit column (normal balance).

In the recording of the second transaction, shown in Figure 7, see if you can identify in order the four steps in the posting process.

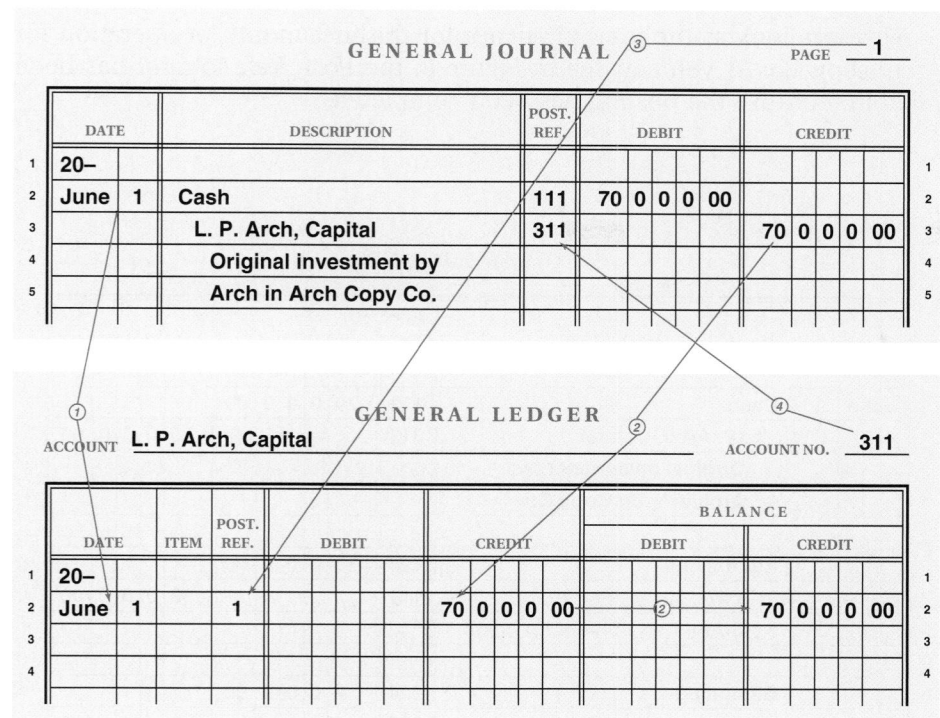

GENERAL JOURNAL   PAGE ___1___

	DATE	DESCRIPTION	POST. REF.	DEBIT	CREDIT	
1	20–					1
2	June 1	Cash	111	70 0 0 0 00		2
3		L. P. Arch, Capital	311		70 0 0 0 00	3
4		Original investment by				4
5		Arch in Arch Copy Co.				5

① *Date of transaction*
② *Amount of transaction*
③ *Page number of the journal*
④ *Ledger account number*

GENERAL LEDGER

ACCOUNT **L. P. Arch, Capital**   ACCOUNT NO. ___311___

	DATE	ITEM	POST. REF.	DEBIT	CREDIT	BALANCE DEBIT	BALANCE CREDIT	
1	20–							1
2	June 1		1		70 0 0 0 00		70 0 0 0 00	2
3								3
4								4

FIGURE 6

FIGURE 7

GENERAL JOURNAL   PAGE ___1___

	DATE	DESCRIPTION	POST. REF.	DEBIT	CREDIT	
7	2	Equipment	124	33 0 0 0 00		7
8		Cash	111		33 0 0 0 00	8
9		Bought equipment for cash.				9
10						10

GENERAL LEDGER

ACCOUNT **Cash**   ACCOUNT NO. ___111___

	DATE	ITEM	POST. REF.	DEBIT	CREDIT	BALANCE DEBIT	BALANCE CREDIT	
1	20–							1
2	June 1		1	70 0 0 0 00		70 0 0 0 00		2
3	2		1		33 0 0 0 00	37 0 0 0 00		3

ACCOUNT **Equipment**   ACCOUNT NO. ___124___

	DATE	ITEM	POST. REF.	DEBIT	CREDIT	BALANCE DEBIT	BALANCE CREDIT	
1	20–							1
2	June 2		1	33 0 0 0 00		33 0 0 0 00		2

REMEMBER!
Do not record account numbers in the Post. Ref. column of the journal until the amounts have been posted to the ledger accounts as either debits or credits.

REMEMBER!
Posting is simply transferring or copying exactly the same date and the debits and credits listed in the journal entry from the journal to the ledger.

Now let's look at the journal entries for the first month of operation for Arch Copy Co. As you can see in Figure 8, the Post. Ref. column has been filled in, because the posting has been completed.

FIGURE 8

GENERAL JOURNAL   PAGE __1__

	DATE		DESCRIPTION	POST. REF.	DEBIT	CREDIT	
1	20–						1
2	June	1	Cash	111	70 0 0 0 00		2
3			L. P. Arch, Capital	311		70 0 0 0 00	3
4			Original investment by				4
5			Arch in Arch Copy Co.				5
6							6
7		2	Equipment	124	33 0 0 0 00		7
8			Cash	111		33 0 0 0 00	8
9			Bought equipment for cash.				9
10							10
11		3	Equipment	124	7 0 0 0 00		11
12			Accounts Payable	221		7 0 0 0 00	12
13			Bought equipment on				13
14			account from Melton Office				14
15			Supply.				15
16							16
17		4	Accounts Payable	221	2 0 0 0 00		17
18			Cash	111		2 0 0 0 00	18
19			Paid Melton Office Supply				19
20			on account.				20
21							21
22		4	Equipment	124	6 2 0 0 00		22
23			L. P. Arch, Capital	311		6 2 0 0 00	23
24			Investment by				24
25			Arch in Arch Copy Co.				25
26							26
27		7	Cash	111	2 5 2 0 00		27
28			Income from Services	411		2 5 2 0 00	28
29			Cash revenue.				29
30							30
31		8	Rent Expense	512	7 0 0 00		31
32			Cash	111		7 0 0 00	32
33			For month ended June 30.				33
34							34
35		10	Supplies Expense	513	6 0 0 00		35
36			Accounts Payable	221		6 0 0 00	36
37			Bought paper and toner				37
38			on account from Nebel				38
39			Computers, Etc.				39
40							40

**FIGURE 8
(continued)**

GENERAL JOURNAL   PAGE ___2___

	DATE		DESCRIPTION	POST. REF.	DEBIT	CREDIT	
1	20–						1
2	June	10	Prepaid Insurance	117	3 6 0 00		2
3			Cash	111		3 6 0 00	3
4			Premium for one-year liability				4
5			insurance policy.				5
6							6
7		14	Advertising Expense	514	2 0 0 00		7
8			Accounts Payable	221		2 0 0 00	8
9			Received bill for advertising				9
10			from City News.				10
11							11
12		15	Accounts Receivable	113	1 0 5 0 00		12
13			Income from Services	411		1 0 5 0 00	13
14			Billed Walker Company for				14
15			services performed.				15
16							16
17		15	Accounts Payable	221	1 8 0 0 00		17
18			Cash	111		1 8 0 0 00	18
19			Paid Melton Office Supply				19
20			on account.				20
21							21
22		18	Utilities Expense	515	1 6 0 00		22
23			Cash	111		1 6 0 00	23
24			Paid bill for utilities, Regional				24
25			Power, Inc.				25
26							26
27		20	Accounts Payable	221	2 0 0 00		27
28			Cash	111		2 0 0 00	28
29			Paid City News in full.				29
30							30
31		24	Wages Expense	511	2 1 3 0 00		31
32			Cash	111		2 1 3 0 00	32
33			Paid wages of part-time				33
34			employee.				34
35							35

GENERAL JOURNAL   PAGE ___3___

	DATE		DESCRIPTION	POST. REF.	DEBIT	CREDIT	
1	20–						1
2	June	26	Equipment	124	3 5 2 0 00		2
3			Cash	111		6 2 0 00	3
4			Accounts Payable	221		2 9 0 0 00	4
5			Bought equipment on				5
6			account from Melton Office				6
7			Supply.				7

FIGURE 8 (continued)

9	30	Cash	111	8 5 0 00		9
10		Accounts Receivable	113		8 5 0 00	10
11		Received from Walker				11
12		Company to apply on				12
13		account.				13
14						14
15	30	Cash	111	4 2 2 0 00		15
16		Income from Services	411		4 2 2 0 00	16
17		Cash revenue.				17
18						18
19	30	L. P. Arch, Drawing	312	2 5 0 0 00		19
20		Cash	111		2 5 0 0 00	20
21		for personal use.				21

FYI

Computerized accounting programs also require journal explanations and will generate posting references.

In making journal entries, you will sometimes find that there are not enough lines at the bottom of a page to record the entire entry. In this case, do not split up the entry; instead, record the entire entry on the next journal page. The ledger accounts and entries for Arch Copy Co. are shown in Figure 9.

FIGURE 9

GENERAL LEDGER

ACCOUNT **Cash** ACCOUNT NO. **111**

	DATE	ITEM	POST. REF.	DEBIT	CREDIT	BALANCE DEBIT	BALANCE CREDIT	
1	20–							1
2	June 1		1	70 0 0 0 00		70 0 0 0 00		2
3	2		1		33 0 0 0 00	37 0 0 0 00		3
4	4		1		2 0 0 0 00	35 0 0 0 00		4
5	7		1	2 5 2 0 00		37 5 2 0 00		5
6	8		1		7 0 0 00	36 8 2 0 00		6
7	10		2		3 6 0 00	36 4 6 0 00		7
8	15		2		1 8 0 0 00	34 6 6 0 00		8
9	18		2		1 6 0 00	34 5 0 0 00		9
10	20		2		2 0 0 00	34 3 0 0 00		10
11	24		2		2 1 3 0 00	32 1 7 0 00		11
12	26		3		6 2 0 00	31 5 5 0 00		12
13	30		3	8 5 0 00		32 4 0 0 00		13
14	30		3	4 2 2 0 00		36 6 2 0 00		14
15	30		3		2 5 0 0 00	34 1 2 0 00		15

ACCOUNT **Accounts Receivable** ACCOUNT NO. **113**

	DATE	ITEM	POST. REF.	DEBIT	CREDIT	BALANCE DEBIT	BALANCE CREDIT	
1	20–							1
2	June 15		2	1 0 5 0 00		1 0 5 0 00		2
3	30		3		8 5 0 00	2 0 0 00		3

**FIGURE 9
(continued)**

ACCOUNT **Prepaid Insurance**   ACCOUNT NO. __117__

			DEBIT	CREDIT	BALANCE	
DATE	ITEM	POST. REF.			DEBIT	CREDIT
20–						
June 10		2	3 6 0 00		3 6 0 00	

ACCOUNT **Equipment**   ACCOUNT NO. __124__

			DEBIT	CREDIT	BALANCE	
DATE	ITEM	POST. REF.			DEBIT	CREDIT
20–						
June 2		1	33 0 0 0 00		33 0 0 0 00	
3		1	7 0 0 0 00		40 0 0 0 00	
4		1	6 2 0 0 00		46 2 0 0 00	
26		3	3 5 2 0 00		49 7 2 0 00	

ACCOUNT **Accounts Payable**   ACCOUNT NO. __221__

			DEBIT	CREDIT	BALANCE	
DATE	ITEM	POST. REF.			DEBIT	CREDIT
20–						
June 3		1		7 0 0 0 00		7 0 0 0 00
4		1	2 0 0 0 00			5 0 0 0 00
10		1		6 0 0 00		5 6 0 0 00
14		2		2 0 0 00		5 8 0 0 00
15		2	1 8 0 0 00			4 0 0 0 00
20		2	2 0 0 00			3 8 0 0 00
26		3		2 9 0 0 00		6 7 0 0 00

ACCOUNT **L. P. Arch, Capital**   ACCOUNT NO. __311__

			DEBIT	CREDIT	BALANCE	
DATE	ITEM	POST. REF.			DEBIT	CREDIT
20–						
June 1		1		70 0 0 0 00		70 0 0 0 00
4		1		6 2 0 0 00		76 2 0 0 00

ACCOUNT **L. P. Arch, Drawing**   ACCOUNT NO. __312__

			DEBIT	CREDIT	BALANCE	
DATE	ITEM	POST. REF.			DEBIT	CREDIT
20–						
June 30		3	2 5 0 0 00		2 5 0 0 00	

FIGURE 9
(continued)

ACCOUNT **Income from Services**   ACCOUNT NO. **411**

	DATE	ITEM	POST. REF.	DEBIT	CREDIT	BALANCE DEBIT	BALANCE CREDIT	
1	20–							1
2	June 7		1		2 5 2 0 00		2 5 2 0 00	2
3	15		2		1 0 5 0 00		3 5 7 0 00	3
4	30		3		4 2 2 0 00		7 7 9 0 00	4
5								5
6								6

ACCOUNT **Wages Expense**   ACCOUNT NO. **511**

	DATE	ITEM	POST. REF.	DEBIT	CREDIT	BALANCE DEBIT	BALANCE CREDIT	
1	20–							1
2	June 24		2	2 1 3 0 00		2 1 3 0 00		2
3								3

ACCOUNT **Rent Expense**   ACCOUNT NO. **512**

	DATE	ITEM	POST. REF.	DEBIT	CREDIT	BALANCE DEBIT	BALANCE CREDIT	
1	20–							1
2	June 8		1	7 0 0 00		7 0 0 00		2

ACCOUNT **Supplies Expense**   ACCOUNT NO. **513**

	DATE	ITEM	POST. REF.	DEBIT	CREDIT	BALANCE DEBIT	BALANCE CREDIT	
1	20–							1
2	June 10		1	6 0 0 00		6 0 0 00		2
3								3

ACCOUNT **Advertising Expense**   ACCOUNT NO. **514**

	DATE	ITEM	POST. REF.	DEBIT	CREDIT	BALANCE DEBIT	BALANCE CREDIT	
1	20–							1
2	June 14		2	2 0 0 00		2 0 0 00		2

ACCOUNT **Utilities Expense**   ACCOUNT NO. **515**

	DATE	ITEM	POST. REF.	DEBIT	CREDIT	BALANCE DEBIT	BALANCE CREDIT	
1	20–							1
2	June 18		2	1 6 0 00		1 6 0 00		2

FIGURE 10

Arch Copy Co.
Trial Balance
June 30, 20—

ACCOUNT NAME	DEBIT	CREDIT
Cash	34 1 2 0 00	
Accounts Receivable	2 0 0 00	
Prepaid Insurance	3 6 0 00	
Equipment	49 7 2 0 00	
Accounts Payable		6 7 0 0 00
L. P. Arch, Capital		76 2 0 0 00
L. P. Arch, Drawing	2 5 0 0 00	
Income from Services		7 7 9 0 00
Wages Expense	2 1 3 0 00	
Rent Expense	7 0 0 00	
Supplies Expense	6 0 0 00	
Advertising Expense	2 0 0 00	
Utilities Expense	1 6 0 00	
	90 6 9 0 00	90 6 9 0 00

Preparation of the Trial Balance

The trial balance is simply a list of the ledger accounts that have balances. A trial balance is presented in Figure 10.

Remember that the trial balance proves only that the total ledger debit balances equal the total ledger credit balances. Even when the debit and credit balances are equal, other types of errors may slip through—for example,

1. Posting the correct debit or credit amounts to the incorrect account.
2. Neglecting to journalize or post an entire transaction.

If the temporary balance of an account happens to be zero, insert long dashes through both the Debit Balance and the Credit Balance columns. We'll use another business, the Becker Company, in this example. Its Accounts Receivable ledger account appears below.

ACCOUNT **Accounts Receivable**   ACCOUNT NO. __113__

DATE	ITEM	POST. REF.	DEBIT	CREDIT	BALANCE DEBIT	BALANCE CREDIT
20–						
Oct. 7		96	1 4 0 00		1 4 0 00	
19		97	2 3 8 00		3 7 8 00	
21		97		1 4 0 00	2 3 8 00	
29		98		2 3 8 00	—	—
31		98	1 6 2 00		1 6 2 00	

Steps in the Accounting Process

1. **Record the transactions of a business in a journal (book of original entry or the day-by-day record of the transactions of a firm).** An entry should be based on some source document or evidence that a transaction has occurred, such as an invoice, a receipt, or a check.
2. **Post entries to the accounts in the ledger.** Transfer the amounts from the journal to the Debit or Credit columns of the specified accounts in the ledger. Use a cross-reference system. Accounts are organized in the ledger according to the account numbers assigned to them in the chart of accounts.
3. **Prepare a trial balance.** Record the balances of the ledger accounts in the appropriate column, Debit or Credit, of the trial balance form. Prove that the total of the debit balances equals the total of the credit balances.

Source Document

A source document can be an invoice, a receipt, a check, etc. We now add an important detail in the recording of a journal entry. This detail consists of listing the related source document number, which is used as a reference for the proof of a transaction. Figure 11 is an example of a source document followed by the journal entry (Figure 12) and ledger accounts (Figure 13). Note how the explanation differs from the one we showed earlier.

FIGURE 11

NEBEL COMPUTERS, ETC.   No. 4-962
220 East Ames Street
Detroit, Michigan 48222

Sold By: __203__   Date: __6/4/20—__
Name: Arch Copy Co.
Address: 1701 East Delaware Street
        Detroit, Michigan 48228
Terms: Net 30 days

QUANTITY	DESCRIPTION	UNIT PRICE		AMOUNT	
20 bx	8 x 11, 20 lb., 10m, copy paper	16	00	320	00
10 ea	No. S2104, toner cartridges	25	14	251	40
	SUBTOTAL			571	40
	SALES TAX			22	86
	SHIPPING			5	74
	TOTAL			600	00

Record in the journal (Figure 12). Note how the explanation includes important information from the source document presented earlier.

GENERAL JOURNAL   PAGE ___1___

	DATE		DESCRIPTION	POST. REF.	DEBIT	CREDIT	
22		10	Supplies Expense	513	6 0 0 00		22
23			Accounts Payable	221		6 0 0 00	23
24			Bought paper and toner				24
25			from Nebel Computers, Etc.,				25
26			Inv. No. 4-962.				26
27							27
28							28
29							29
30							30

FIGURE 12

Post to the ledger (Figure 13).

ACCOUNT **Accounts Payable**   ACCOUNT NO. ___221___

	DATE	ITEM	POST. REF.	DEBIT	CREDIT	BALANCE DEBIT	BALANCE CREDIT	
1	20–							1
2	June 3		1		7 0 0 0 00		7 0 0 0 00	2
3	4		1	2 0 0 0 00			5 0 0 0 00	3
4	10		1		6 0 0 00		5 6 0 0 00	4

Previous postings {

ACCOUNT **Supplies Expense**   ACCOUNT NO. ___513___

	DATE	ITEM	POST. REF.	DEBIT	CREDIT	BALANCE DEBIT	BALANCE CREDIT	
1	20–							1
2	June 10		1	6 0 0 00		6 0 0 00		2
3								3
4								4
5								5

FIGURE 13

CORRECTION OF ERRORS

Errors are occasionally made in recording journal entries and posting to the ledger accounts. Never erase them, because it might look as if you were trying to hide something. The method for correcting errors depends on how and when the errors were made. There are two manual methods for correcting errors; they are

1. The ruling method.
2. The correcting entry method.

Ruling Method—Manual

OBJECTIVE 4
Correct entries using the ruling method.

You can use the ruling method to correct an error in the journal before posting or to correct an error in the ledger after an entry has been posted.

Correcting Errors Before Posting Has Taken Place When an error has been made in recording an account title in a journal entry, draw a line through the incorrect account title in the journal entry, and write the correct account title immediately above. Include your initials with the correction. For example, an entry to record payment of $1,700 rent was incorrectly debited to Salary Expense.

	DATE		DESCRIPTION	POST. REF.	DEBIT	CREDIT	
1	20–						1
2	Mar.	1	~~Salary Expense~~ Rent Expense _DJM_		1 7 0 0 00		2
3			Cash			1 7 0 0 00	3
4			Paid rent for the month.				4

When an error has been made in recording an amount, draw a line through the incorrect amount in the journal entry, and write the correct amount immediately above. For example, an entry for a $230 payment for office supplies was recorded as $320. Include your initials with the correction.

	DATE		DESCRIPTION	POST. REF.	DEBIT	CREDIT	
1	20–				_DJM_ 2 3 0 00		1
2	Apr.	6	Office Supplies		~~3 2 0 00~~	_DJM_ 2 3 0 00	2
3			Cash			~~3 2 0 00~~	3
4			Bought office stationery.				4
5							5

Correcting Errors After Posting Has Taken Place When an entry was journalized correctly but one of the amounts was posted incorrectly, correct the

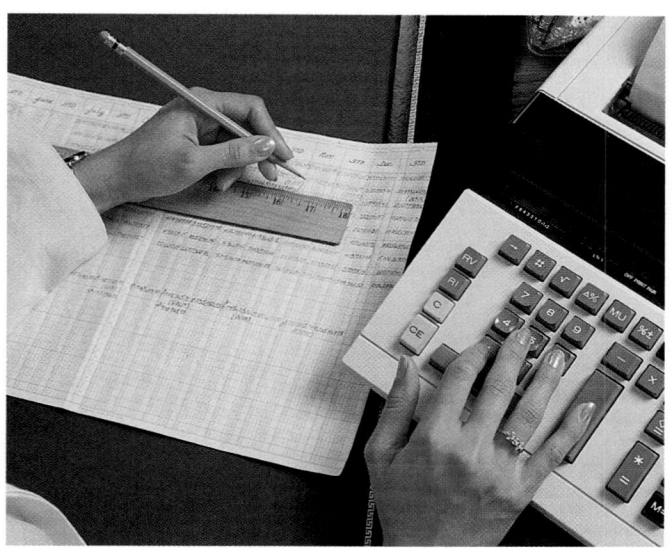

Whether you are preparing accounting records manually or on computer, accuracy is of primary importance. Rapid and accurate ten-key skills are a must for the accountant or bookkeeper.

error by drawing a single line through the amount and recording the correct amount above. For example, an entry to record cash received for professional fees was correctly journalized as $400. However, it was posted as a debit to Cash for $400 and a credit to Professional Fees for $4,000. In the Professional Fees account, draw a line through $4,000 and insert $400 above. Change the running balance of the account and initial the corrections.

FYI
Use a ruler to draw a line through an error.

ACCOUNT	Professional Fees							ACCOUNT NO.	411	

	DATE	ITEM	POST. REF.	DEBIT	CREDIT	BALANCE DEBIT	BALANCE CREDIT	
1	20–				*DJM* ~~4 0 0 0 00~~ 4 0 0 00	*DJM* ~~25 6 0 0 00~~		1
2	Feb. 6		94				29 2 0 0 00	2

Correcting Entry Method—Manual or Computerized

OBJECTIVE 5
Correct entries using the correcting entry method.

You should use the correcting entry method when incorrectly journalized amounts have been posted. There are two correcting entry methods; they are

1. One-step method. Simply make one entry that undoes the error and provides the correct account.
2. Two-step method. The first step reverses the error made by the original entry. The second step includes the correct entry.

The correcting entry should *always* include an explanation. For example, on January 9, a $620 payment for advertising was incorrectly journalized and posted as a debit to Miscellaneous Expense for $620 and a credit to Cash for $620.

FYI
How you correct an error on a computer depends on whether the entry has been posted or not. Before posting, most software programs allow you to replace the incorrect account number or amount. If the entry has been posted, you may have to make a correcting entry to reverse the error, and then record the correct entry.

	DATE	DESCRIPTION	POST. REF.	DEBIT	CREDIT	
1	20–					1
2	Jan. 27	Advertising Expense		6 2 0 00		2
3		Miscellaneous Expense			6 2 0 00	3
4		To correct error of January 9				4
5		in which a payment for				5
6		Advertising Expense was				6
7		debited to Miscellaneous				7
8		Expense.				8

For example, if the original entry was recorded as a debit to Miscellaneous Expense and a credit to Cash, then reverse this entry by debiting Cash and crediting Miscellaneous Expense.

	DATE		DESCRIPTION	POST. REF.	DEBIT	CREDIT	
1	20–						1
2	Jan.	27	Cash		6 2 0 00		2
3			Miscellaneous Expense			6 2 0 00	3
4			To reverse out an incorrect				4
5			entry recorded January 9.				5
6							6
7							7
8							8

	DATE		DESCRIPTION	POST. REF.	DEBIT	CREDIT	
1	20–						1
2	Jan.	27	Advertising Expense		6 2 0 00		2
3			Cash			6 2 0 00	3
4			To correct error of January 9				4
5			in which a payment for				5
6			Advertising Expense was				6
7			debited to Miscellaneous				7
8			Expense.				8

After the correcting entry has been journalized, the accounts are posted as for any other entry. After posting, the account balances should be correct.

CHAPTER REVIEW

Check out ACE for a Review Quiz at

http://college.hmco.com/ accounting/students/.

Review of Performance Objectives

1. Record a group of transactions pertaining to a service enterprise in a two-column general journal.

   Based on source documents, the transactions are analyzed to determine the accounts involved and whether the accounts are debited or credited. For each transaction, total debits must equal total credits. The journal is a book of original entry in which a day-by-day record of business transactions is maintained. The parts of a journal entry consist of the transaction date, the title of the account(s) debited, the title of the account(s) credited, the amounts recorded in the Debit and Credit columns, and an explanation.

2. Post entries from a two-column general journal to general ledger accounts.

The ledger is a book that contains all the accounts, arranged according to the chart of accounts. Posting is the process of transferring information from the journal to the ledger accounts. The posting process consists of four steps:

1. Write the date of the transaction in the account's Date column.
2. Write the amount of the transaction in the Debit or Credit column, and enter the new balance in the Balance columns under Debit or Credit.
3. Write the page number of the journal in the Post. Ref. column of the ledger account.
4. Record the ledger account number in the Post. Ref. column of the journal.

3. Prepare a trial balance from the ledger accounts.

The trial balance consists of a listing of account balances in two columns, one labeled Debit and one labeled Credit. The balances come from the ledger accounts.

4. Correct entries using the ruling method.

The ruling method can be used if an error is discovered before or after an entry has been posted. Draw a line through the incorrect account title or amount, and write the correct account title or amount immediately above. Include your initials with the correction.

5. Correct entries using the correcting entry method.

This method is used if an error is discovered after an incorrectly journalized entry has been posted. If the error consists of the wrong account(s), an entry is made to cancel out or reverse the incorrect account(s) and insert the correct account(s). Initial the correction.

Glossary

Account numbers The numbers assigned to accounts according to the chart of accounts. (78)

Cost principle The principle that a purchased asset should be recorded at its actual cost. (73)

Cross-reference The ledger account number in the Post. Ref. column of the journal and the journal page number in the Post. Ref. column of the ledger account. (80)

General ledger A loose-leaf book containing the activity (by accounts) of a business. (77)

Journal The book in which a person makes the original record of a business transaction; commonly referred to as a *book of original entry*. (69)

Journalizing The process of recording a business transaction in a journal. (69)

Ledger account A complete record of the transactions recorded in an individual account. (77)

Posting The process of transferring figures from the journal to the ledger accounts. (77)

Source documents Business papers, such as checks, invoices, receipts, letters, and memos, that furnish proof that a transaction has taken place. (69)

Two-column general journal A general journal in which there are two amount columns, one used for debit amounts and one used for credit amounts. (69)

QUESTIONS, EXERCISES, AND PROBLEMS

Discussion Questions

1. Why is the journal called a book of original entry?
2. How does the journal differ from the ledger?
3. What is the purpose of providing a ledger account for each account?
4. List by account classification the order of the accounts in the general ledger.
5. Arrange the following steps in the posting process in correct order:
   a. Write the ledger account number in the Post. Ref. column of the journal.
   b. Write the amount of the transaction.
   c. Write the date of the transaction.
   d. Write the page number of the journal in the Post. Ref. column of the ledger account.
6. What does cross-referencing mean in the posting process?
7. Why is a source document important?
8. What is the first number for each of the following accounts in a chart of accounts listed by account number?
   a. Professional Fees
   b. Utilities Expense
   c. J. R. Watson, Capital
   d. Accounts Receivable
   e. Accounts Payable

Exercises

P.O. 1

Label parts of a journal entry.

Exercise 3-1 In the two-column journal below, the capital letters represent where parts of a journal entry appear. Write the numbers 1 through 8 on a piece of paper. After each number, match the capital letter where these items appear with the number of the item.

	GENERAL JOURNAL				PAGE __1__
DATE	DESCRIPTION	POST. REF.	DEBIT	CREDIT	
G					1
H I	J	O	M		2
	K	P		N	3
	L				4
					5

1. Year
2. Month
3. Explanation
4. Title of account debited
5. Ledger account number of account credited
6. Amount of debit
7. Day of the month
8. Title of account credited

P.O. 1

Journalize transactions.

Exercise 3-2 Interior Consulting Service completed the following transactions. Journalize the transactions in general journal form, including brief explanations.

Oct. 7 Received cash on account from Gary Haas, a customer, Inv. No. 312, $930.

15 Paid on account to Morris Brothers, a creditor, $360, Ck. No. 2242.

20 M. Kogle, the owner, withdrew cash for personal use, $900, Ck. No. 2243.

23 Bought store supplies for $98 and office supplies for $64 on account from Warren Office Supply, Inv. No. 1040.

29 M. Kogle, the owner, invested $3,500 cash and $4,500 of his personal equipment.

P.O. 1

Journalize transactions.

Exercise 3-3 Morrow Tutoring Service completed the following transactions. Journalize the transactions in general journal form, including brief explanations.

Mar. 1 Bought equipment for $8,050 from Learning Systems, paying $4,000 in cash and placing the balance on account, Ck. No. 3230.

10 Paid the wages for the first week of March, $1,615, Ck. No. 3231.

15 Sold services for cash to Home School District, $1,230, Sales Inv. 121.

26 Sold services on account to River School, $1,800, Sales Inv. 122.

31 Paid on account to Learning Systems, $650, Ck. No. 3232.

P.O. 2

Post to a ledger account.

Exercise 3-4 The following May journal entries all involved cash.

Increases to Cash—Debits		Decreases to Cash—Credits	
5/1	10,000	5/3	900
5/9	1,700	5/8	700
5/16	5,400	5/12	3,200
5/23	700	5/25	4,600
5/30	4,300		

Post the amounts to the ledger account for Cash, Account No. 111. Assume that all transactions appeared on page 6 of the general journal.

P.O. 2

Determine steps in the posting process.

Exercise 3-5 Arrange the following steps in the posting process in correct order:

a. The amount of the balance of the ledger account is recorded in the Debit Balance or Credit Balance column.

b. The amount of the transaction is recorded in the Debit or Credit column of the ledger account.

c. The ledger account number is recorded in the Post. Ref. column of the journal.

d. The date of the transaction is recorded in the Date column of the ledger account.

e. The page number of the journal is recorded in the Post. Ref. column of the ledger account.

P.O. 3

Prepare a corrected trial balance.

Exercise 3-6 The bookkeeper for Dunn Company has prepared the following trial balance.

Dunn Company
Trial Balance
June 30, 20—

ACCOUNT NAME	DEBIT	CREDIT
Cash		2 5 0 0 00
Accounts Receivable	8 3 0 0 00	
Prepaid Insurance	6 5 0 00	
Equipment	15 3 0 0 00	
Accounts Payable		2 7 0 0 00
M. Dunn, Capital		12 5 0 0 00
M. Dunn, Drawing	4 8 9 0 00	
Professional Fees		17 5 4 0 00
Supplies Expense	6 0 0 00	
Rent Expense	5 0 0 00	
Miscellaneous Expense	1 8 0 0 00	
	32 0 4 0 00	35 2 4 0 00

The bookkeeper has asked for your help. In examining the company's journal and ledger, you discover the following errors. Use this information to construct a corrected trial balance.

a. The debits to the Cash account total $8,000, and the credits total $3,300.
b. A $500 payment to a creditor was entered in the journal correctly but was not posted to the Accounts Payable account.
c. The first two numbers in the balance of the Accounts Receivable account were transposed in copying the balance from the ledger to the trial balance.
d. The $1,500 amount withdrawn by the owner for personal use was debited to Miscellaneous Expense by mistake—it was correctly credited to Cash.

P.O. 4,5

Determine the effect of errors.

Exercise 3-7 Determine the effect of the following errors on a company's total revenue, total expenses, and net income. Indicate the effect by writing O for "Overstated (too much)"; U for "Understated (too little)"; or NA for "Not Affected."

Transactions	Total Revenue	Total Expenses	Net Income
Example: A check for $425 was written to pay on account. The accountant debited Rent Expense for $425 and credited Cash for $425.	NA	O	U
a. $320 was received on account from customers. The accountant debited Cash for $320 and credited Professional Fees for $320.			
b. The owner withdrew $1,000 for personal use. The accountant debited Wages Expense for $1,000 and credited Cash for $1,000.			
c. A check was written for $1,250 to pay the rent. The accountant debited Rent Expense for $1,520 and credited Cash for $1,520.			
d. $1,500 was received on account from customers. The accountant debited Cash for $1,500 and credited the Capital account for $1,500.			
e. A check was written for $125 to pay the phone bill received and recorded earlier in the month. The accountant debited Phone Expense for $125 and credited Cash for $125.			

P.O. 4,5
Journalize correcting entries.

Exercise 3-8 Journalize correcting entries for each of the following errors and include a brief explanation.

a. A cash purchase of office equipment for $510 was journalized as a cash purchase of store equipment for $510. (Use the ruling method; assume the entry has not been posted.)

b. An entry for a $250 payment for office supplies was journalized as $520. (Use the ruling method; assume the entry has not been posted.)

c. A $620 payment for repairs was journalized and posted as a debit to Equipment instead of a debit to Repair Expense. (Use the correcting entry method to journalize the correction.)

d. A $750 bill for vehicle insurance was received and immediately paid. It was journalized and posted as $570. (Use the correcting entry method to journalize the correction.)

REFLECTING ON
THE WORLD WIDE WEB

You have just learned how transactions are recorded in a general journal and then posted to the general ledger. Now, let's go back and apply this to Shaquille O'Neal and his salary. He earned $19.29 million in 2000/2001! (Kevin Garnett with Minnesota earned $19.61 million!)

Questions

1. If you were Shaq's bookkeeper, how would you record the salary he earned for the 2000/2001 year (assuming he gets it all in one paycheck)?

2. Now, let's look at this transaction from the giving end instead of the receiving end. If you were a bookkeeper for the L. A. Lakers, show how you would record the payment made to Shaq for his 2000/2001 salary?

3. You probably need a reality check about now. How much *does* a professional athlete (this means the average person, not Shaquille O'Neal) earn in Los Angeles, California? Go to **http://www.collegegrad.com/salaries/salaries.shtml** to find out.

CONSIDER AND COMMUNICATE

You are the new bookkeeper in a small business. The bookkeeper whose job you are taking is training you on the business's manual system. As he journalizes, he writes the account number into the Post. Ref. column because he thinks it's easier. Then, when he posts, he won't have to be bothered writing the account numbers. How would you explain why he should resist the urge to write the account number in the Post. Ref. column immediately and should instead enter the account number after he has posted the amount to the ledger?

CRITICAL THINKING

You work as an accounting clerk. You have received the following information supplied by a client from the client's bank statement, the client's tax returns, and a variety of other July documents. The client wants you to prepare an income statement, a statement of owner's equity, and a balance sheet for the month of July for Kristin Jay, Jay Company.

Income from Services	8,570	Wages Expense	3,230
Beginning Capital	48,000	Utilities Expense	525
Cash	22,340	Drawing	1,200
Truck	?	Supplies Expense	612
Accounts Payable	?	Equipment	16,148
Rent Expense	1,100	Total Liabilities and Owner's Equity	54,238

PROBLEM SET A

For additional help, see the demonstration problems at the beginning of each chapter in your Working Papers.

P.O. 1

Problem 3-1A The chart of accounts of the Blake School is shown here, followed by the transactions that took place during October of this year:

Assets

111 Cash
113 Accounts Receivable
115 Prepaid Insurance
124 Equipment
127 Furniture

Liabilities

221 Accounts Payable

Owner's Equity

311 R. Blake, Capital
312 R. Blake, Drawing

Revenue

411 Tuition Income

Expenses

511 Salary Expense
512 Rent Expense
513 Gas and Oil Expense
514 Advertising Expense
515 Repair Expense
516 Telephone Expense
517 Utilities Expense
529 Miscellaneous Expense

Oct. 1 Bought liability insurance for one year, $1,650, Ck. No. 1527.
3 Received a bill for advertising from the *Business News*, $420.
4 Paid the rent for the current month, $900, Ck. No. 1528.
7 Received a bill for equipment repair from Quick Service, $188, Inv. No. 436.
10 Received and deposited tuition from students, $5,250.
11 Received and paid the telephone bill, $130, Ck. No. 1529.
15 Bought desks and chairs from Oak Furniture Company, $1,680, paying $800 in cash and placing the balance on account, Ck. No. 1530.
18 Paid on account to the *Business News*, a creditor, $300, Ck. No. 1531.
21 R. Blake withdrew $700 for personal use, Ck. No. 1532.
24 Received a bill for gas and oil from Hess Oil Company, $280, Inv. 682.
25 Received and deposited tuition from students $6,230.

Oct. 27 Paid the salary of the office assistant, $1,010, Ck. No. 1533.

28 Bought a photocopier on account from Discount Office Machines, $1,220, Inv. No. 417.

29 Received $800 tuition from a student who had charged the tuition on account last month.

30 Received and paid the bill for utilities, $460, Ck. No. 1534.

31 Paid for flower arrangements for front office, $52, Ck. No. 1535.

31 R. Blake invested his personal computer and printer, with a fair market value of $1,630, in the business.

Instructions

Record these transactions in the general journal, including a brief explanation for each entry. Number the journal pages 31 and 32.

P.O. 2,3

Problem 3-2A The journal entries for August, Powell Car Care's second month of business, have been journalized in the general journal in your Working Papers. The balances of the accounts as of July 31 have been recorded in the general ledger in your working papers. Notice the word *Balance* in the Item column, the check mark in the Post. Ref. column, and that the amount is in the Balance column only.

Check Figure

Net Income, $9,333

Instructions

1. Write the owner's name, M. Powell, in the Capital and Drawing accounts.
2. Post the general journal entries to the general ledger accounts.
3. Prepare a trial balance as of August 31, 20—.
4. Prepare an income statement for the two months ended August 31, 20—.
5. Prepare a statement of owner's equity for the two months ended August 31, 20—.
6. Prepare a balance sheet as of August 31, 20—.

P.O. 1,2,3

Problem 3-3A Following is the chart of accounts of the K. Haas Clinic.

Assets

111 Cash
113 Accounts Receivable
117 Prepaid Insurance
124 Equipment

Liabilities

221 Accounts Payable

Owner's Equity

311 K. Haas, Capital
312 K. Haas, Drawing

Revenue

411 Professional Fees

Expenses

511 Salary Expense
512 Rent Expense
513 Laboratory Expense
514 Utilities Expense
515 Supplies Expense

Dr. Haas completed the following transactions during July:

July 1 Bought laboratory equipment on account from ALM Surgical Supply Company, $3,460, paying $1,600 in cash and placing the remainder on account, Ck. No. 1730.

3 Paid the office rent for the current month, $1,000, Ck. No. 1731.

5 Received cash on account from patients, $845 (temporary abnormal balance).

6 Bought supplies on account from Ready Supply Company, $318, Inv. 3455.

7 Received and paid the bill for laboratory services, $1,010, Ck. No. 1732.

July 8 Bought insurance for one year, $1,200, Ck. No. 1733.
 12 Performed medical services for patients on account, $3,890.
 15 Performed medical services for patients for cash, $2,320.
 16 Part of the equipment purchased on July 1 was found to be broken. Haas returned the damaged part and received a reduction in his bill, $312, Inv. 3162, Credit Memo No. 141. (Credit Equipment.)
 18 Paid the salary of the part-time nurse, $1,005, Ck. No. 1734.
 24 Received and paid the telephone bill for the month, $152, Ck. No. 1735.
 28 Performed medical services for patients on account, $4,150.
 29 Dr. Haas withdrew cash for his personal use, $1,850, Ck. No. 1736.

Check Figure

Trial balance total, $55,048

Instructions

1. Journalize the transactions for July in the general journal, beginning on page 21.
2. Write the name of the owner next to the Capital and Drawing accounts in the general ledger. The balances of the accounts as of June 30 have been recorded in the general ledger in your Working Papers. Notice the word *Balance* in the Item column, the check mark in the Post. Ref. column, and that the amount is in the Balance column only. This indicates a balance brought forward from a prior page or month.
3. Post the entries to the general ledger accounts.
4. Prepare a trial balance.

Instructions for General Ledger Software

1. Journalize the transactions in the general journal.
2. Post the entries to the general ledger.
3. Print a trial balance as of July 31.

P.O. 1,2,3

Problem 3-4A Jan's Landscaping Service has the following chart of accounts:

Assets

111 Cash
113 Accounts Receivable
117 Prepaid Insurance
124 Equipment

Liabilities

221 Accounts Payable

Owner's Equity

311 J. Dorn, Capital
312 J. Dorn, Drawing

Revenue

411 Landscaping Income

Expenses

511 Salary Expense
512 Rent Expense
513 Gas and Oil Expense
514 Utilities Expense
515 Supplies Expense

The following transactions were completed by Jan's Landscaping Service:

Mar. 1 Dorn deposited $25,000 in a bank account in the name of the business.
 4 Dorn invested her personal gardening equipment, with a fair market value of $1,200, in the business.
 6 Bought a used trailer on account from Rolling Sales, $950, Inv. No. 314.
 7 Paid the rent for the current month, $500, Ck. No. 1000.
 9 Bought a used backhoe from Moving Equipment, $8,200, paying $3,000 in cash and placing the balance on account, Inv. No. 4166, Ck. No. 1001.

Mar. 10 Bought liability insurance for one year, $1,200, Ck. No. 1002.
13 Sold landscaping services on account to Food Chain, $2,320, Inv. 100.
14 Bought supplies on account from Office Fillers, $190, Inv. 5172.
15 Sold landscaping services on account to C. Clayton, $1,460, Inv. 101.
17 Received and paid the bill from Car Care Services for gas and oil for the equipment, $130, Ck. No. 1003.
19 Sold landscaping services for cash to Cass Company, $880, Inv. 102.
22 Paid on account to Moving Sales, a creditor, $500, Inv. 314, Ck. No. 1004.
24 Received on account from Food Chain, a customer, $600, Inv. 100.
28 Sold landscaping services on account to Selger Inc., $1,525, Inv. 103.
29 Received and paid the telephone bill, $194, Ck. No. 1005.
30 Paid the salary of the employee, $2,120, Ck. No. 1006.
31 Dorn withdrew cash for her personal use, $1,200, Ck. No. 1007.

Check Figure

Trial balance total, $38,225

Instructions

1. Journalize the transactions in the general journal, beginning on page 1. Write a brief explanation for each entry.
2. Write the name of the owner on the Capital and Drawing accounts.
3. Post the journal entries to the ledger accounts.
4. Prepare a trial balance dated March 31, 20—.

PROBLEM SET B

For additional help, see the demonstration problem at the beginning of each chapter in your Working Papers.

P.O. 1

Problem 3-1B The chart of accounts of the Alger Academy is shown here, followed by the transactions that took place during December of this year:

Assets

111 Cash
113 Accounts Receivable
115 Prepaid Insurance
124 Equipment
127 Furniture

Liabilities

221 Accounts Payable

Owner's Equity

311 R. Alger, Capital
312 R. Alger, Drawing

Revenue

411 Tuition Income

Expenses

511 Salary Expense
512 Rent Expense
513 Gas and Oil Expense
514 Advertising Expense
515 Repair Expense
516 Telephone Expense
517 Utilities Expense
518 Supplies Expense
529 Miscellaneous Expense

Dec. 1 Bought liability insurance for one year, $1,460, Ck. No. 1627.
11 Received a bill for advertising from the *School News*, $470, Statement No. 4267.
12 Paid the rent for the current month, $1,100, Ck. No. 1628.
13 Received a bill for equipment repair from Electric Services, $260, Inv. No. 547.

16 Received and deposited tuition from students, $3,860.

17 Received and paid the telephone bill, $192, Ck. No. 1629.

18 Bought desks and chairs from School Furniture, $1,420, paying $800 in cash and placing the balance on account, Ck. No. 1630.

20 Paid on account to the *School News*, a creditor, $460, Statement No. 4233, Ck. No. 1631.

21 R. Alger withdrew $850 for personal use, Ck. No. 1632.

26 Received a bill for gas and oil from Otter Oil Company, $184, Inv. 591.

27 Received and deposited tuition from students, $4,572.

31 Paid the salary of the office assistant, $940, Ck. No. 1633.

31 Bought a fax machine on account from Office Machines Company, $692, Inv. 529.

31 Received $820 tuition from a student who had put the tuition on account last month.

31 Received and paid the bill for utilities, $248, Ck. No. 1634.

31 R. Alger invested her personal computer and printer, with a fair market value of $1,475, in the business.

31 Bought supplies, $174, Ck. No. 1635.

Instructions

Record these transactions in the general journal, including a brief explanation for each entry. Number the journal pages 31 and 32.

P.O. 2,3

Problem 3-2B The journal entries for May, Rita's Day Care's second month of business, have been journalized in the general journal in your Working Papers. The balances of the accounts as of April 30 have been recorded in the general ledger in your Working Papers. Notice the word *Balance* in the Item column, the check mark in the Post. Ref. column, and that the amount is in the Balance column only. This indicates a balance brought forward from a prior page or month.

Check Figure

Net Income, $4,994

Instructions

1. Write the owner's name, R. Cederblom, in the Capital and Drawing accounts.
2. Post the general journal entries to the general ledger accounts.
3. Prepare a trial balance as of May 31, 20—.
4. Prepare an income statement for the two months ended May 31, 20—.
5. Prepare a statement of owner's equity for the two months ended May 31, 20—.
6. Prepare a balance sheet as of May 31, 20—.

P.O. 1,2,3

Problem 3-3B Following is the chart of accounts of E. Kennedy, M.D.

Assets

111 Cash
113 Accounts Receivable
117 Prepaid Insurance
124 Equipment

Liabilities

221 Accounts Payable

Owner's Equity

311 E. Kennedy, Capital
312 E. Kennedy, Drawing

Revenue

411 Professional Fees

Expenses

511 Salary Expense
512 Rent Expense
513 Laboratory Expense
514 Utilities Expense
515 Supplies Expense

Dr. Kennedy completed the following transactions during July:

July 1 Bought laboratory equipment on account from Taylor Surgical Supply Company, $3,430, paying $1,430 in cash and placing the remainder on account, Inv. No. 2071, Ck. No. 1930.
3 Paid the office rent for the current month, $1,050, Ck. No. 1931.
5 Received cash on account from patients, $2,653.
6 Bought supplies on account from Fast Supply, $285, Inv. 3455.
9 Received and paid the bill for laboratory services, $895, Ck. No. 1932.
10 Bought insurance for one year, $1,382, Ck. No. 1933.
12 Performed medical services for patients on account, $2,865.
14 Performed medical services for patients for cash, $2,643.
18 Part of the equipment purchased on July 1 was found to be broken. Kennedy returned the damaged part and received a reduction in her bill, $258, Inv. 2071, Credit Memo No. 218. (Credit Equipment.)
20 Paid the salary of the part-time nurse, $995, Ck. No. 1934.
22 Received and paid the telephone bill for the month, $189, Ck. No. 1935.
24 Performed medical services for patients on account, $3,967.
30 Dr. Kennedy withdrew cash for her personal use, $1,200, Ck. No. 1936.

Check Figure

Trial balance total, $38,150

Instructions

1. Journalize the transactions for July in the general journal, beginning on page 21.
2. Write the name of the owner next to the Capital and Drawing accounts in the general ledger. The balances of the accounts as of June 30 have been recorded in the general ledger in your Working Papers. Notice the word *Balance* in the Item column, the check mark in the Post. Ref. column, and that the amount is in the Balance column only. This indicates a balance brought forward from a prior page or month.
3. Post the entries to the general ledger accounts.
4. Prepare a trial balance.

Instructions for General Ledger Software

1. Journalize the transactions in the general journal.
2. Post the entries to the general ledger.
3. Print a trial balance as of July 31.

P.O. 1,2,3

Problem 3-4B Mylo's Landscaping Service maintains the following chart of accounts.

Assets

111 Cash
113 Accounts Receivable
117 Prepaid Insurance
124 Equipment

Liabilities

221 Accounts Payable

Owner's Equity

311 M. Mylo, Capital
312 M. Mylo, Drawing

Revenue

411 Landscaping Income

Expenses

511 Salary Expense
512 Rent Expense
513 Gas and Oil Expense
514 Utilities Expense
515 Supplies Expense

The following transactions were completed by Mylo:

Apr. 1 Mylo deposited $16,000 in a bank account in the name of the business.

   4 Mylo invested his personal gardening equipment, with a fair market value of $1,200, in the business.

   6 Bought a used trailer on account from Discount Sales, $1,100, Inv. No. 415.

   7 Paid the rent for the current month, $610, Ck. No. 100.

   9 Bought a used bulldozer from Brekke Equipment, $9,000, paying $3,000 in cash and placing the balance on account, Inv. No. 3255, Ck. No. 101.

   10 Bought liability insurance for one year, $900, Ck. No. 102.

   13 Sold landscaping services on account to Fulton Homes, $2,363, Inv. 100.

   14 Bought supplies on account from Kreske Supply, $212, Inv. 4281.

   15 Sold landscaping services on account to Baker Inc., $2,941, Inv. 101.

   17 Received and paid the bill from City Tank for gas and oil for the equipment, $95, Ck. No. 103.

   19 Sold landscaping services for cash to Meltor Company, $1,012, Inv. 102.

   22 Paid on account to Discount Sales, a creditor, $500, Inv. 415, Ck. No. 104.

   24 Received on account from Fulton Homes, a customer, $700, Inv. 100.

   28 Sold landscaping services on account to Luis Inc., $1,620, Inv. 103.

   29 Received and paid the telephone bill, $148, Ck. No. 105.

   30 Paid the salary of the employee, $1,874, Ck. No. 106.

   30 Mylo withdrew cash for his personal use, $1,500, Ck. No. 107.

Check Figure

Trial balance total, $31,948

Instructions

1. Journalize the transactions in the general journal that begins on page 1. Write a brief explanation for each entry.
2. Write the name of the owner on the Capital and Drawing accounts.
3. Post the journal entries to the general ledger accounts.
4. Prepare a trial balance dated April 30, 20—.

The Computer Lab

Journalizing, Posting, and Trial Balance

PHASE 1
Meet the New Client

It is June 1. You have been working part time as an accounting clerk. You have just booted up your computer and opened the general ledger package when into your office walks a man. He's wearing a long leather coat and a battered cowboy hat—tools of his trade? He carries a checkbook under one arm and a shoebox under the other arm. The papers sticking out look like invoices.

His first word is "Help! I need someone to make sense of my business!" He introduces himself as Hank Kennedy, the owner and operator of Jeep Jockeys, a local jeep tour company that just began business May 1. Jeep Jockeys is a service business that operates seven days a week through canyons and deserts, giving clients the opportunity to enjoy the sights from the back of a jeep. He employs two full-time drivers (Erica and Brian) and two part-time sales people (Mark and Lindsey) at the kiosk in the middle of town to lure tourists and locals to schedule trips.

PHASE 2
Client Needs

Hank says he needs you and your computer to provide him with two things:

That's an income statement.

1. Financial information at the end of each month (Your general ledger package will provide this.)
   a. How much he earned?
   b. How's his share coming?   A statement of owner's equity!
   c. How is the business doing?

The Balance Sheet!

2. Tour tracking information by month.
   A summary of what tours were taken and how many adults and children participated.

Hmm, Excel

Most income comes from cash and there is no sales tax on services (cash, credit cards, and NO CHECKS except from corporate clients—sometimes conference planners book groups with Jeep Jockeys and pay for the group with corporate funds).

PHASE 3
Information Gathering and Assessment

So far so good, but now you need some data to work with—so you ask to see the checkbook and what's in the box. Hank proudly presents the checkbook and a box full of May's documents: invoices, checks, cash revenue reports summarized by the week, receipts, memos, and notes on envelopes. Hank hands you an adding machine tape listing what he owned and what he owed on May 1. You know you can easily figure out the beginning capital and that what you have in your hand is all you need to create a simple balance sheet. Hank also hands you Jeep Jockeys' brochure, which describes the types of tours available and gives prices for adults and children.

```
Jeep Jockeys
May 1- 20-      0.00*
Cash      4,000.00+
A/R         370.00+
Ppd. Ins. 1,800.00+
Off. Eq.    580.00+
Vehicles 46,000.00+
A/P       6,282.00+
        59,032.00*

H. Kennedy    0.00*
              0.00*
              0.00*
```

As Hank leaves, you shake his hand and assure him that you can do the job and that you will call him when it is ready.

After opening a new client folder for Jeep Jockeys, you begin to organize the documents by date and decide to enter them on an input form before keying them into the general ledger software. As you sort the documents, you see familiar documents—each representing a transaction. You decide to sort them in date order, even though the software will do that automatically. You have before you: the adding machine tape (beginning balances and the start of a chart of accounts).

PHASE 4
Organization and Planning

PHASE 5
Opening Chart of
Accounts and
Beginning Balances

It is clear that the chart of accounts is short to begin with and that you will add account titles as you enter transactions—either manually or from a pick list of Balances accounts. Follow the numbering system set up by your employer.

Assets	100	Revenue	400
Liabilities	200	Expenses	600
Capital	300	(500's will be used later).	

Finally, it is time to enter the beginning chart of accounts and beginning balances into your software. Then you can print a beginning trial balance dated May 1, 20—.

PHASE 6
Enter May's transac-
tions from documents
and/or input form

Key the transactions from the documents. Add account numbers and names as needed according to the numbering system above. SAVE OFTEN.

PHASE 7
Part 1 of Month-End
Wrap-up

Part 1: General Ledger—Unadjusted Financial Statements Print a trial balance dated May 31, 20—. Look at it to see if the numbers make sense, then print the trial balance.

PHASE 7
Part 2 of Month-End
Wrap-up

Part 2: Excel Spreadsheet Jeep Tour Summary Using the information from the four weekly cash revenue reports, devise an Excel spreadsheet headed "JEEP JOCKEYS TOUR SUMMARY" in bold, 16 pt. caps, with a subheading "For the Month of May, 20—" in bold 12 pt. letters. Hank wants to know how many people (adults and children) took which tours this month. You decide to list the three types of tours on the left with Adults and Children as headings under which you will key the numbers. Enter SUM formulas at the bottom of each column and also at the right of each row— essentially cross-footing the spreadsheet (adding both ways).

PHASE 8
Present the information
to Mr. Kennedy

SAVE your file. You decide to include some analysis of the summary below the table to help Hank understand what is on the Excel spreadsheet.

Part of Brochure:

JEEP JOCKEYS TOUR RATES		**Adults**	**Children (under 18)**
			Jeep Jockeys
			340 Jordan Road
			Outback AZ 86336
			928-204-3906
Tour		**Adults**	**Children (under 18)**
Town Tour	1 hour—easy ride with shopping	$15	$8 Must be accompanied by adult
Mild Tour	1 1/2 hours—moderately bumpy with dust	$45 Not recommended for people with bad backs.	$25 Must be accompanied by adult.
Bronco Tour	2 hours—for the hearty and adventurous	$60 Must be fit and free of heart and bone problems.	$40 No children under 12. Must be accompanied by adult.

On all tours bring your camera, sunhat, sun lotion, and water. Our kiosk uptown has cameras, hats, sun lotion, t-shirts, and mugs for your needs, gift, or souvenir buying.

Cash Receipt   5/1/20—
Jeep Jockeys May rent
        $320.00
Check Number 1004

Cash Receipt   5/12/20—
Jeep Jockeys power bill
        $72.00
Check Number 1009

5/7/20—Cash Revenue Report
Week 1
Town 45 Adults, 14 Children
Mild 74 Adults, 6 Children
Bronco 38 Adults,
4 Children
Total week's cash intake
$6,707 (please verify)

Cash Receipt   5/10/20—
Jeep Jockeys May Jeep
payment to Jeep Town
$784.00
Check Number 1008

Cash Receipt   5/1/20—
Jeep Jockeys City Business
License $35
Check Number 1005

Cash Receipt   5/5/20—
Ads in the Outback News, Ck.
No. 1007
        $332.00

5/14/20— Cash Revenue
Report Week 2
Town 48 Adults, 12 Children
Mild 64 Adults, 4 Children
Bronco 42 Adults,
3 Children
Total week's cash intake
$6,436 (please verify)

5/3/20—   0.00*
Supplies Expense
Sun lotion   6.00+
1st Aid Kit   42.00+
                   48.00*
Ck #1006   0.00*
                   0.00*

5/31/20—
Wages paid   0.00*
Ck# 1012   0.◊
Mark   1,600.00+
Lindsey   1,600.00+
Erica   1,764.00+
Brian   1,764.00+
           6,728.00*
                    0.00*

5/31/20—
                    0.00*
Acctg. & Legal   0.00+
Exp.   0.00*
you owe me   179.00+

si   0.00*

5/9/20—
                    0.00*
Outback Office   0.00*
Supply
Office Equipment   0.00*
Scanner   179.00+
                  179.00*
on account
                    0.00*
                    0.00*

5/25/20—
                    0.00*
I took $500
out of the cash   0.00+
register for my
use. Check #1011
hk

Copy of Cash Receipt   5/4
Chamber of Commerce tours
Their Check Number 3005
15 Adults   @ $15 = 225
12 Children @ $ 8 = 96
                   $321.00

Copy of Cash Receipt
                    5/17/20—
Tequa B and B tours   (mild)
Their Check Number 2467
13 Children @ $25 = $325
1 Adult/Complimentary

Cash Receipt   5/16/20—
Jeep Jockeys paid on
account
    $227.00
Check Number 1010

5/21/20—Cash Revenue
Report Week 3
Town 58 Adults, 16 Children
Mild 70 Adults, 8 Children
Bronco 35 Adults, 2
Children
Total week's cash intake
$6,528 (please verify)

Memo   5/19/20-
Harlton Hotel charged tours
on account
31 Adults   @ $15 = 465
12 Children @ $ 8 = 96
                   $561

5/31/20—Cash Revenue
Report Week 4
Town 63 Adults, 10 Children
Mild 72 Adults, 12 Children
Bronco 30 Adults, 4 Children
Total week's cash intake
$6,525 (please verify)

Before a Test Check: Chapters 1–3

PART I: Multiple-choice Questions

_____ 1. Which of the following is not considered an account?

    a. Cash
    b. Prepaid Insurance
    c. Equipment
    d. Assets
    e. Accounts Receivable

_____ 2. In which of the following transactions would an expense be recorded?

    a. Received a bill for utilities.
    b. Paid on an account payable for the electric bill.
    c. Received and paid a bill for repairs.
    d. All of these should be recorded as an expense.
    e. Only a and c should be recorded as an expense.

_____ 3. The ending capital balance appears on which of the following statements?

    a. Statement of owner's equity
    b. Balance sheet
    c. Income statement
    d. Statement of owner's equity and balance sheet
    e. Statement of owner's equity and income statement

_____ 4. On a statement of owner's equity, if beginning capital is $41,000 and there are an additional investment of $6,000, a net loss of $8,000, and owner withdrawals of $15,000, the ending capital amount would be

    a. $70,000.
    b. $24,000.
    c. $40,000.
    d. $54,000.
    e. none of these.

_____ 5. If a $36 cash purchase of supplies is recorded as a $63 debit to Supplies and a $63 credit to Cash, the result will be that

    a. the trial balance will be in balance.
    b. the Supplies account will be overstated.
    c. the Cash account will be understated.
    d. Supplies will be overstated and Cash will be understated.
    e. all of these will be true.

Note: Answers to Before a Test Check begin on page A-1.

____ 6. A person who wanted to know the balance of an account would look
in

    a. the ledger.
    b. the chart of accounts.
    c. the journal.
    d. the source documents.
    e. none of these.

PART II: The Accounting Cycle

Journalizing, Posting, Trial Balance, and Financial Statements

The accounts and their balances, as of December 1 of this year, for Shafer
Services are listed below:

111	Cash	$18,900	311 T. Shafer, Capital	$49,590
112	Accounts Receivable	6,300	312 T. Shafer, Drawing	11,200
114	Prepaid Insurance	1,230	411 Service Income	39,600
124	Equipment	31,200	511 Wages Expense	10,450
221	Accounts Payable	6,340	512 Utilities Expense	2,760
			513 Rent Expense	12,620
			514 Supplies Expense	870

Check Figure

Net Income, $22,040

Instructions

1. Journalize the following December transactions in general journal form on
journal page 31.

    Dec. 1 Sold services for cash, $10,000.
          4 Received and paid the bill for the rent for December, $900, Ck.
            No. 2331.
       11 Received $1,860 on account from customers, Cash Receipt Nos.
            1430–1438.
       19 Sold services on account to J. Lorn, $2,150, Sales Inv. No. 2591.
       22 Received and paid the bill for utilities, $197, Ck. No. 2332.
       23 Bought supplies on account from Office Works, $248, Inv. No.
            2606.
       31 Paid the wages for the month, $1,665, Ck. No. 2333.
       31 Shafer withdrew $1,000 for personal use, Ck. No. 2334.

2. Label T accounts with the above account names.

3. Correctly place the plus and minus signs under all T accounts, and label
the debit and credit sides of each T account.

4. Post the entries to the T accounts by date, and foot and balance the
accounts.

5. Prepare a trial balance as of December 31.

6. Prepare an income statement for the year ended December 31.

7. Prepare a statement of owner's equity for the year ended December 31.

8. Prepare a balance sheet as of December 31.

Adjusting Entries and the Work Sheet

WINDOWS ON THE WORLD WIDE WEB

Whether a small company is doing all its accounting work manually or a large corporation is using a general ledger software package, the process of transforming the information in a company's accounting records into financial statements is the same. Take for instance Activision, a leading producer of video games for systems such as Sony's PlayStation®2, Microsoft's Xbox™, and Nintendo's GameCube™ and Game Boy® Advance. Activision's annual report for 2001 can be viewed at **http://activision.com/en_US/ news_listing_ir/ir_financials_annualreport.html.** Find Activision's balance sheet on page 17 of the annual report. The company reports its property and equipment value as Property and Equipment, net. What does this mean? Review Note 5, Property and Equipment, in the Notes to Consolidated Financial Statements, which begin on page 21. What was the total cost of Activision's property and equipment as of March 31, 2001? How much depreciation had accumulated? As you learn about adjustments for depreciation of equipment, think about the steps that Activision took to determine the amounts reported on the balance sheet in its 2001 annual report. The company used the same process you will learn about here.

In this chapter you will also learn about fiscal periods. After you read about fiscal periods, find out when Activision's fiscal year begins and ends? Where do you find this information in the annual report?

Performance Objectives

REMEMBER!
Accounting steps:

Analyzing: Which accounts are involved?

Classifying: assets, liabilities, capital, revenue, and expenses

Recording: journalizing

Summarizing: financial statements

Interpreting: drawing conclusions

After you have completed this chapter, you will be able to do the following:

1. Define *fiscal period* and *fiscal year.*

2. List the classifications of the accounts that occupy each column of a ten-column work sheet.

3. Complete a work sheet for a service enterprise, involving adjustments for expired insurance, depreciation, and accrued wages.

4. Prepare an income statement, a statement of owner's equity, and a balance sheet for a service business directly from the work sheet.

5. Journalize and post the adjusting entries.

6. Prepare (a) an income statement involving more than one revenue account and a net loss, (b) a statement of owner's equity with an additional investment and either a net income or a net loss, (c) a balance sheet for a business having more than one accumulated depreciation account, and (d) a balance sheet containing the statement of owner's equity information.

A s part of the *summarizing* step in the definition of accounting, here we introduce the work sheet and the financial statements. Now that you are familiar with the classifying and recording phases of accounting for a service business, let's look at the remaining steps in the accounting process.

FISCAL PERIOD

OBJECTIVE 1
Define *fiscal period* and *fiscal year*.

A **fiscal period** is any period of time covering a complete accounting cycle. A **fiscal year** is a fiscal period consisting of twelve consecutive months. It does not have to coincide with the calendar year. If a business has seasonal peaks, it is a good idea to complete the accounting operations at the end of the most active season. At that time, management wants to know the results of the year and where the business stands financially. The fiscal year of a resort that operates during the summer may be from October 1 of one year to September 30 of the next. The government at some levels has a fiscal year from July 1 of one year to June 30 of the following year. Department stores often use a fiscal period from February 1 of one year to January 31 of the next. For income tax purposes, any period of twelve consecutive months may be selected. However, you have to be consistent and use the same fiscal period each year.

THE ACCOUNTING CYCLE

The **accounting cycle** represents the sequence of steps in the accounting process completed during the fiscal period. Figure 1 shows how we introduce these steps on a chapter-by-chapter basis. This outline brings you up to date on what we have accomplished so far and how each chapter fits into the steps in the accounting cycle.

FIGURE 1

REMEMBER!
The yellow color represents source documents, which are evidence of transactions.

Chapter 1
Analysis of Business Transactions
Assets = Liabilities + Owner's Equity
Analysis of Business Transactions
Assets = Liabilities + Owner's Equity + Revenue − Expenses

Chapter 2
Analysis of Business Transactions
Assets = Liabilities + Owner's Equity + Revenue − Expenses
| + | − | | − | + | | − | + | | − | + | | + | − |

Chapter 3
Journalize and Post Business Transactions.
Prepare a Trial Balance.

Chapter 4
Gather the Adjustment Data.
Complete a Work Sheet.
Prepare Financial Statements.
Journalize and Post Adjusting Entries.

Chapter 5
Journalize and Post Closing Entries.
Prepare a Post-Closing Trial Balance.

THE WORK SHEET

FYI
The use of computerized accounting software can eliminate the preparation of the manual work sheet. It does not, however, eliminate the journalizing and posting of the adjusting entries.

The **work sheet** is a working paper used by accountants to record necessary adjustments and provide up-to-date account balances needed to prepare the financial statements. **The work sheet is a tool that accountants use to help in preparing the financial statements.** As a tool, the work sheet serves as a central place for bringing together the information needed to record the adjustments. With up-to-date account balances, the accountant can prepare the financial statements.

First, we present the work sheet form so that you can see the big picture. Next, we describe and show examples of adjustments. Finally, we show how the adjustments are entered on the work sheet and how the work sheet is completed.

For our purposes, we use a ten-column work sheet—so called because two amount columns are provided for each of the work sheet's five major sections. We will explain the function of each of these sections, again basing our discussion on the accounting activities of Arch Copy Co. But first we need to fill in the heading, which consists of three lines: (1) the name of the company, (2) the title of the working paper, and (3) the period of time covered.

Arch Copy Co.
Work Sheet
For Month Ended June 30, 20—

ACCOUNT NAME	TRIAL BALANCE		ADJUSTMENTS		ADJUSTED TRIAL BALANCE		INCOME STATEMENT		BALANCE SHEET	
	DEBIT	CREDIT	DEBIT	CREDIT	DEBIT	CREDIT	DEBIT	CREDIT	DEBIT	CREDIT

Next, we want to point out the account classifications that are placed in each column. We start with the Trial Balance columns and then move across the work sheet, discussing each pair of columns separately.

The Columns of the Work Sheet

OBJECTIVE 2
List the classifications of the accounts that occupy each column of a ten-column work sheet.

Trial Balance Columns When you use a work sheet, you do not have to prepare a trial balance on a separate sheet of paper. Instead, you enter the account balances from the general ledger in the first two amount columns of the work sheet. List the accounts that have balances in the Account Name column in the same order in which they appear in the chart of accounts. Assuming normal balances, the account classifications are listed in the Trial Balance Debit and Credit columns of the work sheet as shown at the top of the next page.

As we move along in this chapter, we will discuss the adjustments. The Adjusted Trial Balance columns contain the same account classifications as the Trial Balance columns. **The Adjusted Trial Balance columns are merely extensions of the Trial Balance columns, plus or minus any adjustment amounts.** If an adjustment is required, the amounts are carried from the Trial Balance columns through the Adjustments columns and into the Adjusted Trial Balance columns.

REMEMBER!
You have already prepared a trial balance. Record the normal balances in the Trial Balance Debit or Credit column.

Account Name	Trial Balance		Adjustments		Adjusted Trial Balance		Income Statement		Balance Sheet	
	Debit	Credit	Debit	Credit	Debit	Credit	Debit	Credit	Debit	Credit
	Assets →				→ Assets					
		Liabilities				→ Liabilities				
		Capital →				→ Capital				
	Drawing →				→ Drawing					
		Revenue →				→ Revenue				
	Expenses →				→ Expenses					

Income Statement Columns An income statement contains the revenues minus the expenses. Revenue accounts have credit balances, so they are recorded in the Income Statement Credit column. Expense accounts have debit balances, so they are recorded in the Income Statement Debit column.

Account Name	Trial Balance		Adjustments		Adjusted Trial Balance		Income Statement		Balance Sheet	
	Debit	Credit	Debit	Credit	Debit	Credit	Debit	Credit	Debit	Credit
	Assets →				→ Assets					
		Liabilities				→ Liabilities				
		Capital →				→ Capital				
	Drawing →				→ Drawing					
		Revenue →				→ Revenue →		→ Revenue		
	Expenses →				→ Expenses →		→ Expenses			

Balance Sheet Columns As you recall, the balance sheet is a statement showing assets, liabilities, and owner's equity. Asset accounts have debit balances, so they are recorded in the Balance Sheet Debit column. Liability accounts have credit balances, so they are recorded in the Balance Sheet credit column. The Capital account has a credit balance, so it is recorded in the Balance Sheet Credit column. Because the Drawing account is a deduction from Capital, it has a debit balance and is recorded in the Balance Sheet Debit column (the opposite column from that in which Capital is recorded).

Account Name	Trial Balance		Adjustments		Adjusted Trial Balance		Income Statement		Balance Sheet	
	Debit	Credit	Debit	Credit	Debit	Credit	Debit	Credit	Debit	Credit
	Assets →				→ Assets →				→ Assets	
		Liabilities				→ Liabilities				→ Liabilities
		Capital →				→ Capital →				→ Capital
	Drawing →				→ Drawing				→ Drawing	
		Revenue →				→ Revenue →		→ Revenue		
	Expenses →				→ Expenses →		→ Expenses			

ADJUSTMENTS

OBJECTIVE 3
Complete a work sheet for a service enterprise, involving adjustments for expired insurance, depreciation, and accrued wages.

Adjustments are a way of updating the ledger accounts. They may be considered *internal transactions*. They have not been recorded in the accounts up to this time because no outside party has been involved. Adjustments are determined after the trial balance has been prepared. Adjustments are a means of fine tuning the accounts to present a more accurate concept of the accounts.

Only a few accounts are adjusted. After you have acquired experience in accounting, these accounts will be easy to recognize. To describe the reasons for making adjustments, let's return to Arch Copy Co. First, we select the accounts that require adjustments. Next, we show the adjustments recorded in T accounts so you can see the effect on the accounts. **However, bear in mind that the adjustments are first recorded on the work sheet.**

Prepaid Insurance

Without adjustments, the financial statements would be out of focus.

The $360 balance in Prepaid Insurance represents the premium paid in advance for a one-year liability insurance policy. One month of the twelve months of premium has now expired, which amounts to $30.

$$12 \text{ months } \overline{)\,\$360}^{\text{\$\,30 per month}}$$

REMEMBER!
Adjustments are recorded in the work sheet first. They will be journalized and posted later in the accounting cycle.

In the adjustment, Arch Copy Co. deducts the expired or used portion from Prepaid Insurance and adds it to Insurance Expense.

REMEMBER!
For the adjustment of insurance, you are given the amount used (expired). So, in the adjusting entry, take the amount used directly out of Prepaid Insurance and put it into Insurance Expense.

	(a)	**Prepaid Insurance**					**Insurance Expense**		
			+	−				+	−
(Old)	Balance		360	Adjusting	30	Adjusting		30	
(New)	Balance		330						

The new balance of Prepaid Insurance, $330 ($360 − $30), represents the cost of insurance that remains paid in advance and should therefore appear in the Balance Sheet Debit column. The $30 amount in Insurance Expense represents the cost of insurance that has expired and should therefore appear in the Income Statement Debit column.

Depreciation of Equipment

FYI
There are several methods of depreciation for assets. Straight-line depreciation is shown here—equal amounts are taken each year. There are also accelerated methods that assign larger amounts to expense in the early years of the life of an asset.

We have followed the policy of recording durable items, such as appliances and fixtures, under Equipment because they will last longer than one year. The benefits of these assets will eventually be used up (the assets will either wear out or become obsolete). Therefore, we should systematically spread out the cost of these assets over their useful lives. That is, we allocate the cost of the equipment as an expense *over its estimated useful life* and call this **depreciation** because such equipment loses its usefulness. A part of this depreciation expense is allotted to each fiscal period. In the case of Arch Copy

Co., the Equipment account has a balance of $49,720. Suppose we estimate that the equipment will have a useful life of seven years, with a trade-in (salvage) value of $6,880 at the end of that time. Using **straight-line depreciation**, we can allocate the cost of an asset, less any trade-in value, evenly over the useful life of the asset. Depreciation for one month is figured like this:

1. Subtract the trade-in (salvage) value from the cost to get the full depreciation.

   $49,720 − $6,880 = $42,840

2. Divide the full depreciation by the number of years in the asset's useful life to get the depreciation for one year.

   $$\frac{\$\ 6,120 \text{ per year}}{7 \text{ years })\$42,840 \text{ full depreciation}}$$

3. Divide the depreciation for one year by 12 to get the depreciation for one month.

   $$\frac{\$\ 510 \text{ per month}}{12 \text{ months })\$6,120}$$

When depreciation is recorded, we do not subtract it directly from the asset account. In asset accounts, such as Equipment or Building, we must keep the original cost recorded in the account. Consequently, the amount of depreciation has to be recorded in another account; that account is Accumulated Depreciation.

Always record the adjusting entry for depreciation as a debit to Depreciation Expense (an income statement item) and a credit to Accumulated Depreciation (a balance sheet item), which increases both accounts. The adjustment in T account form would appear as follows:

(b)

Depreciation Expense, Equipment			Accumulated Depreciation, Equipment	
+	−		−	+
Adjusting 510				Adjusting 510

Accumulated Depreciation, Equipment, is contrary to, or a deduction from, Equipment, so we call it a **contra account**. To show the accounts under their proper headings, let's look at the fundamental accounting equation. Brackets indicate that Accumulated Depreciation, Equipment, is a deduction from the Equipment account. Note that the plus and minus signs are opposite.

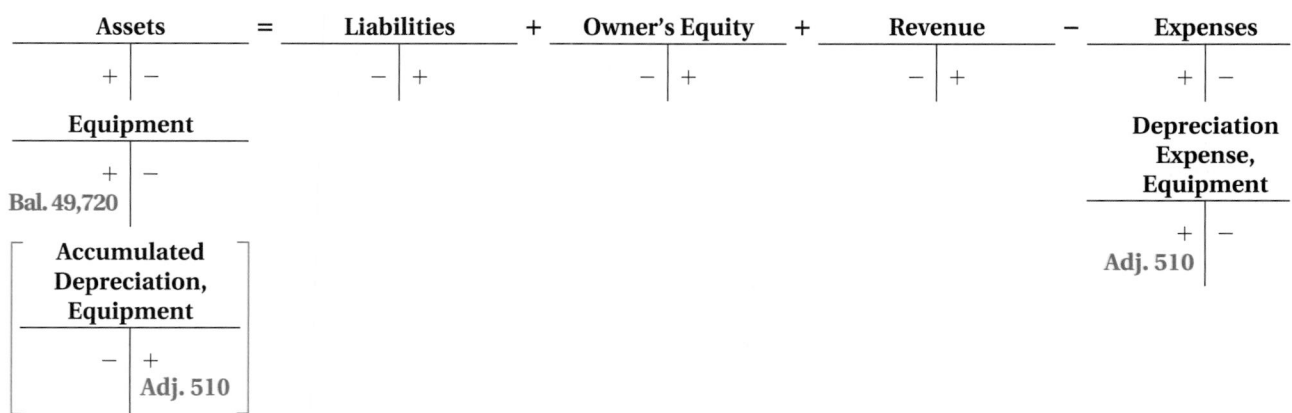

On the work sheet, Equipment (an asset) appears in the Balance Sheet Debit column. Accumulated Depreciation (a deduction from an asset) appears in the opposite column which is the Balance Sheet Credit column.

Accumulated Depreciation, Equipment, as the title implies, is the total depreciation that the company has taken since the original purchase of the asset. Rather than crediting the Equipment account, Arch Copy Co. keeps track of the total depreciation taken since it first acquired the asset in a separate account. The maximum depreciation it could take would be the cost of the equipment, $49,720 less trade-in value of $6,880. So, for the first year, Accumulated Depreciation, Equipment, will increase at the rate of $510 per month, assuming that no additional equipment has been purchased. For example, at the end of the second month, Accumulated Depreciation, Equipment, will amount to $1,020 ($510 + $510).

On the balance sheet, the balance of Accumulated Depreciation is deducted from the balance of the related asset account as illustrated on the following partial balance sheet for Arch Copy Co. The net amount shown, $49,210 is referred to as the book value of the asset. Thus, **book value** (or **carrying value**) is the cost of an asset minus accumulated depreciation.

FYI

If we had a Building account, the adjusting entry would be a debit to Depreciation Expense, Building, and a credit to Accumulated Depreciation, Building. Building and Accumulated Depreciation, Building, would be listed separately on the balance sheet.

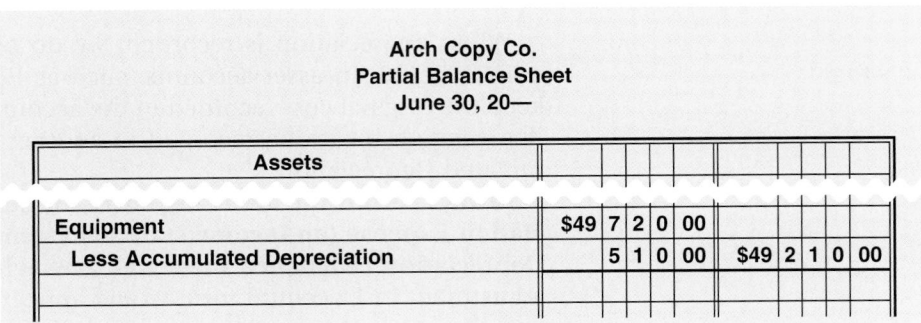

Arch Copy Co.
Partial Balance Sheet
June 30, 20—

Assets			
Equipment	$49 7 2 0 00		
Less Accumulated Depreciation	5 1 0 00	$49 2 1 0 00	

Wages Expense

The end of the fiscal period and the end of the employees' payroll period rarely fall on the same day. A diagram of the situation looks like this:

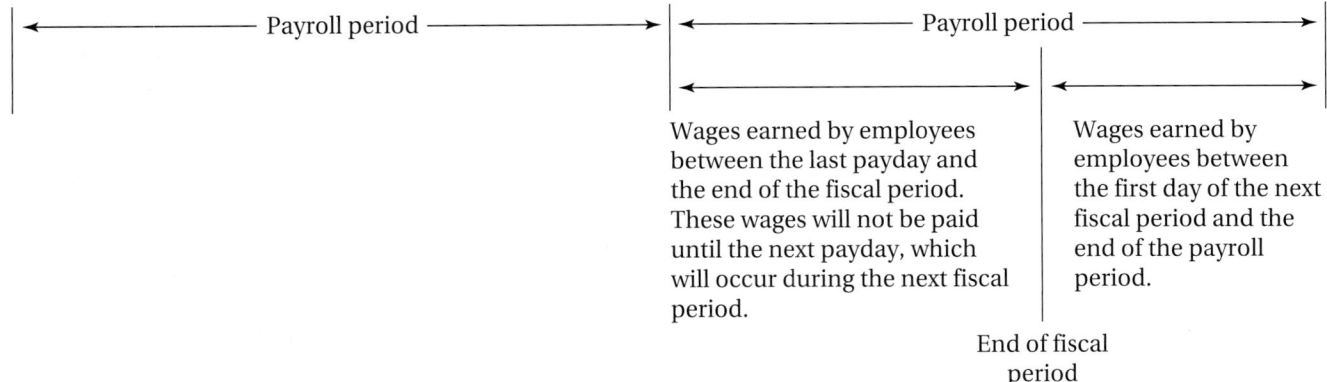

Since the last day of the fiscal period falls in the middle of the payroll period, we have to split up the wages earned in that payroll period between the fiscal period just ending and the next fiscal period. We will use another company for this example.

Assume that this firm pays its employees a total of $400 per day and that payday falls on Friday throughout the year. The employees work a five-day week. When the employees pick up their paychecks on Friday, the amount of the checks includes their wages for that day and for the preceding four days. Suppose that the last day of the fiscal period falls on Wednesday, December 31. The diagram below illustrates this situation.

					End of Fiscal Period				
				Dec. 26	Dec. 29	Dec. 30	Dec. 31	Jan. 1	Jan. 2
Mon	Tue	Wed	Thur	Fri	Mon	Tue	Wed	Thur	Fri
$400	$400	$400	$400	$400	$400	$400	$400	$400	$400
		Payroll period				Payroll period			
				Payday $2,000					Payday $2,000
						$1,200		$800	

December						
S	M	T	W	T	F	S
	1	2	3	4	5	6
7	8	9	10	11	12	13
14	15	16	17	18	19	20
21	22	23	24	25	26	27
28	29	30	31			

— Paydays

To have the Wages Expense account show an accurate balance for the fiscal period, you need to add $1,200 for the cost of labor between the last payday, December 26, and the end of the year, December 31 ($400 for December 29; $400 for December 30; $400 for December 31). Because the $1,200 will not be paid at this time but is owed to the employees as of December 31, you also need to add $1,200 to Wages Payable, a liability account, because the company owes this amount to employees.

REMEMBER!
If the end of the fiscal period (or end of the fiscal year) occurs during the middle of a payroll period, Wages Expense must be adjusted to bring it up to date. In the adjusting entry, add the amount employees have earned between the end of the last payroll period and the end of the fiscal period.

REMEMBER!
In the adjusting entry for accrued wages, increase both the Wages Expense and the Wages Payable accounts.

Wages Expense			**Wages Payable**	
+	−		−	+
(Old) Balance 104,000				Adjusting 1,200
Adjusting 1,200				
(New) Balance 105,200				

Returning to our illustration of Arch Copy Co., the last payday was June 24. Between June 24 and the end of the month, Arch Copy Co. owes an additional $180 in wages to its employee. Accountants refer to this extra amount that has not been recorded at the end of the month as **accrued wages**. In accounting terms, **accrual** means recognition of an expense or a revenue that has been incurred (expense) or earned (revenue) but has not yet been recorded.

(c)	Wages Expense			Wages Payable	
	+	−		−	+
(Old) Balance	2,130				Adjusting 180
Adjusting	180				
(New) Balance	2,310				

Placement of Accounts on the Work Sheet

We have to enter the adjustments on the work sheet, but before doing so, let's briefly discuss the Drawing and Accumulated Depreciation accounts, as well as net income, and their effect on the work sheet.

Capital and Drawing Account Balances The Drawing account is a **contra account** (contrary to Capital). In the statement of owner's equity, Drawing is deducted from Capital. To show one account as a deduction from another, the plus and minus signs are switched around. The T accounts look like this:

L. P. Arch, Capital			L. P. Arch, Drawing	
−	+		+	−
Debit	Credit		Debit	Credit
	Balance		Balance	

The normal balance for the Capital account is recorded in the Credit columns of the Trial Balance, the Adjusted Trial Balance, and the Balance Sheet sections. The normal balance for the Drawing account is recorded in the Debit columns of the Trial Balance, the Adjusted Trial Balance, and the Balance Sheet sections.

Equipment and Accumulated Depreciation, Equipment, Account Balances The Accumulated Depreciation, Equipment, account is a contra account (contrary to Equipment). In the balance sheet, Accumulated Depreciation, Equipment, is deducted from Equipment. The T accounts look like this:

Equipment			Accumulated Depreciation, Equipment	
+	−		−	+
Debit	Credit		Debit	Credit
Balance				Balance

The normal balance for the Equipment account is recorded in the Debit columns of the Trial Balance, the Adjusted Trial Balance, and the Balance Sheet sections. The normal balance for the Accumulated Depreciation, Equipment, account is recorded in the Credit columns of the Trial Balance, the Adjusted Trial Balance, and the Balance Sheet sections.

Net Income

Net income (or net loss) is the difference between revenue and expenses. It is used to balance the Income Statement columns; since revenue is normally larger than expenses, the balancing amount must be added to the expense side. Net income (or net loss) is also used to balance the Balance Sheet columns. On the statement of owner's equity, you add net income to the owner's beginning Capital balance. Since the Capital balance is located in the Balance Sheet Credit column, net income must also be added to that side. The following diagram shows these relationships:

Account Name	Trial Balance		Adjustments		Adjusted Trial Balance		Income Statement		Balance Sheet	
	Debit	Credit	Debit	Credit	Debit	Credit	Debit	Credit	Debit	Credit
	A + Draw. + E	Accum. Depr. + L + Cap. + R			A + Draw. + E	Accum. Depr. + L + Cap. + R	E	R	A + Draw.	Accum. Depr. + L + Cap.
Net Income							NI			NI

On the other hand, if expenses are larger than revenue, the result is a net loss. You must add net loss to the revenue side to balance the Income Statement columns. Also, because a net loss is deducted from the owner's beginning Capital balance, you must include net loss in the debit side of the Balance Sheet columns, thereby balancing these columns. To show this, let's look at the Income Statement and Balance Sheet columns diagramed here.

	Income Statement		Balance Sheet	
	Debit	Credit	Debit	Credit
	E	R	A + Draw.	Accum. Depr. + L + Cap.
Net Loss		NL	NL	

Summary of Adjustments by T Accounts

To test your understanding, describe why the following adjustments are necessary. The answers are shown below the accounts.

(a)

Prepaid Insurance			Insurance Expense		
	+	−		+	−
Balance	360	Adjusting 30	Adjusting	30	

(b)

Depreciation Expense, Equipment			Accumulated Depreciation, Equipment		
	+	−		−	+
Adjusting	510				Adjusting 510

(c)

Wages Expense			Wages Payable		
	+	−		−	+
Balance	2,130				
Adjusting	180				Adjusting 180

a. To record the insurance expired during June, $30.
b. To record the depreciation for the month of June, $510.
c. To record accrued wages owed at the end of June, $180.

Arch Copy Co.
Work Sheet
For Month Ended June 30, 20—

	ACCOUNT NAME	TRIAL BALANCE					ADJUSTMENTS				
		DEBIT		CREDIT			DEBIT		CREDIT		
					Accum. Deprec.						
		A + Draw. + E		+ L + C + R							
1	Cash	34 1 2 0 00									
2	Accounts Receivable	2 0 0 00									
3	Prepaid Insurance	3 6 0 00							(a)	3 0 00	
4	Equipment	49 7 2 0 00									
5	Accounts Payable			6 7 0 0 00							
6	L. P. Arch, Capital			76 2 0 0 00							
7	L. P. Arch, Drawing	2 5 0 0 00									
8	Income from Services			7 7 9 0 00							
9	Wages Expense	2 1 3 0 00					(c) 1 8 0 00				
10	Rent Expense	7 0 0 00									
11	Supplies Expense	6 0 0 00									
12	Advertising Expense	2 0 0 00									
13	Utilities Expense	1 6 0 00									
14		90 6 9 0 00		90 6 9 0 00							
15	Insurance Expense						(a) 3 0 00				
16	Depreciation Expense, Equipment						(b) 5 1 0 00				
17	Accumulated Depreciation, Equipment								(b) 5 1 0 00		
18	Wages Payable								(c) 1 8 0 00		
							7 2 0 00		7 2 0 00		

FIGURE 2

Mixed Accounts At this point, take special notice of the fact that each **adjusting entry contains an income statement account (revenue or expense) and a balance sheet account (asset, contra asset, or liability).** Accountants refer to these accounts as **mixed accounts**—accounts with balances that are partly income statement amounts and partly balance sheet amounts. The income statement and balance sheet accounts involved are separate accounts having a part of their name in common, like Prepaid Insurance and Insurance Expense. Prepaid Insurance is recorded as $360 in the Trial Balance columns but is apportioned as $30 in Insurance Expense in the Income Statement columns and $330 in Prepaid Insurance in the Balance Sheet columns. In other words, portions of these trial balance amounts are recorded in each section.

In the previous examples, we used T accounts to explain how to handle adjustments. T accounts help organize any type of accounting entry into debits and credits. But now it is time to record the adjustments on the work sheet. To help you remember which classifications of accounts appear in each column of the work sheet, we will label the columns with letters specifying each classification of accounts; for example, A for assets and L for liabilities etc., as shown in Figure 2.

Steps in the Completion of the Work Sheet

A completed work sheet is shown on transparency Figures 3 through 6. Before we complete the work sheet, let's list the recommended steps to follow.

1. Complete the Trial Balance columns, total, and rule.
2. Complete the Adjustments columns, total, and rule.
3. Complete the Adjusted Trial Balance columns, total, and rule.
4. Record balances in the Income Statement and Balance Sheet columns and total each column.
5. Record net income or net loss in the Income Statement columns by subtracting the smaller side from the larger side and adding the difference to the smaller side, total, and rule.
6. Record net income or net loss in the Balance Sheet columns by subtracting the smaller side from the larger side and adding the difference to the smaller side (the amount should be the same as the difference between the Income Statement column totals—if not, there is an error), total, and rule.

Step 1: Trial Balance Columns Note that the trial balance in Figure 2 is the same trial balance presented earlier for Arch Copy Co. You will be able to follow the completion of the entire work sheet for Arch Copy Co. in Figures 3 through 6 by turning the transparent pages, thus adding the next stage of its completion. Start with Figure 3.

Step 2: Adjustments Columns When we enter the adjustments, we identify them as **(a), (b), (c),** to indicate the relationships between the debit and credit sides and the sequence of the individual adjusting entries (see Figure 4).

Note that Insurance Expense; Depreciation Expense, Equipment; Accumulated Depreciation, Equipment; and Wages Payable did not appear in the trial balance because there were no balances in the accounts at that time. We wrote them below the Trial Balance totals to complete the work sheet.

Here is a brief review of the adjustments:

a. To record the $30 cost of insurance expired during June.
b. To record $510 depreciation for the month of June.
c. To record $180 of accrued wages owed at the end of June.

Now let's look at the work sheet shown in Figure 7 (pp. 122–123). To reinforce the idea of adjusting entries, see the brief explanation of each adjustment at the right of the work sheet. Again, the completed work sheet is shown on the transparent pages.

After the first fiscal period, Accumulated Depreciation will always have a balance until the related asset is sold or disposed of. Consequently, it will be listed in the Trial Balance columns immediately below the appropriate asset (Equipment, in this case).

Regarding the work sheet, again, we emphasize that it is strictly a working paper or tool used to gather together all the up-to-date information needed to prepare the financial statements. **The adjustments are always recorded in the work sheet first.**

Step 3: Adjusted Trial Balance Columns Once the Adjustments columns are totaled and ruled, extend each Trial Balance amount, plus or minus any adjustment from the Adjustments columns, to the Adjusted Trial Balance columns as shown in Figures 3 through 5.

Step 4: Income Statement and Balance Sheet Columns Extend the balances in the Adjusted Trial Balance columns to either the Income Statement or the Balance Sheet columns (see Figure 6).

FIGURE 7

| ACCOUNT NAME | TRIAL BALANCE | | | |
	DEBIT A + Draw. + E		CREDIT Accum. Deprec. + L + C + R	
1 Cash	34 1 2 0 00			
2 Accounts Receivable	2 0 0 00			
3 Prepaid Insurance	3 6 0 00			
4 Equipment	49 7 2 0 00			
5 Accounts Payable			6 7 0 0 00	
6 L. P. Arch, Capital			76 2 0 0 00	
7 L. P. Arch, Drawing	2 5 0 0 00			
8 Income from Services			7 7 9 0 00	
9 Wages Expense	2 1 3 0 00			
10 Rent Expense	7 0 0 00			
11 Supplies Expense	6 0 0 00			
12 Advertising Expense	2 0 0 00			
13 Utilities Expense	1 6 0 00			
14	90 6 9 0 00		90 6 9 0 00	
15 Insurance Expense				
16 Depreciation Expense, Equipment		*Step 1*		
17 Accumulated Depreciation, Equipment				
18 Wages Payable				
19				
20 *(a) Insurance expired, $30*				
21 *(b) Depreciation of equipment, $510*				
22 *(c) Accrued wages, $180*				

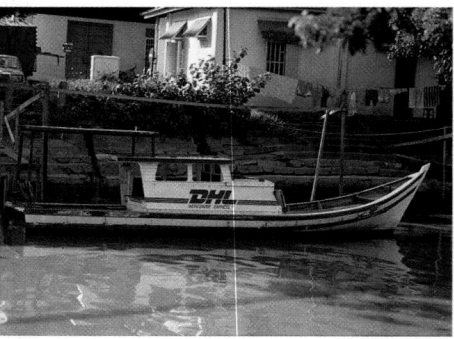

Depreciation can occur from everyday wear and tear or assets can simply become obsolete.

Step 5: Net Income or Net Loss—Income Statement Columns Total each of the two Income Statement columns. Subtract the smaller side from the larger side, and write the difference under the smaller Income Statement column total, total and rule as shown in Figure 6.

Step 6: Net Income or Net Loss—Balance Sheet Columns Total each of the two Balance Sheet columns. Subtract the smaller side from the larger side, and write the difference under the smaller Balance Sheet column total (the amount should be the same as the difference between the Income Statement column totals—if not, there is an error), total and rule as shown in Figure 6.

    If there is a net income, the credit side of the Income Statement columns will be larger than the debit side—more revenue than expenses. In this case, write Net Income in the Account Name column on the same line as the difference you calculated.

    If there is a net loss, the debit side of the Income Statement columns will be larger than the credit side—more expenses than revenue. In this case, write Net Loss in the Account Name column on the same line as the difference you calculated.

Arch Copy Co.
Work Sheet
For Month Ended June 30, 20—

ADJUSTMENTS DEBIT	ADJUSTMENTS CREDIT	ADJUSTED TRIAL BALANCE DEBIT A + Draw. + E	ADJUSTED TRIAL BALANCE CREDIT Accum. Deprec. + L + C + R	INCOME STATEMENT DEBIT E	INCOME STATEMENT CREDIT R	BALANCE SHEET DEBIT A + Draw.	BALANCE SHEET CREDIT Accum. Deprec. + L + C	
		34 1 2 0 00		No adjustment, so carry over amount directly				1
		2 0 0 00		↓				2
	(a) 3 0 00	3 3 0 00		Adjustment involved, subtract $30 (expired) from $360				3
		49 7 2 0 00		No adjustment, so carry over amount directly				4
			6 7 0 0 00					5
			76 2 0 0 00					6
		2 5 0 0 00						7
			7 7 9 0 00	↓				8
(c) 1 8 0 00		2 3 1 0 00		Adjustment involved, add $180 (accrued) to $2,130				9
		7 0 0 00		No adjustment, so carry over amount directly				10
		6 0 0 00						11
		2 0 0 00						12
		1 6 0 00		↓				13
				This line is blank because of the trial balance total				14
(a) 3 0 00		3 0 00		Adjustment involved, carry $30 over to the same column				15
(b) 5 1 0 00		5 1 0 00		Adjustment involved, carry $510 over to the same column				16
	(b) 5 1 0 00		5 1 0 00	Adjustment involved, carry $510 over to the same column				17
	(c) 1 8 0 00		1 8 0 00	Adjustment involved, carry $180 over to the same column				18
7 2 0 00	7 2 0 00	91 3 8 0 00	91 3 8 0 00					19
								20
Step 2		Step 3						21
								22

Work Sheet Requiring Two Pages

If a large number of accounts is involved, it may be necessary to continue the work sheet to a second page.

REMEMBER!
When a work sheet requires two pages, the totals at the bottom of the first sheet do not have to be equal. Debits must equal credits by the end of the last page.

(First Page)

Account Name	Trial Balance		Adjustments	
Wages Expense	3,240 00		(c) 220 50	
Totals carried forward	98,312 00	91,146 10	962 50	126 50

Note that the totals at the bottom of the first page are labeled "Totals carried forward" in the Account Name column. At the top of the second page, the totals are repeated and labeled "Totals brought forward" in the Account Name column. Continue listing account names and balances below the totals brought forward.

(Second Page)

Account Name	Trial Balance		Adjustments	
	Debit	Credit	Debit	Credit
Totals brought forward	98,312 00	91,146 10	962 50	126 50
Wages Payable				(c) 220 50

Finding Errors in the Income Statement and Balance Sheet Columns

As you have seen, the amount of the net income or net loss must be recorded in both an Income Statement column and a Balance Sheet column. Suppose that, after the net income is added to the Balance Sheet Credit column, the Balance Sheet columns are not equal. To find the error, follow this procedure:

1. Check to see that the amount of the net income or loss is recorded in the correct columns. For example, net income is placed in the Income Statement Debit column and the Balance Sheet Credit column.
2. Verify the addition of all the columns.
3. Look to see if the appropriate amounts have been recorded in the Income Statement and Balance Sheet columns. For example, asset amounts should be listed in the Balance Sheet Debit column, expense amounts should be listed in the Income Statement Debit column, and so forth.
4. Verify, by adding or subtracting across each line, that the amounts carried over from the Trial Balance columns through the Adjustments columns into the Adjusted Trial Balance columns are correct.
5. The correct amounts of the revenue and expense accounts are transferred to the income statement columns.
6. The correct amounts of assets, liabilities, and owner's equity accounts are transferred to the balance sheet columns.

Generally, one of these steps will expose the error.

Completion of the Financial Statements

OBJECTIVE 4
Prepare an income statement, a statement of owner's equity, and a balance sheet for a service business directly from the work sheet.

As we stated, the purpose of the work sheet is to help the accountant prepare the financial statements. Since we have completed the work sheet for Arch Copy Co., we can now prepare the income statement, the statement of owner's equity, and the balance sheet by taking the figures directly from the work sheet. These statements are shown in Figure 8 on the facing page.

Note that you record Accumulated Depreciation, Equipment, in the asset section of the balance sheet as a direct deduction from Equipment. As we have said, accountants refer to this as a **contra asset account** because it is contrary to its companion account. The difference, $49,210, is called the book value or carrying value because it represents the cost of the asset after Accumulated Depreciation has been deducted.

When preparing the statement of owner's equity, always remember to check the beginning balance of Capital against the balance shown in the Capital account in the general ledger. An additional investment may have been made during the fiscal period, and you need to record any such additional investment in the statement of owner's equity.

Arch Copy Co.
Income Statement
For Month Ended June 30, 20—

Revenue:						
Income from Services				$7 7 9 0 00	
Expenses:					
Wages Expense	$2 3 1 0 00			
Rent Expense	7 0 0 00			
Supplies Expense	6 0 0 00			
Advertising Expense	2 0 0 00			
Utilities Expense	1 6 0 00			
Insurance Expense	3 0 00			
Depreciation Expense, Equipment	5 1 0 00			
Total Expenses		4 5 1 0 00	
Net Income		$3 2 8 0 00	

Arch Copy Co.
Statement of Owner's Equity
For Month Ended June 30, 20—

L. P. Arch, Capital, June 1, 20—			$76 2 0 0 00
Net Income for June	$3 2 8 0 00	←	
Less Withdrawals for June	2 5 0 0 00		
Increase in Capital		7 8 0 00	
L. P. Arch, Capital, June 30, 20—		$76 9 8 0 00	

Arch Copy Co.
Balance Sheet
June 30, 20—

Assets			
Cash		$34 1 2 0 00	
Accounts Receivable		2 0 0 00	
Prepaid Insurance		3 3 0 00	
Equipment	$49 7 2 0 00		
Less Accumulated Depreciation	5 1 0 00	49 2 1 0 00	
Total Assets		$83 8 6 0 00	
Liabilities			
Accounts Payable	$ 6 7 0 0 00		
Wages Payable	1 8 0 00		
Total Liabilities		$ 6 8 8 0 00	
Owner's Equity			
L. P. Arch, Capital		76 9 8 0 00	←
Total Liabilities and Owner's Equity		$83 8 6 0 00	

FIGURE 8

JOURNALIZING ADJUSTING ENTRIES

OBJECTIVE 5
Journalize and post the adjusting entries.

To change the balance of a ledger account, you need a journal entry as evidence of the change. So far, we have been listing adjustments only in the Adjustments columns of the work sheet. The work sheet is not a journal, so we must make **adjusting entries** to journalize the adjustments to update the ledger accounts. **Take the information for these entries directly from the Adjustments columns of the work sheet, debiting and crediting exactly the same accounts and amounts in the journal entries.**

In the Description column of the general journal, write "Adjusting Entries" before you begin making these entries. This can eliminate the need to write an explanation for each entry. The adjusting entries for Arch Copy Co. are shown in Figure 9.

REMEMBER!
Each adjusting entry consists of an income statement account and a balance sheet account.

GENERAL JOURNAL PAGE 4

	DATE		DESCRIPTION	POST. REF.	DEBIT	CREDIT	
1	20–		**Adjusting Entries**				1
2	June	30	**Insurance Expense**	516	3 0 00		2
3			**Prepaid Insurance**	117		3 0 00	3
4							4
5		30	**Dep. Expense, Equipment**	517	5 1 0 00		5
6			**Accum. Dep., Equipment**	125		5 1 0 00	6
7							7
8		30	**Wages Expense**	511	1 8 0 00		8
9			**Wages Payable**	222		1 8 0 00	9

FIGURE 9

When you post the adjusting entries to the ledger accounts, write the word "Adjusting" in the Item column of the ledger account. The adjusting entry for Prepaid Insurance is posted as follows:

GENERAL LEDGER

ACCOUNT **Prepaid Insurance**   ACCOUNT NO. 117

	DATE		ITEM	POST. REF.	DEBIT	CREDIT	BALANCE DEBIT	BALANCE CREDIT	
1	20–								1
2	June	10		2	3 6 0 00		3 6 0 00		2
3		30	Adj.	4		3 0 00	3 3 0 00		3
4									4

FYI
Many businesses produce monthly financial statements. Adjustments must be made every time a financial statement is done.

ACCOUNT Insurance Expense									ACCOUNT NO. 516	
								BALANCE		
DATE	ITEM	POST. REF.	DEBIT		CREDIT		DEBIT		CREDIT	
20–										1
June 30	Adj.	4	3 0 00				3 0 00			2
										3
										4

Income Statement Involving More than One Revenue Account and a Net Loss

OBJECTIVE 6a
Prepare an income statement involving more than one revenue account and a net loss.

When an organization has more than one distinct source of revenue, a separate revenue account is set up for each source. See, for example, the income statement of Rex Miniature Golf presented in Figure 10. Also note that expenses are greater than revenues, resulting in a net loss.

FIGURE 10

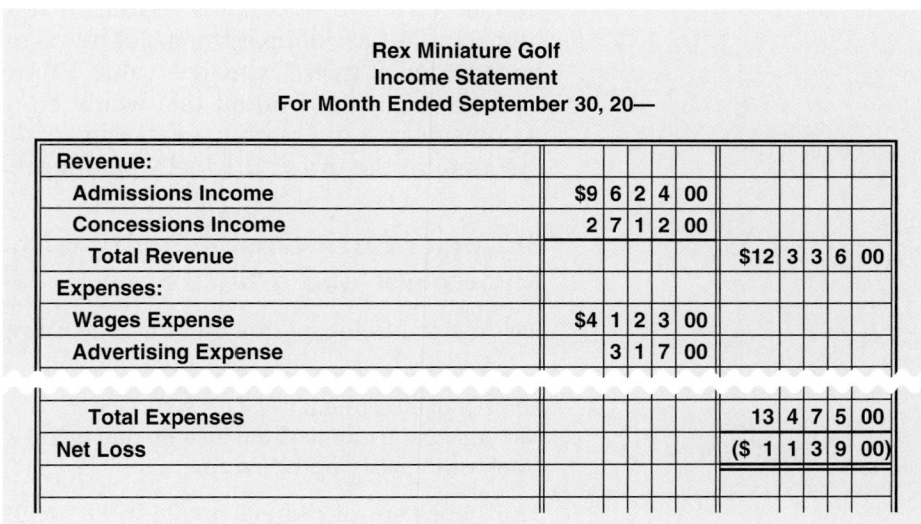

Rex Miniature Golf
Income Statement
For Month Ended September 30, 20—

Revenue:		
Admissions Income	$9 6 2 4 00	
Concessions Income	2 7 1 2 00	
Total Revenue		$12 3 3 6 00
Expenses:		
Wages Expense	$4 1 2 3 00	
Advertising Expense	3 1 7 00	
Total Expenses		13 4 7 5 00
Net Loss		($ 1 1 3 9 00)

REMEMBER!
The amounts in the left column are used to calculate totals. Amounts in the right column are totals or grand totals.

Statement of Owner's Equity with an Additional Investment and a Net Income

OBJECTIVE 6b
Prepare a statement of owner's equity with an additional investment and either a net income or a net loss.

Any additional investment by the owner during the period covered by the financial statements should be shown on the statement of owner's equity, since such a statement should show everything that has affected the Capital account from the *beginning* until the *end* of the period covered by the financial statements. For example, in Figure 11, assume that the following information is true for the L. A. Sloan Company, which has a net income:

Balance of L. A. Sloan, Capital, on April 1	$96,000
Additional investment by L. A. Sloan on April 12	10,000
Net income for the month (from income statement)	5,200
Total withdrawals for the month	4,000

L. A. Sloan Company
Statement of Owner's Equity
For Month Ended April 30, 20—

L. A. Sloan, Capital, April 1, 20—						$ 96	0	0	0	00
Additional Investment, April 12, 20—						10	0	0	0	00
Total Investment						$106	0	0	0	00
Net Income for April	$5	2	0	0	00					
Less Withdrawals for April	4	0	0	0	00					
Increase in Capital						1	2	0	0	00
L. A. Sloan, Capital, April 30, 20—						$107	2	0	0	00

FIGURE 11

The additional investment may be in the form of cash. Or the investment may be in the form of other assets, such as tools, equipment, and similar items. In the case of investments of assets other than cash, the assets should be recorded at their fair market value. Fair market value is the present worth of an asset, or the amount that would be received if the asset were sold to an outsider on the open market. Fair market value may differ greatly from the amount the owner originally paid for the asset.

Statement of Owner's Equity with an Additional Investment and a Net Loss

Assume the following for the J. D. Roy Company, which has a net loss:

J. D. Roy, Capital, on Oct. 1	$70,000
Additional investment by J. D. Roy on Oct. 25	6,000
Net loss for the month (from income statement)	2,500
Total withdrawals for the month	5,100

The statement of owner's equity in Figure 12 shows this information.

FYI

The information normally shown on the statement of owner's equity is sometimes included as part of the owner's equity section of the balance sheet in computerized general ledger systems.

J. D. Roy Company
Statement of Owner's Equity
For Month Ended October 31, 20—

J. D. Roy, Capital, October 1, 20—						$70	0	0	0	00
Additional Investment, October 25, 20—						6	0	0	0	00
Total Investment						$76	0	0	0	00
Less: Net Loss for October	$2	5	0	0	00					
Withdrawals for October	5	1	0	0	00					
Decrease in Capital						7	6	0	0	00
J. D. Roy, Capital, October 31, 20—						$68	4	0	0	00

FIGURE 12

Businesses with More than One Depreciation Expense Account and More than One Accumulated Depreciation Account

OBJECTIVE 6c
Prepare a balance sheet for a business having more than one accumulated depreciation account.

Figures 13 and 14 show the income statement and the balance sheet for Ruiz Veterinary Clinic. In Figure 14, note that the company has two assets subject to depreciation: Building and Equipment. In the financial statements, Depreciation Expense and Accumulated Depreciation must be listed for each asset.

In the adjusted accounts, notice that the intent is to make sure that the expenses recorded match up or compare with the revenues for the same period of time. In other words, for the month of June, we record all the revenues for June and all the expenses for June. Thus the revenues and expenses for the same time period are matched. This is called the **matching principle.**

FIGURE 13

Ruiz Veterinary Clinic
Income Statement
For Year Ended December 31, 20—

Revenues:																
Professional Fees	$335	1	6	0	00											
Boarding Fees	66	1	8	0	00											
Total Revenues							$401	3	4	0	00					
Expenses:																
Salaries Expense	$252	0	0	0	00											
Depreciation Expense, Building	19	4	4	0	00											
Depreciation Expense, Equipment	11	5	2	0	00											
Supplies Expense	11	1	6	0	00											
Insurance Expense	2	1	6	0	00											
Miscellaneous Expense	6	4	8	0	00											
Total Expenses							302	7	6	0	00					
Net Income							$ 98	5	8	0	00					

FIGURE 14

Ruiz Veterinary Clinic
Balance Sheet
December 31, 20—

Assets																
Cash							$ 18	7	2	0	00					
Supplies								6	0	0	00					
Land							13	2	0	0	00					
Building	$353	1	0	0	00											
Less Accumulated Depreciation	109	2	0	0	00		243	9	0	0	00					
Equipment	$127	8	0	0	00											
Less Accumulated Depreciation	87	6	0	0	00		40	2	0	0	00					
Total Assets							$316	6	2	0	00					
Liabilities																
Accounts Payable							$ 8	4	0	0	00					
Owner's Equity																
Rita N. Ruiz, Capital							308	2	2	0	00					
Total Liabilities and Owner's Equity							$316	6	2	0	00					

Land supposedly lasts forever, so land is not depreciated. Adjustments would have been made in the work sheet for depreciation of the equipment and the building. The balance sheet for Ruiz Veterinary Clinic is shown in Figure 14.

Balance Sheet with Statement of Owner's Equity Included

OBJECTIVE 6d
Prepare a balance sheet containing the statement of owner's equity information.

The information normally shown in the statement of owner's equity is sometimes included as part of the owner's equity section of the balance sheet, as shown in Figure 15. The only difference is the elimination of a separate statement and the inclusion of that information on the balance sheet.

FYI

Computerized accounting programs frequently do not produce a separate statement of owner's equity.

FIGURE 15

Arch Copy Co.
Balance Sheet
June 30, 20—

Assets			
Cash			$ 34 1 2 0 00
Accounts Receivable			2 0 0 00
Prepaid Insurance			3 3 0 00
Equipment	$49 7 2 0 00		
Less Accumulated Depreciation	5 1 0 00		49 2 1 0 00
Total Assets			$ 83 8 6 0 00
Liabilities			
Accounts Payable	$ 6 7 0 0 00		
Wages Payable	1 8 0 00		
Total Liabilities			$ 6 8 8 0 00
Owner's Equity			
L. P. Arch, Capital, June 1, 20—			$76 2 0 0 00
Net Income	$ 3 2 8 0 00		
Less L. P. Arch, Drawing	2 5 0 0 00		
Increase in Capital			7 8 0 00
L. P. Arch, Capital, June 30, 20—			$76 9 8 0 00
Total Liabilities and Owner's Equity			$83 8 6 0 00

CHAPTER REVIEW

Check out ACE for a Review Quiz at

http://college.hmco.com/accounting/students/.

Review of Performance Objectives

1. Define *fiscal period* and *fiscal year*.

   A fiscal period is any period of time covering a complete accounting cycle. A fiscal year consists of twelve consecutive months.

2. List the classifications of the accounts that occupy each column of a ten-column work sheet.

Trial Balance Debit	Assets + Drawing + Expenses
Trial Balance Credit	Accum. Deprec. + Liabilities + Capital + Revenue
Adjustments Debit	Expenses

Adjustments Credit	Assets + Liabilities
Adjusted Trial Balance Debit	Assets + Drawing + Expenses
Adjusted Trial Balance Credit	Accum. Deprec. + Liabilities + Capital + Revenue
Income Statement Debit	Expenses
Income Statement Credit	Revenue
Balance Sheet Debit	Assets + Drawing
Balance Sheet Credit	Accumulated Depreciation + Liabilities + Capital

3. Complete a work sheet for a service enterprise, involving adjustments for expired insurance, depreciation, and accrued wages.

Adjustment for expired insurance: debit Insurance Expense and credit Prepaid Insurance.
Adjustment for depreciation: debit Depreciation Expense and credit Accumulated Depreciation.
Adjustment for accrued wages: debit Wages Expense and credit Wages Payable.

4. Prepare an income statement, a statement of owner's equity, and a balance sheet for a service business directly from the work sheet.

Prepare the income statement directly from the amounts listed in the Income Statement Debit and Credit columns. The net income should equal the net income previously determined on the work sheet. For the statement of owner's equity, use the amount of the beginning capital listed in the Balance Sheet Credit column after checking the general ledger for any additional investment(s), the amount of the net income from the Balance Sheet Credit column, and the amount of Drawing from the Balance Sheet Debit column. Prepare the balance sheet directly from the amounts listed in the Balance Sheet Debit and Credit columns (except Drawing and Capital).

5. Journalize and post the adjusting entries.

6. Prepare (a) an income statement involving more than one revenue account and a net loss, (b) a statement of owner's equity with an additional investment and either a net income or a net loss, (c) a balance sheet for a business having more than one accumulated depreciation account, and (d) a balance sheet containing the statement of owner's equity information.

(a) An income statement containing more than one revenue account requires an additional line for each type of revenue, followed by a total amount of revenue.

(b) A statement of owner's equity involving an additional investment requires a line for each additional investment beneath the beginning capital amount, followed by a total amount of investment.

(c) Businesses that have more than one source of revenue or more than one type of asset that is subject to depreciation must show a separate account for each on the income statement and the balance sheet.

(d) A balance sheet sometimes contains in the owner's equity section the information normally placed in a separate statement of owner's equity. The section would contain the beginning capital, plus the amount of net income (or minus the net loss), minus total withdrawals. The result is the same amount that would be calculated in a separate statement of owner's equity—the ending capital.

Glossary

Accounting cycle The sequence of steps in the accounting process completed during the fiscal period. (111)

Accrual Recognition of an expense or a revenue that has been incurred or earned but has not yet been recorded. (117)

Accrued wages The amount of unpaid wages owed to employees for the time between the end of the last pay period and the end of the fiscal period. (117)

Adjusting entries Entries that bring the books up to date at the end of the fiscal period. (126)

Adjustments Internal transactions that bring ledger accounts up to date, as a planned part of the accounting procedure. They are first recorded in the Adjustments columns of the work sheet. (114)

Book value or carrying value The cost of an asset minus the accumulated depreciation. (116)

Contra account An account that is contrary to, or a deduction from, another account; for example, Accumulated Depreciation is listed as a deduction from Equipment. (115)

Contra asset account An account that is contrary to or a deduction from its companion asset account. (124)

Depreciation An expense based on the expectation that an asset will gradually decline in usefulness due to time, wear and tear, or obsolescence; the cost of the asset is therefore spread out over its estimated useful life. A part of depreciation expense is apportioned to each fiscal period. (114)

Fiscal period Any period of time covering a complete accounting cycle, generally consisting of twelve consecutive months. (111)

Fiscal year A fiscal period consisting of twelve consecutive months. (111)

Matching principle The principle that the revenue for one time period is matched up or compared with the related expenses for the same time period. (129)

Mixed accounts Certain accounts that appear on the trial balance with balances that are partly income statement amounts and partly balance sheet amounts—for example, Prepaid Insurance and Supplies. (120)

Straight-line depreciation A means of calculating depreciation in which the cost of an asset, less any trade-in value, is allocated evenly over the useful life of the asset. (115)

Work sheet A working paper used by accountants to record necessary adjustments and provide up-to-date account balances needed to prepare the financial statements. (112)

QUESTIONS, EXERCISES, AND PROBLEMS

Discussion Questions

1. What is the purpose of a work sheet?
2. What is the purpose of adjusting entries?
3. What is a mixed account? Give an example. What is a contra account? Give an example.
4. In which column of the work sheet—Income Statement (IS), Balance Sheet (BS)—would the adjusted balances of the following accounts appear?

Account	IS or BS?	Account	IS or BS?
a. Prepaid Insurance		e. Accumulated Depreciation, Equipment	
b. Depreciation Expense		f. T. Ogleby, Drawing	
c. Wages Payable		g. Insurance Expense	
d. Income from Services		h. Depreciation Expense, Equipment	

5. Why is it necessary to make an adjustment if wages for work performed for the pay period Monday through Friday are paid on Friday and the accounting period ends on a Wednesday?
6. Define depreciation as it relates to a truck you bought for your business.
7. Define an internal transaction and provide an example.
8. Why is it necessary to journalize and post adjusting entries that you have prepared on the work sheet?

Exercises

P.O. 2

List account classifications in work sheet columns.

Exercise 4-1 List the following classifications of accounts in all the columns in which they appear on the work sheet, with the exception of the Adjustments columns. (Example: Assets.)

Assets
Accumulated Depreciation (with previous balance)
Liabilities
Capital
Drawing
Revenue
Expenses

Write Net Income in the appropriate columns.

Account Name	Trial Balance		Adjustments		Adjusted Trial Balance		Income Statement		Balance Sheet	
	Debit	Credit	Debit	Credit	Debit	Credit	Debit	Credit	Debit	Credit
	Assets				Assets				Assets	
Net Income										

P.O. 2

Classify accounts and indicate normal balances and statement columns.

Exercise 4-2 Classify each of the accounts listed below as assets (A), liabilities (L), owner's equity (OE), revenue (R), or expenses (E). Indicate the normal debit or credit balance of each account. Indicate whether each account will appear in the Income Statement columns (IS) or the Balance Sheet columns (BS) of the work sheet. Item 0 is given as an example.

Account	Classification	Normal Balance	IS or BS Columns
0. Example: Wages Expense	E	Debit	IS
a. Prepaid Insurance			
b. Accounts Payable			
c. T. Robbins, Capital			
d. Accounts Receivable			
e. Accumulated Depreciation, Building			
f. T. Robbins, Drawing			
g. Rental Income			
h. Equipment			
i. Depreciation Expense, Equipment			
j. Supplies Expense			

P.O. 3

Choose accounts that require adjustment.

Exercise 4-3 Place a check mark next to any account(s) requiring adjustment. Explain why those accounts must be adjusted.

✓	Account Name (in trial balance order)	Reason for Adjusting This Account
	a. Cash	
	b. Accounts Receivable	
	c. Prepaid Insurance	
	d. Equipment	
	e. Accumulated Depreciation, Equipment	
	f. Accounts Payable	
	g. L. Johnson, Capital	
	h. L. Johnson, Drawing	
	i. Wages Expense	

P.O. 3

Prepare adjustments on the work sheet.

Exercise 4-4 Below is a partial work sheet for Meg's Place. Prepare the following adjustments on this work sheet for the month ended June 30, 20—.

a. Expired or used-up insurance, $300.
b. Depreciation expense on equipment, $850—remember to credit the Accumulated Depreciation account for equipment, not Equipment.
c. Wages accrued or earned since the last payday, $124 (owed and to be paid on the next payday).

	ACCOUNT NAME	TRIAL BALANCE		ADJUSTMENTS	
		DEBIT	CREDIT	DEBIT	CREDIT
1	Cash	5 6 2 1 00			
2	Prepaid Insurance	9 0 0 00			
3	Equipment	4 6 8 0 00			
4	Accumulated Depreciation, Equipment		1 2 5 0 00		
5	Accounts Payable		2 6 4 9 00		
6	M. Ryan, Capital		4 6 2 4 00		
7	M. Ryan, Drawing	2 2 0 0 00			
8	Service Income		6 8 4 7 00		
9	Rent Expense	9 5 6 00			
10	Supplies Expense	3 8 5 00			
11	Wages Expense	5 6 0 00			
12	Miscellaneous Expense	6 8 00			
13		15 3 7 0 00	15 3 7 0 00		
14					

P.O. 3

Prepare adjustments and adjusted trial balance.

Exercise 4-5 Complete the work sheet through the adjusted trial balance using the following adjustment information:

a. Expired or used-up insurance, $450.
b. Depreciation expense on equipment, $970—remember to credit theAccumulated Depreciation account for equipment, not Equipment.
c. Wages accrued or earned since the last payday, $221 (owed and to be paid on the next payday).

	ACCOUNT NAME	TRIAL BALANCE		ADJUSTMENTS		ADJUSTED TRIAL BALANCE	
		DEBIT	CREDIT	DEBIT	CREDIT	DEBIT	CREDIT
1	Cash	4 6 2 0 00					
2	Prepaid Insurance	1 1 0 0 00					
3	Equipment	5 6 7 8 00					
4	Accumulated Depreciation,						
5	Equipment		1 4 5 6 00				
6	Accounts Payable		1 9 7 5 00				
7	D. Von, Capital		6 1 2 6 00				
8	D. Von, Drawing	1 8 0 0 00					
9	Service Fees		5 7 3 6 00				
10	Rent Expense	8 6 5 00					
11	Supplies Expense	3 6 7 00					
12	Wages Expense	7 8 5 00					
13	Miscellaneous Expense	7 8 00					
14		15 2 9 3 00	15 2 9 3 00				
15							

P.O. 3

Calculate the missing adjustments.

Exercise 4-6 Journalize the three adjusting entries from the partial work sheet below for the month ended May 31. (*Hint:* Use what you know about opening new accounts for adjusting entries.)

	ACCOUNT NAME	INCOME STATEMENT DEBIT	INCOME STATEMENT CREDIT	BALANCE SHEET DEBIT	BALANCE SHEET CREDIT	
1	Cash			4 7 3 1 00		1
2	Prepaid Insurance			8 4 1 00		2
3	Equipment			5 8 3 2 00		3
4	Accumulated Depreciation, Equipment				1 8 2 0 00	4
5	Accounts Payable				9 8 5 00	5
6	B. Ray, Capital				6 8 1 0 00	6
7	B. Ray, Drawing			2 1 5 0 00		7
8	Professional Fees		8 6 7 3 00			8
9	Salary Expense	2 7 8 7 00				9
10	Rent Expense	1 2 0 0 00				10
11	Supplies Expense	3 8 4 00				11
12	Miscellaneous Expense	1 3 4 00				12
13						13
14	Insurance Expense	1 8 5 00				14
15	Depreciation Expense, Equipment	3 6 4 00				15
16	Salaries Payable				3 2 0 00	16
17		5 0 5 4 00	8 6 7 3 00	13 5 5 4 00	9 9 3 5 00	17
18	Net Income	3 6 1 9 00			3 6 1 9 00	18
19		8 6 7 3 00	8 6 7 3 00	13 5 5 4 00	13 5 5 4 00	19
20						20

P.O. 5

Journalize adjusting entries from the work sheet.

Exercise 4-7 Journalize the adjustments for James Company as of August 31.

	ACCOUNT NAME	TRIAL BALANCE DEBIT	TRIAL BALANCE CREDIT	ADJUSTMENTS DEBIT	ADJUSTMENTS CREDIT
1	Cash	3 9 7 1 00			
2	Prepaid Insurance	4 8 7 3 00			(a) 2 6 5 00
3	Equipment	5 6 7 8 00			
4	Accumulated Depreciation, Equipment		6 4 5 00		(b) 2 0 6 00
5	Accounts Payable		8 4 3 00		
6	L. Max, Capital		12 7 5 2 00		
7	L. Max, Drawing	2 0 0 0 00			
8	Service Fees		4 6 8 3 00		
9	Rent Expense	7 9 5 00			
10	Supplies Expense	6 6 3 00			
11	Wages Expense	8 6 5 00		(c) 1 6 8 00	
12	Miscellaneous Expense	7 8 00			
13		18 9 2 3 00	18 9 2 3 00		
14	Insurance Expense			(a) 2 6 5 00	
15	Depreciation Expense, Equipment			(b) 2 0 6 00	
16	Wages Payable				(c) 1 6 8 00
17				6 3 9 00	6 3 9 00
18					

P.O. 5
Journalize adjusting entries.

Exercise 4-8 Journalize the following adjusting entries that were included on the work sheet for the month ended December 31. Assume the financial statements have been prepared.

Dec. 31 Salaries for two days are unpaid at December 31, $1,600 (verify). Salaries are $4,000 for a five-day week.
  31 Insurance was bought on September 1 for $1,800 for 12 months' coverage. Four months' coverage has expired, $600 (verify).
  31 Depreciation for the month on equipment, $50, based on an asset costing $4,500 with a trade-in value of $1,500 and an estimated life of 5 years (verify).

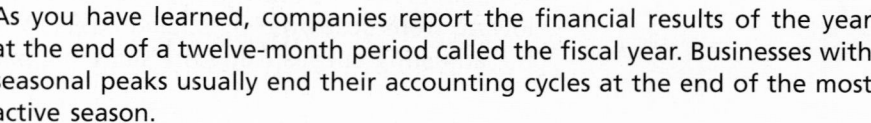

REFLECTING ON
THE WORLD WIDE WEB

As you have learned, companies report the financial results of the year at the end of a twelve-month period called the fiscal year. Businesses with seasonal peaks usually end their accounting cycles at the end of the most active season.

1. Is Activision a company that might have seasonal peaks and that would want a fiscal year that is different from the calendar year? What is its fiscal year and where do you find this information in the annual report? (Access their annual report for 2001 at **http://activision.com/ en_US/news_listing_ir/ir_financials_annualreports.html.**

2. In this chapter, financial information entered into the general journal is transformed into the financial statements. Let's go back to Activision and analyze the Property and Equipment account on its balance sheet. This account is listed as Property and Equipment, *net* on the balance sheet on page 17. What does this mean?

3. If Property and Equipment, net was $15,240,000 as of March 31, 2001, what was the total cost of Activision's property and equipment? (*Hint:* What was Accumulated Depreciation, Property and Equipment as of March 31, 2001? Review Note 5, Property and Equipment, in the Notes to Consolidated Financial Statements, which begin on page 21 of the annual report.)

CONSIDER AND COMMUNICATE

You are the bookkeeper for a busy small business. You have asked the owner for the information you need in order to make adjusting entries for depreciation, insurance, and wages. He says he's really busy, and what you've done so far is "close enough." Explain the need for adjusting entries and how they affect his balance sheet and the "bottom line" on the income statement.

A MATTER OF ETHICS

Your client is preparing financial statements to show the bank. You know that he has incurred a computer repair expense during the month, but you see no such expense on the books. When you question the client, he tells you that he has not received the official bill, although he knows the expense was $1,250. Your client is on the accrual basis of accounting. He does not want the computer repair expense on the books as of the end of the month because he wants his profits to look good for the bank. Is your client behaving ethically by suggesting that the computer repair expense not be booked until the official bill is presented? Are you behaving ethically if you go along with the client's request? What principle is involved here?

CRITICAL THINKING

Your supervisor just finished a work sheet, but all the columns except the following were destroyed by spilled coffee. You have been asked to journalize the adjusting entries using the surviving partial work sheet.

	ACCOUNT NAME	INCOME STATEMENT		BALANCE SHEET	
		DEBIT	CREDIT	DEBIT	CREDIT
1	Cash			8 4 7 6 00	
2	Accounts Receivable			1 4 8 6 00	
5	Equipment			12 3 6 7 00	
6	Accumulated Depreciation, Equipment				3 6 1 0 00
7	Accounts Payable				2 8 1 3 00
8	G. Kramer, Capital				11 7 0 7 00
9	G. Kramer, Drawing			1 1 0 0 00	
10	Income from Services		11 2 1 6 00		
11	Rent Expense	1 4 0 0 00			
12	Supplies Expense	1 1 1 0 00			
13	Wages Expense	2 4 6 7 00			
14	Insurance Expense	2 1 0 00			
15	Depreciation Expense, Equipment	7 5 0 00			
16	Wages Payable				6 2 0 00
17		5 9 3 7 00	11 2 1 6 00	24 0 2 9 00	18 7 5 0 00

PROBLEM SET A

For additional help, see the demonstration problem at the beginning of each chapter in your Working Papers.

P.O. 3

Problem 4-1A The trial balance for the Milor Insurance Agency as of August 31, after the firm has completed its first month of operations follows:

Milor Insurance Agency Trial Balance August 31, 20—													
ACCOUNT NAME		DEBIT					CREDIT					
Cash		3	4	2	7	00						
Accounts Receivable		1	3	1	9	00						
Prepaid Insurance			3	6	2	00						
Office Equipment		4	9	3	9	00						
Accounts Payable								1	0	7	1	00
C. Milor, Capital								9	0	2	0	00
C. Milor, Drawing			9	0	0	00						
Commissions Earned								2	5	2	0	00
Rent Expense			6	9	5	00						
Travel Expense			2	2	5	00						
Supplies Expense			4	9	2	00						
Utilities Expense			1	9	8	00						
Miscellaneous Expense				5	4	00						
		12	6	1	1	00		12	6	1	1	00

Check Figure

Net Income, $70

Instructions

1. Record the amounts in the Trial Balance columns of the work sheet.
2. Complete the work sheet by making the following adjustments and lettering each adjustment:
   a. Expired or used-up insurance, $86.
   b. Depreciation expense on office equipment, $700—remember to credit the Accumulated Depreciation account for office equipment, not Office Equipment.

P.O. 4,5

Problem 4-2A The completed work sheet for J. West Design for the month of March is in your Working Papers.

Check Figure

Total Assets, $15,164

Instructions

1. Prepare an income statement.
2. Prepare a statement of owner's equity. Assume that no additional investments were made in March.
3. Prepare a balance sheet.
4. Journalize the adjusting entries.

P.O. 3,5

Problem 4-3A The trial balance of The Design Center for the month ended September 30 is presented on the following page.

The Design Center
Trial Balance
September 30, 20—

ACCOUNT NAME	DEBIT	CREDIT
Cash	2 3 7 8 00	
Prepaid Insurance	1 3 4 5 00	
Equipment	32 9 7 8 00	
Accumulated Depreciation, Equipment		16 2 3 5 00
Accounts Payable		2 7 5 1 00
C. Bock, Capital		45 2 0 8 00
C. Bock, Drawing	22 4 4 5 00	
Income from Services		43 7 9 1 00
Wages Expense	29 7 6 1 00	
Rent Expense	14 9 3 2 00	
Supplies Expense	8 6 4 00	
Utilities Expense	1 5 7 3 00	
Telephone Expense	1 2 7 1 00	
Miscellaneous Expense	4 3 8 00	
	107 9 8 5 00	107 9 8 5 00

Data for the adjustments are as follows:

a. Expired or used-up insurance, $320.
b. Depreciation expense on equipment, $2,800—remember to credit the Accumulated Depreciation account for equipment, not Equipment.
c. Wages accrued or earned since the last payday, $468 (owed and to be paid on the next payday).

Check Figure

Net Loss, $8,636

P.O. 3,4,5,6

Instructions

1. Complete the work sheet.　　2. Journalize the adjusting entries.

Problem 4-4A See the trial balance for Wyn's Putt Putt Golf on June 30 below.

Wyn's Putt Putt Golf
Trial Balance
June 30, 20—

ACCOUNT NAME	DEBIT	CREDIT
Cash	4 5 3 2 00	
Prepaid Insurance	1 2 8 4 00	
Equipment	23 6 8 7 00	
Accumulated Depreciation, Equipment		1 2 7 8 00
Repair Equipment	6 2 8 9 00	
Accumulated Depreciation, Repair Equipment		1 4 8 5 00
Accounts Payable		9 6 0 00
R. Wyn, Capital		23 0 1 0 00
R. Wyn, Drawing	1 5 6 5 00	
Golf Fees Income		12 3 8 7 00
Concessions Income		2 8 6 3 00
Wages Expense	2 1 6 3 00	
Rent Expense	1 3 5 0 00	
Utilities Expense	3 5 7 00	
Repair Expense	2 7 1 00	
Supplies Expense	3 4 6 00	
Miscellaneous Expense	1 3 9 00	
	41 9 8 3 00	41 9 8 3 00

Data for month-end adjustments are as follows:

a. Expired or used-up insurance, $350.
b. Depreciation expense on Equipment, $800 (remember to credit the Accumulated Depreciation account for equipment, not Equipment).
c. Depreciation expense on Repair Equipment, $1,240 (remember to credit the Accumulated Depreciation account for repair equipment, not Repair Equipment).
d. Wages accrued or earned since the last payday, $385 (owed and to be paid on the next payday).

Check Figure

Net Income, $7,849

Instructions

1. Complete the work sheet for the month.
2. Prepare an income statement, a statement of owner's equity, and a balance sheet. Assume that no additional investments were made during June.
3. Journalize the adjusting entries.

Instructions for General Ledger Software

1. Journalize the adjusting entries in the general journal. (No work sheet is required.)
2. Post the adjusting entries.
3. Print an income statement, a statement of owner's equity, and a balance sheet. Assume that no additional investments were made during the month.

PROBLEM SET B

For additional help, see the demonstration problem at the beginning of each chapter in your Working Papers.

P.O. 3

Problem 4-1B The trial balance of the Marian Insurance Agency as of September 30, after the firm has completed its first month of operations, follows:

Marian Insurance Agency
Trial Balance
September 30, 20—

ACCOUNT NAME	DEBIT	CREDIT
Cash	3 5 3 7 00	
Accounts Receivable	1 2 2 8 00	
Prepaid Insurance	6 7 5 00	
Office Equipment	5 2 4 6 00	
Accounts Payable		1 2 6 7 00
S. Marian, Capital		9 6 2 8 00
S. Marian, Drawing	1 1 0 0 00	
Commissions Earned		2 8 4 3 00
Rent Expense	7 8 5 00	
Supplies Expense	3 8 7 00	
Travel Expense	4 8 8 00	
Utilities Expense	2 2 7 00	
Miscellaneous Expense	6 5 00	
	13 7 3 8 00	13 7 3 8 00

Check Figure

Net Income, $191

Instructions

1. Record the amounts in the Trial Balance columns of the work sheet.
2. Complete the work sheet by making the following adjustments and lettering each adjustment:
   a. Expired or used-up insurance, $100.
   b. Depreciation expense on office equipment, $600—remember to credit the Accumulated Depreciation account for office equipment, not Office Equipment.

P.O. 4,5

Problem 4-2B The completed work sheet for Ono Design for the month of March is in your Working Papers.

Check Figure

Total Assets, $20,134

Instructions

1. Prepare an income statement.
2. Prepare a statement of owner's equity. Assume no additional investments were made in March.
3. Prepare a balance sheet.
4. Journalize the adjusting entries.

P.O. 3,5

Problem 4-3B The trial balance of Gentle Cleaners for the month ended September 30 is presented below.

Gentle Cleaners
Trial Balance
September 30, 20—

ACCOUNT NAME	DEBIT	CREDIT
Cash	2 4 8 9 00	
Prepaid Insurance	1 2 3 6 00	
Equipment	22 7 5 2 00	
Accumulated Depreciation, Equipment		14 3 5 7 00
Accounts Payable		2 6 4 7 00
D. Stevens, Capital		28 1 6 9 00
D. Stevens, Drawing	20 3 5 9 00	
Income from Services		40 8 5 0 00
Wages Expense	24 9 8 3 00	
Rent Expense	10 6 7 3 00	
Utilities Expense	1 1 5 4 00	
Supplies Expense	7 5 2 00	
Telephone Expense	1 2 4 4 00	
Miscellaneous Expense	3 8 1 00	
	86 0 2 3 00	86 0 2 3 00

Data for the adjustments are as follows:

a. Expired or used-up insurance, $895.
b. Depreciation expense on equipment, $3,200 (remember to credit the Accumulated Depreciation account for equipment, not Equipment).
c. Wages accrued or earned since the last payday, $595 (owned and to be paid on the next payday).

Instructions

1. Complete the work sheet.
2. Journalize the adjusting entries.

Problem 4-4B The trial balance for Game Town on July 31 is shown below. Data for month-end adjustments are as follows:

Game Town
Trial Balance
July 31, 20—

ACCOUNT NAME	DEBIT	CREDIT
Cash	3 6 2 1 00	
Prepaid Insurance	1 2 9 5 00	
Equipment	28 6 4 2 00	
Accumulated Depreciation, Equipment		2 3 8 7 00
Repair Equipment	1 8 6 5 00	
Accumulated Depreciation, Repair Equipment		7 8 0 00
Accounts Payable		8 4 2 00
A. Wata, Capital		23 9 7 1 00
A. Wata, Drawing	1 0 0 0 00	
Game Fees Income		8 9 5 4 00
Concessions Income		2 7 5 2 00
Wages Expense	1 2 6 8 00	
Rent Expense	9 8 0 00	
Utilities Expense	2 4 6 00	
Repair Expense	3 8 0 00	
Supplies Expense	2 5 7 00	
Miscellaneous Expense	1 3 2 00	
	39 6 8 6 00	39 6 8 6 00

a. Expired or used-up insurance, $245.
b. Depreciation expense on equipment, $650 (remember to credit the Accumulated Depreciation account for equipment, not Equipment).
c. Depreciation expense on repair equipment, $450 (remember to credit the Accumulated Depreciation account for repair equipment, not Repair Equipment).
d. Wages accrued or earned since the last payday, $315 (owed and to be paid on the next payday).

Instructions

1. Complete the work sheet for the month.
2. Prepare an income statement, a statement of owner's equity, and a balance sheet. Assume that no additional investments were made during July.
3. Journalize the adjusting entries.

Instructions for General Ledger Software

1. Journalize the adjusting entries in the general journal. (No work sheet is required.)
2. Post the adjusting entries.
3. Print an income statement, a statement of owner's equity, and a balance sheet. Assume no additional investments were made during the month.

The Computer Lab

PHASE 9
Month-end Adjusting
Entries

And no work sheet on the computer.

Adjustments

While you have printed out preadjusted statements to get an idea of how Jeep Jockeys is doing, some adjusting entries are required to make the picture even clearer.

Adjustment a: You have done some research on depreciation and have determined that Jeep Jockeys' jeeps costing $46,000 will have a trade-in or salvage value of $1,000 and have about 3 years of usefulness.

Adjustment b: You also need to depreciate the office equipment by the straight-line method. It cost $759 with a salvage value of $80 and expected to last 5 years.

Adjustment c: Prepaid insurance was bought May 1 and one month has expired. Jeep Jockeys paid $1,800 for the 12-month liability insurance policy.

Adjustment d: The company owes the employees two days of wages that they earned in the month of May. So, the Wages Expense and Wages Payable need to be increased by $293.

Time to print the financial statements for Mr. Kennedy.

1. Print an income statement for the month ended May 31, 20—.
2. Print a statement of owner's equity for the month ended May 31, 20—.
3. Print a balance sheet as of May 31, 20—.

APPENDIX

A Methods of Depreciation

Performance Objectives

After you have completed this appendix, you will be able to do the following:

1. Prepare a schedule of depreciation using the straight-line method.

2. Prepare a schedule of depreciation using the double-declining-balance method.

3. Prepare a schedule of depreciation for five-year property under the Modified Accelerated Cost Recovery System.

Two methods of depreciation will be illustrated using the example of a delivery truck. Assume that the truck was bought at the beginning of Year 1 and at a cost of $24,000. The truck is estimated to have a useful life of five years and a trade-in value of $6,000 at the end of the five-year period. The two methods to be described are straight-line and double-declining-balance.

STRAIGHT-LINE METHOD

OBJECTIVE 1
Prepare a schedule of depreciation using the straight-line method.

We showed this method in Chapter 4, providing for an equal amount of depreciation each year.

$$\text{Yearly depreciation} = \frac{\text{Cost of asset} - \text{Trade-in value}}{\text{Years of life}} = \frac{\$24,000 - \$6,000}{5 \text{ years}}$$

$$= \frac{\$18,000}{5 \text{ years}} = \$3,600 \text{ per year}$$

Year	Depreciation for the Year	Accumulated Depreciation	Book Value (Cost Less Accumulated Depreciation)
1	$18,000 ÷ 5 years = $ 3,600	$ 3,600	$24,000 − $ 3,600 = $20,400
2	18,000 ÷ 5 years = 3,600	$ 3,600 + $3,600 = 7,200	24,000 − 7,200 = 16,800
3	18,000 ÷ 5 years = 3,600	7,200 + 3,600 = 10,800	24,000 − 10,800 = 13,200
4	18,000 ÷ 5 years = 3,600	10,800 + 3,600 = 14,400	24,000 − 14,400 = 9,600
5	18,000 ÷ 5 years = 3,600	14,400 + 3,600 = 18,000	24,000 − 18,000 = 6,000
	$18,000		

Double-Declining-Balance Method

The term *double* refers to double the straight-line rate. With an estimated useful life of five years, the straight-line rate is ⅕, or 0.2. Twice, or double, the straight-line rate is ⅖ (⅕ × 2) or 0.4. The trade-in value is not taken into account until the end of the schedule. Multiply *book value* at beginning of year by twice the straight-line rate.

Year	Depreciation for the Year	Accumulated Depreciation	Book Value (Cost Less Accumulated Depreciation)
1	$24,000 × 0.4 = $ 9,600	$ 9,600	$24,000 − $ 9,600 = $14,400
2	$14,400 × 0.4 = 5,760	$ 9,600 + $5,760 = 15,360	24,000 − 15,360 = 8,640
3	$8,640 − $6,000 = 2,640	15,360 + 2,640 = 18,000	24,000 − 18,000 = 6,000
4	0	18,000	24,000 − 18,000 = 6,000
5	0	18,000	24,000 − 18,000 = 6,000
	$18,000		

If the schedule is continued for Year 3, depreciation expense would be $3,456 ($8,640 × 0.4). Accumulated depreciation would be $18,816 ($15,360 + $3,456). And book value would be $5,184 ($24,000 − $18,816). However, the book value can not drop below the established trade-in value of $6,000. So for Year 3 an adjustment must be made limiting the depreciation for the year to $2,640, which will bring the accumulated depreciation up to $18,000. Consequently, the book value at the end of the year will be $6,000 ($24,000 cost − $18,000 accumulated depreciation).

TAX REQUIREMENT—MACRS

Modified Tax Recovery System (MACRS) is the title given by the Internal Revenue Service for a variety of tax rate schedules. The term *recovery* is used because MACRS is a means of recovering or deducting the cost of an asset. According to MACRS, property is divided into nine classes, as follows:

3-year property—certain horses and tractor units for use over the road

5-year property—autos, trucks, computers, typewriters, and copiers

7-year property—office furniture and fixtures and any property that does not have a class life and that is not, by law, in any other class

10-year property—vessels, barges, tugs, and similar water transportation equipment

15-year property—wharves, roads, fences, and any municipal wastewater treatment plants

20-year property—certain farm buildings and municipal sewers

27.5-year residential rental property—rental houses and apartments

31.5-year real property—office buildings and warehouses

39-year property—nonresidential real property placed in service after May 13, 1993

only straight line · no double

Under MACRS, trade-in value is ignored. The following table lists the depreciation rates that a business typically may use for tax purposes.

	Depreciation for Recovery Period			
Year	3-Year	5-Year	7-Year	10-Year
1	33.33%	20.00%	14.29%	10.00%
2	44.45	32.00	24.49	18.00
3	14.81	19.20	17.49	14.40
4	7.41	11.52	12.49	11.52
5		11.52	8.93	9.22
6		5.76	8.92	7.37
7			8.93	6.55
8			4.46	6.55
9				6.56

Our light truck qualifies as five-year property.

Year	Depreciation for the Year	Accumulated Depreciation	Book Value (Cost Less Accumulated Depreciation)
1	$24,000 × 0.20 = $ 4,800.00	$ 4,800.00	$24,000.00 − $ 4,800.00 = $19,200.00
2	24,000 × 0.32 = 7,680.00	$ 4,800.00 + $7,680.00 = 12,480.00	24,000.00 − 12,480.00 = 11,520.00
3	24,000 × 0.192 = 4,608.00	12,480.00 + 4,608.00 = 17,088.00	24,000.00 − 17,088.00 = 6,912.00
4	24,000 × 0.1152 = 2,764.80	17,088.00 + 2,764.80 = 19,852.80	24,000.00 − 19,852.80 = 4,147.20
5	24,000 × 0.1152 = 2,764.80	19,852.80 + 2,764.80 = 22,617.60	24,000.00 − 22,617.60 = 1,382.40
6	24,000 × 0.0576 = 1,382.40	22,617.60 + 1,382.40 = 24,000.00	24,000.00 − 24,000.00 = 0
	$24,000.00		

PROBLEMS

P.O. 1
Check Figure
Year 1 depreciation, $3,000

P.O. 4
Check Figure
Year 3 depreciation, $2,850

Problem A-1 A delivery van was bought for $15,000. The estimated life of the van is four years. The trade-in value at the end of four years is estimated to be $3,000. Prepare a depreciation schedule for the four-year period using the straight-line method.

Problem A-2 Assume the van is 5-year property. Using the information in Problem A-1, prepare a schedule of depreciation under MACRS.

5

Closing Entries and the Post-Closing Trial Balance

Performance Objectives

After you have completed this chapter, you will be able to do the following:

1. List the steps in the accounting cycle.

2. Journalize and post closing entries for a service enterprise.

3. Prepare a post-closing trial balance.

4. Define the following methods of accounting: accrual basis and modified cash basis.

5. Prepare interim statements.

Let's review the steps in the accounting cycle for an entire fiscal period. Remember that a fiscal period is generally twelve consecutive months, but can also consist of other time frames like three months or six months.

OBJECTIVE 1
List the steps in the accounting cycle.

1. **Analyze source documents and record business transactions in a journal.**
2. **Post journal entries to the accounts in the ledger.**
3. **Prepare a trial balance.**
4. **Gather adjustment data and record the adjusting entries on a work sheet.**
5. **Complete the work sheet.**
6. **Prepare financial statements from the data on the work sheet.**
7. **Journalize and post the adjusting entries from the data on the work sheet.**

8. **Journalize and post the closing entries.**
9. **Prepare a post-closing trial balance.**

This chapter explains the procedure for completing the final steps: closing entries and the post-closing trial balance.

Adjusting entries, closing entries, and a post-closing trial balance are prepared at the end of a fiscal period. The number of months in a fiscal period varies. To introduce you to these final steps in the accounting cycle, we assume here that the fiscal period for Arch Copy Co. is one month. We make this assumption so that we can thoroughly cover the material and give you a chance to practice its application. The entire accounting cycle is outlined in Figure 1.

FIGURE 1

CLOSING ENTRIES

To help you understand the reason for the closing entries, let's repeat the fundamental accounting equation:

Assets = Liabilities + Owner's Equity + Revenue − Expenses

We know that the income statement, as stated in the third line of its heading, covers a period of time. The income statement consists of revenue minus expenses for this period of time only. So, when the next fiscal period begins, we should start with zero balances. We start all over again each period.

Closing entries empty or zero out temporary owner's equity accounts and prepare the accounts for the new accounting period—emptying out folders for one year so they can be filled with the new year's revenue and expenses.

REMEMBER!
The matching principle is why we close revenue, expense, and Drawing accounts.

O B J E C T I V E   2
Journalize and post closing entries for a service enterprise.

Purpose of Closing Entries

This brings us to the *purpose* of the **closing entries**, which is to close (or zero) the temporary-equity or nominal accounts (revenue, expense, and drawing accounts). We do this because their balances apply to only one fiscal period. Closing entries are made after the last adjusting entry. With the coming of the next fiscal period, we want to start from zero, recording revenue and expenses for the new fiscal period. The closing entries also update the owner's Capital account.

Accountants also refer to closing the accounts as clearing the accounts. For income tax purposes, this is certainly understandable. No one wants to pay income tax more than once on the same income, and the Internal Revenue Service doesn't allow you to count an expense more than once. So now we have this:

$$\text{Assets} = \text{Liabilities} + \text{Owner's Equity} + \overset{\text{(closed)}}{\cancel{\text{Revenue}}} - \overset{\text{(closed)}}{\cancel{\text{Expenses}}}$$
$$\text{(Capital)}$$

The assets, the liabilities, and the owner's Capital account remain open. The balance sheet gives the present balances of these accounts. The accountant carries the asset, liability, and Capital account balances over to the next fiscal period.

Procedure for Closing

The procedure for closing is simply to balance off the account; in other words, to make the balance *equal to zero*. This meets our objective, which is to start from zero in the next fiscal period. Let's illustrate this first with T accounts. Suppose an account to be closed has a debit balance of $960; then, to make the balance equal to zero, we *credit* the account for $960.

Debit		Credit	
Balance	960	Closing	960

Now suppose an account to be closed has a credit balance of $1,200; then, to make the balance equal to zero, we *debit* the account for $1,200.

Debit		Credit	
Closing	1,200	Balance	1,200

Remember, every entry must have both a debit and a credit. So, to record the other half of the closing entry, we bring into existence the **Income Summary Account**. The Income Summary Account does not have plus and minus signs, just debit and credit.

At the end of a fiscal period, closing entries allow a business to start a new income statement period with a clean slate. Revenue and expense accounts are closed.

There are four steps in the closing procedure:

1. **Close the revenue accounts into Income Summary.**
2. **Close the expense accounts into Income Summary.**
3. **Close the Income Summary account into the Capital account, transferring the net income or loss to the Capital account.**
4. **Close the Drawing account into the Capital account.**

To illustrate, we return to Arch Copy Co. For the purpose of the illustration, assume that Arch Copy Co.'s fiscal period consists of one month. We have the following T account balances in the revenue and expense accounts after the adjustments have been posted.

Income from Services		
−	+	
	Balance	7,790

Advertising Expense		
+	−	
Balance 200		

Wages Expense		
+	−	
Balance 2,310		

Utilities Expense		
+	−	
Balance 160		

Rent Expense		
+	−	
Balance 700		

Insurance Expense		
+	−	
Balance 30		

Supplies Expense		
+	−	
Balance 600		

Depreciation Expense, Equipment		
+	−	
Balance 510		

Step 1 **Close the revenue account or accounts into Income Summary.** In order to make the balance of Income from Services equal to zero, we *balance it off,* or debit it, in the amount of $7,790. Because we need an offsetting credit, we credit Income Summary for the same amount. Notice that there

are no signs in Income Summary, only Debit and Credit like the other accounts.

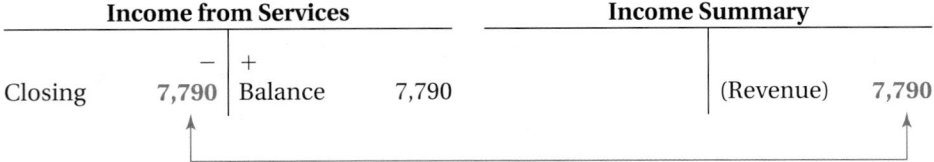

The balance of Income from Services is transferred to Income Summary.

Step 2 Close the expense accounts into Income Summary. To make the balances of the expense accounts equal to zero, we need to balance them off, or credit them. Again the T accounts are useful for formulating this journal entry.

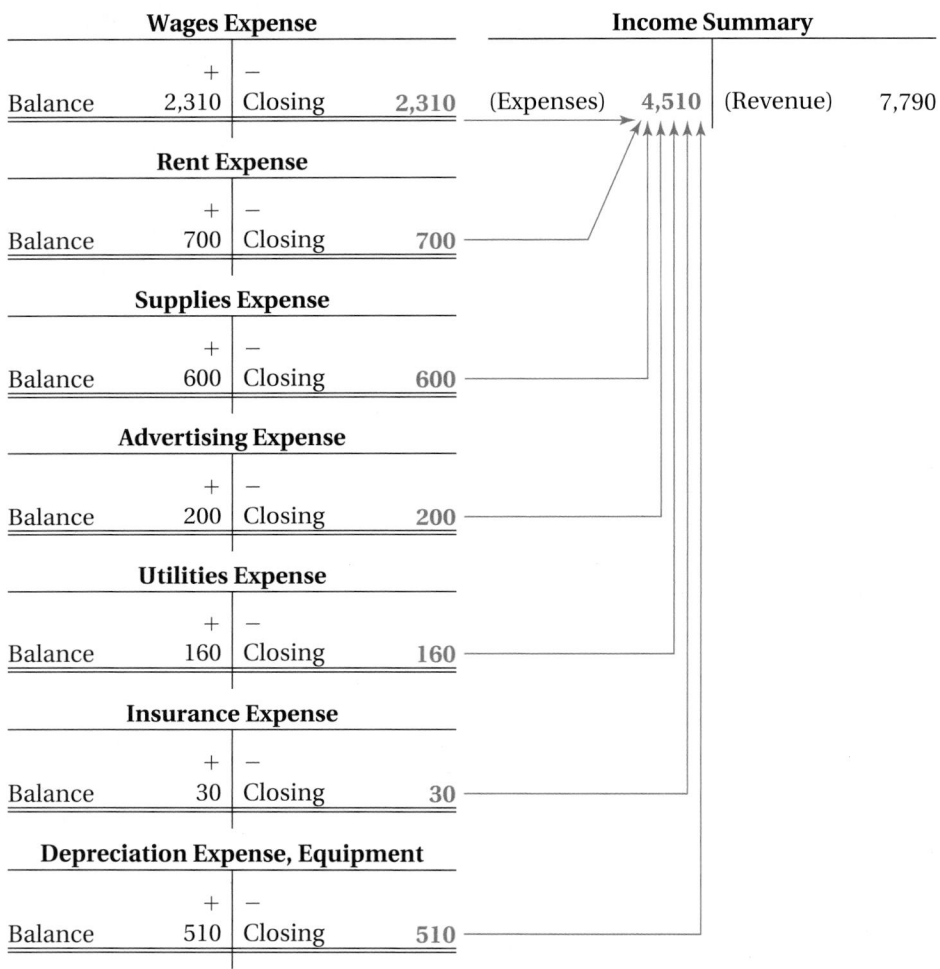

Step 3 Recall that we created Income Summary so that we could have a debit and a credit in each closing entry. Now that it has done its job, we close it out. We use the same procedure as before, in that we make the balance equal to zero, or balance off the account. We transfer, or close, the balance of the Income Summary account into the Capital account, as shown in the T accounts and in Figure 2.

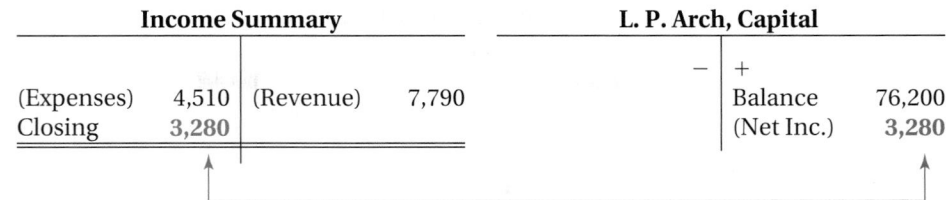

Income Summary is always closed into the Capital account by the amount of the net income (Revenue minus Expenses) or the net loss. Comparing net income or net loss on the work sheet with the closing entry for Income Summary can serve as a check point or verification for you.

FIGURE 2

GENERAL JOURNAL   PAGE ___4___

	DATE	DESCRIPTION	POST. REF.	DEBIT	CREDIT	
14	Step	**Closing Entries**				14
15	1 30	Income from Services		7 7 9 0 00		15
16		Income Summary			7 7 9 0 00	16
17						17
18	30	Income Summary		4 5 1 0 00		18
19		Wages Expense			2 3 1 0 00	19
20		Rent Expense			7 0 0 00	20
21	Step	Supplies Expense			6 0 0 00	21
22	2	Advertising Expense			2 0 0 00	22
23		Utilities Expense			1 6 0 00	23
24		Insurance Expense			3 0 00	24
25		Depreciation Expense,				25
26		Equipment			5 1 0 00	26
27						27
28	30	Income Summary		3 2 8 0 00		28
29		L. P. Arch, Capital			3 2 8 0 00	29

Net income is added (credited) to the Capital account because, as shown in the statement of owner's equity, net income is treated as an addition. Net loss, on the other hand, is subtracted from (debited) to the Capital account,

because net loss is treated as a deduction in the statement of owner's equity. Here's how to close Income Summary for J. Doe Company (net loss of $200):

The entry to close Income Summary into Doe's Capital account would look like the following.

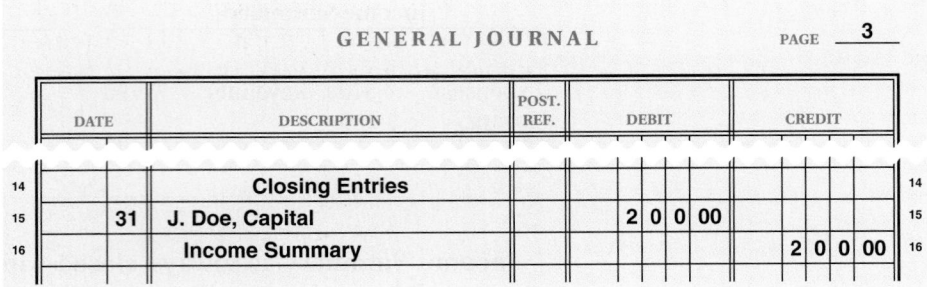

Step 4 Let's return to the example of Arch Copy Co. The Drawing account applies to only one fiscal period, and so it too must be closed. Drawing is not an expense because it did not help the business generate revenue. And because Drawing is not an expense, it cannot affect net income or net loss. It appears in the statement of owner's equity as a deduction from the Capital account, so it is closed directly into the Capital account. We balance off the Drawing account, or make the balance of it equal to zero. The balance of Drawing is transferred to the Capital account.

The journal entries in the closing procedure are shown in Figure 3.

FIGURE 3

| | | | | | | GENERAL JOURNAL | | | | | | PAGE 4 | | |

GENERAL JOURNAL   PAGE 4

	DATE	DESCRIPTION	POST. REF.	DEBIT	CREDIT	
14	Step	**Closing Entries**				14
15	1 30	Income from Services	411	7 7 9 0 00		15
16		Income Summary	313		7 7 9 0 00	16
17						17
18	30	Income Summary	313	4 5 1 0 00		18
19		Wages Expense	511		2 3 1 0 00	19
20		Rent Expense	512		7 0 0 00	20
21	Step	Supplies Expense	513		6 0 0 00	21
22	2	Advertising Expense	514		2 0 0 00	22
23		Utilities Expense	515		1 6 0 00	23
24		Insurance Expense	516		3 0 00	24
25		Depreciation Expense,				25
26		Equipment	517		5 1 0 00	26
27						27
28	Step 30	Income Summary	313	3 2 8 0 00		28
29	3	L. P. Arch, Capital	311		3 2 8 0 00	29
30						30
31	Step 30	L. P. Arch, Capital	311	2 5 0 0 00		31
32	4	L. P. Arch, Drawing	312		2 5 0 0 00	32

FYI

As a memory tool for the sequence of steps in the closing procedure, use the letters of the closing elements, **REID**: Revenue, Expenses, Income Summary, Drawing.

These closing entries show that Arch Copy Co. has net income of $3,280, the owner has withdrawn $2,500 for personal expenses, and $780 has been retained in the business, thereby increasing capital.

Closing Entries Taken Directly from the Work Sheet

You can gather the information for the closing entries either directly from the ledger accounts or from the work sheet. Since the Income Statement columns of the work sheet consist entirely of revenues and expenses, you can pick up the figures for three of the four closing entries from these columns. Figure 4 shows a partial work sheet for Arch Copy Co.

	ACCOUNT NAME	TRIAL BALANCE DEBIT	TRIAL BALANCE CREDIT	ADJUSTMENTS DEBIT	ADJUSTMENTS CREDIT	INCOME STATEMENT DEBIT	INCOME STATEMENT CREDIT
1	Cash	34 1 2 0 00					
2	Accounts Receivable	2 0 0 00					
3	Prepaid Insurance	3 6 0 00			(a) 3 0 00		
4	Equipment	49 7 2 0 00					
5	Accounts Payable		6 7 0 0 00				
6	L. P. Arch, Capital		76 2 0 0 00				
7	L. P. Arch, Drawing	2 5 0 0 00					
8	Income from Services		7 7 9 0 00				7 7 9 0 00
9	Wages Expense	2 1 3 0 00		(c) 1 8 0 00		2 3 1 0 00	
10	Rent Expense	7 0 0 00				7 0 0 00	
11	Supplies Expense	6 0 0 00				6 0 0 00	
12	Advertising Expense	2 0 0 00				2 0 0 00	
13	Utilities Expense	1 6 0 00				1 6 0 00	
14		90 6 9 0 00	90 6 9 0 00				
15	Insurance Expense			(a) 3 0 00		3 0 00	
16	Depreciation Expense,						
17	Equipment			(b) 5 1 0 00		5 1 0 00	
18							
19	Accumulated Dep.,						
20	Equipment				(b) 5 1 0 00		
21	Wages Payable				(c) 1 8 0 00		
22				7 2 0 00	7 2 0 00	4 5 1 0 00	7 7 9 0 00
23	Net Income					3 2 8 0 00	
24						7 7 9 0 00	7 7 9 0 00
25							
26							

FIGURE 4

You may plan the closing entries by balancing off all the figures that appear in the Income Statement columns. For example, in the Income Statement Credit column, there is a credit for $7,790 (Income from Services), so we debit that account for $7,790 and credit Income Summary for $7,790.

There are debits for $2,310, $700, $600, $200, $160, $30, and $510 (expense accounts). So now we *credit* these accounts for the same amounts, and we debit Income Summary for their total ($4,510).

Next, we close Income Summary into Capital, using the net income figure already shown on the work sheet in Figure 4.

We do, of course, have to get the last closing entry from the Balance Sheet columns to close Drawing.

Incidentally, accountants call the accounts that are to be closed (such as revenue, expenses, Income Summary, and Drawing) **nominal** or **temporary-equity accounts.** These accounts are *temporary* in that their balances apply to only one fiscal period. The *equity* aspect pertains because these accounts all come under the umbrella of owner's equity.

On the other hand, accountants call the accounts that remain open (such as assets, liabilities, and Capital) **real** or **permanent accounts.** These accounts have balances that will be carried over to the next fiscal period. They are *permanent* because as long as the company exists, there will be balances in these accounts.

Posting the Closing Entries

In the Item column of the ledger account, we write the word *Closing.* To show that the balance of an account is zero, we draw a line through both the Debit Balance and the Credit Balance columns.

After we have posted the closing entries, the Capital, Drawing, Income Summary, revenue, and expense accounts of Arch Copy Co. appear as follows:

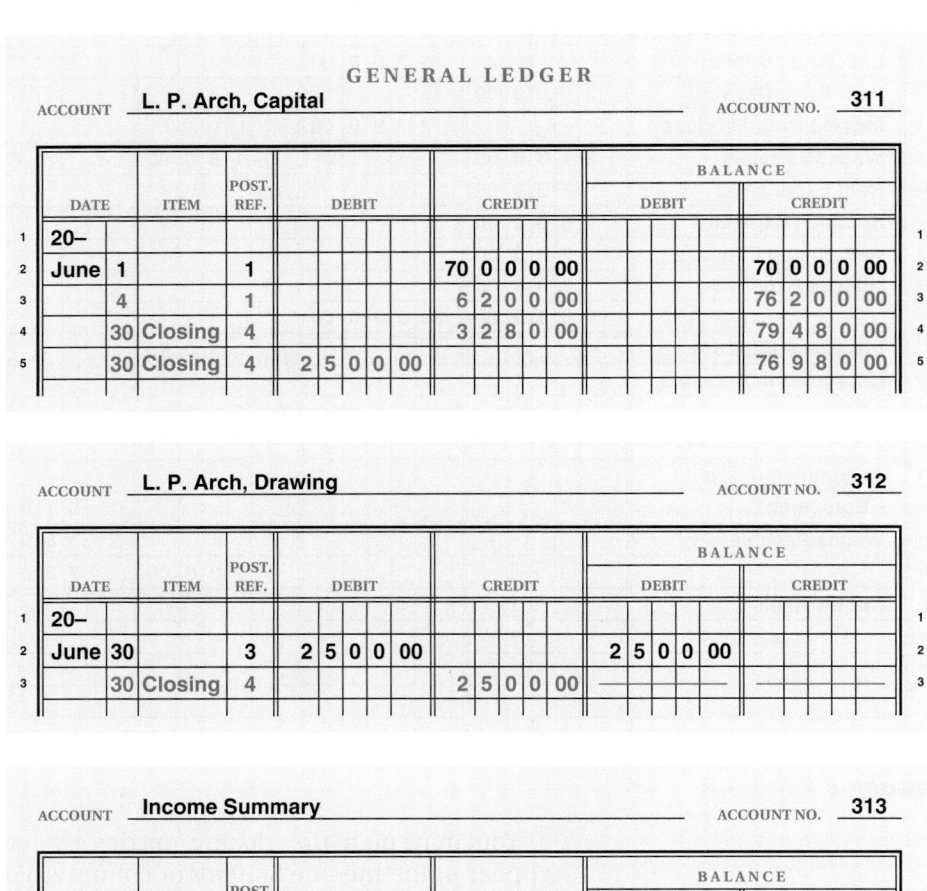

GENERAL LEDGER

ACCOUNT **L. P. Arch, Capital**   ACCOUNT NO. **311**

	DATE	ITEM	POST. REF.	DEBIT	CREDIT	BALANCE DEBIT	BALANCE CREDIT	
1	20–							1
2	June 1		1		70 0 0 0 00		70 0 0 0 00	2
3	4		1		6 2 0 0 00		76 2 0 0 00	3
4	30	Closing	4		3 2 8 0 00		79 4 8 0 00	4
5	30	Closing	4	2 5 0 0 00			76 9 8 0 00	5

ACCOUNT **L. P. Arch, Drawing**   ACCOUNT NO. **312**

	DATE	ITEM	POST. REF.	DEBIT	CREDIT	BALANCE DEBIT	BALANCE CREDIT	
1	20–							1
2	June 30		3	2 5 0 0 00		2 5 0 0 00		2
3	30	Closing	4		2 5 0 0 00	—	—	3

ACCOUNT **Income Summary**   ACCOUNT NO. **313**

	DATE	ITEM	POST. REF.	DEBIT	CREDIT	BALANCE DEBIT	BALANCE CREDIT	
1	20–							1
2	June 30	Closing	4		7 7 9 0 00		7 7 9 0 00	2
3	30	Closing	4	4 5 1 0 00			3 2 8 0 00	3
4	30	Closing	4	3 2 8 0 00		—	—	4

ACCOUNT Income from Services   **ACCOUNT NO.** 411

	DATE		ITEM	POST. REF.	DEBIT	CREDIT	BALANCE DEBIT	BALANCE CREDIT	
1	20–								1
2	June	7		1		2 5 2 0 00		2 5 2 0 00	2
3		15		2		1 0 5 0 00		3 5 7 0 00	3
4		30		3		4 2 2 0 00		7 7 9 0 00	4
5		30	Closing	4	7 7 9 0 00				5
6									6

ACCOUNT Wages Expense   **ACCOUNT NO.** 511

	DATE		ITEM	POST. REF.	DEBIT	CREDIT	BALANCE DEBIT	BALANCE CREDIT	
1	20–								1
2	June	24		2	2 1 3 0 00		2 1 3 0 00		2
3		30	Adj.	4	1 8 0 00		2 3 1 0 00		3
4		30	Closing	4		2 3 1 0 00			4

ACCOUNT Rent Expense   **ACCOUNT NO.** 512

	DATE		ITEM	POST. REF.	DEBIT	CREDIT	BALANCE DEBIT	BALANCE CREDIT	
1	20–								1
2	June	8		1	7 0 0 00		7 0 0 00		2
3		30	Closing	4		7 0 0 00			3

ACCOUNT Supplies Expense   **ACCOUNT NO.** 513

	DATE		ITEM	POST. REF.	DEBIT	CREDIT	BALANCE DEBIT	BALANCE CREDIT	
1	20–								1
2	June	10		1	6 0 0 00		6 0 0 00		2
3		30	Closing	4		6 0 0 00			3

ACCOUNT Advertising Expense   **ACCOUNT NO.** 514

	DATE		ITEM	POST. REF.	DEBIT	CREDIT	BALANCE DEBIT	BALANCE CREDIT	
1	20–								1
2	June	14		2	2 0 0 00		2 0 0 00		2
3		30	Closing	4		2 0 0 00			3

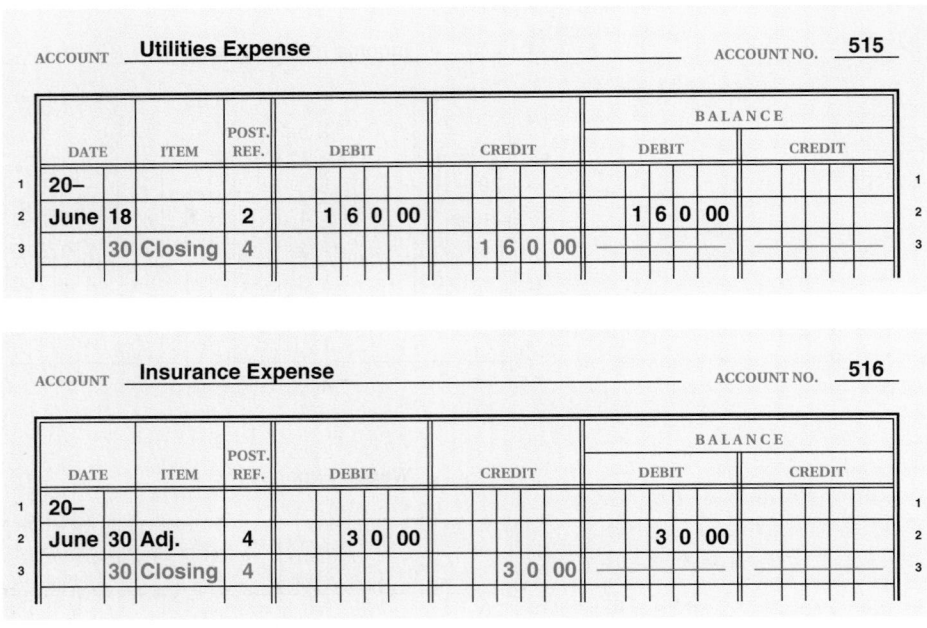

ACCOUNT	Utilities Expense					ACCOUNT NO.	515	
			POST.				BALANCE	
DATE	ITEM	REF.	DEBIT	CREDIT		DEBIT	CREDIT	
20–								
June 18		2	1 6 0 00			1 6 0 00		
30	Closing	4		1 6 0 00		—		

ACCOUNT	Insurance Expense					ACCOUNT NO.	516	
			POST.				BALANCE	
DATE	ITEM	REF.	DEBIT	CREDIT		DEBIT	CREDIT	
20–								
June 30	Adj.	4	3 0 00			3 0 00		
30	Closing	4		3 0 00		—		

ACCOUNT	Depreciation Expense, Equipment					ACCOUNT NO.	517	
			POST.				BALANCE	
DATE	ITEM	REF.	DEBIT	CREDIT		DEBIT	CREDIT	
20–								
June 30	Adj.	4	5 1 0 00			5 1 0 00		
30	Closing	4		5 1 0 00		—		

Office supplies—such as those supplied by major chains like Staples and Office Max—consist of a wide variety of items that are used up and reordered frequently in the course of doing business.

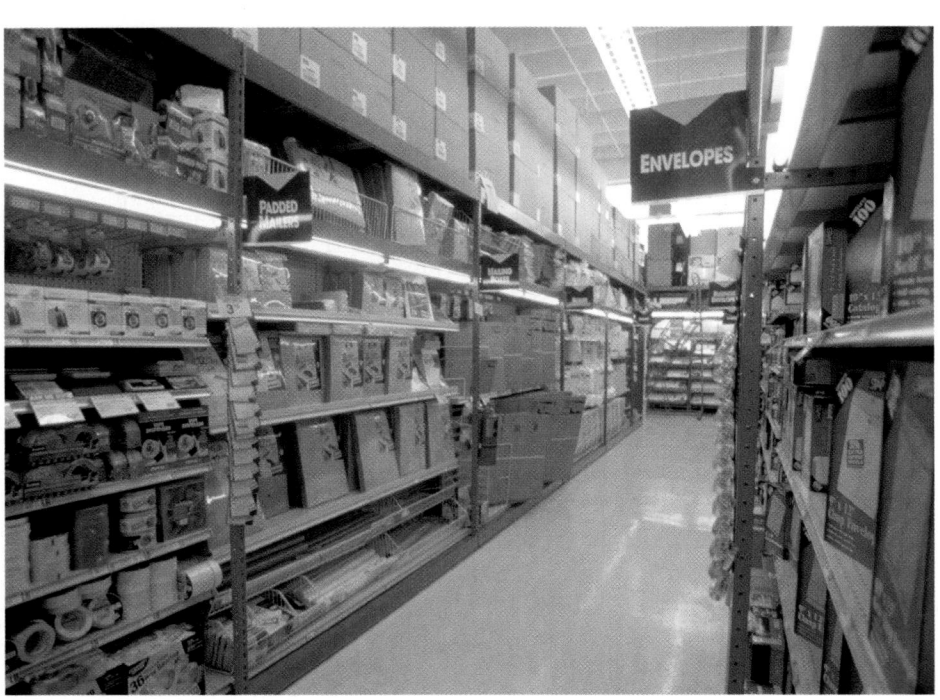

THE POST-CLOSING TRIAL BALANCE

OBJECTIVE 3
Prepare a post-closing trial balance.

After posting the closing entries and before going on to the next fiscal period, verify the balances of the accounts that remain open. To do so, prepare a **post-closing trial balance**, using the final balance figures from the ledger accounts. The purpose of the post-closing trial balance is to make sure that the debit balances equal the credit balances.

Note that the accounts listed in the post-closing trial balance (assets, liabilities, and Capital) are the *real* or *permanent accounts* (see Figure 5). The accountant carries forward the balances of the permanent accounts from one fiscal period to another.

FIGURE 5

Arch Copy Co.
Post-Closing Trial Balance
June 30, 20—

ACCOUNT NAME	DEBIT	CREDIT
Cash	34 1 2 0 00	
Accounts Receivable	2 0 0 00	
Prepaid Insurance	3 3 0 00	
Equipment	49 7 2 0 00	
Accumulated Depreciation, Equipment		5 1 0 00
Accounts Payable		6 7 0 0 00
Wages Payable		1 8 0 00
L. P. Arch, Capital		76 9 8 0 00
	84 3 7 0 00	84 3 7 0 00

Contrast this to the handling of *nominal* or *temporary-equity accounts* (revenue, expenses, Income Summary, and Drawing), which are closed at the end of each fiscal period.

If the total debits and total credits of the post-closing trial balance are not equal, here's a recommended procedure for tracking down the error.

1. Re-add the trial balance columns.
2. Check to see that the figures were correctly transferred from the ledger accounts to the post-closing trial balance.
3. Verify the posting of the adjusting entries and the recording of the new balances.
4. Make sure that the closing entries have been posted and that all revenue, expense, Income Summary, and Drawing accounts have zero balances.

THE BASIS OF ACCOUNTING: CASH, MODIFIED CASH, AND ACCRUAL

OBJECTIVE 4
Define the following methods of accounting: accrual basis and modified cash basis.

The basis of accounting that a company chooses has a direct effect on the company's net income and the company's income tax. Guidelines for the three bases are set by the Internal Revenue Service.

Under the cash basis revenue is counted when it is received in cash, and expenses are counted when they are paid in cash. Individuals' personal income taxes are recorded on the cash basis.

FYI

Availability of the cash method is expanded by the IRS in Notice 2001–76. Most small service businesses with average annual gross receipts of $1 million or less will be allowed to use the cash method rather than the accrual method, which is more complicated and time consuming. For purposes of this text and ease of learning with smaller numbers, we have avoided transactions in the hundreds of thousands and millions. For more detail on this important change, see the IRS website at **www.irs.gov/smallbiz**.

Under the **modified cash basis** exceptions are made for expenditures on items having economic lives of more than one year and on some prepaid items. Examples of such expenditures are equipment and insurance. Costs of these items must be prorated or spread out over their useful lives. Consequently adjustments are made for depreciation of equipment and the expiration of insurance. The IRS publications refer to this basis as a hybrid method, because it combines some of the characteristics of both the cash basis and the accrual basis.

Under the **accrual basis**, revenue is recorded when it is earned, and expenses are recorded when they are incurred. For example, in the sale of goods revenue is counted by the seller when the buyer accepts delivery. Expenses are recorded by the seller of the goods when the costs are incurred. This is called the *matching* principle, since revenue in one fiscal period is matched up with expenses incurred in the same period.

INTERIM STATEMENTS

OBJECTIVE 5
Prepare interim statements.

As we said previously, a firm's fiscal year generally consists of twelve consecutive months. However, it is understandable that the owner of the business does not want to wait until the end of the twelve-month period to determine whether the company made a profit or a loss. Instead, most owners want financial statements at the end of each month. Financial statements prepared during the fiscal year, for periods of less than twelve months, are called **interim statements**. (They are given this name because they are prepared within the fiscal period.) For example, a business may prepare the income statement, the statement of owner's equity, and the balance sheet *monthly*. These statements provide up-to-date information about the results and status of operations. For example, a company might have the following interim statements:

In this case, the accountant would prepare a work sheet at the end of each month. Next, based on these work sheets, he or she would prepare the financial statements. *However, the remaining steps—journalizing the adjusting and closing entries and preparing the post-closing trial balance—would be performed only at the end of the year.*

CHAPTER REVIEW

Review of Performance Objectives

1. List the steps in the accounting cycle.

   1. Analyze source documents and record business transactions in a journal.
   2. Post journal entries to the accounts in the ledger.
   3. Prepare a trial balance.
   4. Gather adjustment data and record the adjusting entries on a work sheet.
   5. Complete the work sheet.
   6. Prepare financial statements from the data on the work sheet.
   7. Journalize and post the adjusting entries from the data on the work sheet.
   8. Journalize and post the closing entries.
   9. Prepare a post-closing trial balance.

2. Journalize and post closing entries for a service enterprise.

   The four steps in the closing procedure are as follows:

   1. Close the revenue accounts into Income Summary.
   2. Close the expense accounts into Income Summary.
   3. Close the Income Summary account into the Capital account, transferring the net income or loss to the Capital account.
   4. Close the Drawing account into the Capital account.

3. Prepare a post-closing trial balance.

   A post-closing trial balance consists of the final balances of the accounts remaining open. It is the final proof that the debit balances equal the credit balances before the posting for the new fiscal period begins.

4. Define the following methods of accounting: accrual basis and modified cash basis.

   Under the *accrual basis* of accounting, revenue is recorded when earned, even if cash is received at a later date, and expenses are recorded when incurred, even if cash is to be paid at a later date.

   Under the *modified cash basis*, revenue is recorded only when cash is received, and most expenses are recorded only when paid in cash. However, exceptions are made for certain expenses, such as depreciation and insurance expired, requiring adjusting entries.

5. Prepare interim statements.

   Interim statements consist of year-to-date income statements, statements of owner's equity, and balance sheets as of various dates during the fiscal period.

Glossary

Accrual basis An accounting method under which revenue is recorded when it is earned, regardless of when it is received, and expenses are recorded when they are incurred, regardless of when they are paid. (160)

Closing entries Entries made at the end of a fiscal period to close off the revenue, expense, and drawing accounts—that is, to make the balances of the temporary-equity accounts equal to zero. Closing is also called *clearing the accounts*. (150)

Income Summary Account An account brought into existence in order to have a debit and credit in each closing entry. The revenue and expense account balances are transferred to this account to allow calculations of net income or net loss. (150)

Interim statements Financial statements prepared during the fiscal year, covering a period of time less than twelve months. (160)

Modified cash basis An accounting method under which revenue is recorded only when it is received in cash. Most expenses are recorded only when they are paid in cash. However, exceptions are made for expenditures on items having a useful life of more than one year and for certain prepaid items. Expenditures for insurance premiums can be *prorated*, or spread out, over the fiscal periods covered. Expenditures for long-lived items are recorded as assets and later depreciated as an expense over their useful lives. (160)

Nominal or **temporary-equity accounts** Accounts that apply to only one fiscal period and that are to be closed at the end of that fiscal period, such as revenue, expense, Income Summary, and Drawing accounts. This category may also be described as all accounts except assets, liabilities, and the Capital account. (156)

Post-closing trial balance The listing of the final balances of the real accounts at the end of the fiscal period. (159)

Real or **permanent accounts** The accounts that remain open (assets, liabilities, and the Capital account in owner's equity) and that have balances that will be carried over to the next fiscal period. (156)

QUESTIONS, EXERCISES, AND PROBLEMS

Discussion Questions

1. Number in order the following steps in the accounting cycle.
   a. Prepare a trial balance on the first two columns of the work sheet.
   b. Post journal entries to accounts in the ledger.
   c. Journalize and post adjusting entries.
   d. Analyze source documents and record transactions in the journal.
   e. Prepare financial statements.
   f. Gather adjusting data and write adjusting entries on the work sheet.

g. Journalize and post closing entries.

h. Prepare a post-closing trial balance.

i. Complete the work sheet.

2. List the steps in the closing procedure in the correct order.

3. What is the purpose of closing entries? Consider the consequence of forgetting to make closing entries.

4. What are the two sources from which you can make closing entries?

5. What are real accounts? What are nominal accounts? Give examples of each.

6. What is the purpose of the Income Summary Account, and how does it relate to the revenue and expense accounts?

7. What is the purpose of the post-closing trial balance? What is the difference between a trial balance and a post-closing trial balance?

8. Write the third closing entry to transfer the profit or loss to the B. Thomas, Capital account, assuming the following:

a. A profit of $3,874 during the first quarter (Jan.–Mar.)

b. A loss of $1,278 during the second quarter (Apr.–Jun.)

Exercises

P.O. 2

Classify accounts and show where they are listed on the work sheet.

Exercise 5-1 Classify the accounts listed below as real (permanent) or nominal (temporary), and indicate with an X whether the account is closed. Also, indicate the financial statement in which each account will appear. The Building account is given as an example.

Account Title	Real	Nominal	Closed Yes	Closed No	Income Statement	Balance Sheet
0. Example: Building	X			X		X
a. Prepaid Insurance						
b. Accounts Payable						
c. Wages Payable						
d. Services Income						
e. Rent Expense						
f. Supplies Expense						
g. Accum. Depr., Equip.						

P.O. 2

Journalize closing entries from T account balances.

Exercise 5-2 Number the closing entries as steps 1 through 4. Journalize the following closing entries.

Assets	=	Liabilities	+	Owner's Equity	+	Revenue	−	Expenses
Dr. | Cr.		Dr. | Cr.		Dr. | Cr.		Dr. | Cr.		Dr. | Cr.
+ | −		− | +		− | +		− | +		+ | −

Prepaid Insurance

Bal. 990 | (c)   360
Bal. 630 |

Accum. Depr., Equipment

| Bal. 3,200
| (b)   700
3,900 Bal. |

Wages Payable

| (a)   210

J. Jenson, Capital

560 | Bal.
500 | 24,000
| Bal. 22,940

J. Jenson, Drawing

Bal. 500 | 500

Income Summary

4,210 | 3,650
| 560

Professional Fees

3,650 | Bal. 3,650

Wages Expense

Bal. 2,800 | 3,010
(a)   210 |
Bal. 3,010 |

Insurance Expense

(c)   360 | 360

Depr. Expense, Equipment

(b)   700 | 700

Misc. Expense

Bal. 140 | 140

P.O. 2

Journalize closing entries from account balances.

Exercise 5-3 As of December 31, the end of the current year, the ledger of Heron Company contained the following account balances after adjustment. All accounts have normal balances. Journalize the closing entries.

Cash	$ 8,540	H. Heron, Drawing	$1,698
Equipment	11,486	Professional Fees	6,875
Accumulated Depreciation,		Wages Expense	1,468
Equipment	2,687	Rent Expense	990
Accounts Payable	1,574	Depreciation Expense,	
Wages Payable	658	Equipment	1,243
H. Heron, Capital	13,876	Miscellaneous Expense	245

P.O. 2

Journalize closing entries from work sheet columns—a profit.

Exercise 5-4 The Income Statement columns of the work sheet of Dryer Company for the fiscal year ended June 30 appear below. During the year, N. Dryer withdrew $4,200. Journalize the closing entries.

	ACCOUNT NAME	INCOME STATEMENT	
		DEBIT	CREDIT
1	Service Income		6 8 9 7 00
2	Rental Income		3 6 7 6 00
3	Rent Expense	2 7 0 0 00	
4	Wages Expense	1 9 5 4 00	
5	Utilities Expense	3 6 5 00	
6	Miscellaneous Expense	1 5 9 00	
7		5 1 7 8 00	10 5 7 3 00
8	Net Income	5 3 9 5 00	
9		10 5 7 3 00	10 5 7 3 00

P.O. 2

Journalize closing entries from work sheet columns—a loss.

Exercise 5-5 The Income Statement columns of the work sheet of Mandy Company for the fiscal year ended December 31 appear on the following page. During the year, S. Mandy withdrew $18,000. Journalize the closing entries.

	ACCOUNT NAME	INCOME STATEMENT	
		DEBIT	CREDIT
1	Service Income		32 7 4 0 00
2	Rental Income		12 0 0 0 00
3	Wages Expense	43 5 2 0 00	
4	Utilities Expense	4 6 3 0 00	
5	Miscellaneous Expense	9 2 0 0 00	
6		57 3 5 0 00	44 7 4 0 00
7	Net Loss		12 6 1 0 00
8		57 3 5 0 00	57 3 5 0 00

P.O. 2

Journalize closing entries three and four from account balances.

Exercise 5-6 After all revenue and expenses have been closed at the end of the fiscal period ended December 31, Income Summary has a debit of $45,450 and a credit of $35,430. On the same date, E. Morris, Drawing, has a debit balance of $14,300, and E. Morris, Capital, had a beginning credit balance of $65,320.

a. Journalize the entries necessary to close the remaining temporary accounts.
b. What is the new balance of E. Morris, Capital, after closing the remaining temporary accounts? Show your calculations.

P.O. 5

Place accounts on financial statements.

Exercise 5-7 Indicate with an X whether each of the following would appear on the income statement, statement of owner's equity, or balance sheet. The first item is provided as an example.

Item	Income Statement	Statement of Owner's Equity	Balance Sheet
0. Example: The total liabilities of the business at the end of the year.			X
a. The amount of the owner's Capital balance at the end of the year.			
b. The amount of depreciation expense on equipment during the year.			
c. The amount of the company's net income for the year.			
d. The book value of the equipment.			
e. Total insurance expired during the year.			
f. Total accounts receivable at the end of the year.			
g. Total withdrawals by the owner.			
h. The cost of supplies used during the year.			
i. The amount of the owner's Capital balance at the beginning of the year.			

P.O. 5

Prepare a statement of owner's equity from T accounts.

Exercise 5-8 Prepare a statement of owner's equity for The Beren Clinic for the year ended December 31. P. Beren's capital amount on January 1 was $120,000, and there was an additional investment of $7,000 on May 12 and withdrawals of $29,500 for the year. Net income for the year was $18,310.

REFLECTING ON
THE WORLD WIDE WEB

You just learned about the methods of accounting a company can use when recording transactions, such as sales. This would be a good time to review the methods discussed in Objective 4. Then, see if you can answer some questions about Tommy Hilfiger Corporation. Use the financial statements that begin on page 25 of the 2002 annual report **http://www.tommypr.com/media/downloads/TH02.pdf**

1. What method of accounting does Tommy Hilfiger Corporation use? Can you tell by looking at its financial statements?
2. For 2002, how much is net sales (assume that all revenue is from sales) on Tommy Hilfiger's income statement? How much is Accounts Receivable on the balance sheet? What can you tell from these two amounts?

CONSIDER AND COMMUNICATE

Your friend owns a small sole proprietorship. He does his own bookkeeping, although he didn't finish the chapter on closing entries before he went to work. He mentions to you that closing entries look like they take a long time. He wonders why he should bother to do them, because all he really looks at is the checkbook anyway. Convince him that closing entries are necessary.

CRITICAL THINKING

Following is the post-closing trial balance submitted to you by the bookkeeper. Assume that the debit total ($41,048) is correct.

a. Analyze the work and prepare a response to what you have reviewed.
b. Journalize the closing entries.
c. What is the net income or net loss?
d. Is there an increase or a decrease in Capital?
e. What would be the ending amount of Capital?
f. What is the new balance of the post-closing trial balance?

Wicker Consulting Company
Post-Closing Trial Balance
December 31, 20—

ACCOUNT NAME	DEBIT	CREDIT
Cash	3 4 1 2 00	
Accounts Receivable	1 6 9 3 00	
Prepaid Insurance	2 1 4 7 00	
Accounts Payable		
C. Wicker, Capital		13 8 1 8 00
C. Wicker, Drawing	6 3 6 0 00	
Consulting Income		25 6 0 3 00
Wages Expense	11 9 9 4 00	
Rent Expense	9 6 0 0 00	
Advertising Expense	2 5 8 2 00	
Supplies Expense	9 1 4 00	
Insurance Expense	1 6 1 0 00	
Miscellaneous Expense	7 3 6 00	
	41 0 4 8 00	41 0 4 8 00

A MATTER OF ETHICS

You are completing the accounting cycle for the company for which you work. You have made a post-closing trial balance, but it doesn't balance. You are tired, and besides, you don't think they pay you for this kind of headache. You decide to increase the balance of an asset account to make the totals balance. Discuss this behavior and whether it is ethical or illegal.

WHAT'S WRONG WITH THIS PICTURE?

The bookkeeper has completed a work sheet and has journalized and posted the closing entries, but he forgot to journalize and post the adjusting entries from the work sheet. What are the effects of these actions and omissions? How would these actions and omissions affect the accounting records and the resulting financial statements?

PROBLEM SET A

For additional help, see the demonstration problem at the beginning of each chapter in your Working Papers.

P.O. 2

Problem 5-1A After the accountant posted the adjusting entries for M. Ward, Designer, the general ledger contained the following account balances on May 31:

	ACCOUNT NAME	ADJUSTED TRIAL BALANCE DEBIT A + Draw. + E	CREDIT Accum. Deprec. + L + C + R
1	Cash	2 3 1 8 00	
2	Accounts Receivable	1 4 0 8 00	
3	Prepaid Insurance	9 8 7 00	
4	Office Equipment	5 7 9 0 00	
5	Accumulated Depreciation, Office Equipment		1 3 6 4 00
6	Accounts Payable		8 8 0 00
7	M. Ward, Capital		8 2 4 7 00
8	M. Ward, Drawing	1 8 0 0 00	
9	Commissions Earned		3 8 9 7 00
10	Rent Expense	7 9 0 00	
11	Supplies Expense	3 8 1 00	
12	Depreciation Expense, Office Equipment	5 2 0 00	
13	Utilities Expense	2 7 6 00	
14	Miscellaneous Expense	1 1 8 00	
15		14 3 8 8 00	14 3 8 8 00

Check Figure

Net Income, $1,812

Instructions

a. Write the owner's name on the Capital and Drawing T accounts.
b. Record the account balances in the T accounts for owner's equity, revenue, and expenses.
c. Journalize the closing entries with the four steps in correct order. Number the closing entries 1–4.
d. Post the closing entries to the T accounts right after you journalize each one to see the effect of the closing entries. Number the closing entries 1–4.

P.O. 2

Problem 5-2A The partial work sheet for Kingly Consulting for the month of May is as follows:

	ACCOUNT NAME	INCOME STATEMENT DEBIT E	INCOME STATEMENT CREDIT R	BALANCE SHEET DEBIT A + Draw.	BALANCE SHEET CREDIT Accum. Depr. + L + C	
1	Cash			2 2 4 8 00		1
2	Prepaid Insurance			8 5 9 00		2
3	Equipment			5 7 3 1 00		3
4	Accumulated Depreciation, Equipment				2 3 7 9 00	4
5	Accounts Payable				8 4 1 00	5
6	K. Kingly, Capital				2 4 1 5 00	6
7	K. Kingly, Drawing			1 8 0 0 00		7
8	Consulting Income		8 5 4 6 00			8
9	Rent Expense	8 0 0 00				9
10	Wages Expense	1 6 3 3 00				10
11	Supplies Expense	3 6 5 00				11
12	Miscellaneous Expense	1 6 8 00				12
13						13
14	Insurance Expense	2 6 4 00				14
15	Depreciation Expense, Equipment	7 0 0 00				15
16	Wages Payable				3 8 7 00	16
17		3 9 3 0 00	8 5 4 6 00	10 6 3 8 00	6 0 2 2 00	17
18	Net Income	4 6 1 6 00			4 6 1 6 00	18
19		8 5 4 6 00	8 5 4 6 00	10 6 3 8 00	10 6 3 8 00	19
20						20

Check Figure

Debit to Income Summary, second entry, $3,930

Instructions

a. Write the owner's name on the Capital and Drawing T accounts.
b. Record the account balances in the T accounts for owner's equity, revenue, and expenses.
c. Journalize the closing entries with the four steps in correct order. Number the closing entries 1 through 4.
d. Post the closing entries to the T accounts right after you journalize each one to see the effect of the closing entries. Number the closing entries 1 through 4.

P.O. 1,2,3

Problem 5-3A The completed work sheet for Dunn's Tour Company as of December 31 is presented in your Working Papers, along with the general ledger as of December 31 before adjustments.

Check Figure

Post-closing trial balance total, $7,408

Instructions

1. Write the name of the owner in the Capital and Drawing accounts.
2. Write the balances from the unadjusted trial balance in the general ledger.
3. Journalize and post the adjusting entries.
4. Journalize and post the closing entries with the four steps in the correct order.
5. Prepare a post-closing trial balance.

P.O. 1,2,3

Problem 5-4A The account balances of Top Tutoring Service as of June 30, 20—, the end of the current fiscal year, are as follows:

| | ACCOUNT NAME | TRIAL BALANCE | |
		DEBIT	CREDIT
1	Cash	5 4 9 1 00	
2	Accounts Receivable	6 2 4 00	
3	Prepaid Insurance	1 2 8 0 00	
4	Equipment	6 4 9 7 00	
5	Accumulated Depreciation, Equipment		2 6 7 2 00
6	Van	18 6 7 4 00	
7	Accumulated Depreciation, Van		4 3 6 8 00
8	Accounts Payable		1 0 3 6 00
9	B. Morrow, Capital		4 8 4 8 00
10	B. Morrow, Drawing	12 0 0 0 00	
11	Fees Earned		53 2 8 0 00
12	Salary Expense	18 0 0 0 00	
13	Advertising Expense	1 2 0 0 00	
14	Van Operating Expense	6 0 5 00	
15	Utilities Expense	1 2 4 8 00	
16	Supplies Expense	3 2 7 00	
17	Miscellaneous Expense	2 5 8 00	
18		66 2 0 4 00	66 2 0 4 00

Check Figure

Net Income, $28,288

Instructions

1. Complete the work sheet:

   Data for the adjustments:

   a. Expired or used up insurance, $320.
   b. Depreciation expense on equipment, $890 (remember to credit the Accumulated Depreciation account for equipment, not Equipment).
   c. Depreciation expense on the van, $1,860 (remember to credit the Accumulated Depreciation account for the van, not Van).
   d. Salary accrued (earned) since the last payday, $284 (owed and to be paid on the next payday).

2. Prepare an income statement.
3. Prepare a statement of owner's equity; assume there was an additional investment of $2,000 on July 10.
4. Prepare a balance sheet.
5. Journalize the adjusting entries.
6. Journalize the closing entries with the four steps in the correct sequence.

Instructions for General Ledger Software

1. Print a trial balance.
2. Journalize the adjusting entries in the general journal and post to the general ledger. (No work sheet is required on the computer.)

3. Print an income statement, a statement of owner's equity, and a balance sheet.
4. Journalize the closing entries in the general journal.
5. Post the closing entries.
6. Print a post-closing trial balance.

PROBLEM SET B

For additional help, see the demonstration problem at the beginning of each chapter in your Working Papers.

P.O. 2

Problem 5-1B After the accountant posted the adjusting entries for C. Lorn, Designer, the general ledger contained the following account balances on May 31:

	ACCOUNT NAME	ADJUSTED TRIAL BALANCE	
		DEBIT	CREDIT Accum. Deprec.
		A + Draw. + E	+ L + C + R
1	Cash	2 4 2 9 00	
2	Accounts Receivable	8 8 6 00	
3	Prepaid Insurance	1 4 6 0 00	
4	Equipment	4 6 7 2 00	
5	Accumulated Depreciation, Equipment		1 2 5 3 00
6	Accounts Payable		9 4 3 00
7	C. Lorn, Capital		6 5 2 0 00
8	C. Lorn, Drawing	1 6 5 0 00	
9	Commissions Earned		4 6 7 9 00
10	Rent Expense	8 9 5 00	
11	Depreciation Expense, Equipment	4 6 7 00	
12	Supplies Expense	5 7 0 00	
13	Utilities Expense	2 6 4 00	
14	Miscellaneous Expense	1 0 2 00	
15		13 3 9 5 00	13 3 9 5 00

Check Figure

Net Income, $2,381

Instructions

a. Write the owner's name on the Capital and Drawing T accounts.
b. Record the account balances in the T accounts for owner's equity, revenue, and expenses.
c. Journalize the closing entries with the four steps in correct order. Number the closing entries 1 through 4.
d. Post the closing entries to the T accounts right after you journalize each one to see the effect of the closing entries. Number the closing entries 1 through 4.

P.O. 2

Problem 5-2B The partial work sheet for Kuntz Consulting for the month of June is as follows.

	ACCOUNT NAME	INCOME STATEMENT DEBIT (E)	INCOME STATEMENT CREDIT (R)	BALANCE SHEET DEBIT (A + Draw.)	BALANCE SHEET CREDIT Accum. Depr. + L + C	
1	Cash			6 1 0 4 00		1
2	Prepaid Insurance			1 3 4 4 00		2
3	Equipment			6 7 5 1 00		3
4	Accumulated Depreciation, Equipment				3 3 9 3 00	4
5	Accounts Payable				1 3 5 6 00	5
6	L. Kuntz, Capital				1 3 6 7 00	6
7	L. Kuntz, Drawing			2 4 0 0 00		7
8	Consulting Income		15 0 6 0 00			8
9	Rent Expense	1 1 0 0 00				9
10	Wages Expense	1 9 0 8 00				10
11	Miscellaneous Expense	2 4 0 00				11
12						12
13	Supplies Expense	4 3 2 00				13
14	Insurance Expense	3 4 5 00				14
15	Depreciation Expense, Equipment	9 0 0 00				15
16	Wages Payable				3 4 8 00	16
17		4 9 2 5 00	15 0 6 0 00	16 5 9 9 00	6 4 6 4 00	17
18	Net Income	10 1 3 5 00			10 1 3 5 00	18
19		15 0 6 0 00	15 0 6 0 00	16 5 9 9 00	16 5 9 9 00	19
20						20

Check Figure

Debit to Income Summary, second entry, $4,925

Instructions

a. Write the owner's name on the Capital and Drawing T accounts.
b. Record the account balances in the T accounts for owner's equity, revenue, and expenses.
c. Journalize the closing entries with the four steps in correct order. Number the closing entries 1 through 4.
d. Post the closing entries to the T accounts right after you journalize each one to see the effect of the closing entries. Number closing entries 1–4.

P.O. 1,2,3

Problem 5-3B The completed work sheet for Mann Insurance Agency as of December 31 is presented in your Working Papers, along with the general ledger as of December 31 before adjustments.

Check Figure

Post-closing trial balance total, $8,889.60

Instructions

1. Write the name of the owner in the Capital and Drawing accounts.
2. Write the balances from the unadjusted trial balance in the general ledger.
3. Journalize and post the adjusting entries.
4. Journalize and post the closing entries with the four steps in the correct order.
5. Prepare a post-closing trial balance.

P.O. 1,2,3

Problem 5-4B The account balances of BRB Company as of June 30, the end of the current fiscal year, are as follows.

	ACCOUNT NAME	DEBIT	CREDIT
1	Cash	4 3 8 1 00	
2	Accounts Receivable	5 7 8 00	
3	Prepaid Insurance	1 1 3 8 00	
4	Equipment	5 7 1 3 00	
5	Accumulated Depreciation, Equipment		2 4 8 7 00
6	Van	12 6 7 8 00	
7	Accumulated Depreciation, Van		3 3 1 8 00
8	Accounts Payable		9 9 7 00
9	B. Miles, Capital		5 9 6 4 00
10	B. Miles, Drawing	18 0 0 0 00	
11	Fees Earned		48 3 1 7 00
12	Salary Expense	16 0 0 0 00	
13	Advertising Expense	8 8 7 00	
14	Supplies Expense	3 9 7 00	
15	Van Operating Expense	4 6 2 00	
16	Utilities Expense	6 8 5 00	
17	Miscellaneous Expense	1 6 4 00	
18		61 0 8 3 00	61 0 8 3 00

Check Figure

Net income, $26,838

Instructions

1. Complete the work sheet.

   Data for the adjustments:
   a. Expired or used up insurance, $582.
   b. Depreciation expense on equipment, $590 (remember to credit the Accumulated Depreciation account for equipment, not Equipment).
   c. Depreciation expense on the van, $1,032 (remember to credit the Accumulated Depreciation account for the van, not Van).
   d. Salary accrued (earned) since the last payday, $680 (owed and to be paid on the next payday).

2. Prepare an income statement.
3. Prepare a statement of owner's equity; assume there was an additional investment of $3,000 on October 10.
4. Prepare a balance sheet.
5. Journalize the adjusting entries.
6. Journalize the closing entries with the four steps in the proper sequence.

Instructions for General Ledger Software

1. Print a trial balance.
2. Journalize the adjusting entries in the general journal and post to the general ledger. (No work sheet is required on the computer.)
3. Print an income statement, a statement of owner's equity, and a balance sheet.
4. Journalize the closing entries in the general journal.
5. Post the closing entries.
6. Print a post-closing trial balance.

The Computer Lab

Closing Entries

PHASE 10
Month-End-Closing
Entries

First, back up (make a copy of) your files before closing. Make sure you have printed the statements you want to print. If you find later on that you have a numerical error in a prior period, you can go to the backup file, correct it, and reprint the statements affected.

You need to find out whether your computer software does automatic closing entries or whether you must key the four closing entries. Either way you need to **close:**

Revenue to Income Summary (credit)

Expenses to Income Summary (debit)

Income Summary and transfer the profit or loss to the Capital account

Drawing to the Capital account (debit)

> Now why was it that I have to print a post-closing trial balance and what am I supposed to look for?

As you look at the statements you've prepared, you try to remember why you need to prepare a post-closing trial balance. You think to yourself: I'll print a trial balance after closing and maybe it will come to me. Ah ha! When I look at this post-closing trial balance, I see that it only lists accounts that have balances greater than zero. Those are the assets, the liabilities, and Mr. Kennedy's Capital account. The closing entries zeroed out all revenue and expense accounts and put the profit into Mr. Kennedy's Capital account as well as closing the Drawing account into the Capital account. Now Jeep Jockeys' temporary owner's equity accounts (revenue, expenses, and Drawing) are cleared and are ready to accept new transactions for June. The matching principle really does work.

Before a Test Check: Chapters 4–5

PART I: Multiple-Choice Questions

_____ 1. The net income appears on all of the following statements except

   a. the statement of owner's equity.
   b. the balance sheet.
   c. the income statement.
   d. all of these.
   e. none of these.

_____ 2. Which of the following entries records the withdrawal of cash for personal use by Dolan, the owner of a business firm?

   a. Debit Cash and credit Drawing.
   b. Debit Salary Expense and credit Cash.
   c. Debit Cash and credit Salary Expense.
   d. Debit Drawing and credit Cash.
   e. None of these.

_____ 3. Which of the following errors, considered individually, would cause the trial balance totals to be unequal?

   a. A payment of $62 for supplies was posted as a debit of $62 to Supplies and a credit of $26 to Cash.
   b. A payment of $763 to a creditor was posted as a debit of $763 to Accounts Payable and a debit of $763 to Cash.
   c. Cash received from customers on account was posted as a debit of $480 to Cash and a credit of $48 to Accounts Receivable.
   d. All of these.
   e. None of these.

_____ 4. The balance in the Prepaid Insurance account before adjustment at the end of the year is $480. This represents six months' insurance paid on November 1. The adjusting entry required on December 31 is

   a. debit Insurance Expense, $160; credit Prepaid Insurance, $160.
   b. debit Prepaid Insurance, $80; credit Insurance Expense, $80.
   c. debit Prepaid Insurance, $420; credit Insurance Expense, $420.
   d. debit Insurance Expense, $420; credit Prepaid Insurance, $420.
   e. none of these.

_____ 5. If an accountant fails to make an adjusting entry to record expired insurance at the end of a fiscal period, the omission will cause

   a. total expenses to be understated.
   b. total revenue to be understated.
   c. total assets to be understated.
   d. all of these.
   e. none of these.

Note: Answers to Before a Test Check begin on page A-1.

_____ 6. Farmer Company bought equipment on January 2 of this year for $7,600. At the time of purchase, the equipment was estimated to have a useful life of eight years and a trade-in value of $400 at the end of eight years. Using the straight-line method, the amount of depreciation for the first year is

a. $1,000.
b. $900.
c. $800.
d. $950.
e. none of these.

_____ 7. If expenses are greater than revenue, the Income Summary account will be closed by a debit to

a. Cash and a credit to Income Summary.
b. Income Summary and a credit to Cash.
c. Capital and a credit to Income Summary.
d. Income Summary and a credit to Capital.
e. none of these.

_____ 8. In preparing closing entries, it is helpful to refer to which of the following columns of the work sheet first?

a. The Balance Sheet columns
b. The Adjusted Trial Balance columns
c. The Income Statement columns
d. Both the Adjusted Trial Balance and the Income Statement columns
e. None of these

PART II: Practical Application

On December 31, the ledger accounts of Karl's Upholstery Shop have the following balances after all adjusting entries have been posted.

Cash	$ 1,200
Equipment	15,400
Accumulated Depreciation, Equipment	1,100
Accounts Payable	300
K. Pitts, Capital	16,500
K. Pitts, Drawing	16,400
Income Summary	
Income from Services	35,900
Wages Expense	11,500
Rent Expense	2,400
Utilities Expense	1,000
Depreciation Expense, Equipment	500
Supplies Expense	4,100
Miscellaneous Expense	900

Instructions

Journalize the four closing entries in the proper order.

PART III: Matching Questions

____ 1. Creditor

____ 2. Business entity

____ 3. Fundamental accounting equation

____ 4. Income statement

____ 5. Owner's equity

____ 6. Accounts Receivable

____ 7. Net loss

____ 8. Ledger

____ 9. Credit

____ 10. Compound entry

____ 11. Trial balance

____ 12. Journalizing

____ 13. Posting

____ 14. Cross-reference

____ 15. Journal

____ 16. Work sheet

____ 17. Book value

____ 18. Depreciation

____ 19. Accounting cycle

____ 20. Fiscal year

____ 21. Contra account

____ 22. Mixed accounts

____ 23. Temporary-equity accounts

____ 24. Real accounts

____ 25. Debit

a.   The book of original entry

b.   One to whom money is owed

c.   Accounts that are partly income statement and partly balance sheet accounts

d.   Assets − Liabilities

e.   A listing of the ending balances of all ledger accounts that proves the equality of total debits and total credits

f.   The process of recording transactions in a journal

g.   The left side of a T account

h.   A business enterprise, separate and distinct from the person who owns its assets

i.   The process of transferring accounts and amounts from the journal to the ledger

j.   An account that is deducted from another account

k.   Amounts owed by charge customers

l.   Balance sheet accounts

m.   Assets = Liabilities + Owner's Equity

n.   A bookkeeping device for referring from journal to ledger or ledger to journal

o.   The right side of a T account

p.   Allocation of the cost of a plant asset over its estimated life

q.   Financial statement that shows the net results of operations

r.   Accounts that belong to only one fiscal period and are closed out at the end of each fiscal period

s.   A transaction that has two or more debits and/or credits

t.   Paper used to record adjustments and provide balances to prepare financial statements

u.   Excess of total expenses over total revenues

v.   A period of 12 consecutive months

w.   A book containing all the accounts of a business

x.   The cost of an asset minus its accumulated depreciation

y.   Steps in the accounting process, completed during the fiscal period

Accounting Cycle Review Problem A

This problem is designed to enable you to apply the knowledge you have acquired in the preceding chapters. In accounting, the ultimate test is being able to handle data in real-life situations. This problem will give you valuable experience.

Chart of Accounts

Assets

111 Cash
112 Accounts Receivable
114 Prepaid Insurance
121 Land
125 Pool Structure
126 Accumulated Depreciation,
    Pool Structure
127 Fan System
128 Accumulated Depreciation,
    Fan System
129 Sailboats
130 Accumulated Depreciation,
    Sailboats

Liabilities

221 Accounts Payable
222 Wages Payable
223 Mortgage Payable

Owner's Equity

311 R. Elly, Capital
312 R. Elly, Drawing
313 Income Summary

Revenue

411 Income from Services
412 Concessions Income

Expenses

511 Sailboat Rental Expense
512 Wages Expense
513 Advertising Expense
514 Utilities Expense
515 Interest Expense
516 Insurance Expense
517 Depreciation Expense, Pool Structure
518 Depreciation Expense, Fan System
519 Depreciation Expense, Sailboats
522 Miscellaneous Expense

You are to record transactions in a two-column general journal. Assume that the fiscal period is one month. You will then be able to complete all the steps in the accounting cycle.

When you are analyzing the transactions, think them through by visualizing the T accounts or by writing them down on scratch paper. For unfamiliar types of transactions, specific instructions for recording them are included. However, reason them out for yourself as well. Check off each transaction as it is recorded.

June   1   Elly deposited $84,200 in a bank account for the purpose of buying Wind Chasers, a business offering the use of small sailboats to the public at a large indoor pool with a fan system that provides wind.

         2   Bought Wind Chasers in its entirety for a total price of $216,100. The assets include sailboats, $22,800; fan system, $8,300; pool structure, $145,000; land, $40,000. Paid $64,000 down, and signed a mortgage note for the remainder. (Debit each asset and credit Cash and Mortgage Payable.)

June 3 Received and paid bill for newspaper advertising, $150.

3 Received and paid bill for a one-year premium for insurance, $12,000.

3 Bought additional boats from J and K Manufacturing Co. for $7,200, paying $3,200 down, with the remainder due in thirty days.

3 Signed a contract with a vending machine service to lease space for vending machines. The rental income agreed upon is 10 percent of the sales generated from the machines, with the estimated total rental income payable in advance. Received estimated cash payment for June, $200. (Debit Cash and credit Concessions Income.)

3 Received bill from Quick Printing for promotional handouts, $360 (Advertising Expense).

3 Signed a contract for leasing sailboats from Kelly Boat Co. and paid rental fee for June, $700.

5 Paid cash for miscellaneous expenses, $93.50.

8 Received $2,632.50 in cash as income for the use of the boats.

9 Bought an addition for the fan system on account from Stanly Pool Supply, $845.

15 Paid wages to employees for the period ending June 14, $4,100.

16 Paid on account for promotional handouts already recorded on June 3, $360.

16 Elly withdrew cash for personal use, $1,050.

16 Bought additional sails from Burgur Products, Inc., $850; payment due in thirty days. (Debit Sailboats.)

16 Received $3,250 in cash as income for the use of the boats.

19 Paid cash for miscellaneous expenses, $40.45.

20 Paid cash to J and K Manufacturing Co. as part payment on account, $1,100.

22 Received $7,230 in cash for the use of the boats (Income from Services).

23 Received a reduction in the outstanding bill from J and K Manufacturing Co. for a boat received in a damaged condition, $472. (Debit Accounts Payable, credit Sailboats.)

24 Received and paid telephone bill, $184.

29 Paid wages for period June 15 through 28, $4,235.

30 Paid cash to Stanly Pool Supply to apply on account, $463.

30 Received and paid electric bill, $145.

30 Paid cash as an installment payment on the mortgage, $1,936. Of this amount, $685 represents a reduction in the principal, and the remainder is interest. (Debit Mortgage Payable, debit Interest Expense, and credit Cash.)

30 Received and paid water bill, $488.

30 Bought additional boats from Plinski and Son for $4,974, paying $1,450 down, with the remainder due in thirty days.

30 Elly withdrew cash for personal use, $1,100.

30 Received $4,832 in cash as income for the use of the boats.

30 Sales from vending machines for the month amounted to $2,653. Ten percent of $2,653 equals $265. Since you have already recorded $200 as concessions income, list the additional $65 revenue earned from the vending machine operator. (Cash was not received.)

Check Figures

Net income, $3,197.55; total of
post-closing trial balance,
$246,111.55

Instructions

1. Journalize the transactions, starting on page 1 of the general journal.
2. Post the transactions to the ledger accounts.
3. Prepare a trial balance in the first two columns of the work sheet.
4. Complete the work sheet. Data for the adjustments are as follows:
   a. Insurance expired during the month, $1,000 (rounded off).
   b. Depreciation of pool structure for the month, $615.
   c. Depreciation of fan system for the month, $160.
   d. Depreciation of sailboats for the month, $800.
   e. Wages accrued at June 30, $690.
5. Prepare the income statement.
6. Prepare the statement of owner's equity.
7. Prepare the balance sheet.
8. Journalize adjusting entries.
9. Post adjusting entries to the ledger accounts.
10. Journalize closing entries.
11. Post closing entries to the ledger accounts.
12. Prepare a post-closing trial balance.

Accounting Cycle Review Problem B

This problem is designed to enable you to apply the knowledge you have acquired in the preceding chapters. In accounting, the ultimate test is being able to handle data in real-life situations. This problem will give you valuable experience.

Chart of Accounts

Assets

111 Cash
112 Accounts Receivable
114 Prepaid Insurance
121 Land
122 Building
123 Accumulated Depreciation, Building
124 Pool/Slide Facility
125 Accumulated Depreciation, Pool/Slide Facility
126 Pool Furniture
127 Accumulated Depreciation, Pool Furniture

Liabilities

221 Accounts Payable
222 Wages Payable
223 Mortgage Payable

Owner's Equity

311 W. Macy, Capital
312 W. Macy, Drawing
313 Income Summary

Revenue

411 Income from Services
412 Concessions Income

Expenses

511 Pool Maintenance Expense
512 Wages Expense
513 Advertising Expense
514 Utilities Expense
515 Interest Expense
517 Insurance Expense
518 Depreciation Expense, Building
519 Depreciation Expense, Pool/Slide Facility
520 Depreciation Expense, Pool Furniture
522 Miscellaneous Expense

You are to record transactions in a two-column general journal. Assume that the fiscal period is one month. You will then be able to complete all the steps in the accounting cycle.

When you are analyzing the transactions, think them through by visualizing the T accounts or by writing them down on scratch paper. For unfamiliar types of transactions, specific instructions for recording them are included. However, reason them out for yourself as well. Check off each transaction as it is recorded.

July

1   Macy deposited $160,000 in a bank account for the purpose of buying Waterwings. The business is a public recreation area offering three large waterslides (called "tubes"), one children's slide, an inner tube run, and a hot tub area.

2   Bought Waterwings in its entirety for a total price of $540,800. The assets include pool furniture, $2,800; the pool/slide facility (includes filter system, pools, pump, and slides), $149,800; building, $95,200; and land, $293,000. Paid $130,000 down and signed a mortgage note for the remainder. (Debit the assets, and credit Cash and Mortgage Payable.)

July 2 Received and paid the bill for a one-year premium for insurance, $10,360.

2 Bought 125 inner tubes from Well's Tires for $3,225, paying $1,500 down, with the remainder due in twenty days. (Debit Pool/Slide Facility.)

3 Signed a contract with a video game company to lease space for video games and to provide a food concession. The rental income agreed upon is 10 percent of the revenues generated from the machines and food, with the estimated monthly rental income paid in advance. Received cash payment for July, $230. (Debit Cash and credit Concessions Income.)

5 Received bills totaling $1,220 for the grand opening/Fourth of July party. The bill from Party Promotions for the promotional hand-outs, balloons, decorations, and prizes was $520, and the newspaper advertising bills from the *City Star* were $700. (These expenses should all be considered advertising expense.)

6 Signed a one-year contract for the pool maintenance with Pool Clean Maintenance and paid the maintenance fee for July of $600.

6 Paid cash for employee picnic food and beverages, $112.48. (Debit Miscellaneous Expense.)

7 Received $14,086 in cash as income for the use of the facilities.

9 Bought parts for the filter system on account from Arley's Pool Supply, $846. (Debit Pool Maintenance Expense.)

14 Received $10,138 in cash as income for the use of the facilities.

15 Paid wages to employees for the period ending July 14, $10,978.

16 Paid $1,220 on account for promotional expenses recorded on July 5.

16 Macy withdrew cash for personal use, $2,000.

17 Bought additional pool furniture from Pool Products for $2,200; payment due in thirty days.

18 Paid cash to seamstress for alterations and repairs to the character costumes, $148.30. (Debit Miscellaneous Expense.)

21 Received $11,330 in cash as income for the use of the facilities.

21 Paid cash to Well's Tires as partial payment on account, $800.

23 Received a $325 reduction of our account from Pool Products for lawn chairs received in damaged condition.

25 Received and paid telephone bill, $192.

29 Paid wages for the period July 15 through 28 of $10,886.

31 Received $12,970 in cash as income for the use of the facilities.

31 Paid cash to Arley's Pool Supply to apply on account, $460.

31 Received and paid water bill, $794.

31 Paid cash as an installment payment on the mortgage, $3,788. Of this amount, $1,610 represents a reduction in the principal, and the remainder is interest. (Debit Mortgage Payable, debit Interest Expense, and credit Cash.)

31 Received and paid electric bill, $924.

31 Bought additional inner tubes from Well's Tires for $580, paying $100 down, with the remainder due in thirty days.

31 Macy withdrew cash for personal use, $2,125.

31 Sales for the video and food concessions amounted to $5,741, and 10 percent of $5,741 equals $574. Since you have already recorded $230 as concessions income, record the additional $344 revenue due from the concessionaire (cash was not received).

Check Figures

Trial balance total, $621,954.00;
net income, $17,513.89

Instructions

1. Journalize the transactions, starting on page 1 of the general journal.
2. Post the transactions to the ledger accounts.
3. Prepare a trial balance in the first two columns of the work sheet.
4. Complete the work sheet. Data for the adjustments are as follows:
   a. Insurance expired during the month, $863.33 (rounded off).
   b. Depreciation of building for the month, $380.
   c. Depreciation of pool/slide facility for the month, $575.
   d. Depreciation of pool furniture for the month, $60.
   e. Wages accrued at July 31, $827.
5. Prepare the income statement.
6. Prepare the statement of owner's equity.
7. Prepare the balance sheet.
8. Journalize adjusting entries.
9. Post adjusting entries to the ledger accounts.
10. Journalize closing entries.
11. Post closing entries to the ledger accounts.
12. Prepare a post-closing trial balance.

6

Accounting for Professional Enterprises: The Combined Journal (Optional)

Accounting systems for professional companies such as architecture firms, law firms, and physician's offices require users to document such items as fees for services rendered, utility bills, travel expenses, supplies, and insurance. But each type of profession uses an individualized set of accounts to record business transactions. These professionals would probably find that a combined journal, which has special columns to record frequently used accounts, is more efficient than a general journal. As you learn about combined journals in this chapter, think about how the accounts you would commonly use in your accounting records might differ if you were an architect or a doctor.

A little later in this chapter, you will also learn how the entries in the combined journal (or general journal) are transformed into financial statements, which are prepared for professional enterprises as well as major corporations. How does Dr. Olsen's balance sheet in this chapter differ from Best Buy's balance sheet? How is it the same? Best Buy's 2002 balance sheet can be found at **http://www.bestbuy.com/About/ InvestorRelations/index.asp?m=435&cat=437** on pages 36 and 37 of the 2002 annual report. Follow the link to Financials on the Investor Relations page.

Performance Objectives

After you have completed this chapter, you will be able to do the following:

1. Describe the accounting records for a professional enterprise.

2. Record transactions for both a professional and a service enterprise in a combined journal.

3. Post from the combined journal and determine the cash balance.

4. Prepare a work sheet for a professional enterprise.

5. Prepare financial statements for a professional enterprise.

6. Record adjusting and closing entries in a combined journal.

A professional enterprise offers a specialized service for a fee. The fee may be charged on a per hour basis, a per visit basis, or a per job or task basis. **Professional enterprises** include practices of medicine, dentistry, law, architecture, engineering, optometry, and so forth. Your knowledge of accounting procedures can be readily applied to professional enterprises. Professional enterprises generally use a modified cash basis.

EXAMPLE: RECORDS OF A DENTIST

OBJECTIVE 1
Describe the accounting records for a professional enterprise.

To understand the modified cash system used by a professional enterprise, let's look at the records of Dr. S. A. Olsen, a dentist. The basic records used in his office are the appointment record and the patient's ledger record. Following is the chart of accounts for the office:

Chart of Accounts

Assets

111 Cash
115 Prepaid Insurance
121 Dental Equipment
122 Accumulated Depreciation, Dental Equipment
123 Office Furniture and Equipment
124 Accumulated Depreciation, Office Furniture and Equipment

Liabilities

211 Notes Payable

Owner's Equity

311 S. A. Olsen, Capital
312 S. A. Olsen, Drawing
313 Income Summary

Revenue

411 Professional Fees

Expenses

511 Dental Instruments Expense
512 Laundry and Cleaning Expense
513 Salary Expense
514 Laboratory Expense
515 Dental Supplies Expense
516 Rent Expense
517 Depreciation Expense, Dental Equipment
518 Depreciation Expense, Office Furniture and Equipment
519 X-ray Supplies Expense
521 Office Supplies Expense
522 Insurance Expense
523 Telephone Expense
524 Utilities Expense
525 Repairs and Maintenance Expense
526 Miscellaneous Expense

Appointment Record

The dentist's receptionist keeps a daily appointment record, showing the time of each appointment and the name of the patient, and gives a copy of the appointment record to the dentist the day before the scheduled appointments. Dr. Olsen's appointment record is shown in Figure 1.

FIGURE 1

APPOINTMENT RECORD

DATE 12/1/20—

HOUR	PATIENT	SERVICE RENDERED	FEES	RECEIPTS
8:00	Ella Berger			
15	John Lyons			
30				
45	Carlos Reyes			
9:00				
15				
30				
45	Donna Heller			
10:00	L. A. Curtis			
15				
30				
45	Ralph Warfield			
11:00	Peter Smithson			
15				
30				
45				
1:00	Donald C. Kraft			
15				
30	N. C. Byers			
45				
2:00	Mrs. N. D. West			
15				
30	John F. Piper			
45	Nolan F. Sanderson			
3:00				
15	Nancy Stacy			
30				
45	C. D. Harper			
4:00				
15	Ardis Holcomb			

Patient's Ledger Record

The receptionist also maintains a **patient's ledger record** card for each patient. One side of this card shows a daily record of the services performed, amount of any cost estimate given, plan of payment, and information regarding collections. This side of the card is shown in Figure 2.

The other side of the card contains a diagram of the patient's teeth and a space for personal information about the patient.

After Dr. Olsen completes the work, he (or an assistant) describes the services performed and writes the amount of the fees in the debit column. The card is returned to the receptionist, who records the services rendered and the fees charged on the appointment record.

The patient's ledger record for L. A. Curtis is shown in Figure 2. **As with Accounts Receivable, debits mean increases in the amounts owed by patients, and credits mean decreases in the amounts owed by patients.** The

FIGURE 2

L. A. Curtis
2416 Bryan Ave., E
Chicago, IL 60644

360-365-2619
Account No. 46-4128

DATE		SERVICE RENDERED	TIME	DEBIT			CREDIT			BALANCE			
June	15	#31—M.O.D. (4)	10:00	1	0	5	00				1	0	5	00
July	4	Ck.						1	0	5	00			
	16	#27—D.O. (Amal.)	9:15		9	4	00					9	4	00
Aug.	5	Ck.							9	4	00			
Sept.	24	#25—P.J.C.	10:00	7	4	0	00					7	4	0	00
Oct.	6	Ck.						1	2	0	00	6	2	0	00
	18	#24—D. (Porc.)	9:00		8	0	00					7	0	0	00
Nov.	3	Ck.						1	2	0	00	5	8	0	00
	9	#18—full gold crown	10:00	5	5	0	00				1	1	3	0	00
Dec.	1	B. W. X-rays (6)	10:00		9	6	00				1	2	2	6	00
		Full upper denture		9	0	0	00				2	1	2	6	00
	1	Ck.						2	0	0	00	1	9	2	6	00

PLAN OF SERVICE		PLAN OF PAYMENT	COLLECTION EFFORTS
1–2 surf. ⎫ 2–3 surf. ⎬	amalgam 1 full gold crown	30-day basis or $100 per month	
1–1 surf. ⎭	1 ceramic crown		
2 anterior porcelain			

ESTIMATE IF ANY		
$900 upper denture (6 appt.)	$150 per month	

Balance column shows the amount owed by the patient at the time of the latest entry.

The services to be performed may require a number of appointments. Some patients may make partial payments each time they have an appointment. Others may pay the entire amount at—or after—the last appointment. Patients' bills are compiled directly from the patient's ledger record. The dentist or receptionist regularly reviews the patients' ledger records to determine which accounts are past due. Figure 3 on page 188 shows the statement that was mailed to L. A. Curtis at the end of December.

Receipt of Payments from Patients

REMEMBER!
The fees charged are not recorded in the Professional Fees account until they are received in cash when using the cash basis.

Depending on the size of the office, the person who receives payments may be the receptionist or the cashier in the accounting office. Whoever receives the payments issues a written receipt for all incoming cash, filled out in duplicate, sending the first copy to the patient and filing the second copy as evidence of the transaction. Receipts should be prenumbered so that they can be accounted for. The payment is recorded in the Receipts column of the appointment record.

When a patient sends in a payment, the receptionist records the amount on the appointment record and on the patient's ledger record in the credit column on the day the payment was received.

FIGURE 3

S. A. OLSEN, D.D.S.
1710 CARTER AVE., E
CHICAGO, IL 60642

STATEMENT

L. A. Curtis
2416 Bryan Ave., E
Chicago, IL 60644

December 31, 20—
Account No. 46-4128

DATE	PROFESSIONAL SERVICE	CHARGES		PAYMENTS		BALANCE	
6/15	#31—MOD (4)	105	00			105	00
7/4	Ck.			105	00	—	
7/16	#27—DO (Amal.)	94	00			94	00
8/5	Ck.			94	00	—	
9/24	#25—PJC	740	00			740	00
10/6	Ck.			120	00	620	00
10/18	#24—D (Porc.)	80	00			700	00
11/3	Ck.			120	00	580	00
11/9	#18—full gold crown	550	00			1,130	00
12/1	B.W. X-rays (6)	96	00			1,226	00
	Full upper denture	900	00			2,126	00
12/1	Ck.			200	00	1,926	00

PAY LAST AMOUNT IN BALANCE COLUMN. ✦

The form in Figure 4 is a typical appointment record for a day, showing services rendered, fees (recorded by the dentist on the patients' ledger records), and payments received (recorded by the receptionist). The receptionist deposits $1,349 in the bank. A journal entry would now be made debiting Cash and crediting Professional Fees for $1,349.

Summary of Procedures

1. Patients request appointments.
2. Receptionist records appointments on appointment record: date, time, and name of patient.
3. Receptionist furnishes dentist with appointment record for the day, plus the patients' ledger records.
4. Dentist performs services and records descriptions of the services performed on each patient's ledger card, listing the fees to be charged in the Debit column.
5. Receptionist accepts payments from patients both in the office and through the mail and records receipt of payments in the Receipts column of the appointment record. Any difference between the fee charged amount and the insurance company approved amount for the services rendered can be shown in the Debit column and a note made in the Service Rendered column. (For purposes of this text, cash receipts are recorded weekly.)
6. At the end of the day, receptionist deposits cash received in the bank.

FIGURE 4

APPOINTMENT RECORD

DATE 12/1/20—

HOUR	PATIENT	SERVICE RENDERED	FEES		RECEIPTS	
8:00	Ella Berger	Extraction	50	00		
15	John Lyons	Three amalgam fillings				
30		D.O. (3)	306	00	70	00
45	Carlos Reyes	Gold inlay filling	425	00		
9:00						
15						
30						
45	Donna Heller	Amalgam filling D.O.	92	00		
10:00	L. A. Curtis	B.W. X-rays (6)	96	00	200	00
15		Denture—full upper				
30		(6 appointments)	900	00		
45	Ralph Warfield	Prophylaxis	72	00	72	00
11:00	Peter Smithson	Endodontia treatment	220	00	50	00
15						
30						
45						
1:00	Donald C. Kraft	Amalgam filling M.O.D.	104	00	52	00
15						
30	N. C. Byers	Ceramco crown	585	00		
45						
2:00	Mrs. N. D. West	Extraction	50	00		
15						
30	John F. Piper	Amalgam filling 1 surf.	75	00		
45	Nolan F. Sanderson	Prophylaxis and full-				
3:00		mouth X-ray (14)	134	00		
15	Nancy Stacy	Fixed bridge 3 units				
30		(Gold) (5 appointments)	1,640	00	125	00
45	C. D. Harper	Prophylaxis & bitewing				
4:00		X-rays	92	00		
15	Ardis Holcomb	Periodontal treatment	284	00		
30						
45						
5:00						
15						
	Ronald T. McCaw				120	00
	Helen Bower				110	00
	Eugene Sampson				136	00
	Sidney Weeks				54	00
	C. D. Sanderson				186	00
	Roger Lindsay				74	00
	Gilbert Rae				100	00
			5,125	00	1,349	00

7. Receptionist lists the description of services and the amount charged on the appointment record.
8. Receptionist records payments received on the patients' ledger cards in the Credit column. The source is the appointment record.

9. Receptionist compiles monthly statements directly from patient's ledger records.

This procedure may vary, depending on the size of the office staff. Also, the monthly statement may consist of a duplicate copy of the patient's ledger card. If the size of the office staff is sufficiently large, the function of accepting and depositing money should be separated from the function of recording payments.

Here is a list of Dr. Olsen's transactions for December, the last month of the fiscal period. **To save time and space, cash receipts are recorded on a weekly basis.**

Dec.	1	Issued Ck. No. 416 for rent for December, $2,000.
	1	Issued Ck. No. 417 for telephone bill for November, $71.
	1	Issued Ck. No. 418 for electric bill for November, $112.
	3	Issued Ck. No. 419 to First-Rate Printing for patient statement forms, $132.
	5	Issued Ck. No. 420 to Milner Dental Supply for drills, $254.
	5	Total cash received from patients during the week, $7,144.
	8	Issued Ck. No. 421 to Garcia Office Supply for repair of copier, $92.
	9	Issued Ck. No. 422 to S. A. Olsen for personal use, $750.
	11	Issued Ck. No. 423 to Ready Cleaning Service for janitorial service, $140.

We will first record these transactions in general journal form (Figure 5). However, since our objective is to introduce the combined journal, we will also record the same transactions in a combined journal.

FIGURE 5

GENERAL JOURNAL

DATE		DESCRIPTION	POST. REF.	DEBIT	CREDIT
20—					
Dec.	1	Rent Expense		2 0 0 0 00	
		Cash			2 0 0 0 00
		Rent for December,			
		Ck. No. 416.			
	1	Telephone Expense		7 1 00	
		Cash			7 1 00
		Telephone bill for November,			
		Ck. No. 417.			
	1	Utilities Expense		1 1 2 00	
		Cash			1 1 2 00
		Electric bill for November,			
		Ck. No. 418.			
	3	Office Supplies Expense		1 3 2 00	
		Cash			1 3 2 00
		First-Rate Printing for			
		statement forms, Ck. No. 419.			

**FIGURE 5
(continued)**

5	Dental Instruments Expense		2 5 4 00			
	Cash			2 5 4 00		
	Milner Dental Supply for					
	drills, Ck. No. 420.					
5	Cash	7 1 4 4 00				
	Professional Fees			7 1 4 4 00		
	For period Dec. 1 through 5.					
8	Repairs and Maint. Expense		9 2 00			
	Cash			9 2 00		
	Garcia Office Supply, for					
	repair of copier, Ck. No. 421.					
9	S. A. Olsen, Drawing		7 5 0 00			
	Cash			7 5 0 00		
	For personal use, Ck. No. 422.					
11	Laundry and Cleaning Expense		1 4 0 00			
	Cash			1 4 0 00		
	Ready Cleaning Service,					
	Ck. No. 423.					

THE COMBINED JOURNAL

OBJECTIVE 2
Record transactions for both a professional and a service enterprise in a combined journal.

The **combined journal** is designed to make the recording and posting of transactions more efficient. It is used widely by professional and service enterprises, where **it replaces the general journal.** No explanations are given in the combined journal. **Special columns** are set up to record accounts that are used frequently by a particular business. Most transactions can be recorded on one line.

Compare the first nine transactions in the combined journal in Figure 6 (pages 192–193) with the same transactions recorded in the general journal in Figure 5. In the first transaction (paid rent for the month, $2,000), the entry is a debit to Rent Expense and a credit to Cash. There is a Cash Credit column in the combined journal, so you list $2,000 in this column; that $2,000 will be posted as part of the column total. The Other Accounts columns are used to record any accounts for which there are no special columns. Since there is no Rent Expense Debit column, the $2,000 debit to Rent Expense must be recorded in the Other Accounts Debit column. Notice that the Other Accounts column does not tell you where to post the $2,000. Therefore, you need to write the title of the account to be posted in the Account Name column. This amount is posted separately.

In the December 5 entry to record professional fees received in cash, special columns are available to handle both the debit to Cash and the credit to Professional Fees. In cases where the special columns can handle both the entire debit and credit amounts, it is not necessary to use the Account Name

COMBINED JOURNAL

	CASH				CK. NO.	DATE	ACCOUNT NAME	POST. REF.	OTHER ACCOUNTS				
	DEBIT		CREDIT						DEBIT		CREDIT		
1						20—							
2			2 0 0 0 00		416	Dec. 1	Rent Expense	516	2 0 0 0 00				
3			7 1 00		417	1	Telephone Expense	523	7 1 00				
4			1 1 2 00		418	1	Utilities Expense	524	1 1 2 00				
5			1 3 2 00		419	3	Office Supplies Expense	521	1 3 2 00				
6			2 5 4 00		420	5	Dental Instruments Expense	511	2 5 4 00				
7	7 1 4 4 00					5	———————————	–					
8			9 2 00		421	8	Repairs and Maintenance Expense	525	9 2 00				
9			7 5 0 00		422	9	S. A. Olsen	–					
10			1 4 0 00		423	11	Ready Cleaning Service	–					
11	2 4 1 1 00					12	———————————	–					
12			4 3 2 00		424	16	Davies Dental Supply	–					
13			9 7 0 00		425	16	C. R. Jarvis	–					
14			9 7 0 00		426	16	D. C. Smith	–					
15						19	Dental Equipment	121	5 7 7 9 00				
16			1 7 7 9 00		427	19	Notes Payable	211			4 0 0 0 00		
17	1 1 2 0 00					19	———————————	–					
18			8 1 0 00		428	22	S. A. Olsen	–					
19			2 9 6 00		429	23	Nollen Dental Laboratory	–					
20			4 0 0 00		430	23	Notes Payable	211	4 0 0 00				
21	1 3 9 6 00					27	———————————	–					
22			2 2 6 00		431	29	Briggs Automotive	–					
23			2 1 9 00		432	31	Milner Dental Supply	–					
24			9 7 0 00		433	31	C. R. Jarvis	–					
25			9 7 0 00		434	31	D. C. Smith	–					
26			1 1 9 0 00		435	31	S. A. Olsen	–					
27			5 4 00		436	31	Jersey Publishers Service	–					
28			8 4 00		437	31	Clement Linen Supply	–					
29	1 9 7 6 00					31	———————————	–					
30	14 0 4 7 00		12 9 2 1 00			31			8 8 4 0 00		4 0 0 0 00		
31	(1 1 1)		(1 1 1)						(X)		(X)		
32													
33													
34													

END OF MONTH
Post the column totals to the Cash account in the general ledger at the end of the month. The account number in parentheses at the foot of each column indicates that posting has been completed.

DAILY
Post each amount in the Other Accounts columns to an account in the general ledger. The account number recorded in the Post. Ref. column indicates that posting has been completed. The (X) indicates that the column total is not to be posted.

FIGURE 6

			DENTAL SUPPLIES EXPENSE	S. A. OLSEN, DRAWING	PROFESSIONAL FEES	LAUNDRY AND CLEANING EXPENSE	SALARY EXPENSE	LABORATORY EXPENSE	MISC. EXPENSE	
			DEBIT	DEBIT	CREDIT	DEBIT	DEBIT	DEBIT	DEBIT	
										1
										2
										3
										4
										5
										6
					7 1 4 4 00					7
										8
				7 5 0 00						9
						1 4 0 00				10
					2 4 1 1 00					11
			4 3 2 00							12
							9 7 0 00			13
							9 7 0 00			14
										15
										16
					1 1 2 0 00					17
				8 1 0 00						18
								2 9 6 00		19
										20
					1 3 9 6 00					21
				2 2 6 00						22
			2 1 9 00							23
							9 7 0 00			24
							9 7 0 00			25
				1 1 9 0 00						26
									5 4 00	27
						8 4 00				28
					1 9 7 6 00					29
			6 5 1 00	2 9 7 6 00	14 0 4 7 00	2 2 4 00	3 8 8 0 00	2 9 6 00	5 4 00	30
			(5 1 5)	(3 1 2)	(4 1 1)	(5 1 2)	(5 1 3)	(5 1 4)	(5 2 6)	31
										32
										33
										34

END OF MONTH
Post the column totals to their general ledger accounts. Account numbers in parentheses indicate that posting has been completed.

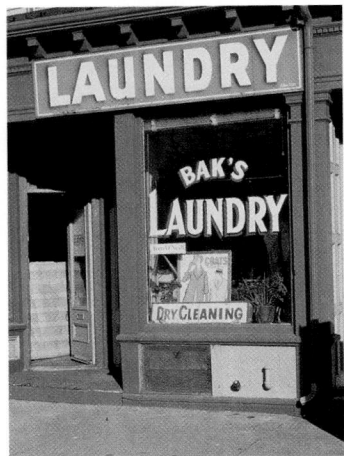

Owners of dry cleaners and service stations as well as doctors and lawyers can buy premade combined journals targeted directly for their own professions. These combined journals are set up to help channel routine transactions into the journal.

column except to write the name of the check payee. To show that the Account Name column has not been overlooked, we draw a long line through it and put a dash in the Post. Ref. column. The individual amounts are posted as parts of the totals of the special columns. The rest of the month's transactions follow:

Dec. 12 Total cash received from patients during the week, $2,411.

16 Issued Ck. No. 424 to Davies Dental Supply for miscellaneous dental supplies, $432.

16 In payment of salaries, issued Ck. No. 425 to C. R. Jarvis, $970 and Ck. No. 426 to D. C. Smith, $970. (Use two lines.)

19 Bought new dental chair from Milner Dental Supply, $5,779. Issued Ck. No. 427 as a downpayment, $1,779. The balance is to be paid in ten monthly payments of $400 each (Notes Payable). (Use two lines.)

19 Total cash received from patients during the week, $1,120.

22 Issued Ck. No. 428 to S. A. Olsen for personal use, $810.

23 Issued Ck. No. 429 to Nollen Dental Laboratory for laboratory expense, $296.

23 Issued Ck. No. 430 to Milner Dental Supply as a contract payment (Notes Payable) on dental equipment purchased in October, $400.

27 Total cash received from patients during the week, $1,396.

29 Olsen wrote Ck. No. 431 payable to Briggs Automotive for repairing his car, $226 (to be recorded as Drawing).

31 Issued Ck. No. 432 to Milner Dental Supply for miscellaneous dental supplies, $219.

31 In payment of salaries, issued Ck. No. 433 to C. R. Jarvis, $970 and Ck. No. 434 to D. C. Smith, $970. (Use two lines.)

31 Issued Ck. No. 435 to S. A. Olsen for personal use, $1,190.

31 Issued Ck. No. 436 to Jersey Publishers Service for magazines for the office, $54.

31 Issued Ck. No. 437 to Clement Linen Supply for laundry services, $84.

31 Total cash received from patients this week up until last day of year, $1,976.

After you have added all columns at the end of the month, prove on scratch paper that the sum of the debit totals equals the sum of the credit totals.

Column	Debit totals	Credit totals
Cash	$14,047.00	$12,921.00
Other Accounts	8,840.00	4,000.00
S. A. Olsen, Drawing	2,976.00	
Professional Fees		14,047.00
Dental Supplies Expense	651.00	
Laundry and Cleaning Expense	224.00	
Salary Expense	3,880.00	
Laboratory Expense	296.00	
Miscellaneous Expense	54.00	
	$30,968.00	$30,968.00

Posting from the Combined Journal

OBJECTIVE 3
Post from the combined journal and determine the cash balance.

REMEMBER!
Special columns are posted as one total. Amounts in Other Accounts columns are posted individually.

The person who keeps records posts items in the Other Accounts columns individually, usually daily, using the specific transaction date. **After posting the ledger account, the person records the ledger account number in the Post. Ref. column of the combined journal.** This procedure is similar to posting from a general journal.

Special columns, used only for debits or credits to specific accounts, are posted as totals at the end of the month. **After posting the ledger account, you record the ledger account number in the special column immediately below the total.** The account number is placed in parentheses. The total of the Cash Debit column in Figure 6 on pages 192–193 is an example. After the Cash account in the general ledger has been debited for $14,047.00, the account number of Cash (111) is placed in parentheses below the total of the Cash Debit column in the combined journal. Notice the X's in parentheses below the totals of the Other Accounts columns. These totals were not posted because the individual amounts recorded in the columns were posted separately. The separate amounts listed in the Other Accounts columns should not be posted twice.

The Cash, Dental Supplies Expense, and Rent Expense accounts from Dr. Olsen's completed general ledger are shown in Figure 7 to illustrate the posting process.

FIGURE 7

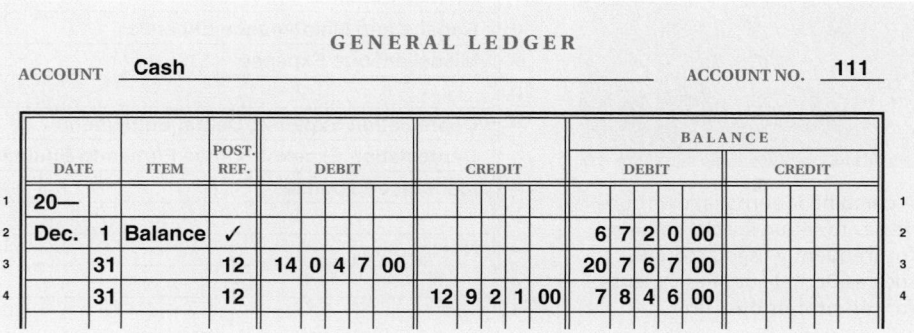

GENERAL LEDGER

ACCOUNT Cash   ACCOUNT NO. 111

DATE		ITEM	POST. REF.	DEBIT	CREDIT	BALANCE DEBIT	BALANCE CREDIT
20—							
Dec.	1	Balance	✓			6 7 2 0 00	
	31		12	14 0 4 7 00		20 7 6 7 00	
	31		12		12 9 2 1 00	7 8 4 6 00	

ACCOUNT Dental Supplies Expense   ACCOUNT NO. 515

DATE		ITEM	POST. REF.	DEBIT	CREDIT	BALANCE DEBIT	BALANCE CREDIT
20—							
Dec.	1	Balance	✓			4 8 2 9 00	
	31		12	6 5 1 00		5 4 8 0 00	

ACCOUNT Rent Expense   ACCOUNT NO. 516

DATE		ITEM	POST. REF.	DEBIT	CREDIT	BALANCE DEBIT	BALANCE CREDIT
20—							
Dec.	1	Balance	✓			16 0 0 0 00	
	1		12	2 0 0 0 00		18 0 0 0 00	

FIGURE 8

ACCOUNT NAME	TRIAL BALANCE DEBIT	TRIAL BALANCE CREDIT
1 Cash	7 8 4 6 00	
2 Prepaid Insurance	2 4 4 8 00	
3 Dental Equipment	115 2 3 4 00	
4 Accumulated Depreciation, Dental Equipment		17 2 0 0 00
5 Office Furniture and Equipment	7 8 0 0 00	
6 Accum. Depr., Office Furniture and Equipment		4 2 0 0 00
7 Notes Payable		7 6 0 0 00
8 S. A. Olsen, Capital		71 4 9 8 00
9 S. A. Olsen, Drawing	46 2 8 0 00	
10 Professional Fees		161 0 2 4 00
11 Dental Instruments Expense	1 9 8 2 00	
12 Laundry and Cleaning Expense	3 0 2 4 00	
13 Salary Expense	40 8 0 0 00	
14 Laboratory Expense	5 8 5 6 00	
15 Dental Supplies Expense	5 4 8 0 00	
16 Rent Expense	18 0 0 0 00	
17 X-ray Supplies Expense	1 3 0 8 00	
18 Office Supplies Expense	2 7 6 2 00	
19 Telephone Expense	4 1 2 00	
20 Utilities Expense	7 7 8 00	
21 Repairs and Maintenance Expense	8 8 8 00	
22 Miscellaneous Expense	6 2 4 00	
23	261 5 2 2 00	261 5 2 2 00
24 Depreciation Expense, Dental Equipment		
25 Depreciation Expense, Office Furn. and Equipment		
26 Insurance Expense		
27		
28 Net Income		
29		

A combined journal allows businesses to set up special columns for frequently used accounts, such as Dental Supplies Expense, for this professional firm.

Determining Cash Balance

The cash balance may be determined at any time during the month by taking the beginning balance of cash, adding the total cash debits so far during the month, and subtracting the total cash credits so far during the month. For example, to determine the balance of cash on December 5:

Beginning balance (Dec. 1)	$ 6,720
Add cash debits	7,144
Total	$13,864
Less cash credits	2,569
Ending balance (Dec. 5)	$11,295

COMBINED JOURNAL   PAGE **12**

CASH DEBIT	CASH CREDIT	CK. NO.	DATE	ACCOUNT NAME
1			20—	
2	2 0 0 0 00	416	Dec. 1	Rent Expense
3	7 1 00	417	1	Telephone Expense
4	1 1 2 00	418	1	Utilities Expense
5	1 3 2 00	419	3	Office Supplies Expense
6	2 5 4 00	420	5	Dental Instruments Expense
7 7 1 4 4 00			5	————————
8 7 1 4 4 00	2 5 6 9 00			

S. A. Olsen, D.D.S.
Work Sheet
For Year Ended December 31, 20—

	ADJUSTMENTS		ADJUSTED TRIAL BALANCE		INCOME STATEMENT		BALANCE SHEET		
	DEBIT	CREDIT	DEBIT	CREDIT	DEBIT	CREDIT	DEBIT	CREDIT	
1			7 8 4 6 00				7 8 4 6 00		1
2		(c) 1 8 3 6 00	6 1 2 00				6 1 2 00		2
3			115 2 3 4 00				115 2 3 4 00		3
4	(a) 8 4 0 0 00			25 6 0 0 00				25 6 0 0 00	4
5			7 8 0 0 00				7 8 0 0 00		5
6		(b) 1 5 2 0 00		5 7 2 0 00				5 7 2 0 00	6
7				7 6 0 0 00				7 6 0 0 00	7
8				71 4 9 8 00				71 4 9 8 00	8
9			46 2 8 0 00				46 2 8 0 00		9
10				161 0 2 4 00		161 0 2 4 00			10
11			1 9 8 2 00		1 9 8 2 00				11
12			3 0 2 4 00		3 0 2 4 00				12
13			40 8 0 0 00		40 8 0 0 00				13
14			5 8 5 6 00		5 8 5 6 00				14
15			5 4 8 0 00		5 4 8 0 00				15
16			18 0 0 0 00		18 0 0 0 00				16
17			1 3 0 8 00		1 3 0 8 00				17
18			2 7 6 2 00		2 7 6 2 00				18
19			4 1 2 00		4 1 2 00				19
20			7 7 8 00		7 7 8 00				20
21			8 8 8 00		8 8 8 00				21
22			6 2 4 00		6 2 4 00				22
23									23
24	(a) 8 4 0 0 00		8 4 0 0 00		8 4 0 0 00				24
25	(b) 1 5 2 0 00		1 5 2 0 00		1 5 2 0 00				25
26	(c) 1 8 3 6 00		1 8 3 6 00		1 8 3 6 00				26
27	11 7 5 6 00	11 7 5 6 00	271 4 4 2 00	271 4 4 2 00	93 6 7 0 00	161 0 2 4 00	177 7 7 2 00	110 4 1 8 00	27
28					67 3 5 4 00			67 3 5 4 00	28
29					161 0 2 4 00	161 0 2 4 00	177 7 7 2 00	177 7 7 2 00	29
30									30

Work Sheet for a Professional Enterprise

OBJECTIVE 4
Prepare a work sheet for a professional enterprise.

Assume that Dr. Olsen's receptionist posted the journal entries to the ledger accounts and recorded the trial balance in the first two columns of the work sheet. Dr. Olsen uses the modified cash basis of accounting, recording revenue only when he has received it in cash and recording expenses only when he has paid for them in cash. However, when Dr. Olsen buys an item that is going to last a number of years, he records this item as an asset and writes it off or depreciates it by making an adjusting entry each year of its useful life. He also makes adjusting entries for expired insurance. Data for the adjustments are given below.

a. Additional depreciation on dental equipment, $8,400.
b. Additional depreciation on office furniture and equipment, $1,520.
c. Insurance expired, $1,836.

With these adjusting entries, the rest of the work sheet can be completed as shown in Figure 8. First the balances of the accounts that were adjusted are brought up to date in the Adjusted Trial Balance columns. Then these amounts are carried forward to the remaining columns.

Medical professionals have their uniforms or lab coats cleaned by outside services. Their work sheets are likely to include an account for Laundry and Cleaning Expenses.

Financial Statements

From the work sheet, Dr. Olsen's accountant prepares the financial statements shown in Figure 9. In this case, there was no additional investment made by S. A. Olsen during the year.

FIGURE 9

S. A. Olsen, D.D.S.
Income Statement
For Year Ended December 31, 20—

Revenue:			
Professional Fees			$161 0 2 4 00
Expenses:			
Dental Instruments Expense	$ 1 9 8 2 00		
Laundry and Cleaning Expense	3 0 2 4 00		
Salary Expense	40 8 0 0 00		
Laboratory Expense	5 8 5 6 00		
Dental Supplies Expense	5 4 8 0 00		
Rent Expense	18 0 0 0 00		
Depreciation Expense, Dental			
Equipment	8 4 0 0 00		
Depreciation Expense, Office			
Furniture and Equipment	1 5 2 0 00		
X-ray Supplies Expense	1 3 0 8 00		
Office Supplies Expense	2 7 6 2 00		
Insurance Expense	1 8 3 6 00		
Telephone Expense	4 1 2 00		
Utilities Expense	7 7 8 00		
Repairs and Maintenance Expense	8 8 8 00		
Miscellaneous Expense	6 2 4 00		
Total Expenses			93 6 7 0 00
Net Income			$ 67 3 5 4 00

S. A. Olsen, D.D.S.
Statement of Owner's Equity
For Year Ended December 31, 20—

S. A. Olsen, Capital, January 1, 20—					$71	4 9 8	00
Net Income for Year	$67	3 5 4	00				
Less Withdrawals for Year	46	2 8 0	00				
Increase in Capital					21	0 7 4	00
S. A. Olsen, Capital, December 31, 20—					$92	5 7 2	00

S. A. Olsen, D.D.S.
Balance Sheet
December 31, 20—

Assets				
Cash			$ 7 8 4 6	00
Prepaid Insurance			6 1 2	00
Dental Equipment	$115 2 3 4	00		
Less Accumulated Depreciation	25 6 0 0	00	89 6 3 4	00
Office Furniture and Equipment	$ 7 8 0 0	00		
Less Accumulated Depreciation	5 7 2 0	00	2 0 8 0	00
Total Assets			$100 1 7 2	00
Liabilities				
Notes Payable			$ 7 6 0 0	00
Owner's Equity				
S. A. Olsen, Capital			92 5 7 2	00
Total Liabilities and Owner's Equity			$100 1 7 2	00

Adjusting and Closing Entries

Dr. Olsen (or his receptionist) records the adjusting and closing entries entirely in the Other Accounts columns of the combined journal. These entries must be posted individually, so the special columns are never used for them.

The adjusting and closing entries are shown in Figure 10 on page 200, two pages of a shortened combined journal. These adjusting and closing entries are shown here on two pages to make the concept clear. In practice, the closing entries would be written right below the adjusting entries. Be careful not to split up any individual entry between two pages. The totals are included because it is customary to show totals of all columns of a combined journal. In the Account Name column, accounts to be credited do not have to be indented.

COMBINED JOURNAL

	CASH		CK. NO.	DATE	ACCOUNT NAME	POST. REF.	OTHER ACCOUNTS	
	DEBIT	CREDIT					DEBIT	CREDIT
1				20—	**Adjusting Entries**			
2				Dec. 31	Depr. Expense, Dental Equipment	517	8 4 0 0 00	
3					Accum. Depr., Dental Equipment	122		8 4 0 0 00
4				31	Depreciation Expense, Office			
5					Furniture and Equipment	518	1 5 2 0 00	
6					Accumulated Depreciation, Office			
7					Furniture and Equipment	124		1 5 2 0 00
8				31	Insurance Expense	522	1 8 3 6 00	
9					Prepaid Insurance	115		1 8 3 6 00
10				31			11 7 5 6 00	11 7 5 6 00
11							(X)	(X)
12								
13								
14								
15								
16								
17								

COMBINED JOURNAL

	CASH		CK. NO.	DATE	ACCOUNT NAME	POST. REF.	OTHER ACCOUNTS	
	DEBIT	CREDIT					DEBIT	CREDIT
1				20—	**Closing Entries**			
2				Dec. 31	Professional Fees	411	161 0 2 4 00	
3					Income Summary	313		161 0 2 4 00
4				31	Income Summary	313	93 6 7 0 00	
5					Dental Instruments Expense	511		1 9 8 2 00
6					Laundry and Cleaning Expense	512		3 0 2 4 00
7					Salary Expense	513		40 8 0 0 00
8					Laboratory Expense	514		5 8 5 6 00
9					Dental Supplies Expense	515		5 4 8 0 00
10					Rent Expense	516		18 0 0 0 00
11					Depr. Expense, Dental Equipment	517		8 4 0 0 00
12					Depr. Expense, Office Furniture			
13					and Equipment	518		1 5 2 0 00
14					X-ray Supplies Expense	519		1 3 0 8 00
15					Office Supplies Expense	521		2 7 6 2 00
16					Insurance Expense	522		1 8 3 6 00
17					Telephone Expense	523		4 1 2 00
18					Utilities Expense	524		7 7 8 00
19					Repairs and Maintenance Expense	525		8 8 8 00
20					Miscellaneous Expense	526		6 2 4 00
21				31	Income Summary	313	67 3 5 4 00	
22					S. A. Olsen, Capital	311		67 3 5 4 00
23				31	S. A. Olsen, Capital	311	46 2 8 0 00	
24					S. A. Olsen, Drawing	312		46 2 8 0 00
25				31			368 3 2 8 00	368 3 2 8 00
26							(X)	(X)

FIGURE 10

DESIGNING A COMBINED JOURNAL

Since the combined journal is widely used in professional offices and service business firms, it is interesting to look over the varieties of combined journals available at stores selling office supplies. Some are bound journals; others are loose-leaf books. The number of columns varies from six to twenty, and they are available with or without column headings. Those that have printed column headings represent a "canned" type of combined journal. These journals are available for service stations, dry cleaners, doctors' offices, and many other types of businesses.

Combined journals with blank columns can be customized to meet the specific requirements of a given business. Prior to labeling the columns, first study the operations of the business and make up a chart of accounts. Next, identify those accounts that are likely to be used frequently to record typical transactions of the business. Naturally, if these accounts are used over and over, you need to set up special columns for them.

CHAPTER REVIEW

Review of Learning Objectives

1. Describe the accounting records for a professional enterprise.

The records for a professional enterprise generally consist of an appointment record, a recording of charges levied for services rendered, and patients' or clients' (customers') ledger cards. A combined journal is generally used to record transactions that are posted to a general ledger.

2. Record transactions for both a professional and a service enterprise in a combined journal.

Special columns are set up to record transactions involving frequently used accounts. Transactions involving other accounts are recorded in the Other Accounts columns. A long line in the Account Name column and a dash in the Post. Ref. column indicate that all debits and credits for a transaction have been entered in special columns.

3. Post from the combined journal and determine the cash balance.

Combined Journal
Posting Procedure

Amounts in the Other Accounts columns are posted separately, usually on a daily basis.

Amounts in the special columns are posted as column totals at the end of the month.

An account number in the Post. Ref. column indicates that the amount in the Other Accounts column has been posted; a dash in that column indicates that the amount is being posted as part of a column total. Below the totals of the Other Accounts columns, an X in parentheses indicates that the column total was not posted; accounts were posted individually. Below the totals of the special columns, the account numbers in parentheses indicate that each column has been posted.

4. Prepare a work sheet for a professional enterprise.

The work sheet for a professional enterprise is the same as the work sheet presented in Chapter 4 for a service enterprise.

5. Prepare financial statements for a professional enterprise.

The financial statements for professional enterprises are the same as the financial statements presented previously for service enterprises, except for some new account titles.

6. Record adjusting and closing entries in a combined journal.

Adjusting and closing entries are recorded in the Account Name column and the Other Accounts Debit and Credit columns. The closing entries may be recorded immediately below the adjusting entries. However, if it is necessary to carry over any one entry to a second page, you should not split up the entry.

Glossary

Combined journal A journal format widely used by professional and service enterprises in place of a general journal; designed to make the recording and posting of transactions more efficient. (191)

Patient's ledger record A record of amounts charged to patients, amounts received from patients, estimates given, and the remaining amounts owed by patients, which are called debit balances. In the event that a patient overpaid, the remainder is called a credit balance, which indicates a liability exists to the patient. (186)

Professional enterprise A business that provides a highly specialized service for a fee. (185)

Special columns Columns in a journal that are used to record amounts that occur frequently. (191)

QUESTIONS, EXERCISES, AND PROBLEMS

Discussion Questions

1. Why do small businesses find the combined journal convenient to use?
2. Name four columns that should always appear in a combined journal.
3. What types of transactions are recorded in the Other Accounts Debit and Other Accounts Credit columns?
4. In the Post. Ref. column of a combined journal, what does a dash signify and what does a number indicate?
5. What is the meaning of X's and numbers in parentheses under the column totals of a combined journal?
6. When an amount is placed in the Other Accounts Debit or Other Accounts Credit column, why is it necessary to complete the Account Name column?
7. You have been asked to design a combined journal for Andrea's Hair Salon. Customers pay in cash only. The business buys supplies on account from

creditors. Rent and utilities are paid monthly. Employees are paid wages weekly. The owner, Andrea Wilke, makes withdrawals weekly. The firm advertises frequently. List the special columns needed plus the four columns that always appear in a combined journal.

8. Describe the process of proving the combined journal at the end of the month.

Exercises

P.O. 1

Record receipt of cash under modified cash basis.

Exercise 6-1 On June 4, the appointment record for a chiropractor shows that the total of the fees column is $326 and the total of the receipts column is $197. At the end of the day, $197 is deposited in the bank. Record the journal entry for the deposit in the general journal. Assume that the modified cash basis is used.

P.O. 2

List the columns to record transactions.

Exercise 6-2 The Brandon Advertising Agency uses a combined journal with the following columns. Assume that the accrual basis of accounting is used.

Cash Debit
Cash Credit
Ck. No.
Date
Account Name
Post. Ref.
Other Accounts Debit
Other Accounts Credit

Accounts Receivable Debit
Accounts Receivable Credit
Accounts Payable Debit
Accounts Payable Credit
Commissions Income Credit
Salary Expense Debit
Utilities Expense Debit

List the columns in which each of the following would be recorded.

a. Payment of rent for the month.
b. Charging a client a commission.
c. Payment of an electric bill.
d. Investment of equipment by the owner.

P.O. 2

Designate columns to record transactions.

Exercise 6-3 T. L. Lee, an attorney, uses a combined journal with the columns listed below. Indicate which columns would be used to enter the following transactions.

a. Cash Debit
b. Cash Credit
c. Other Accounts Debit
d. Other Accounts Credit
e. Accounts Receivable Debit
f. Accounts Receivable Credit
g. Fees Earned Credit
h. Office Supplies Expense Debit
i. Salary Expense Debit
j. Travel Expense Debit

1. Issued a check for $249 for the purchase of a filing cabinet.
2. Sold services on account, $5,440.
3. Received and paid the electric bill, $98.
4. Received and paid the bill for airline ticket, $356.
5. Sold services for cash, $100.
6. Received and paid the bill for rent for the month, $1,000.
7. Received $4,200 on account from customers.

8. T. L. Lee withdrew $1,500 for personal use.
9. Issued a check for $50 payment of court fees on behalf of a client (client owes us).

Exercise 6-4 The books of Binyon and Associates, Certified Public Accountants, are kept on a modified cash basis. The client record of Alice Benson is presented below.

BINYON AND ASSOCIATES
CERTIFIED PUBLIC ACCOUNTANTS
242 SELVA AVENUE
MIAMI, FLORIDA 32906

CLIENT RECORD

Alice Benson
1429 Garfield Avenue
Miami, Florida 32909

DATE		SERVICE	CHG		REC		BAL	
20—								
May	6	Tax prep.	164	00			164	00
June	2				90	00	74	00

Record the June 2 transaction in a combined journal.

Exercise 6-5 Assume that on June 14, Binyon and Associates issues business check number 311 for $950 to Miami National Bank for payment on N. Binyon's home mortgage. Explain how the transaction would be recorded in a combined journal.

Exercise 6-6 Baxter Dental Laboratory maintains charge accounts for nine dentists. The owner is R. A. Baxter. Frequent payments include supplies, salaries, delivery, and owner's withdrawals. List the special columns you would suggest for a combined journal.

Exercise 6-7 Kroyer Landscaping Services uses a combined journal that includes the following columns:

Cash Debit
Cash Credit
Other Accounts Debit
Other Accounts Credit
Fees Income Credit
Truck Expense Debit
Supplies Expense Debit
Wages Expense Debit
Miscellaneous Expense Debit

Indicate the columns that are posted individually and those that are posted as a column total. Indicate the columns that are posted daily and those that are posted at the end of the month.

P.O. 3
Determine up-to-date cash balance.

Exercise 6-8 Determine the cash balance after November 11.

Cash

Beginning Nov. 1 Bal. 642.50	

	CASH		CK. NO.	DATE
	DEBIT	CREDIT		
1				20—
2	9 2 1 64			Nov. 1
3		7 5 42	121	3
4	3 8 9 00			5
5		4 1 6 20	122	8
6	8 4 0 00	2 1 9 00	123	9
7		8 4 59	124	11

REFLECTING ON
THE WORLD WIDE WEB

Now that you have learned about recording transactions in a combined journal and preparing financial statements, let's go back to the questions we asked at the beginning of the chapter.

1. How would the accounts you would commonly use in a combined journal differ for an architect and a doctor?
2. Give some examples of how Dr. Olsen's balance sheet in this chapter differs from Best Buy's balance sheet (found on pages 36 and 37 of the 2002 annual report by following the Financials link at **http://www.bestbuy.com/About/InvestorRelations/index.asp?m=435 &cat=437**)?
3. The information found on the Internet seems endless. Choose any professional enterprise you know about and see if you can find its financial statements online.

CONSIDER AND COMMUNICATE

You do the bookkeeping for a veterinarian. She has no formal accounting system yet, but she does save all source documents.

1. Convince her of the benefits of a combined journal.
2. Design the format for a combined journal with debit and credit columns and headings to accommodate the entries for a veterinarian using the modified cash basis.

WHAT'S WRONG WITH THIS PICTURE? ━━━━━━━━━━━━━━━━━━━ ▪▪▪

Your friend has been using a general journal for his sole proprietorship business. He needs a better journal solution because he does the accounting himself. Discuss how you think a combined journal could be the answer he is looking for.

A MATTER OF ETHICS ━━━━━━━━━━━━━━━━━━━━━━━━━━━━━━━ ▪▪▪

It is Friday at 5 P.M. It is your responsibility to count the money in the cash register, prepare the deposit slip for the bank, and lock up. You have counted the money, prepared the bank deposit, and cleared the cash register, when a customer comes in to buy something. You finish the sale for $9.50. The customer had the exact change. You are in a hurry and do not want to redo the deposit, so you put the $9.50 in your bag (the safe is locked and you don't have the combination). You intend to add it to Monday's deposit. Over the weekend you run out of gas and need the $9.50 for gas. Discuss the situation.

▪ PROBLEM SET A

For additional help, see the demonstration problem at the beginning of each chapter in your Working Papers.

P.O. 2

Problem 6-1A M. L. Janes, M.D., uses the following chart of accounts:

Assets

111 Cash
121 Medical Equipment
122 Accumulated Depreciation, Medical Equipment
123 Office Furniture and Equipment
124 Accumulated Depreciation, Office Furniture and Equipment
125 Vehicle
126 Accumulated Depreciation, Vehicle

Liabilities

211 Notes Payable

Owner's Equity

311 M. L. Janes, Capital
312 M. L. Janes, Drawing
313 Income Summary

Revenue

411 Professional Fees

Expenses

511 Nurse Salary Expense
512 Office Salary Expense
513 Equipment Rental Expense
514 Rent Expense
515 Medical Supplies Expense
516 X-ray Supplies Expense
517 Laboratory Expense
518 Cleaning Expense
519 Office Supplies Expense
521 Depreciation Expense, Medical Equipment
522 Depreciation Expense, Office Furniture and Equipment
523 Depreciation Expense, Vehicle
524 Vehicle Expense
525 Insurance Expense
526 Telephone Expense
527 Utilities Expense
528 Miscellaneous Expense

Dr. Janes's records consist of an appointment record book, examination and charge reports, patients' ledger records, a combined journal, and a general ledger. The doctor fills out an examination and charge report each time a patient visits. The report contains a description or listing of the treatments and tests administered, and also the amounts of the charges. The charges are then recorded in the patient's ledger record. Monthly statements based on the patient's ledger record are mailed to the patient. Dr. Janes's books are kept on the modified cash basis. These transactions took place during April:

Apr.

1 Paid Krebs Realty for rent for the month, $1,680 (Ck. No. 636).
2 Paid salary to M. Lewis (part-time office person), $875 (Ck. No. 637).
4 Bought medical supplies for cash from Pike Medical Supply Co., $460 (Ck. No. 638).
6 Received cash from patients during week, $7,920.
9 Paid telephone bill to Acme Telephone Company, $97 (Ck. No. 639).
12 Paid Techno-Labs for laboratory expense, $465 (Ck. No. 640).
13 Total cash received from patients during week, $5,470.
15 Dr. M. L. Janes withdrew $850 for personal use (Ck. No. 641).
17 Bought x-ray supplies for cash from Tilly Supply Company, $214 (Ck. No. 642).
18 Paid Terry's Service Station for gas and oil for vehicle used in business, $87 (vehicle expense) (Ck. No. 643).
20 Received cash from patients during week, $2,986.
23 Bought postage stamps for cash at post office, $10 (Miscellaneous Expense) (Ck. No. 644).
24 Paid $104 for laundry service to Crystal Laundry (Cleaning Expense) (Ck. No. 645).
27 Paid King News Service for magazines, $76.75 (Miscellaneous Expense) (Ck. No. 646).
30 Paid salary for the month to C. Doane (nurse), $2,010 (Ck. No. 647).
30 Paid Best Janitorial, $132 (Cleaning Expense) (Ck. No. 648).
30 Received cash from patients (April 21 through 30), $2,158.
30 Dr. M. L. Janes withdrew $1,820 for personal use (Ck. No. 649).

Check Figure
Total debits, $27,414.75

Instructions

1. Record these transactions on page 9 of the combined journal. Insert the name of the Drawing account.
2. Prove the equality of the debit and credit totals in the Account Name column below the totals.

P.O. 6

Problem 6-2A The completed work sheet for S. R. Lindell, Psychologist, is shown in Figure 11 on pages 208 and 209.

Check Figure
Total Other Accounts Debit column, $172,626.20

Instructions

Record the adjusting and closing entries in the combined journal. Remember to total the columns and insert an X in parentheses below each total.

P.O. 2,3

Problem 6-3A Dr. Terrence T. Cascone operates the Cascone Allergy Clinic. The transactions were completed during September of this year. Following is his chart of accounts.

FIGURE 11

	ACCOUNT NAME	TRIAL BALANCE		
		DEBIT	CREDIT	
1	Cash	6 2 7 0 00		
2	Office Equipment	56 4 1 0 25		
3	Accumulated Depreciation, Office Equipment		16 9 8 4 16	
4	S. R. Lindell, Capital		38 8 7 2 94	
5	S. R. Lindell, Drawing	24 7 8 5 00		
6	Professional Fees		70 9 2 9 20	
7	Salary Expense	16 3 2 4 60		
8	Advertising Expense	4 5 7 5 10		
9	Rent Expense	7 6 7 0 00		
10	Vehicle Expense	2 0 6 2 75		
11	Travel Expense	2 2 4 1 32		
12	Entertainment Expense	7 9 6 12		
13	Supplies Expense	5 2 6 0 00		
14	Miscellaneous Expense	3 9 1 16	126 7 8 6 30	
15		126 7 8 6 30		
16	Depreciation Expense, Office Equipment			
17				
18	Net Income			
19				
20				

Assets

111 Cash
112 Accounts Receivable
114 Prepaid Insurance
121 Equipment
122 Accumulated Depreciation,
    Equipment

Liabilities

221 Accounts Payable

Owner's Equity

311 T. T. Cascone, Capital
312 T. T. Cascone, Drawing
313 Income Summary

Revenue

411 Professional Fees

Expenses

511 Salary Expense
512 Rent Expense
513 Laboratory Expense
514 Utilities Expense
515 Depreciation Expense,
    Equipment
516 Supplies Expense
517 Miscellaneous Expense

Sept. 2 Bought medical equipment on account, $1,680, from Wing Medical Supplies. (Use two lines.)

2 Paid Jayco Realty for office rent for month, $1,050 (Ck. No. 516).

2 Received cash on account from patients, $829: D. R. Calvin, $152.50; Diane Stillman, $272; Jackson Niles, $317; Teresa Garrett, $87.50. (Dr. Cascone uses the accrual basis. Use four lines,

S. R. Lindell, Psychologist
Work Sheet
For Year Ended December 31, 20—

	ADJUSTMENTS		ADJUSTED TRIAL BALANCE		INCOME STATEMENT		BALANCE SHEET		
	DEBIT	CREDIT	DEBIT	CREDIT	DEBIT	CREDIT	DEBIT	CREDIT	
			6 2 7 0 00				6 2 7 0 00		1
			56 4 1 0 25				56 4 1 0 25		2
		(a) 5 9 8 2 80		22 9 6 6 96				22 9 6 6 96	3
				38 8 7 2 94				38 8 7 2 94	4
			24 7 8 5 00				24 7 8 5 00		5
				70 9 2 9 20		70 9 2 9 20			6
			16 3 2 4 60		16 3 2 4 60				7
			4 5 7 5 10		4 5 7 5 10				8
			7 6 7 0 00		7 6 7 0 00				9
			2 0 6 2 75		2 0 6 2 75				10
			2 2 4 1 32		2 2 4 1 32				11
			7 9 6 12		7 9 6 12				12
			5 2 6 0 00		5 2 6 0 00				13
			3 9 1 16		3 9 1 16				14
									15
	(a) 5 9 8 2 80		5 9 8 2 80		5 9 8 2 80				16
	5 9 8 2 80	5 9 8 2 80	132 7 6 9 10	132 7 6 9 10	45 3 0 3 85	70 9 2 9 20	87 4 6 5 25	61 8 3 9 90	17
					25 6 2 5 35			25 6 2 5 35	18
					70 9 2 9 20	70 9 2 9 20	87 4 6 5 25	87 4 6 5 25	19
									20

recording individual amounts in both the Cash Debit column and the Accounts Receivable Credit column. List each patient's name in the Account Name column.)

Sept. 3   Received cash for professional services rendered, $2,419.

5   Received and paid electric bill to Mid-State Power, $147.52 (Ck. No. 517).

8   Received and paid telephone bill to Western Telephone Company for month, $73 (Ck. No. 518).

9   Recorded fees charged to patients on account for professional services rendered $766.50: F. Radewan, $396.50; M. Parkhill, $370. (Use two lines.)

15   Paid salary of L. Macy (assistant), $757.50 (Ck. No. 519).

19   Received cash for professional services, $598.

23   Returned part of the equipment purchased on September 2 and received a reduction on the bill, $75.

28   Billed patients on account for professional services rendered, $1,133: C. C. Robbins, $575; Meredith Capwell, $316.50; Drew Hanson, $241.50.

30   Paid salary of C. Bates (part-time assistant), $820.75 (Ck. No. 520).

30   Paid salary of R. Cato (receptionist), $1,120 (Ck. No. 521).

30   Dr. Cascone withdrew $1,688.50 cash for personal use (Ck. No. 522).

Check Figure

Total debits, $13,157.77

Instructions

1. Record these transactions in the combined journal, page 37.
2. Prove the equality of the debit and credit totals in the Account Name column below the totals.
3. Fill in owner's equity accounts and post to the accounts in the general ledger.
4. Prepare a trial balance.

P.O. 2

Problem 6-4A On September 1 of this year, T. W. Binford started a limousine service serving the local area. The following transactions related to Luxury Limousine Service were completed during September.

Sept.		
	1	Binford opened an account in the Golden State Bank in the name of the business and deposited $34,000.
	2	Bought two used limousines from Laughlin Motors for $80,900, paying $20,900 down, with the balance payable in 30 days (Ck. No. 1).
	3	Bought heavy-duty vacuum and car-cleaning equipment for $359 from Gehrig E. Schaums, paying cash (Ck. No. 2).
	4	Paid Valley Service for gas and oil for limousines, $172 (Ck. No. 3).
	5	Paid rent for subletting office space, $235 (Ck. No. 4).
	7	Paid wages to L. Bain, $454 (Ck. No. 5).
	7	Received revenue for the week, $1,214.
	9	Paid for city business license, $86 (Ck. No. 6).
	11	Bought desk and filing cabinet on account from Murray Office Supply, $279.
	14	Paid for telephone answering service for the month, $136 (Ck. No. 7).
	14	Paid wages to L. Bain, $469 (Ck. No. 8).
	14	Binford withdrew $750 for personal use (Ck. No. 9).
	14	Received revenue for the week, $1,340.
	17	Paid Laughlin Motors $3,000 as part payment on account (Ck. No. 10).
	18	Paid $142 for advertising in the telephone directory (Ck. No. 11).
	18	Paid Valley Service for gas and oil for limousines, $214 (Ck. No. 12).
	20	Paid utilities for the month, $106 (Ck. No. 13).
	21	Received revenue for the week $1,439.
	23	Paid wages to L. Bain, $471 (Ck. No. 14).
	30	Received revenue for the week, $1,010.
	30	Paid Security Insurance Agency for vehicle insurance for six months, $757.
	30	Paid wages to L. Bain, $444 (Ck. No. 15).
	30	Binford withdrew $1,000 for personal use (Ck. No. 16).

Check Figure

Total debits, $128,977

Instructions

1. By reviewing the transactions for Luxury Limousine Service, develop a chart of accounts. The company will use the modified cash basis. All revenue is in the form of cash.
2. Label the appropriate columns in the combined journal. Next to the Date column, list a Ck. No. column and record checks beginning with number 1.
3. Record the transactions in the combined journal beginning with page 1.
4. Show proof of the equality of debit and credit totals in the Account Name column below the totals.

PROBLEM SET B

For additional help, see the demonstration problem at the beginning of each chapter in your Working Papers.

P.O. 2

Problem 6-1B The following chart of accounts is used by C. Stevenson, M.D.:

Assets

111 Cash
121 Medical Equipment
122 Accumulated Depreciation, Medical Equipment
123 Office Furniture and Equipment
124 Accumulated Depreciation, Office Furniture and Equipment
125 Vehicle
126 Accumulated Depreciation, Vehicle

Liabilities

211 Notes Payable

Owner's Equity

311 C. Stevenson, Capital
312 C. Stevenson, Drawing
313 Income Summary

Revenue

411 Professional Fees

Expenses

511 Salary Expense
512 Rent Expense
513 Equipment Rental Expense
514 Medical Supplies Expense
515 X-ray Supplies Expense
516 Laboratory Expense
517 Cleaning Expense
518 Office Supplies Expense
519 Depreciation Expense, Medical Equipment
521 Depreciation Expense, Office Furniture and Equipment
522 Depreciation Expense, Vehicle
523 Vehicle Expense
524 Insurance Expense
525 Telephone Expense
526 Utilities Expense
527 Miscellaneous Expense

Dr. Stevenson's records consist of an appointment record book, examination and charge reports, patients' ledger records, a combined journal, and a general ledger. The doctor fills out an examination and charge report each time a patient visits. The reports contain a description or listing of the treatments and tests administered, along with the amounts of the charges. The charges are then recorded in the patient's ledger record. Monthly statements based on the patients' ledger records are mailed to patients. Dr. Stevenson's books are kept on the modified cash basis.

The following transactions took place during November:

Nov. 1 Bought medical supplies for cash from Mason Surgical Supply, $521.50 (Ck. No. 214).

1 Paid Kelsey Realty for rent for the month, $1,350 (Ck. No. 215).

4 Paid salary to C. Ortiz (part-time office person), $935 (Ck. No. 216).

6 Received cash from patients during the week, $8,412.

7 Bought an examination table from Shelly Surgical Supply, costing $1,680, paying $480 in cash and agreeing by contract to pay the balance in three monthly installments of $400 each (credit Notes Payable). (Issued Ck. No. 217.)

8 Paid Ruiz Laboratories for laboratory expense, $354 (Ck. No. 218).

9 Paid telephone bill to Region Telephone Company, $96 (Ck. No. 219).

FIGURE 12

	ACCOUNT NAME	TRIAL BALANCE	
		DEBIT	CREDIT
1	Cash	8 1 0 5 00	
2	Equipment	35 2 1 9 00	
3	Accumulated Depreciation, Equipment		7 4 9 0 00
4	T. R. Berman, Capital		27 9 4 5 40
5	T. R. Berman, Drawing	14 8 8 0 00	
6	Professional Fees		65 9 5 2 00
7	Salary Expense	31 3 1 5 00	
8	Advertising Expense	1 0 6 0 80	
9	Rent Expense	1 8 3 0 00	
10	Vehicle Expense	1 9 7 5 00	
11	Travel Expense	3 1 2 4 60	
12	Entertainment Expense	9 3 5 00	
13	Supplies Expense	2 2 4 2 40	
14	Miscellaneous Expense	7 0 0 60	
15		101 3 8 7 40	101 3 8 7 40
16	Depreciation Expense, Equipment		
17			
18	Net Income		
19			
20			

Nov. 13 Total cash received from patients during the week, $6,111.
16 Dr. C. Stevenson withdrew $1,000 for personal use (Ck. No. 220).
16 Bought x-ray supplies for cash from Saling's Supply Company, $198.50 (Ck. No. 221).
20 Total cash received from patients during the week, $2,595.
23 Bought postage stamps for cash at post office, $15 (Miscellaneous Expense) (Ck. No. 222).
26 Paid Sharkie's Service Station for gas and oil, $100.25 (Vehicle Expense) (Ck. No. 223).
28 Paid Strong and Company for janitorial service, $85 (Cleaning Expense) (Ck. No. 224).
30 Paid salary to L. Mackey (nurse), $2,305 (Ck. No. 225).
30 Dr. C. Stevenson withdrew $1,620 for personal use (Ck. No. 226).
30 Received cash from patients (November 21 through 30), $3,000.
30 Paid $102.10 to Economy Laundry for laundry service through November 30 (Cleaning Expense) (Ck. No. 227).

Check Figure

Total debits, $30,480.35

Instructions

1. Record these transactions in the combined journal, page 26. Insert the name in the Drawing account.
2. Prove the equality of the debits and credits in the Account Name column below the totals.

P.O. 6

Problem 6-2B The completed work sheet for Berman Development Company is shown in Figure 12 above.

Berman Development Company
Work Sheet
For Month Ended December 31, 20—

	ADJUSTMENTS		ADJUSTED TRIAL BALANCE		INCOME STATEMENT		BALANCE SHEET		
	DEBIT	CREDIT	DEBIT	CREDIT	DEBIT	CREDIT	DEBIT	CREDIT	
			8 1 0 5 00				8 1 0 5 00		1
			35 2 1 9 00				35 2 1 9 00		2
		(a) 1 2 2 1 00		8 7 1 1 00				8 7 1 1 00	3
				27 9 4 5 40				27 9 4 5 40	4
			14 8 8 0 00				14 8 8 0 00		5
				65 9 5 2 00		65 9 5 2 00			6
			31 3 1 5 00		31 3 1 5 00				7
			1 0 6 0 80		1 0 6 0 80				8
			1 8 3 0 00		1 8 3 0 00				9
			1 9 7 5 00		1 9 7 5 00				10
			3 1 2 4 60		3 1 2 4 60				11
			9 3 5 00		9 3 5 00				12
			2 2 4 2 40		2 2 4 2 40				13
			7 0 0 60		7 0 0 60				14
									15
	(a) 1 2 2 1 00		1 2 2 1 00		1 2 2 1 00				16
	1 2 2 1 00	1 2 2 1 00	102 6 0 8 40	102 6 0 8 40	44 4 0 4 40	65 9 5 2 00	58 2 0 4 00	36 6 5 6 40	17
					21 5 4 7 60			21 5 4 7 60	18
					65 9 5 2 00	65 9 5 2 00	58 2 0 4 00	58 2 0 4 00	19
									20

Check Figure

Total Other Accounts Debit column, $148,005

P.O. 2,3

Instructions

Record the adjusting and closing entries in the combined journal. Remember to total the columns and insert an X in parentheses below each total.

Problem 6-3B Teresa K. Muller, D.C., operates the Muller Chiropractic Clinic. The transactions described on page 214 were completed during September of this year. Her chart of accounts is as follows:

Assets

111 Cash
112 Accounts Receivable
114 Prepaid Insurance
121 Equipment
122 Accumulated Depreciation, Equipment

Liabilities

221 Accounts Payable

Owner's Equity

311 T. K. Muller, Capital
312 T. K. Muller, Drawing
313 Income Summary

Revenue

411 Professional Fees

Expenses

511 Salary Expense
512 Rent Expense
513 Laboratory Expense
514 Utilities Expense
515 Depreciation Expense, Equipment
516 Supplies Expense
517 Miscellaneous Expense

Sept. 1 Bought x-ray equipment on account from Radiological Associates, $1,680. (Use two lines.)

2 Paid N. Barnes for office rent for the month, $925 (Ck. No. 423).

2 Received cash on account from patients, $816: Ralph Whitehall, $285; Eileen Butterick, $321; Anthony Clark, $210. (Dr. Muller uses the accrual basis. Use three lines, recording individual amounts in both the Cash Debit column and the Accounts Receivable Credit column. List each patient's name in the Account Name column.)

4 Received cash for professional services rendered, $1,890.50.

6 Received and paid electric bill to Universal Electric, $135.50 (Ck. No. 424).

7 Received and paid telephone bill for month to Southern Telephone Company, $42 (Ck. No. 425).

9 Recorded fees charged to patients on account for professional services rendered, $891.50: T. R. Swenson, $420; Hubert Cooke, $471.50. (Use two lines.)

15 Paid salary of A. Olivera (assistant), $1,120 (Ck. No. 426).

19 Received cash for professional services, $585.

22 Returned part of equipment purchased on September 1 and received a reduction on the bill, $175.

27 Billed patients on account for professional services rendered, $690: N. R. Cranston, $160; J. R. Perez, $285; S. N. Appleton, $245.

30 Paid salary of D. Curry (part-time assistant), $522.50 (Ck. No. 427).

30 Paid salary of V. Green (receptionist), $1,040 for the month (Ck. No. 428).

30 Dr. Muller withdrew $1,520 cash for personal use (Ck. No. 429).

Check Figure

Total debits, $12,033

Instructions

1. Record these transactions in the combined journal, page 43.
2. Prove the equality of the debit and credit totals in the Account Name column below the money column totals.
3. Fill in owner's equity accounts and post to the accounts in the general ledger.
4. Prepare a trial balance.

P.O. 2

Problem 6-4B On July 1 of this year, K. A. Boehm started a landscaping business. The following transactions relating to Boehm's Landscaping were completed during July.

July 1 Boehm opened an account at the Carter National Bank in the name of the business and deposited $15,000.

1 Paid rent for office and warehouse space for the month, $525 (Ck. No. 1).

2 Bought a used truck from Nielsen Motors for $18,200, paying $4,000 as a downpayment, with the balance on account due in 30 days (Ck. No. 2).

3 Bought landscaping equipment from Greene Equipment for $3,500, paying $1,500 as a downpayment, with the balance due in 30 days (Ck. No. 3).

3 Paid Zippie's Fast Serve for gas and oil for the truck, $149 (Ck. No. 4).

4 Received and paid bill for advertising from the *City Lights Review*, $158 (Ck. No. 5).

July   4   Bought fertilizers on account from Date's Lawn and Garden Store, $1,060 (Supplies Expense).

4   Bought beauty bark from O&P Distributing Company on account, $300 (Supplies Expense).

6   Received revenue for the week, $1,492.

7   Paid wages to part-time employee, $292 (Ck. No. 6).

7   Paid for telephone answering service for the week, $144 (Ck. No. 7).

10   Paid Zippie's Fast Serve for gas and oil for the truck, $135 (Ck. No. 8).

13   Received revenue for the week, $1,601.

17   Boehm withdrew $1,020 for personal use (Ck. No. 9).

20   Received revenue for the week, $1,288.

21   Paid wages to part-time employee, $312 (Ck. No. 10).

27   Paid $67 for city business license (Ck. No. 11).

27   Paid utilities for the month, $126 (Ck. No. 12).

30   Paid Nielsen Motors $2,000 to apply on account (Ck. No. 13).

30   Paid Zippie's Fast Serve for gas and oil for the truck, $45, plus $95 for a tune-up (Ck. No. 14).

31   Received revenue for the period July 21–31, $1,625.

31   Paid wages to part-time employee, $321 (Ck. No. 15).

31   Boehm withdrew $850 for personal use (Ck. No. 16).

Check Figure

Total debits, $50,305

Instructions

1. By reviewing the transactions for Boehm's Landscaping, formulate a chart of accounts. Boehm will use the modified cash basis of accounting.
2. Label the appropriate columns in the combined journal. Next to the Date column, list a Ck. No. column and record checks beginning with number 1.
3. Record the transactions in the combined journal beginning with page 1.
4. Show proof of the equality of debit and credit totals in the Account Name column below the totals.

7 Bank Accounts and Cash Funds

WINDOWS ON
THE WORLD WIDE WEB

Managing your money online is easier than ever. You can manage your checking and savings accounts, apply for loans, and handle your investments over the Internet. Most banks and credit unions offer remote banking online. Customers can view their bank statements; they can also view their account balances, make transfers, pay bills, and more. But, how do you find out which institutions provide the best online customer service or are easiest to use? The Gomez™ Internet Quality Measurement™ website ranks the services of banking institutions. This information can be used to help consumers decide which institution might be best for them. Their scorecard for banking institutions can be found at **http://www.gomez.com**.

If you wanted to bank online, what factors would be important to you when choosing an institution? What do you think some advantages and disadvantages of banking online might be?

Performance Objectives

After you have completed this chapter, you will be able to do the following:

1. Describe the procedure for depositing checks.

2. Reconcile a bank statement.

3. Record the required journal entries directly from the bank reconciliation.

4. Record journal entries to establish and reimburse a Petty Cash Fund.

5. Complete petty cash vouchers and petty cash payments records.

6. Record the journal entries to establish a Change Fund.

7. Record journal entries for transactions involving Cash Short and Over.

A very important aspect of any system of financial accounting, either for an individual or for a business enterprise, is the accurate and efficient management of cash. For a business of any size, all cash received during a work day should be deposited at the end of the day, and all disbursements—with the exception of payments from Petty Cash—should be made by check. When we talk about cash, we mean currency, coins, checks, money orders, traveler's checks, and bank drafts or bank cashier's checks. Personal checks are accepted conditionally—that is, based on the condition that they are valid. In other words, we consider checks to be good until they are otherwise proven not to be good.

216

Internal control of cash is a critical activity in a business. Divide the cash activities among several people to deter mishandling.

In this chapter, besides discussing bank accounts, we are going to talk about **cash funds**—petty cash funds and change funds—which are separately held reserves of cash set aside for specific purposes.

USING A CHECKING ACCOUNT

Although you may be familiar with the process of opening a checking account, making deposits, and writing checks, let's review these and other procedures associated with opening and maintaining a business checking account. We will discuss signature cards, deposit slips, automated teller machines, night deposits, and endorsements.

Signature Card

FYI

As a means of preventing employee theft, many companies require more than one signature on their checks.

When Marsha C. Bell founded Bell Video, she opened a checking account in the name of the business. When she made her first deposit, she filled out a **signature card** for the bank's files. Bell gave her assistant, Alicia C. Hecata, the right to sign checks too, so the assistant also signed the card. The signature card gives the bank a copy of the official signatures of any persons authorized to sign checks. The bank can use it to verify the signatures on any checks of Bell Video presented for payment. This card helps the bank detect forgeries. Figure 1 shows a typical signature card.

FIGURE 1

Title					Account Number
Bell Video					5008-3007

In consideration of the acceptance by   BESSETT NATIONAL BANK   of my/our account of the type indicated below, I/we agree to be bound by such rules and regulations and/or such schedules of interest, fees and charges applicable to such account as may now or hereafter be adopted by and in effect at said Bank, and also by the provisions printed hereon. It is understood that the acceptance by said Bank of my/our account is subject to the receipt by said Bank of satisfactory credit information.

(1) Sign Here   *Marsha C. Bell*

(2) Sign Here   *Alicia C. Hecata*

Address   **625 Harper Avenue**

City   **San Diego**   State   **California**   Zip   **92109**

☑ CHECKING   ☐ MULTIPLE MATURITY   ☐ CASH MANAGER

☐ SAVINGS   ☐ GUARANTEED INTEREST (Multiple Maturity)   ☐ SAFE DEPOSIT   ☐ OTHER _____

IF THIS IS A JOINT ACCOUNT, BOTH OWNERS MUST SIGN ABOVE

Each of the signers guarantees the genuineness of the signature of the other. Each signer also agrees with the other and the Bank that deposits now or hereafter made to this account may be withdrawn in whole or part by either or survivor, and that each may endorse for deposit to this account any instrument payable to the order of either or both. Provisions respecting this agreement shall be modified only upon receipt by the Bank of written notice, signed by both.

Deposit Slips

O B J E C T I V E   1
Describe the procedure for depositing checks.

The bank provides printed **deposit slips** or deposit tickets on which customers record the amount of coins and currency they are depositing and list each individual check being deposited. A typical deposit slip is shown in Figure 2.

FIGURE 2

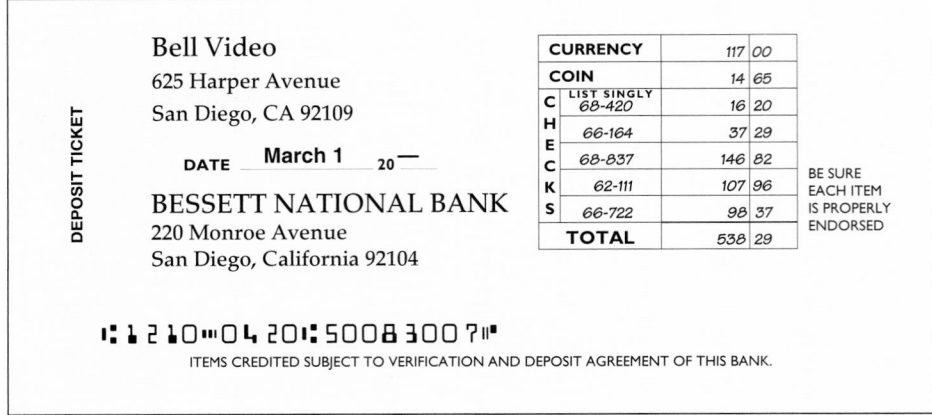

Each check should be listed according to its American Bankers Association (ABA) transit number. The **ABA number** is the small fraction located in the upper right corner of a check. The numerator (top of the fraction) indicates the city or state in which the bank is located and the specific bank on which the check is drawn. The denominator (bottom of the fraction) indicates the Federal Reserve District in which the check is cleared and the routing number used by the Federal Reserve Bank. For example,

$$\frac{68\text{-}420}{1210}$$

FYI

The 12 in the denominator represents the Twelfth Federal Reserve District, and the 10 represents the routing number used by the Federal Reserve Bank.

The 68 identifies the city or state, and the 420 indicates the specific bank within that area (see Figures 3 and 5).

For a business account, the depositor fills out the deposit slip in duplicate, giving the original to the bank teller and keeping the copy. (This procedure may vary from bank to bank.)

When the bank receives the deposited checks, it prints the amount of each check on the lower right side of the check in a very distinctive script called **MICR**, which stands for *magnetic ink character recognition*. The routing number (as well as the depositor's number) used by the Federal Reserve Bank was printed on the lower left side of the blank check before it was sent to the account holder. The reason banks use this MICR script is that the electronic equipment used to process the checks is able to rapidly read the script identifying the bank on which the check is drawn and the amount of the check.

Automated Teller Machines

Deposits, withdrawals, and transfers can be made at all hours at banks with **ATMs** (automated teller machines). Each depositor uses a plastic card that contains a code number. The amount to be deposited, withdrawn, or transferred is keyed in by the depositor. To make a deposit, the customer inserts an envelope containing cash and/or checks and a copy of the deposit slip into the ATM. To make a withdrawal, the customer requests an amount, the ATM dispenses it, and the customer removes the cash. In addition to deposits and withdrawals, a customer may transfer amounts from one account to another (for example, from savings to checking).

Night Deposits

Most banks also provide night depositories so that firms and individuals can make deposits after regular banking hours. Depositories are secured chutes into which a firm's representative can drop a bag of cash and checks, knowing that the day's receipts will be safe until the bank opens in the morning.

Endorsements

The bank may not accept for deposit a check made out to a firm until someone from the firm has endorsed the check. The endorsement may be made by signature or by stamp. The endorsement should appear on the back of the left end of a check, as it does in Figure 3. The **endorsement** (1) transfers title to the money and (2) authorizes the payment of the check. In other words, if the check is not good, NSF (not sufficient funds), then the bank, in order to protect itself, will deduct the amount of the check from the depositor's account.

FIGURE 3

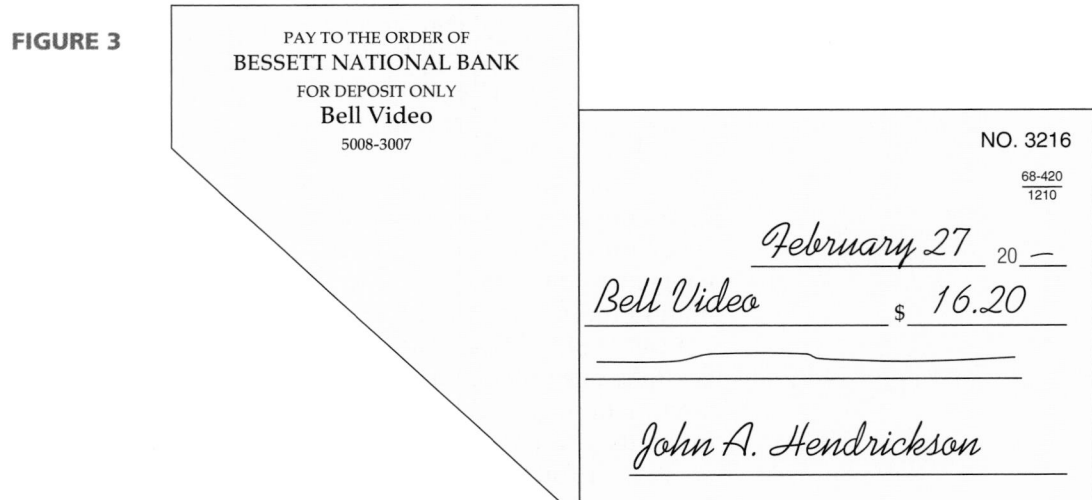

Restrictive Endorsement All checks made payable to Bell Video are endorsed by stamping on the back of the checks "Pay to the Order of Bessett National Bank, For Deposit Only, Bell Video." This is called a **restrictive endorsement** because it restricts or limits any further transfer of the check. This endorsement also forces the deposit of the check, because the endorsement is not valid for any other purpose.

Blank Endorsement When the party to whom a check is made payable (the payee) endorses the check by signing only her or his name on the back of the check, this is known as a **blank endorsement** (Figure 4). With a blank endorsement, there are no restrictions attached.

FIGURE 4

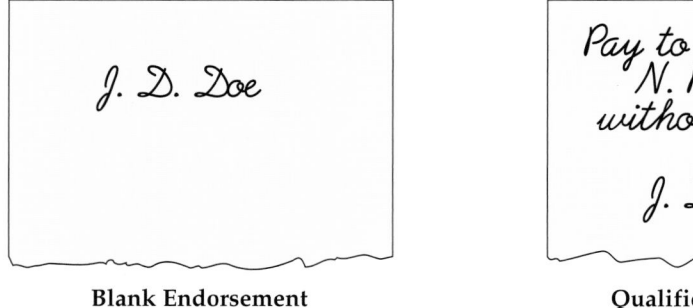

Blank Endorsement   Qualified Endorsement

Qualified Endorsement A third type of endorsement is a **qualified endorsement** (see Figure 4), which generally includes the phrase "Pay to the order of," followed by the name of the person to whom the check is being transferred, and then followed by the phrase "without recourse." Such an endorsement frees the endorser from future liability in case the drawer of the check does not have sufficient funds to cover the check.

WRITING CHECKS

People generally use a check to withdraw money from a bank checking account. The party who writes the check is called the **drawer**. A check represents an order by the drawer, directing the bank to pay a designated person or company. The party to whom payment is to be made is the **payee**.

The checks may be attached to check stubs. Each stub has spaces for recording the check number and amount, the date and payee, the purpose of the check, and the beginning and ending balances of cash. *Note:* The information recorded on the check stub is the basis for the journal entry, so check stubs are vitally important. A person in a hurry or under pressure sometimes neglects to fill in the check stubs. Therefore, it is best to record all the information on the check stub *before making out the check.*

Checks should be written carefully so that no dishonest person can successfully alter them. Write the payee's name on the first long line. Write the amount of the check in figures close to the dollar sign, then write the amount in words at the extreme left of the line provided for this information. Write cents as a fraction of 100. For example, write $727.50 as "seven hundred twenty-seven and 50/100," or $89.00 as "eighty-nine and NO/100." From a legal standpoint, if there is a discrepancy between the amount in figures and the written amount, the written amount prevails. However, as a general practice, the bank gets in touch with the drawer and asks what the correct amount should be.

Computerized firms print their checks electronically. Some firms use a **check writer**, which is a machine that imprints the amount in figures and words on the check itself. Using this machine neatly prevents anyone from altering the amount of the check.

Finally, the drawer's signature on the face of the check should match that on the signature card on file at the drawer's bank.

Figure 5 is a check, with the accompanying stub, drawn on the account of Bell Video.

A description of the script appears in Figure 6.

FIGURE 5

FIGURE 6

BANK STATEMENTS

Once a month the bank sends each of its customers a **bank statement**. The statement provides the following information about customers' cash accounts:

- The balance at the beginning of the month
- Additions in the form of deposits and credit memos
- Deductions in the form of checks and debit memos
- The final balance at the end of the month

A bank statement for Bell Video is shown in Figure 7 on page 222. The following legend of symbols is listed on the bottom of the statement:

- **CM (credit memo)** Increases in or credits to the account, such as notes or accounts left with the bank for collection.
- **DM (debit memo)** Decreases in or debits to the account, such as NSF checks, ATM withdrawals, and service charges. Service charges are based on the number of items processed and the average account balance. Special charges may also be levied against the account for collections and other services performed, including check printing.
- **PBP (pay by phone)** Transactions made by telephone using the number keypad instead of writing checks.

BESSETT NATIONAL BANK
220 Monroe Avenue
San Diego, California 92104

STATEMENT OF ACCOUNT	**Bell Video** **625 Harper Avenue** **San Diego, CA 92109**	ACCOUNT NUMBER **5008-3007** STATEMENT DATE **September 30, 20 — – October 31, 20 —** TAX ID NUMBER **83-424 9732**

	SUMMARY	Balance Last Statement	$7,089.13
		Amount of Checks and Debits	$25,154.91
		Number of Checks	66
		Amount of Deposits and Credits	$27,031.78
		Number of Deposits	23
		Balance This Statement	$8,966.00

CHECKS/ OTHER DEBITS	CHECKS	CHECK NUMBER	DATE POSTED	AMOUNT	CHECK NUMBER	DATE POSTED	AMOUNT
		1952	10-01	50.00	1988	10-17	61.22
		1953	10-01	200.00	1989	10-17	463.29
		1954	10-01	400.00	1990	10-18	520.00
		1955	10-02	46.00	1991	10-19	14.57
		1956	10-02	174.23	1992	10-19	23.98
		1957	10-02	671.74	1993	10-19	115.16
		1958	10-03	846.20	1994	10-20	117.37
		1984	10-14	664.56	2018	10-30	126.70
		1985	10-15	719.00	2019	10-30	943.64
		1986	10-16	61.68	2020	10-31	843.17
		1987	10-16	591.84	2021	10-31	21.92

	OTHER DEBITS	DESCRIPTION	DATE POSTED	AMOUNT
		DM NSF check from D. M. Scott	10-15	125.00
		DM Automated Teller Trans. 062142 customer N3162241 at terminal 30962—cash	10-16	20.00
		DM Service charge	10-31	5.50

DEPOSITS/ OTHER CREDITS	DEPOSITS	DATE POSTED	AMOUNT	DATE POSTED	AMOUNT
		10-01	921.00	10-17	873.19
		10-02	1,476.22	10-18	946.78
		10-03	463.62	10-21	329.49
		10-04	789.44	10-22	1,116.27
		10-07	1,063.14	10-23	734.13
		10-08	1,211.96	10-26	227.69
		10-14	992.27	10-28	439.45
		10-15	759.41	10-29	611.12
		10-16	641.33	10-30	764.35

	OTHER CREDITS	DESCRIPTION	DATE POSTED	AMOUNT
		CM Note collected, principal $600, interest $6	10-29	606.00

PLEASE EXAMINE THIS STATEMENT CAREFULLY. REPORT ANY POSSIBLE ERRORS IN 10 DAYS.

CODE SYMBOLS

CM Credit Memo	OD Overdraft
DM Debit Memo	EC Error Correction
PBP Pay by Phone	

FIGURE 7

- **OD (overdraft)** The withdrawal of more than the cash balance in the account, resulting in a negative balance.
- **EC (error correction)** Corrections of errors made by the bank, such as mistakes in transferring figures.

The bank statement is a valuable aid to efficiency and accuracy because it provides a double record of the Cash account. If a business entity deposits all cash receipts in the bank and makes all payments by check, then the bank is keeping an independent record of the firm's cash. You might think that the two balances—the firm's and the bank's—should be equal, but this is unlikely. Some transactions may have been recorded in the firm's account before being entered in the bank's records. In addition, there are unavoidable delays (by either the firm or the bank) in recording transactions. Ordinarily, there is a delay of one or more days between the date on which a check is written and the date when it is presented to the bank for payment. Also, banks may not record deposits until the following business day. During this time lag, deposits made or checks written are recorded in the firm's checkbook, but they are not yet listed on the bank statement.

The bank mails statements to its depositors each month. The **canceled checks** (checks that have been paid or cleared by the bank) are listed on the bank statement. They are called *canceled checks* because they are canceled by a stamp or perforation, indicating that they have been paid. Debit or credit memos are generally mailed with the statement.

REMEMBER!
Debit memos represent deductions from and credit memos represent additions to a bank account.

Recording Deposits or Withdrawals

Each business entity keeps its accounts from its *own* point of view. As far as the bank is concerned, each customer's deposits are liabilities, in that the bank owes the customer the amount of the deposits. Using T accounts, it looks like this:

When the bank receives a cash deposit from a customer, the bank credits Deposits Payable, because it owes more to its customer. When the bank cashes a check (pays out) for a customer, the bank debits Deposits Payable, because it owes less to its customer.

The customer, on the other hand, uses the account titled Cash, or Cash in Bank, or simply the name of the bank. Deposits are recorded as debits, and withdrawals are recorded as credits in the account. On a bank reconciliation, the balance of the account is listed as the **ledger balance of cash** before reconciliation with the bank statement.

MENTOR PROFILE

JERRY DUNN

Co-founder, Co-owner, and President of Aviation Finance Group

How do you go from reconciling bank statements to owning a company that finances private jets for high-net-worth individuals on a nationwide basis? Jerry Dunn says you apply common sense and problem-solving skills as you learn accounting rather than relying on rote memorization. He believes that the successful accounting student and businessperson must understand the "big picture" of the business transaction before applying accounting procedures and principles. In other words, you mustn't get buried in the procedures and lose sight of what the numbers mean, where they are going, and what impact they have on the business as a whole.

"The statement of cash flows is king in business along with the fundamental foundation of successful business—INTEGRITY."

Jerry believes that *cash flow is king* in business and that *integrity is essential*—beliefs shared by many successful businesses and individuals. Integrity is a fundamental foundation of a successful business. And building on these beliefs, Jerry's career has taken an exciting path. After working on Wall Street in the finance industry, he later became an entrepreneur. Although he has never prepared financial statements, he certainly uses them almost every day. There's that solid accounting foundation and big-picture combination again; they are inseparable.

Besides selling jets to high-net-worth people, as president of the Aviation Finance Group, Jerry is responsible for the day-to-day internal operations of the company—human resources, operations, and systems. Part of that responsibility includes managing the financial health of the company. It is very hard to stay in any business without a healthy cash flow. And without his accounting and finance background, he wouldn't be able to balance the responsibilities involved with financing jets and keeping up his own company's cash flow and monetary return.

Need for Reconciling Bank Balance and Ledger Balance

OBJECTIVE 2
Reconcile a bank statement.

Since the bank statement balance and the ledger balance of cash are not equal, a firm prepares a **bank reconciliation** to uncover the reasons for the difference between the two balances and to correct any errors that may have been made by either the bank or the firm. This makes it possible to arrive at the same balance in each account, which is called the *adjusted balance,* or *true balance,* of the Cash account.

There are a variety of reasons for differences between the bank statement balance and the customer's cash balance. Here are some of the more common ones:

FYI

When a bank agrees to accept payments on behalf of a customer, the fee the bank charges does not necessarily mean that the bank will follow up on collection of a payment or notify the customer that the payment is late.

- **Deposit in transit** A deposit made after the bank statement was issued. The depositor has naturally already added the amount to the Cash account in his or her books, but the deposit has not been recorded by the bank (this is also called a *late deposit*).
- **Outstanding checks** Checks that have been written by the company but not yet received for payment by the time the bank sends out its statement. The company employee, when writing checks, deducted the amounts from the Cash account in the company's books, which explains the difference.

- **Collections** When the bank acts as a collection point for its customers by accepting payments on their behalf, it adds the proceeds to the customer's bank account and sends a credit memorandum to notify the customer of the transaction or includes it on the next bank statement.
- **Interest income** Some checking accounts are interest bearing or earning. The depositor will not learn how much interest the bank has credited to the bank account until the bank statement is received.
- **NSF (not sufficient funds) check** When a bank customer deposits a check, it is recorded as cash on the customer's books. Occasionally, however, a check is not paid (bounces). When the bank notifies the customer of this, the customer must make a deduction from the Cash account. Simultaneously, the depositor records an increase in accounts receivable because the client's debt to the depositor remains unpaid. An NSF check may also be called a *dishonored check.*
- **Service charge** A bank charge for services rendered: for handling checks, for collecting money, for receiving payment of notes turned over to it by the customer for collection, for check printing, and for other such services. The bank immediately deducts the fee from the balance of the bank account and notifies the depositor with a debit memorandum.
- **Errors** In spite of internal controls and systems designed to double-check to prevent errors, sometimes either the customer or the bank makes a mistake. Often these errors do not become evident until the bank reconciliation is performed.

Steps in Reconciling the Bank Statement

Follow these steps to reconcile a bank statement:

1. **Canceled checks**
   a. Compare the amount of each canceled check with the bank statement and note any differences. The amount of the machine-readable characters should appear at the lower right-hand corner of the check, which should match the amount written on the check and the bank statements.
   b. In the checkbook beside the check number, list the date of the bank statement. In some cases, a bank may not pay a check until one or two months after it was written. If a question arises as to whether or not you have paid a particular bill, you can look at the checkbook. Then you can refer directly to the bank statement to pick up the accompanying canceled check as proof of payment.
2. **Deposits**
   a. Compare the deposits in transit (not recorded by the bank at the time of the statement) listed on last month's bank reconciliation with the deposits shown on the bank statement. All of last month's deposits in transit should be listed on this month's bank statement. If they are not, notify the bank immediately.
   b. Compare the remaining deposits listed on this month's bank statement with deposits written in the company's accounting records. Consider any deposits not shown on the bank statement as deposits in transit.
3. **Outstanding checks**
   a. Arrange the canceled checks in order by check number.
   b. Look over the list of outstanding checks left over from last month's bank reconciliation, and note the checks that have now been returned or cleared.

Besides their core activities of providing financial transactions, many banks are actively committed to community service by supporting various causes, such as Chase Manhattan Bank's sponsorship of the Chase Corporate Challenge.

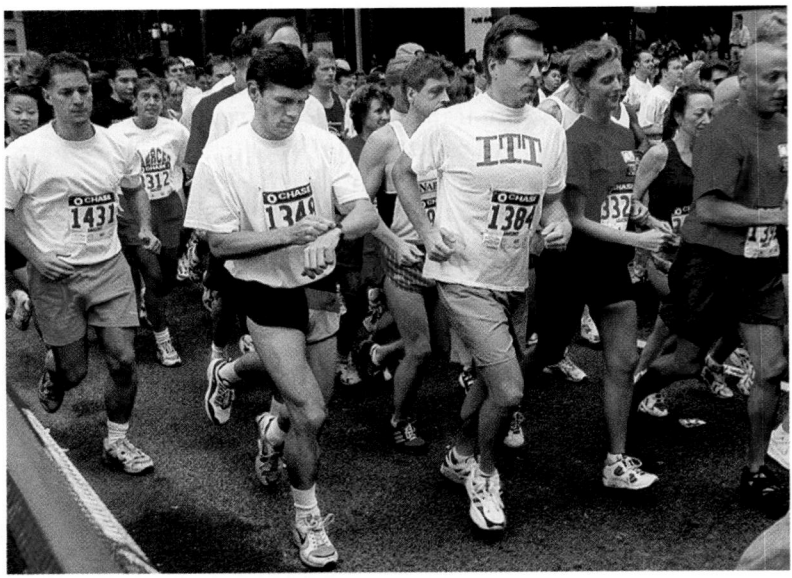

c. For each canceled check, compare the amount recorded in MICR numbers at the lower right-hand corner of the check with the amount recorded in the checkbook. Next, compare the canceled checks with the numerical listing in the statement. Use a check mark (✓) to indicate that the check has been paid and that the amount is correct. Any payments that have not been marked off, including the outstanding checks from last month's bank reconciliation, are the present outstanding checks.

d. Review the endorsements on the backs of the checks to verify that money has been sent to the correct payee.

4. **Bank memoranda** Trace the credit memos and debit memos to the journal. If the memos have not been recorded, make separate entries for them.

A large firm should require that the reconciliation be prepared by an employee who is not involved in recording business transactions or in handling cash receipts and disbursements.

Examples of Bank Reconciliations

Let's go through the reconciliation process for two firms, L. A. Compton Company and Bell Video.

L. A. Compton Company The bank statement of L. A. Compton Company indicates a balance of $4,238 as of March 31. The balance of the Cash account in Compton's ledger as of that date is $3,104. Compton's accountant has taken the following steps:

1. Verified that canceled checks were recorded correctly on the bank statement.
2. Noted that the deposit made on March 31 was not recorded on the bank statement, $1,524.
3. Noted outstanding checks: no. 921, $1,252; no. 985, $138; no. 986, $876.
4. Noted credit memo: note collected by the bank from S. Ellers, $400, not recorded in the journal.
5. Noted debit memo: collection charge and service charge not recorded in the journal, $8.

The note received from S. Ellers is called a promissory note. A **promissory note** is a written promise to pay a definite amount at a definite future time. Let's assume that L. A. Compton Company received the sixty-day non-interest-bearing note from S. Ellers for services performed. In recording the transaction, Compton's accountant debited Notes Receivable and credited Income from Services. (The account Notes Receivable is similar to Accounts Receivable. However, Accounts Receivable is reserved for customer charge accounts, with payments usually due in thirty days.) Next, L. A. Compton Company turned the note over to its bank for collection.

The bank will use a credit memo form to notify L. A. Compton Company that the note has been collected and that the company's bank account has been increased by the amount of the note. Based on the credit memo, Compton's accountant will make a journal entry debiting Cash and crediting Notes Receivable.

Think of the bank reconciliation in terms of the following:

1. Bring the bank statement balance up to date by recording the events that we knew about but the bank did not know about when it prepared the statement (deposits in transit and outstanding checks as shown in our checkbook, for example).
2. Bring the balance of the Cash account up to date by recording the events that the bank knew about but we did not know about until we received the statement (debit memos and credit memos as shown on the bank statement, for example).

The bank reconciliation may be prepared on a separate sheet of paper or on the back of the bank statement. Figure 8 shows L. A. Compton's bank reconciliation. The items in the reconciliation that require journal entries are shown in color, and the entries are shown below.

FIGURE 8

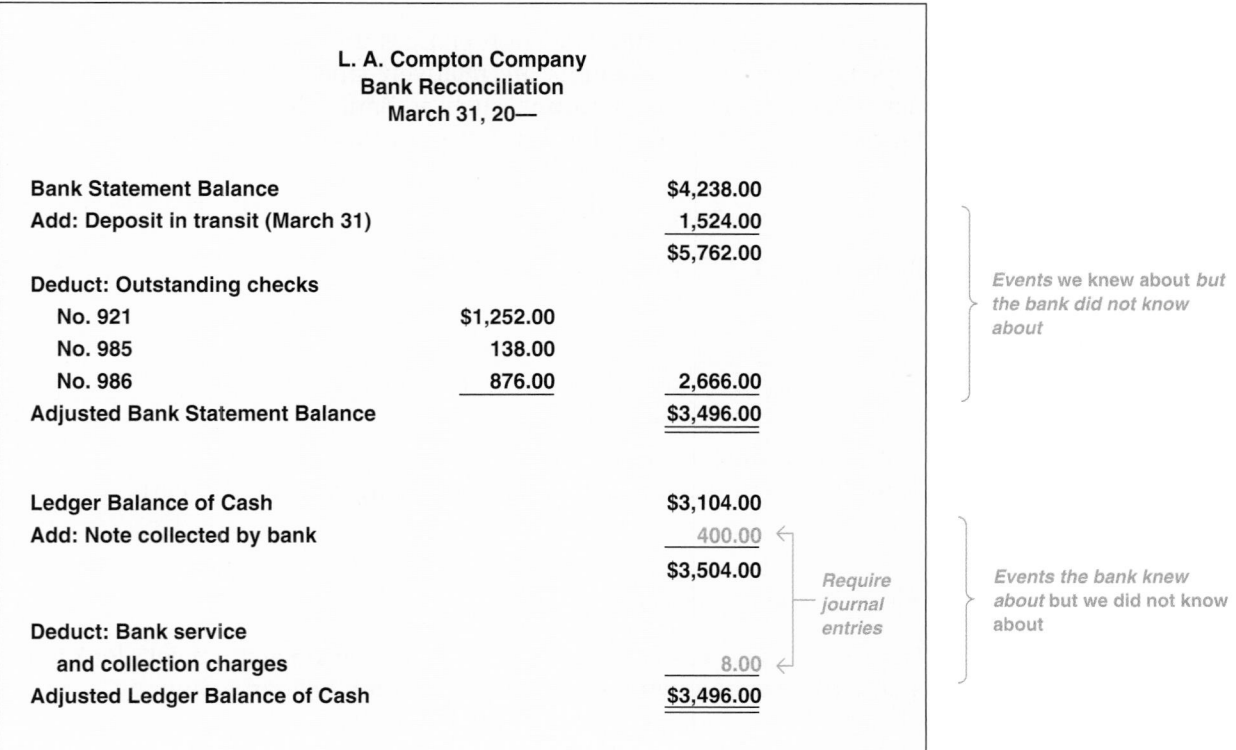

L. A. Compton Company Bank Reconciliation March 31, 20—			
Bank Statement Balance		$4,238.00	
Add: Deposit in transit (March 31)		1,524.00	
		$5,762.00	Events we knew about but the bank did not know about
Deduct: Outstanding checks			
No. 921	$1,252.00		
No. 985	138.00		
No. 986	876.00	2,666.00	
Adjusted Bank Statement Balance		$3,496.00	
Ledger Balance of Cash		$3,104.00	
Add: Note collected by bank		400.00	Events the bank knew about but we did not know about
		$3,504.00	Require journal entries
Deduct: Bank service and collection charges		8.00	
Adjusted Ledger Balance of Cash		$3,496.00	

Note that the journal entries are based on the items used to adjust the ledger balance of Cash. These items represent the transactions that the bank has knowledge of but the firm does not. According to the bank reconciliation, the true balance of Cash is $3,496, which is the balance we wish to show on the firm's books. We can't change the balance of an account unless we first make a journal entry and then post the entry to the accounts involved. **Consequently, we have to make journal entries for items in the Ledger Balance of Cash section of the bank reconciliation.** In the Ledger Balance of Cash section, the additions are debited to the Cash account, and the deductions are credited to the Cash account. L. A. Compton Company records the entries in its general journal:

		GENERAL JOURNAL			PAGE _____	
DATE		DESCRIPTION	POST. REF.	DEBIT	CREDIT	
20—						
Mar.	31	Cash		4 0 0 00		
		Notes Receivable			4 0 0 00	
		Non-interest-bearing note				
		signed by S. Ellers was				
		collected by the bank.				
	31	Miscellaneous Expense		8 00		
		Cash			8 00	
		Service charge and collection				
		charge levied by bank.				

Here bank service and collection charges are recorded in Miscellaneous Expense because the amounts are relatively small. Some accountants may use a separate expense account, such as Bank Charge Expense. After the entries have been posted, the T account for Cash looks like this:

Cash

Balance	3,104	Mar. 31	8
Mar. 31	400		
	3,504		
Bal.	3,496		

Note that the balance in the T account is now equal to both the adjusted bank statement balance and the adjusted ledger balance of cash.

Form of Bank Reconciliation

Now that you have seen an example of a bank reconciliation, let's look at the standard form of a bank reconciliation for an imaginary company.

Bank Statement Balance (last figure on the statement)		$4,000
Add		
Deposits in transit (deposits made after the bank statement was issued and already added to the ledger balance of Cash)	$300	
Bank errors (that understate balance)	20	320
		$4,320
Deduct		
Outstanding checks (they have already been deducted from the Cash account)	$960	
Bank errors (that overstate balance)	40	1,000
Adjusted Bank Statement Balance (the true balance of Cash)		$3,320
Ledger Balance of Cash (the latest balance of the Cash account if it has been posted up to date; otherwise take the beginning balance of Cash, plus cash receipts, minus cash payments)		$2,850
Add		
Credit memos (additions by the bank not recorded in the Cash account, such as collections of notes)	$500	
Book errors (that understate balance)	40	540
		$3,390
Deduct		
Debit memos (deductions by the bank not recorded in the Cash account, such as service charges or collection charges and NSF checks)	$ 20	
Book errors (that overstate balance)	50	70
Adjusted Ledger Balance of Cash (the true balance of Cash)		$3,320

Bell Video The bank statement of Bell Video shows a final balance of $8,966 as of October 31 (see Figure 9 on page 230). The present balance of the Cash account in the ledger, after Bell's accountant has posted from the journal, is $8,330.50. The accountant took the following steps:

1. Verified that canceled checks were recorded correctly on the bank statement.
2. Discovered that a deposit of $1,303 made on October 31 was not recorded on the bank statement.
3. Noted outstanding checks: no. 1916, $461; no. 2022, $119; no. 2023, $827; no. 2024, $67.
4. Noted that a credit memo for a note collected by the bank from Lee and Brock, $600 principal plus $6 interest, was not recorded in the journal.
5. Found that check no. 2001 for $523, payable to Davis, Inc., on account, was recorded in the journal as $532. (The correct amount is $523.)
6. Noted that a debit memo for a collection charge and service charge of $5.50 was not recorded in the journal.

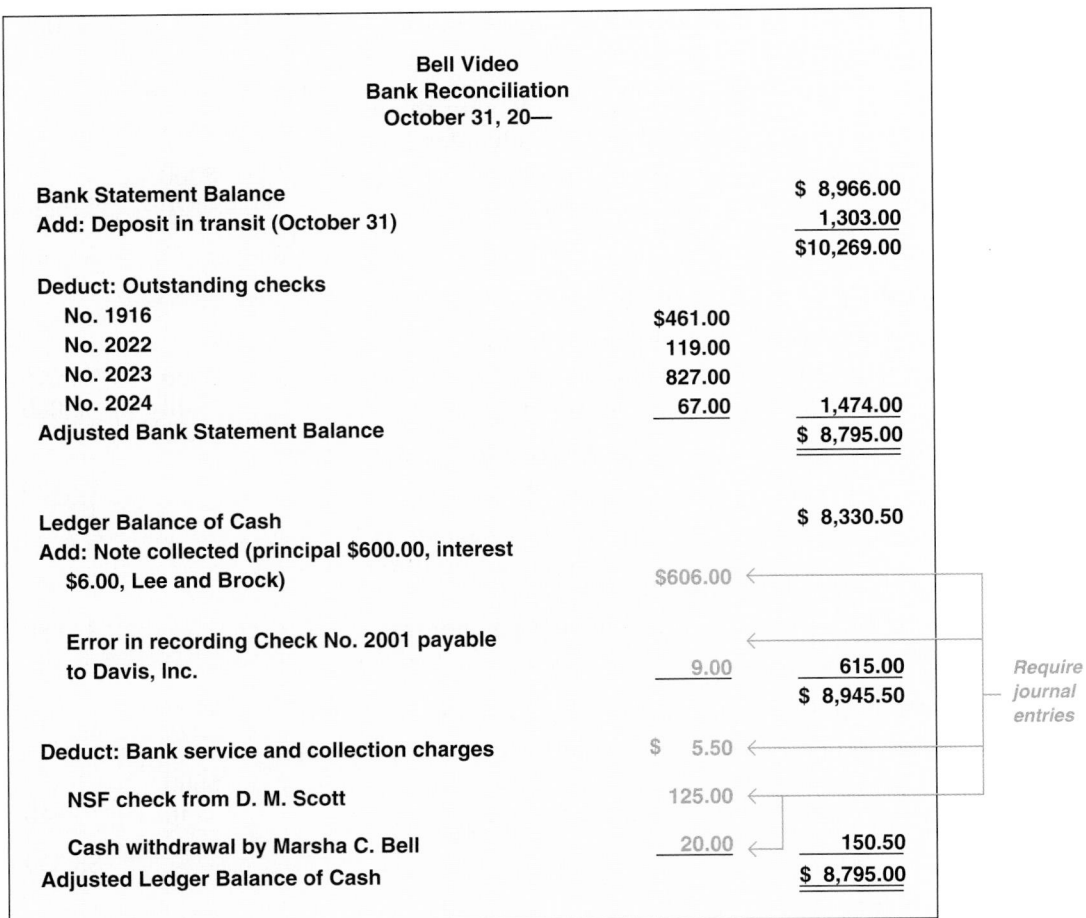

FIGURE 9

7. Noted that a debit memo for an NSF check for $125 from D. M. Scott was not recorded.
8. Noted that a $20 personal withdrawal by Marsha C. Bell, the owner, using an ATM, was not recorded.

Look at Figure 9 to see how each step relates to the bank reconciliation.

The accountant makes journal entries for the items indicated in Figure 9 to change the balance of the Cash account from its present balance of $8,330.50 to the true balance of $8,795.00. Again, those items that require journal entries are highlighted in Figure 9 and shown in Figure 10.

The account Interest Income is classified as a revenue account. It represents the amount received on the promissory note that is over and above the face value of the note.

As for the NSF check, upon being notified by the bank, Bell Video calls its customer (D. M. Scott). Scott can now take steps to cover the check. Let's back up and review Bell's transaction with D. M. Scott. In return for service provided, Bell received Scott's check for $125. At that time, Bell's accountant recorded the transaction as a debit to Cash for $125 and a credit to Income from Services for $125. Then the bank, through its debit memorandum, notifies Bell Video about Scott's NSF check. To avoid overdrawing its own bank account, Bell makes an entry crediting Cash (to correct its record of Cash)

FIGURE 10

GENERAL JOURNAL   PAGE _____

DATE		DESCRIPTION	POST. REF.	DEBIT	CREDIT
20—					
Oct.	31	Cash		6 0 6 00	
		Notes Receivable			6 0 0 00
		Interest Income			6 00
		Bank collected note signed			
		by Lee and Brock.			
	31	Cash		9 00	
		Accounts Payable			9 00
		Error in recording check no.			
		2001 payable to Davis, Inc.			
	31	Miscellaneous Expense		5 50	
		Cash			5 50
		Bank service charge and			
		collection charge.			
	31	Accounts Receivable		1 2 5 00	
		Cash			1 2 5 00
		NSF check received from			
		D. M. Scott.			
	31	Marsha C. Bell, Drawing		2 0 00	
		Cash			2 0 00
		Withdrawal for personal use.			

and debiting Accounts Receivable (to put the amount into Accounts Receivable). Since D. M. Scott owes the money, it is logical to add the amount to Accounts Receivable.

A bank reconciliation form is ordinarily printed on the back of the bank statement. The adjusted balance of the ledger balance of cash has already been determined. Consequently, the bank form is provided only for calculating the adjusted bank statement balance of the bank reconciliation. The bank form for Bell Video is shown in Figure 11 on page 232.

THE PETTY CASH FUND

Day after day, business firms are confronted with transactions requiring small immediate payments, such as paying for delivery charges, a birthday card, or a new toner cartridge. If the firm had to go through the usual procedure of making all payments by check, the time consumed would be frustrating and the whole process would be unduly expensive. For many firms, the cost of writing each check is more than $10; this includes the cost of an

**THIS FORM IS PROVIDED TO HELP YOU BALANCE
YOUR BANK STATEMENT**

CHECKS OUTSTANDING—NOT
CHARGED TO ACCOUNT

NO.			
1916	$	461	00
2022		119	00
2023		827	00
2024		67	00
TOTAL	$	1,474	00

BEFORE YOU START—

PLEASE BE SURE YOU HAVE ENTERED IN YOUR CHECKBOOK ALL AUTOMATIC TRANSACTIONS SHOWN ON THE FRONT OF YOUR STATEMENT.

YOU SHOULD HAVE ADDED IF ANY OCCURRED:

1. Loan advances.
2. Credit memos.
3. Other automatic deposits.

YOU SHOULD HAVE SUBTRACTED IF ANY OCCURRED:

1. Automatic loan payments.
2. Automatic savings transfers.
3. Service charges.
4. Debit memos.
5. Other automatic deductions and payments.

BANK BALANCE SHOWN
ON THIS STATEMENT $ 8,966.00

ADD

DEPOSITS NOT SHOWN
ON THIS STATEMENT
(IF ANY) $ 1,303.00

_____

_____

TOTAL $ 10,269.00

SUBTRACT—

►CHECKS OUTSTANDING $ 1,474.00

BALANCE $ 8,795.00

SHOULD AGREE WITH YOUR CHECKBOOK
BALANCE AFTER DEDUCTING SERVICE CHARGE
(IF ANY) SHOWN ON THIS STATEMENT.

Please examine immediately and report if incorrect. If no reply
is received within 15 days the account will be considered correct.

FIGURE 11

employee's time for writing and reconciling the check. Suppose you buy five stamps from an employee for $1.65, and you want to reimburse her for that money. To write a check would not be practical. It only makes sense to pay in cash, using the **Petty Cash Fund**. *Petty* means "small," so the firm sets a maximum amount that can be paid immediately out of petty cash. Payments that exceed this maximum must be processed by regular check through the journal.

Establishing the Petty Cash Fund

After the firm has set the maximum amount of a payment from petty cash, the next step is to estimate how much cash will be needed during a given period of time, such as a month. It is also important to consider the element of security when keeping cash in the office. If the risk is great, the amount kept in the fund should be small. Bell Video decides to establish a Petty Cash Fund of $70 and put it under the control of the assistant. Accordingly, Bell's accountant writes a check, cashes it at the bank, and records this transaction in the journal as follows:

GENERAL JOURNAL   PAGE _____

	DATE		DESCRIPTION	POST. REF.	DEBIT	CREDIT	
1	20—						1
2	Sept.	1	Petty Cash Fund		7 0 00		2
3			Cash			7 0 00	3
4			Established a Petty Cash				4
5			Fund.				5

T accounts for the entry look like this:

Petty Cash Fund	Cash
+ | −	+ | −
70 |	| 70

Because the Petty Cash Fund is an asset account, it is listed on the balance sheet immediately below Cash.

Once the fund has been created, it is not debited again unless the original amount is not large enough to handle the necessary transactions. In that case, the accountant has to increase the Petty Cash Fund—perhaps from $70 to $100. **But, barring such a change in the size of the fund, Petty Cash Fund is debited only once.**

The check is written to the assistant, "Al Hecata, Petty Cash Fund." He converts it into convenient **denominations**, which are varieties of coins and currency, such as quarters and dimes and $1 and $5 bills. Then the assistant puts the money in a locked drawer and will not pay anything larger than $5 (or whatever is the agreed-upon amount) out of petty cash.

Payments from the Petty Cash Fund

The assistant now takes the responsibility for the Petty Cash Fund. He is designated as the only person who can make payments from it. In case of his or her illness, some other employee should be named as stand-in. A **petty cash voucher** must be used to account for every payment from the fund. The voucher constitutes a receipt signed by the person who authorized the payment and by the person who received payment as well as the purpose of the petty cash payment. Thus, even for small payments of $5 or less, there would have to be collusion between the payee and the assistant for any theft to occur. Figure 12 is a petty cash voucher.

FIGURE 12

PETTY CASH VOUCHER	
No. 1	Date September 2, 20—
Paid to Mark Delivery Service	$ 2.00
For Delivery	
Account Delivery Expense	
Approved by	*Payment received by*
A. Hecata	D. Stanton

Petty Cash Payments Record

Some firms prefer to have a written record on one sheet of paper, so they keep a **petty cash payments record**. In a petty cash payments record, petty cash vouchers and the accounts that are to be charged are listed as well as

FIGURE 13

Petty Cash Payments Record
Month of September 20—

	DATE	VOU. NO.	EXPLANATION	PAYMENTS	OFFICE SUPPLIES	
1	Sept. 1		Establish fund, check no. 90, $70			
2	2	1	Mark Delivery Service	2 00		
3	3	2	Pencils and pens	3 09	3 09	
4	5	3	Local newspaper	5 00		
5	7	4	Postage on incoming mail	2 90		
6	10	5	Marsha C. Bell	5 00		
7	14	6	Reimburse employee for stamps	1 65		
8	21	7	Stick-on tabs	4 10	4 10	
9	22	8	Mark Delivery Service	3 00		
10	26	9	Postage for mailings	3 80		
11	27	10	Fast Way Delivery	3 50		
12	29	11	Memo pads	4 40	4 40	
13	29	12	Making duplicate keys	2 60		
14	30	13	Mark Delivery Service	3 20		
15	30	14	Trash removal	5 00		
16	30		Totals	4 9 24	1 1 59	
17			Balance in Fund $20.76			
18			Reimburse fund, check no. 136 49.24			
19			Total $70.00			
20						
21						

the purpose of the expenditure. Special columns for frequent types of expenditures are included in the Distribution of Payments section. The petty cash payments record is not a journal.

Bell Video made the following payments from its Petty Cash Fund during September:

Sept. 2 Paid $2 to Mark Delivery Service, voucher no. 1.
3 Bought pencils and pens, $3.09, voucher no. 2.
5 Paid local newspaper for advertising, $5, voucher no. 3.
7 Paid postage on incoming packages, $2.90, voucher no. 4.
10 Marsha C. Bell, the owner, withdrew $5 for personal use, voucher no. 5.
14 Reimbursed employee for stamps, $1.65, voucher no. 6.
21 Bought stick-on tabs, $4.10, voucher no. 7.
22 Paid $3 to Mark Delivery Service, voucher no. 8.
26 Paid for mailing packages, $3.80, voucher no. 9.
27 Paid $3.50 to Fast Way Delivery, voucher no. 10.
29 Bought memo pads, $4.40, voucher no. 11.
29 Paid for making duplicate keys, $2.60, voucher no. 12.
30 Paid $3.20 to Mark Delivery Service, voucher no. 13.
30 Paid for trash removal, $5, voucher no. 14.

Figure 13 below shows how these payments are recorded.

PAGE 1

	DELIVERY EXPENSE	MISCELLANEOUS EXPENSE	OTHER ACCOUNTS	
			ACCOUNT	AMOUNT
1				
2	2 00			
3				
4			Advertising Expense	5 00
5	2 90			
6			M. C. Bell, Drawing	5 00
7		1 65		
8				
9	3 00			
10	3 80			
11	3 50			
12				
13		2 60		
14	3 20			
15		5 00		
16	1 8 40	9 25		1 0 00
17				
18				
19				
20				
21				

DISTRIBUTION OF PAYMENTS

A petty cash fund is an effective and efficient way to deal with small cash payments that need to be made immediately. These caterers, delivering food for an office party, can be paid on the spot, saving their own company the expense of billing and the recipient the expense of writing a check.

Reimbursement of the Petty Cash Fund

To bring the fund back up to the original amount when it is nearly exhausted (for instance, at the end of the month), the accountant reimburses the fund for expenditures made. Consequently, the Petty Cash Fund may be considered a revolving fund. If the amount initially put in the Petty Cash Fund is $70 and at the end of the month only $20.76 is left, the accountant puts $49.24 in the fund as a reimbursement, thereby bringing the fund back up to $70 to start the new month.

Bear in mind that the petty cash payments record is only a supplementary record for gathering information. A less formal way of compiling the information concerning petty cash payments might consist of collecting one month's petty cash vouchers, then sorting them by accounts, such as Office Supplies Expense, Delivery Expense, and the like. Then run a calculator tape for each account. At the end of the month, the accountant makes a summarizing entry to officially journalize the transactions that have taken place. The journal and T accounts of Bell Video are shown below.

Note that, in the summarizing entry, the accountant debits the accounts on whose behalf the payments were made and credits the Cash account. She or he leaves the Petty Cash Fund account alone. Then the assistant cashes a check for $49.24 and puts the cash in a locked place, thereby restoring the amount in the Petty Cash Fund to the original $70.

REMEMBER!
The petty cash payments record or calculator tapes are not journals; they are simply used as a basis for compiling information for the journal entry. Remember, to change an account, we have to make a journal entry.

GENERAL JOURNAL   PAGE _____

	DATE		DESCRIPTION	POST. REF.	DEBIT	CREDIT	
1	20—						1
2	Sept.	30	Office Supplies Expense		1 1 59		2
3			Delivery Expense		1 8 40		3
4			Miscellaneous Expense		9 25		4
5			Advertising Expense		5 00		5
6			M. C. Bell, Drawing		5 00		6
7			Cash			4 9 24	7
8			Reimbursed the Petty Cash				8
9			Fund, Ck. No. 136.				9
10							10

Cash		**M. C. Bell, Drawing**		**Miscellaneous Expense**	
+	−	+	−	+	−
	49.24	5.00		9.25	

Office Supplies		**Delivery Expense**		**Advertising Expense**	
+	−	+	−	+	−
11.59		18.40		5.00	

THE CHANGE FUND

Anyone who has ever tried to pay for a small item with a $20 bill knows that any firm that carries out numerous cash transactions needs a **Change Fund**.

Establishing the Change Fund

OBJECTIVE 6
Record the journal entries to establish a Change Fund.

Before setting up a Change Fund, you have to decide two things: (1) how much money needs to be in the fund, and (2) what denominations of bills and coins are needed. Like the Petty Cash Fund, **the Change Fund is debited only once: when it is established.** It is left at the initial figure unless the person in charge decides to make it larger. The Change Fund account, like the Petty Cash Fund account, is an asset. It is recorded in the balance sheet immediately below Cash. If the Petty Cash Fund account is larger than the Change Fund account, it precedes the Change Fund.

The owner of Bell Video, Marsha C. Bell, decides to establish a change fund; she decides this at the same time she sets up the company's petty cash fund. The entries for the two transactions look like this:

GENERAL JOURNAL   PAGE _____

DATE		DESCRIPTION	POST. REF.	DEBIT	CREDIT
20—					
Sept.	1	Petty Cash Fund		7 0 00	
		Cash			7 0 00
		Established a petty cash fund.			
	1	Change Fund		1 2 0 00	
		Cash			1 2 0 00
		Established a change fund.			

The T accounts for establishing the fund are as follows:

Change Fund		Cash	
+	−	+	−
120			120

Bell cashes a check for $120 and gets the money in several denominations. She is now prepared to make change for any normal business transactions.

Depositing Cash

At the end of each business day, Bell deposits the cash taken in during the day, but she holds back the amount of the Change Fund, being sure that it is in convenient denominations. Let's say that on September 1, Bell Video had $425 on hand at the end of the day.

```
$425   Total cash count
−  120   Change fund
─────
$305   New cash deposit  ────────────────────────────
```

The T accounts look like this:

Cash	Video Rental Income
+ −	− +
305	305

The day's receipts are journalized as follows:

GENERAL JOURNAL   PAGE _____

	DATE		DESCRIPTION	POST. REF.	DEBIT	CREDIT	
1	20—						1
2	Sept.	1	Cash		3 0 5 00		2
3			Video Rental Income			3 0 5 00	3
4			To record revenue earned				4
5			during the day.				5
6							6

The amount of the cash deposit is the total cash count less the amount of the Change Fund. This should be equal to the income earned.

On September 9, the cash count is $537. So Bell deposits $417 ($537 − $120). Bell's accountant makes the following entry to record the day's receipts:

GENERAL JOURNAL   PAGE _____

	DATE		DESCRIPTION	POST. REF.	DEBIT	CREDIT	
1	20—						1
2	Sept.	9	Cash		4 1 7 00		2
3			Video Rental Income			4 1 7 00	3
4			To record revenue earned				4
5			during the day.				5
6							6

Some businesses label the Cash account *Cash in Bank* and label the Change Fund *Cash on Hand*.

CASH SHORT AND OVER

There is an inherent danger in making change: Human beings make mistakes, especially when there are many customers to be waited on or when the business is temporarily short-handed. Because mistakes do happen, accounting records must be set up to cope with the situation. One reason that a business uses a cash register is to detect mistakes in handling cash. **If, after removing the Change Fund, the day's receipts are less than the register reading, then a cash shortage exists. Conversely, when the day's receipts are greater than the register reading, a cash overage exists.** Both shortages and overages are recorded in the same account, which is called Cash Short and Over. Shortages are considered an expense of operating a business, and therefore shortages are recorded on the debit side of the account. Overages are treated as another form of revenue, and therefore overages are recorded on the credit side of the account.

Let's say that on September 14, Bell Video is faced with the following situation:

Cash Register Tape	Cash Count	Amount of the Change Fund
$490	$607	$120

After deducting the $120 in the Change Fund, Bell will deposit $487 ($607 − $120). Note that this amount is $3 less than the amount indicated by the cash register ($490 − $487); therefore, a $3 cash shortage exists. The following T accounts show how Bell entered this transaction into the books:

Cash		Video Rental Income		Cash Short and Over
+	−	−	+	
487			490	3

The next day, September 15, the pendulum happens to swing in the other direction:

Cash Register Tape	Cash Count	Amount of the Change Fund
$559	$680	$120

The amount to be deposited is $560 ($680 − $120). This figure is $1 greater than the $559 in video rental income indicated by the cash register tape. Thus, there is a $1 cash overage ($560 − $559). The analysis of this transaction is shown in the following T accounts:

Cash		Video Rental Income		Cash Short and Over
+	−	−	+	
560			559	1

Bell Video's revenue for September 14 and 15 is recorded in the general journal as follows:

			GENERAL JOURNAL				PAGE _____	
	DATE		DESCRIPTION	POST. REF.	DEBIT	CREDIT		
1	20—							1
2	Sept.	14	Cash		4 8 7 00			2
3			Cash Short and Over		3 00			3
4			Video Rental Income			4 9 0 00		4
5			To record revenue earned					5
6			for the day involving a					6
7			cash shortage of $3.					7
8								8
9		15	Cash		5 6 0 00			9
10			Video Rental Income			5 5 9 00		10
11			Cash Short and Over			1 00		11
12			To record revenue earned					12
13			during the day involving a					13
14			cash overage of $1.					14

A scanner can speed customer checkout, or taking inventory of goods still on the shelves. The scanner, however, is only as accurate as the amount for each item entered in the computer.

As far as errors are concerned, one would think that shortages would be offset by overages. However, customers receiving change are more likely to report shortages than overages. **Consequently, the firm usually experiences a greater number of shortages.** A firm may set a tolerance level for the cashiers. If the shortages consistently exceed the level of tolerance, either fraud is being committed or somebody is making entirely too many careless mistakes.

Now let's summarize our discussion of the Cash Short and Over account by drawing the following conclusions from the illustration:

1. At the close of the business day, the firm deposits the difference between the amount in the cash drawer and the amount in the Change Fund.
2. The firm records the amount shown on the cash register tape as its video rental income.
3. If the amount of the cash deposit disagrees with the record of receipts, Cash Short and Over makes up the difference. In the first situation just described, there was a shortage of $3, and so there was a debit to Cash Short and Over. In the second situation, there was an overage of $1, and so there was a credit to Cash Short and Over. It is apparent that, as a result of these transactions, the account looks like this:

Cash Short and Over

Shortage	3	1	Overage

Throughout any fiscal period, the accountant must continually record shortages and overages in the Cash Short and Over account. Let's say that

Bell's final balance is $21 on the debit side. Bell winds up with a net shortage of $21.

At the end of the fiscal period, **if the account has a debit balance or net shortage, the accountant classifies it as an expense and credits Cash Short and Over and debits Miscellaneous Expense, so that the amount is put in the income statement under Miscellaneous Expense.** The T account would look like this:

Cash Short and Over

Short	3	1		Over
	4	1		
	3	2		
	7	2		
	5	1		
	2	2		
	3	1		
	4	10		
	31			
Bal.	21			

Conversely, **if the account has a credit balance or net overage, the accountant classifies it as a revenue account and debits Cash Short and Over and credits Miscellaneous Income, so that the amount is put in the income statement under Miscellaneous Income.** This is an exception to the policy of recording accounts under their exact account title in financial statements. Rather than attaching plus and minus signs to the Cash Short and Over account immediately, we wait until we find out its final balance, then make a journal entry to send the balance to the correct account classification.

CHAPTER REVIEW

Check out ACE for a Review Quiz at

http://college.hmco.com/ accounting/students/.

ACE self-test

Review of Performance Objectives

1. Describe the procedure for depositing checks.

   The procedure for depositing checks consists of first endorsing each check and then completing a deposit slip. On the deposit slip, record the date, the amount of currency to be deposited, the amount and ABA number of each check, and the total amount to be deposited. The checks to be deposited should accompany the deposit slip.

2. Reconcile a bank statement.

   The standard form for a bank reconciliation is as follows:

   Bank Statement Balance

   Add

   Deposits in transit
   Bank errors that understate bank statement balance

   Deduct

   Outstanding checks
   Bank errors that overstate bank statement balance

Adjusted Bank Statement Balance

Ledger Balance of Cash

Add

Notes collected
Interest income earned
Checkbook errors that understate the ledger balance of cash
Bank credit memos

Deduct

Bank service charges
Checkbook errors that overstate the ledger balance of cash
NSF checks
Bank debit memos

Adjusted Ledger Balance of Cash

3. Record the required journal entries directly from the bank reconciliation.

   Journal entries for the Ledger Balance of Cash section are required. The entry for notes and interest collected is a debit to Cash and credits to Notes Receivable and Interest Income. The entry for a bank service charge is a debit to Miscellaneous Expense and a credit to Cash. The entry for an NSF check is a debit to Accounts Receivable and a credit to Cash.

4. Record journal entries to establish and reimburse a Petty Cash Fund.

   The entry to establish a Petty Cash Fund is a debit to Petty Cash Fund and a credit to Cash. The entry to reimburse the Petty Cash Fund consists of debits to the items for which payments from the Petty Cash Fund were made and one credit to Cash for the total payments.

5. Complete petty cash vouchers and petty cash payments records.

   A petty cash voucher is made out for each payment from the Petty Cash Fund. In the petty cash payments record, each voucher is listed and a notation is made concerning the accounts involved; also, an explanation of why the money was paid out is recorded. The petty cash payments record is used as a source of information for making the journal entry to reimburse the Petty Cash Fund.

6. Record the journal entries to establish a Change Fund.

   The entry to establish the Change Fund is a debit to Change Fund and a credit to Cash.

7. Record journal entries for transactions involving Cash Short and Over.

   The Cash Short and Over account provides a way to keep a record of errors in making change. A debit balance in Cash Short and Over denotes a shortage, which is listed as Miscellaneous Expense; the entry is a debit to Miscellaneous Expense and a credit to Cash Short and Over. A credit balance in Cash Short and Over denotes an overage, which becomes Miscellaneous Income; the entry is a debit to Cash Short and Over and a credit to Miscellaneous Income.

Glossary

ABA number The number assigned by the American Bankers Association to a given bank. The first part of the numerator denotes the city or state in which the bank is located; the second part denotes the bank on which the check is drawn. The denominator indicates the Federal Reserve District in which the check is cleared and the routing number used by the Federal Reserve Bank. (218)

ATM (automated teller machine) A machine that enables depositors to make deposits, withdrawals, and transfers using a coded plastic card. (218)

Bank reconciliation A process by which an accountant determines whether and why there is a difference between the balance shown on the bank statement and the balance of the Cash account in the firm's general ledger. The object is to determine the adjusted (or true) balance of the Cash account. (224)

Bank statement A periodic statement that a bank sends to the drawer/depositor of a checking account listing deposits received and checks paid by the bank, debit and credit memos, and beginning and ending balances. (221)

Blank endorsement An endorsement in which the holder (payee) of a check simply signs her or his name on the back of the check. There are no restrictions attached. (219)

Canceled checks Checks issued by the depositor that have been paid (cleared) by the bank and listed on the bank statement. They are called canceled checks because they are canceled by a stamp or perforation, indicating that they have been paid. (223)

Cash funds Separately held reserves of cash set aside for specific purposes. (217)

Change Fund A cash fund used by a firm to make change for customers who pay cash for goods or services. (237)

Check writer A machine that imprints the amount of a check in figures and words on the check itself. (220)

Collections Payments collected by the bank and added to the customer's bank account in the form of a credit memorandum. (225)

Denominations Varieties of coins and currency, such as quarters, dimes, and nickels and $1 and $5 bills and so on. (233)

Deposit in transit A deposit not recorded on the bank statement because the deposit was made between the time of the bank's closing date for compiling items for its statement and the time the statement is received by the depositor; also known as a *late deposit.* (224)

Deposit slips Printed forms provided by a bank on which customers can list all items being deposited; also known as *deposit tickets.* (218)

Drawer The party who writes the check. (220)

Endorsement The process by which the payee transfers ownership of the check to a bank or another party. A check must be endorsed when deposited in a bank, because the bank must have legal title to it in order to collect payment from the drawer of the check (the person or firm who wrote the check). In case the check cannot be collected, the endorser guarantees all subsequent holders (*exception:* an endorsement "without recourse"). (219)

Interest income The amount earned from lending money to another person or business. (225)

Ledger balance of cash The balance of the Cash account in the general ledger before it is reconciled with the bank statement. (223)

MICR Magnetic ink character recognition; the characters the bank uses to print the number of the depositor's account and the bank's number at the bottom of checks and deposit slips. The bank also prints the amount of the check in MICR when the check is deposited. A number written in these characters can be read by electronic equipment used by banks in clearing checks. (218)

NSF (not sufficient funds) checks Checks drawn against an account in which there are *not sufficient funds* and returned by the payee's bank to the drawer's bank because of nonpayment; also known as *dishonored checks.* (225)

Outstanding checks Checks that have been written by the drawer and deducted on his or her records but have not reached the bank for payment and are not deducted from the bank balance by the time the bank issues its statement. (224)

Payee The person to whom a check is payable. (220)

Petty Cash Fund A cash fund used to make small immediate cash payments. (232)

Petty cash payments record A record indicating the amount of each petty cash voucher, the accounts to which it should be charged, and the purpose of the expenditure. (234)

Petty cash voucher A form stating who requested cash from the Petty Cash Fund, signed by (1) the person in charge of the fund and (2) the person who received the cash, and indicating the purpose of the petty cash payment. (233)

Promissory note A written promise to pay a definite sum at a definite future time. (227)

Qualified endorsement An endorsement in which the holder (payee) of a check avoids future liability, in case the drawer of the check does not have sufficient funds to cover the check, by adding the words "Pay to the order of" and "without recourse" to the endorsement on the back of the check. (220)

Restrictive endorsement An endorsement, such as "Pay to the order of (name of bank), for deposit only," that restricts or limits any further negotiation of a check. It forces the check's deposit, because the endorsement is not valid for any other purpose. (219)

Service charge The fee the bank charges for handling checks, collections, and other items. It is in the form of a debit memorandum. (225)

Signature card The form a depositor signs to give the bank a copy of the official signatures of any persons authorized to sign checks. The bank can use it to verify the depositors' signatures on checks. (217)

QUESTIONS, EXERCISES, AND PROBLEMS

Discussion Questions

1. Why does a bank keep a signature card on file for your account(s)?

2. What is the purpose served by endorsing a check?

3. Why is there generally a difference between the balance in the Cash account on the company's books and the balance on the bank statement?

4. On the bank statement reconciliation, what is the similarity between outstanding checks and NSF checks?

5. Indicate whether the following items in a bank reconciliation should be (1) added to the Cash account balance, (2) deducted from the Cash account balance, (3) added to the bank statement balance, or (4) deducted from the bank statement balance.
   a. NSF check
   b. Deposit in transit
   c. Outstanding check
   d. Bank error charging the firm's account with another company's check
   e. Bank service charge

6. Why is it necessary to make general journal entries for the ledger balance side of the bank reconciliation?

7. a. Explain the purpose served by a Petty Cash Fund.
   b. Write the entries to establish and reimburse the fund.

8. a. What does a debit balance in Cash Short and Over represent?
   b. Where does a debit balance in Cash Short and Over appear in the financial statements?
   c. What does a credit balance in Cash Short and Over represent?
   d. Where does a credit balance in Cash Short and Over appear in the financial statements?

Exercises

P.O. 2

Determine missing amounts on a bank reconciliation.

Exercise 7-1 Fill in the missing amounts for the following bank reconciliation:

Bank Reconciliation
March 31, 20—

Bank Statement Balance		$3,754.00
Add: Deposit in transit		(a)
		$4,021.00
Deduct: Outstanding checks		
No. 210	$210.00	
No. 224	(b)	
No. 227	320.00	851.00
Adjusted Bank Statement Balance		(c)
Ledger Balance of Cash		$2,840.00
Add: Note collected by bank		427.00
		(d)
Deduct: Bank service and collection charge	(e)	
NSF check from customer	85.00	97.00
Adjusted Ledger Balance of Cash		(f)

P.O. 3

Journalize entries from a bank reconciliation.

Exercise 7-2 The Ledger Balance of Cash section of the bank reconciliation for Jeon Company for July 31 is shown on the following page.

Ledger Balance of Cash		$6,357.00
Add: Note collected (principal, $700.00, interest		
$41, signed by L. Hyde)	$741.00	
Error in recording Ck. No. 2225 payable to		
Fenton Company (recorded check for		
$18 too much)	18.00	759.00
		$7,116.00
Deduct: NSF check from J. Kelton	$ 85.00	
Bank service and collection charges	21.00	106.00
Adjust ledger balance of cash		$7,010.00

Journalize the entries required to bring the general ledger up to date as of July 31 of this year.

P.O. 2

Determine amount of outstanding checks.

Exercise 7-3 When the bank statement is received on December 3, it shows a balance of $3,000 as of November 30, before reconciliation. After reconciliation, the adjusted balance is $2,500. If there was one deposit in transit amounting to $500, what was the total of the outstanding checks, assuming that there were no other adjustments to be made to the bank statement?

P.O. 2

Place items on a bank reconciliation.

Exercise 7-4 Write a check mark in the column that indicates the location of each item that would be found on a bank reconciliation. The checks are written correctly.

Item	Add to Bank Statement Balance	Subtract from Bank Statement Balance	Add to Ledger Balance of Cash	Subtract from Ledger Balance of Cash
a. A check-printing charge				
b. An outstanding check				
c. A deposit for $187 listed incorrectly on the bank statement as $178				
d. A collection charge the bank made for a note it collected for its depositor				
e. A check written for $40.73 and recorded incorrectly in the checkbook as $40.37				
f. A deposit in transit				
g. An NSF check received from a customer				
h. A check written for $72.39 and recorded incorrectly in the checkbook as $720.39				

P.O. 2

Determine the adjusted ledger balance of cash.

Exercise 7-5 The Mysung Company's Cash account shows a balance of $752.00 as of August 31 of this year. The balance on the bank statement on that date is $1,250.50. Checks for $263.70, $437.05, and $327.00 are out-standing. The bank statement shows a check issued by another depositor for $237.25 (in other words, the bank made an error and charged Mysung Company for a check written by another company). The bank statement also shows an NSF check for $280.00 received from one of Mysung's customers. Service charges for the month were $12.00. What is the adjusted ledger balance of cash as of August 31?

P.O. 4

Journalize entries pertaining to a Petty Cash Fund.

Exercise 7-6 Make entries in general journal form to record the following:

a. Established a Petty Cash Fund, $150. Issued Ck. No. 857.
b. Reimbursed the Petty Cash Fund for expenditures of $102: Store Supplies Expense, $28; Office Supplies Expense, $36; Miscellaneous Expense, $38. Issued Ck. No. 889.
c. Increased the amount of the fund by an additional $25. Issued Ck. No. 891.
d. Reimbursed the Petty Cash Fund for expenditures of $91.84: Store Supplies Expense, $45.92; Delivery Expense, $36.00; Miscellaneous Expense, $9.92. Issued Ck. No. 936.

P.O. 7

Journalize entry for the receipt of cash.

Exercise 7-7 At the end of the day, the cash register tape lists $827.27 as total income from services. Cash on hand consists of $15.27 in coins, $694.00 in currency, $80 in traveler's checks, and $236.00 in customers' checks. The amount of the Change Fund is $200. In general journal form, record the entry to record the day's cash revenue.

P.O. 6,7

Describe entries related to the Change Fund and Cash Short and Over.

Exercise 7-8

a. Describe the entries that have been posted to the following accounts after the Change Fund was established.

Change Fund		Sales		Cash	
200			1,521 Jan. 3	Jan. 3 1,523	
			1,420 4	4 1,419	
			1,663 6	6 1,660	

Cash Short and Over	
Jan. 4 1	2 Jan. 3
6 3	

b. How will the balance of Cash Short and Over be reported on the income statement?

REFLECTING ON
THE WORLD WIDE WEB

You have just learned about checking accounts, reconciling bank statements, and managing petty cash funds. Using an online banking service can provide many advantages to managing your cash.

1. What advantages are there to having access to your bank statement online?
2. What are the disadvantages, if any?

CONSIDER AND COMMUNICATE

As the new bookkeeper at a small business, you find the petty cash fund operation to be unorganized and ineffective. The amount of cash does not match the recorded amount of the fund, and there is no evidence how it was spent. Explain how the petty cash fund operation can be made more efficient in order to maintain an accurate accounting of its changes.

CRITICAL THINKING

John Page, a college student, plans to provide typing services to graduate students at the university near his home. He must determine how much money to deposit initially in his business account to cover the start-up of the new business. The deposit must cover the start-up costs and leave him with a balance of $5,000 in his business account. He plans to buy a computer/printer and a copier for $4,500 cash. The fax machine and the telephone system he needs are available for $2,500, and he will put down $300. He will buy paper for the copier for $275 on account. How much should John's investment be on June 1 if he is to meet his goal of having $5,000 in his business account after his anticipated transactions?

1. Use the practice grid to complete each transaction. Balance the fundamental accounting equation after each transaction.

	Quality Typing Service				
	Cash	+ Equipment =	Accounts Payable	+ J. Page, Capital	− Supplies Expense
(a) Make unknown beginning investment.					
Balance					
(b) Buy equipment for cash, $4,500.					
Balance					
(c) Buy equipment, $2,500, paying $300 down.					
Balance					
(d) Buy supplies on account, $275.					
Balance					

2. Prepare a balance sheet for John's business as of June 10, 20—.

WHAT'S WRONG WITH THIS PICTURE? ▬▬▬▬▬▬▬▬▬▬▬▬▬▬▬▬ ▪▪▪

You work as a cashier in a service business. Some days you are short of cash at the end of the day, and some days you have more cash than the cash register tape says was earned. You are embarrassed when your cash is short and don't want the owner to know, so you take money from your wallet and make up the difference. On days when you are over, you keep the difference to help pay back what you paid to cover your shortages. Comment on this practice.

■ PROBLEM SET A

P.O. 2,3

Problem 7-1A Mario's Men's Shop deposits all receipts in the bank each evening and makes all payments by check. On November 30 its Cash in Bank account has a balance of $1,967.65. The bank statement of November 30 shows a balance of $2,122.25. Use the following information to reconcile the bank statement:

a. The reconciliation for October, the previous month, showed three checks outstanding on October 31: no. 1416 for $85, no. 1419 for $76.50, and no. 1420 for $126. Checks no. 1416 and 1420 were returned with the November bank statement; however, check no. 1419 was not returned.

b. Checks no. 1499 for $39, no. 1516 for $21.60, no. 1517 for $101.50, and no. 1518 for $17 were written during November and have not been returned by the bank.

c. A deposit of $410 was placed in the night depository on November 30 and did not appear on the bank statement.

d. The canceled checks were compared with the entries in the checkbook, and it was observed that check no. 1487, for $78, was written correctly, payable to M. A. Gallo, the owner, for personal use, but was recorded in the checkbook as $87.

e. A bank debit memo for service charges, $3.

f. A bank credit memo for collection of a note signed by T. R. Schultz, $303, including $300 principal and $3 interest.

Check Figure

Adjusted ledger balance of cash, $2,276.65

Instructions

1. Prepare a bank reconciliation as of November 30, assuming that the debit and credit memos have not been recorded.
2. Record the necessary entries in general journal form.

P.O. 4,5

Problem 7-2A On May 1 of this year, Berger and Company established a Petty Cash Fund. The following petty cash transactions took place during the month:

May 1 Cashed check no. 956 for $70 to establish a Petty Cash Fund, and put the $70 in a locked drawer in the office.
3 Bought postage stamps, $6, voucher no. 1 (Miscellaneous Expense).
4 Issued voucher no. 2 for taxi fare, $4 (Miscellaneous Expense).
6 Issued voucher no. 3 for delivery charges on outgoing parts, $8.
9 N. Berger withdrew $9.50 for personal use, voucher no. 4.
13 Paid $7 for postage, voucher no. 5 (Miscellaneous Expense).
19 Bought pens for office, $7.74, voucher no. 6.

May   23   Paid $2 for a box of staples, voucher no. 7.
    28   Paid $9 for window cleaning service, voucher no. 8 (Miscellaneous Expense).
    29   Paid $1.82 for pencils for office, voucher no. 9.
    31   Issued for cash check no. 1098 for $55.06 to reimburse Petty Cash Fund.

Check Figure

Office Supplies Expense, $11.56

Instructions

1. Journalize the entry establishing the Petty Cash Fund in the general journal.
2. Record the disbursements of petty cash in the petty cash payments record.
3. Journalize the summarizing entry to reimburse the Petty Cash Fund.

P.O. 7

Problem 7-3A Errol Horn, owner of Horn's Dry Cleaners, makes bank deposits in the night depository at the close of each business day. The following information for the last three days of July is available.

	July		
	29	**30**	**31**
Cash register tape	$867.20	$724.50	$ 921.60
Cash count	965.50	823.60	1,023.40

Check Figure

Cash Short and Over, July 31, $1.80 over

Instructions

In general journal form, record the cash deposit for each day, assuming that there is a $100 Change Fund.

P.O. 2,3

Problem 7-4A On August 31, Bronski and Company receives its bank statement (on the following page). The company deposits its receipts in the bank and makes all payments by check. The debit memo for $49 is for an NSF check written by N. Collins. Check no. 924 for $37, payable to Johnson Company (a creditor), was recorded in the checkbook and journal as $73.

The balance of the Cash account as of August 31 is $1,237. Outstanding checks as of August 31 are: no. 928, $119; no. 929, $243. The accountant notes that the deposit of August 31 for $261 did not appear on the bank statement.

Check Figure

Adjusted ledger balance of cash, $1,222

Instructions

1. Prepare a bank reconciliation as of August 31, assuming that the debit memos have not been recorded.
2. Record the necessary journal entries.
3. Complete the bank form to determine the adjusted balance of cash.

Instructions for General Ledger Software

1. Prepare a bank reconciliation as of August 31. Errors made by the company or the bank, as well as service charges, must be entered as debit or credit memos.
2. Print the bank reconciliation.
3. Record the necessary journal entries.
4. Print the journal entries.

PEABODY NATIONAL BANK

Bronski and Company
416 Seneca Avenue
Kansas City, Missouri 64102

ACCOUNT NO.
152-6 55-217

STATEMENT DATE
August 1–31, 20—

SUMMARY		
	Balance Last Statement	$ 961.00
	Amount of Checks and Debits	$2,289.00
	Number of Checks	11
	Amount of Deposits and Credits	$2,651.00
	Number of Deposits	7
	Balance This Statement	$1,323.00

CHECKS/OTHER DEBITS

CHECKS	CHECK NUMBER	DATE POSTED	AMOUNT	CHECK NUMBER	DATE POSTED	AMOUNT
	917	8-04	172.00	923	8-09	621.00
	918	8-04	76.00	924	8-17	37.00
	919	8-05	146.00	925	8-17	14.00
	920	8-07	206.00	926	8-23	533.00
	921	8-07	139.00	927	8-28	94.00
	922	8-08	200.00			

OTHER DEBITS	DESCRIPTION	DATE POSTED	AMOUNT
	DM NSF check	8-31	49.00
	DM Service charge	8-31	2.00

DEPOSITS/OTHER CREDITS

DEPOSITS	DATE POSTED	AMOUNT	DATE POSTED	AMOUNT
	8-02	326.00	8-18	419.00
	8-05	412.00	8-24	398.00
	8-09	437.00	8-28	291.00
	8-14	368.00		

PLEASE EXAMINE THIS STATEMENT CAREFULLY. REPORT ANY POSSIBLE ERRORS IN 10 DAYS.

CODE SYMBOLS

CM Credit Memo   DM Debit Memo   OD Overdraft   EC Error Correction

PROBLEM SET B

P.O. 2,3

Problem 7-1B The Mallon Company deposits all receipts in the bank and makes all payments by check. On November 30 its Cash account has a balance of $2,829.42. The bank statement on November 30 shows a balance of $2,999.42. You are given the following information with which to reconcile the bank statement:

a. A deposit of $319.23 was placed in the night depository on November 30 and did not appear on the bank statement.

b. The reconciliation for October, the previous month, showed three checks outstanding on October 31: no. 727 for $81.30, no. 730 for $127.40, and no. 732 for $38.46. Checks no. 727 and 730 were returned with the November bank statement; however, check no. 732 was not returned.

c. Checks no. 742 for $31, no. 743 for $19.20, no. 744 for $106, and no. 745 for $14.56 were written during November but were not returned by the bank.

d. You compare the canceled checks with the entries in the checkbook and find that check no. 737 for $48 was written correctly, payable to C. R. Mallon, the owner, for her personal use. However, the check was recorded in the checkbook as $84.

e. Included in the bank statement was a bank debit memo for service charges, $2.99.

f. A bank credit memo was also enclosed for the collection of a note signed by L. B. Leman, $247, including $244 principal and $3 interest.

P.O. 4,5

Instructions

1. Prepare a bank reconciliation as of November 30, assuming that the debit and credit memos have not been recorded.
2. Record the necessary entries in general journal form.

Problem 7-2B On March 1 of this year, the Stenn Company established a Petty Cash Fund, and the following petty cash transactions took place during the month:

Mar. 1 Cashed check no. 314 for $60 to establish a Petty Cash Fund, and put the $60 in a locked drawer in the office.

4 Issued voucher no. 1 for taxi fare, $4 (Miscellaneous Expense).

7 Issued voucher no. 2 for memo pads, $6.20 (Office Supplies Expense).

9 Paid $7.50 for an advertisement in a college basketball program, voucher no. 3.

16 Bought postage stamps, $6, voucher no. 4 (Miscellaneous Expense).

20 Paid $8.50 to have snow removed from office front sidewalk, voucher no. 5 (Miscellaneous Expense).

25 Issued voucher no. 6 for delivery charge, $4.45.

28 R. C. Stenn, the owner, withdrew $9 for personal use, voucher no. 7.

29 Paid $1.72 for postage, voucher no. 8 (Miscellaneous Expense).

30 Paid $5.40 for delivery charge, voucher no. 9.

31 Issued for cash check no. 372 for $52.77 to reimburse Petty Cash Fund.

Instructions

1. Journalize the entry establishing the Petty Cash Fund in the general journal.
2. Record the disbursements of petty cash in the petty cash payments record.
3. Journalize the summarizing entry to reimburse the Petty Cash Fund.

P.O. 7

Problem 7-3B Betty Rice, owner of Betty's Beauty Salon, makes bank deposits in the night depository at the close of each business day. The following information for the first three days of April is available.

	April		
	1	2	3
Cash register tape	$304.75	$480.25	$428.00
Cash count	373.50	551.25	496.00

Instructions

In general journal form, record the cash deposit for each day, assuming that there is a $70 Change Fund.

P.O. 2,3

Problem 7-4B On August 2, Northway Hotel receives its bank statement (on the following page). The company deposits its receipts in the bank and makes all payments by check. The debit memo for $37 is for an NSF check written by T. N. Rankin. Check no. 1617 for $72.50, payable to Melville Company (a creditor), was incorrectly recorded in the checkbook and journal as $27.50.

The balance of the Cash account as of July 31 is $1,482.46. Outstanding checks as of July 31 are: no. 1631, $110; no. 1632, $71.19; no. 1633, $163.20. The accountant notes that the July 31 deposit of $165.69 did not appear on the bank statement.

Check Figure

Adjusted ledger balance of cash, $1,397.36

Instructions

1. Prepare a bank reconciliation as of July 31, assuming that the debit memos have not been recorded.
2. Record the necessary journal entries.
3. Complete the bank form to determine the adjusted balance of cash.

STANTON NATIONAL BANK

Northway Hotel
410 W. Lang Street
Rockford, Illinois 61104

ACCOUNT NO.
761-145-792
STATEMENT DATE
July 1–31, 20—

SUMMARY		
Balance Last Statement	$1,153.80
Amount of Checks and Debits	$2,105.91
Number of Checks	14
Amount of Deposits and Credits	$2,528.17
Number of Deposits	7
Balance This Statement	$1,576.06

CHECKS/OTHER DEBITS

CHECKS	CHECK NUMBER	DATE POSTED	AMOUNT	CHECK NUMBER	DATE POSTED	AMOUNT
	1617	7-03	72.50	1624	7-08	120.00
	1618	7-03	167.00	1625	7-09	429.60
	1619	7-03	124.20	1626	7-12	37.40
	1620	7-05	137.20	1627	7-14	38.49
	1621	7-06	236.25	1628	7-22	182.71
	1622	7-06	159.89	1629	7-25	96.87
	1623	7-08	244.50	1630	7-26	19.20

OTHER DEBITS

	DESCRIPTION	DATE POSTED	AMOUNT
DM	NSF check	7-22	37.00
DM	Service charge	7-31	3.10

DEPOSITS/OTHER CREDITS

DEPOSITS	DATE POSTED	AMOUNT	DATE POSTED	AMOUNT
	7-03	491.50	7-15	291.76
	7-06	415.72	7-18	142.90
	7-09	439.16	7-28	368.93
	7-11	378.20		

PLEASE EXAMINE THIS STATEMENT CAREFULLY. REPORT ANY POSSIBLE ERRORS IN 10 DAYS.

CODE SYMBOLS

CM Credit Memo   DM Debit Memo   OD Overdraft   EC Error Correction

Instructions for General Ledger Software

1. Prepare a bank reconciliation as of July 31. Errors made by the company or the bank, as well as service charges, must be entered as debit or credit memos.
2. Print the bank reconciliation.
3. Record the necessary journal entries.
4. Print the journal entries.

B Bad Debts

Performance Objectives

After you have completed this appendix, you will be able to do the following:

1. Prepare the adjusting entry for bad debts using the allowance method, based on a percentage of credit sales.

2. Prepare the entry to write off an account as uncollectible when the allowance method is used.

3. Prepare the entry to write off an account as uncollectible when the specific charge-off method is used.

As you know, not all credit customers pay their bills. In this appendix, we turn our attention to the accounts receivable that will not be collected. There are two basic methods of providing for writing or charging off credit customers' accounts that are considered uncollectible. They are the allowance method and the specific charge-off method.

ALLOWANCE METHOD

The allowance method provides for bad debt losses in advance, by estimating them. Though there are a number of ways to estimate the amount of future losses from open accounts, we will base our estimate on a percentage of credit sales.

For example, based on its experience with bad debt losses, the Dorian Company estimates that 1 percent of its revenue from services on account for the year will be uncollectible. Obviously, Dorian does not know which credit customers will not pay their bills. If the company were certain that a particular customer would not pay his or her bill, then it wouldn't perform services without requiring cash in advance.

Adjusting Entry and Writing Off an Account

OBJECTIVE 1
Prepare the adjusting entry for bad debts using the allowance method, based on a percentage of credit sales.

Dorian's total income from services on account for last year was $500,000. One percent of $500,000 is $5,000. On its work sheet, Dorian makes an adjusting entry. We show this in T account form.

Bad Debts Expense		Allowance for Doubtful Accounts	
+	−	−	+
Dec. 31			Dec. 31
Adjusting 5,000		5,000	Adjusting

Allowance for Doubtful Accounts is treated as a deduction from Accounts Receivable. Consequently, Allowance for Doubtful Accounts is a contra account. The adjusting entry is similar to the entry for depreciation in that there is a debit to an expense account and a credit to a contra account. In T account form, the adjustment for depreciation looks like this:

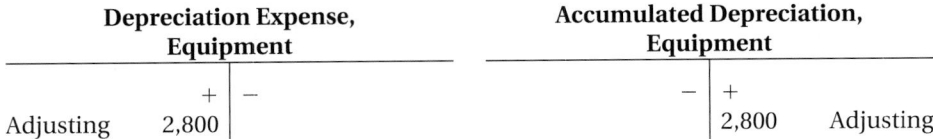

Depreciation Expense, Equipment			Accumulated Depreciation, Equipment		
	+	−		−	+
Adjusting	2,800				2,800 Adjusting

Assume that Dorian Company's balance of Accounts Receivable is $90,000 and its balance of Equipment is $75,000. Let's show the accounts and the adjusting entries in T account form.

Assets	=	Liabilities	+	Owner's Equity	+	Revenue	−	Expenses
+ −		− +		− +		− +		+ −

Accounts Receivable

+	−
Bal. 90,000	

Allowance for Doubtful Accounts

−	+
	Bal. 170
	Adj. 5,000
	Bal. 5,170

Equipment

+	−
Bal. 75,000	

Accumulated Depreciation, Equipment

−	+
	Bal. 7,000
	Adj. 2,800
	Bal. 9,800

Income from Services

−	+
	Bal. 500,000

Bad Debts Expense

+	−
Adj. 5,000	

Depreciation Expense, Equipment

+	−
Adj. 2,800	

The Depreciation Expense, Equipment, account comes into existence as an adjusting entry at the end of the year. It is closed immediately after being brought into existence. The same thing happens to Bad Debts Expense; it comes into existence as an adjusting entry, and then it is immediately closed during the closing process.

OBJECTIVE 2
Prepare the entry to write off an account as uncollectible when the allowance method is used.

As certain charge customers' accounts are determined to be uncollectible and are written off, the losses are taken out of Allowance for Doubtful Accounts. Think of the Allowance for Doubtful Accounts as a reservoir. By means of the adjusting entry, the account is filled up at the end of the year and then is gradually drained off (reduced) during the next year by write-offs of charge customer accounts. The $170 balance in Allowance for Doubtful Accounts at the end of the year indicates that less accounts receivable were actually written off as uncollectible during the year than previously estimated. As a result, Bad Debts Expense in the period was overstated and therefore net income understated.

Let's go on to the next year. On January 2, the Dorian Company finally gives up on its attempts to collect $720 from its credit customer A. N. Brady, which is included in Accounts Receivable. The Dorian Company now writes off the account in the amount of $720, shown below in T account form.

Accounts Receivable				Allowance for Doubtful Accounts			
	+	−			−	+	
Bal.	90,000			Jan. 2		5,170	Bal.
		720	Jan. 2 (write-off)	(write-off)	720		
Bal.	89,280					4,450	Bal.

As you can see, the write-off has reduced both the balance of Accounts Receivable and the balance of Allowance for Doubtful Accounts but has not changed the net realizable value of accounts receivable. The general journal entry is shown below.

PAGE _____

DATE		DESCRIPTION	POST. REF.	DEBIT	CREDIT
20—					
Jan.	2	Allowance for Doubtful Accounts		720 00	
		Accounts Receivable			720 00
		Wrote off the account of			
		A. N. Brady as uncollectible.			

An Advantage and a Disadvantage of the Allowance Method

The allowance method is consistent with the accrual basis of accounting in that it matches revenues of one year with expenses of the same year. The bad-debt loss potential is provided in the same year in which the revenue is earned. The conformity with the matching principle places the allowance method in compliance with generally accepted accounting principles as recognized by the FASB. However, the allowance method cannot be used for federal income tax purposes. This means that if a business uses the allowance method, the net income shown on the company's income statement will differ from the net income shown on its federal income tax return.

SPECIFIC CHARGE-OFF METHOD

Under the specific charge-off method, when a credit customer's account is determined to be uncollectible, the account is simply written off. The terms *write-off* and *charge-off* mean the same thing. No allowance account is used with the specific charge-off method because no estimate of uncollectible accounts receivable is calculated. As an illustration, Walton Company uses the specific charge-off method. On May 5, Walton Company writes off the account of L. C. Garber, $220. For the purpose of this example, we will use a separate Accounts Receivable account for L. C. Garber. T accounts pertaining to Garber's account look like this:

Accounts Receivable				Bad Debts Expense		
	+	−			+	−
Balance	220		May 5	May 5		
		220	(write-off)	(write-off)	220	

The general journal entry is shown below.

PAGE _____

	DATE		DESCRIPTION	POST. REF.	DEBIT	CREDIT	
1	20—						1
2	May	5	Bad Debts Expense		2 2 0 00		2
3			Accounts Receivable			2 2 0 00	3
4			Wrote off the account of				4
5			L. C. Garber as uncollectible.				5
6							6

Under this method, entries will be made directly into the Bad Debts Expense account during the year. No adjusting entry is needed, and Allowance for Doubtful Accounts is not used.

Advantage of the Specific Charge-off Method

The main advantage is that the method may be used for federal income tax purposes. It is not necessary to make an adjusting entry. Also, one less account (Allowance for Doubtful Accounts) is required.

Disadvantage of the Specific Charge-off Method

This method is not consistent with the accrual basis of accounting (recognizing revenue when it is earned and expenses when they are incurred). The method does not match up the revenue of one year with the expense of the same year. This lack of conformity with the matching principle places the specific charge-off method in violation of generally accepted accounting principles. For example, the sale of services on account to L. C. Garber could have been made four years ago. Since the account receivable will never be collected, the revenue for that year was too high (overstated). Consequently, net income is also overstated during that year. Now, four years later, $220 is written off as an expense. So net income for this year is too low (understated) because of the added expense.

PROBLEMS

P.O. 1,2
Check Figure
Adjusting entry amount, $3,620

Problem B-1 Ramos Company's total sales on account for the year amounted to $362,000. The company, which uses the allowance method, estimated bad debts at 1 percent of its charge sales. Journalize the following selected entries:

2005
Dec. 31 The adjusting entry.

2006
Mar. 2 Write-off of the account of B. L. Hulse as uncollectible, $264.

June 6 Write-off of the account of A. P. Tolland as uncollectible, $341.

P.O. 1,2
Check Figure
Adjusting entry amount,
$1,431.53

Problem B-2 Harron's Landscape Service's total revenue on account for 2003 amounted to $286,305. The company, which uses the allowance method, estimates bad debts at ½ percent of total revenue on account. Journalize the following selected entries:

2005
Dec. 12 Performed services on account for D. A. Wagner, $114.
31 The adjusting entry for Bad Debts Expense.
31 The closing entry for Bad Debts Expense.

2006
Feb. 18 Wrote off the account of D. A. Wagner as uncollectible, $114.

P.O. 3
Check Figure
Name of debit account, Bad
Debts Expense

Problem B-3 Jump City uses the specific charge-off method for recording bad debts. Journalize the following selected entries:

2005
Apr. 10 Write-off of the account of J. C. Sonja as uncollectible, $195.

July 27 Write-off of the account of B. R. West as uncollectible, $142.

8 Employee Earnings and Deductions

WINDOWS ON
THE WORLD WIDE WEB

When you graduate from college, where will you work? If you move to another state, will that affect the amount of taxes deducted from your paycheck? As you learn about recording payroll deductions, think about how these deductions affect you. You can learn more about payroll tax information for each state at Payroll-taxes.com **http://www.payroll-taxes. com/**. How does your state compare to one you might want to move to, as far as payroll deductions for income taxes are concerned? You can find out by using the paycheck calculator provided at this site. Also, visit the IRS web site at **www.irs.gov** to view the wage-bracket tax tables in Circular E as you cover the material under Objective 3.

Performance Objectives

After you have completed this chapter, you will be able to do the following:

1. Understand the role of laws that affect payroll deductions and contributions.

2. Calculate total earnings based on an hourly, piece-rate, or commission basis.

3. Determine deductions using tables of employees' income tax withholding.

4. Complete a payroll register.

5. Journalize the payroll entry from a payroll register.

6. Maintain employees' individual earnings records.

U p to now, we've been recording employees' earnings as a debit to Salary or Wages Expense and a credit to Cash, but we've really been talking only about **gross pay**: the total amount of an employee's pay before deductions. We haven't mentioned the various deductions that we all know are taken out of our gross pay before we get to the **net pay**, or take-home pay. In this chapter, we talk about types of deductions and how to enter them in the payroll records, and about journal entries to record the payroll and pay the employees.

OBJECTIVES OF PAYROLL RECORDS AND ACCOUNTING

There are two primary reasons to maintain accurate payroll records. First, we must collect the data necessary to compute the compensation for each employee for each payroll period.

Second, we must provide the information needed to complete the various government reports—federal and state—required of all employers. All business enterprises, both large and small, are required by law to withhold certain amounts from employees' pay for taxes, to make payments to government agencies by specific deadlines, and to submit reports on official forms. Because governments impose penalties if the requirements are not met, employers are vitally concerned with payroll accounting. Anyone going into accounting or involved with the management of any business should be thoroughly acquainted with payroll accounting.

The employer is required to keep records of the following information:

1. **Personal data on employee** Name, address, Social Security number, date of birth

2. **Data on wage payments** Dates and amounts of payments, and payroll periods

3. **Amount of taxable wages paid** Dates and amount earned year to date for the calendar year involved

4. **Amount of tax withheld from each employee's earnings by pay period**

EMPLOYER/EMPLOYEE RELATIONSHIPS

FYI

Examples of independent contractors include a self-employed appliance repair person, plumber, or CPA.

Payroll accounting is concerned with employees and their compensation, withholdings, records, reports, and taxes. There is a distinction between an employee and an independent contractor. An **employee** is one who is under the direction and control of the employer, such as a secretary, bookkeeper, salesclerk, vice president, controller, and so on. An **independent contractor** is engaged for a definite job or service and may choose her or his own means of doing the work. Payments made to independent contractors are in the form of fees or charges. Independent contractors submit bills or invoices for the work they do. The payment is not subject to any withholding or payroll taxes by the person or firm paying that invoice.

LAWS AFFECTING EMPLOYEES' PAY DEDUCTIONS

Both federal and state laws require the employer to act as a collecting agent and deduct specified amounts from employees' gross earnings. The employer sends the withholdings to the appropriate government agencies, along with reports substantiating the figures. Let's look at some of the more important laws that pertain to employees' pay.

Fair Labor Standards Act

OBJECTIVE 1
Understand the role of laws that affect payroll deductions and contributions.

The **Fair Labor Standards Act** of 1938 is referred to as "the Act" or "FLSA." The Act provides for minimum standards for both wages and overtime. Included in the Act are also provisions related to child labor and equal pay for equal work. In addition, the Act exempts specified employees or groups of employees from the application of certain of its provisions. Details of the Act may be read at **http://www.opm.gov.**

Federal Income Tax Withholding

The **Current Tax Payment Act** requires employers not only to withhold the tax and then pay it to the U.S. Treasury, but to keep records of the names and addresses of persons employed, their earnings and withholdings, and the amounts and dates of payment. The employer has to submit reports to the Internal Revenue Service on a quarterly basis (Form 941) and to the employee on an annual basis (W-2 form). With few exceptions, this requirement applies to employers of one or more persons. We will discuss these reports and the related deposits in Chapter 9.

FICA Tax (Employees' Share)

The **Social Security Act of 1935** began as an attempt to provide retired workers with benefits based upon their work history. Several amendments have added benefits for spouses and minor children of retired workers, disability insurance, lowering the age when benefits may be collected, Medicare, and supplemental security income.

Currently FICA consists of Social Security and Medicare. Employees contribute 6.2 percent (.062) on the first $84,900 earned in a calendar year for Social Security. Employees contribute 1.45 percent (.0145) on all earnings in a calendar year with no limit for Medicare.

LAWS AFFECTING EMPLOYER'S PAYROLL TAX CONTRIBUTIONS (PAYROLL TAX EXPENSE)

Certain payroll taxes, based on the total wages paid to employees, are levied on the employer. Let's look at some of the more important laws that pertain to the pay of employees.

FICA Tax (Employer's Share)

The employer has to match the amount of FICA tax withheld from the employees' wages, and the employer's share is recorded under Payroll Tax Expense. Every three months the employer has to submit reports to the U.S. Treasury, recording the information on Form 941, the same form that is used to report the income tax withheld. The employer's payment to the Internal Revenue Service consists of (1) the employee's share of the FICA tax, (2) the employer's matching portion of the FICA tax, and (3) the employee's income tax withheld. We will talk about this in detail in Chapter 9.

State Unemployment Taxes (SUTA)

Each state is responsible for paying its own unemployment compensation benefits. The revenue provided by **state unemployment taxes** is used exclusively for this purpose. However, there is considerable variation among the states concerning the tax rates and the amount of taxable income. **This tax is paid by employers only.** Most states, under a State Unemployment Tax Act, charge their employers a percentage (5.4 percent of the first $7,000 in this text) based on the taxable income stipulated in the Federal Unemployment Tax Act. States require employers to file reports on a quarterly, or three-month, basis. Included in these reports are a listing of employees' names, Social Security numbers, amounts of wages paid to each employee, and computations of unemployment taxes.

Federal Unemployment Tax Act (FUTA)

The purpose of the Federal Unemployment Tax Act is to provide financial support for the maintenance of government-run employment offices throughout the country. **FUTA taxes are paid by employers only.** Generally this includes all employers except nonprofit schools and institutions.

The federal unemployment tax is based on the total earnings of each employee during the calendar year. Congress has frequently changed the rates and the taxable income base.

For the examples and problems in this text, we will assume that employers pay an effective federal unemployment tax rate of 0.8 percent (.008) of the first $7,000 of earnings of each employee during the calendar year.

Reports to the federal government (Form 940) must be submitted annually. We will discuss these reports in Chapter 9.

Workers' Compensation Laws

Workers' compensation laws protect employees and their dependents against losses due to death or injury incurred on the job. Most states require employers either to contribute to a state compensation insurance fund or to buy similar insurance from a private insurance company. The employer ordinarily pays the cost of the insurance premiums. The premium rates vary according to the degree of danger inherent in each job category and the employer's number of accidents. The employer has to keep records of job descriptions and classifications as well as claims of insured persons.

HOW EMPLOYEES GET PAID

Employees may be paid salaries or wages, depending on the type of work and the period of time covered. Money paid to a person for managerial or administrative services is usually called a salary, and the time period covered is generally a month or a year. Money paid for either skilled or unskilled labor is usually called wages, and the time period covered is hours or weeks. Wages may also be paid on a piecework basis. A company may supplement an employee's salary or wage by commissions, bonuses, cost-of-living adjustments, and profit-sharing plans. As a rule, employees are paid by check, in cash, or by a direct deposit to their bank account. However, their compensation may take the form of merchandise, lodging, meals, or other property as well. When the compensation is in these forms, you have to determine the fair value of the property or service given in payment for an employee's labor.

Calculating Total Earnings

OBJECTIVE 2
Calculate total earnings based on an hourly, piece-rate, or commission basis.

When compensation is based on the amount of time worked, the accountant has to have a record of the number of hours worked by each employee. When there are only a few employees, this can be accomplished by means of a time book. When there are many employees, time clocks or other electronic time-keeping systems are used.

Employees may be paid weekly, biweekly, semimonthly, or monthly. Biweekly is every two weeks. Semimonthly is twice a month.

Wages

Consider Matte E. Asino, who works for Greg Company. His regular rate of pay is $22.84 per hour. The company pays time-and-a-half for hours worked in excess of 40 per week. In addition, it pays him double time for any work he does on Sundays and holidays. Asino has a ½-hour lunch break during an 8½-hour day. He is not paid for the lunch break nor is he paid for minutes before 8 AM or after 4:30 PM unless hours of overtime were authorized in advance. His time card for the week is shown in Figure 1.

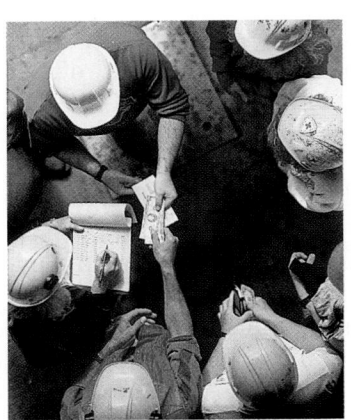

Although wages are more often paid by check or direct deposit, some industries or companies still pay employees in cash. From an internal control point of view, however, it is better to have a permanent record, which a check or direct deposit slip provides.

FIGURE 1

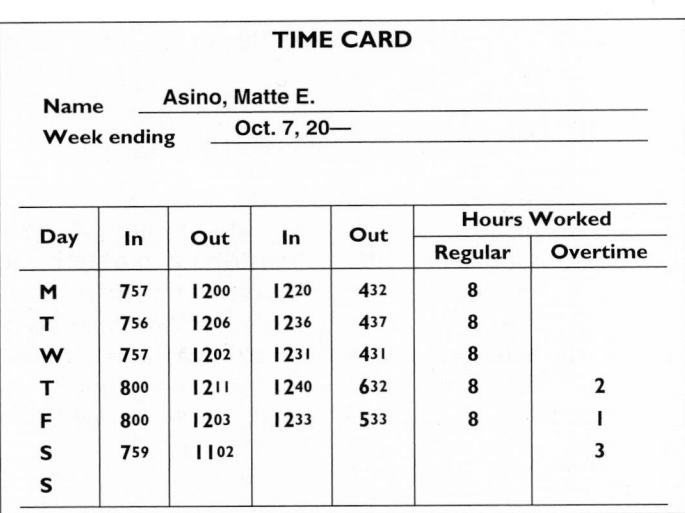

TIME CARD

Name: Asino, Matte E.
Week ending: Oct. 7, 20—

Day	In	Out	In	Out	Hours Worked Regular	Hours Worked Overtime
M	757	1200	1220	432	8	
T	756	1206	1236	437	8	
W	757	1202	1231	431	8	
T	800	1211	1240	632	8	2
F	800	1203	1233	533	8	1
S	759	1102				3
S						

Asino's gross wages can be computed by one of two methods. The first method works like this:

40 hours at straight time	40 × $22.84 per hour =	$ 913.60
2 hours overtime on Thursday	2 × $34.26 per hour =	68.52
1 hour overtime on Friday	1 × $34.26 per hour =	34.26
3 hours overtime on Saturday	3 × $34.26 per hour =	102.78
Total gross wages	46	$1,119.16

The second method of calculating gross wages is often used when it is necessary to identify or track overtime premium.

46 hours at straight time: $46 \times \$22.84$ per hour = $1,050.64
Overtime premium:
6 hours $\times$ $11.42 per hour premium =   68.52

Total gross wages $1,119.16

Salaries

Employees who are paid a regular salary may also be entitled to extra pay for overtime. It is necessary to figure out their regular hourly rate of pay before you can determine their overtime rate. Consider R. Helvi, who gets a salary of $2,250 per month. She is entitled to overtime pay for all hours worked in excess of 40 during a week at the rate of 1½ times her regular hourly rate. This past week she worked 44 hours, so we calculate her overtime pay as follows:

$2,250 per month $\times$ 12 months = $27,000 per year
$27,000 per year $\div$ 52 weeks = $519.23 per week
$519.23 per week $\div$ 40 hours = $12.98 per regular hour

Earnings for 44 hours:
40 hours at straight time $40 \times \$12.98 = \$519.20$
4 hours overtime $4 \times \$19.47 = \$\ 77.88$

Total gross earnings $597.08

Piece Rate

Workers under the piece-rate system are paid at the rate of so much per unit of production. For example, Bob Faulk, a pear picker, gets paid $9 for picking a bin of pears. If he picks 6 bins during the day, his total earnings are $6 \times \$9 = \$54$.

Workers paid by the piece-rate system are paid according to how much they produce. The number of heads of lettuce picked or shirts sewn determines the worker's total compensation.

Commissions

Some salespersons are paid on a purely commission basis. However, a more common arrangement is a salary plus a commission or bonus. Assume that Lena Breski receives an annual salary of $18,000. Her employer agrees to pay her a 5 percent commission on all sales during the year in excess of $100,000. Her sales for the year total $240,000. Her commission is $7,000 ($140,000 × 0.05). Therefore, her total earnings are $25,000 ($18,000 + $7,000).

DEDUCTIONS FROM TOTAL EARNINGS

Anyone who has ever earned a paycheck has encountered some of the many types of deductions. Total earnings minus deductions equal net pay. The most usual deductions are for

1. Federal income tax withholding
2. State income tax withholding
3. FICA tax (Social Security and Medicare), employee's share
4. Purchase of U.S. savings bonds
5. Union dues
6. Medical and life insurance premiums
7. Contributions to a charitable organization
8. Repayment of personal loans from the company credit union
9. Savings through the company credit union

Employees' Federal Income Tax Withholding

FYI

Federal tax rates change frequently, but the procedure stays the same. We will use the tax table given in this chapter for all computations.

Employers are required not only to withhold employees' taxes and then pay them to the U.S. Treasury, but also to keep records of the names and addresses of persons employed, their **taxable earnings** (the earnings subject to tax) and withholdings, and the amounts and dates of payment.

The amount of federal income tax withheld from an employee's earnings depends on the amount of her or his total earnings, marital status, and the number of withholding allowances claimed. A **withholding allowance** is an amount of an individual's earnings that is exempt from income taxes (nontaxable). An employee is entitled to one personal allowance for the taxpayer, one for his or her spouse, and one for each dependent. An **exemption** is an amount of an employee's annual earnings not subject to income tax. Each employee has to fill out an **Employee's Withholding Allowance Certificate (Form W-4)**, shown in Figure 2.

The employer retains this form as authorization to withhold money for the employee's federal income tax.

Circular E, Employer's Tax Guide

OBJECTIVE 3
Determine deductions using tables of employees' income tax withholding.

Circular E contains withholding tables for federal income, Social Security, and Medicare taxes, along with the rules for depositing these taxes. It is regularly updated to reflect changes in tax laws and withholding rates. It also describes filing requirements for official employer reports. Circular E is provided free of charge by the Internal Revenue Service. Accountants responsible for preparation of payroll registers and forms should be familiar with the contents of Circular E.

Form **W-4** Department of the Treasury Internal Revenue Service	**Employee's Withholding Allowance Certificate** ▶ **For Privacy Act and Paperwork Reduction Act Notice, see page 2.**	OMB No. 1545-0010 **20XX**

1 Type or print your first name and middle initial **Matte E.**	Last name **Asino**	2 Your social security number **5 4 3 2 4 1 6 8 0**

Home address (number and street or rural route)
6242 Baxter Drive

3 ☐ Single ☒ Married ☐ Married, but withhold at higher Single rate.
Note: *If married, but legally separated, or spouse is a nonresident alien, check the Single box.*

City or town, state, and ZIP code
Bangor, Maine 04412

4 If your last name differs from that on your social security card, check
here. **You** must call 1-800-772-1213 for a new card . . . ▶ ☐

5 Total number of allowances you are claiming (from line H above or from the worksheets on page 2 if they apply) . | 5 | **0**

6 Additional amount, if any, you want withheld from each paycheck . . . . | 6 | $

7 I claim exemption from withholding for 1999, and I certify that I meet **BOTH** of the following conditions for exemption:
  • Last year I had a right to a refund of **ALL** Federal income tax withheld because I had **NO** tax liability **AND**
  • This year I expect a refund of **ALL** Federal income tax withheld because I expect to have **NO** tax liability.
  If you meet both conditions, write "EXEMPT" here . . . . ▶ | 7 |

Under penalties of perjury, I certify that I am entitled to the number of withholding allowances claimed on this certificate, or I am entitled to claim exempt status.
Employee's signature
(Form is not valid
unless you sign it) ▶ *Matte E. Asino*   Date ▶ *October 7, 20—*

8 Employer's name and address (Employer: Complete 8 and 10 only if sending to the IRS)	9 Office code (optional)	10 Employer identification number

FIGURE 2

The **wage-bracket tax tables** cover monthly, semimonthly, biweekly, weekly, and daily payroll periods. The tables are also subdivided on the basis of marital status. First locate the wage bracket in the first two columns of the table. Next, find the column for the number of allowances claimed and read down this column until you get to the appropriate wage-bracket line. A portion of the weekly federal income tax withholding table for married persons is reproduced in Figure 3 on page 268.

Assume that Matte E. Asino, who claims zero allowances as of the October 7 payroll, has gross wages of $1,119.16 for the week. As $1,119.16 falls in the $1,110–$1,120 bracket, you can see from the table that $150 should be withheld.

Note the headings of the bracket columns: "At least" and "But less than." A strict interpretation of the $1,110–$1,120 bracket really means $1,110–$1,119.99. Therefore, if Asino's salary were $1,120, it would fall into the $1,120–$1,130 bracket.

Employees' State Income Tax Withholding

Many states that levy state income taxes also furnish employers with withholding tables. Other states use a fixed percentage of the federal income tax withholding as the amount to be withheld for state taxes. In our illustration, we assume that the amount of each employee's state income tax deduction is 20 percent of that employee's federal income tax deduction.

Employees' FICA Tax Withholding (Social Security and Medicare)

The Federal Insurance Contributions Act provides for retirement pensions after a worker reaches age 62, disability benefits for any worker who becomes disabled (and for her or his dependents), and a health insurance program

MARRIED Persons—WEEKLY Payroll Period
(For Wages Paid in 2003)

If the wages are—		And the number of withholding allowances claimed is—										
At least	But less than	0	1	2	3	4	5	6	7	8	9	10
		The amount of income tax to be withheld is—										
$750	$760	$83	$74	$66	$57	$48	$39	$30	$22	$16	$10	$4
760	770	85	76	67	58	49	41	32	23	17	11	5
770	780	86	77	69	60	51	42	33	25	18	12	6
780	790	88	79	70	61	52	44	35	26	19	13	7
790	800	89	80	72	63	54	45	36	28	20	14	8
800	810	91	82	73	64	55	47	38	29	21	15	9
810	820	92	83	75	66	57	48	39	31	22	16	10
820	830	94	85	76	67	58	50	41	32	23	17	11
830	840	95	86	78	69	60	51	42	34	25	18	12
840	850	97	88	79	70	61	53	44	35	26	19	13
850	860	98	89	81	72	63	54	45	37	28	20	14
860	870	100	91	82	73	64	56	47	38	29	21	15
870	880	101	92	84	75	66	57	48	40	31	22	16
880	890	103	94	85	76	67	59	50	41	32	23	17
890	900	104	95	87	78	69	60	51	43	34	25	18
900	910	106	97	88	79	70	62	53	44	35	26	19
910	920	107	98	90	81	72	63	54	46	37	28	20
920	930	109	100	91	82	73	65	56	47	38	29	21
930	940	110	101	93	84	75	66	57	49	40	31	22
940	950	112	103	94	85	76	68	59	50	41	32	24
950	960	113	104	96	87	78	69	60	52	43	34	25
960	970	115	106	97	88	79	71	62	53	44	35	27
970	980	116	107	99	90	81	72	63	55	46	37	28
980	990	118	109	100	91	82	74	65	56	47	38	30
990	1,000	119	110	102	93	84	75	66	58	49	40	31
1,000	1,010	121	112	103	94	85	77	68	59	50	41	33
1,010	1,020	123	113	105	96	87	78	69	61	52	43	34
1,020	1,030	126	115	106	97	88	80	71	62	53	44	36
1,030	1,040	128	116	108	99	90	81	72	64	55	46	37
1,040	1,050	131	118	109	100	91	83	74	65	56	47	39
1,050	1,060	134	119	111	102	93	84	75	67	58	49	40
1,060	1,070	137	121	112	103	94	86	77	68	59	50	42
1,070	1,080	139	123	114	105	96	87	78	70	61	52	43
1,080	1,090	142	126	115	106	97	89	80	71	62	53	45
1,090	1,100	145	129	117	108	99	90	81	73	64	55	46
1,100	1,110	147	132	118	109	100	92	83	74	65	56	48
1,110	1,120	150	134	120	111	102	93	84	76	67	58	49
1,120	1,130	153	137	121	112	103	95	86	77	68	59	51
1,130	1,140	155	140	124	114	105	96	87	79	70	61	52
1,140	1,150	158	142	127	115	106	98	89	80	71	62	54
1,150	1,160	161	145	129	117	108	99	90	82	73	64	55
1,160	1,170	164	148	132	118	109	101	92	83	74	65	57
1,170	1,180	166	150	135	120	111	102	93	85	76	67	58
1,180	1,190	169	153	137	121	112	104	95	86	77	68	60
1,190	1,200	172	156	140	124	114	105	96	88	79	70	61
1,200	1,210	174	159	143	127	115	107	98	89	80	71	63
1,210	1,220	177	161	145	130	117	108	99	91	82	73	64
1,220	1,230	180	164	148	132	118	110	101	92	83	74	66
1,230	1,240	182	167	151	135	120	111	102	94	85	76	67
1,240	1,250	185	169	154	138	122	113	104	95	86	77	69
1,250	1,260	188	172	156	140	125	114	105	97	88	79	70
1,260	1,270	191	175	159	143	127	116	107	98	89	80	72
1,270	1,280	193	177	162	146	130	117	108	100	91	82	73
1,280	1,290	196	180	164	148	133	119	110	101	92	83	75
1,290	1,300	199	183	167	151	135	120	111	103	94	85	76
1,300	1,310	201	186	170	154	138	122	113	104	95	86	78
1,310	1,320	204	188	172	157	141	125	114	106	97	88	79
1,320	1,330	207	191	175	159	143	128	116	107	98	89	81
1,330	1,340	209	194	178	162	146	130	117	109	100	91	82
1,340	1,350	212	196	181	165	149	133	119	110	101	92	84
1,350	1,360	215	199	183	167	152	136	120	112	103	94	85
1,360	1,370	218	202	186	170	154	138	123	113	104	95	87
1,370	1,380	220	204	189	173	157	141	125	115	106	97	88
1,380	1,390	223	207	191	175	160	144	128	116	107	98	90
1,390	1,400	226	210	194	178	162	147	131	118	109	100	91

$1,400 and over   Use Table 1(b) for a **MARRIED person** on page 34. Also see the instructions on page 32.

FIGURE 3

after age 65 (Medicare). Both the employee and the employer have to pay **FICA taxes**, which are commonly referred to as **Social Security taxes** and **Medicare taxes**. The employer withholds FICA taxes from employees' wages and pays them to the U.S. Treasury.

FICA tax rates apply to the gross earnings of an employee during the **calendar year** (January 1 through December 31). After an employee has paid Social Security tax on the maximum taxable earnings, the employer stops deducting Social Security tax until the next calendar year begins. Congress has frequently changed the schedule of rates and taxable incomes.

In this text, we assume a Social Security rate of 6.2 percent of the first $84,900 for each employee and a Medicare rate of 1.45 percent of all earnings for each employee. Both tax rates apply to earnings during the calendar year. (Tables for Social Security and Medicare tax withholdings are available in the Internal Revenue Service Circular E, Employer's Tax Guide, also called Publication 15.)

Let's return to Matte E. Asino, who had gross wages of $1,119.16 for the week ending October 7. Suppose that his total accumulated gross wages earned this year prior to this payroll period are $32,890. Asino's total gross wages including this payroll period were $34,009.16 ($32,890 + $1,119.16). Since the Social Security tax applies to the first $84,900 and the Medicare tax applies to all earnings, Asino's earnings are subject to both taxes. For Asino's Social Security tax, multiply $1,119.16 by 6.2 percent ($1,119.16 × 0.062 = $69.39). For Asino's Medicare tax, multiply $1,119.16 by 0.0145 = $16.23.

Here's another example. Assume that Sharlet Wilson had cumulative earnings of $84,600 at the beginning of the pay period. During this pay period, she earned $2,886.24. Since her cumulative earnings are $300 less than $84,900, she must pay Social Security tax on $300, or $18.60 ($300 × 0.062). However, because the Medicare tax applies to all earnings, she is not exempt from any Medicare tax. Her Medicare tax is $41.85 ($2,886.24 × 0.0145).

PAYROLL REGISTER

O B J E C T I V E 4
Complete a payroll register.

The **payroll register** is a multicolumn form prepared for each payroll period listing the earnings, deductions, and net pay for each employee. In Figure 4 (shown on the next page) we see a payroll register that shows the data for each employee on a separate line. This would be suitable for a firm, like Greg Company, that has a small number of employees.

First, we'll show the entire payroll register, then we'll break it down and explain it column by column. The number at the foot of each column refers to the related text description.

The payroll period shown in Figure 4 covers October 1 through October 7. The first part consists of employees' names, hours worked, beginning cumulative earnings, and taxable earnings.

(1) **Total Hours**—Taken from employees' time cards.

(2) **Beginning Cumulative Earnings**—The amount each employee has earned between January 1 and September 30 (the last day of the previous payroll period). It is taken from each employee's individual earnings record. (See Figure 7, pages 276–277.)

(3) **Regular Earnings**—Earnings for hours worked up to and including 40. In other words, the first 40 hours multiplied by each employee's regular hourly rate.

	NAME	TOTAL HOURS	BEGINNING CUMULATIVE EARNINGS	EARNINGS REGULAR	EARNINGS OVERTIME	EARNINGS TOTAL	ENDING CUMULATIVE EARNINGS	UNEMPLOYMENT
1	Asino, Matte E.	46	32 8 9 0 00	9 1 3 60	2 0 5 56	1 1 1 9 16	34 0 0 9 16	
2	Boritsky, Olga	45	6 1 9 2 00	6 1 9 20	1 1 6 10	7 3 5 30	6 9 2 7 30	7 3 5 30
3	Dray, Greg G.	49	6 8 4 6 00	6 8 4 60	2 3 1 05	9 1 5 65	7 7 6 1 65	1 5 4 00
4	Foulkes, Bob L.	40	38 6 3 7 00	1 0 7 3 25	0 00	1 0 7 3 25	39 7 1 0 25	
5	Groyer, Milli K.	40	68 0 0 0 00	1 8 8 8 89	0 00	1 8 8 8 89	69 8 8 8 89	
6	Kramer, Ada A.	40	68 1 0 0 00	1 8 9 1 67	0 00	1 8 9 1 67	69 9 9 1 67	
7	Minkowitz, John L.	55	36 8 4 0 00	1 0 2 3 33	5 7 5 63	1 5 9 8 96	38 4 3 8 96	
8	Orleons, Janet C.	40	45 7 8 3 00	1 2 7 1 75	0 00	1 2 7 1 75	47 0 5 4 75	
9	Pinkovich, Mark S.	44	46 9 7 0 00	1 3 0 4 72	1 9 5 71	1 5 0 0 43	48 4 7 0 43	
10	Romero, Sheila J.	45	54 9 7 8 00	1 5 2 7 17	2 8 6 34	1 8 1 3 51	56 7 9 1 51	
11	Tivoli, Jake T.	40	42 0 7 8 00	1 1 6 8 83	0 00	1 1 6 8 83	43 2 4 6 83	
12	Wilson, Sharlet D.	52	84 6 0 0 00	1 9 9 0 56	8 9 5 68	2 8 8 6 24	87 4 8 6 24	
13			531 9 1 4 00	15 3 5 7 57	2 5 0 6 07	17 8 6 3 64	549 7 7 7 64	8 8 9 30
14		(1)	(2)	(3)	(4)	(5)	(6)	(7 A)
15								

15,357.57 + 2,506.07 = 17,863.64

531,914.00 + 17,863.64 = 549,777.64

FIGURE 4

(4) **Overtime Earnings**—Hours in excess of 40 (relative to a 40-hour week) worked by each employee, multiplied by that employee's overtime rate.

(5) **Total Earnings**—Regular earnings plus overtime earnings.

(6) **Ending Cumulative Earnings**—Beginning Cumulative Earnings plus Total Earnings.

(7) **Taxable Earnings**—The amount of earnings subject to taxation, **not the tax itself.** We'll use these columns later to figure the amount of each tax. In other words, **Taxable Earnings is the base on which to figure the tax. Taxable Earnings multiplied by the tax rate equals the amount of the tax.**

(7A) **Unemployment Taxable Earnings**—In our illustration, we are using a maximum of $7,000 for unemployment tax liability on the employer for each employee. This column represents the previously untaxed portion remaining of the $7,000 for the individual employees. **Unemployment tax is paid only by the employer in most states. An unemployment tax may be paid both to the state and to the federal government.** Actually, states may use different maximum earnings and different rates than does the federal government. However, many states use $7,000, which at the time of this writing is the amount used by the federal government. There are three possibilities for Unemployment Taxable Earnings, as follows:

a. **Employee's cumulative earnings including this pay period have not reached $7,000.** When an employee's cumulative earnings so far during the calendar year (since January 1) are less than $7,000, we record the total earnings for the payroll period in the Unemployment Taxable Earnings column. For example, Olga Boritsky's cumulative earnings before this

PAYROLL REGISTER FOR WEEK ENDED   October 7, 20—

(7) TAXABLE EARNINGS		(8) DEDUCTIONS					
SOCIAL SECURITY	MEDICARE	FEDERAL INCOME TAX	STATE INCOME TAX	SOCIAL SECURITY TAX	MEDICARE TAX	MEDICAL INSURANCE	OTHER
1119 16	1119 16	150 00	30 00	69 39	16 23	11 19	0 00
735 30	735 30	80 00	16 00	45 59	10 66	11 03	UW 12 00
915 65	915 65	107 00	21 40	56 77	13 28	13 73	UW 15 00
1073 25	1073 25	123 00	24 60	66 54	15 56	16 10	0 00
1888 89	1888 89	394 00	78 80	117 11	27 39	28 33	0 00
1891 67	1891 67	395 00	79 00	117 28	27 43	28 38	UW 10 00
1598 96	1598 96	312 00	62 40	99 14	23 18	23 98	UW 12 00
1271 75	1271 75	193 00	38 60	78 85	18 44	19 08	UW 20 00
1500 43	1500 43	284 00	56 80	93 03	21 76	22 51	0 00
1813 51	1813 51	372 00	74 40	112 44	26 30	27 20	AR 50 00
1168 83	1168 83	164 00	32 80	72 47	16 95	17 53	UW 25 00
300 00	2886 24	665 00	133 00	18 60	41 85	41 44	UW 30 00
15277 40	17863 64	3239 00	647 80	947 21	259 03	260 50	174 00
(7B)	(7C)	(8A)	(8B)	(8C)	(8D)	(8E)	(8F)

3,289.00 + 647.80 + 947.21 + 259.03 + 260.50 + 174.00 = 5,527.54   5,527.54+

PAGE   68

	(9) PAYMENTS			(10) EXPENSE ACCOUNT DEBITED		
TOTAL	NET AMOUNT	CK. NO.	SALES WAGES EXPENSE	OFFICE WAGES EXPENSE		
276 81	842 35	931	1119 16		1
175 28	560 02	932	735 30		2
227 18	688 47	933	915 65		3
245 80	827 45	934		1073 25	4
645 63	1243 26	935	1888 89		5
657 09	1234 58	936		1891 67	6
532 70	1066 26	937	1598 96		7
367 97	903 78	938		1271 75	8
478 10	1022 33	939	1500 43		9
662 34	1151 17	940	1813 51		10
328 75	840 08	941	1168 83		11
929 89	1956 35	942	2886 24		12
5527 54	12336 10		13626 97	4236 67	13
(8G)	(9A)	(9B)	(10A)	(10B)	14
					15

12,336.10 = 17,863.64   13,626.97 + 4,236.67 = 17,863.64

FYI
Social Security and Medicare taxes are recorded separately in the payroll register because there is no limit on Medicare as there is on Social Security.

week were $6,192. Olga's cumulative earnings after this week are $6,927.30 ($6,192 + $735.30). Because Olga's cumulative earnings are still less than $7,000, the entire $735.30 in wages earned during this pay period is listed in the Unemployment Taxable Earnings column.

b. **Employee's cumulative earnings were less than $7,000 before this week and are more than $7,000 after this week.** Look at the line for Greg Dray and notice that his cumulative earnings before this week were $6,846. Dray's new cumulative earnings (ending) are $7,761.65 ($6,846 + $915.65), putting him over the $7,000 maximum. Therefore, to bring Dray up to the $7,000 limit, $154 ($7,000 − $6,846) of his earnings for the week are taxable. After this week, none of Dray's earnings for the remainder of this calendar year will be taxable for unemployment.

c. **Employee's cumulative earnings before this week were more than $7,000.** After an employee's earnings top $7,000 during the calendar year, record a dash in the Unemployment Taxable Earnings column to indicate that the column has not been forgotten or overlooked. For example, Matte Asino's total earnings before the payroll period ended October 7 (beginning) were $32,890 (as shown in his individual earnings record in Figure 7). Since he had previously earned more than $7,000 this year, we record a dash in the Unemployment Taxable Earnings column.

(7B) **Social Security Taxable Earnings**—The first $84,900 for each employee. We assume a Social Security tax rate of 6.2 percent of the first $84,900 paid to each employee during the calendar year.

a. **Employee's cumulative earnings including this pay period have not reached $84,900.** When an employee's cumulative earnings so far during the year are less than $84,900, we record the total earnings for the payroll period in the Social Security Taxable Earnings column. For example, Olga Boritsky's cumulative earnings so far this year amount to $6,192. Because Olga's total earnings are less than $84,900 the entire $735.30 of wages earned during this pay period is listed in the Social Security Taxable Earnings column. Note that this is true of all the employees except Sharlet Wilson.

b. **Employee's cumulative earnings before the week were more than $84,900.** After an employee's earnings top $84,900 during the calendar year, record a dash to indicate that the column has not been forgotten or overlooked. (Use the same procedure as for the Unemployment Taxable Earnings column.) For example, Sharlet Wilson's cumulative earnings before the payroll period ended October 7 were $84,600. Since she is $300 below the limit of $84,900, we record $300 in the Social Security Taxable Earnings column.

(7C) **Medicare Taxable Earnings**—All earnings for this period. We have assumed a Medicare tax rate of 1.45 percent on all earnings that are paid to each employee during the calendar year. Therefore, all earnings for this period are taxable and are recorded in the Medicare Taxable Earnings column.

(8) **Deductions**—Amounts taken away (withheld) from total earnings.

(8A) **Federal Income Tax Deductions**—The amount of the federal income tax deduction for each employee can be located directly on the wage bracket tables or calculated on a percentage basis.

(8B) **State Income Tax Deductions**—States that impose income taxes also provide wage-bracket tables. The state tax deduction for each employee can be located directly in the appropriate table. As stated previously, we are assuming a rate of 20 percent of the federal income tax.

(8C) **Social Security Tax Deductions**—For each employee's Social Security tax deduction, we first go to the Social Security Taxable Earnings column and note the amount subject to tax. Next, we multiply the Social Security taxable earnings by 6.2 percent. For example, Boritsky's taxable earnings are $735.30, and her Social Security tax deduction is $45.59 ($735.30 × .062).

(8D) **Medicare Tax Deductions**—For each employee's Medicare tax deduction, we go to the Medicare Taxable Earnings column and note the amount subject to tax. Next, we multiply the Medicare taxable earnings by 1.45 percent. For example, Boritsky's taxable earnings are $735.30, and her Medicare tax deduction is $10.66 ($735.30 × .0145).

(8E) **Medical Insurance Deductions**—Premiums paid by the employee through payroll withholding. The amount of the premium for each employee depends on the number of dependents claimed, among other things. For example, Boritsky's premium is $11.03 per week.

(8F) **Other Deductions**—Employees' voluntary withholdings. In our illustration, UW represents the United Way, and AR stands for Accounts Receivable (employee pays charge account to the company). For example, Sheila Romero paid $50 on her charge account.

(8G) **Total Deductions**—The combined total of each employee's deductions for taxes, insurance, and other. For example, Boritsky's total deduction is $175.28 ($80.00 + $16.00 + $45.59 + $10.66 + $11.03 + $12.00).

(9) **Payments**—The amount of each employee's payroll check (take-home pay).

(9A) **Net Amount**—Each employee's Total Earnings minus Total Deductions. For example, Boritsky's net amount is $560.02 ($735.30 − $175.28).

(9B) **Ck. No.**—The number of each employee's payroll check.

(10) **Expense Account Debited**—Columns used for distributing each amount into the appropriate wages expense account. Greg Company uses Sales Wages Expense and Office Wages Expense. The sum of these two columns equals the total earnings.

(10A) **Sales Wages Expense**—Amounts earned by employees involved in sales activities.

(10B) **Office Wages Expense**—Amounts earned by employees involved in office activities.

THE PAYROLL ENTRY

Because the payroll register summarizes the payroll data for the period, it is used as the basis for recording the payroll in the ledger accounts. Since the payroll register does not have the status of a journal, a journal entry is necessary. Figure 5 on page 274 shows the entry in general journal form.

GENERAL JOURNAL   PAGE **31**

DATE		DESCRIPTION	POST. REF.	DEBIT	CREDIT	
20–						1
Oct.	7	Sales Wages Expense		13 6 2 6 97		2
		Office Wages Expense		4 2 3 6 67		3
		Employees' Federal Income				4
		Tax Payable			3 2 3 9 00	5
		FICA Tax Payable			1 2 0 6 24	6
		Employees' State Income Tax				7
		Payable			6 4 7 80	8
		Employees' Medical Insurance				9
		Payable			2 6 0 50	10
		Employees' United Way				11
		Payable			1 2 4 00	12
		Accounts Receivable			5 0 00	13
		Wages Payable			12 3 3 6 10	14
		Payroll register, page 68,				15
		for week ended October 7.				16

FIGURE 5

REMEMBER!
The totals from the payroll register are the amounts used in the payroll entry.

Note that the accountant records the total cost to the company for services of employees as debits to the Wages Expense accounts.

Also note that the total Social Security tax deductions ($947.21) and the total Medicare tax deductions ($259.03) are combined to become FICA Tax Payable of $1,206.24 ($947.21 + $259.03). The two tax deductions are combined into the one liability account because they are paid together at the same time. Social Security and Medicare taxes are recorded separately in the payroll register because they must be listed separately on each employee's W-2 form (Wage and Tax Statement).

To pay the employees from the company's regular checking account, the accountant now makes the following journal entry:

REMEMBER!
The amount shown as Wages Payable is the employees' take-home pay.

				DEBIT	CREDIT	
	8	Wages Payable		12 3 3 6 10		17
		Cash—M. Asino			8 4 2 35	18
		Cash—O. Boritsky			5 6 0 62	19
		Cash—G. Dray			6 8 8 47	20
		Cash—B. Foulkes			8 2 7 45	21
		Cash—M. Groyer			1 2 4 3 26	22
		Cash—A. Kramer			1 2 3 4 58	23
		Cash—J. Minkowitz			1 0 6 6 26	24
		Cash—J. Orleons			9 0 3 78	25
		Cash—M. Pinkovich			1 0 2 2 33	26
		Cash—S. Romero			1 1 5 1 17	27
		Cash—J. Tivoli			8 4 0 08	28
		Cash—S. Wilson			1 9 5 6 35	29

Special Payroll Bank Account—An Alternative

A firm with a large number of employees would probably open a special **payroll bank account** with its bank. One check drawn on the regular bank account is made payable to the special payroll account for the amount of the total net pay for a payroll period. All payroll checks for the period are then written on the special payroll account. To record this, the accountant makes the following journal entry. In this book, assume the entry to debit Cash—Payroll Bank Account and to credit Cash has already been made.

GENERAL JOURNAL   PAGE **1**

DATE	DESCRIPTION	POST. REF.	DEBIT	CREDIT
8	Wages Payable		12 3 3 6 10	
	Cash—Payroll Bank Account			12 3 3 6 10
	Paid wages for week			
	ended October 7.			

Paycheck

All the data needed to make out a payroll check are available in the payroll register. Matte E. Asino's paycheck is shown in Figure 6.

FIGURE 6

EMPLOYEE	TOTAL HOURS	O.T. HOURS	REG. PAY	O.T. PREM. PAY	GROSS PAY	FED INC. TAX	STATE INC. TAX	SOCIAL SECURITY TAX	MEDICARE TAX	MEDICAL INSURANCE	OTHER	TOTAL DED.	NET PAY
Matte E. Asino	46	6	913.60	205.56	1119.16	150.00	30.00	69.39	16.23	11.19	—	276.81	842.35

CENTRAL NATIONAL BANK   98-461 / 252

Payroll Account

Greg Company
610 First Avenue
Bangor, Maine 04412

October 8 20 — No. 931

PAY TO THE ORDER OF Matte E. Asino $ 842.35

Eight hundred forty-two and 35/100 _____ DOLLARS

Ellen D. Greg

⑆252⑈0461⑆

EMPLOYEE'S INDIVIDUAL EARNINGS RECORD

NAME __Matte E. Asino__   EMPLOYEE NO. __5__

ADDRESS __6242 Baxter Drive__   SOC. SEC. NO. __543-24-1680__

__Bangor, Maine 04412__   PAY RATE __$22.84__

MALE __X__   FEMALE _____   EQUIVALENT HOURLY RATE __$22.84__

MARRIED __X__   SINGLE _____   DATE TERMINATED _____

PHONE NO. __663-2556__   DATE OF BIRTH __9/19/72__   CLASSIFICATION FOR WORKERS' COMPENSATION INSURANCE __Sales floor__

	PERIOD ENDED	DATE PAID	HOURS WORKED REG	O.T.	EARNINGS REGULAR	OVERTIME	TOTAL	ENDING CUMULATIVE EARNINGS	FEDERAL INCOME TAX	STATE INCOME TAX
40	9/3	9/4	40	8	9 1 3 60	2 7 4 08	1 1 8 7 68	28 7 2 1 70	1 6 9 00	3 3 80
41	9/10	9/11	40	2	9 1 3 60	6 8 52	9 8 2 12	29 7 0 3 82	1 1 8 00	2 3 60
42	9/17	9/18	40	2	9 1 3 60	6 8 52	9 8 2 12	30 6 8 5 94	1 1 8 00	2 3 60
43	9/24	9/25	40	5	9 1 3 60	1 7 1 30	1 0 8 4 90	31 7 7 0 84	1 4 2 00	2 8 40
44	9/30	10/1	40	6	9 1 3 60	2 0 5 56	1 1 1 9 16	32 8 9 0 00	1 5 0 00	3 0 00
45	10/7	10/8	40	6	9 1 3 60	2 0 5 56	1 1 1 9 16	34 0 0 9 16	1 5 0 00	3 0 00

FIGURE 7

OBJECTIVE 6
Maintain employees' individual earnings records.

Employees' Individual Earnings Records

To comply with government regulations, a firm has to keep current data on each employee's accumulated earnings, deductions, and net pay. The information contained in the payroll register is recorded each payday in each **employee's individual earnings record**. Figure 7 shows a portion of the earnings record for Matte E. Asino.

CHAPTER REVIEW

Check out ACE for a Review Quiz at

http://college.hmco.com/accounting/students/.

ACE self-test

Review of Performance Objectives

1. Understand the role of laws that affect payroll deductions and contributions.

   Those employees and employers involved in the computation and paying of employees for their work must understand the laws, know the percentages and limits involved, and when and to whom to submit the funds deducted from employees and contributed by employees.

2. Calculate total earnings based on an hourly, piece-rate, or commission basis.

   Earnings calculated on an *hourly basis* equal the hourly rate multiplied by the number of hours worked. Earnings calculated on a *piece-rate basis* equal the total number of products produced multiplied by the rate per unit of product. Earnings calculated on a *commission basis* equal the total number of units sold or the price of units sold multiplied by the commission rate.

3. Determine deductions using tables of employees' income tax withholding.

   Using the appropriate income tax withholding table in IRS Circular E, first determine marital status and payroll period and then locate the wage bracket containing the amount of earnings. Next, on the same horizontal line, select the vertical column containing the number of allowances claimed.

4. Complete a payroll register.

   List the employees' names, hours worked, and beginning cumulative earnings. Add the total earnings to the beginning cumulative earnings to get ending cumu-

DATE EMPLOYED __2/1/—__

NO. OF EXEMPTIONS __0__

PER HOUR __X__   PER DAY _____

PER WEEK _____   PER MONTH _____

	DEDUCTIONS						PAID	
SOCIAL SECURITY TAX	MEDICARE TAX	MEDICAL INSURANCE	CODE	OTHER AMOUNT	TOTAL	NET AMOUNT	CK. NO.
7 3 64	1 7 22	1 1 19	UW	5 00	3 0 9 85	8 7 7 83	871
6 0 89	1 4 24	1 1 19	UW		2 2 7 92	7 5 4 20	883
6 0 89	1 4 24	1 1 19	UW	5 00	2 3 2 92	7 4 9 20	895
6 7 26	1 5 73	1 1 19	UW		2 6 4 58	8 2 0 32	907
6 9 39	1 6 23	1 1 19	UW	5 00	2 8 1 81	8 3 7 35	919
6 9 39	1 6 23	1 1 19	UW		2 7 6 81	8 4 2 35	931

lative earnings. The Unemployment Taxable Earnings column is used for the first $7,000 of each employee's earnings for FUTA and SUTA. The Social Security Taxable Earnings column is used for an assumed first $84,900. The Medicare Taxable Earnings column is used for all earnings. Under the Deductions columns, list the income taxes withheld, the Social Security taxes withheld, the Medicare taxes withheld, and other deductions. The Social Security tax deduction equals the Social Security taxable earnings multiplied by an assumed rate of 6.2 percent. The Medicare tax deduction equals the Medicare taxable earnings multiplied by an assumed rate of 1.45 percent. Net amount equals total (gross) earnings minus total deductions. The Expense Account Debited columns are used to distribute salaries and wages expense to the appropriate accounts.

5. Journalize the payroll entry from a payroll register.

Totals are taken directly from the payroll register. For the following entry, assume that one check is made payable to a special payroll bank account. The entry to transfer the cash to the payroll bank account is not shown here.

GENERAL JOURNAL   PAGE __31__

DATE		DESCRIPTION	POST. REF.	DEBIT	CREDIT
20—					
Oct.	7	Sales Wages Expense		13 6 2 6 97	
		Office Wages Expense		4 2 3 6 67	
		Employees' Federal Income			
		Tax Payable			3 2 3 9 00
		FICA Tax Payable			1 2 0 6 24
		Employees' State Income Tax			
		Payable			6 4 7 80
		Employees' Medical Insurance			
		Payable			2 6 0 50
		Employees' United Way			
		Payable			1 2 4 00
		Accounts Receivable			5 0 00
		Wages Payable			12 3 3 6 10
		Payroll register, page 68,			
		for week ended October 7.			

The following entry is used to pay the employees:

	8	Wages Payable		12 3 3 6 10			18
19		Cash			12 3 3 6 10		19
20		Paid wages for week					20
21		ended October 7.					21
22							22
23							23
24							24

6. Maintain employees' individual earnings records.

In the employees' individual earnings records, list the personal data for each employee. Based on the information contained in the payroll register, record the earnings and deductions for each payroll period.

Glossary

Calendar year A twelve-month period beginning on January 1 and ending on December 31 of the same year. (269)

Current Tax Payment Act (Income Tax Withholding) An act to require employers to withhold and pay to the U.S. Treasury employee funds. (262)

Employee One who works for compensation under the direction and control of the employer. (261)

Employee's individual earnings record A supplementary record for each employee showing personal payroll data and yearly cumulative earnings, deductions, and net pay. (276)

Employee's Withholding Allowance Certificate (Form W-4) A form that specifies the number of allowances claimed by each employee and gives the employer the authority to withhold money for an employee's federal income taxes and FICA taxes. (266)

Exemption An amount of an employee's annual earnings not subject to income tax for the taxpayer, taxpayer's spouse, and dependents (usually children). (266)

Fair Labor Standards Act (FLSA) The act of 1938 that provides for minimum standards for wages and overtime, including provisions related to child labor and equal pay for equal work. (262)

FICA taxes Social Security taxes plus Medicare taxes, paid by both employee and employer under the provisions of the Federal Insurance Contributions Act. The proceeds are used to pay old-age and disability pensions and to fund the Medicare program. (269)

Gross pay The total amount of an employee's pay before any deductions. (260)

Independent contractor Someone who is engaged for a definite job or service, and who may choose her or his own means of doing the work. This person is not an employee of the firm for which the service is provided. (261)

Medicare taxes Federal government taxes levied on employees and employers; proceeds are used for medical insurance for eligible people age 65 or over. (269)

Net pay Gross pay minus deductions. Also called *take-home pay*. (260)

Payroll bank account A special checking account used to pay a company's employees. (275)

Payroll register A multicolumn form prepared for each payroll period listing the earnings, deductions, and net pay for each employee. (269)

Social Security Act of 1935 An act to provide for worker retirement funding through deductions from their wages and matching amounts from the employers. (262)

Social Security taxes Federal government taxes levied on employees and employers; proceeds are used for old-age pensions and disability benefits. (269)

Taxable earnings The amount of an employee's earnings subject to a tax. (266)

Wage-bracket tax tables A chart providing the amounts to be deducted for income taxes based on amount of earnings, marital status, and number of allowances claimed. (267)

Withholding allowance An amount of an employee's annual earnings not subject to income tax. (266)

Workers' compensation laws Laws that protect employees and dependents against losses due to death or injury incurred on the job. (263)

QUESTIONS, EXERCISES, AND PROBLEMS

Discussion Questions

1. What is the purpose of the employee's individual earnings record, and how is it related to the payroll register?
2. What is the purpose of the payroll register?
3. What information is included in an employee's individual earnings record?
4. Explain how gross earnings differ from net earnings for a payroll period.
5. Describe how a special payroll bank account is useful in paying the wages and salaries of employees.
6. List three required deductions and four voluntary deductions from an employee's total earnings.
7. What is the difference between an employee and an independent contractor? List three examples of an independent contractor.
8. What information is included in a wage-bracket withholding table? Are there overlapping amounts of gross earnings in the table?

Exercises

P.O. 1,2

Calculate gross pay.

Exercise 8-1 Determine the gross pay for each employee listed below.

a. Greg Dunn is paid time-and-a-half for all hours over forty. He worked forty-five hours during the week. His regular pay rate is $10.80 per hour.
b. Mia Nye worked fifty-two hours during the week. She is entitled to time-and-a-half for all hours in excess of forty per week. Her regular pay rate is $12.50 per hour.
c. Linda Morgan is paid a commission of 9 percent of her sales, which amounted to $10,885.

d. Mary Beson's yearly salary is $40,800. During the week, Beson worked forty-two hours, and she is entitled to time-and-a-half for all hours over forty.

P.O. 1,2,3

Determine gross pay and withholding.

Exercise 8-2 Lupe Martin works for Paul Company, which pays its employees time-and-a-half for all hours worked in excess of forty per week. Martin's pay rate is $16.00 per hour. Her wages are subject to federal income tax, a Social Security tax deduction at the rate of 6.2 percent, and a Medicare tax deduction at the rate of 1.45 percent. She is married and claims three allowances. Martin has a half-hour lunch break during an eight-and-one-half-hour day. She is paid for hours between 8 and 4:30 and overtime for increments greater than 30 minutes on a given day. Martin's beginning cumulative earnings are $36,827.

Complete the following using Martin's time card shown below:

a. _____ hours at straight time × $16.00
   per hour $_____
b. _____ hours overtime × $_____
   per hour   _____
c. Total gross pay $_____
d. Federal income tax withholding (from tax
   tables in Figure 3, page 268) $_____
e. Social Security tax withholding at 6.2 percent   _____
f. Medicare tax withholding at 1.45 percent   _____
g. Total withholding   _____
h. Net pay $_____

TIME CARD

Name   Martin, Lupe

Week ending   March 11, 20—

Day	In	Out	In	Out	Hours Worked Regular	Hours Worked Overtime
M	7 56	12 09	12 39	4 32	8	
T	7 52	12 05	12 35	5 04	8	½
W	7 59	12 20	12 40	5 03	8	½
T	8 00	12 08	12 38	4 34	8	
F	7 56	12 09	12 39	6 33	8	2
S	8 00	12 01	12 40	3 40		7
S						

FIGURE 8

NAME	BEGINNING CUMULATIVE EARNINGS	EARNINGS REGULAR	EARNINGS OVERTIME	EARNINGS TOTAL	ENDING CUMULATIVE EARNINGS	TAXABLE EARNINGS UNEMPLOYMENT	TAXABLE EARNINGS SOCIAL SECURITY	TAXABLE EARNINGS MEDICARE
	245 75 4 00	6 72 4 00	1 2 20 00	7 49 4 00	253 24 8 00	2 4 56 00	7 94 4 00	7 94 4 00

P.O. 1,2,3,4

Determine net pay.

Exercise 8-3 Using the income tax withholding table in Figure 3, page 268, for each employee of Molor Company, determine the net pay for the week ended January 21. Assume a Social Security tax of 6.2 percent and a Medicare tax of 1.45 percent. All employees have cumulative earnings of less than $84,900. Assume all employees are married.

Employee	Allowances	Total Earnings	Social Security Tax Withheld	Medicare Tax Withheld	Federal Income Tax Withheld	Union Dues Withheld	Medical Insurance Withheld	Net Pay
a. Alison, C. A.	1	$ 880	$	$	$	$ 25	$ 30	$
b. Door, R. N.	2	820				25	26	
c. Fenn, T. C.	3	1,010				—	30	
d. Harris, L. O.	0	1,075				25	30	
e. Nguyen, M. E.	2	930				25	30	
Totals		$4,715	$	$	$	$100	$146	$

P.O. 1,4

Locate errors in a payroll register.

Exercise 8-4 For the week ended September 7, the totals of the payroll register for Bender, Inc., are presented in Figure 8. The regular and overtime earnings are correct. List six errors that exist. All earnings are subject to Social Security and Medicare taxes.

P.O. 1,4

Determine taxable earnings.

Exercise 8-5 For tax purposes, assume that the maximum taxable earnings are $84,900 for Social Security and $7,000 for the unemployment tax, and that all earnings are taxable for Medicare. For the payroll register for the month of November in Figure 9 (page 282), determine the taxable earnings for each employee.

P.O. 1,4,5

Determine FICA withholdings and journalize payroll entry.

Exercise 8-6 On January 21, the column totals of the payroll register for Cray Company showed that its sales employees had earned $14,580, its trucking employees had earned $9,870, and its office employees had earned

	DEDUCTIONS					PAYMENTS		WAGES EXPENSE
FEDERAL INCOME TAX	SOCIAL SECURITY TAX	MEDICARE TAX	UNION DUES	MEDICAL INSURANCE	TOTAL	NET AMOUNT	CK. NO.	DEBIT
9 4 9 00	4 2 9 53	1 1 5 19	1 9 3 00	2 9 2 00	2 0 8 3 00	5 4 5 6 00		7 4 9 4 00

EMPLOYEE	BEGINNING CUMULATIVE EARNINGS	TOTAL EARNINGS	ENDING CUMULATIVE EARNINGS	TAXABLE EARNINGS		
				UNEMPLOYMENT	SOCIAL SECURITY	MEDICARE
Aldon, J.	84 3 5 0 00	4 2 3 7 00	88 5 8 7 00			
Ellis, E.	33 2 1 9 00	3 8 3 0 00	37 0 4 9 00			
Glade, C.	30 5 5 0 00	2 7 3 0 00	33 2 8 0 00			
Johns, M.	3 7 5 1 00	1 4 6 3 00	5 2 1 4 00			
Newkirk, J.	5 4 3 6 00	1 2 8 4 00	6 7 2 0 00			

FIGURE 9

$7,684. Social Security taxes were withheld at an assumed rate of 6.2 percent, and Medicare taxes were withheld at an assumed rate of 1.45 percent. Other deductions consisted of federal income tax, $3,745; medical insurance, $1,560; union dues, $496. Determine the amount of Social Security and Medicare taxes withheld, and record the general journal entry for the payroll, crediting Salaries Payable for the net pay. All earnings were taxable.

P.O. 1,2,3

Determine missing amounts.

Exercise 8-7 Lien Labs has two employees. The information shown below was taken from their individual earnings records for the month of September. Determine the missing amounts, assuming that the Social Security tax is 6.2 percent and the Medicare tax is 1.45 percent. All earnings are subject to Social Security and Medicare taxes. Round amounts to nearest dollar.

	Bailey	**Rinken**	**Total**
Regular earnings	$1,650	$?	$?
Overtime earnings	?	110	?
Total earnings	$1,740	$?	$?
Federal income tax withheld	$ 332	$?	$?
State income tax withheld	?	86	?
Social Security tax withheld	108	92	?
Medicare tax withheld	25	22	?
Medical insurance withheld	104	98	?
Total deductions	$ 681	$ 477	$?
Net pay	$?	$1,013	$?

P.O. 5
Journalize the payroll entry.

Exercise 8-8 Assume that the employees in Exercise 8-7 are paid from the company's regular bank account (check numbers 931 and 932). Prepare the entry to record and pay the payroll in general journal form, dated September 30.

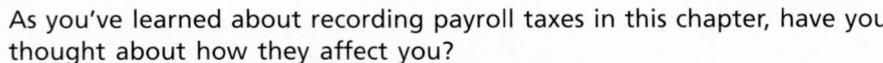

REFLECTING ON
THE WORLD WIDE WEB

As you've learned about recording payroll taxes in this chapter, have you thought about how they affect you?

Find out whether you would have more or less deducted from your paycheck if you moved from Massachusetts to New Mexico. Use the paycheck calculator provided at Payroll-taxes.com (**http://www.paycheckcity. com/copayroll-taxes/netpaycalculator.asp**). Assume it is the 2003 tax year, you are single, you would make $2,000 per week in either state, and you claim no federal or state exemptions or other deductions. If the amounts differ, why do they differ?

CONSIDER AND COMMUNICATE

Nathan Company pays its employees weekly by issuing checks on its regular bank account. The owner thinks it would be too much trouble to have a second checking account. Respond to the owner's concern.

WHAT'S WRONG WITH THIS PICTURE?

You have just completed the payroll register for this week's payroll. You have crossfooted the register—that is, you have added the columns vertically and horizontally. There is just one problem: The total of the Net Amount column does not equal the total of the Gross Amount column minus the total of the Total Deductions column. How could this happen? What would you do to obtain correctly crossfooted totals?

A MATTER OF ETHICS

An employee who is married and has two children submits a W-4 form to his employer indicating that he is single and claims zero deductions. Is this action ethical, unethical, or illegal? Explain your reasoning.

PROBLEM SET A

For additional help, see the demonstration problem at the beginning of each chapter in your Working Papers.

P.O. 1,2,3

Problem 8-1A Vickie Roe, an employee of Vance Company, worked forty-six hours during the week of February 9 through 15. Her rate of pay is $16.50 per hour, and she gets time-and-a-half for work in excess of forty hours per week. She is married and claims one allowance on her W-4 form. Her wages are subject to the following deductions:

a. Federal income tax (use the table in Figure 3, page 268).
b. Social Security tax at 6.2 percent.
c. Medicare tax at 1.45 percent.
d. Union dues, $20.00.
e. Medical insurance, $22.00.

Check Figure

Net pay, $622.65

Instructions

Compute her regular pay, overtime pay, gross pay, and net pay.

P.O. 1,2,4,5

Problem 8-2A Ridge Homes has the following payroll information for the week ended February 21:

| Name | Earnings at End of Previous Week | Daily Time | | | | | | | Pay Rate | Federal Income Tax |
		S	M	T	W	T	F	S		
Aig, A. C.	1,920.00	8	8	8	8	8			11.65	130.00
Ball, D. R.	2,030.00			8	8	8	8	8	11.50	137.00
Caan, H. A.	2,064.00	8	8	8			8	8	11.95	139.00
Dorn, G. L.	628.00				8	8			21.00	115.00
Ellen, L. B.	2,597.00	8	8	8			8	8	11.90	147.00
Fitz, G. W.	2,075.00	8	8		8	8	8	8	11.00	127.00

Taxable earnings for Social Security are based on the first $84,900. Taxable earnings for Medicare are based on all earnings. Taxable earnings for federal and state unemployment are based on the first $7,000. Employees are paid time-and-a-half for work in excess of forty hours per week.

Check Figure

Net Amount, $1,779.73

Instructions

1. Complete the payroll register, page 37. The Social Security tax rate is 6.2 percent, and the Medicare tax rate is 1.45 percent.

2. Prepare a general journal entry to record the payroll. The firm's general ledger contains a Wages Expense account and a Wages Payable account.

3. Assuming that the firm transfers funds from its regular bank account to its special payroll bank account, and that that entry has been made, prepare a general journal entry to record the payment of wages. Begin payroll checks with no. 208.

P.O. 1,2,3,4,5

Problem 8-3A The Utter Company pays its employees time-and-a-half for hours worked in excess of forty per week. The information available from time cards and employees' individual earnings records for the pay period ended October 14 is shown in the chart below.

Name	Earnings at End of Previous Week	Daily Time						Pay Rate	Income Tax Allowances
		M	T	W	T	F	S		
Bender, J. C.	42,827.00	8	8	8	8	8	0	20.30	2
Cory, A. K.	43,539.00	8	8	8	8	10	8	20.60	1
Dunn, W. L.	43,225.00	8	8	10	8	8	0	20.50	1
Greg, S. P.	83,630.00	8	8	8	8	8	0	48.00	3
Norr, M. B.	44,985.00	8	8	8	8	8	4	20.40	3
Odin, N. B.	41,131.00	8	8	8	8	8	0	20.00	1
Rich, J. B.	6,529.00	8	8	8	8	8	4	19.50	1
Singh, P. W.	43,013.00	8	8	8	8	8	4	20.25	2

Taxable earnings for Social Security are based on the first $84,900. Taxable earnings for Medicare are based on all earnings. Taxable earnings for federal and state unemployment are based on the first $7,000.

Check Figure

Net Amount, $6,814.73

Instructions

1. Complete the payroll register, page 72, using the wage-bracket income tax withholding table in Figure 3 (page 268). The Social Security tax rate is 6.2 percent, and the Medicare tax rate is 1.45 percent. Assume that all employees are married. Greg's federal income tax is $240.

2. Prepare a general journal entry to record the payroll. The firm's general ledger contains a Wages Expense account and a Wages Payable account.

3. Assuming that the firm has transferred funds from its regular bank account to its special payroll bank account, and that this entry has been made, prepare a general journal entry to record the payment of wages. In the payroll register, begin payroll checks with number 945.

P.O. 1,4,5

Problem 8-4A The information for the Trago Company, shown in the chart below, is available from Trago's time cards and the employees' individual earnings records for the pay period ended December 22.

Name	Hours Worked	Earnings at End of Previous Week	Total Earnings	Class.	Federal Income Tax	Other Deduct.	
Cro, C. E.	44	32,950	1,750	Sales	203.00	UW	16.50
Dan, V. A.	40	37,410	1,850	Sales	216.00	AR	80.00
Finn, J. P.	40	36,860	1,838	Sales	208.00	UW	16.50
Gray, N. D.	44	32,490	1,735	Office	191.00	UW	15.00
Jory, J. W.	48	36,980	1,840	Office	213.00	UW	16.00
Lind, D. C.	40	84,240	2,000	Office	250.00	UW	12.00
Ming, R. G.	40	36,860	1,836	Sales	208.00	AR	54.00
Nye, P. M.	40	36,750	1,830	Sales	204.00	UW	16.00
Ott, T. B.	44	33,480	1,760	Sales	206.00	UW	16.50
Tory, K. C.	42	47,000	1,070	Sales	118.00	UW	18.00

Taxable earnings for Social Security are based on the first $84,900. Taxable earnings for Medicare are based on all earnings. Taxable earnings for federal and state unemployment are based on the first $7,000.

Check Figure

Net Amount, $13,975.12

Instructions

1. Complete the payroll register, page 56, using a Social Security tax rate of 6.2 percent and a Medicare tax rate of 1.45 percent. (The total of Social Security tax deduction and Medicare tax deduction for D. C. Lind is $69.92. Concerning Other Deductions, AR refers to Accounts Receivable and UW refers to United Way. Begin payroll checks in the payroll register with number 914.
2. Prepare the general journal entry to record the payroll.
3. Prepare the general journal entry to pay the payroll. Assume that funds for this payroll have been transferred to Cash—Payroll Bank Account and that this entry has been made.

PROBLEM SET B

For additional help, see the demonstration problem at the beginning of each chapter in your Working Papers.

P.O. 1,2,3

Problem 8-1B Ida Penn, an employee of Kellen Company, worked forty-four hours during the week of October 11 through 17. Her rate of pay is $18.50

per hour, and she receives time-and-a-half for all work in excess of forty hours per week. Penn is married and claims two allowances on her W-4 form. Her wages are subject to the following deductions:

a. Federal income tax (use the table in Figure 3, page 268).
b. Social Security tax at 6.2 percent.
c. Medicare tax at 1.45 percent.
d. Union dues, $25.25.
e. Medical insurance, $44.75.

Check Figure

Net pay, $634.90

Instructions

Compute her regular pay, overtime pay, gross pay, and net pay.

P.O. 1,2,4,5

Problem 8-2B Hagen Company has the following payroll information for the pay period ended May 14:

| Name | Earnings at End of Previous Week | Daily Time | | | | | | Pay Rate | Federal Income Tax |
		M	T	W	T	F	S		
Grim, N. C.	7,455.00	8	8	8	8	8	0	19.00	127.00
Hart, A. L.	6,513.00	8	8	8	8	8	0	18.50	133.00
Lord, D. R.	6,843.00	0	8	8	8	8	8	18.60	125.00
Moe, N. A.	9,536.00	8	8	8	0	8	8	19.80	141.00
Sorkin, B. M.	6,632.00	8	8	8	8	8	8	18.90	136.00
Tigh, P. R.	7,467.00	0	8	8	8	8	8	19.20	121.00

Taxable earnings for Social Security are based on the first $84,900. Taxable earnings for Medicare are based on all earnings. Taxable earnings for federal and state unemployment are based on the first $7,000. Employees are paid time-and-a-half for work in excess of forty hours per week.

Check Figure

Net Amount, $3,637.61

Instructions

1. Complete the payroll register, page 34. The Social Security tax rate is 6.2 percent, and the Medicare tax rate is 1.45 percent.
2. Prepare a general journal entry to record the payroll.
3. Assuming that the firm has transferred funds from its regular bank account to its special payroll bank account, and that this entry has been made, prepare a journal entry to record the payment of wages. Begin payroll checks with No. 744.

P.O. 1,2,3,4,5

Problem 8-3B The Worelle Company pays its employees time-and-a-half for hours worked in excess of forty per week. The information in the chart on page 288 is available from time cards and employees' individual earnings records for the pay period ended September 21.

Name	Earnings at End of Previous Week	Daily Time						Pay Rate	Income Tax Allowances
		M	T	W	T	F	S		
Bolt, A. C.	6,665.00	8	8	8	10	8	0	19.70	1
Drew, B. N.	35,430.00	8	8	8	8	8	0	24.90	2
Gill, A. J.	33,520.00	8	10	8	8	8	0	23.50	2
Iber, D. G.	83,956.00	8	8	8	8	8	4	52.00	3
Jenn, H. O.	34,655.00	8	8	8	8	8	0	24.50	0
Kelt, J. E.	28,827.00	8	8	9	8	8	0	19.50	2
Olin, D. W.	6,843.00	8	8	8	9	9	4	20.10	1
Wolf, W. L.	26,386.00	8	8	10	8	8	0	20.20	1

Taxable earnings for Social Security are based on the first $84,900. Taxable earnings for Medicare are based on all earnings. Taxable earnings for federal and state unemployment are based on the first $7,000.

Check Figure

Net Amount, $7,482.20

Instructions

1. Complete the payroll register, page 72, using the wage-bracket income tax withholding table in Figure 3 (page 268). The Social Security tax rate is 6.2 percent, and the Medicare tax rate is 1.45 percent. Assume that all employees are married. Iber's federal income tax deduction is $130.
2. Prepare a general journal entry to record the payroll. The firm's general ledger contains a Wages Expense account and a Wages Payable account.
3. Assuming that the firm has transferred funds from its regular bank account to its special payroll bank account, and that this entry has been made, prepare a general journal entry to record the payment of wages. In the payroll register, begin payroll checks with Ck. No. 863.

P.O. 1,4,5

Problem 8-4B For the Marley Company, the information in the chart on the following page is available from the time books and employees' individual earnings records for the pay period ended December 29.

Taxable earnings for Social Security are based on the first $84,900. Taxable earnings for Medicare are based on all earnings. Taxable earnings for federal and state unemployment are based on the first $7,000.

Check Figure

Net Amount, $13,645.82

Instructions

1. Complete the payroll register, page 56, using a Social Security tax rate of 6.2 percent and a Medicare tax rate of 1.45 percent. (The total of Social Security tax deduction and Medicare tax deduction for D. C. Long is $57.74.) Concerning Other Deductions, AR refers to Accounts Receivable, and UW refers to United Way. Begin payroll checks in the payroll register with check no. 914.

Name	Hours Worked	Earnings at End of Previous Week	Total Earnings	Class.	Federal Income Tax	Other Deduct.	
Choy, C. E.	44	33,700	1,750.00	Sales	179.00	AR	75.00
Diggs, V. A.	42	38,260	1,910.00	Sales	211.00	UW	16.50
Fenn, J. P.	40	37,698	1,838.00	Sales	199.00	UW	16.50
Grant, N. D.	44	33,225	1,735.00	Office	185.00		——
John, J. W.	48	37,820	1,840.00	Office	288.00	UW	16.00
Long, D. C.	40	84,350	1,630.00	Office	295.00	UW	12.00
Mort, R. G.	43	37,696	1,926.00	Sales	205.00	UW	16.00
Nat, P. M.	40	37,580	1,830.00	Sales	207.00		——
Orr, T. B.	44	34,240	1,760.00	Sales	196.00	AR	16.50
Tye, K. C.	42	48,070	1,070.00	Sales	236.00	UW	18.00

2. Prepare the general journal entry to record the payroll.
3. Prepare the general journal entry to pay the payroll. Assume that funds for this payroll have been transferred to Cash—Payroll Bank Account and that this entry has been made.

9 Employer Taxes, Payments, and Reports

Performance Objectives

After you have completed this chapter, you will be able to do the following:

1. Calculate the amount of payroll tax expense and journalize the related entry.

2. Journalize the entry for the deposit of employees' federal income taxes withheld and FICA taxes (both employees' withheld and employer's matching share) and prepare the deposit coupon.

3. Journalize the entries for the payment of employer's state and federal unemployment taxes.

4. Journalize the entry for the deposit of employees' state income taxes withheld.

5. Complete Employer's Quarterly Federal Tax Return, Form 941.

6. Prepare W-2 and W-3 forms and Form 940.

7. Calculate the premium for workers' compensation insurance, and prepare the entry for payment in advance.

8. Determine the amount of the end-of-the-year adjustments for (a) workers' compensation insurance and (b) accrued salaries and wages, and record the adjustments.

We have talked about computing and recording such payroll data as gross pay, employees' income tax withheld, employees' FICA tax withheld, and various deductions requested by employees. Now we will pay these withholding liabilities and the taxes levied on the employer based on the total payroll.

EMPLOYER IDENTIFICATION NUMBER

Everyone who works must have a Social Security number, a vital part of federal income tax returns. An employer's counterpart to the Social Security number is the **employer identification number** assigned by the Internal Revenue Service. Employers of one or more persons are required to have such a number, and it must be listed on all reports and payments of employees' federal income tax withholding and FICA taxes.

EMPLOYER'S PAYROLL TAXES

An employer's payroll taxes are based on the gross wages paid to employees. Payroll taxes—like property taxes—are an expense of doing business. Greg Company records these taxes in the **Payroll Tax Expense** account and debits the account for the company's portion of FICA taxes and for state and federal unemployment taxes. In T account form, Payroll Tax Expense for Greg Company would look like the following example.

Payroll Tax Expense

+	−
FICA tax (employer's matching portion) State unemployment tax Federal unemployment tax	Closed at the end of the year along with all other expense accounts

The skyrocketing costs of Medicare have caused Congress to try to make sweeping reforms. The issues are far-reaching. Medicare affects a large percentage of the population—who fear their benefits may be reduced.

As you can see, **FICA tax (employer's share), state unemployment tax, and federal unemployment tax are included under the umbrella of Payroll Tax Expense.** In most states, the unemployment taxes are levied on the employer only.

Employer's Matching Portion of FICA Tax (Social Security Plus Medicare)

FICA tax is imposed equally on both employer and employee. After the firm's accountant deducts the employee's share from gross wages and records it in the payroll entry under FICA Tax Payable, he or she then determines the employer's share by multiplying the employer's tax rates (assumed to be 6.2 percent for Social Security and 1.45 percent for Medicare) by the taxable earnings (assumed to be a maximum of $84,900 for Social Security and all earnings for Medicare). The same tax rates apply to both the employer and the employees.

The accountant gets the Social Security and Medicare taxable earnings amounts from the payroll register. In Figure 1, on the following page, we present the Taxable Earnings columns taken from the payroll register for the week ended October 7.

Amount of employees'
earnings for the period
that has not, as yet,
been taxed as part of the
$7,000 maximum liability

Amount of employees'
earnings that are less
than $84,900 per
employee for the year

Amount of
all employees'
earnings

	NAME	TOTAL HOURS	TOTAL	ENDING CUMULATIVE EARNINGS	(7) TAXABLE EARNINGS UNEMPLOYMENT	SOCIAL SECURITY	MEDICARE
1	Asino, Matte E.	46	1119.16	34009.16		1119.16	1119.16
2	Boritsky, Olga	45	735.30	6927.30	735.30	735.30	735.30
3	Dray, Greg G.	49	915.65	7761.65	154.00	915.65	915.65
4	Foulkes, Bob L.	40	1073.25	39710.25		1073.25	1073.25
5	Groyer, Milli K.	40	1888.89	69888.89		1888.89	1888.89
6	Kramer, Ada A.	40	1891.67	69991.67		1891.67	1891.67
7	Minkowitz, John L.	55	1598.96	38438.96		1598.96	1598.96
8	Orleons, Janet C.	40	1271.75	47054.75		1271.75	1271.75
9	Pinkovich, Mark S.	44	1500.43	48470.43		1500.43	1500.43
10	Romero, Sheila J.	45	1813.51	56791.51		1813.51	1813.51
11	Tivoli, Jake T.	40	1168.83	43246.83		1168.83	1168.83
12	Wilson, Sharlet D.	52	2886.24	87486.24		300.00	2886.24
13			17863.64	549777.64	889.30	15277.40	17863.64

FIGURE 1

Employer's state
unemployment tax
$889.30 × .054 = $48.02

Employer's
Social Security tax
$15,277.40 × .062 = $947.21

Employer's
Medicare tax
$17,863.64 × .0145 =
$259.03

Employer's federal
unemployment tax
$889.30 × .008 = $7.11

Combined Employer's FICA tax
($947.21 + $259.03) = $1,206.24

Before we look at the journal entry to record the employer's share of FICA tax, let's look at the entry in T account form.

Note particularly that the FICA Tax Payable account is often used for both the tax liability of the employer and the amounts withheld from the employees. This is logical because both FICA taxes are paid at the same time and to the same place. There may be a slight difference between the employer's and the employees' share of FICA taxes because of the rounding process. For the employees' share, the accountant uses the total of the employees' Social Security and Medicare tax deductions. For the employer's share, the accountant multiplies the total taxable earnings (Social Security and Medicare) by the tax rates.

Employer's State Unemployment Tax

The state unemployment tax (SUTA) **is levied only on the employer in most states, the proceeds to be used to pay subsistence benefits to unemployed workers.** The rate of the state unemployment tax varies considerably among the states. Assume that Greg Company is subject to a rate of 5.4 percent of the first $7,000 of each employee's earnings (the same base amount as for the federal unemployment tax). As shown in the portion of the payroll register illustrated in Figure 1, $889.30 of earnings are subject to the state unemployment tax. Accordingly, by T accounts, the state unemployment tax based on taxable earnings is as follows.

Payroll Tax Expense		State Unemployment Tax Payable	
+	−	−	+
(889.30 × .054)			(889.30 × .054)
48.02			48.02

Employer's Federal Unemployment Tax

The federal unemployment tax (FUTA) **is paid only by the employer.** Congress may from time to time change the rate. Let's assume a rate of 0.8 percent (.008) of the first $7,000 earned by each employee during the calendar year. For the weekly payroll period for Greg Company, the tax liability is $7.11 ($889.30 of unemployment taxable earnings, taken from the payroll register, multiplied by .008, the tax rate). The T account is as follows:

Payroll Tax Expense		Federal Unemployment Tax Payable	
+	−	−	+
(889.30 × .008)			(889.30 × .008)
7.11			7.11

OBJECTIVE 1
Calculate the amount of payroll tax expense and journalize the related entry.

To make things clearer, figures for the employer's three payroll taxes have been presented separately. Now let's combine all of this information into one entry, which follows the regular payroll entry. Greg Company pays its employees weekly, so it also makes its Payroll Tax Expense entry weekly.

	DATE		DESCRIPTION	POST. REF.	DEBIT	CREDIT	
17	Oct.	7	Payroll Tax Expense		1 2 6 1 37		17
18			FICA Tax Payable			1 2 0 6 24	18
19			State Unemployment Tax				19
20			Payable			4 8 02	20
21			Federal Unemployment Tax				21
22			Payable			7 11	22
23			To record employer's share				23
24			of FICA tax and employer's				24
25			state and federal				25
26			unemployment taxes.				26
27							27
28							28

JOURNAL ENTRIES FOR RECORDING PAYROLL

At this point, let's restate in general journal form the entries that have already been recorded. We'll do this so that you can see the sequence of the payroll entries. First, the entry to record the payroll is journalized.

	DATE		DESCRIPTION	POST. REF.	DEBIT	CREDIT	
1	20–						1
2	Oct.	7	Sales Wages Expense		13 6 2 6 97		2
3			Office Wages Expense		4 2 3 6 67		3
4			Employees' Federal Income				4
5			Tax Payable			3 2 3 9 00	5
6			FICA Tax Payable			1 2 0 6 24	6
7			Employees' State Income Tax				7
8			Payable			6 4 7 80	8
9			Employees' Medical Insurance				9
10			Payable			2 6 0 50	10
11			Employees' United Way				11
12			Payable			1 2 4 00	12
13			Accounts Receivable			5 0 00	13
14			Wages Payable			12 3 3 6 10	14
15			Payroll register, page 68,				15
16			for week ended October 7.				16
17							17

Next, the entry to record the employer's payroll taxes is journalized.

REMEMBER!
The sequence of steps for recording the payroll entries is: (1) record the payroll for the present period in the payroll register; (2) based on the payroll register, record the payroll entry in the journal; (3) based on the Taxable Earnings columns of the payroll register, record Payroll Tax Expense in the journal; (4) make a journal entry to pay the employees.

	DATE		DESCRIPTION	POST. REF.	DEBIT	CREDIT	
17		7	Payroll Tax Expense		1 2 6 1 37		17
18			FICA Tax Payable			1 2 0 6 24	18
19			State Unemployment Tax				19
20			Payable			4 8 02	20
21			Federal Unemployment Tax				21
22			Payable			7 11	22
23			To record employer's share				23
24			of FICA tax and employer's				24
25			state and federal				25
26			unemployment taxes.				26
27							27

Finally, the entry to pay the employees is journalized. Greg Company issues one check payable to a payroll bank account. To pay its employees, it will draw separate payroll checks on this payroll account. (The entry to transfer cash to the payroll bank account is not shown here.)

DATE		DESCRIPTION	POST. REF.	DEBIT	CREDIT	
27	8	Wages Payable		12 3 3 6 10		27
28		Cash—Payroll Bank Account			12 3 3 6 10	28
29		Paid salaries for week				29
30		ended October 7.				30
31						31

As stated previously, in the first payroll entry, small employers will credit Cash directly instead of Wages Payable. These employers issue separate checks out of their regular bank accounts for each employee.

Next, we describe the entries for paying withholdings for employees' federal income tax and FICA tax and the employer's matching share of FICA tax. We also show the entries for paying the federal and state unemployment taxes and the withholdings for employees' state income tax.

PAYMENTS OF FICA TAX AND EMPLOYEES' FEDERAL INCOME TAX WITHHOLDING

OBJECTIVE 2
Journalize the entry for the deposit of employees' federal income taxes withheld and FICA taxes (both employees' withheld and employer's matching share) and prepare the deposit coupon.

FYI
There are penalties applied for late deposits of federal taxes.

After paying employees, the employer must make payments in the form of federal tax deposits. A deposit includes the combined total of three items: (1) employees' federal income taxes withheld, (2) employees' FICA taxes withheld, and (3) employer's share of FICA taxes. Employers make these deposits on a pay-as-you-go basis.

Deposits are made to authorized commercial banks or Federal Reserve banks. The deposits are forwarded to the U.S. Treasury. The timing of these deposits depends on the amounts owed. The calendar year is broken into days, semiweekly periods, months, and **quarters** (3 consecutive months).

Employers submit a return, Form 941, every quarter. The due dates for filing this return are as follows:

Quarter	Ending Date of Quarter	Due Date for Form 941
January–February–March	March 31	April 30
April–May–June	June 30	July 31
July–August–September	September 30	October 31
October–November–December	December 31	January 31

Federal Tax Deposit Coupon

FYI
We will show a Form 941 later in this chapter.

Let's go back to Greg Company, where taxes were previously paid up to date. From the payroll of October 7, the following federal taxes are owed:

Employees' federal income taxes withheld	$3,239.00
Employees' FICA taxes withheld	1,206.24
Employer's share of FICA taxes	1,206.24
Total federal undeposited taxes	$5,651.48

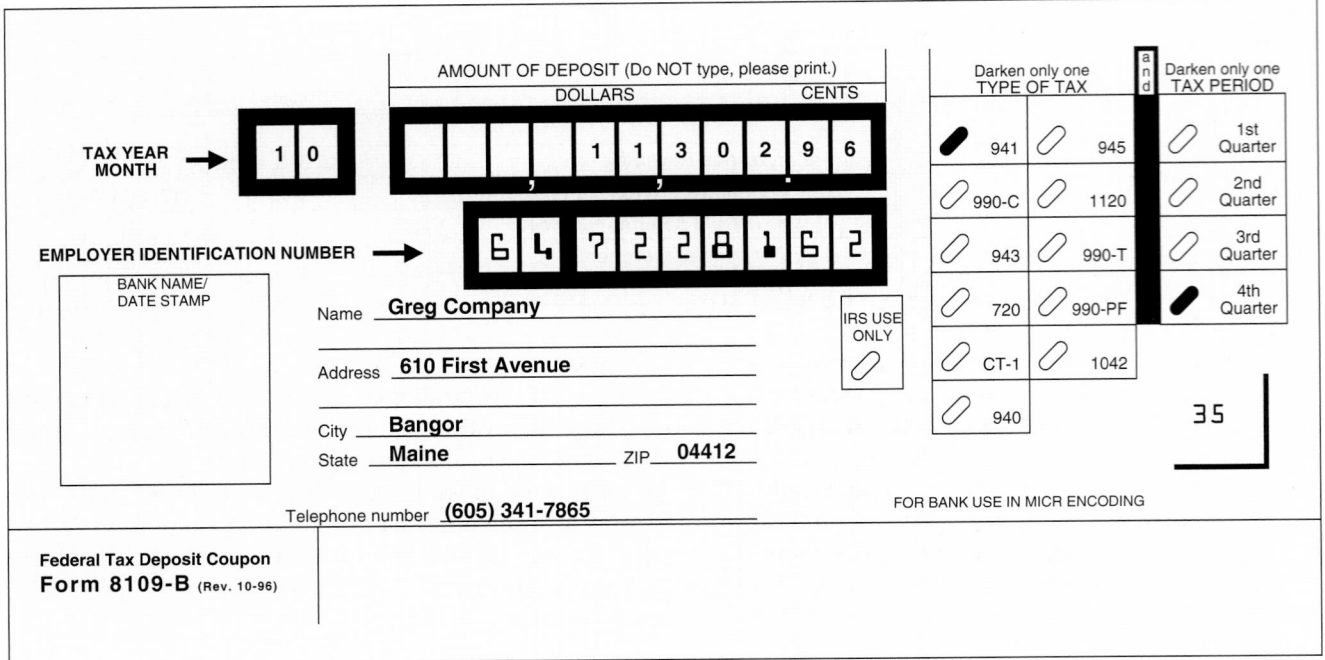

FIGURE 2

We continue on for the next payroll period, ended October 14:

	Oct. 7	Oct. 14	Total
Employees' federal income taxes withheld	$3,239.00	$3,239.00	$ 6,478.00
Employees' FICA taxes withheld	1,206.24	1,206.24	2,412.48
Employer's share of FICA taxes	1,206.24	1,206.24	2,412.48
Total federal undeposited taxes	$5,651.48	$5,651.48	$11,302.96

Greg Company, which deposits monthly, receives a federal tax deposit card (printed with the company's name and tax number) from the Internal Revenue Service (Figure 2).

The accountant records the amount of the deposit, the employer identification number, the type of tax, the tax period, and the name and address of the company. The entry in general journal form to record the deposit of two weeks' taxes looks like the following.

FYI

Because of rounding differences, the employee and employer amounts of FICA taxes may differ slightly. Line 9 of the 941 Form accommodates this difference.

	DATE		DESCRIPTION	POST. REF.	DEBIT	CREDIT	
1	20–						1
2	Nov.	15	Employees' Federal Income Tax				2
3			Payable		6 4 7 8 00		3
4			FICA Tax Payable		4 8 2 4 96		4
5			Cash			11 3 0 2 96	5
6			Issued check for federal tax				6
7			deposit, Bangor Bank.				7
8							8

Employers must deposit the taxes they withhold from employees' paychecks, as well as the employer's share of FICA taxes, in an authorized commercial bank or Federal Reserve bank. These deposits are then forwarded to the U.S. Treasury.

PAYMENTS OF STATE UNEMPLOYMENT INSURANCE

OBJECTIVE 3
Journalize the entries for the payment of employer's state and federal unemployment taxes.

As we stated before, states differ with regard to both the rate and the taxable base for unemployment insurance. In our example, we assume that the state tax is 5.4 percent of the first $7,000 paid to each employee during the calendar year. **The state tax is usually paid quarterly and is due by the end of the month following the end of the quarter (the same as the due dates for Form 941).** Here's the entry in general journal form made by Greg Company for the first quarter (covering the months of January, February, and March). We assume that $60,436 was taxable for the quarter. The amount of the tax is $3,263.54 ($60,436 × 0.054).

	DATE		DESCRIPTION	POST. REF.	DEBIT	CREDIT	
1	20–						1
2	Apr.	30	State Unemployment Tax				2
3			Payable		3 2 6 3 54		3
4			Cash			3 2 6 3 54	4
5			Issued check for payment of				5
6			state unemployment tax.				6
7							7

The T accounts are as follows:

Cash		State Unemployment Tax Payable	
+	−	−	+
	Apr. 30 3,263.54	Apr. 30 3,263.54	Mar. 31 Balance 3,263.54

The balance in State Unemployment Tax Payable is the result of weekly entries recording the state unemployment portion of payroll tax expense.

PAYMENTS OF FEDERAL UNEMPLOYMENT TAX

The FUTA tax is calculated quarterly, during the month following the end of each calendar quarter and is used to administer the funds. **If the accumulated tax liability is greater than $100, the tax is deposited in a commercial bank or Federal Reserve bank, accompanied by a preprinted federal tax deposit card** like that used to deposit employees' federal income tax withholding and FICA taxes. The due date for this deposit is the last day of the month following the end of the quarter, the same as the due dates for the Employer's Quarterly Federal Tax Return and for state unemployment taxes.

Here is the entry in general journal form made by Greg Company for the first quarter. In our example, since the FUTA and state unemployment taxable earnings are the same (the first $7,000 for each employee), we assume that $60,436 was taxable for the quarter. The amount of the tax is $483.49 ($60,436 × 0.008).

	DATE		DESCRIPTION	POST. REF.	DEBIT	CREDIT	
1	20–						1
2	Apr.	30	Federal Unemployment Tax				2
3			Payable		4 8 3 49		3
4			Cash			4 8 3 49	4
5			Issued check for deposit of				5
6			federal unemployment tax.				6
7							7

The T accounts are as follows:

Cash			Federal Unemployment Tax Payable		
+	–		–	+	
	Apr. 30	483.49		Mar. 31	
			Apr. 30	483.49	Balance	483.49

The balance in Federal Unemployment Tax Payable is the result of weekly entries recording the federal unemployment portion of payroll tax expense.

DEPOSITS OF EMPLOYEES' STATE INCOME TAX WITHHOLDING

OBJECTIVE 4
Journalize the entry for the deposit of employees' state income taxes withheld.

Assume that the withholdings for employees' state income taxes are deposited on a quarterly basis, payable at the same time as state unemployment tax. Also, as of March 31, the credit balance of Employees' State Income Tax Payable is $1,526.08. The entry in general journal form to record the payment for the first quarter looks like the following form.

	DATE		DESCRIPTION	POST. REF.	DEBIT	CREDIT	
1	20–						1
2	Apr.	30	Employees' State Income Tax				2
3			Payable		1 5 2 6 08		3
4			Cash			1 5 2 6 08	4
5			Issued check for state				5
6			income tax deposit.				6
7							7

The T accounts are as follows:

Cash			Employees' State Income Tax Payable		
+	–			–	+
	Apr. 30	1,526.08			Mar. 31
			Apr. 30 1,526.08		Balance 1,526.08

EMPLOYER'S QUARTERLY FEDERAL TAX RETURN (FORM 941)

OBJECTIVE 5
Complete Employer's Quarterly Federal Tax Return, Form 941.

The purpose of **Form 941** is to report the tax liability for withholdings of employees' federal income tax and FICA taxes, and also the employer's share of FICA taxes. Total tax deposits are also listed. As the title implies, the time period is three months. Remember that the due dates for the calendar year are: first quarter, April 30; second quarter, July 31; third quarter, October 31; fourth quarter, January 31.

A completed Form 941 for Greg Company is shown in Figure 3 on page 300. Note that there are three main sections, which may be completed in the order presented below. (The Internal Revenue Service has frequently changed the arrangement and questions on Form 941.)

Heading

Once an employer has secured an identification number and has filed her or his first return, the Internal Revenue Service sends forms directly to the employer. These forms have the employer's name, address, and identification number filled in.

Monthly Summary of Federal Tax Liability

For each month, list the combined total of employees' federal income and FICA taxes withheld and employer's share of FICA.

Questions Listed on Form 941 (Figure 3)

Read each question line by line.

1. Total number of employees.
2. Total wages and tips, plus other compensation, subject to federal tax withholding.

Form **941** (Rev. October 2000) Department of the Treasury Internal Revenue Service	**Employer's Quarterly Federal Tax Return** ▶ See separate instructions for information on completing this return. Please type or print.	

OMB No. 1545-0029

Enter state code for state in which deposits were made ONLY if different from state in address to the right ▶ ☐⋮ (see page 2 of instructions).

Name (as distinguished from trade name)

Trade name, if any
Greg Company

Address (number and street)
610 First Avenue

Date quarter ended
December 31, 20—

Employer identification number
64-7228162

City, state, and ZIP code
Bangor, Maine 04412

T	
FF	
FD	
FP	
I	
T	

If address is different from prior return, check here ▶ ☐

IRS Use

1 1 1 1 1 1 1 1 1 1   2   3 3 3 3 3 3 3   4 4   5 5 5
6   7   8 8 8 8 8 8 8   9 9 9 9 9   10 10 10 10 10 10 10 10 10 10

If you do not have to file returns in the future, check here ▶ ☐ and enter date final wages paid ▶ _____

If you are a seasonal employer, see **Seasonal employers** on page 1 of the instructions and check here ▶ ☐

1	Number of employees in the pay period that includes March 12th . ▶	**1**	12	
2	Total wages and tips, plus other compensation	**2**	216,252	00
3	Total income tax withheld from wages, tips, and sick pay	**3**	39,768	00
4	Adjustment of withheld income tax for preceding quarters of calendar year	**4**	—	
5	Adjusted total of income tax withheld (line 3 as adjusted by line 4—see instructions) . . .	**5**	39,768	00

6	Taxable social security wages	**6a**	130,080	00	× 12.4% (.124) =	**6b**	16,129	92
	Taxable social security tips	**6c**			× 12.4% (.124) =	**6d**	—	
7	Taxable Medicare wages and tips . . .	**7a**	216,252	00	× 2.9% (.029) =	**7b**	6,271	31

8	Total social security and Medicare taxes (add lines 6b, 6d, and 7b). Check here if wages are not subject to social security and/or Medicare tax . . . . ▶ ☐	**8**	22,401	23
9	Adjustment of social security and Medicare taxes (see instructions for required explanation) Sick Pay $ _____ ± Fractions of Cents $ _____ ± Other $ _____ =	**9**	—	
10	Adjusted total of social security and Medicare taxes (line 8 as adjusted by line 9—see instructions)	**10**	22,401	23
11	**Total taxes** (add lines 5 and 10)	**11**	62,169	23
12	Advance earned income credit (EIC) payments made to employees	**12**	—	
13	Net taxes (subtract line 12 from line 11). **If $1,000 or more, this must equal line 17, column (d) below (or line D of Schedule B (Form 941))**	**13**	62,169	23
14	Total deposits for quarter, including overpayment applied from a prior quarter	**14**	62,169	23
15	**Balance due** (subtract line 14 from line 13). See instructions	**15**	—0—	
16	**Overpayment.** If line 14 is more than line 13, enter excess here ▶ $ _____			

and check if to be: ☐ Applied to next return **OR** ☐ Refunded.

- **All filers:** If line 13 is less than $1,000, you need not complete line 17 or Schedule B (Form 941).
- **Semiweekly schedule depositors:** Complete Schedule B (Form 941) and check here . . . . ▶ ☐
- **Monthly schedule depositors:** Complete line 17, columns (a) through (d), and check here . . . . . . ▶ ☑

17	**Monthly Summary of Federal Tax Liability.** Do not complete if you were a semiweekly schedule depositor.			
	(a) First month liability	**(b)** Second month liability	**(c)** Third month liability	**(d)** Total liability for quarter
	18,236.45	20,956.56	22,976.22	62,169.23

Sign Here

Under penalties of perjury, I declare that I have examined this return, including accompanying schedules and statements, and to the best of my knowledge and belief, it is true, correct, and complete.

Signature ▶ *Ellen D. Greg*   Print Your Name and Title ▶ *Ellen D. Greg, Owner*   Date ▶ *Jan. 31, 20—*

For Privacy Act and Paperwork Reduction Act Notice, see back of form.   Cat. No. 17001Z   Form **941** (Rev. 10-2000)

FIGURE 3

3. Total federal income tax withheld—shown as credits in the Employees' Federal Income Tax Payable account.
4. Adjustment of withheld income tax for preceding quarters of calendar year.
5. Adjusted total of income tax withheld—the total of income tax withheld after any adjustment for withheld income tax for preceding quarters.
6. Taxable Social Security wages paid—total of the Social Security Taxable Earnings listed in the payroll register for the three-month quarter; 12.4 percent equals the employees' 6.2 percent plus the employer's 6.2 percent.

   Taxable Social Security tips—refers to customer tips reported by employees; the employer withholds 6.2 percent.
7. Taxable Medicare wages and tips—total of the Medicare Taxable Earnings listed in the payroll register for the three-month quarter; 2.9 percent equals the employees' 1.45 percent plus the employer's 1.45 percent.
8. Total Social Security and Medicare taxes—shown as credits in the FICA Tax Payable account.
9. Adjustment of Social Security and Medicare taxes—used to record corrections in Social Security taxes reported on earlier returns and for rounding differences.
10. Adjusted total of Social Security and Medicare taxes.
11. Total taxes—the total of various taxes withheld from employees' pay and the taxes imposed on the employer.
12. Advance earned income credit (EIC) payments—payments made in advance to qualified employees for earned income credit. For qualifying low-income taxpayers, the earned income credit is a deduction from income tax owed.
13. Net taxes—the total federal tax liability for the quarter (this is the same amount as the total of the Monthly Summary of Federal Tax Liability section).
14. Total deposits for quarter—total of the debits to the Employees' Federal Income Tax Payable and the FICA Tax Payable accounts for the three-month quarter.
15. Balance due.
16. Overpayment.

The amount of wages subject to tax may differ in blocks 2, 6, and 7. Qualified employee contributions to retirement plans, such as 401k and 403b plans, reduce the amount of wages subject to federal income tax but not Social Security tax or Medicare tax. Whether employee retirement contributions reduce taxable state and local wages depends upon the appropriate state and local laws.

Wage Withholding Statements for Employees (Form W-2)

OBJECTIVE 6
Prepare W-2 and W-3 forms and Form 940.

After the end of a year (December 31) and by the following January 31, the employer must furnish for each employee a Wage and Tax Statement, known as **Form W-2**. This form contains information about the employee's earnings and tax deductions for the year. The source of the information used to complete Form W-2 is the employee's individual earnings record. The amounts used to complete Matte E. Asino's W-2 form (in Figure 4 on page 302) represent the amounts taken from his earnings record at the end of the calendar year, December 31.

a Control number				Safe, accurate, FAST! Use	IRS e-file	Visit the IRS Web Site at **www.irs.gov**.

b Employer identification number 64-7228162	**1** Wages, tips, other compensation 46,330 **2** Federal income tax withheld 8,573

OMB No. 1545-0008

c Employer's name, address, and ZIP code

Greg Company
610 First Avenue
Bangor, Maine 04412

3 Social security wages 46,330	**4** Social security tax withheld 2,872.46
5 Medicare wages and tips 46,330	**6** Medicare tax withheld 671.79
7 Social security tips 0	**8** Allocated tips

d Employee's social security number
543-24-1680

9 Advance EIC payment 0	**10** Dependent care benefits 0

e Employee's first name and initial   Last name

Matte E. Asino
6243 Baxter Drive
Bangor, Maine 04412

11 Nonqualified plans 0	**12a** See instructions for box 12
13 Statutory employee ☐ Retirement plan ☐ Third-party sick pay ☐	**12b**
14 Other	**12c**
	12d

f Employee's address and ZIP code

15 State Employer's 'state ID number 464-729	**16** State wages, tips, etc. 46,330	**17** State income tax 1,715	**18** Local wages, tips, etc. 0	**19** Local income tax 0	**20** Locality name 0

Form **W-2** **Wage and Tax Statement**
20___
Department of the Treasury—Internal Revenue Service

Copy B To Be Filed with Employee s FEDERAL Tax Return.
This information is being furnished to the Internal Revenue Service.

FIGURE 4

Block 9 shows the total paid to the employee as advance earned income credit (EIC) payments. Block 13 is used for miscellaneous items, such as sick pay that is not included in income because the employee contributed to the sick pay plan. This box is also used for employer-provided group term life insurance in excess of $50,000. Box 14 may include the value of noncash fringe benefits, such as providing a vehicle for the employee. In box 13, statutory employees are life insurance and traveling salespersons, and legal representatives include attorneys and parents.

The accountant will prepare at least four copies of the W-2 form for each employee.

Copy A—Employer sends to the Social Security Administration.
Copy B—Employer gives to employee to be attached to the employee's individual federal income tax return.
Copy C—Employer gives to employee to be kept for his or her personal records.
Copy D—Employer keeps this copy as a record of payments made.

If state and local income taxes are withheld, the employer prepares additional copies to be sent to the appropriate tax agency.

FYI

A copy is also sent (if applicable) to the state and/or local tax department, and a copy is given to the employee to attach to the state/local tax return.

Employer's Annual Federal Income Tax Reports (Form W-3)

Accompanying copy A of the employees' W-2 forms, Greg Company sends Form W-3, Transmittal of Wage and Tax Statements, to the Social Security Administration. This form is due on February 28, following the end of the calendar year.

For all employees, Form W-3 shows the total wages and tips, total federal income tax withheld, total Social Security and Medicare taxable wages, total Social Security and Medicare tax withheld, and other information. These amounts must be the same as the grand totals of the W-2 forms and the four quarterly 941 forms for the year. Greg Company's completed Form W-3 is presented in Figure 5.

FIGURE 5

DO NOT STAPLE

a Control number	33333	For Official Use Only ▶ OMB No. 1545-0008		
b Kind of Payer ▶	941 [X] Military [ ] 943 [ ] CT-1 [ ] Hshld. emp. [ ] Medicare govt. emp. [ ]	1 Wages, tips, other compensation **865,008**	2 Federal income tax withheld **103,801**	
		3 Social security wages **778,836**	4 Social security tax withheld **48,287.83**	
c Total number of Forms W-2 **12**	d Establishment number ———	5 Medicare wages and tips **865,008**	6 Medicare tax withheld **12,542.62**	
e Employer identification number **64-7228162**		7 Social security tips **0**	8 Allocated tips **0**	
f Employer's name **Greg Company**		9 Advance EIC payments **0**	10 Dependent care benefits **0**	
610 First Avenue **Bangor, Maine 04412**		11 Nonqualified plans **0**	12 Deferred compensation **0**	
		13		
		14		
g Employer's address and ZIP code				
h Other EIN used this year **0**		15 Income tax withheld by third-party payer **0**		
i Employer's state I.D. no. **464-729**				

Contact person **Ellen D. Greg**	Telephone number **(605) 341-7865**	Fax number **(605) 341-1463**	E-mail address **GregCo@not.com**

Under penalties of perjury, I declare that I have examined this return and accompanying documents, and, to the best of my knowledge and belief, they are true, correct, and complete.

Signature ▶ *Ellen D. Greg*   Title ▶ *Owner*   Date ▶ *2/27/20—*

Form **W-3** Transmittal of Wage and Tax Statements 2 0 ___   Department of the Treasury Internal Revenue Service

Send this entire page with the entire Copy A page of Forms W-2 to the Social Security Administration. Photocopies are NOT acceptable.
Do not send any remittance (cash, checks, money orders, etc.) with FORMS W-2 and W-3.

Some boxes deserve an explanation. Box d, establishment number, may be used for a company that has separate establishments, with each establishment filing W-2 and W-3 forms separately. Box 9 is used for recording the amount of advance earned income credits shown on W-2 forms for qualified employees. Box h is used by a company that had more than one employer identification number (EIN) during the year.

To sum up thus far: The employer must submit the following at the end of the calendar year: Employer's Quarterly Federal Tax Return, Form 941, for the fourth quarter by January 31; Wage and Tax Statements, Form W-2, for all employees by January 31; Transmittal of Wage and Tax Statements, Form W-3, by February 28.

REPORTS AND PAYMENTS OF FEDERAL UNEMPLOYMENT TAX

REMEMBER!
If the accumulated FUTA tax liability at the end of a quarter is greater than $100, a deposit must be made.

As we stated previously, generally all employers are subject to the Federal Unemployment Tax Act. These employers must submit an Employer's Annual Federal Unemployment Tax Return, Form 940, not later than January 31 following the close of the calendar year. This deadline may be extended until February 10 if the employer has made deposits paying the FUTA tax liability in full. **Form 940** shows total wages paid to employees, total wages subject to federal unemployment tax, and other information.

Using Greg Company as our example, federal unemployment taxable earnings by quarter are as follows:

Federal Unemployment Tax	1st Quarter	2nd Quarter	3rd Quarter	4th Quarter	Cumulative Total
Taxable earnings	$60,436	$9,536	$10,427	$3,601	$84,000
Tax rate	× .008	× .008	× .008	× .008	× .008
Tax liability	$483.49	$76.29	$ 83.42	$28.81*	$672.00

* Rounding

We now repeat the journal entry for the first quarter, in which $483.49 was deposited on April 30.

	DATE		DESCRIPTION	POST. REF.	DEBIT	CREDIT	
1	20–						1
2	Apr.	30	Federal Unemployment Tax				2
3			Payable		4 8 3 49		3
4			Cash			4 8 3 49	4
5			Issued check for deposit of				5
6			federal unemployment tax.				6
7							7

During the second quarter, many employees' total earnings passed the $7,000 limit of taxable earnings, and the firm's tax liability was reduced accordingly. Because Greg's total accumulated liability ($76.29) was less than $100, a deposit covering that quarter was not made. However, because of an expansion of the company, three new employees were hired during the middle of the quarter.

For the third quarter, the tax liability amounted to $83.42. The total cumulative tax liability was now $159.71 ($76.29 second quarter plus $83.42 third quarter). Consequently, $159.71 was deposited on October 31.

By the end of the fourth quarter, each of the twelve employees' earnings passed the $7,000 mark. The total liability for the quarter is $28.80. This amount will be paid by January 31, accompanied by the completed Employer's Annual Federal Unemployment Tax Return, Form 940.

The T account for Federal Unemployment Tax Payable follows. The credits to the account were part of the entries to record the federal unemployment tax portion of Payroll Tax Expense for each payroll period.

Federal Unemployment Tax Payable

	−	+	
Apr. 30 deposit	483.49	1st quarter (liability)	483.49
Oct. 31 deposit	159.71	2nd quarter (liability)	76.29
		3rd quarter (liability)	83.42
Jan. 31 deposit	28.80	4th quarter (liability)	28.80

Employer's Annual Federal Unemployment (FUTA) Tax Return (Form 940)

Figure 6, on page 306, shows a completed Form 940-EZ for Greg Company. This form has three sections. (Bear in mind that this form changes from time to time.)

Part I   Line 1   Record total wages paid.

Line 2   Record certain exempt wages—this includes such items as agricultural labor, family employment, and the value of meals and lodging.

Line 3   Record exempt wages paid—wages paid to each employee over and above $7,000 for the calendar year.

Line 4   Total exempt payments.

Line 5   Total taxable wages.

Line 6   Computation of tax due.

Line 7   Total FUTA tax deposited.

Line 8   Balance due.

Line 9   Overpayment.

Part II   Record of Quarterly Federal Unemployment Tax Liability.

Form **940-EZ**	**Employer's Annual Federal Unemployment (FUTA) Tax Return**	OMB No. 1545-1110

Department of the Treasury
Internal Revenue Service   (99)

▶ See separate **Instructions for Form 940-EZ** for information on completing this form.

20 _ _

	T	
	FF	
	FD	
	FP	
	I	
	T	

Name (as distinguished from trade name)

Calendar year
20—

Trade name, if any
Greg Company

Address and ZIP code
**610 First Avenue
Bangor, Maine 04412**

Employer identification number
64 ⋮ 7228162

Answer the questions under **Who May Use Form 940-EZ** *on page 2. If you cannot use Form 940-EZ, you must use Form 940.*

A   Enter the amount of contributions paid to your state unemployment fund. (See separate instructions.) . . . ▶ $ ....

B   (1) Enter the name of the state where you have to pay contributions . . . . ▶ ....

   (2) Enter your state reporting number as shown on your state unemployment tax return ▶ ....

If you will not have to file returns in the future, check here (see **Who Must File** in separate instructions), **and complete and sign the return.** ▶ ☐

If this is an Amended Return, check here . . . . ▶ ☐

Part I   **Taxable Wages and FUTA Tax**

1	Total payments (including payments shown on lines 2 and 3) during the calendar year for services of employees	1	865,008	00
2	Exempt payments. (Explain all exempt payments, attaching additional sheets if necessary.) ▶	2		
3	Payments of more than $7,000 for services. Enter only amounts over the first $7,000 paid to each employee. Do not include any exempt payments from line 2. The $7,000 amount is the Federal wage base. Your state wage base may be different. **Do not use your state wage limitation**	3	781,008	00
4	Total exempt payments (add lines 2 and 3)	4	781,008	00
5	**Total taxable wages** (subtract line 4 from line 1) . . . . ▶	5	84,000	00
6	**FUTA tax.** Multiply the wages on line 5 by .008 and enter here. **(If the result is over $100, also complete Part II.)**	6	672	00
7	Total FUTA tax deposited for the year, including any overpayment applied from a prior year	7	672	00
8	**Balance due** (subtract line 7 from line 6). Pay to the "United States Treasury" . . . . ▶	8	———	
	If you owe more than $100, see **Depositing FUTA tax** in separate instructions.			
9	**Overpayment** (subtract line 6 from line 7). Check if it is to be: ☐ **Applied to next return or** ☐ **Refunded ▶**	9	———	

Part II   **Record of Quarterly Federal Unemployment Tax Liability** (Do not include state liability.) **Complete only if line 6 is over $100.**

Quarter	First (Jan. 1 – Mar. 31)	Second (Apr. 1 – June 30)	Third (July 1 – Sept. 30)	Fourth (Oct. 1 – Dec. 31)	Total for year
Liability for quarter	483.49	76.29	83.42	28.80	672.00

Under penalties of perjury, I declare that I have examined this return, including accompanying schedules and statements, and, to the best of my knowledge and belief, it is true, correct, and complete, and that no part of any payment made to a state unemployment fund claimed as a credit was, or is to be, deducted from the payments to employees.

Signature ▶ *Ellen D. Greg*   Title (Owner, etc.) ▶ *Owner*   Date ▶ *1/31/20—*

For Privacy Act and Paperwork Reduction Act Notice, see separate instructions.   Cat. No. 10983G   Form **940-EZ** (2000)

DETACH HERE

FIGURE 6

WORKERS' COMPENSATION INSURANCE

OBJECTIVE 7
Calculate the premium for workers' compensation insurance, and prepare the entry for payment in advance.

Most states require employers to provide **workers' compensation insurance** or industrial accident insurance for employees killed or injured on the job, either through plans administered by the state or through private insurance companies authorized by the state. The employer usually has to pay all the premiums. The premium rate varies with the amount of risk the job entails and the company's claims history. For example, handling molten steel ingots is much more dangerous than typing reports. Thus, it is very important that employees be identified properly in terms of the insurance premium classi-fications. The rates as percentages of the payroll may be 0.15 percent for office work, 0.5 percent for sales work, and 3.5 percent for industrial labor in heavy manufacturing. These same rates may be expressed as $0.15 per $100 of the salaries or wages for office work, $0.50 per $100 for sales work, and $3.50 per $100 for industrial labor.

Generally, the employer pays a premium in advance, based on the esti-mated payroll for the year. After the year ends, the employer knows the exact amount of the payroll and can calculate the exact premium. At that time, depending on the difference between the estimated and the exact premium, the employer either pays an additional premium or gets a credit for over-payment.

At Greg Company, there are two work classifications: office work and sales work. At the beginning of the year, the firm's accountant computed the esti-mated annual premium as follows:

Classification	Predicted Payroll	Rate (Percent)	Estimated Premium
Office work	$187,000	.15	$187,000 × .0015 = $ 280.50
Sales work	663,000	.50	663,000 × .0050 = 3,315.00
			Total estimated premium $3,595.50

As shown by T accounts, the accountant made the following entry.

Prepaid Insurance, Workers' Compensation			Cash	
+	−		+	−
Jan. 10 3,595.50				3,595.50 Jan. 10

Then, at the end of the calendar year, the accountant calculated the exact premium:

Classification	Exact Payroll	Rate (Percent)	Exact Premium
Office work	$192,000	.15	$192,000 × .0015 = $ 288.00
Sales work	673,000	.50	673,000 × .0050 = 3,365.00
			Total exact premium $3,653.00

Therefore, the amount of the unpaid premium is

$3,653.00	Total exact premium
$3,595.50	Less total estimated premium paid
$ 57.50	Additional premium owed

Workers' compensation premiums are based on the level of risk involved. A decimal rating is given to the employer for each type of job.

OBJECTIVE 8a
Determine the amount of the end-of-the-year adjustment for workers' compensation insurance, and record the adjustment.

Now the accountant makes an adjusting entry, similar to the adjusting entry for expired insurance; this entry appears on the work sheet. The accountant then makes an additional adjusting entry for the extra premium owed. By T accounts, the entries are as follows:

Prepaid Insurance, Workers' Compensation				Workers' Compensation Insurance Payable		
	+	−			−	+
Jan. 10 Bal.	3,595.50					57.50

Dec. 31 Adj. (right side of Prepaid Insurance): 3,595.50

Workers' Compensation Insurance Payable: 57.50 — Dec. 31 Adj.

Workers' Compensation Insurance Expense

	+	−
Dec. 31 Adj.	3,595.50	
Dec. 31 Adj.	57.50	

FYI
Workers' compensation premiums are based on the level of risk involved. A rating is given to the employer for each type of job.

Greg Company will pay $57.50, the amount of unpaid premium, in January, together with the estimated premium for the next year.

ADJUSTING FOR ACCRUED SALARIES AND WAGES

OBJECTIVE 8b
Determine the amount of the end-of-the-year adjustment for accrued salaries and wages, and record the adjustment.

Assume that $1,000 of salaries accrue for the time between the last payday and the end of the year. An adjusting entry is necessary.

	DATE		DESCRIPTION	POST. REF.	DEBIT	CREDIT	
1	20–		**Adjusting Entry**				1
2	Dec.	31	**Salary Expense**		1 0 0 0 00		2
3			**Salaries Payable**			1 0 0 0 00	3
4							4

Salaries Payable is considered a liability account, as are employees' withholding taxes and deductions payable. Federal income tax and FICA tax levied on employees do not become legal obligations until the employees are paid. Therefore, for the purpose of recording the adjusting entry, the entire liability of the gross salaries and wages is included under Salaries Payable or Wages Payable. In other words, in the adjusting entry, such accounts as Employees' Federal Income Tax Payable, FICA Tax Payable (employees' share), and Employees' Union Dues Payable are not used.

Adjusting Entry for Accrual of Payroll Taxes

As you have seen, the following taxes come under the umbrella of the Payroll Tax Expense account: the employer's share of the FICA tax, the state unemployment tax, and the federal unemployment tax. The employer becomes liable for these taxes only when the employees are actually paid, rather than at the time the liability to the employees is incurred. From the standpoint of legal liability, there should be no adjusting entry for Payroll Tax Expense.

TAX CALENDAR

Now let's put it all together. To keep up with the task of paying and reporting the various taxes, the accountant compiles a chronological list of the due dates. We are including only the payroll taxes here, but sales taxes and property taxes should also be listed. When you think about the penalties for nonpayment of taxes by the due dates, this chronological list seems to be well worth the effort. The employer is a monthly depositor for the federal tax deposit.

Jan. 10 Pay estimated annual premium for workers' compensation insurance. (This is an approximate date, as it varies among the states.)

15 Make federal tax deposit for employees' income tax withholding, employees' FICA taxes withheld, and employer's FICA taxes for wages paid during the month of December.

31 Complete Employer's Quarterly Federal Tax Return, Form 941, for the fourth quarter.

31 Issue copies B and C of Wage and Tax Statement, Form W-2, to employees.

31 Pay state unemployment tax liability for the previous quarter, and submit state return, employer's tax report.

31 Pay any remaining federal unemployment tax liability for the previous year, and submit Form 940, Employer's Annual Federal Unemployment Tax Return.

31 Make state deposit for employees' state income tax withholding and submit any required state payroll reports. (Timing and required reports may differ from state to state.)

Feb. 15 Make federal tax deposit for employees' income tax withholding, employees' FICA tax withholding, and employer's FICA tax for wages paid during the month of January.

28 Complete Transmittal of Wage and Tax Statements, Form W-3, and attach copy A of W-2 forms for employees.

Compiling a chronological list of tax due dates helps accountants keep up with paying and reporting the various taxes.

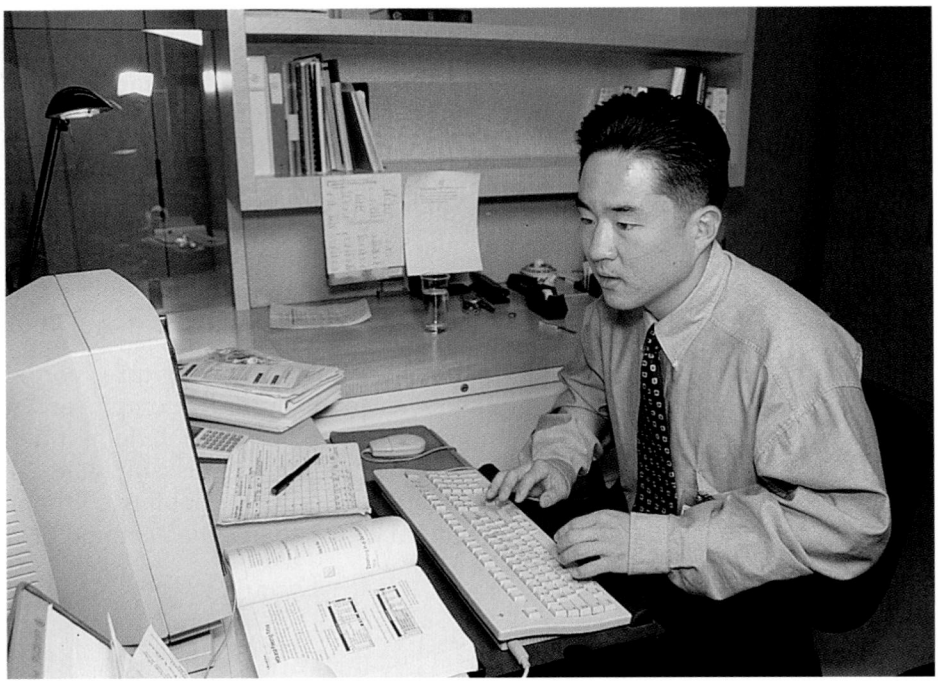

Mar.   15   Make federal tax deposit for employees' income tax withholding, employees' FICA tax withholding, and employer's FICA tax for wages paid during the month of February.

Apr.   15   Make federal tax deposit for employees' income tax withholding, employees' FICA tax withholding, and employer's FICA tax for wages paid during the month of March.

         30   Pay state unemployment tax liability for the previous quarter and submit state return, employer's tax report.

         30   Complete Employer's Quarterly Federal Tax Return, Form 941, for the first quarter.

         30   Make federal tax deposit for federal unemployment tax liability if it exceeds $100.

         30   Make state deposit for employees' state income tax withholding.

CHAPTER REVIEW

Check out ACE for a Review Quiz at

http://college.hmco.com/ accounting/students/.

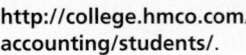

Review of Performance Objectives

1. Calculate the amount of payroll tax expense and journalize the related entry.

Payroll tax expense consists of the employer's matching portion of FICA taxes, plus the state unemployment tax, plus the federal unemployment tax. The *FICA tax* consists of Social Security and Medicare taxes. *Social Security tax* equals total Social Security taxable earnings multiplied by .062 (6.2 percent assumed rate) on the taxable earnings. For this text, the maximum taxable is assumed to be $84,900.

Total *Medicare tax* equals Medicare taxable earnings multiplied by .0145 (1.45 percent assumed rate). There is no maximum limit for Medicare—all earnings are taxable. *State unemployment tax* equals unemployment taxable earnings multiplied by .054 (5.4 percent assumed rate). *Federal unemployment tax* equals unemployment taxable earnings multiplied by .008 (.8 percent assumed rate). The related journal entry is as follows:

	DATE		DESCRIPTION	POST. REF.	DEBIT	CREDIT	
17	Oct.	7	Payroll Tax Expense		1 2 6 1 37		17
18			FICA Tax Payable			1 2 0 6 24	18
19			State Unemployment Tax				19
20			Payable			4 8 02	20
21			Federal Unemployment Tax				21
22			Payable			7 11	22
23			To record employer's share				23
24			of FICA tax and employer's				24
25			state and federal				25
26			unemployment taxes.				26
27							27

2. Journalize the entry for the deposit of employees' federal income taxes withheld and FICA taxes (both employees' withheld and employer's matching share) and prepare the deposit coupon.

	DATE		DESCRIPTION	POST. REF.	DEBIT	CREDIT	
1	20–						1
2	Nov.	15	Employees' Federal Income Tax				2
3			Payable		6 4 7 8 00		3
4			FICA Tax Payable		4 8 2 4 96		4
5			Cash			11 3 0 2 96	5
6			Issued check for federal tax				6
7			deposit, Bangor Bank.				7
8							8
9							9
10							10
11							11

3. Journalize the entries for the payment of employer's state and federal unemployment taxes.

State unemployment tax is paid on a quarterly basis. Payment is due by the end of the next month following the end of the calendar quarter.

	DATE		DESCRIPTION	POST. REF.	DEBIT		CREDIT	
1	20–							1
2	Apr.	30	State Unemployment Tax					2
3			Payable		3 2 6 3 54			3
4			Cash				3 2 6 3 54	4
5			Issued check for payment of					5
6			state unemployment tax.					6
7								7
8								8
9								9
10								10

If the amount of the accumulated federal unemployment tax liability exceeds $100 at the end of any quarter, the tax is due by the end of the next month following the end of the quarter. If the federal unemployment tax payable is less than $100 at the end of the year, it is due by January 31 of the next year.

	DATE		DESCRIPTION	POST. REF.	DEBIT		CREDIT	
1	20–							1
2	Apr.	30	Federal Unemployment Tax					2
3			Payable		4 8 3 49			3
4			Cash				4 8 3 49	4
5			Issued check for deposit of					5
6			federal unemployment tax.					6
7								7

4. Journalize the entry for the deposit of employees' state income taxes withheld.

Employees' state income taxes withheld are paid on a quarterly basis or as required by your state. Payment may be due by the end of the next month following the end of the calendar quarter.

	DATE		DESCRIPTION	POST. REF.	DEBIT		CREDIT	
1	20–							1
2	Apr.	30	Employees' State Income Tax					2
3			Payable		1 5 2 6 08			3
4			Cash				1 5 2 6 08	4
5			Issued check for state					5
6			income tax deposit.					6
7								7

5. Complete Employer's Quarterly Federal Tax Return, Form 941.

   Form 941 is illustrated on page 300.

6. Prepare W-2 and W-3 forms and Form 940.

   W-2 form (Wage and Tax Statement) is illustrated on page 302. W-3 form (Transmittal of Wage and Tax Statements) is illustrated on page 303. Form 940 is illustrated on page 306.

7. Calculate the premium for workers' compensation insurance, and prepare the entry for payment in advance.

   Rates vary depending on the degree of physical risk involved in different occupations. The amount of the premium equals the predicted annual payroll multiplied by the premium rate. The entry is a debit to Prepaid Insurance, Workers' Compensation, and a credit to Cash.

8. Determine the amount of the end-of-the-year adjustments for (a) workers' compensation insurance and (b) accrued salaries and wages, and record the adjustments.

   When the total annual payroll is known, the exact cost of workers' compensation insurance can be determined by multiplying the total payroll by the premium rate. Two adjusting entries are required. The first adjusting entry records the expired insurance as a debit to Workers' Compensation Insurance Expense and a credit to Prepaid Insurance, Workers' Compensation. The second adjusting entry records the difference between the estimated and the actual premiums. If the actual premium is greater than the premium that was paid in advance, the entry is a debit to Workers' Compensation Insurance Expense and a credit to Workers' Compensation Insurance Payable. The adjustment for accrued salaries and wages accounts for the additional amount of salaries or wages paid in the next payroll that are incurred in the current fiscal period—a debit to Wages (or Salaries) Expense. The credit to Salaries (or Wages) Payable accounts for the additional amount of liability incurred in the current period that will be paid with the next payroll that occurs in the following fiscal period.

Glossary

Employer identification number The number assigned each employer by the Internal Revenue Service for use in the submission of reports and payments for FICA taxes and federal income tax withheld. (291)

Federal unemployment tax (FUTA) A tax levied only on the employer, equal to 0.8 percent of the first $7,000 of total earnings paid to each employee during the calendar year. This tax is used to administer the funds. (293)

Form 940 An annual report filed by employers showing total wages paid to employees, total wages subject to federal unemployment tax, total federal unemployment tax, and other information. Also called the *Employer's Annual Federal Unemployment Tax Return*. (304)

Form 941 A quarterly report showing the tax liability for withholdings of employees' federal income tax and FICA tax and the employer's share of FICA tax. Total tax deposits made in the quarter are also listed on this Employer's Quarterly Federal Tax Return. (299)

Form W-2 A form containing information about employee earnings and tax deductions for the year. Also called *Wage and Tax Statement*. (301)

Form W-3 An annual report sent to the Social Security Administration listing the total wages and tips, total federal income tax withheld, total Social

Security and Medicare taxable wages, total Social Security and Medicare tax withheld, and other information for all employees of a firm. Also called the *Transmittal of Wage and Tax Statements*. (303)

Payroll Tax Expense A general expense account used for recording the employer's matching portion of the FICA tax, the federal unemployment tax, and the state unemployment tax. (291)

Quarters Three consecutive months, also referred to as *calendar quarters*. (295)

State unemployment tax (SUTA) A tax levied only on the employer in most states. Rates differ among the various states; however, they are generally 5.4 percent or higher of the first $7,000 of total earnings paid to each employee during the calendar year. The proceeds are used to pay subsistence benefits to unemployed workers. (293)

Workers' compensation insurance This insurance, primarily paid for by the employer, provides benefits for employees injured or killed on the job. The rates vary according to the degree of risk inherent in the job. The plans may be sponsored by states or by private firms. The employer pays the premium in advance at the beginning of the year, based on the estimated payroll. The rates are adjusted after the exact payroll is known. (306)

QUESTIONS, EXERCISES, AND PROBLEMS

Discussion Questions

1. What payroll taxes are included under the Payroll Tax Expense account?
2. List the correct sequence of the steps for recording payroll entries, and identify the specific source of information for each entry.
3. Explain the deposit requirement for federal unemployment tax.
4. What is the purpose of Form 941? How often is it prepared, and what are the due dates?
5. How many copies are made of a Form W-2, and who uses the copies of the W-2 form?
6. What is the purpose of Form 940? How often is it prepared, and what is the due date?
7. Generally, what is the time schedule for payment of workers' compensation insurance premiums?
8. Explain the advantage of establishing a tax calendar.

Exercises

P.O. 1

Journalize the entry for payroll tax expense.

Exercise 9-1 West Company's partial payroll register for the week ended January 7 is shown on page 315.

Assume that the payroll is subject to a Social Security tax of 6.2 percent of the first $84,900 and a Medicare tax of 1.45 percent on all earnings. Also assume that the federal unemployment tax is 0.8 percent of the first $7,000, and the state unemployment tax is 5.4 percent of the first $7,000. Give the entry in general journal form to record the payroll tax expense.

	BEGINNING CUMULATIVE EARNINGS	TOTAL EARNINGS	ENDING CUMULATIVE EARNINGS	TAXABLE EARNINGS		
NAME				UNEMPLOYMENT	SOCIAL SECURITY	MEDICARE
1 Bonney, R. S.		9 3 2 00	9 3 2 00	9 3 2 00	9 3 2 00	9 3 2 00
2 Fisk, M. C.		5 6 7 00	5 6 7 00	5 6 7 00	5 6 7 00	5 6 7 00
3 Hayes, W. O.		4 8 3 00	4 8 3 00	4 8 3 00	4 8 3 00	4 8 3 00
4 Lee, L. B.		6 7 9 00	6 7 9 00	6 7 9 00	6 7 9 00	6 7 9 00
5 Parks, S. J.		5 7 8 00	5 7 8 00	5 7 8 00	5 7 8 00	5 7 8 00
6 Tempy, E. B.		5 4 6 00	5 4 6 00	5 4 6 00	5 4 6 00	5 4 6 00
7		3 7 8 5 00	3 7 8 5 00	3 7 8 5 00	3 7 8 5 00	3 7 8 5 00

P.O. 1

Journalize the entry for payroll tax expense.

Exercise 9-2 On January 14, at the end of the second week of the year, the totals of Casey Company's payroll register showed that its store employees' wages amounted to $31,432 and its warehouse wages amounted to $11,360. Withholdings consisted of federal income taxes, $4,052; Social Security taxes at the rate of 6.2 percent of the first $84,900 and no employee has reached the limit; Medicare taxes at the rate of 1.45 percent on all earnings; union dues, $815.

a. Calculate the amount of Social Security and Medicare taxes to be withheld, and write the general journal entry to record the payroll.
b. Write the general journal entry to record the employer's payroll taxes, assuming that the federal unemployment tax is 0.8 percent of the first $7,000, that the state unemployment tax is 5.4 percent of the same base, and that no employee has surpassed the $7,000 limit.

P.O. 1

Journalize the payroll entries.

Exercise 9-3 Fenn Systems had the following payroll data for wages for the week ended February 5. These calculations for state income tax (20% of federal income tax) are exceptions.

TOTAL EARNINGS	ENDING CUMULATIVE EARNINGS	TAXABLE EARNINGS			DEDUCTIONS			
		UNEMPLOYMENT	SOCIAL SECURITY	MEDICARE	FEDERAL INCOME TAX	STATE INCOME TAX	SOCIAL SECURITY TAX	MEDICARE TAX
6 7 7 0 00	72 8 5 0 00	6 7 7 0 00	6 7 7 0 00	6 7 7 0 00	8 2 4 00	1 5 7 00	4 1 9 74	9 8 17

a. Write the general journal entry to record the payroll.
b. Write the general journal entry to record the employer's payroll taxes. Assume rates of 0.8 percent for federal unemployment tax and 5.4 percent for state unemployment tax based on the first $7,000 for each employee and that no employee has earned more than $7,000.

P.O. 1

Journalize the entry for payroll tax expense.

Exercise 9-4 The following information on earnings and deductions for the pay period ended December 14 is from Ladry Company's payroll records:

Name	Gross Pay	Beginning Cumulative Earnings
Brent, A. F.	$ 310	$ 6,620
Digger, L. D.	760	38,100
Spark, C. R.	1,693	84,650
Rendy, L. W.	290	38,700
Carcy, M. E.	590	62,400
Stevens, D. H.	950	6,810

For each employee, the Social Security tax is 6.2 percent of the first $84,900 and the Medicare tax is 1.45 percent on all earnings. The federal unemployment tax is 0.8 percent of the first $7,000 of earnings of each employee. The state unemployment tax is 5.4 percent of the same base. Determine the total taxable earnings for unemployment, Social Security, and Medicare. Prepare a general journal entry to record the employer's payroll taxes.

P.O. 2

Journalize entries for payment of federal payroll taxes.

Exercise 9-5 Selected columns of Lin Company's payroll register for the month of January are as follows. The employees' FICA taxes are matched by the employer.

Payment Date	Employees' Federal Income Tax	Employees' Social Security Tax	Employees' Medicare Tax
Jan. 7	1,092.00	485.00	114.25
14	1,124.00	512.14	123.31
21	1,215.00	562.62	126.24
28	1,431.00	581.27	141.26

Lin Company deposits taxes monthly. Record the entry for payment of FICA and federal income taxes for employees and employer in general journal form.

P.O. 2,3

Journalize entries for payment of payroll taxes.

Exercise 9-6 On September 30, Karl Company's selected account balances are as follows:

Employees' Federal Income Tax Payable	$ 2,269.00
FICA Tax Payable (employer and employee)	2,504.46
State Unemployment Tax Payable	1,350.00 } (Some employees have
Federal Unemployment Tax Payable	200.00 } reached the limit.)
Salaries Payable	29,216.77
Salary Expense	32,738.00
Payroll Tax Expense	2,802.23

In general journal form, prepare the entries to record the following:

Oct. 15 Payment of liabilities for FICA and federal income tax.
31 Payment of liability for state unemployment tax.
31 Payment of liability for federal unemployment tax.

P.O. 2,3

Journalize entries for payment of payroll taxes.

Exercise 9-7 On September 30, Michael Company's selected payroll accounts are as follows.

FICA Tax Payable		State Unemployment Tax Payable	
−	+	−	+
	Sept. 30 2,213.86		Sept. 30 1,217.83
	Sept. 30 2,213.86		

Federal Unemployment Tax Payable		Employees' Federal Income Tax Payable	
−	+	−	+
	Sept. 30 201.14		Sept. 30 3,312.74

Prepare general journal entries to record the following:

Oct. 15 Payment of federal tax deposit of FICA and federal income tax.
31 Payment of state unemployment tax.
31 Payment of federal unemployment tax.

P.O. 7,8

Journalize entries for workers' compensation insurance.

Exercise 9-8 Mayeno Company received and paid a premium notice on January 2 for workers' compensation insurance stating the rates for the new year. Estimated employees' earnings for the year are as follows:

Classification	Estimated Wages and Salaries	Rate Per Hundred	Estimated Premium
Office clerical	$ 91,000	.11	$ 100.10
Warehouse work	28,000	.92	257.60
Manufacturing	265,000	1.20	3,180.00
			$3,537.70

At the end of the year, the exact figures for the payroll are as follows:

Classification	Estimated Wages and Salaries	Rate Per Hundred	Exact Premium
Office clerical	$ 92,000	.11	$ 101.20
Warehouse work	27,000	.92	248.40
Manufacturing	268,000	1.20	3,216.00
			$3,565.60

a. Record the entry in general journal form for payment of the estimated premium.
b. Record the adjusting entries on December 31 for the insurance expired and for the additional premium.

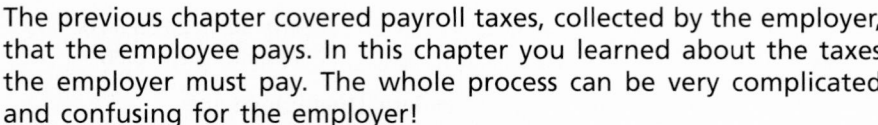

REFLECTING ON
THE WORLD WIDE WEB

The previous chapter covered payroll taxes, collected by the employer, that the employee pays. In this chapter you learned about the taxes the employer must pay. The whole process can be very complicated and confusing for the employer!

Are any methods other than Form 8109-B available for making deposits? See if you can find out by visiting the IRS website at **www.irs.gov**. If so, what are they and how are they used?

WHAT'S WRONG WITH THIS PICTURE?

The payroll clerk is working on the payroll register, specifically the Taxable Earnings columns for federal and state unemployment taxes and FICA taxes. The problem is that several employees' gross earnings are about to exceed the limits for unemployment and FICA taxes. For each employee whose cumulative earnings were near the limit, the payroll clerk multiplied the tax rate by the amount by which the employee's earnings exceeded the tax ceiling (not the amount between the beginning cumulative earnings and the tax limit). Comment on this procedure.

CRITICAL THINKING

It is December 15, and you are the payroll clerk for Lindon Company. The owner has come to you for help; two employees have asked for a 4 percent pay raise, and the owner wants to know how much more such a raise will cost her next year. Present gross salaries are as follows:

Employee A
$40,000/year   Married, with 2 allowances   Paid weekly
Employee B
$42,000/year   Married, with 1 allowance   Paid weekly

Assume the following tax rates and limits:

Social Security, 6.2 percent with a limit of $84,900
Medicare, 1.45 percent with no limit (all earnings taxable)
SUTA, 5.4 percent with a limit of $7,000
FUTA, 0.8 percent with a limit of $7,000

What will be the cost to the employer of giving Employee A and Employee B the pay raise?

A MATTER OF ETHICS

An employer prepares the payroll and correctly computes the necessary withholding taxes. The employer pays accumulated employment taxes on the fifteenth of the next month. Payday is the last day of the month. However, between the end of one month and the fifteenth day of the next month, the balance in the employer's business bank account has been getting smaller and smaller. The employer has used the funds withheld from employees to pay some of the business's bills. He anticipates that enough of the customers who owe him money will pay their outstanding debts. If this assumption is true, the checking account will have enough in it to pay the federal deposit on the fifteenth of the month. Is the employer acting ethically, because he intends to have enough money in the account for the deposit?

PROBLEM SET A

For additional help, see the demonstration problem at the beginning of each chapter in your Working Papers.

P.O. 1

Problem 9-1A Milano Labs had the following payroll for the week ended February 28:

Salaries		Deductions	
Technicians' salaries	$6,855.00	Federal income tax withheld	$ 694.00
Office salaries	2,060.00	Social Security tax withheld	552.73
		Medicare tax withheld	129.27
Total	$8,915.00	Union dues withheld	160.00
		Medical insurance	450.00
		Total	$1,986.00

Assumed tax rates are as follows:

a. FICA: Social Security, 6.2 percent (.062) on the first $84,900 for each employee, and Medicare, 1.45 percent (.0145) on all earnings for each employee.
b. State unemployment tax, 5.4 percent (.054) on the first $7,000 for each employee.
c. Federal unemployment tax, 0.8 percent (.008) on the first $7,000 for each employee.

Check Figure
Payroll Tax Expense, $1,073.84

Instructions

Record the following entries in general journal form:

1. The payroll entry as of February 28.
2. The entry to record the employer's payroll taxes as of February 28, assuming that the total payroll is subject to the FICA tax (combined Social Security and Medicare) and that $6,320.00 is subject to unemployment taxes.

3. The payment of the employees on March 2 (assume that the company has transferred cash to Cash—Payroll Bank Account for this payroll).

P.O. 1

Problem 9-2A Temp Services has the following payroll information for the week ended December 7. These calculations for state income tax (20% of federal income tax) are exceptions.

	NAME	BEGINNING CUMULATIVE EARNINGS	TOTAL EARNINGS	DEDUCTIONS FEDERAL INCOME TAX	DEDUCTIONS STATE INCOME TAX
1	Baker, T. L.	6 8 2 0 00	4 8 0 00	4 6 00	5 52
2	Ellen, R. M.	6 8 4 0 00	4 7 0 00	4 5 00	5 40
3	Fink, J. M.	36 3 2 0 00	7 4 0 00	8 5 00	1 0 20
4	King, R. L.	26 2 0 0 00	5 4 0 00	5 5 00	6 60
5	Lincoln, M. N.	84 2 5 4 00	1 7 2 0 00	2 8 9 00	3 4 68
6	Mork, P. O.	28 4 2 6 00	6 0 5 00	6 4 00	7 68
7					
8					
9					
10					
11					
12					
13					
14					

Assumed tax rates are as follows:

a. FICA: Social Security, 6.2 percent (.062) on the first $84,900 for each employee, and Medicare, 1.45 percent (.0145) on all earnings for each employee.
b. State unemployment tax, 5.4 percent (.054) on the first $7,000 for each employee.
c. Federal unemployment tax, 0.8 percent (.008) on the first $7,000 for each employee.

Check Figure
Payroll Tax Expense, $302.95

Instructions

1. Complete the payroll register, page 72.
2. Prepare a general journal entry to record the payroll as of December 7.
3. Prepare a general journal entry to record the payroll taxes as of December 7.
4. Journalize the entry to pay the payroll on December 9. (Assume that the company has transferred cash to the Cash—Payroll Bank Account for this payroll.) Payroll checks begin with Ck. No. 714 in the payroll register.

P.O. 5

Problem 9-3A For the third quarter of the year, Jordon Company, 6227 Circle Avenue, Chicago, Illinois 60652, received Form 941 from the Internal Revenue Service. The identification number of Jordon Company is 76-4213171. Its payroll for the quarter ended September 30 is as follows.

	TOTAL EARNINGS	TAXABLE EARNINGS		DEDUCTIONS		
NAME		SOCIAL SECURITY	MEDICARE	FEDERAL INCOME TAX	SOCIAL SECURITY TAX	MEDICARE TAX
1 Barker, D. D.	6 6 2 9 00	6 6 2 9 00	6 6 2 9 00	8 4 3 00	4 1 1 00	9 6 12
2 Carey, L. R.	8 5 2 8 00	8 5 2 8 00	8 5 2 8 00	8 2 5 00	5 2 8 74	1 2 3 66
3 Domzalski, T. P.	4 6 6 5 00	4 6 6 5 00	4 6 6 5 00	6 8 9 00	2 8 9 23	6 7 64
4 Grisson, R. O.	3 7 2 1 00	3 7 2 1 00	3 7 2 1 00	4 7 8 00	2 3 0 70	5 3 95
5 Tyler, J. L.	7 4 0 6 00	7 4 0 6 00	7 4 0 6 00	8 6 5 00	4 5 9 17	1 0 7 39
6 Vardic, K. R.	5 2 8 7 00	5 2 8 7 00	5 2 8 7 00	7 9 5 00	3 2 7 79	7 6 66
7	36 2 3 6 00	36 2 3 6 00	36 2 3 6 00	4 4 9 5 00	2 2 4 6 63	5 2 5 42
8						

The company has had six employees throughout the year. Assume that the Social Security tax is 6.2 percent of the first $84,900 and that the Medicare tax is 1.45 percent of all earnings. The employer matches the employees' FICA (Social Security and Medicare) taxes. There are no taxable tips, adjustments, backup withholding, or earned income credits. Jordon Company has submitted the following federal tax deposits and written the accompanying checks:

On August 15 for the July Payroll

Employees' income tax withheld	$1,380.00
Employees' Social Security and Medicare tax withheld	851.10
Employer's Social Security and Medicare tax contributed	851.10
	$3,082.20

On September 15 for the August Payroll

Employees' income tax withheld	$1,892.00
Employees' Social Security and Medicare tax withheld	875.92
Employer's Social Security and Medicare tax contributed	875.92
	$3,643.84

On October 15 for the September Payroll

Employees' income tax withheld	$1,223.00
Employees' Social Security and Medicare tax withheld	1,045.03
Employer's Social Security and Medicare tax contributed	1,045.03
	$3,313.06

Check Figure
Total taxes, $10,039.10

P.O. 1,2,3

Instructions

Complete Form 941 dated October 31 for the owner, Maxwell Jordon.

Problem 9-4A The Leighton Company has the following balances in its general ledger as of June 1 of this year:

a. FICA Tax Payable (liability for May), $1,709.42 (employee and employer).
b. Employees' Federal Income Tax Payable (liability for May), $988.00.
c. Federal Unemployment Tax Payable (liability for April and May), $179.00.
d. State Unemployment Tax Payable (liability for April and May), $1,208.25.
e. Employees' Medical Insurance Payable (liability for April and May), $1,295.00.

The company completed the following transactions involving the payroll during June and July:

June 13 Issued check for $2,697.42 payable to Security Bank, for the monthly deposit of May FICA taxes and employees' federal income tax withheld.

30 Recorded the payroll entry in the general journal from the payroll register for June. The payroll register has the following column totals:

Sales salaries	$10,380.00	
Office salaries	4,168.00	
Total earnings		$14,548.00
Employees' federal income tax deductions	$ 1,522.00	
Employees' Social Security tax deductions	901.98	
Employees' Medicare tax deductions	210.95	
Employees' medical insurance deductions	720.00	
Total deductions		3,354.93
Net pay		$11,193.07

30 Recorded payroll taxes. Employer matches the employees' FICA taxes. State unemployment tax is 5.4 percent, and federal unemployment tax is 0.8 percent. At this time, all employees' earnings are taxable for FICA and unemployment taxes.

30 Issued check for $11,193.07 from Cash—Payroll Bank Account to pay salaries for the month.

July 14 Issued check for $2,015, payable to Careso Insurance Company, in payment of employees' medical insurance for April, May, and June.

14 Issued check for $3,747.86, payable to Security Bank, for the monthly deposit of June FICA taxes (employee and employer matching) and employees' federal income tax withheld.

31 Issued check for $1,993.84, payable to the State Tax Commission, for state unemployment tax for April, May, and June. The check was accompanied by the quarterly tax return.

31 Issued check for $295.38 payable to Security Bank, for the deposit of federal unemployment tax for the months of April, May, and June.

Check Figure
Payroll Tax Expense, $2,014.90

Instructions

Record the transactions in the general journal, pages 77–78.

Instructions for General Ledger Software

1. Record the transactions in the general journal.
2. Print the journal entries.

PROBLEM SET B

For additional help, see the demonstration problem at the beginning of each chapter in your Working Papers.

P.O. 1

Problem 9-1B Kovach Company had the following payroll for the week ended March 21:

Salaries		Deductions	
Sales salaries	$7,520.00	Federal income tax withheld	$ 794.00
Office salaries	1,798.00	Social Security tax withheld	577.72
		Medicare tax withheld	135.11
Total	$9,318.00	Union dues withheld	188.00
		Medical insurance	200.00
		Total	$1,894.83

Assumed tax rates are as follows:

a. FICA: Social Security, 6.2 percent (.062) on the first $84,900 for each employee, and Medicare, 1.45 percent (.0145) on all earnings for each employee.
b. State unemployment tax, 5.4 percent (.054) on the first $7,000 for each employee.
c. Federal unemployment tax, .8 percent (.008) on the first $7,000 for each employee.

Check Figure
Payroll Tax Expense, $1,013.53

Instructions

Record the following entries in general journal form:

1. The payroll entry as of March 21.
2. The entry to record the employer's payroll taxes as of March 21, assuming that the total payroll is subject to the FICA tax (combined Social Security and Medicare) and that $4,850 is subject to unemployment taxes.
3. The payment of the employees on March 23. (Assume that the company has transferred cash to Cash—Payroll Bank Account for this payroll.)

P.O. 1

Problem 9-2B Kye Agency has the following information for the week ended December 14. These calculations for state income tax (20% of federal income tax) are exceptions.

	NAME	BEGINNING CUMULATIVE EARNINGS	TOTAL EARNINGS	DEDUCTIONS	
				FEDERAL INCOME TAX	STATE INCOME TAX
1	Bern, R. E.	10 6 5 0 00	4 6 0 00	4 3 00	5 00
2	Gertz, T. S.	38 8 2 0 00	9 7 0 00	1 2 3 00	2 7 00
3	Jenks, E. G.	84 5 0 0 00	1 6 9 0 00	2 0 5 00	7 6 00
4	Ling, P. D.	6 7 5 0 00	3 8 5 00	3 1 00	1 5 00
5	Phel, S. D.	31 6 7 0 00	6 9 4 00	7 8 00	1 8 00
6	Quid, D. L.	48 9 6 1 00	1 0 4 0 00	1 4 3 00	3 5 00
7					

Assumed tax rates are as follows:

a. FICA: Social Security, 6.2 percent (0.062) on the first $84,900 for each employee, and Medicare, 1.45 percent (0.0145) on all earnings for each employee.

b. State unemployment tax, 5.4 percent (0.054) on the first $7,000 for each employee.

c. Federal unemployment tax, 0.8 percent (0.008) on the first $7,000 for each employee.

Check Figure

Payroll Tax Expense, $336.31

Instructions

1. Complete the payroll register, page 72.
2. Prepare a general journal entry to record the payroll as of December 14. The company's general ledger contains a Salary Expense account and a Salaries Payable account.
3. Prepare a general journal entry to record the payroll taxes as of December 14.
4. Journalize the entry to pay the payroll on December 16. (Assume that the company has transferred cash to the Cash—Payroll bank account for this payroll.) Payroll checks begin with Ck. No. 923 in the payroll register.

P.O. 5

Problem 9-3B For the third quarter of the year, Forman Construction, of 7144 Stone Boulevard, San Francisco, California 94421, received Form 941 from the District Office of the Internal Revenue Service. The identification number for Forman Construction is 77-6271161. Its payroll for the quarter ended September 30 is as follows:

| | NAME | TOTAL EARNINGS | TAXABLE EARNINGS | | DEDUCTIONS | | |
			SOCIAL SECURITY	MEDICARE	FEDERAL INCOME TAX	SOCIAL SECURITY TAX	MEDICARE TAX
1	Brinnon, D. L.	3 3 8 7 00	3 3 8 7 00	3 3 8 7 00	3 1 0 00	2 0 9 99	4 9 11
2	Finn, J. A.	6 7 5 3 00	6 7 5 3 00	6 7 5 3 00	7 0 4 00	4 1 8 69	9 7 92
3	Harrell, N. E.	7 7 8 0 00	7 7 8 0 00	7 7 8 0 00	8 2 0 00	4 8 2 36	1 1 2 81
4	Kelly, T. L.	6 2 4 3 00	6 2 4 3 00	6 2 4 3 00	6 6 0 00	3 8 7 07	9 0 52
5	Morton, S. M.	4 2 1 5 00	4 2 1 5 00	4 2 1 5 00	3 8 4 00	2 6 1 33	6 1 12
6	Rieck, A. J.	10 2 6 4 00	10 2 6 4 00	10 2 6 4 00	1 2 2 4 00	6 3 6 37	1 4 8 83
7		38 6 4 2 00	38 6 4 2 00	38 6 4 2 00	4 1 0 2 00	2 3 9 5 81	5 6 0 31

The company has had six employees throughout the year. Assume that the Social Security tax is 6.2 percent of the first $84,900, and that the Medicare tax is 1.45 percent of all earnings. The employer matches the employees' FICA (Social Security and Medicare) taxes. There are no taxable tips, adjustments, backup withholding, or earned income credits. Forman Construction has submitted the following federal tax deposits and written the accompanying checks:

On August 15 for the July Payroll

Employees' income tax withheld	$1,440.00
Employees' Social Security and Medicare tax withheld	984.80
Employer's Social Security and Medicare tax contributed	984.80
	$3,409.60

On September 15 for the August Payroll

Employees' income tax withheld	$1,394.00
Employees' Social Security and Medicare tax withheld	1,138.40
Employer's Social Security and Medicare tax contributed	1,138.40
	$3,670.80

On October 15 for the September Payroll

Employees' income tax withheld	$1,268.00
Employees' Social Security and Medicare tax withheld	832.92
Employer's Social Security and Medicare tax contributed	832.92
	$2,933.84

Check Figure
Total taxes, $10,014.23

P.O. 1,2,3

Instructions

Complete Form 941 dated October 29 for the owner, Tom Forman.

Problem 9-4B The DeGrut Company has the following balances in its general ledger as of March 1 of this year:

a. FICA Tax Payable (liability for February), $1,408.80 (employee and employer).
b. Employees' Federal Income Tax Payable (liability for February), $845.00.
c. State Unemployment Tax Payable (liability for January and February), $961.20.
d. Federal Unemployment Tax Payable (liability for January and February), $142.40.
e. Employees' Medical Insurance Payable (liability for January and February), $945.00.

The company completed the following transactions involving the payroll during March and April:

Mar. 12 Issued check for $2,253.80 payable to Coastal Bank, for monthly deposit of February FICA taxes and employees' federal income tax withheld.

31 Recorded the payroll entry in the general journal from the payroll register for March. The payroll register had the following column totals:

Sales salaries	$7,528.00	
Office salaries	1,886.00	
Total earnings		$9,414.00
Employees' federal income tax deductions	$ 750.00	
Employees' Social Security tax deductions	583.67	
Employees' Medicare tax deductions	136.50	
Employees' medical insurance deductions	495.00	
Total deductions		1,965.17
Net pay		$7,448.83

Mar. 31 Recorded payroll taxes. Employer matches the employees' FICA taxes. State unemployment tax is 5.4 percent. Federal unemployment tax is 0.8 percent. At this time, all employees' earnings are taxable for FICA and unemployment taxes.

31 Issued check for $7,448.83 from Cash—Payroll Bank Account to pay the salaries for the month.

Apr. 3 Issued check for $1,440, payable to Angel Insurance Company, for employees' medical insurance for January, February, and March.

14 Issued check for $2,190.34, payable to Coastal Bank, for monthly deposit of March FICA taxes and employees' federal income tax withheld.

30 Issued check for $1,469.56, payable to State Department of Revenue, for state unemployment tax for January, February, and March. The check was accompanied by the quarterly tax return.

30 Issued check, payable to Coastal Bank, for deposit of federal unemployment tax for January, February, and March, $217.71.

Check Figure
Payroll Tax Expense, $1,303.84

Instructions

Record the transactions in the general journal, pages 77 and 78.

Instructions for General Ledger Software

1. Record the transactions in the general journal.
2. Print the journal entries.

Before a Test Check: Chapters 7–9

PART I: Completion

1. Checks issued by the depositor that have been paid or have cleared the bank are called _____ checks.

2. A deposit that is not recorded on the bank statement because it was made after the bank's closing date for preparation of bank statements is called a(n) _____.

3. The process by which the payee transfers ownership of the check to a bank or other party is called a(n) _____.

4. The person to whom a check is payable is called the _____.

5. A cash fund used to make small immediate cash payments is called a(n) _____.

PART II: Application

1. Cora Thomas's salary is $1,775 per month. If she works more than 40 hours in one week, she is entitled to overtime pay at the rate of $1\frac{1}{2}$ times her regular hourly rate. During the current week, she worked 45 hours. Calculate her gross pay.

2. On June 30, the column totals of Midway Cleaning's payroll register showed that its cleaning employees had earned $9,000 and its office employees had earned $3,000. Social Security taxes were withheld at 6.2 percent, and Medicare taxes were withheld at 1.45 percent. All earnings are taxable. Other deductions consisted of federal income tax, $1,500; U.S. savings bonds, $500; and medical insurance, $962. Determine the amount of Social Security and Medicare taxes that should be withheld. Record the general journal entry to record the payroll, crediting Salaries Payable for the net pay.

3. Rensel Company's payroll for the week ended December 31 is as follows:

Gross earnings of employees	$155,000
Social Security taxable earnings	143,000
Medicare taxable earnings	155,000
Federal unemployment taxable earnings	22,000
State unemployment taxable earnings	22,000

Assume that the payroll is subject to Social Security tax of 6.2 percent (0.062), Medicare tax of 1.45 percent (0.0145), federal unemployment tax of 0.8 percent (0.008), and state unemployment tax of 5.4 percent (0s.054). Write the entry in general journal form to record the employer's payroll tax expense.

Note: Answers to Before a Test Check begin on page A-1.

PART III: True/False

T   F   1. There is no limit on the amount of taxable earnings for Medicare.

T   F   2. When journalizing the entry to reimburse the Petty Cash Fund, include a credit to Petty Cash Fund.

T   F   3. When journalizing the entry to account for a customer's NSF check, debit Accounts Payable.

T   F   4. An employee's net pay is the result of subtracting his or her deductions from gross pay.

T   F   5. The gross pay for an employee who works 45 hours, earns $8.50 per hour, and receives time and a half for hours worked past 40 hours is $402.75.

10

The Sales Journal and the Purchases Journal

Performance Objectives

After you have completed the chapter, you will be able to do the following:

1. Describe the specific accounts used by a merchandising firm.

2. Journalize transactions in a sales journal.

3. Post sales journal transactions to an accounts receivable ledger and a general ledger.

4. Prepare a schedule of accounts receivable.

5. Journalize sales returns and allowances, including credit memorandums and returns involving sales tax, in a general journal, and post to the accounts receivable ledger and general ledger.

6. Journalize transactions in a three-column purchases journal.

7. Post purchases journal transactions to an accounts payable ledger and a general ledger.

8. Prepare a schedule of accounts payable.

9. Journalize transactions involving purchases returns and allowances in a general journal, and post to the accounts payable ledger and general ledger.

10. Describe the procedures for handling freight charges on merchandise and other goods.

329

o increase your accounting knowledge, let's introduce accounting systems for merchandising enterprises. This chapter describes specific accounts of merchandising firms; a merchandising firm can be anything from a dress shop to a supermarket.

SPECIAL JOURNALS

Special journals are books of original entry in which specialized types of repetitive transactions are recorded. The four most commonly used special journals are:

Sales journal (S) To record sales of merchandise on account *only*.
Purchases journal (P) To record purchases of merchandise on account *only*.
Cash receipts journal (CR) To record cash received.
Cash payments journal (CP) To record cash paid out.

All other transactions are recorded in the general journal (J). A business need use only the journal(s) that best serve its purposes.

SPECIFIC ACCOUNTS FOR MERCHANDISING FIRMS

OBJECTIVE 1
Describe the specific accounts used by a merchandising firm.

Merchandise inventory consists of a stock of goods that a company buys and intends to resell, in the same physical condition, at a profit. Merchandise should be differentiated from other assets, such as equipment and supplies, that are acquired for use in the business and are not for resale. Here is the fundamental accounting equation with the T accounts for merchandising businesses.

The **Sales account** is a revenue account used for recording sales of merchandise.

The **Purchases account** is used strictly to record the cost of merchandise bought for resale. The plus and minus signs are the same as the signs for Merchandise Inventory. Purchases is placed under the heading of Expenses only because the accountant closes it along with the expense accounts at the end of the fiscal period.

The **Sales Returns and Allowances account** is used to record the physical return of merchandise by customers or a reduction in a bill because merchandise was damaged. It is treated as a deduction from Sales.

The **Sales Tax account** is a tax levied by a state or city government on the retail sale of goods and services. The tax is paid by the consumer, but collected by the retailer.

The **Purchases Returns and Allowances account** is used to record the company's returns of merchandise it had purchased from suppliers or reductions in bills because of damaged merchandise. It is treated as a deduction from Purchases.

The **Sales Discount account** and **Purchases Discount account** are used to record cash discounts granted for prompt payments, in accordance with the credit terms.

The **Freight In account** is used to record the transportation charges on incoming merchandise intended for resale. Debits to this account increase the cost of purchases.

The T accounts for returns and allowances and for discounts are shown in green to emphasize that we are treating them as deductions from the related accounts placed above them. We list these accounts as deductions because they appear as deductions in the financial statements. Their relationship is similar to that between the Drawing account and the Capital account; remember that we deduct Drawing from Capital in the statement of owner's equity. These same types of accounts pertain to both retail and wholesale businesses.

RECORDING SALES ON ACCOUNT

A sale of merchandise on account is recorded as a debit to Accounts Receivable and a credit to Sales.

In a retail business, a salesperson usually prepares a sales ticket in either duplicate or triplicate for a sale on account. One copy goes to the customer and another to the accounting department, where it serves as the basis for an entry in the sales journal. A third copy may be used as a record of sales—to compute sales commissions or control inventory, for example.

In a wholesale business, the company usually receives a written order from a customer or from a salesperson who obtained the order from the customer. The credit department approves the order, then sends it to the billing department, where the sales invoice is prepared.

Invoices are prepared in multiple copies. Figure 1, on page 332, shows one possible distribution of sales invoice copies to various parties.

Just as we used Arch Copy Co. as a continuous example of a service business, we will use Dodson Plumbing Supply as a continuous example of a merchandising business. Dodson Plumbing Supply is a wholesaler.

MENTOR PROFILE

TRACY L. NEWKIRK

Production Traffic Manager, External Affairs,
Experience Music Project, Seattle

Tracy never thought she'd end up using her accounting skills as a production coordinator in a marketing department—let alone for a museum whose corporate offices are in Seattle, Washington, near the Space Needle. And it is not just any museum; it is the Experience Music Project, a nonprofit, interactive and experiential museum that celebrates American popular music. While the structure of the corporate office building looks quite normal, the museum's unorthodox architecture is as unusual as what you will find inside.

Tracy works as the production/traffic manager in the external affairs department, where they produce all of the museum's marketing materials and signage. She works with a great variety of people, including other marketing and promotions professionals, talent booking agents, curators, technology people, sales representatives, sponsorship organizations, educational groups, and of course, the finance department.

But it's not all marketing and finance. Since the museum celebrates American popular music, there are frequent visitors from the music industry—professionals and artists tour the museum and perform on its stage. Museum visitors can explore the dynamic galleries, learn how to play instruments, record their own CDs, or "perform" in a simulated concert venue.

Each day brings something new in Tracy's nonprofit corporate world, intertwining marketing and accounting with the ever-changing face of the museum and its galleries. She always loved accounting because she could crunch the numbers and make the balance sheet balance—and that has landed her in the exciting world of music past and present. Who would ever think debits and credits could be such fun?

> *"Absorb all that you can in accounting and hang onto it so that you can apply it in your everyday life. Put it on your resume. If you can sit in a room with the controller and/or director of finance and hold your own in a budget discussion, you'll be doing very well. Not many people can do that."*

FIGURE 1

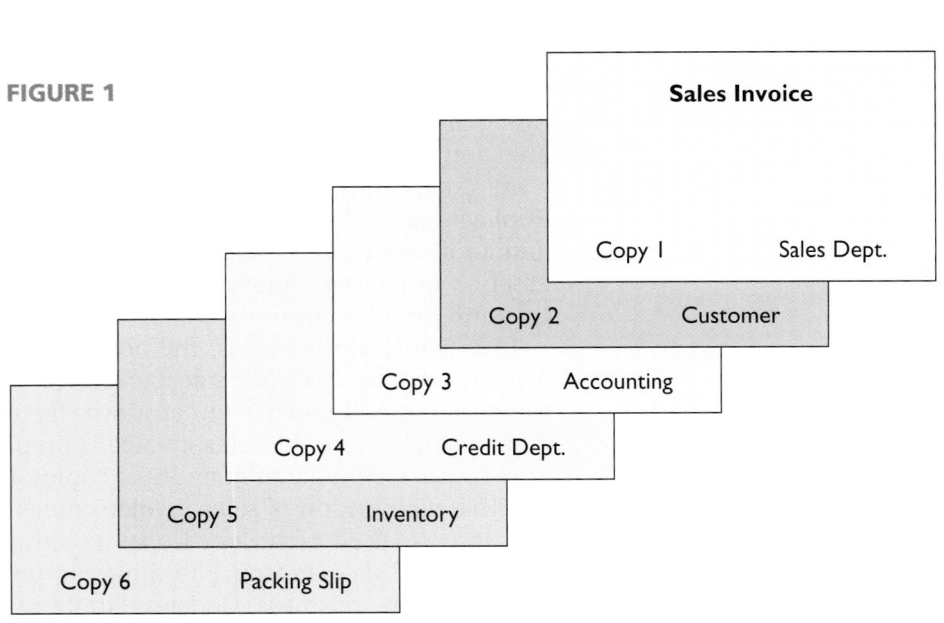

We will introduce the sales journal by looking at three transactions on the books of Dodson Plumbing Supply:

Aug. 1 Sold merchandise on account to C. P. Landis Company, invoice no. 320, $580.92.

3 Sold merchandise on account to Milne, Inc., invoice no. 321, $116.

6 Sold merchandise on account to Alvarez Construction, invoice no. 322, $394.

Here's how the accounts appear in the fundamental accounting equation.

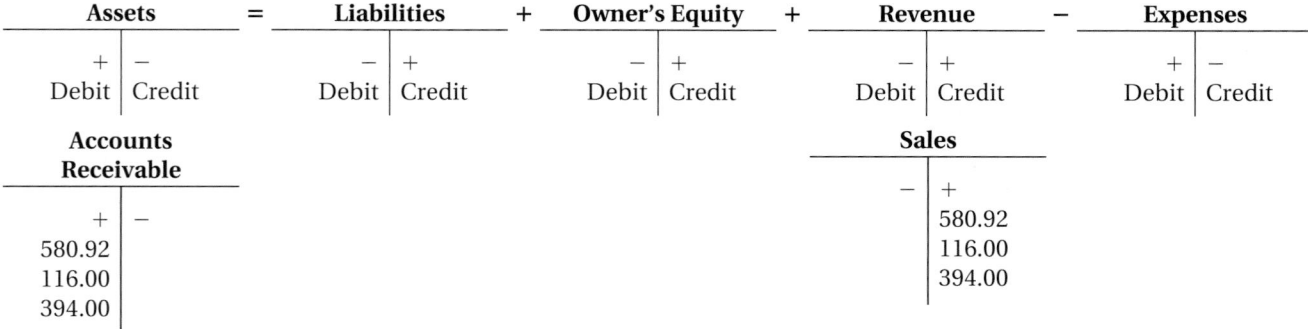

The sales invoice for the sale to C. P. Landis Company is shown in Figure 2.

FIGURE 2

REMEMBER!
Stress that the sales invoice is a source document and as such is evidence that serves as the basis for recording a transaction.

Dodson Plumbing Supply
1400 Jackson Avenue
San Diego, California 92102

INVOICE

SOLD TO C. P. Landis Company
5120 Gilman Avenue
San Diego, CA 92102

DATE: August 1, 20–
INVOICE NO.: 320
ORDER NO.: 5384
SHIPPED BY: Their truck
TERMS: 2/10, n/30

QUANTITY	DESCRIPTION	UNIT PRICE	TOTAL
6	Olin single-control tub shower faucet #44B652	51 50	309 00
6	Olin dual-control washerless lavoratory faucet #59B641	22 20	133 20
12	Olin massage shower head, antique brass #37B411	11 56	138 72
	TOTAL		580 92

THE SALES JOURNAL

The **sales journal** records sales of merchandise **on account only.** This specialized type of transaction calls for debits to Accounts Receivable and credits to Sales. Let's see how to record the three transactions for Dodson Plumbing Supply in the sales journal *instead of* in the general journal.

SALES JOURNAL   PAGE 38

	DATE		INV. NO.	CUSTOMER'S NAME	POST. REF.	ACCOUNTS RECEIVABLE DR. SALES CR.	
1	20–						1
2	Aug.	1	320	C. P. Landis Company		5 8 0 92	2
3		3	321	Milne, Inc.		1 1 6 00	3
4		6	322	Alvarez Construction		3 9 4 00	4
5							5

Because *one* money column is headed Accounts Receivable Dr./Sales Cr., each transaction requires only a single line. Repetition is avoided, and all entries for sales of merchandise on account are found in one place. Listing the invoice number makes it easier to check the details of a particular sale at a later date.

The amount of each sale will be posted daily to the account of each charge customer in the accounts receivable ledger. The accounts receivable ledger is introduced on page 336.

Posting from the Sales Journal

Using the sales journal also saves time and space in posting to the ledger accounts. The transactions involving the sales of merchandise on account for the entire month of August are shown in Figure 3.

Because every entry is a debit to Accounts Receivable and a credit to Sales, you can make a single posting to these accounts for the amount of the total as of the last day of the month. This entry is called a **summarizing entry** because it summarizes one month's transactions. In the Post. Ref. columns of the ledger accounts, the letter S designates the sales journal.

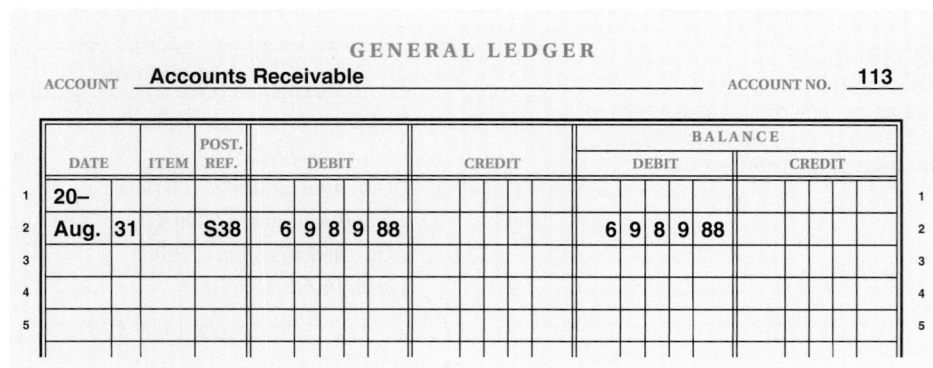

GENERAL LEDGER

ACCOUNT **Accounts Receivable**   ACCOUNT NO. 113

	DATE	ITEM	POST. REF.	DEBIT	CREDIT	BALANCE DEBIT	BALANCE CREDIT	
1	20–							1
2	Aug. 31		S38	6 9 8 9 88		6 9 8 9 88		2
3								3
4								4
5								5

| | | | | ACCOUNT _Sales_ | | | | | | | ACCOUNT NO. _411_ | | | | | | |

			POST.							BALANCE						
	DATE	ITEM	REF.	DEBIT				CREDIT		DEBIT			CREDIT		
1	20–															1
2	Aug. 31		S38					6 9 8 9 88					6 9 8 9 88		2
3																3
4																4
5																5

REMEMBER!
The purpose of posting reference numbers is to tell where in the ledger an amount was posted or the journal from which it came.

After posting the total of the sales journal to the Accounts Receivable account in the general ledger, write the account number of Accounts Receivable at the left below the total of the sales journal. Repeat the process of posting for the total of the sales journal to the Sales account in the general ledger, placing the account number of Sales at the right below the total of the sales journal. **Don't record these account numbers until you have completed the postings.**

FIGURE 3

REMEMBER!
The sales journal is used to record the sales of merchandise (goods) on account only.

				SALES JOURNAL		PAGE _38_	
		INV.			POST.	ACCOUNTS RECEIVABLE DR.	
	DATE	NO.	CUSTOMER'S NAME		REF.	SALES CR.	
1	20–						1
2	Aug. 1	320	C. P. Landis Company			5 8 0 92	2
3	3	321	Milne, Inc.			1 1 6 00	3
4	6	322	Alvarez Construction			3 9 4 00	4
5	9	323	Mitchell Service Company			9 6 1 00	5
6	11	324	Cozart Hardware			7 7 2 24	6
7	16	325	Hewitt and Sons, Inc.			4 4 1 00	7
8	20	326	Hazen Plumbing and Heating			7 1 0 00	8
9	23	327	Barlow Building Supplies			3 8 4 00	9
10	24	328	Cozart Hardware			2 9 3 22	10
11	28	329	Hewitt and Sons, Inc.			4 8 7 00	11
12	30	330	Barlow Building Supplies			6 1 4 00	12
13	31	331	C. P. Landis Company			3 7 5 50	13
14	31	332	F. A. Barnes, Inc.			8 6 1 00	14
15	31					6 9 8 9 88	15
16						(113)(411)	16
17							17

Sales Journal Provision for Sales Tax

Most states and some cities levy a **sales tax** on retail sales of goods and services. The retailer collects the sales tax from customers and later pays it to the tax authorities.

When goods or services are sold on credit, the sales tax is charged to the customer and recorded at the time of the sale. The sales journal must be designed to handle this type of transaction. For example, if a retail store sells an item for $100 and the sales tax is 7 percent, the transaction would be recorded in T accounts like this:

Accounts Receivable	Sales	Sales Tax Payable
+ | −	− | +	− | +
107 |	| 100	| 7

Incidentally, when the sales tax is paid to the state, the accountant debits Sales Tax Payable and credits Cash.

Because we want to illustrate a sales journal for a retail merchandising firm operating in a state that has a sales tax, we will talk about the transactions of Fiel Toy Center, another company. Its sales journal is shown in Figure 4.

FIGURE 4

SALES JOURNAL   PAGE __96__

	DATE	INV. NO.	CUSTOMER'S NAME	POST. REF.	ACCOUNTS RECEIVABLE DEBIT	SALES TAX PAYABLE CREDIT	SALES CREDIT	
1	20–							1
2	Apr. 1	9382	D. E. Bates		1 6 64	64	1 6 00	2
3	1	9383	Center Child Care		2 2 88	88	2 2 00	3
4	1	9384	Randy Kelley		5 2 00	2 00	5 0 00	4
5	2	9385	R. M. Kale		1 2 48	48	1 2 00	5
18	30	10121	L. O. Link		1 2 4 80	4 80	1 2 0 00	18
19	30				2 5 1 8 80	9 6 80	2 4 2 2 00	19
20					(1 1 3)	(2 1 4)	(4 1 1)	20
21								21
22								22

REMEMBER!
With a sales journal that has more than one column, use the column totals to prove that the total debits equal the total credits. Do this before posting to the general ledger accounts.

Column totals would be posted as a debit to Accounts Receivable, a credit to Sales Tax Payable, and a credit to Sales. After posting, the respective account numbers are recorded in parentheses below the totals.

THE ACCOUNTS RECEIVABLE LEDGER

In order to know how much each charge customer owes a business, the firm maintains an **accounts receivable ledger**. This ledger is a separate book or record containing a list of the charge customers with their respective balances listed in either alphabetical order or by account number. If the company's accounting system is not computerized, accountants prefer a loose-leaf binder, so that they can insert accounts for new customers and remove closed accounts.

The Accounts Receivable account in the general ledger should still be maintained. When all the postings are up to date, the balance of this

account should equal the total of all the charge customers' individual account balances. The Accounts Receivable account in the general ledger is called a controlling account. The accounts receivable *ledger,* containing the accounts of all the charge customers, is really a special ledger, called a subsidiary ledger. Figure 5 diagrams the interrelationship of these ledgers.

The accountant posts the individual amounts to the accounts receivable ledger every day, so that this ledger will have up-to-date information. At the end of the month, the accountant posts the sales journal total of $2,900 (in Figure 5) to the general ledger accounts as a debit to the Accounts Receivable controlling account and a credit to the Sales account. The schedule of accounts receivable is merely a listing of charge customers' individual account balances.

REMEMBER!
The balance of the Accounts Receivable controlling account at the end of the month must equal the total of the balances of the charge customer accounts in the accounts receivable ledger.

FIGURE 5

In the simplified illustration in Figure 5, it just so happens that, since no payments were received from charge customers, the total of the sales journal equals the balance of Accounts Receivable. However, if $1,200 had been received from charge customers, both the balance of the Accounts Receivable controlling account and the total of the schedule of accounts receivable would be $1,700 ($2,900 − $1,200). The total of the sales journal would still be $2,900.

After you post an amount from the sales journal to a charge customer's account in the accounts receivable ledger, put a check mark (✓) in the Post. Ref. column of the sales journal. Figure 6 shows the posting procedure for a single-column sales journal.

Let's go back to the sales journal of Dodson Plumbing Supply for August. We will cover the daily postings that its accountant has made to the accounts receivable ledger. Then we'll see the schedule of accounts receivable. These entries are shown in Figure 6 and the ledger accounts that follow. Note that the ruling consists of a single line under the amount column and double lines extended through the Date, Post. Ref., and Amount columns. The last day of the month is recorded on the same line as the total.

FIGURE 6

REMEMBER!
The check marks (✓) indicate that each amount has been posted to a charge customer's account.

SALES JOURNAL PAGE **38**

	DATE	INV. NO.	CUSTOMER'S NAME	POST. REF.	ACCOUNTS RECEIVABLE DR. SALES CR.	
1	20–					1
2	Aug. 1	320	C. P. Landis Company	✓	5 8 0 92	2
3	3	321	Milne, Inc.	✓	1 1 6 00	3
4	6	322	Alvarez Construction	✓	3 9 4 00	4
5	9	323	Mitchell Service Company	✓	9 6 1 00	5
6	11	324	Cozart Hardware	✓	7 7 2 24	6
7	16	325	Hewitt and Sons, Inc.	✓	4 4 1 00	7
8	20	326	Hazen Plumbing and Heating	✓	7 1 0 00	8
9	23	327	Barlow Building Supplies	✓	3 8 4 00	9
10	24	328	Cozart Hardware	✓	2 9 3 22	10
11	28	329	Hewitt and Sons, Inc.	✓	4 8 7 00	11
12	30	330	Barlow Building Supplies	✓	6 1 4 00	12
13	31	331	C. P. Landis Company	✓	3 7 5 50	13
14	31	332	F. A. Barnes, Inc.	✓	8 6 1 00	14
15	31				6 9 8 9 88	15
16					(113)(411)	16
17						17

ACCOUNTS RECEIVABLE LEDGER

NAME **Alvarez Construction**
ADDRESS **3680 Paseo Avenue**
San Diego, CA 92103

DATE	ITEM	POST. REF.	DEBIT	CREDIT	BALANCE
20–					
Aug. 6		S38	3 9 4 00		3 9 4 00

FIGURE 6
(continued)

NAME **Barlow Building Supplies**
ADDRESS **2242 Mission Avenue**
San Diego, CA 92103

DATE		ITEM	POST. REF.	DEBIT	CREDIT	BALANCE
20–						
Aug.	23		S38	3 8 4 00		3 8 4 00
	30		S38	6 1 4 00		9 9 8 00

NAME **F. A. Barnes, Inc.**
ADDRESS **424 Fifteenth Street**
San Diego, CA 92104

DATE		ITEM	POST. REF.	DEBIT	CREDIT	BALANCE
20–						
Aug.	31		S38	8 6 1 00		8 6 1 00

NAME **Cozart Hardware**
ADDRESS **2168 Tenth Street**
San Diego, CA 92103

DATE		ITEM	POST. REF.	DEBIT	CREDIT	BALANCE
20–						
Aug.	11		S38	7 7 2 24		7 7 2 24
	24		S38	2 9 3 22		1 0 6 5 46

NAME **Hazen Plumbing and Heating**
ADDRESS **1620 Salazar Road**
San Diego, CA 92105

DATE		ITEM	POST. REF.	DEBIT	CREDIT	BALANCE
20–						
Aug.	20		S38	7 1 0 00		7 1 0 00

(continued)

FIGURE 6
(continued)

NAME   Hewitt and Sons, Inc.

ADDRESS   4142 Lucientes Avenue

San Diego, CA 92105

DATE		ITEM	POST. REF.	DEBIT	CREDIT	BALANCE
20–						
Aug.	16		S38	4 4 1 00		4 4 1 00
	28		S38	4 8 7 00		9 2 8 00

NAME   C. P. Landis Company

ADDRESS   5120 Gilman Avenue

San Diego, CA 92102

DATE		ITEM	POST. REF.	DEBIT	CREDIT	BALANCE
20–						
Aug.	1		S38	5 8 0 92		5 8 0 92
	31		S38	3 7 5 50		9 5 6 42

NAME   Milne, Inc.

ADDRESS   1457 Megler Avenue

San Diego, CA 92103

DATE		ITEM	POST. REF.	DEBIT	CREDIT	BALANCE
20–						
Aug.	3		S38	1 1 6 00		1 1 6 00

NAME   Mitchell Service Company

ADDRESS   5196 Eighteenth Street

San Diego, CA 92104

DATE		ITEM	POST. REF.	DEBIT	CREDIT	BALANCE
20–						
Aug.	9		S38	9 6 1 00		9 6 1 00

OBJECTIVE 4
Prepare a schedule of accounts receivable.

Next, the accountant prepares a schedule of accounts receivable, like the one shown in Figure 7 on the following page, listing each charge customer's account balance.

FIGURE 7

Dodson Plumbing Supply
Schedule of Accounts Receivable
August 31, 20—

Alvarez Construction	$	3	9	4	00
Barlow Building Supplies		9	9	8	00
F. A. Barnes, Inc.		8	6	1	00
Cozart Hardware	1	0	6	5	46
Hazen Plumbing and Heating		7	1	0	00
Hewitt and Sons, Inc.		9	2	8	00
C. P. Landis Company		9	5	6	42
Milne, Inc.		1	1	6	00
Mitchell Service Company		9	6	1	00
Total Accounts Receivable	$ 6	9	8	9	88

We assume that there were no previous balances in the customers' accounts. Under this circumstance, the Accounts Receivable controlling account in the general ledger will have the same balance, $6,989.88, as the schedule of accounts receivable.

GENERAL LEDGER

ACCOUNT **Accounts Receivable**   ACCOUNT NO. **113**

	DATE	ITEM	POST. REF.	DEBIT	CREDIT	BALANCE DEBIT	BALANCE CREDIT	
1	20—							1
2	Aug. 31		S38	6 9 8 9 88		6 9 8 9 88		2
3								3

REMEMBER!
Posting to the Accounts Receivable account from the sales journal took place at the end of the month.

SALES RETURNS AND ALLOWANCES

OBJECTIVE 5
Journalize sales returns and allowances, including credit memorandums and returns involving sales tax, in a general journal, and post to the accounts receivable ledger and general ledger.

The Sales Returns and Allowances account handles two types of transactions having to do with merchandise that has previously been sold. A *return* is a physical return of the goods. An *allowance* is a reduction from the original price because the goods were defective or damaged. It may not be economically worthwhile to have customers return the goods; each situation is a special case. To avoid writing a separate letter each time to inform customers of their account adjustments, businesses use a special form called a **credit memorandum**. A credit memorandum (Figure 8 on page 342) is a written statement indicating a seller's willingness to reduce the amount of a buyer's debt.

The Sales Returns and Allowances account is a deduction from Sales. Using an account separate from Sales provides a better record of the total

FIGURE 8

Dodson Plumbing Supply
1400 Jackson Avenue
San Diego, California 92102

CREDIT MEMORANDUM   No. 69

CREDIT TO: *Barlow Building Supplies*   DATE: *September 2, 20–*
2242 Mission Avenue
San Diego, CA 92103

WE CREDIT YOUR ACCOUNT AS FOLLOWS:

QUANTITY	DESCRIPTION	TOTAL
1	*Olin pop-up tub drain antique finish* *1½-inch brass overflow tube #46C72*	*54 00*

FYI

A company must manage its return policy carefully. Customers often take advantage of return privileges, creating significant handling costs for the merchant.

returns and allowances. Accountants deduct Sales Returns and Allowances from Sales on the income statement.

Using T accounts, here's an example of a return. The original sale is shown first, followed by the issuance of a credit memorandum.

Transaction (a) On August 30, Dodson Plumbing Supply sold merchandise on account to Barlow Building Supplies, $614, and recorded the sale in the sales journal.

Transaction (b) On September 2, Barlow Building Supplies returned $54 worth of the merchandise. Dodson Plumbing Supply issued credit memorandum no. 69 (see Figure 8).

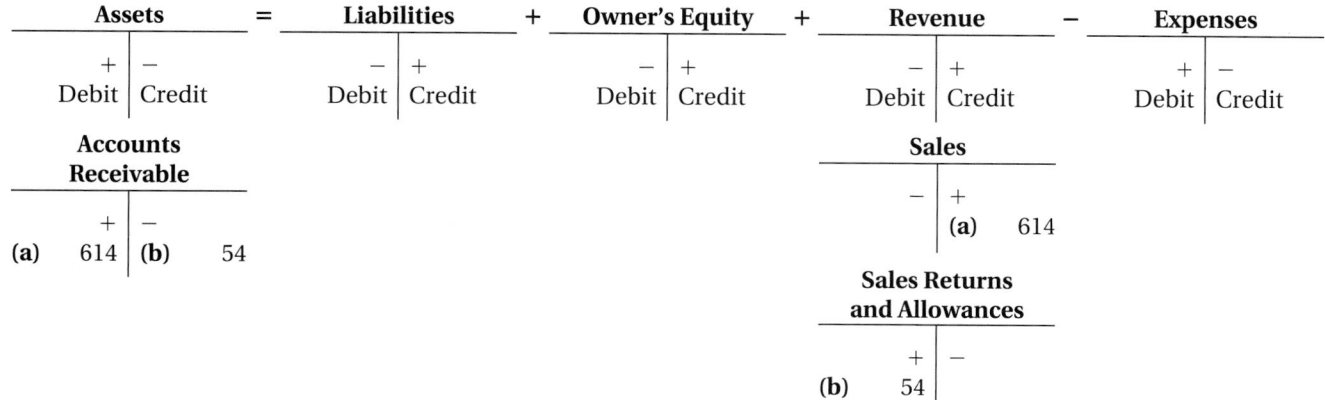

Dodson Plumbing Supply's accountant debits Sales Returns and Allowances, because Dodson Plumbing has more returns and allowances than it had before. The accountant credits Accounts Receivable because the charge customer, Barlow Building Supplies, owes less than before.

The general journal entry serves as the posting source for crediting the Accounts Receivable controlling account in the general ledger. It also serves as the posting source for updating the accounts receivable ledger and therefore includes the name of the charge customer. If the balance of the Accounts Receivable controlling account is to equal the total of the individual account balances in the accounts receivable ledger, one must post to *both* the Accounts Receivable account in the general ledger *and* the account of Barlow Building Supplies in the accounts receivable ledger. To take care of this double posting, draw a slanted line in the Post. Ref. column. When the amount has been posted as a credit to the general ledger account, the accountant writes the account number of Accounts Receivable in the left part of the Post. Ref. column. After the account of Barlow Building Supplies has been posted as a credit, the accountant puts a check mark in the right portion of the Post. Ref. column. Sales Returns and Allowances is posted in the usual manner. Here is the entry after posting is complete:

GENERAL JOURNAL   PAGE __27__

	DATE		DESCRIPTION	POST. REF.	DEBIT	CREDIT	
1	20–						1
2	Sept.	2	Sales Returns and Allowances	412	5 4 00		2
3			Accounts Receivable, Barlow				3
4			Building Supplies	113 ✓		5 4 00	4
5			Issued credit memo no. 69.				5
6							6

GENERAL LEDGER

ACCOUNT **Accounts Receivable**   ACCOUNT NO. __113__

	DATE	ITEM	POST. REF.	DEBIT	CREDIT	BALANCE DEBIT	BALANCE CREDIT	
1	20–							1
2	Aug. 31		S38	6 9 8 9 88		6 9 8 9 88		2
3	Sept. 2		J27		5 4 00	6 9 3 5 88		3
4								4

ACCOUNT **Sales Returns and Allowances**   ACCOUNT NO. __412__

	DATE	ITEM	POST. REF.	DEBIT	CREDIT	BALANCE DEBIT	BALANCE CREDIT	
1	20–							1
2	Sept. 2		J27	5 4 00		5 4 00		2
3								3

ACCOUNTS RECEIVABLE LEDGER

NAME **Barlow Building Supplies**

ADDRESS **2242 Mission Avenue**

San Diego, CA 92103

DATE		ITEM	POST. REF.	DEBIT	CREDIT	BALANCE
20–						
Aug.	23		S38	3 8 4 00		3 8 4 00
	30		S38	6 1 4 00		9 9 8 00
Sept.	2		J27		5 4 00	9 4 4 00

Sales Return Involving a Sales Tax

If a customer who returns merchandise to a retail store was originally charged a sales tax, the sales tax must be returned to the customer. Refer back to the sales journal of Fiel Toy Center on page 336, which included sales taxes. On April 3, assume that D. E. Bates returns the merchandise bought on April 1 for $16 plus $0.64 sales tax. Following is the general journal entry required for this type of return:

GENERAL JOURNAL   PAGE __12__

	DATE		DESCRIPTION	POST. REF.	DEBIT	CREDIT	
1	20–						1
2	Apr.	3	Sales Returns and Allowances		1 6 00		2
3			Sales Tax Payable		64		3
4			Accounts Receivable, D. E. Bates			1 6 64	4
5			Issued credit memo no. 371.				5
6							6
7							7

PURCHASING PROCEDURES

In a small retail store, the owner may do the buying. In large retail and whole-sale concerns, department heads or division managers do the buying, after which the Purchasing Department goes into action: It places purchase orders, follows up the orders, and sees that deliveries are made to the right departments. The Purchasing Department also acts as a source of information on current prices, price trends, quality of goods, prospective suppliers, and reliability of suppliers.

The Purchasing Department normally requires that any requests to buy merchandise be in writing, in the form of a **purchase requisition**. After the purchase requisition is approved, the Purchasing Department sends a purchase order to the supplier. A **purchase order** is the company's written offer to buy certain goods. The accountant does not make any entry at this point because the supplier has not yet indicated acceptance of the order. A purchase order has at least four copies. The original goes to the supplier; copies go to the Purchasing Department (as proof of what was ordered), the department that issued the requisition (telling it that the goods it wanted have been

FIGURE 9

Dodson Plumbing Supply

No. C-726

1400 Jackson Avenue
San Diego, California 92102

PURCHASE REQUISITION

DEPARTMENT ___Fixtures___

DATE OF REQUEST ___July 2, 20–___

ADVISE ON DELIVERY ___C. Fenwick___

DATE REQUIRED ___Aug. 5, 20–___

QUANTITY	DESCRIPTION
50	Drominex shower heads #772R

APPROVED BY _D. M. Bruce_

REQUESTED BY _J. C. Garcia_

FOR PURCHASING DEPT. USE ONLY

PURCHASE ORDER NO. ___7918___

ISSUED TO: Colvin, Inc.

DATE ___July 5, 20–___

1614 Olivera Street
San Francisco, CA 94129

ordered), the Accounting Department, and a blind copy (with quantities omitted) goes to Receiving.

To continue with the accounts of Dodson Plumbing Supply, the Fixtures Department submits a purchase requisition to the Purchasing Department, as shown in Figure 9.

The Purchasing Department completes the rest of the purchase requisition and then sends out the purchase order shown in Figure 10.

FIGURE 10

Dodson Plumbing Supply

1400 Jackson Avenue
San Diego, California 92102

PURCHASE ORDER

TO: Colvin, Inc.
1614 Olivera Street
San Francisco, CA 94129

DATE: July 5, 20–
ORDER NO.: 7918
SHIPPED BY:
TERMS: 2/10, n/30

QUANTITY	DESCRIPTION	UNIT PRICE	TOTAL
50	Drominex shower heads #772R	14 20	710 00
	Total		710 00

D. M. Bruce

The seller then sends an **invoice** to the buyer as shown in Figure 11. This invoice should arrive in advance of the goods (or at least *with* the goods).

FIGURE 11

Colvin, Inc.
No. 2706

1614 Olivera Street
San Francisco, CA 94129

INVOICE

SOLD TO *Dodson Plumbing Supply*	**DATE:** *July 31, 20–*
1400 Jackson Avenue	**ORDER NO.:** *7918*
San Diego, CA 92102	**SHIPPED BY:** *Western Freight Line*
	TERMS: *2/10, n/30*

YOUR ORDER NO.	SALESPERSON	TERMS
7918	*C. L.*	*2/10, n/30*
DATE SHIPPED	**SHIPPED BY**	**FOB**
July 31, 20–	*Western Freight Line*	*San Francisco*

QUANTITY	DESCRIPTION	UNIT PRICE	TOTAL
50	*Drominex shower heads #772R*	14	20	710	00
	Freight			49	00
	Total			759	00

Colvin, Inc. (the seller) prepaid the freight cost and added the $49 to the bill, listing it separately; this is similiar to buying something by mail order. Freight In is discussed in more detail on pages 353–354. The transaction is recorded in T accounts below.

Purchases		Freight In		Accounts Payable	
+	–	+	–	–	+
Aug. 2 710		Aug. 2 49			Aug. 2 759

PURCHASES JOURNAL (THREE-COLUMN)

OBJECTIVE 6
Journalize transactions in a three-column purchases journal.

Here's the **purchases journal** for Dodson Plumbing Supply for the month of August. By including a separate column for each account, we can record a typical purchase of merchandise on account on one line.

Terms means the terms of payment. For example, 2/10, n/30 means that if we pay the amount due within 10 days, we will receive a 2 percent discount; otherwise, all is due in 30 days.

PURCHASES JOURNAL   PAGE __29__

	DATE		SUPPLIER'S NAME	INVOICE NO.	INVOICE DATE	TERMS	POST. REF.	ACCOUNTS PAYABLE CREDIT	FREIGHT IN DEBIT	PURCHASES DEBIT	
1	20–										1
2	Aug.	2	Colvin, Inc.	2706	7/31	2/10, n/30		7 5 9 00	4 9 00	7 1 0 00	2
3		3	Richter and Son	982	8/2	n/30		8 2 9 00	5 7 00	7 7 2 00	3
4		5	Adams Manufacturing Co.	10611	8/3	2/10, n/30		5 6 4 00		5 6 4 00	4
5		9	Spargo Products Co.	B643	8/6	1/10, n/30		1 6 5 00	1 0 00	1 5 5 00	5
6		18	L. C. Waters	46812	8/17	n/60		2 2 8 00		2 2 8 00	6
7		25	Delaney and Cox	1024	8/23	2/10, n/30		3 7 6 00	1 4 00	3 6 2 00	7
8		26	Colvin, Inc.	2801	8/25	2/10, n/30		4 0 6 00	2 2 00	3 8 4 00	8
9		31						3 3 2 7 00	1 5 2 00	3 1 7 5 00	9
10								(2 1 2)	(5 1 4)	(5 1 1)	10
11											11
12											12

Posting from the Purchases Journal to the General Ledger

OBJECTIVE 7
Post purchases journal transactions to an accounts payable ledger and a general ledger.

Figures 12 and 13 show the journal entries for all transactions involving the purchase of merchandise on account for August and the related ledger accounts for the same time period. In the Post. Ref. column of the ledger accounts, P designates the purchases journal. After posting the column totals for the month to the ledger accounts, the accountant goes back to the purchases journal and records the account numbers in parentheses directly below the total.

FIGURE 12

REMEMBER!
Transactions involving the buying of supplies or other assets should not be journalized in the three-column purchases journal, because this purchases journal may be used only for purchases of merchandise for resale.

GENERAL LEDGER

ACCOUNT **Accounts Payable**   ACCOUNT NO. __212__

	DATE	ITEM	POST. REF.	DEBIT	CREDIT	BALANCE DEBIT	BALANCE CREDIT	
1	20–							1
2	Aug. 1	Balance	✓				5 0 4 00	2
3	31		P29		3 3 2 7 00		3 8 3 1 00	3
4								4

ACCOUNT **Purchases**   ACCOUNT NO. __511__

	DATE	ITEM	POST. REF.	DEBIT	CREDIT	BALANCE DEBIT	BALANCE CREDIT	
1	20–							1
2	Aug. 1	Balance	✓			20 6 1 2 00		2
3	31		P29	3 1 7 5 00		23 7 8 7 00		3
4								4

(continued)

FIGURE 12 (continued)

ACCOUNT Freight In   ACCOUNT NO. __514__

	DATE	ITEM	POST. REF.	DEBIT	CREDIT	BALANCE DEBIT	BALANCE CREDIT	
1	20–							1
2	Aug. 1	Balance	✓			1 5 0 2 00		2
3	31		P29	1 5 2 00		1 6 5 4 00		3
4								4

PURCHASES JOURNAL   PAGE __29__

	DATE	SUPPLIER'S NAME	INVOICE NO.	INVOICE DATE	TERMS	POST. REF.	ACCOUNTS PAYABLE CREDIT	FREIGHT IN DEBIT	PURCHASES DEBIT	
1	20–									1
2	Aug. 2	Colvin, Inc.	2706	7/31	2/10, n/30	✓	7 5 9 00	4 9 00	7 1 0 00	2
3	3	Richter and Son	982	8/2	n/30	✓	8 2 9 00	5 7 00	7 7 2 00	3
4	5	Adams Manufacturing Co.	10611	8/3	2/10, n/30	✓	5 6 4 00		5 6 4 00	4
5	9	Spargo Products Co.	B643	8/6	1/10, n/30	✓	1 6 5 00	1 0 00	1 5 5 00	5
6	18	L. C. Waters	46812	8/17	n/60	✓	2 2 8 00		2 2 8 00	6
7	25	Delaney and Cox	1024	8/23	2/10, n/30	✓	3 7 6 00	1 4 00	3 6 2 00	7
8	26	Colvin, Inc.	2801	8/25	2/10, n/30	✓	4 0 6 00	2 2 00	3 8 4 00	8
9	31						3 3 2 7 00	1 5 2 00	3 1 7 5 00	9
10							(2 1 2)	(5 1 4)	(5 1 1)	10

FIGURE 13

THE ACCOUNTS PAYABLE LEDGER

REMEMBER!
Creditors are companies or individuals to whom we owe money.

REMEMBER!
Increases in Accounts Payable are recorded in the Credit column. Decreases in Accounts Payable are recorded in the Debit column.

Previously, we called the Accounts Receivable account in the general ledger a **controlling** account, and we saw that the accounts receivable ledger consists of an individual account for each charge customer. We also saw that the accountant posts to the accounts receivable ledger every day.

Accounts Payable is a parallel case; it, too, is a controlling account in the general ledger. The accounts payable ledger **is a subsidiary ledger, and it consists of individual accounts for all the creditors.** Again, posting to the accounts payable ledger is usually done daily. After posting to the individual creditors' accounts, the accountant puts a check mark (✓) in the Post. Ref. column of the purchases journal. After the accountant has finished the posting to the controlling account at the end of the period, the total of the schedule of accounts payable should equal the balance of the Accounts Payable (controlling) account. The three-column form is used for the accounts payable ledger.

Now let's look at the purchases journal (Figure 13) and the postings to the ledger. Note that in the accounts payable ledger—as in the accounts receivable ledger—the accounts of the individual creditors are listed in either alphabetical or numerical order. Firms that handle all of their bookkeeping and accounting on computer may assign an account number to each individual account.

REMEMBER!

Signs for Accounts Payable

Debit	Credit
−	+

Columns for Accounts Payable Ledger

DEBIT	CREDIT	BALANCE
−	+	

ACCOUNTS PAYABLE LEDGER

NAME **Adams Manufacturing Company**

ADDRESS **254 Calle Mancha**

Los Angeles, CA 90025

DATE		ITEM	POST. REF.	DEBIT	CREDIT	BALANCE
20–						
Aug.	5		P29		5 6 4 00	5 6 4 00

NAME **Colvin, Inc.**

ADDRESS **1614 Olivera Street**

San Francisco, CA 94129

DATE		ITEM	POST. REF.	DEBIT	CREDIT	BALANCE
20–						
Aug.	2		P29		7 5 9 00	7 5 9 00
	26		P29		4 0 6 00	1 1 6 5 00

NAME **Delaney and Cox**

ADDRESS **2426 Reilly Way, N.E.**

Seattle, WA 98102

DATE		ITEM	POST. REF.	DEBIT	CREDIT	BALANCE
20–						
Aug.	25		P29		3 7 6 00	3 7 6 00

NAME **Richter and Son**

ADDRESS **142 Grant Road**

Cleveland, OH 44102

DATE		ITEM	POST. REF.	DEBIT	CREDIT	BALANCE
20–						
July	27		P28		1 8 0 00	1 8 0 00
Aug.	3		P29		8 2 9 00	1 0 0 9 00

NAME **Spargo Products Company**

ADDRESS **2154 Springer St.**

Boston, MA 02107

DATE		ITEM	POST. REF.	DEBIT	CREDIT	BALANCE
20–						
Aug.	9		P29		1 6 5 00	1 6 5 00

NAME   L. C. Waters

ADDRESS   1620 Minard St.

San Jose, CA 95101

DATE		ITEM	POST. REF.	DEBIT	CREDIT	BALANCE
20–						
July	29		P28		3 2 4 00	3 2 4 00
Aug.	18		P29		2 2 8 00	5 5 2 00

Schedule of Accounts Payable

Assuming that no other transactions involved Accounts Payable, the schedule of accounts payable would appear as shown in Figure 14. Note that the balance of Adams Manufacturing Company is taken from the accounts payable ledger.

The Accounts Payable controlling account in the general ledger below is now posted up to date.

GENERAL LEDGER

ACCOUNT   Accounts Payable   ACCOUNT NO.   212

	DATE		ITEM	POST. REF.	DEBIT	CREDIT	BALANCE DEBIT	BALANCE CREDIT	
1	20–								1
2	Aug.	1	Balance	✓				5 0 4 00	2
3		31		P29		3 3 2 7 00		3 8 3 1 00	3
4									4

FIGURE 14

Dodson Plumbing Supply
Schedule of Accounts Payable
August 31, 20—

Adams Manufacturing Company	$ 5 6 4 00
Colvin, Inc.	1 1 6 5 00
Delaney and Cox	3 7 6 00
Richter and Son	1 0 0 9 00
Spargo Products Company	1 6 5 00
L. C. Waters	5 5 2 00
Total Accounts Payable	$3 8 3 1 00

PURCHASES RETURNS AND ALLOWANCES

OBJECTIVE 9
Journalize transactions involving purchases returns and allowances in a general journal and post to the accounts payable ledger and general ledger.

As its title implies, the Purchases Returns and Allowances account handles either a return of merchandise previously purchased or an allowance made for merchandise that arrived in damaged condition. In both cases there is a reduction in the amount owed to the supplier. The buyer sends a letter or printed form to the supplier, who acknowledges the reduction by sending a **credit memorandum**. The buyer should wait for notice of the agreed deduction before making an entry.

The Purchases Returns and Allowances account is considered to be a deduction from Purchases. Using a separate account provides a better record of the total returns and allowances. Purchases Returns and Allowances is deducted from the Purchases account on the income statement. (We'll talk about this point later.) For now, let's look at an example consisting of a return on the books of Dodson Plumbing Supply.

Transaction (a) On September 5, bought merchandise on account from Adams Manufacturing Company, $564. Journalized this entry as a debit to Purchases and a credit to Accounts Payable.

Transaction (b) On September 8, received credit memorandum no. 629 from Adams Manufacturing Company for $70. Journalized this as a debit to Accounts Payable and a credit to Purchases Returns and Allowances.

Purchases Returns and Allowances is credited because Dodson Plumbing Supply has more returns and allowances than before. Accounts Payable is debited because Dodson Plumbing Supply owes less than before. The related entry including the postings is shown below. Note that Accounts Payable is followed by the name of the individual creditor's account. **The accountant must post the amount to both the Accounts Payable controlling account and the individual creditor's account in the accounts payable ledger.** The account numbers in the Post. Ref. column indicate postings to the accounts in the general ledger, and the check marks indicate postings to the accounts in the accounts payable ledger.

GENERAL JOURNAL   PAGE ___27___

	DATE		DESCRIPTION	POST. REF.	DEBIT	CREDIT	
1	20–						1
2	Sept.	8	Accounts Payable, Adams				2
3			Manufacturing Company	212 ✓	7 0 00		3
4			Purchases Returns and				4
5			Allowances	512		7 0 00	5
6			Credit memo no. 629 for				6
7			return of merchandise.				7
8							8

GENERAL LEDGER

ACCOUNT   **Accounts Payable**   ACCOUNT NO.   __212__

	DATE		ITEM	POST. REF.	DEBIT	CREDIT	BALANCE DEBIT	BALANCE CREDIT	
1	20–								1
2	Sept.	1	Balance	✓				3 8 3 1 00	2
3		8		J27	7 0 00			3 7 6 1 00	3
4									4

ACCOUNT   **Purchases Returns and Allowances**   ACCOUNT NO.   __512__

	DATE		ITEM	POST. REF.	DEBIT	CREDIT	BALANCE DEBIT	BALANCE CREDIT	
1	20–								1
2	Sept.	1	Balance	✓				6 4 0 00	2
3		8		J27		7 0 00		7 1 0 00	3
4									4

ACCOUNTS PAYABLE LEDGER

NAME   **Adams Manufacturing Company**

ADDRESS   **254 Calle Mancha**

          Los Angeles, CA 90025

DATE		ITEM	POST. REF.	DEBIT	CREDIT	BALANCE
20–						
Sept.	1	Balance	✓			5 6 4 00
	8		J27	7 0 00		4 9 4 00

FREIGHT CHARGES ON INCOMING MERCHANDISE

Companies use the Freight In account to keep a record of all separately charged delivery costs on incoming merchandise.

Freight costs are expressed as FOB (free on board) destination or shipping point. **(Destination is the buyer's location; shipping point is the seller's location.)** In both cases, the supplier loads the goods free on board the carrier. Beyond that point, there must be an understanding as to who is responsible for paying the freight charges. **If the seller assumes the entire cost of transportation, without any reimbursement from the buyer, the terms are FOB destination.** In this case, title or ownership changes hands when the buyer receives the goods. **If the buyer is responsible for paying the freight cost, the shipping terms are called FOB shipping point.** In this case, title or ownership changes hands when goods are transferred to a common carrier (freight company).

Briefly, when goods are shipped FOB destination, the freight charges are not stated, and the seller simply pays the amount of the freight. Suppose Dodson Plumbing Supply (remember, it's in San Diego) buys merchandise from a supplier in Chicago with shipping terms of FOB San Diego listed on the invoice. The total of the invoice is $1,740, and there is no separate listing of freight charges. In other words, the seller has included the transportation costs in the price.

On the other hand, when goods are shipped FOB shipping point, with the buyer responsible for paying the freight charges, transportation costs may be handled in two ways:

1. The buyer may pay the freight charges directly to the transportation company. For example, an automobile dealer in Houston buys cars FOB Detroit. In this case, the automobile dealer makes one check payable to the manufacturer and another check payable to the carrier for the freight charges. (FOB Detroit is the same as FOB shipping point.)

2. The transportation costs may be listed separately on the invoice. For example, suppose a person orders a refrigerator from a mail order company. The mail order company has prepaid (paid in advance) the freight charges as a favor or convenience for the buyer. However, the freight

To record the transportation costs of merchandise purchased for resale such as automobiles, accountants use an expense account called Freight In (also called Transportation In).

charges are listed on the bill or invoice, and the buyer is responsible for reimbursing the mail order company for the freight charges. Similarly, when a business buys merchandise, the amount of the freight charges may be prepaid by the seller and listed separately on the invoice.

Look again at the invoice of Colvin, Inc. Note that the freight cost is listed separately, and so the terms are FOB shipping point (San Francisco). Colvin paid the transportation cost; Dodson must reimburse Colvin for this cost.

Let's proceed with three other transactions for Dodson Plumbing Supply. We first record the transactions in a general journal. Then, as a means of reemphasizing the advantages of special journals as opposed to a general journal, we record the same transactions in a special journal. In practice, the transactions would be recorded *in only one journal, not both.*

During the first week in August, the following transactions took place:

Aug. 2 Bought merchandise on account from Colvin, Inc., $710, its invoice no. 2706, dated July 31; terms 2/10, n/30; FOB San Francisco; freight prepaid and added to the invoice, $49 (total $759).

3 Bought merchandise on account from Richter and Son, $772, its invoice no. 982 dated August 2; terms net 30 days; FOB Cleveland; freight prepaid and added to the invoice, $57 (total $829).

5 Bought merchandise on account from Adams Manufacturing Company, $564, its invoice no. 10611 dated August 3; terms 2/10, n/30; FOB Los Angeles.

Notice that the transactions with Colvin, Inc., and Richter and Son are both FOB shipping point with the freight charges listed separately. Consequently, the buyer (Dodson) must reimburse the sellers for the transportation costs by paying the total of the invoices. However, in the transaction with Adams Manufacturing, which is FOB shipping point without freight charges listed, the buyer (Dodson) must pay the freight costs separately, perhaps when the goods are delivered.

TRANSPORTATION CHARGES ON THE BUYING OF GOODS AND SERVICES OTHER THAN MERCHANDISE

Any freight charges incurred when buying any other assets, such as supplies or equipment, should be debited to the respective asset accounts. Let's return to Dodson Plumbing Supply and assume that this company bought display cases on account from Coster Cabinet Shop, at a cost of $2,700 plus freight charges of $90. The seller of the display cases prepaid the transportation costs for Dodson Plumbing Supply and then added the $90 to the invoice price of the cases. Let's visualize this with T accounts.

Store Equipment		Accounts Payable	
+	−	−	+
2,790			2,790

If Dodson Plumbing Supply had paid the freight charges separately, the entry for the payment would be a debit to Store Equipment for $90 and a credit to Cash for $90.

INTERNAL CONTROL

You know that the efficient management of cash is critical to a firm. All payments should be made either by check or from the petty cash fund, and all cash received should be deposited in the bank at the end of the day. The handling of cash in this manner is an example of **internal control**. Internal control embraces plans and procedures for the control of operations as a part of the accounting system. This is necessary when the owner or management must delegate authority. The owner has to take measures to (1) protect assets against fraud and waste, (2) provide for accurate accounting data, (3) promote an efficient operation, and (4) encourage adherence to management policies.

Internal Control of Purchases

Purchases is one of the areas in which internal control is essential. Efficiency and security require most companies to work out careful procedures for buying and paying for goods. This is understandable, as large sums of money are usually involved. The control aspect generally involves the following measures:

1. Purchases are made only after proper authorization is given. Purchase requisitions and purchase orders are all prenumbered, so that each form can be accounted for.
2. The receiving department carefully checks all goods upon receipt for count, damages, and description. Later, the report of the receiving department is verified against the purchase order and the purchase invoice.
3. The person who authorizes the payment is neither the person doing the ordering nor the person actually writing the check. Payment is authorized only after verifying the purchase invoice data with the receiving report and purchase order.
4. The person who actually writes the check has not been involved in any of the foregoing purchasing procedures.

CHAPTER REVIEW

Check out ACE for a Review Quiz at

http://college.hmco.com/accounting/students/.

Picture the T accounts involved in transactions. Here are examples of transactions. Sold merchandise on account to Barlow Building Supplies, $384.

Assets		=	Liabilities		+	Owner's Equity		+	Revenue		–	Expenses	
+	–		–	+		–	+		–	+		+	–
Debit	Credit		Debit	Credit		Debit	Credit		Debit	Credit		Debit	Credit

Accounts Receivable	
+	–
384	

REMEMBER!
Always think of the T accounts involved in each transaction. Get and stay in the T account habit.

Sales	
–	+
	384

Sold merchandise on account to D. E. Bates, $16.00 plus sales tax $0.64.

Assets	=	Liabilities	+	Owner's Equity	+	Revenue	−	Expenses
+ | −		− | +		− | +		− | +		+ | −
Debit | Credit		Debit | Credit		Debit | Credit		Debit | Credit		Debit | Credit

Accounts Receivable		Sales Tax Payable				Sales		
+ | −		− | +				− | +		
16.64 |		| 0.64				| 16.00		

Barlow Building Supplies returned $54 of merchandise.

Assets	=	Liabilities	+	Owner's Equity	+	Revenue	−	Expenses
+ | −		− | +		− | +		− | +		+ | −
Debit | Credit		Debit | Credit		Debit | Credit		Debit | Credit		Debit | Credit

Accounts Receivable		REMEMBER! Sales Returns and Allowances are a deduction from Sales.				Sales Returns and Allowances		
+ | −						+ | −		
| 54						54 |		

Purchased merchandise from Spargo Products Co., $155 plus $10 freight, total $165.

Assets	=	Liabilities	+	Owner's Equity	+	Revenue	−	Expenses
+ | −		− | +		− | +		− | +		+ | −
Debit | Credit		Debit | Credit		Debit | Credit		Debit | Credit		Debit | Credit

		Accounts Payable						Purchases
		− | +						+ | −
		| 165						155 |

								Freight In
								+ | −
								10 |

Returned merchandise to Adams Manufacturing Co., $70, and received a credit memorandum.

Assets	=	Liabilities	+	Owner's Equity	+	Revenue	−	Expenses
+ | −		− | +		− | +		− | +		+ | −
Debit | Credit		Debit | Credit		Debit | Credit		Debit | Credit		Debit | Credit

		Accounts Payable						Purchases Returns and Allowances
		− | +						− | +
		70 |						| 70

Review of Performance Objectives

1. Describe the specific accounts used by a merchandising firm.

   The Merchandise Inventory account is an asset account representing the cost of goods bought for resale. The Sales Tax Payable account is a liability account representing amounts owed to state or city governments. The Sales account is a revenue account representing the total sales of merchandise. The Sales Returns and Allowances account is a deduction from the Sales account, representing amounts allowed for returns of merchandise and damaged goods. The Sales Discount account is a deduction from the Sales account, representing amounts deducted for prompt payments. The Purchases account is a cost (expense) account representing the costs of goods bought for resale. The Purchases Returns and Allowances account is a deduction from the Purchases account, representing amounts granted by suppliers for the return of merchandise or damaged goods. The Purchases Discount account is a deduction from the Purchases account, representing amounts suppliers allow for prompt payments. The Freight In account is a cost representing the transportation charges on incoming merchandise.

2. Journalize transactions in a sales journal.

   The sales journal is used to record sales of merchandise on account only.

   The entries are posted daily to the accounts receivable ledger. At the end of the month, the total is posted to the general ledger as a debit to the Accounts Receivable controlling account and a credit to the Sales account.

3. Post sales journal transactions to an accounts receivable ledger and a general ledger.

   During the month, as customers charge merchandise, the amounts must be posted to their individual accounts as debits and a running balance maintained.

   At the end of the month, the total of the amounts charged by customers for purchase of merchandise must be posted to the general ledger as a Debit to Accounts Receivable and a Credit to Sales.

4. Prepare a schedule of accounts receivable.

   The schedule of accounts receivable consists of a listing of the individual account balances of the charge customers taken from the accounts receivable ledger.

5. Journalize sales returns and allowances, including credit memorandums and returns involving sales tax, in a general journal, and post to the accounts receivable ledger and general ledger.

   When a customer returns merchandise, or when his or her bill is reduced owing to an allowance for defective or damaged merchandise, the Sales Returns and Allowances account is debited and the Accounts Receivable account is credited. The entry is recorded in the general journal and posted to both the general ledger and the accounts receivable ledger.

6. Journalize transactions in a three-column purchases journal.

   The three-column purchases journal handles the purchase of merchandise on account and freight charges that are prepaid by the seller and included in the invoice total.

7. Post purchases journal transactions to an accounts payable ledger and a general ledger.

   Amounts in the Accounts Payable Credit column are posted daily to the accounts payable ledger. At the end of the month, the totals are posted to the general ledger as a debit to Purchases, a debit to Freight In, and a credit to Accounts Payable.

8. Prepare a schedule of accounts payable.

   A schedule of accounts payable, listing the balance of each individual creditor's account, is prepared from the accounts payable ledger.

9. Journalize transactions involving purchases returns and allowances in a general journal, and post to the accounts payable ledger and general ledger.

   When a credit memo is received for the return of merchandise or as an allowance for damaged merchandise, the buyer credits Purchases Returns and Allowances. If the merchandise was bought on account, the buyer debits Accounts Payable. The transaction is journalized in the general journal.

10. Describe the procedures for handling freight charges on merchandise and other goods.

    The Freight In account is debited for the cost of transportation charges on incoming merchandise intended for resale. Freight costs that apply to assets purchased are added to the asset account which applies. For example, $300 freight on a large freezer for a restaurant would be debited to that freezer account—part of the cost of that asset.

Glossary

Accounts payable ledger A subsidiary ledger that lists the individual accounts of creditors in either alphabetical or numerical order with their respective balances. (348)

Accounts receivable ledger A subsidiary ledger that lists the individual accounts of charge customers in either alphabetical or numerical order, with their respective transactions and balances. (336)

Controlling account An account in the general ledger that summarizes the balances of a subsidiary ledger. (337)

Credit memorandum A written statement indicating a seller's willingness to reduce the amount of a buyer's debt. The seller records the amount of the credit memorandum in the Sales Returns and Allowances account. (341)

FOB destination Shipping terms under which the seller pays the freight charges and includes them in the selling price. Title or ownership changes hands when the buyer receives the goods. (353)

FOB shipping point Shipping terms under which the buyer pays the freight charges between the point of shipment and the destination. Payment may be made directly to the carrier upon receiving the goods or to the supplier, if the supplier prepaid the freight charges on behalf of the buyer. Title or ownership changes hands when goods are transferred to the freight company. (353)

Freight In account The account used to record transportation charges on incoming merchandise intended for resale. (331)

Internal control Plans and procedures built into the accounting system with the following objectives: (1) to protect assets against fraud and waste; (2) to provide accurate accounting data; (3) to promote an efficient operation; and (4) to encourage adherence to management policies. (355)

Invoices Business forms prepared by the seller that list the items shipped, their cost, the terms of the sale, and the mode of shipment. They may also state the freight charges. The buyer considers them purchase invoices; the seller considers them sales invoices. (331)

Merchandise inventory A stock of goods (an asset account) that a company buys and intends to resell, in the same physical condition, at a profit. (330)

Purchase order A written order from the buyer of goods to the supplier, listing the items wanted and the terms of the transaction. (344)

Purchase requisition A form used to request that the Purchasing Department buy something. This form is intended for internal use within a company. (344)

Purchases account An account for recording the cost of merchandise acquired for resale. (331)

Purchases Discount account An account that records cash discounts granted by suppliers in return for prompt payment; it is treated as a deduction from Purchases. (331)

Purchases journal A special journal used to record the buying of goods on account only. It may be used to record the purchase of merchandise only. (346)

Purchases Returns and Allowances account An account that records a company's return of merchandise it has purchased or a reduction in the bill because of damaged merchandise; it is treated as a deduction from Purchases. (331)

Sales account A revenue account for recording the sale of merchandise. (331)

Sales Discount account An account that records a deduction from the original price, granted by the seller to the buyer for the prompt payment of an invoice. (331)

Sales journal A special journal for recording the sale of merchandise on account only. (334)

Sales Returns and Allowances account The account a seller uses to record the physical return of merchandise by customers or a reduction in a bill because merchandise was damaged. Sales Returns and Allowances is treated as a deduction from Sales. This account is usually evidenced by a credit memorandum issued by the seller. (331)

Sales Tax account A tax levied by a state or city government on the retail sale of goods and services. The tax is paid by the consumer but collected by the retailer. (331)

Special journals Books of original entry in which specialized types of repetitive transactions are recorded. (330)

Subsidiary ledger A group of accounts representing individual subdivisions showing the debits of a controlling account. (337)

Summarizing entry An entry made to post the column totals of a special journal to the appropriate accounts in the general ledger. It is also used when individual sales invoices are posted directly to the accounts receivable ledger. (334)

QUESTIONS, EXERCISES, AND PROBLEMS

Discussion Questions

1. Describe the posting procedures and rules for totaling and ruling the:
   a. Sales journal
   b. Purchases journal
2. What is the purpose of a:
   a. Schedule of accounts receivable?
   b. Schedule of accounts payable?
3. Describe the procedure for posting:
   a. from the sales journal to the accounts receivable ledger.
   b. from the purchases journal to the accounts payable ledger.
4. How are sales returns and allowances and purchases returns and allowances two sides of the same coin?
5. Explain the meaning and importance of the shipping terms FOB destination and FOB shipping point. Who has title to the goods once they have been shipped?
6. Why is an accounts receivable ledger or an accounts payable ledger necessary for a business with large numbers of charge customers or large numbers of vendors/suppliers?
7. Why is it a good practice to post daily to the accounts receivable or the accounts payable ledgers?
8. Describe the four procedures that most companies follow to maintain internal control of purchases of merchandise?

Exercises

P.O. 3,4,7,8

Post to general and subsidiary ledgers; prepare schedules of accounts receivable and accounts payable.

Exercise 10-1 Milcer Company has completed October's sales and purchases journals. Your job is to:

a. Total and post the journals to the general ledger and to the accounts receivable and accounts payable ledgers.
b. Complete a schedule of accounts receivable for October 31, 20—.
c. Complete a schedule of accounts payable for October 31, 20—.
d. Compare the balances of the schedules with their respective general ledger accounts. If they are not the same, find and correct the error(s).

SALES JOURNAL   PAGE __18__

	DATE	INV. NO.	CUSTOMER'S NAME	POST. REF.	ACCOUNTS RECEIVABLE DR. SALES CR.	
1	20–					1
2	Oct. 3	414	Anderson Company		4 4 3 24	2
3	4	415	R. T. Holcomb		1 4 2 6 90	3
4	7	416	Gray and Malo		1 6 4 7 00	4
5	11	417	Mercer Mobil		3 1 1 2 16	5
6	16	418	J. L. Anthony		2 1 3 0 00	6
7	22	419	C. A. Goldschmidt		1 9 4 4 05	7
8	31	420	F. A. Baumann		2 7 9 1 00	8
9	31					9
10					( )( )	10

PURCHASES JOURNAL

PAGE __10__

	DATE	SUPPLIER'S NAME	INVOICE NO.	INVOICE DATE	TERMS	POST. REF.	ACCOUNTS PAYABLE CREDIT	FREIGHT IN DEBIT	PURCHASES DEBIT	
1	20–									1
2	Oct. 2	Colter, Inc.	2706	7/31	2/10, n/30		7 5 9 00	4 9 00	7 1 0 00	2
3	3	Thomas and Son	982	8/2	n/30		8 2 9 00	5 7 00	7 7 2 00	3
4	5	Archer Manufacturing Co.	10611	8/3	2/10, n/30		5 6 4 00		5 6 4 00	4
5	9	Spence Products Co.	B643	8/6	1/10, n/30		1 6 5 00	1 0 00	1 5 5 00	5
6	18	L. C. Walter	46812	8/17	n/60		2 2 8 00		2 2 8 00	6
7	25	Delaney and Cox	1024	8/23	2/10, n/30		3 7 6 00	1 4 00	3 6 2 00	7
8	26	Colter, Inc.	2801	8/25	2/10, n/30		4 0 6 00	2 2 00	3 8 4 00	8
9	31									9
10							( )	( )	( )	10

Accounts Receivable Ledger

Anderson Company

J. L. Anthony

F. A. Baumann

C. A. Goldschmidt

Gray and Malo

R. T. Holcomb

Mercer Mobil

General Ledger

Accounts Receivable 113

Accounts Payable 212

Sales 411

Purchases 511

Freight In 514

Accounts Payable Ledger

Archer Mfg.

Colter, Inc.

Delaney and Cox

Spence Products Co.

Thomas and Son

L. C. Walter

SCHEDULE OF ACCOUNTS RECEIVABLE

SCHEDULE OF ACCOUNTS RECEIVABLE

P.O. 3

Describe transactions involving a sale, a return, and a payment.

Exercise 10-2 Describe the transactions recorded in the following T accounts:

Cash		Sales Tax Payable		Sales Returns and Allowances	
(c) 541.00		(b) 8.20	(a) 49.20	(b) 100.00	

Accounts Receivable		Sales	
(a) 649.20	(b) 108.20		(a) 600.00
	(c) 541.00		

P.O. 3

Record entries involving a sale, a return, and a receipt of cash.

Exercise 10-3 Record the following transactions in general journal form:

a. Sold merchandise on account to C. C. Hall, $360 plus $18.00 sales tax (invoice no. D446).
b. Hall returned $90 of the merchandise. Issued credit memo no. 114 for $94.50 ($90 for the amount of the sale plus $4.50 for the amount of the sales tax).
c. Received $283.50 from C. C. Hall in full payment of account.

P.O. 5

Post to general and accounts receivable ledgers.

Exercise 10-4 Post the following entry to the general ledger and subsidiary ledger:

GENERAL JOURNAL PAGE 52

	DATE		DESCRIPTION	POST. REF.	DEBIT	CREDIT	
1	20–						1
2	June	16	Sales Returns and Allowances		2 4 1 27		2
3			Accounts Receivable, R. D. Moen			2 4 1 27	3
4			Issued credit memo no. 131.				4
5							5

GENERAL LEDGER

ACCOUNT **Accounts Receivable** ACCOUNT NO. 113

DATE		ITEM	POST. REF.	DEBIT	CREDIT	BALANCE DEBIT	BALANCE CREDIT
20–							
June	1	Balance	✓			6 5 1 1 19	

ACCOUNT	Sales Returns and Allowances					ACCOUNT NO.	**412**		

DATE	ITEM	POST. REF.	DEBIT	CREDIT	BALANCE DEBIT	BALANCE CREDIT
20–						
June 1	Balance	✓			3 1 4 60	

ACCOUNTS RECEIVABLE LEDGER

NAME   R. D. Moen

ADDRESS   416 Fifth Avenue

Dallas, Texas   75204

DATE	ITEM	POST. REF.	DEBIT	CREDIT	BALANCE
20–					
May 31		S26	3 1 2 60		3 1 2 60

P.O. 5,9

Record a sales return and a
purchases return.

Exercise 10-5 Using the following source document (credit memo issued by Heald Electronics), record the transaction in general journal form on the books of Heald Electronics, then on the books of The Merchandise Mart.

Heald Electronics
4160 Broad Street
Chicago, Illinois 60627

CREDIT MEMORANDUM   No.   **121**

DATE: **November 6, 20—**

CREDIT TO:

   The Merchandise Mart

   2241 Sullivan Street

   Chicago, Illinois   60632

Your account has been credited for:

   1 Benton 27" color TV (1xf27)   **$623.00**

P.O. 9

Describe entries involving a
purchase and return.

Exercise 10-6 Describe the transactions in the T accounts.

Cash						Purchases		
		(c)	750		(a)	760		

Accounts Payable						Purchases Returns and Allowances		
(b)	50	(a)	800				(b)	50
(c)	750					Freight In		
					(a)	40		

P.O. 9

Record journal entries for a purchase and return.

Exercise 10-7 Journalize the following transactions in general journal form:

a. Bought merchandise on account from Westro, Inc., invoice no. C229; net 30 days; FOB destination, $1,010.
b. Received credit memo no. 117 from Westro, Inc., for merchandise returned, $102.
c. Issued a check to Westro, Inc., in full payment of account.

P.O. 9

Post to accounts payable ledger and general ledger.

Exercise 10-8 Post the following entry to the general ledger and the subsidiary ledger:

GENERAL JOURNAL PAGE 92

	DATE		DESCRIPTION	POST. REF.	DEBIT	CREDIT	
1	20–						1
2	July	14	Accounts Payable, Bullock and				2
3			Hendricks		1 9 2 30		3
4			Purchases Returns and				4
5			Allowances			1 9 2 30	5
6			Credit memo no. 942 for				6
7			return of merchandise.				7
8							8

GENERAL LEDGER

ACCOUNT **Accounts Payable** ACCOUNT NO. 212

	DATE		ITEM	POST. REF.	DEBIT	CREDIT	BALANCE DEBIT	BALANCE CREDIT	
1	20–								1
2	July	1	Balance	✓				2 7 6 1 24	2
3									3

ACCOUNT **Purchases Returns and Allowances** ACCOUNT NO. 512

	DATE		ITEM	POST. REF.	DEBIT	CREDIT	BALANCE DEBIT	BALANCE CREDIT	
1	20–								1
2	July	1	Balance	✓				2 3 0 16	2
3									3

ACCOUNTS PAYABLE LEDGER

NAME **Bullock and Hendricks**

ADDRESS **542 Roselle Blvd.**

Richmond, CA 94879

DATE		ITEM	POST. REF.	DEBIT	CREDIT	BALANCE
20–						
June	13		P73		2 1 8 00	2 1 8 00

THE WORLD WIDE WEB

Sales Returns at Wal-Mart

You have just learned about recording transactions related to a company's sales. Sales returns and allowances, as well as discounts, affect the amount of a company's net sales.

1. Can you tell from looking at Wal-Mart's financial statements, how much merchandise was returned during a year? You can view Wal-Mart's financial statements at **http://www.walmartstores.com/wmstore/ wmstores/Mainnews.jsp?pagetype=news&categoryOID= -8775&template=DisplayAllContents.jsp.**

2. Wal-Mart is a merchandising company. The company purchases merchandise inventory and then resells it. In Wal-Mart's chart of accounts, which accounts are related to the purchase and sale of merchandise inventory?

3. Would these accounts appear in the chart of accounts for a professional enterprise? (Go back and review Chapter 6.)

In Chapter 5, we discussed Tommy Hilfiger Corporation's net sales and accounts receivable amounts. Now that you have learned about recording sales on account, let's go back to the same question and take another look. Use the financial statements that begin on page 27 of the 2002 annual report. They can be found at **http://www.tommypr.com/media/ downloads/TH02.pdf.**

4. For 2002, how much is net sales (assume that all revenue is from sales) on Tommy Hilfiger's income statement? How much is accounts receivable on the balance sheet? What can you tell from these two amounts? What is their relation to each other?

CONSIDER AND COMMUNICATE

You are the bookkeeper at a small merchandising firm. You are comparing the income statements from the last three years. You notice that the Purchases Returns and Allowances account (as a percentage of net sales) has been increasing at an alarming rate. If you were a manager, who would you speak to in the organization to help you understand why so much merchandise is being returned.

CRITICAL THINKING

<table>
<tr><td>TO:</td><td>Accounting Clerk</td><td>SUBJECT:</td><td>Errors in trial balance</td></tr>
<tr><td>FROM:</td><td>Senior Accountant</td><td>DATE:</td><td>April 1, 20—</td></tr>
</table>

Following is a trial balance prepared just before you were hired. There are two accounts missing, and the amount for Sales is off. Here are a few facts to consider. Our business is in a state that collects sales tax. I ran some totals, and we collected $1,800 in sales tax. Customers returned $900 in goods, which would reduce the above sales tax by $70. Our books need to reflect these events. The former accounting clerk said she did record every-thing—somewhere. She said she may have credited the $1,800 sales tax to Sales and not to Sales Tax Payable. Plus, she looked confused when Sales Returns and Allowances was mentioned. She asked, "why not just debit Sales?" Please determine the two missing accounts and correct the accounts that are off.

Cox Retail Outlet
Trial Balance
March 31, 20—

ACCOUNT NAME	DEBIT	CREDIT
Cash	8 9 4 0 00	
Accounts Receivable	4 8 0 00	
Supplies	1 7 5 00	
Store Equipment	9 4 6 0 00	
Accounts Payable		9 5 8 00
D. Cox, Capital		11 9 5 9 00
D. Cox, Drawing	4 4 8 0 00	
Sales		18 0 0 0 00
Rent Expense	2 4 0 0 00	
Wages Expense	4 8 6 4 00	
Miscellaneous Expense	1 1 8 00	
	30 9 1 7 00	30 9 1 7 00

1. Think about where these amounts might have been put, think about what accounts are missing, and use T accounts to solve the problems.
2. Prepare a corrected trial balance.

A MATTER OF ETHICS

Ms. Wynn, an employee, accidentally dropped a pallet of boxes containing microwaves off the forklift she was driving in the warehouse. No one saw what happened. She couldn't see (or hear) any damage to the microwaves, so she reloaded the boxes and did not tell her supervisor. Is Ms. Wynn behaving in an ethical manner when she withholds this information? Assume that the microwaves were damaged and were delivered to customers. How might this damage affect the income statement?

PROBLEM SET A

For additional help, see the demonstration problem at the beginning of each chapter in your Working Papers.

P.O. 2,3,4,5

Problem 10-1A Bradley Company sells electrical supplies on a wholesale basis. The following transactions took place during April of this year:

Apr. 1 Sold merchandise on account to Mayfair Company, invoice no. 761, $561.24.

  5 Sold merchandise on account to L. R. Friedman Company, invoice no. 762, $297.11.

  6 Issued credit memo no. 50 to Mayfair Company for merchandise returned, $42.72.

  10 Sold merchandise on account to Danforth Hardware, invoice no. 763, $193.35.

  14 Sold merchandise on account to Berg and Hobart, invoice no. 764, $740.16.

  17 Sold merchandise on account to Poe and Roberts, invoice no. 765, $472.12.

  21 Issued credit memo no. 51 to Berg and Hobart for merchandise returned, $67.77.

  24 Sold merchandise on account to Overmeier Company, invoice no. 766, $482.87.

  26 Sold merchandise on account to Danforth Hardware, invoice no. 767, $761.19.

  30 Issued credit memo no. 52 to Danforth Hardware for damage to merchandise, $91.50.

Check Figure

Accounts Receivable account balance, $4,475.47 debit

Instructions

1. Record these sales of merchandise on account in the sales journal (page 39). Record the sales returns and allowances in the general journal (page 74).
2. Immediately after recording each transaction, post to the accounts receivable ledger.
3. Post the amounts from the general journal daily. Post the sales journal amounts as a total at the end of the month; Accounts Receivable 113, Sales 411, Sales Returns 412, and Allowances.
4. Prepare a schedule of accounts receivable. Compare the balance of the Accounts Receivable controlling account with the total of the schedule of accounts receivable.

Instructions for General Ledger Software

1. Record these transactions in either the sales journal or the general journal and post.
2. Print the entries from the general journal.
3. Print the entries from the sales journal.
4. Print a schedule of accounts receivable and compare its total with the Accounts Receivable controlling account.

P.O. 2,3,4,5

Problem 10-2A Mancini Florists sells flowers on a retail basis. Most of the sales are for cash; however, a few steady customers have charge accounts. Mancini's sales staff fills out a sales slip for each sale. The state government levies a 5 percent retail sales tax, which is collected by the retailer. The following represent Mancini Florists' charge sales for March:

Mar. 4 Sold potted plant on account to C. Mills, sales slip no. 242, $18, plus sales tax of $0.90, total $18.90.

6 Sold floral arrangement on account to R. Drake, sales slip no. 267, $36, plus sales tax of $1.80, total $37.80.

12 Sold corsage on account to B. Cater, sales slip no. 279, $14, plus sales tax of $0.70, total $14.70.

16 Sold wreath on account to American League, sales slip no. 296, $68, plus sales tax of $3.40, total $71.40.

18 Sold floral arrangements on account to Town Funeral Home, sales slip no. 314, $240 plus sales tax of $12, total $252.00.

21 Town Funeral Home returned a flower spray. Delivery of the spray occurred after the funeral was over. Mancini allowed full credit on the sale of $44 and the sales tax of $2.20, credit memo no. 27.

23 Sold flower arrangements on account to Peninsula Savings and Loan Association for their anniversary, sales slip no. 337, $160 plus sales tax of $8, total $168.

24 Allowed Peninsula Savings and Loan Association credit, $18, plus sales tax of $0.90, because of withered blossoms in floral arrangements, credit memo no. 28.

Check Figure

Schedule of Accounts Receivable total, $608.92

Instructions

1. Record these transactions in either the sales journal (page 23) or the general journal (page 57).
2. Immediately after recording each transaction, post to the accounts receivable ledger.
3. Post the amounts from the general journal daily. Post the sales journal amounts as a total at the end of the month; Accounts Receivable 113, Sales Tax Payable 214, Sales 411, Sales Returns and Allowances 412.
4. Prepare a schedule of accounts receivable and compare its total with the Accounts Receivable controlling account.

P.O. 6,7,8

Problem 10-3A Minard Appliance uses a three-column purchases journal. The company is located in Fresno, California. On January 1 of this year, the balances of the ledger accounts are Accounts Payable, $559.06; Purchases, zero; Freight In, zero. In addition to a general ledger, Minard Appliance also uses an accounts payable ledger. Transactions for January related to the buying of merchandise are as follows:

Jan. 2 Bought eighty 12-inch, 3-speed Brighton Oscillating Fans from Sweat and Allen, $1,680, invoice no. 268J, dated January 2; terms net 60 days; FOB Fresno.

4 Bought ten 35-pint-capacity Coster Humidifiers from Shannon Company, $2,100, invoice no. 39426, dated January 2; terms 2/10, n/30; FOB Denver, freight prepaid and added to the invoice, $80 (total $2,180).

7 Bought ten 16-inch Apex Window Fans from Tedder, Inc., $380, invoice no. 452AD, dated January 6; terms 1/10, n/30; FOB Fresno.

10 Bought twenty-four 4-blade Tempo Ceiling Fans, Model 2760, from Ulrich Company, $3,648, invoice no. D7742, dated January 7; terms 2/10, n/30; FOB Napa, freight prepaid and added to the invoice, $97 (total $3,745).

Jan. 14 Bought four Champion Electric Hedge Trimmers from Fowler Products Company, $164, invoice no. 2542, dated January 13; terms net 30 days; FOB Fresno.

22 Bought forty Larkin Electric Bug Killers from Sweat and Allen, $2,480, invoice no. 392J, dated January 22; terms net 60 days; FOB Fresno.

28 Bought ten Champion Electric Blowers from Fowler Products Company, $640, invoice no. 2691, dated January 27; terms net 30 days; FOB Fresno.

30 Bought ten King Powered Attic Ventilators from Pollard Manufacturing Company, $345, invoice no. 664CC, dated January 27; terms 2/10, n/30; FOB Seattle, freight prepaid and added to the invoice, $45 (total $390).

Check Figure

Accounts Payable account balance, $12,218.06 credit

Instructions

1. Open the following accounts in the accounts payable ledger and record the balances, if any, as given as of January 1: Fowler Products Company; Pollard Manufacturing Company, $163.17; Shannon Company, $167.19; Sweat and Allen; Tedder, Inc., $228.70; Ulrich Company. For the accounts having balances, write "Balance" in the Item column and place a check mark in the Post. Ref. column.

2. Record the balance of $559.06 in the Accounts Payable controlling account as of January 1. Write "Balance" in the Item column and place a check mark in the Post. Ref. column.

3. Record the transactions in the purchases journal beginning on page 81.

4. Post to the accounts payable ledger daily.

5. Post to the general ledger at the end of the month.

6. Prepare a schedule of accounts payable, and compare the balance of the Accounts Payable controlling account with the total of the schedule of accounts payable.

P.O. 2,3,4,5,6,7,8,9

Problem 10-4A The following transactions relate to the Broderick Company of Atlanta during April of this year. Terms of sale are 2/10, n/30.

Apr. 2 Sold merchandise on account to Slocum and Company, invoice no. 1126, $942.

4 Bought merchandise on account from Padrow Manufacturing Company, invoice no. 16521, $568; terms 1/10, n/30; dated April 2; FOB Atlanta.

9 Sold merchandise on account to Pittman and Lowe, invoice no. 1127, $1,376.

12 Bought merchandise on account from Vinson Company, invoice no. L8552, $2,363; terms 2/10, n/30; dated April 11; FOB Rome, freight prepaid and added to the invoice, $59 (total $2,422).

15 Received credit memo no. 79 for merchandise returned to Kreiger and Company, for $118.

17 Sold merchandise on account to C. N. Howell, Inc., invoice no. 1128, $959.

19 Issued credit memo no. 34 to Pittman and Lowe for merchandise returned, $86.

26 Bought merchandise on account from M. R. Pace, Inc., invoice no. 7447, $1,697; terms 2/10, n/30; dated April 23; FOB Macon, freight prepaid and added to the invoice, $47 (total $1,744).

29 Bought office supplies on account from Tiffany Stationery Company, invoice no. S336, dated April 29, $134; terms net 30 days.

Apr. 30 Sold merchandise on account to Schmidt and Maki, invoice no. 1129, $2,557.

30 Issued credit memo no. 35 to Schmidt and Maki for merchandise returned, $162.

Check Figure

Accounts Payable account balance, $5,128.00 credit

Instructions

1. Open the following accounts in the accounts receivable ledger and record the balances as of April 1: C. N. Howell, Inc.; Pittman and Lowe, $426; Schmidt and Maki, $974; Slocum and Company. For the accounts having balances, write "Balance" in the Item column and place a check mark in the Post. Ref. column.
2. Open the following accounts in the accounts payable ledger and record the balances as of April 1: Kreiger and Company, $262; M. R. Pace, Inc., $116; Padrow Manufacturing Company; Tiffany Stationery Company; Vinson Company. For the accounts having balances, write "Balance" in the Item column and place a check mark in the Post. Ref. column.
3. Record the transactions in the sales, purchases, or general journal, as appropriate.
4. Post the entries to the accounts receivable ledger daily.
5. Post the entries to the accounts payable ledger daily.
6. Post the entries in the general journal immediately after you make each journal entry.
7. Post the totals from the special journals at the end of the month.
8. Prepare a schedule of accounts receivable.
9. Prepare a schedule of accounts payable.
10. Compare the totals of the schedules with the balances of the controlling accounts.

Instructions for General Ledger Software

1. Record the transactions in the sales, purchases, or general journals.
   a. For efficiency, analyze the transactions, indicate into which journal each transaction goes, and key the entries in three batches—the sales journal, the purchases journal, and the general journal.
   b. If the program uses a single-column purchases journal, add the amount of the freight to the amount of purchases.
2. Print the journals.
3. Post the amounts from the sales, purchases, and general journals.
4. Print the general ledger.
5. Print a schedule of accounts receivable and compare the total with the balance of the Accounts Receivable controlling account.
6. Print a schedule of accounts payable and compare the total with the balance of the Accounts Payable controlling account.

PROBLEM SET B

For additional help, see the demonstration problem at the beginning of each chapter in your Working Papers.

P.O. 2,3,4,5

Problem 10-1B C. H. Brighton Company sells electrical supplies on a wholesale basis. The following transactions took place during April of this year.

Apr.   3   Sold merchandise on account to Mayfair Company, invoice no. 822, $641.20.

7   Sold merchandise on account to L. R. Friedman Company, invoice no. 823, $378.53.

8   Sold merchandise on account to Danforth Hardware, invoice no. 824, $193.25.

13   Issued credit memo no. 61 to L. R. Friedman Company for merchandise returned, $46.50.

15   Sold merchandise on account to Berg and Hobart, invoice no. 825, $814.77.

21   Sold merchandise on account to Poe and Roberts, invoice no. 826, $681.64.

24   Issued credit memo no. 62 to Berg and Hobart for merchandise returned, $78.31.

26   Sold merchandise on account to Overmeier Company, invoice no. 827, $587.16.

28   Issued credit memo no. 63 to Danforth Hardware for damage to merchandise, $43.67.

30   Sold merchandise on account to Danforth Hardware, invoice no. 828, $740.04.

Check Figure

Accounts Receivable account balance, $5,037.53 debit

Instructions

1. Record these sales of merchandise on account in the sales journal (page 39). Record the sales returns and allowances in the general journal (page 74).
2. Immediately after recording each transaction, post to the accounts receivable ledger.
3. Post the amounts from the general journal daily. Post the sales journal amount as a total at the end of the month; Accounts Receivable 113, Sales 411, Sales Returns and Allowances 412.
4. Prepare a schedule of accounts receivable. Compare the balance of the Accounts Receivable controlling account with the total of the schedule of accounts receivable.

Instructions for General Ledger Software

1. Record these transactions in either the sales journal or the general journal and post.
2. Print the entries from the general journal.
3. Print the entries from the sales journal.
4. Print a schedule of accounts receivable and compare its total with the balance of Accounts Receivable.

P.O. 2,3,4,5

Problem 10-2B Nguyen Florists sells flowers on a retail basis. Most of the sales are for cash; however, a few steady customers have charge accounts. Nguyen's sales staff fills out a sales slip for each sale. The state government levies a 5 percent retail sales tax, which is collected by the retailer. Nguyen Florists' charge sales for March are as follows:

Mar.   4   Sold floral arrangement on account to R. Drake, sales slip no. 236, $32, plus sales tax of $1.60, total $33.60.

7   Sold potted plant on account to C. Mills, sales slip no. 272, $18, plus sales tax of $0.90, total $18.90.

Mar. 12 Sold wreath on account to American League, sales slip no. 294, $64, plus sales tax of $3.20, total $67.20.

17 Sold floral arrangements on account to Town Funeral Home, sales slip no. 299, $180, plus sales tax of $9.00, total $189.00.

20 Town Funeral Home returned a flower spray. Delivery of the spray occurred after the funeral was over. Nguyen allowed full credit on the sale of $36 and the sales tax of $1.80, credit memo no. 27.

21 Sold flower arrangements on account to Peninsula Savings and Loan Association for their anniversary, sales slip no. 310, $236, plus sales tax of $11.80, total $247.80.

22 Allowed Peninsula Savings and Loan Association credit, $20 plus sales tax of $1.00, because of withered blossoms in floral arrangements, credit memo no. 28.

27 Sold corsage on account to B. Cater, sales slip no. 332, $16.80, plus sales tax of $0.84, total $17.64.

Check Figure

Schedule of Accounts Receivable total, $626.56

Instructions

1. Record these transactions in either the sales journal (page 23) or the general journal (page 57).
2. Immediately after recording each transaction, post to the accounts receivable ledger.
3. Post the amounts from the general journal daily. Post the sales journal amount as a total at the end of the month; Accounts Receivable 113, Sales Tax Payable 214, Sales 411, Sales Returns and Allowances 412.
4. Prepare a schedule of accounts receivable and compare its total with the balance of Accounts Receivable.

P.O. 6,7,8

Problem 10-3B The Suburban Bicycle Shop uses a three-column purchases journal. The company is located in Topeka, Kansas. On January 1 of this year, the balances of the ledger accounts are Accounts Payable, $423.08; Purchases, zero; Freight In, zero. In addition to a general ledger, the company also uses an accounts payable ledger. Transactions for January related to the purchase of merchandise are as follows:

Jan. 4 Bought sixty 10-speed bicycles from Nakata Company, $5,980, invoice no. 26145, dated January 3; terms net 60 days; FOB Topeka.

7 Bought tires from Berger Tire Company, $486, invoice no. 9763, dated January 5; terms 2/10, n/30; FOB Topeka.

8 Bought bicycle lights and reflectors from Goddard Products Company, $272, invoice no. 17317, dated January 6; terms net 30 days; FOB Topeka.

11 Bought hand brakes from Brady, Inc., $270, invoice no. 291GE, dated January 9; terms 1/10, n/30; FOB Kansas City, freight prepaid and added to the invoice, $24 (total $294).

19 Bought handle grips from Goddard Products Company, $74.50, invoice no. 17520, dated January 17; terms net 30 days; FOB Topeka.

24 Bought thirty 5-speed bicycles from Nakata Company, $1,396, invoice no. 26942, dated January 23; terms net 60 days; FOB Topeka.

29 Bought knapsacks from Duncan Manufacturing Company, $299.42, invoice no. 762AC, dated January 26; terms 2/10, n/30; FOB Topeka.

Jan. 31   Bought locks from Lincoln Security, $311.47, invoice no. 27712, dated January 26; terms 2/10, n/30; FOB Dodge City, freight prepaid and added to the invoice, $19 (total $330.47).

Check Figure

Accounts Payable account balance, $9,555.47 credit

Instructions

1. Open the following creditor accounts in the accounts payable ledger and record the January 1 balances, if any, as given: Berger Tire Company, $156; Brady, Inc.; Duncan Manufacturing Company, $82.88; Goddard Products Company; Lincoln Security, $184.20; Nakata Company. For the accounts having balances, write "Balance" in the Item column and place a check mark in the Post. Ref. column.
2. Record the balance of $423.08 in the Accounts Payable controlling account as of January 1. Write "Balance" in the Item column and place a check mark in the Post. Ref. column.
3. Record the transactions in the purchases journal beginning with page 81.
4. Post to the accounts payable ledger daily.
5. Post to the general ledger at the end of the month.
6. Prepare a schedule of accounts payable, and compare the balance of the Accounts Payable controlling account with the total of the schedule of accounts payable.

P.O. 2,3,4,5,6,7,8,9

Problem 10-4B The following transactions relate to King Metal Products during April of this year. Terms of sale are 2/10, n/30. The company is located in Los Angeles.

Apr. 1   Sold merchandise on account to Howard Hardware, invoice no. 5522, $584.00.

  4   Bought merchandise on account from Sanger Manufacturing Company, invoice no. C1142, $528; terms 1/10, n/30; dated April 2; FOB San Diego, freight prepaid and added to the invoice, $33 (total $561).

  9   Sold merchandise on account to Buckley Department Store, invoice no. 5523, $994.

  11   Bought merchandise on account from Beale Products Company, invoice no. 8990, $1,893.65; terms 2/10, n/30; dated April 11; FOB San Francisco, freight prepaid and added to the invoice, $79 (total $1,972.65).

  16   Sold merchandise on account to B. R. Anders, invoice no. 5524, $856.70.

  19   Issued credit memo no. 32 to Buckley Department Store for merchandise returned, $92.

  24   Bought merchandise on account from Ashford Manufacturing Company, invoice no. P1981, $1,401.50; terms 2/10, n/30; dated April 22; FOB Santa Rosa, freight prepaid and added to the invoice, $81 (total $1,482.50).

  27   Bought office supplies on account from Chandler and Dunn, invoice no. E621A, dated April 25, $78.40; net 30 days.

  28   Sold merchandise on account to Goddard Specialty Company, invoice no. 5525, $3,852.00.

  29   Issued credit memo no. 33 to B. R. Anders for allowance on damaged merchandise, $86.

  30   Received credit memo no. 356 for merchandise returned to Bonwell, Inc., for $152.22.

Check Figure

Accounts Payable account balance, $4,320.33 credit

Instructions

1. Open the following accounts in the accounts receivable ledger and record the balances as of April 1: B. R. Anders; Buckley Department Store, $352.50; Goddard Specialty Company, $225.50; Howard Hardware, $822.00. For the accounts having balances, write "Balance" in the Item column and place a check mark in the Post. Ref. column.
2. Open the following accounts in the accounts payable ledger and record the balances as of April 1: Ashford Manufacturing Company; Beale Products Company, $122.46; Bonwell, Inc., $255.54; Chandler and Dunn; Sanger Manufacturing Company. For the accounts having balances, write "Balance" in the Item column and place a check mark in the Post Ref. column.
3. Record the transactions in the sales, purchases, or general journal, as appropriate.
4. Post the entries to the accounts receivable ledger daily.
5. Post the entries to the accounts payable ledger daily.
6. Post the entries in the general journal immediately after you make each journal entry.
7. Post the totals from the special journals at month end.
8. Prepare a schedule of accounts receivable.
9. Prepare a schedule of accounts payable.
10. Compare the totals of the schedules with the balances of the controlling accounts.

Instructions for General Ledger Software

1. Record the transactions in the sales, purchases, or general journals.
   a. For efficiency, analyze the transactions, indicate into which journal each transaction goes, and key the entries in three batches—the sales journal, the purchases journal, and the general journal.
   b. If the program uses a single-column purchases journal, add the amount of the freight to the amount of purchases.
2. Print the journals.
3. Post the amounts from the sales, purchases, and general journals.
4. Print the general ledger.
5. Print a schedule of accounts receivable and compare the total with the balance of the Accounts Receivable controlling account.
6. Print a schedule of accounts payable and compare the total with the balance of the Accounts Payable controlling account.

The Computer Lab

Sales and Purchases Journals

New journals for more efficiency!

Mr. Kennedy of Jeep Jockeys called and said that he has decided to supplement his service business, which provides sightseeing and thrill jeep rides, by adding several merchandise items, specifically logo mugs, logo T-shirts, disposable cameras, logo baseball caps, and suntan lotion. He believes he will be able to increase his profits significantly. He will bring over what he has purchased and sold in June, as well as a summary of the service revenues, operating expenses, and other accounting activity that occurred in June.

The first thing you want to do is to open your general ledger accounting software package and bring up the May 31, 20— trial balance for Jeep Jockeys.

Egad! What happened to the revenue, expense, and drawing accounts? Oh yes, I closed them at the end of May—the books are ready for June's transactions.

Jeep Jockeys
Post-Closing Trial Balance
May 31, 20—

ACCOUNT NAME	DEBIT	CREDIT
Cash	21 7 9 6 00	
Accounts Receivable	9 3 1 00	
Prepaid Insurance	1 6 5 0 00	
Office Equipment	7 5 9 00	
Accumulated Depreciation, Office Equipment		1 1 32
Vehicles	46 0 0 0 00	
Accumulated Depreciation, Vehicles		1 2 5 0 00
Accounts Payable		5 6 2 9 00
Wages Payable		2 9 3 00
H. Kennedy, Capital		63 9 5 2 68
	71 1 3 6 00	71 1 3 6 00

I'll need to follow directions carefully!

Mr. Kennedy has delivered the following information to you:

A list of merchandise purchase invoices for June—he wants you to open a purchases journal for purchases of merchandise for resale bought on account.

A list of merchandise sales invoices for June—he wants you to open a sales journal for sales of merchandise sold on account—mostly to corporate clients.

A summary of the other transactions occurring in June, including other purchases of goods that are not for resale.

List of purchase invoices of merchandise bought for resale on account

Date	Supplier's Name	Invoice No.	Invoice Date	Terms	Details of Purchase
June 1	Mug Shots	32655-A	June 1	2/10, n/30	24 cases logo mugs (12 mugs per case) @ $24/case plus $20.86 freight charge (Hank didn't have time to extend the totals.)
1	T-Mart	989-C	June 1	2/10, n/30	20 cases logo T-shirts (12 shirts per case: 2 child, 1 small, 3 med., 7 lg., 7 x-lg.) @ $84/case plus $156.80 freight charge
2	Cost-Less	520600	June 2	n/30	6 cases disposable cameras (12 cameras per case), 35 mm, 24 shot @ $72/case plus $17.40 freight charge
3	CapCo	6-36344	June 3	2/10, n/30	7 cases logo baseball caps, (12 caps per case), adjustable @ $108/case plus $27.60 freight charge
3	TanShine	361777-6	June 3	n/30	4 cases 25 SPF suntan lotion (twelve 12-oz. bottles per case) @ $60/case plus $10.90 freight charge

List of sales invoices of merchandise bought on account

Date	Invoice No.	Detail of Sale	Amount
June 5	1	Chamber of Commerce, 2 cases lotion (12 bottles per case) @ $9.99/bottle; 2 cases logo mugs (12 mugs per case) @ $7.99/mug (Hank wants you to extend the totals because he didn't have time to do it.)	
7	2	Harlton Hotel, 3 cases T-shirts—1 lg., 2 x-lg. (12 shirts per case) @ $16.99/shirt	
11	3	Morgan B and B, 1 case disposable cameras (12 cameras per case) @ $10.99/camera	
15	4	Wilkins' Reunion Party, 3 cases T-shirts—1 child, 1 lg., 1 x-lg. (12 shirts per case) @ $16.99/shirt; 3 cases of caps (12 caps per case) @ $14.99/cap	
19	5	Mikels' Wedding, 2 cases disposable cameras (12 cameras per case) @ $10.99/camera; 2 cases of T-shirts—1 lg., 1 x-lg. (12 shirts per case) @ $16.99/shirt	
23	6	Simms' Sales Conference, 3 cases T-shirts—2 lg., 1 x-lg. (12 shirts per case) @ $16.99/shirt	
28	7	Drake Car Rally, 4 cases caps (12 caps per case) @ $14.99/cap	
30	8	Welcomer's Luncheon, 10 cases logo mugs (12 mugs per case) @ $7.99/mug	

June's other transactions

Date		Amount
June 1	Rent Ck. No. 1013	320.00
1	Advertising Expense—June ad w/photo, Ck. No. 1014.	410.00
3	Miscellaneous Expense—Chamber of Commerce Membership, Ck. No. 1015.	75.00
5	Bought supplies—2 cases of bottled water for clients, Ck. No. 1016. (Debit Supplies instead of Supplies Expense—this will be explained in chapter 12.)	21.00
6	5 display cases @ $89.95 plus $28.94 freight charge on account from Store Depot (debit Kiosk Equipment—new account).	
8	1 neon OPEN sign @ $288.95 plus $18.40 freight charge on account from Sign Masters (debit Advertising Expense).	
10	10 strings small white lights for kiosk at $3.99 per string, no freight—picked it up at Wilmart, Ck. No. 1017 (debit Advertising Expense).	
15	Paid Outback Office Supply on account, Ck. No. 1018.	179.00
18	Made Jeep payment to Jeep Town, Ck. No. 1019.	784.00
21	Harlton Hotel paid on account.	561.00
27	H. Kennedy withdrew funds for personal use, Ck. No. 1020.	750.00
30	Paid month's wages, Ck. No. 1021. (We have not yet covered reversing entries, which would eliminate the debit to Wages Payable you see at the right. We will discuss them in Chapter 13.)	Debit Wages Payable 293.00, Debit Wages Expense 6,435.00, credit Cash 6,728.00
30	Accounting and Legal Expense, accounting fees, Ck. No. 1022.	150.00
30	Tour Revenue received in cash.	18,364.00

30	Tour Revenue received on account (verify total)
	  Wilkins' Reunion $3,200.00
	  Mikels' Wedding $4,000.00
	  Simms' Sales Conference $3,400.00
	  Drake Car Rally $1,100.00
		11,700.00

30	Returned 1 string of lights (reduce Advertising Expense).	3.99
30	Returned 1 case of broken mugs.	24.00 and 0.87 freight
30	Morgan B and B returned one defective camera.	10.99
30	Paid utility bill for June, Ck. No. 1023.	87.00

I'll have to review how to journalize the purchase of goods NOT FOR RESALE. I know I have to treat freight on these purchases differently from freight on merchandise for resale.

It looks like you may need a calculator to figure out or verify the amount of Purchases debit (and Accounts Payable credit) as well as Sales credit (and Accounts Receivable debit) in the sales journal. You will also need to make some calculations to complete the other non–special journal entries.

I must remember—journalize a transaction in only one journal!

A large amount of information—where do I begin? Let's see, I'll do the Other June transactions first because they are familiar. I'll use the general journal—because none of those transactions are purchases of goods for resale on account or sales of goods on account. Later, I'll journalize those entries in the new purchases journal and the new sales journal—I'm sure I saw those tabs on the software.

Clues and check figures for calculations:

First, I'll calculate the June 6 purchase of five display cases @ $89.95 each plus $28.94 freight. These are to be debited to the new account, Kiosk Equipment. The price of the freight is added to the cost of the display cases (5 × $89.95 = $449.75 plus $28.94 = $478.69). No Freight In is involved since this is not a purchase of merchandise for resale.

Next, I'll calculate one of the purchase invoices. Let's see, I'll try the June 1 invoice no. 32655-A from Mug Shots: 24 cases of mugs @ $24 per case = 24 × $24 = $576 plus $20.86 freight charge = $596.86. When I get to the purchases journal, I'll debit Purchases for $576, debit Freight In for $20.86, and credit Accounts Payable (the amount we owe for goods and freight) $596.86.

Finally, before I go to the computer, I'll see if the sales invoices are just as easy to calculate. I'll try invoice No. 1 from June 5 where the Chamber of Commerce bought two cases of lotions with 12 bottles per case (2 × 12 = 24 bottles × $9.99 per bottle = $239.76). They also bought two cases of logo mugs with 12 mugs per case (2 × 12 = 24 mugs × $7.99/mug = $191.76). Add $239.76 to $191.76 and I get $431.52 that was sold to the Chamber of Commerce. When I get to the sales journal, I'll credit Sales for $431.52 and debit Accounts Receivable (Chamber of Commerce) for $431.52. If I do the rest of the calculations as I have done these three practice calculations and fill in the blanks Hank left, I should be okay on the computer.

Whew, I've journalized everything. Now what?

Let's see, I've journalized all the transactions in the sales journal, the purchases journal, and the general journal—thank goodness my software automatically posts to the general ledger, the accounts receivable ledger, and the accounts payable ledger.

I'll run a trial balance before I do the schedules for the subsidiary ledgers.

All that's left to do is print a schedule of accounts receivable for June 30, 20— and compare the total to the Accounts Receivable account balance in the general ledger. They should match—if they don't, I'll track down the error, correct it, and reprint the trial balance. The same for the schedule of accounts payable for June 30, 20—. That total should match the Accounts Payable account balance in the general ledger.

I'll call Mr. Kennedy to report my progress and fax him the schedules.

11

The Cash Receipts Journal and the Cash Payments Journal

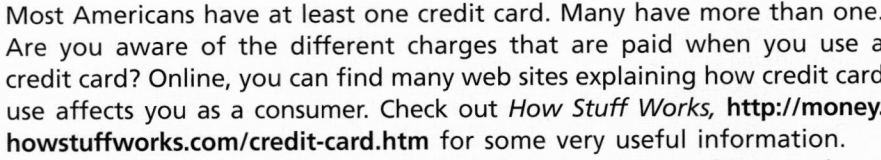
Performance Objectives

After you have completed this chapter, you will be able to do the following:

1. Journalize transactions for a retail merchandising business in a cash receipts journal.

2. Post from a cash receipts journal to a general ledger and an accounts receivable ledger.

3. Determine cash discounts according to credit terms, and record cash receipts from charge customers who are entitled to deduct the cash discount.

4. Journalize transactions in a cash payments journal for a service enterprise.

5. Post from a cash payments journal to a general ledger and an accounts payable ledger.

6. Journalize transactions involving cash discounts in a cash payments journal for a merchandising enterprise.

7. Journalize transactions in a check register.

8. Journalize transactions involving trade discounts.

W e have seen that using a sales journal and a purchases journal enables an accountant to carry out the journalizing and posting processes much more efficiently. These special journals make it possible to post column totals rather than individual figures. They also make the division of labor more efficient because the journalizing functions can be delegated to different persons. The *cash receipts journal* and the *cash payments journal* further extend these advantages.

THE CASH RECEIPTS JOURNAL

OBJECTIVE 1
Journalize transactions for a retail merchandising business in a cash receipts journal.

The **cash receipts journal** contains all transactions in which cash is received, or increases. When a cash receipts journal is used, all transactions in which cash is debited *must* be recorded in it. It may be used for a service as well as a merchandising business. Let's list some typical transactions of a retail merchandising business that result in an increase in cash. To get a better picture of the transactions, let's first record them in T accounts.

May 3 Sold Merchandise for cash, $100, plus $8 sales tax.

Cash	Sales Tax Payable	Sales
+ −	− +	− +
108	8	100

May 4 Sold merchandise, $100, plus $8 sales tax, and the customer used a bank charge card. The bank issuing the card bills the customer directly each month. The business, on the other hand, deposits the bank credit card receipts every day. The bank *deducts a discount* and credits the firm's account with cash. We will assume that the discount is 4 percent. The firm therefore records the amount of the discount under Credit Card Expense: $108.00 × .04 = $4.32 credit card expense; $100.00 + $8.00 − $4.32 = $103.68.

Cash	Sales Tax Payable	Sales	Credit Card Expense
+ −	− +	− +	+ −
103.68	8.00	100.00	4.32

May 5 Collected cash on account from L. R. Reed, a charge customer, $216.

Cash	Accounts Receivable
+ −	+ −
216	216

May 7 The owner, G. H. Hall, invested cash in the business, $4,000.

Cash	G. H. Hall, Capital
+ −	− +
4,000	4,000

Cash transactions can take place anywhere in the world through an ATM machine, with clients never entering their banks.

May 8 Sold equipment for cash at cost, $150.

The same transactions are shown in general journal form as follows:

		GENERAL JOURNAL				PAGE _____	
	DATE	DESCRIPTION	POST. REF.	DEBIT		CREDIT	
1	20–						1
2	May 3	Cash		1 0 8 00			2
3		Sales				1 0 0 00	3
4		Sales Tax Payable				8 00	4
5		Sold merchandise for cash.					5
6							6
7	4	Cash		1 0 3 68			7
8		Credit Card Expense		4 32			8
9		Sales				1 0 0 00	9
10		Sales Tax Payable				8 00	10
11		Sold merchandise involving					11
12		a bank charge card.					12
13							13
14	5	Cash		2 1 6 00			14
15		Accounts Receivable, L. R. Reed				2 1 6 00	15
16		Collected cash on account.					16
17							17
18	7	Cash		4 0 0 0 00			18
19		G. H. Hall, Capital				4 0 0 0 00	19
20		Owner invested cash.					20
21							21
22	8	Cash		1 5 0 00			22
23		Equipment				1 5 0 00	23
24		Sold equipment at cost.					24
25							25

Now let's analyze these five transactions: The first three would occur frequently; the last two would occur less frequently. When designing a cash receipts journal, it is logical to include a Cash Debit column because all the transactions involve an increase in cash. If a business regularly collects cash from charge customers, there should be an Accounts Receivable Credit column. If a firm often sells merchandise for cash and collects a sales tax, there should be a Sales Credit column and a Sales Tax Payable Credit column. If the business honors bank charge cards and wants to record the amount of the discount at the time of each transaction, there should be a Credit Card Expense Debit column for the amount deducted by the bank.

However, the credit to G. H. Hall, Capital, and the credit to Equipment occur very seldom, so it would not be practical to set up special columns for

CASH RECEIPTS JOURNAL   PAGE __41__

DATE		ACCOUNT CREDITED	POST. REF.	CASH DEBIT	CREDIT CARD EXPENSE DEBIT	ACCOUNTS RECEIVABLE CREDIT	SALES CREDIT	SALES TAX PAYABLE CREDIT	OTHER ACCOUNTS CREDIT	
1	20–									1
2	May	3	——————		1 0 8 00			1 0 0 00	8 00		2
3		4	——————		1 0 3 68	4 32		1 0 0 00	8 00		3
4		5	L. R. Reed		2 1 6 00		2 1 6 00				4
5		7	G. H. Hall,								5
6			Capital		4 0 0 0 00					4 0 0 0 00	6
7		8	Equipment		1 5 0 00					1 5 0 00	7
8											8

FIGURE 1

these credits. They can be handled adequately by an Other Accounts Credit column, which can be used for credits to all accounts that have no special column.

Now let's record these transactions in a cash receipts journal (see Figure 1). First, we repeat the transactions:

May 3 Sold merchandise for cash, $100, plus $8 sales tax.
  4 Sold merchandise, $100, plus $8 sales tax, and the customer used a bank charge card. Discount charged by the bank is 4 percent of the total of sales plus sales tax.
  5 Collected cash on account from L. R. Reed, a charge customer, $216.
  7 The owner, G. H. Hall, invested cash in the business, $4,000.
  8 Sold equipment for cash at cost, $150.

As an alternative, many firms postpone recording the amount of bank credit card expense until they actually receive notification from their bank on their bank statement. For example, total credit card sales for a restaurant for a time period amount to $1,600 plus 6 percent sales tax. The entry is as follows:

Cash		Sales Tax Payable		Sales	
+	–	–	+	–	+
1,696			96		1,600

The restaurant's next bank statement includes a debit memorandum for credit card charges of $67.84, using an assumed 4 percent discount rate ($1,696.00 × .04). The firm handles this in a similar manner to a check service charge:

Credit Card Expense		Cash	
+	–	+	–
67.84			67.84

Posting from the Cash Receipts Journal

Here are some other transactions made during the month that involve increases in cash. (Remember that these transactions are for a retail business.)

May 11 Borrowed $300 from the bank, receiving cash and giving the bank a promissory note.

16 Sold merchandise for cash, $200, plus $16 sales tax.

21 Sold merchandise, $50, plus $4 sales tax; customer used a bank charge card. Credit card expense charge is 4 percent of sales plus sales tax.

26 Collected cash from B. Sanchez, a charge customer, on account, $62.40.

28 Sold merchandise for cash, $40, plus $3.20 sales tax.

31 Sold merchandise, $150, plus $12 sales tax; customer used a bank charge card. Credit card expense charge is 4 percent of sales plus sales tax.

31 Collected cash from T. Nguyen, a charge customer, on account, $26.

In the transaction of May 11, in which $300 was borrowed from the bank, the bank was given a **promissory note** (a written promise to pay a specified amount at a specified time) as evidence of the debt. The account **Notes Payable**, instead of Accounts Payable, is used to represent the amount owed on the promissory note. The Accounts Payable account is reserved for charge accounts with creditors, which are normally paid on a thirty-day basis.

OBJECTIVE 2
Post from a cash receipts journal to a general ledger and an accounts receivable ledger.

Let's assume that all the month's transactions involving debits to Cash have now been recorded in the cash receipts journal. The cash receipts journal (see Figure 2 on the following page) and the T accounts following it illustrate the postings to the general ledger and the accounts receivable ledger.

Individual amounts in the Accounts Receivable Credit column of the cash receipts journal are usually posted daily to the accounts receivable ledger. Individual amounts in the Other Accounts Credit column are usually posted daily.

At the end of the month, we can post the special column totals in the cash receipts journal to the general ledger accounts. These columns include Credit Card Expense Debit, Cash Debit, Accounts Receivable Credit, Sales Credit, and Sales Tax Payable Credit.

FYI
The dash is a placeholder indicating that nothing has been left out or forgotten.

In the Post. Ref. column, the check marks (✓) indicate that the amounts in the Accounts Receivable Credit column have been posted to the individual charge customers' accounts as credits. The account numbers show that the amounts in the Other Accounts Credit column have been posted separately to the accounts described in the Account Credited column. An (X) goes under the total of the Other Accounts Credit column; it means "do not post—the figures have already been posted separately." This column is totaled to make it easier to prove that the debits equal the credits.

Note the ruling. A single rule is placed above the column totals, and double rules extend through all but the Account Credited column. Also, on the last line, the last day of the month is recorded in the Date column.

Let's say it's the end of the month. Total the columns first. Then begin crossfooting the journal by proving that the sum of the debit totals equals the sum of the credit totals. This process must be done before you post the totals to the general ledger accounts.

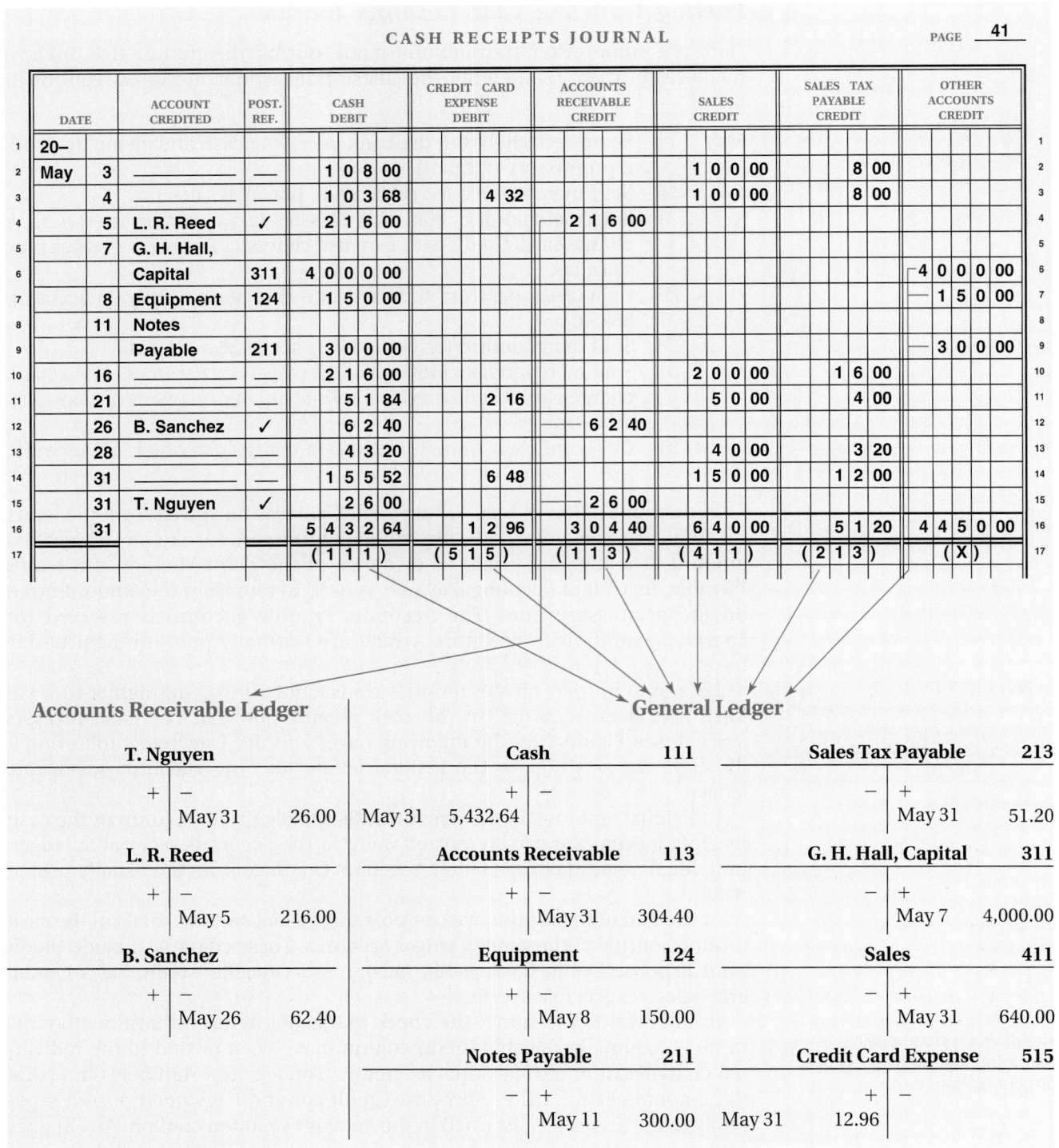

FIGURE 2

Debit Totals		Credit Totals	
Cash	$5,432.64	Accounts Receivable	$ 304.40
Credit Card Expense	12.96	Sales	640.00
		Sales Tax Payable	51.20
		Other Accounts	4,450.00
	$5,445.60		$5,445.60

Post the special column totals to the general ledger, using the letters CR as the posting reference. Next, write the general ledger account number in parentheses below the total in the appropriate column.

Advantages of a Cash Receipts Journal

1. Transactions generally can be recorded on one line.
2. All transactions involving debits to Cash are recorded in one place.
3. It eliminates much repetition in posting when there are numerous transactions involving Cash debits. The Cash Debit side can be posted as one total.
4. Special columns can be used for specialized transactions and posted as one total.

CREDIT TERMS

OBJECTIVE 3
Determine cash discounts according to credit terms, and record cash receipts from charge customers who are entitled to deduct the cash discount.

The cash receipts journal and the cash payments journal are used by both service and merchandising businesses to record all transactions in which cash comes into or goes out of the business.

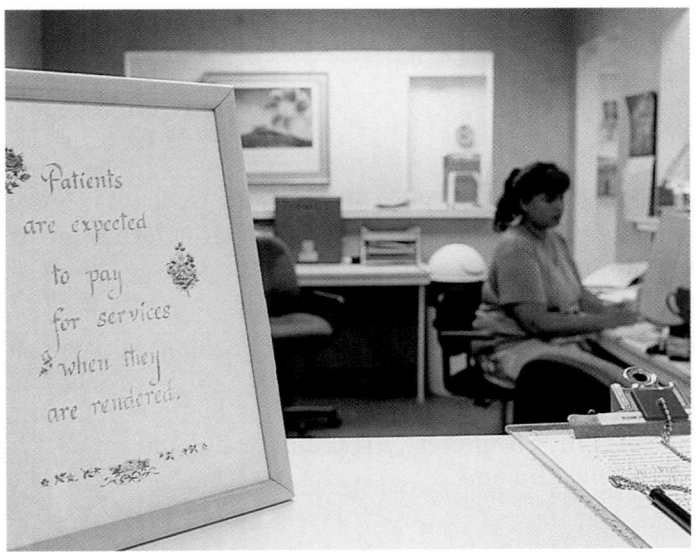

The seller always stipulates credit terms: How much credit can a customer be allowed? And, how much time should the customer be given to pay the full amount? The **credit period** is the time the seller allows the buyer before full payment has to be made. Retailers generally allow twenty-five to thirty days.

Wholesalers and manufacturers often specify a **cash discount** in their credit terms. A cash discount is an amount that a customer can deduct if a bill is paid within a specified time. The discount is based on the *total amount of the invoice after any returns and allowances and freight charges billed on the invoice have been deducted.* Naturally, this discount acts as an incentive for charge customers to pay their bills promptly.

Let's say that a wholesaler offers customers credit terms of 2/10, n/30. These terms mean that the customer gets a 2 percent discount if the bill is paid within ten days after the invoice date. The discount period begins the day after the invoice date. If the bill is not paid within the ten days, the entire amount is due within thirty days after the invoice date. Other cash discounts that may be used are the following:

- **1/15, n/60** The seller offers a 1 percent discount if the bill is paid within fifteen days after the invoice date, and the whole bill must be paid within sixty days after the invoice date.
- **2/10, EOM, n/60** The seller offers a 2 percent discount if the bill is paid within ten days after the end of the month, and the whole bill must be paid within sixty days after the last day of the month.

A wholesaler or manufacturer that offers a cash discount adopts a single cash discount as a credit policy and makes this available to all its customers. The seller considers cash discounts as sales discounts; the buyer, on the other hand, considers cash discounts as purchases discounts. In this section we are concerned with the sales discount. *The Sales Discounts account, like Sales Returns and Allowances, is a deduction from Sales.*

To illustrate, we return to Dodson Plumbing Supply. We will record the following transactions in T accounts.

Transaction (a) August 1: Sold merchandise on account to C. P. Landis Company, invoice no. 320; terms 2/10, n/30, $580.92.

Transaction (b) August 10: Received check from C. P. Landis Company for $569.30 in payment of invoice no. 320, less cash discount ($580.92 × .02 = $11.62; $580.92 − $11.62 = $569.30).

Since Dodson Plumbing Supply offers this cash discount to all its customers, and since charge customers often pay their bills within the discount period, Dodson Plumbing sets up a Sales Discounts Debit column in the cash receipts journal. Note that Dodson Plumbing Supply is a wholesaler. Therefore, a column for Sales Tax Payable is not used since few states levy a tax on sales at the wholesale level.

CASH RECEIPTS JOURNAL PAGE __18__

	DATE	ACCOUNT CREDITED	POST. REF.	CASH DEBIT	SALES DISCOUNTS DEBIT	ACCOUNTS RECEIVABLE CREDIT	SALES CREDIT	OTHER ACCOUNTS CREDIT	
1	20–								1
2	Aug. 10	C. P. Landis Co.		5 6 9 30	1 1 62	5 8 0 92			2
3									3

Several other transactions of Dodson Plumbing Supply involve increases in cash during August. Remember that the standard credit terms for all charge customers are 2/10, n/30.

Aug. 15 Cash sales for first half of the month, $1,460.
16 Received check from Alvarez Construction for $386.12 in payment of invoice no. 322, less cash discount ($394.00 − $7.88 = $386.12).
17 Received payment on a promissory note given by John R. Bryant, $300 principal, plus $3 interest. (The amount of the interest is recorded in Interest Income.)

Aug. 21 Received check from Cozart Hardware for $756.80 in payment of invoice no. 324, less cash discount ($772.24 − $15.44 = $756.80).

23 Sold equipment for cash at cost, $126.

26 L. E. Dodson, the owner, invested an additional $4,000 cash in the business.

26 Received a check from Hewitt and Sons, Inc., for $432.18 in payment of invoice no. 325 less the cash discount ($441.00 − $8.82 = $432.18).

30 Received check from Hazen Plumbing and Heating for $695.80 in payment of invoice no. 326, less cash discount ($710.00 − $14.20 = $695.80).

31 Cash sales for second half of the month, $1,620.

31 Received check from Milne, Inc., in payment of invoice no. 321, for $116. (This is longer than the ten-day period, so they missed the cash discount.)

Dodson Plumbing records these transactions in its cash receipts journal (Figure 3).

After that has been done, the company's accountant proves the equality of debits and credits:

REMEMBER!
When journalizing a cash receipt involving a sales discount, be sure to credit Accounts Receivable for the total amount of the sales transaction.

Debit Totals

Cash	$10,465.20
Sales Discounts	57.96
	$10,523.16

Credit Totals

Accounts Receivable	$ 3,014.16
Sales	3,080.00
Other Accounts	4,429.00
	$10,523.16

FIGURE 3

CASH RECEIPTS JOURNAL   PAGE ___18___

	DATE	ACCOUNT CREDITED	POST. REF.	CASH DEBIT	SALES DISCOUNTS DEBIT	ACCOUNTS RECEIVABLE CREDIT	SALES CREDIT	OTHER ACCOUNTS CREDIT	
1	20–								1
2	Aug. 10	C. P. Landis Co.	✓	5 6 9 30	1 1 62	5 8 0 92			2
3	15	_____	—	1 4 6 0 00			1 4 6 0 00		3
4	16	Alvarez Construction	✓	3 8 6 12	7 88	3 9 4 00			4
5	17	Notes Receivable	112					3 0 0 00	5
6		Interest Income	422	3 0 3 00				3 00	6
7	21	Cozart Hardware	✓	7 5 6 80	1 5 44	7 7 2 24			7
8	23	Equipment	124	1 2 6 00				1 2 6 00	8
9	26	L. E. Dodson, Capital	311	4 0 0 0 00				4 0 0 0 00	9
10	26	Hewitt and Sons, Inc.	✓	4 3 2 18	8 82	4 4 1 00			10
11	30	Hazen Plumbing and Heating	✓	6 9 5 80	1 4 20	7 1 0 00			11
12	31	_____	—	1 6 2 0 00			1 6 2 0 00		12
13	31	Milne, Inc.	✓	1 1 6 00		1 1 6 00			13
14	31			10 4 6 5 20	5 7 96	3 0 1 4 16	3 0 8 0 00	4 4 2 9 00	14
15				(1 1 1)	(4 1 3)	(1 1 3)	(4 1 1)	(X)	15
16									16
17									17

SALES RETURNS AND ALLOWANCES AND SALES DISCOUNTS ON AN INCOME STATEMENT

In the fundamental accounting equation, to be consistent with the income statement, we placed Sales Returns and Allowances and Sales Discounts under Sales with the plus and minus signs reversed. Both accounts are contra revenue accounts, so we subtract their totals from Sales on the income statement. Here is the Revenue from Sales section of the annual income statement of Jackson Electric Supply.

Jackson Electric Supply
Income Statement
For Year Ended December 31, 20—

Revenue from Sales:			
Sales		$235 1 8 0 00	
Less: Sales Returns and Allowances	$ 8 4 0 00		
Sales Discounts	1 8 8 0 00	2 7 2 0 00	
Net Sales			$232 4 6 0 00

THE CASH PAYMENTS JOURNAL: SERVICE ENTERPRISE

The **cash payments journal**, as the name implies, is a special journal used to record all transactions in which cash goes out, or decreases. When the cash payments journal is used, all transactions in which cash is credited *must* be recorded in it. This journal may be used for either a service or a merchandising business.

To get acquainted with the cash payments journal, let's list some typical transactions of a service firm (such as a dry cleaner or a bowling alley) or a professional enterprise (such as a lawyer's office) that result in a decrease in cash. To illustrate, we record the following transactions in T accounts:

May 2 Paid L. N. Brown Company, a creditor, on account, Ck. No. 63, $1,220.

Accounts Payable		Cash	
−	+	+	−
1,220			1,220

May 4 Paid cash for liability insurance, Ck. No. 64, $890.

Prepaid Insurance		Cash	
+	−	+	−
890			890

May 5 Paid wages for two weeks, Ck. No. 65, $3,220 (previously recorded in the payroll entry).

Wages Payable		Cash	
−	+	+	−
3,220			3,220

May 6 Paid rent for the month, Ck. No. 66, $1,950.

Rent Expense		Cash	
+	−	+	−
1,950			1,950

The same transactions are now shown in general journal form.

GENERAL JOURNAL   PAGE _____

	DATE		DESCRIPTION	POST. REF.	DEBIT	CREDIT	
1	20–						1
2	May	2	Accounts Payable,				2
3			L. N. Brown Co.		1 2 2 0 00		3
4			Cash			1 2 2 0 00	4
5			Paid on account, Ck. No. 63.				5
6							6
7		4	Prepaid Insurance		8 9 0 00		7
8			Cash			8 9 0 00	8
9			Paid cash for liability				9
10			insurance, Ck. No. 64.				10
11							11
12		5	Wages Payable		3 2 2 0 00		12
13			Cash			3 2 2 0 00	13
14			Paid wages for two weeks,				14
15			Ck. No. 65.				15
16							16
17		6	Rent Expense		1 9 5 0 00		17
18			Cash			1 9 5 0 00	18
19			Paid rent for month,				19
20			Ck. No. 66.				20

Let's analyze these four transactions. The first one would occur frequently, as payments to creditors are made several times a month. Of the last three transactions, the debit to Wages Payable might occur twice a month, the debit to Rent Expense once a month, and the debit to Prepaid Insurance only occasionally.

It is logical to include a Cash Credit column in a cash payments journal because all transactions recorded in this journal involve a decrease in cash. Since payments to creditors are made often, there should also be an

OBJECTIVE 4
Journalize transactions in a cash payments journal for a service enterprise.

Accounts Payable Debit column. You can set up any other column that is used often enough to warrant it. Otherwise, an Other Accounts Debit column takes care of all the other transactions.

Now let's record these same transactions in a cash payments journal and include a column titled Ck. No. If you think a moment, you will see that this is consistent with good management of cash. All expenditures except Petty Cash expenditures should be paid for by check. Let's repeat the transactions.

May 2 Paid L. N. Brown Company, a creditor, on account, Ck. No. 63, $1,220.
4 Paid cash for liability insurance, Ck. No. 64, $890.
5 Paid wages for two weeks, Ck. No. 65, $3,220 (previously recorded in the payroll entry).
6 Paid rent for the month, Ck. No. 66, $1,950.

CASH PAYMENTS JOURNAL PAGE 62

	DATE	CK. NO.	ACCOUNT DEBITED	POST. REF.	OTHER ACCOUNTS DEBIT	ACCOUNTS PAYABLE DEBIT	CASH CREDIT	
1	20–							1
2	May 2	63	L. N. Brown Co.			1 2 2 0 00	1 2 2 0 00	2
3	4	64	Prepaid Insurance		8 9 0 00		8 9 0 00	3
4	5	65	Wages Payable		3 2 2 0 00		3 2 2 0 00	4
5	6	66	Rent Expense		1 9 5 0 00		1 9 5 0 00	5
6								6

Other transactions involving decreases in cash during May are as follows:

May 7 Paid a one-year premium for fire insurance, Ck. No. 67, $360.
9 Paid Morris, Inc., a creditor, on account, Ck. No. 68, $418.
11 Issued Ck. No. 69 in payment of delivery expense, $62.
14 Paid Russet and Son, a creditor, on account, Ck. No. 70, $110.
16 Issued Ck. No. 71 to the Logan State Bank for a Note Payable, $660, $600 on the principal and $60 interest.
19 Voided Ck. No. 72.
19 Bought equipment from Snyder Company for $200. Issued Ck. No. 73.
20 Paid wages for two weeks, Ck. No. 74, $1,340 (previously recorded in the payroll entry).
22 Issued Ck. No. 75 to Scheel Advertising Agency for advertising, $94 (not previously recorded).
26 Paid telephone bill, Ck. No. 76, $26.
31 Issued check for freight bill on equipment purchased on May 19, Ck. No. 77, $28.
31 Paid Lynn and Trask, a creditor, on account, Ck. No. 78, $160.

You should list all checks in consecutive order, even those checks that must be voided. In this way, *every* check is accounted for, which is necessary for internal control.

These transactions are recorded in the cash payments journal illustrated in Figure 4. Notice that an (X) is placed under the Other Accounts column. That means "do not post—the individual figures have already been posted."

FIGURE 4

CASH PAYMENTS JOURNAL PAGE __62__

	DATE	CK. NO.	ACCOUNT DEBITED	POST. REF.	OTHER ACCOUNTS DEBIT	ACCOUNTS PAYABLE DEBIT	CASH CREDIT	
1	20–							1
2	May 2	63	L. N. Brown Co.	✓		1 2 2 0 00	1 2 2 0 00	2
3	4	64	Prepaid Insurance	113	8 9 0 00		8 9 0 00	3
4	5	65	Wages Payable	214	3 2 2 0 00		3 2 2 0 00	4
5	6	66	Rent Expense	512	1 9 5 0 00		1 9 5 0 00	5
6	7	67	Prepaid Insurance	114	3 6 0 00		3 6 0 00	6
7	9	68	Morris, Inc.	✓		4 1 8 00	4 1 8 00	7
8	11	69	Delivery Expense	513	6 2 00		6 2 00	8
9	14	70	Russet and Son	✓		1 1 0 00	1 1 0 00	9
10	16	71	Notes Payable	211	6 0 0 00			10
11			Interest Expense	518	6 0 00		6 6 0 00	11
12	19	72	Void	—				12
13	19	73	Equipment	121	2 0 0 00		2 0 0 00	13
14	20	74	Wages Payable	214	1 3 4 0 00		1 3 4 0 00	14
15	22	75	Advertising					15
16			Expense	515	9 4 00		9 4 00	16
17	26	76	Telephone					17
18			Expense	516	2 6 00		2 6 00	18
19	31	77	Equipment	121	2 8 00		2 8 00	19
20	31	78	Lynn and Trask	✓		1 6 0 00	1 6 0 00	20
21	31				8 8 3 0 00	1 9 0 8 00	10 7 3 8 00	21
22					(X)	(2 1 2)	(1 1 1)	22

At the end of the month, after totaling the columns, check the accuracy of the footings by proving that the sum of the debit totals equals the sum of the credit totals. Since you have posted the individual amounts in the Other Accounts Debit column to the general ledger, the only posting that remains is the credit to the Cash account for $10,738 and the debit to the Accounts Payable (controlling) account for $1,908.

Debit Totals		Credit Totals	
Accounts Payable	$ 1,908.00	Cash	$10,738.00
Other Accounts	8,830.00		
	$10,738.00		$10,738.00

OBJECTIVE 5
Post from a cash payments journal to a general ledger and an accounts payable ledger.

The posting process for the cash payments journal is similar to the posting process for the cash receipts journal. Individual amounts in the Accounts Payable Debit column are usually posted daily to the subsidiary ledger. After posting, put a check mark (✓) in the Post. Ref. column. Individual amounts in the Other Accounts Debit column are usually posted daily to the general ledger. Post these figures individually, then place the account number in the Post. Ref. column. Totals of the Cash Credit column and the Accounts Payable Debit column are posted to the general ledger accounts at the end of the month. Write the appropriate general ledger account number in parentheses below the column totals. Print an (X) below the total of the Other Accounts Debit column to indicate that the total amount is not posted. The posting letter designation for the cash payments journal is CP.

The advantages of the cash payments journal are similar to the advantages of the cash receipts journal:

1. Transactions generally can be recorded on one line.
2. All the transactions involving credits to Cash are recorded in one place.
3. For numerous transactions involving Cash credits, the Cash Credit side can be posted as one total.
4. Special columns can be used for specialized transactions and posted as one total.

THE CASH PAYMENTS JOURNAL: MERCHANDISING ENTERPRISE

OBJECTIVE 6
Journalize transactions involving cash discounts in a cash payments journal for a merchandising enterprise.

There is one slight difference between the cash payments journal for a merchandising enterprise and that for a service enterprise. This difference has to do with the cash discounts available to a merchandising business. Recall that a cash discount is the amount that the buyer may deduct from the bill; this acts as an incentive to get the buyer to pay the bill promptly. The buyer considers the cash discount to be a purchases discount, because it relates to the buyer's purchase of merchandise. The Purchases Discounts account, like Purchases Returns and Allowances, is treated as a deduction from Purchases on the buyer's income statement.

Let us return to Dodson Plumbing Supply and assume that the following transactions take place. To demonstrate the debits and credits, let's show some typical transactions in the form of T accounts.

Transaction (a) August 2: Bought merchandise on account from Colvin, Inc., $710, their invoice no. 2706, dated July 31; terms 2/10, n/30; FOB San Francisco; freight prepaid and added to the invoice, $49 (total $759).

Transaction (b) August 8: Issued Ck. No. 76 to Colvin, Inc., in payment of invoice no. 2706 less the cash discount of $14.20, $744.80 ($759 − $14.20), which is recorded in the cash payments journal. Notice that the discount applies only to the amount billed for the merchandise (2 percent of $710). Here are the transactions shown in T accounts:

Any well-managed business takes advantage of a purchases discount whenever possible. So, if a discount is generally available to the business, it is worthwhile to set up a special Purchases Discounts Credit column in the cash payments journal. Transaction (b), August 8, looks like this in the cash payments journal:

CASH PAYMENTS JOURNAL PAGE __26__

	DATE	CK. NO.	ACCOUNT DEBITED	POST. REF.	OTHER ACCOUNTS DEBIT	ACCOUNTS PAYABLE DEBIT	CASH CREDIT	PURCHASES DISCOUNTS CREDIT	
1	20–								1
2	Aug. 8	76	Colvin, Inc.			7 5 9 00	7 4 4 80	1 4 20	2
3									3

Here are some other transactions of Dodson Plumbing Supply involving decreases in cash during August. Note that credit terms vary among the different creditors. Detailed information on the purchase invoices paid below is available in the purchases journal on page 347.

Aug. 10 Paid wages for two-week period, Ck. No. 77, $1,680 (previously recorded in the payroll entry).

11 Issued Ck. No. 78 to Adams Manufacturing Company, in payment of invoice no. 10611 ($564), less return ($70); less cash discount, 2/10, n/30; $484.12 ($564 − $70 = $494; $494.00 × .02 = $9.88; $494.00 − $9.88 = $484.12).

12 Bought supplies for cash; issued Ck. No. 79 payable to Davenport Office Supplies, $70.

15 Issued Ck. No. 80 to Spargo Products Company in payment of their invoice no. B643 ($165) less return ($42); less cash discount, 1/10, n/30; $121.87 [$165 − $42 = $123; freight charges totaled $10.00 ($123 − $10 = $113); $113.00 × .01 = $1.13; $123.00 − $1.13 = $121.87].

16 Bought merchandise for cash, Ck. No. 81, payable to Jones and Son, $200.

19 Received bill and issued Ck. No. 82 to Monroe Express for freight charges on merchandise purchased earlier from Adams Manufacturing Company, $60.

23 Voided Ck. No. 83.

23 Issued Ck. No. 84 to American Fire Insurance Company for insurance premium for one year, $420.

25 Paid wages for two-week period, Ck. No. 85, $1,750 (previously recorded in the payroll entry).

27 Paid F. P. Franz for merchandise he returned on a cash sale, Ck. No. 86, $51.

31 Issued Ck. No. 87 to Richter and Son in payment of invoice no. 902, net 30 days, $180.

The transaction of August 19 paying the freight bill to Monroe Express increases the Freight In account, as the transportation charges are for merchandise purchased.

CASH PAYMENTS JOURNAL

PAGE ___26___

	DATE	CK. NO.	ACCOUNT DEBITED	POST. REF.	OTHER ACCOUNTS DEBIT	ACCOUNTS PAYABLE DEBIT	CASH CREDIT	PURCHASES DISCOUNTS CREDIT	
1	20–								1
2	Aug. 8	76	Colvin, Inc.	✓		7 5 9 00	7 4 4 80	1 4 20	2
3	10	77	Wages Payable	213	1 6 8 0 0 00		1 6 8 0 0 00		3
4	11	78	Adams Manufacturing Company	✓		4 9 4 00	4 8 4 12	9 88	4
5	12	79	Supplies	115	7 0 00		7 0 00		5
6	15	80	Spargo Products Company	✓		1 2 3 00	1 2 1 87	1 13	6
7	16	81	Purchases	511	2 0 0 00		2 0 0 00		7
8	19	82	Freight In	514	6 0 00		6 0 00		8
9	23	83	Void	—					9
10	23	84	Prepaid Insurance	116	4 2 0 00		4 2 0 00		10
11	25	85	Wages Payable	213	1 7 5 0 00		1 7 5 0 00		11
12	27	86	Sales Returns and Allowances	412	5 1 00		5 1 00		12
13	31	87	Richter and Son	✓		1 8 0 00	1 8 0 00		13
14	31				4 2 3 1 00	1 5 5 6 00	5 7 6 1 79	2 5 21	14
15					(X)	(212)	(111)	(513)	15
16									16

NOTE: The Supplies account is explained in Chapter 12.

FIGURE 5

Now let's record these transactions in the cash payments journal (Figure 5). After that has been done, Dodson Plumbing's accountant proves the equality of debits and credits:

Debit Totals		Credit Totals	
Accounts Payable	$1,556.00	Cash	$5,761.79
Other Accounts	4,231.00	Purchases Discounts	25.21
	$5,787.00		$5,787.00

PURCHASES RETURNS AND ALLOWANCES, PURCHASES DISCOUNTS, AND FREIGHT IN ON AN INCOME STATEMENT

In the fundamental accounting equation, to be consistent with the income statement, we placed Purchases Returns and Allowances and Purchases Discounts under Purchases with the plus and minus signs reversed. Both accounts are considered contra accounts and are subtracted from Purchases on the income statement. Since Freight In increases the cost of purchases, it must be added. A portion of the Cost of Goods Sold section of the annual income statement of Dodson Plumbing Supply, as well as the Revenue from Sales section (taken from the illustration in Chapter 13), is shown in Figure 6.

Dodson Plumbing Supply
Income Statement
For Year Ended December 31, 20—

Revenue from Sales:					
Sales			$195 1 8 0 00		
Less: Sales Returns and Allowances	$ 8 4 0 00				
Sales Discounts	1 8 8 0 00		2 7 2 0 00		
Net Sales				$192 4 6 0 00	
Cost of Goods Sold:					
Merchandise Inventory, January 1, 20—			$ 67 0 0 0 00		
Purchases	$87 1 4 0 00				
Less: Purchases Returns and					
Allowances	$ 832.00				
Purchases Discounts	1,248.00	2 0 8 0 00			
Net Purchases		$85 0 6 0 00			
Add Freight In		2 4 6 0 00			
Delivered Cost of Purchases			87 5 2 0 00		
Goods Available for Sale			$154 5 2 0 00		

FIGURE 6

CHECK REGISTER

OBJECTIVE 7
Journalize transactions in a check register.

Instead of using a cash payments journal as a book of original entry, you can use a check register. The **check register** is merely a large checkbook with perforations that make it easy to tear out the checks. The page opposite the checks has columns labeled for special accounts, such as Bank Credit (in place of Cash), Accounts Payable Debit, and so on. The checks are prenumbered, and each check issued is recorded on the columnar sheet. This is common practice for a small business in which the owner writes the checks personally. Transactions are posted directly from the check register.

Suppose Dodson Plumbing Supply had used a check register instead of the cash payments journal. Its August transactions would appear as they do in Figure 7 on page 396.

You can see that the difference between the cash payments journal and the check register is minor. The Bank Credit column substitutes for the Cash Credit column. The check register lists the payee of the check.

Two additional columns, Deposits and Bank Balance, can be added to give the current balance of the City Bank or Cash account. The posting process for each book of original entry is the same.

REMEMBER!
In the Post. Ref. column, a check mark indicates that the amount has been posted to the creditor's account in the accounts payable ledger; below the total of the Other Accounts Debit column, an (X) indicates that the total is not to be posted.

In a small business, the owner or manager usually signs all the checks. However, if the owner delegates the authority to sign checks to some other person, that person should *not* have access to the accounting records. Why? This helps prevent fraud, because a dishonest employee could conceal a cash disbursement in the accounting records. In other words, for a medium- to large-size business, a manager should keep a separate book, which in this case is the cash payments journal. One person writes the checks; another person records the checks in the cash payments journal; and a third person does the bank reconciliation. In this way, each person acts as a control on the others. There would have to be cooperation among the three people for

DATE	CK. NO.	PAYEE	ACCOUNT DEBITED	POST. REF.	OTHER ACCOUNTS DEBIT	ACCOUNTS PAYABLE DEBIT	PURCHASES DISCOUNTS CREDIT	CITY BANK CREDIT
20–								
Aug. 8	76	Colvin, Inc.	Colvin, Inc.	✓		7 5 9 00	1 4 20	7 4 4 80
10	77	Payroll	Wages Payable	213	1 6 8 0 00			1 6 8 0 00
11	78	Adams Manufacturing Co.	Adams Manufacturing Co.	✓		4 9 4 00	9 88	4 8 4 12
12	79	Davenport Office Supplies	Supplies	115	7 0 00			7 0 00
15	80	Spargo Products Co.	Spargo Products Co.	✓		1 2 3 00	1 13	1 2 1 87
16	81	Jones and Son	Purchases	511	2 0 0 00			2 0 0 00
19	82	Monroe Express	Freight In	514	6 0 00			6 0 00
23	83	Void	————	—				
23	84	American Fire Ins. Co.	Prepaid Insurance	116	4 2 0 00			4 2 0 00
25	85	Payroll	Wages Payable	213	1 7 5 0 00			1 7 5 0 00
27	86	F. P. Franz	Sales Ret. and Allowances	412	5 1 00			5 1 00
31	87	Richter and Son	Richter and Son	✓		1 8 0 00		1 8 0 00
31					4 2 3 1 00	1 5 5 6 00	2 5 21	5 7 6 1 79
					(X)	(2 1 2)	(5 1 3)	(1 1 1)

NOTE: The Supplies account is explained in Chapter 12.

FIGURE 7

embezzlement to take place. This precaution is consistent with a good system of internal control, because more than one person is involved in the process of recording cash payments. This system also provides protection against errors. One person can double-check the other person's work.

Comparison of Transactions for Two Companies' Purchases and Sales

REMEMBER!
To the seller, a cash discount is a sales discount and is recorded in the cash receipts journal as a debit. To the purchaser, a cash discount is a purchases discount and is recorded in the cash payments journal as a credit.

Purchaser's Books— Able Company	Seller's Books— Baker Company
Bought merchandise from Baker Company, $500; terms 2/10, n/30.	Sold merchandise to Able Company, $500; terms 2/10, n/30.

Dr. Purchases, 500
  Cr. Accounts Payable, 500
	Dr. Accounts Receivable, 500
	  Cr. Sales, 500

Received credit memo from Baker Company for return of merchandise, $100.	Issued credit memo to Able Company for return of merchandise, $100.

Dr. Accounts Payable, 100
  Cr. Purchases Returns and
    Allowances, 100
	Dr. Sales Returns and Allowances, 100
	  Cr. Accounts Receivable, 100

Paid Baker Company within the discount period, $392 ($500 − $100 = $400; $400 × .02 = $8; $400 − $8 = $392).	Received cash from Able Company within the discount period, $392.

Dr. Accounts Payable, 400
  Cr. Cash, 392
  Cr. Purchases Discounts, 8
	Dr. Cash, 392
	Dr. Sales Discounts, 8
	  Cr. Accounts Receivable, 400

TRADE DISCOUNTS

OBJECTIVE 8
Journalize transactions involving
trade discounts.

Manufacturers and wholesalers of many lines of products publish annual
catalogs listing their products at retail prices. These organizations offer their
customers substantial reductions (often as much as 40 percent) from the list
or catalog prices. The reductions from the list prices are called **trade discounts**. Trade discounts are not journalized. Remember, firms grant cash discounts for prompt payment of invoices. Trade discounts are *not related* to
cash payments. Manufacturers and wholesalers use trade discounts to avoid
the high cost of reprinting catalogs when selling prices change. To change
prices, the manufacturer or wholesaler simply issues a sheet showing a new
list of trade discounts to be applied to the catalog prices. Trade discounts can
also be used to differentiate between classes of customers. For example, a
manufacturer may use one schedule of trade discounts for wholesalers and
another schedule for retailers.

Firms may quote trade discounts as a single percentage. *Example:* A distributor of furnaces grants a single discount of 40 percent off the listed catalog price of $8,000. In this case, the selling price is calculated as follows:

List or catalog price	$8,000
Less trade discount of 40% ($8,000 × .4)	3,200
Selling price	$4,800

**Neither the seller nor the buyer records trade discounts in the accounts;
they enter only the selling price.** Using T accounts, the furnace distributor
records the sale like this:

Accounts Receivable			Sales	
+	−		−	+
4,800				4,800

The buyer records the purchase as follows:

Purchases			Accounts Payable	
+	−		−	+
4,800				4,800

Firms may also quote trade discounts as a chain, or series, of percentages.
For example, a distributor of automobile parts grants discounts of 30 percent, 10 percent, and 10 percent off the listed catalog price of $900. In this
case, the selling price is calculated as follows:

List or catalog price	$900.00
Less first trade discount of 30% ($900 × .3)	270.00
Remainder after first discount	$630.00
Less second trade discount of 10% ($630 × .1)	63.00
Remainder after second discount	$567.00
Less third discount of 10% ($567 × .1)	56.70
Selling price	$510.30

Using T accounts, the automobile parts distributor records the sale as follows:

Accounts Receivable		Sales	
+	−	−	+
510.30			510.30

The buyer records the purchase as follows:

Purchases		Accounts Payable	
+	−	−	+
510.30			510.30

In the situation involving a chain of discounts, the additional discounts are granted for large-volume transactions, either in dollar amount or in size of shipment, such as carload lots.

Cash discounts could also apply in situations involving trade discounts. *Example:* Suppose that the credit terms of the preceding sale include a cash discount of 2/10, n/30, and that the buyer pays the invoice within ten days. The seller applies the cash discount to the selling price. The seller records the transaction as shown in the following T accounts.

Cash		Sales Discounts		Accounts Receivable	
+	−	+	−	+	−
500.09		10.21			510.30

The buyer records the transaction as follows:

Cash		Purchases Discounts		Accounts Payable	
+	−	−	+	−	+
	500.09		10.21	510.30	

COMPARISON OF THE FIVE TYPES OF JOURNALS

We have now looked at four special journals and the general journal. It is very important for a business to select and use the journals that provide the most efficient accounting system possible. Figure 8 summarizes the applications of the journals we have discussed and the correct procedures for using them.

Recommended Order of Posting to the Subsidiary Ledgers and the General Ledger

To avoid errors and negative balances in accounts, post from the special journals in this order:

1. Sales journal
2. Purchases journal
3. Cash receipts journal
4. Cash payments journal

Types of Transactions				
Sale of merchandise on account	Purchase of merchandise on account	Receipt of cash	Payment of cash	All other
Evidenced by Source Documents				
Sales invoice	Purchase invoice	Credit card receipts Cash Checks	Check stub	Miscellaneous
Types of Journals				
Sales journal	Purchases journal	Cash receipts journal	Cash payments journal	General journal
Posting to Ledger Accounts				
Individual amounts posted daily to the accounts receivable ledger and the total posted monthly to the general ledger.	*Individual amounts posted daily to the accounts payable ledger and the totals of the special columns posted monthly to the general ledger.*	*Individual amounts in the Accounts Receivable Credit column posted daily to the accounts receivable ledger.* *Individual amounts in the Other Accounts columns posted daily to the general ledger.* *Totals of special columns posted monthly to the general ledger.*	*Individual amounts in the Accounts Payable Debit column posted daily to the accounts payable ledger.* *Individual amounts in the Other Accounts columns posted daily to the general ledger.* *Totals of special columns posted monthly to the general ledger.*	*Entries posted daily to the subsidiary ledgers and the general ledger.*

FIGURE 8

Posting of general journal entries depends on the dates of the specific transactions.

Picture the T accounts involved in transactions. Here are examples of the transactions we have introduced.

Sold merchandise $100, plus $8 sales tax, and customer used a bank credit card. Bank discount rate is 4 percent.

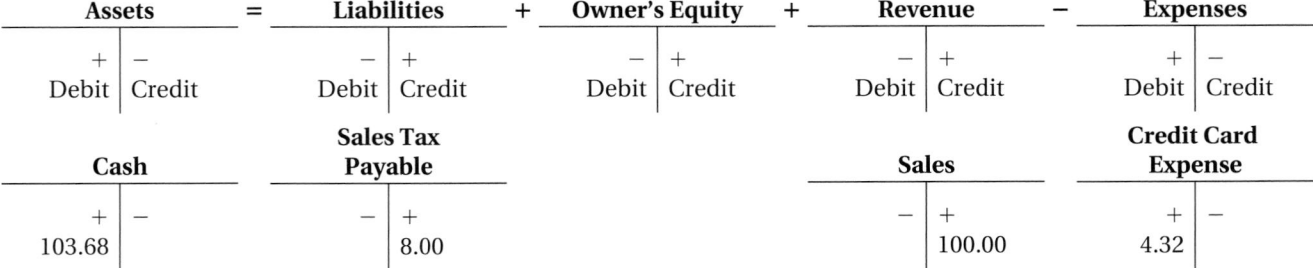

Received check from C. P. Landis Company for $569.30 in payment of $580.92 invoice less $11.62 cash discount.

Issued check to Colvin, Inc. in payment of bill, $759 less $14.20 cash discount.

Assets	=	Liabilities	+	Owner's Equity	+	Revenue	–	Expenses
+ | –		– | +		– | +		– | +		+ | –
Debit | Credit		Debit | Credit		Debit | Credit		Debit | Credit		Debit | Credit

Cash

+ | –
 | 744.80

Accounts Payable

– | +
759.00 |

REMEMBER!
Purchases Discounts is a deduction from Purchases.

Purchases Discounts

– | +
 | 14.20

CHAPTER REVIEW

Review of Performance Objectives

1. Journalize transactions for a retail merchandising business in a cash receipts journal.

   A transaction for a retail merchandising business can be recorded on one line in a cash receipts journal. The cash receipts journal usually contains the following columns: Date, Account Credited, Post. Ref., Other Accounts Credit, Accounts Receivable Credit, Sales Credit, Sales Tax Payable Credit, Credit Card Expense Debit, and Cash Debit.

2. Post from a cash receipts journal to a general ledger and an accounts receivable ledger.

   The accountant posts daily from the Accounts Receivable Credit column to the individual charge customers' accounts in the accounts receivable ledger. After posting, the accountant puts a check mark (✓) in the Post. Ref. column. The accountant also posts the amounts in the Other Accounts Credit column daily and records the account numbers in the Post. Ref. column. The special columns are posted as totals at the end of the month. The accountant then writes the account numbers in parentheses under the totals. An (X) below the total of the Other Accounts Credit column shows that amounts are posted individually and the total is not posted.

3. Determine cash discounts according to credit terms, and record cash receipts from charge customers who are entitled to deduct the cash discount.

The same cash discount is available to all the supplier's customers. The amount of the discount is determined by multiplying the invoice total (excluding freight charges and any returns and allowances) by the cash discount rate (usually 1 or 2 percent). The amount of the discount is recorded as a debit to Sales Discounts.

4. Journalize transactions in a cash payments journal for a service enterprise.

   A cash payment by a service enterprise can be handled on one line in a cash payments journal. The cash payments journal usually contains the following columns: Date, Ck. No., Account Debited, Post. Ref., Other Accounts Debit, Accounts Payable Debit, and Cash Credit.

5. Post from a cash payments journal to a general ledger and an accounts payable ledger.

   The accountant posts daily from the Accounts Payable Debit column to the individual suppliers' accounts in the accounts payable ledger. After posting, the accountant puts a check mark (✓) in the Post. Ref. column. The accountant also posts the amounts in the Other Accounts Debit column daily and records the account numbers in the Post. Ref. column. The special columns are posted as totals at the end of the month. The accountant then writes the account numbers in parentheses under the totals. An (X) below the total of the Other Accounts Debit column shows that amounts are posted individually and the total is not posted.

6. Journalize transactions involving cash discounts in a cash payments journal for a merchandising enterprise.

   A cash payment by a merchandising enterprise that includes a purchase discount can be recorded on one line in a cash payments journal. The cash payments journal usually contains the following columns: Date, Ck. No., Account Debited, Post. Ref., Other Accounts Debit, Accounts Payable Debit, Purchases Discounts Credit, and Cash Credit.

7. Journalize transactions in a check register.

   Transactions can be recorded on one line in a check register. The check register is similar to the cash payments journal. However, the check register has an additional column entitled Payee, and instead of a Cash Credit column there is often a column with the name of the bank (City Bank Credit, for example).

8. Journalize transactions involving trade discounts.

   In transactions involving trade discounts, the trade discounts are deducted from the list prices to arrive at the selling prices. Both sellers and buyers record the transactions at the selling prices.

Glossary

Bank charge card A bank credit card, like the credit cards used by millions of private citizens. The cardholder pays what she or he owes directly to the issuing bank. The business firm deposits the credit card receipts; the amount of the deposit equals the total of the receipts, less a discount deducted by the bank. (380)

Cash discount The amount a customer can deduct for paying a bill within a specified period of time; used to encourage prompt payment. Not all sellers offer cash discounts. (385)

Cash payments journal A special journal used to record all transactions involving cash payments or decreases. (388)

Cash receipts journal A special journal used to record all transactions involving cash receipts or increases. (380)

Check register A journal in which checks are listed as they are written. A check register replaces a cash payments journal. (395)

Credit period The time the seller allows the buyer before full payment on a charge sale has to be made. (383)

Notes Payable The account containing the balance of promissory notes. (383)

Promissory note A written promise to pay a specified amount at a specified time. (383)

Trade discount A substantial discount from the list or catalog prices of goods, granted by the seller; not recorded by the buyer or the seller. (397)

QUESTIONS, EXERCISES, AND PROBLEMS

Discussion Questions

1. What are the normal balances of (a) Purchases? (b) Sales Discounts? (c) Purchases Returns and Allowances? (d) Sales? (e) Purchases Discounts? (f) Sales Returns and Allowances?
2. What does an X under the total of a special journal's Other Accounts column signify?
3. Explain the following credit terms: (a) n/30, (b) 2/10, n/60, (c) 1/15, EOM, n/30.
4. In a cash receipts journal, both the Accounts Receivable Credit column and the Cash Debit column were mistakenly underadded by $700. How will this error be discovered?
5. If a cash payments journal is supposed to save writing, why are there so many entries in the Other Accounts Debit column?
6. Describe the posting procedure for a cash payments journal with an Other Accounts Debit column and several special columns, including an Accounts Payable Debit column.
7. An electronics business purchased speakers for resale. The total of the invoice is $2,440, and it is subject to trade discounts of 15 percent, 10 percent, and 5 percent. Compute the amount the dealer will pay for the speakers.
8. What is the difference between a cash discount and a trade discount?

Exercises

P.O. 1

Describe a recorded transaction involving sale of merchandise with sales tax, paid by credit card.

Exercise 11-1 Describe the transaction recorded.

Cash	Sales Tax Payable	Sales	Credit Card Expense
322.56	16.00	320.00	13.44

P.O. 1,3

Label column headings.

Exercise 11-2 Label the blanks in the column heads as either debit or credit.

CASH RECEIPTS JOURNAL   PAGE ____

DATE	ACCOUNT CREDITED	POST. REF.	OTHER ACCOUNTS	ACCOUNTS RECEIVABLE	SALES	SALES DISCOUNTS	CASH

P.O. 6

Describe posted transactions.

Exercise 11-3 Describe the transactions recorded in the following T accounts:

Cash		Accounts Payable			Purchases	
(c) 1,176	(b) 150	(c) 1,200	(a) 1,350	(a) 1,350	

Purchases Returns and Allowances		Purchases Discounts	
(b) 150	(c) 24	

P.O. 6

Calculate amounts paid for merchandise purchases involving returns and cash discounts.

Exercise 11-4 For the following purchases of merchandise, determine the amount of cash to be paid:

Purchase	Invoice Date	Credit Terms	FOB	Amount of Purchase	Freight Charges	Total Invoice Amount	Returns and Allowances	Date Paid
a.	June 1	2/10, n/30	Destination	$450	—	$ 450	—	June 30
b.	June 12	1/10, n/30	Destination	600	—	600	$100	June 21
c.	June 14	2/10, n/30	Shipping point	940	$60	1,000	—	June 20
d.	June 21	n/30	Shipping point	830	70	900	130	July 12
e.	June 24	1/10, n/30	Shipping point	760	50	810	90	July 3

P.O. 1,6

Designate the appropriate journal.

Exercise 11-5 Indicate the journal in which each of the following transactions should be recorded. Assume a three-column purchases journal.

Transaction	S	P	CR	CP	J
a. Paid a creditor on account.					
b. Bought merchandise on account.					
c. Sold merchandise for cash.					
d. Adjusted for insurance expired.					
e. Received payment on account from a charge customer.					
f. Received a credit memo for merchandise returned.					
g. Bought equipment on credit.					
h. Sold merchandise on account.					
i. Recorded a customer's NSF check.					
j. Invested personal noncash assets in the business.					
k. Withdrew cash for personal use.					

P.O. 3

Journalize transactions involving sales and purchases of merchandise with returns and cash discounts.

Exercise 11-6 Record the following transactions in general journal form:

May

4   Sold merchandise on account to Seymour, Inc.; 2/10, n/30; $640.

10   Purchased merchandise on account from the Mann Company; 1/10, n/60; FOB shipping point; $760.

11   Paid freight bill on merchandise purchased from the Mann Company, $22, to Golina Freight Lines.

13   Received full payment from Seymour, Inc.

14   Received a credit memo from the Mann Company for defective merchandise returned, $94.

19   Paid the Mann Company in full within the discount period.

28   Bought merchandise on account from Bean Company, $900; 2/10, n/30; freight prepaid and added to the invoice, $47 (total, $947).

P.O. 3

Journalize transactions involving sale and purchase of merchandise, a return, and a cash discount.

Exercise 11-7 Record the following transactions in general journal form, first on the books of the seller (Fry Company) and then on the books of the buyer (Lee Company).

Fry Company

a. Sold merchandise on account to Lee Company; 2/10, n/30; $1,500.

b. Issued a credit memo to Lee Company for damaged merchandise, $100.

c. Lee Company paid the account in full within the discount period.

Lee Company

a. Purchased merchandise on account from Fry Company; 2/10, n/30; $1,500.

b. Received a credit memo from Fry Company for damaged merchandise, $100.

c. Paid the Fry Company account in full within the discount period.

P.O. 8

Make correcting entries involving freight charges, returns, and trade discounts.

Exercise 11-8 Record general journal entries to correct the errors described below. Assume that the incorrect entries were posted in the same period in which the errors occurred.

a. A freight cost of $57 incurred on equipment purchased for use in the business was debited to Freight In.

b. The issuance of a credit memo to Merino Company for $126 for merchandise returned was recorded as a debit to Purchases Returns and Allowances and a credit to Accounts Receivable, Merino Company.

c. A cash purchase of $114 of store supplies for the business was recorded as office supplies.

d. A cash sale of $92 to M. A. Marx was recorded as a sale on account.

e. A purchase of merchandise from Ames Company in the amount of $1,000 with a 30 percent trade discount was recorded as a debit to Purchases and a credit to Accounts Payable of $1,000 each.

REFLECTING ON THE WORLD WIDE WEB

1. Who pays for, and who receives money from, a credit card transaction?
2. Fleet Bank pays the merchant 98 percent of the sale amount. How might the grocer record the sale in its cash receipts journal?

CONSIDER AND COMMUNICATE

You are the manager of the Accounts Receivable Department for a merchandising business. Your billing clerk sent a bill for $2 to a customer who had charged $100 in goods (including sales tax) with terms 2/10, n/30. The customer has called and indicated his displeasure; he can't understand an error like this, since he paid on time. Explain to your billing clerk why Accounts Receivable is credited for $100 and not $98. How was permission given to send less than the full amount?

WHAT'S WRONG WITH THIS PICTURE?

Suppose we collected cash from a charge customer, and our debit was to Cash and the credit to Sales. How and when would this error be discovered?

CRITICAL THINKING

You work for Gibson Plumbing Supply. You are responsible for training a new accounting clerk. He has the following questions for you to answer about this invoice:

Gibson Plumbing Supply   No. 320
14 Indiana Avenue
Chicago, Illinois 60612

INVOICE

SOLD TO: C. P. Lander Company
5210 Gilman Avenue
San Diego, CA 92102

DATE: August 1, 20–
ORDER NO.: 5384
SHIPPED BY: Faster Freight
TERMS: 2/10, n/30
SALESPERSON: H. T.

QUANTITY	DESCRIPTION	UNIT PRICE	TOTAL
6	Olin single-control tub shower faucet #44B652	51 50	309 00
6	Olin dual-control washerless lavatory faucet #59B641	22 20	133 20
12	Olin massage shower head, antique brass #37B411	11 56	138 72
	Subtotal		580 92
	Freight		63 80
	Total		644 72

---

1. Who is the buyer?
2. Who is paying the freight?

3. What is the customer's order number?
4. What percentage of the goods bought is the cost of the freight?
5. What are the credit terms and what do they mean?
6. How much will the buyer actually have to pay if the money is received within ten days?
7. What is the dollar amount of the discount?
8. Who receives the discount?
9. What is the due date for payment to get the discount?
10. Why would a seller give a buyer a discount?

A MATTER OF ETHICS

When the new accountant started to work, the owner took him out to lunch each Friday to discuss problems, progress, and suggestions to improve the business. One Friday, the owner couldn't go to lunch with the accountant. The accountant took the money for his lunch from petty cash and charged it to the owner's drawing account. He reasoned that the owner always took him to lunch on Friday, and he didn't have money for lunch. This happened several Fridays during the year. Was this a fair assumption for the accountant to make? Was it ethical?

PROBLEM SET A

P.O. 1,2

Problem 11-1A Walters and Company, a retail carpet store, sells on the bases of (1) cash, (2) charge accounts, and (3) bank credit cards. The following transactions involved cash receipts for the firm during May of this year. The state imposes a 4 percent sales tax on retail sales. The bank charges 4 percent on the total of the credit card sales plus sales tax. (For all sales involving credit cards, record credit card expense at the time of the sale.)

May 8 Total cash sales for the week, $1,350, plus $54 sales tax.
8 Total sales for the week paid for by bank credit cards, $1,200, plus $48 sales tax.
11 D. C. Walters, the owner, invested an additional $3,000.
11 Collected cash from N. D. Pryor, a charge customer, $71.70.
12 Sold store equipment at cost for cash, $240.
15 Total cash sales for the week, $1,650, plus $66 sales tax.
15 Total sales for the week paid for by bank credit cards, $900, plus $36 sales tax.
19 Borrowed $2,400 from the bank, receiving the same in cash and giving the bank a promissory note.
21 Collected cash from R. Branch, a charge customer, $78.
22 Total sales for the week paid for by bank credit cards, $1,050, plus $42 sales tax.
22 Total cash sales for the week, $2,400, plus $96 sales tax.
24 Received cash as refund for the return of merchandise purchased, $135.
26 Collected cash from C. Feller, a charge customer, $156.
31 Total sales for the week paid for by bank credit cards, $240, plus $9.60 sales tax.

May 31 Collected cash from R. D. Thorp, a charge customer, $109.20.
31 Total cash sales for the remainder of the month, $2,325, plus $93 sales tax.

Check Figure

Total Sales Credit, $11,115

Instructions

1. Open the following accounts in the accounts receivable ledger and record the May 1 balances as given: R. Branch, $78; C. Feller, $186; S. R. Pratt, $114.72; N. D. Pryor, $71.70; R. D. Thorp, $176.47; F. N. Weeks, $79.52. Place a check mark in the Post. Ref. column.
2. Record a balance of $706.41 in the Accounts Receivable controlling account as of May 1.
3. Record the transactions in the cash receipts journal beginning with page 62.
4. Post daily to the accounts receivable ledger.
5. Total and rule the cash receipts journal.
6. Prove the equality of debit and credit totals.
7. Post to the Accounts Receivable controlling account in the general ledger.

P.O. 1,3

Problem 11-2A Peterson Company sells candy wholesale to vending machine operators. Terms of sales on account are 2/10, n/30, FOB shipping point. The following transactions involving cash receipts and sales of merchandise took place in May of this year:

May 1 Received $980 cash from L. Riggan in payment of April 22 invoice of $1,000 less cash discount.
4 Received $792 cash in payment of $720 note receivable and interest of $72.
7 Received $686 cash from K. L. Shafer in payment of April 29 invoice of $700, less cash discount.
8 Sold merchandise on account to D. Perry, invoice no. 272, $486.
16 Cash sales for first half of May, $3,284.
17 Received cash from D. Perry in payment of invoice no. 272, less cash discount.
20 Received $321 cash from L. N. Sharp in payment of April 16 invoice, no discount.
21 Sold merchandise on account to R. O. Weinstein, invoice no. 285, $836.
24 Received $318 cash refund for return of defective equipment that was originally bought for cash.
27 Sold merchandise on account to R. Johnston, invoice no. 292, $540.
31 Cash sales for second half of May, $3,462.

Check Figure

Total sales on account, $1,862

Instructions

1. Journalize the transactions for May in the cash receipts journal and the sales journal.
2. Total and rule the journals.
3. Prove the equality of debit and credit totals.

P.O. 7

Problem 11-3A The Macklin Bookshop uses a check register to keep track of expenditures. The following transactions occurred during February of this year.

Feb. 3 Issued check no. 4312, $705.60, to Kentworth Company for the amount of their invoice no. 68172 recorded previously for $720, less 2 percent cash discount.

4 Paid freight bill to Keller Express Company, $48, for books purchased, issued check no. 4313.

6 Paid rent for the month, $320; check no. 4314, to Moore Land Company.

11 Received and paid bill for advertising in the *Northside News,* $58, check no. 4315.

11 Paid Collins Book Company $930.60, check no. 4316, for their invoice no. A3322 recorded previously for $940 less 1 percent cash discount.

17 Paid wages recorded previously for first half of February, $480; check no. 4317.

21 R. D. Macklin, the owner, withdrew $600 for personal use; check no. 4318.

26 Made payment on bank loan, $550; check no. 4319, consisting of $500 on the principal and $50 interest, Coast National Bank.

27 Paid Garrett Publishing Company $926, check no. 4320, for their invoice no. 7768 recorded previously (no discount).

28 Voided check no. 4321.

28 Paid wages expense recorded previously for second half of February, $480; check no. 4322.

Check Figure

Total First Nat'l Bank Credit, $5,098.20

Instructions

1. Record the transactions in the check register.
2. Total and rule the check register.
3. Prove the equality of the debit and credit totals.

P.O. 1,2,3,5,6

Problem 11-4A The following transactions were completed by Hammonds Auto Supply during January, which is the first month of this fiscal year. Terms of sale are 2/10, n/30.

Jan. 2 Paid rent for the month, $600; check no. 6981.

2 J. Hammonds, the owner, invested an additional $2,200 in the business.

4 Bought merchandise on account from Vaughn and Company, $2,840; their invoice no. A691, dated January 2; terms 2/10, n/30.

4 Received check from Vessey Appliance for $980 in payment of $1,000 invoice less discount.

4 Sold merchandise on account to L. Parker, $750, invoice no. 6483.

6 Received check from Peterson, Inc., for $637 in payment of $650 invoice less discount.

7 Issued check no. 6982, $490, to Franklin and Son, in payment of their invoice no. C1272 for $500 less discount.

7 Bought supplies on account from Duncan Office Supply, $98, their invoice no. 1906B; terms net 30 days. (Debit Supplies—Chapter 12 explains when to use the asset account Supplies.)

7 Sold merchandise on account to English and Cole, $890, invoice no. 6484.

9 Issued credit memo no. 43 to L. Parker, $50, for merchandise returned.

11 Cash sales for January 1 to January 10, $4,514.

11 Paid Vaughn and Company $2,783.20; check no. 6983, in payment of $2,840 invoice less discount.

Jan. 14 Sold merchandise on account to Vessey Appliance, $1,950, invoice no. 6485.

18 Bought merchandise on account from Crosby Products, $4,780; their invoice no. 7281D, dated January 16; FOB shipping point, freight prepaid and added to the invoice $150 (total $4,930); terms 2/10, n/60.

21 Issued check no. 6984, $282, to *The Shopper* for advertising not recorded previously (Miscellaneous Expense).

21 Cash sales for January 11 to January 20, $3,990.

23 Received and paid invoice from Ball Fast Freight, check no. 6985, $86, for freight charges on merchandise purchased on January 4.

23 Received credit memo no. 163, $425, from Crosby Products for merchandise returned.

29 Sold merchandise on account to Bryan Supply, $1,940, invoice no. 6486.

31 Cash sales, January 21 to January 31, $4,428.

31 Issued check no. 6986 for $49 payable to M. Dole for miscellaneous expenses.

31 Recorded payroll entry from the payroll register; total salaries, $6,100; employees' federal income tax withheld, $854; FICA tax withheld, $466.65.

31 Recorded the payroll taxes: FICA, $466.65; state unemployment tax, $329.40; federal unemployment tax, $48.80.

31 Issued check no. 6987, $4,779.35, for salaries for the month.

31 J. Hammonds, the owner, withdrew $950 for personal use, check no. 6988.

Check Figure

Trial balance totals, $63,022.30

Instructions

1. Record the transactions for January, using a sales journal, page 73; a purchases journal, page 56; a cash receipts journal, page 38; a cash payments journal, page 45; a general journal, page 100. The chart of accounts is as follows:

111 Cash	311 J. Hammonds, Capital
113 Accounts Receivable	312 J. Hammonds, Drawing
114 Merchandise Inventory	
115 Supplies	411 Sales
116 Prepaid Insurance	412 Sales Returns and Allowances
121 Equipment	413 Sales Discounts
212 Accounts Payable	
215 Salaries Payable	511 Purchases
216 Employees' Federal Income Tax Payable	512 Purchases Returns and Allowances
217 FICA Tax Payable	513 Purchases Discounts
218 State Unemployment Tax Payable	514 Freight In
	521 Salary Expense
219 Federal Unemployment Tax Payable	522 Payroll Tax Expense
	527 Rent Expense
	531 Miscellaneous Expense

2. Post daily all entries involving customer accounts to the accounts receivable ledger.

3. Post daily all entries involving creditor accounts to the accounts payable ledger.

4. Post daily those entries involving the Other Accounts columns and the general journal to the general ledger. Write the owner's name in the Capital and Drawing accounts.

5. Add the columns of the special journals, and prove the equality of debit and credit totals on scratch paper.
6. Post the appropriate totals of the special journals to the general ledger.
7. Prepare a trial balance.
8. Prepare a schedule of accounts receivable and a schedule of accounts payable. Do the totals equal the balances of the related controlling accounts?

Instructions for General Ledger Software

1. Record the transactions in the sales journal, purchases journal, cash receipts journal, cash payments journal, and general journal.
   a. For efficiency, analyze the transactions, indicate what journal each transaction goes into, and key the entries in five groups or batches, one for each journal.
   b. Because the program uses a single-column purchases journal, add the amount of the freight to the amount of purchases.
2. Print the journals.
3. Post the amounts from the sales, purchases, cash receipts, cash payments, and general journals.
4. Print a trial balance.
5. Print a schedule of accounts receivable and compare the total with the balance of the Accounts Receivable controlling account.
6. Print a schedule of accounts payable and compare the total with the balance of the Accounts Payable controlling account.

PROBLEM SET B

P.O. 1,2

Problem 11-1B Budget Furniture, a home furnishings store, sells on the bases of (1) cash, (2) charge accounts, and (3) bank credit cards. The following transactions involve cash receipts for the firm for November of this year. The state imposes a 4 percent sales tax on retail sales. The bank charges 4 percent of the total credit card sales plus tax. (For all sales involving credit cards, record credit card expense at the time of the sale.)

Nov. 7 Total cash sales for the week, $1,700, plus $68 sales tax.
   7 Total sales from bank credit cards for the week, $1,800, plus $72 sales tax.
   11 M. R. Vance, the owner, invested an additional $4,728.
   12 Sold office equipment for cash at cost, $366.
   12 Collected cash from T. R. Allison, a charge customer, $53.84.
   14 Total cash sales for the week, $2,593.04, plus $103.72 sales tax.
   14 Total sales from bank credit cards for the week, $1,440 plus $57.60 sales tax.
   18 Collected cash from N. P. Thorne, a charge customer, $78.52.
   19 Borrowed $5,560 from the bank, receiving the same in cash and giving the bank a promissory note.
   21 Total cash sales for the week, $3,254, plus $130.16 sales tax.
   21 Total sales from bank credit cards for the week, $1,480, plus $59.20 sales tax.
   22 Collected cash from C. E. Barnes, a charge customer, $233.52.
   24 Budget Furniture received cash as a refund for the return of merchandise it purchased, $372.

27   Collected cash from O. Hauff, a charge customer, $143.12.
30   Total sales from bank credit cards for the week, $352.80, plus $14.11 sales tax.
30   Total cash sales for the week, $3,955.68, plus $158.23 sales tax.

Check Figure

Total Sales Credit, $16,575.52

Instructions

1. Open the following accounts in the accounts receivable ledger and record the November 1 balances as given: T. R. Allison, $193.84; C. E. Barnes, $233.52; L. R. Cain, $106.46; L. P. Dunn, $179.52; O. Hauff, $143.12; N. P. Thorne, $78.52. Place a check mark in the Post. Ref. column.
2. Record a balance of $934.98 in the Accounts Receivable controlling account as of November 1.
3. Record the transactions in the cash receipts journal beginning with page 16.
4. Post daily to the accounts receivable ledger.
5. Total and rule the cash receipts journal.
6. Prove the equality of debit and credit totals.
7. Post to the Accounts Receivable controlling account in the general ledger.

P.O. 1,3

Problem 11-2B The C. R. Michaels Company sells candy wholesale, primarily to vending machine operators. Terms of sales on account are 2/10, n/30, FOB shipping point. The following transactions involving cash receipts and sales of merchandise took place in May of this year:

May   2   Received $686 cash from N. Roche in payment of April 23 invoice of $700 less cash discount.
5   Received $990 cash in payment of $900 note receivable and interest of $90.
8   Sold merchandise on account to G. Selleck, invoice no. 862, $420.
9   Received $784 in cash from D. Morton in payment of April 30 invoice of $800, less cash discount.
15   Received cash from G. Selleck in payment of invoice no. 862, less discount.
16   Cash sales for first half of May, $3,447.
19   Received $253 in cash from R. O. Huff in payment of April 14 invoice, no discount.
22   Sold merchandise on account to N. T. Jackson, invoice no. 887, $585.
25   Received $326 cash refund for return of defective equipment bought in April for cash.
28   Sold merchandise on account to M. E. Murray, invoice no. 910, $728.
31   Cash sales for the second half of May, $3,394.

Check Figure

Total sales on account, $1,733

Instructions

1. Journalize the transactions for May in the cash receipts journal and the sales journal.
2. Total and rule the journals.
3. Prove the equality of debit and credit totals.

P.O. 7

Problem 11-3B Jefferson Company uses a check register to keep track of expenditures. The following transactions occurred during February of this year:

Feb.   1   Issued check no. 4311 to Bennett Company for their invoice no. 3113E recorded previously; $640 less cash discount of $12.80, $627.20.

Feb. 2 Paid freight bill to Baxter Express Company, $53, for merchandise purchased, issuing check no. 4312.

4 Paid rent for month of February, $345; check no. 4313 to Dixon Realty.

9 Received and paid bill for advertising in *Neighborhood News;* check no. 4314, $48.

10 Paid Dietrich Company $990, check no. 4315, for their invoice no. D642 recorded previously in the amount of $1,000 less 1 percent cash discount.

15 Paid wages for first half of month, $1,538; check no. 4316 (payroll entry was previously recorded).

19 R. Kelly, the owner, withdrew $500 for personal use; check no. 4317.

25 Made payment on bank loan, $930; check no. 4318, consisting of $900 on principal and $30 interest, Second National Bank.

27 Issued to Lattimer Company check no. 4319, $429, for their invoice no. 6317 recorded previously (no discount).

28 Voided check no. 4320.

28 Paid wages recorded previously for the second half of month, $1,538; check no. 4321.

28 Received and paid telephone bill, $56; check no. 4322, payable to Central Telephone Company.

Check Figure

Total First Nat'l Bank Credit, $7,054.20

Instructions

1. Record the transactions in the check register.
2. Total and rule the check register.
3. Prove the equality of the debit and credit totals.

P.O. 1,2,3,5,6

Problem 11-4B The following transactions were completed by Yu Restaurant Equipment during January, the first month of this fiscal year. Terms of sale are 2/10, n/30.

Jan. 2 Paid rent for the month, $550; check no. 6981.

2 E. Yu, the owner, invested an additional $2,240 in the business.

4 Bought merchandise on account from Vaughn and Company, $2,710; their invoice no. A694, terms 2/10, n/30; dated January 2.

4 Received check from Vessey Appliance for $980 in payment of invoice for $1,000 less discount.

4 Sold merchandise on account to L. Parker, $650, invoice no. 6483.

6 Received check from Peterson, Inc., for $637 in payment of $650 invoice less discount.

7 Issued check no. 6982, $588, to Franklin and Son in payment of their invoice no. C127 for $600, less discount.

7 Bought supplies on account from Duncan Office Supply, $84.80, their invoice no. 190B; terms net 30 days. (Debit Supplies—Chapter 12 explains when to use the asset account Supplies.)

7 Sold merchandise on account to English and Cole, $850, invoice no. 6484.

9 Issued credit memo no. 43 to L. Parker, $30, for merchandise returned.

11 Cash sales for January 1 to January 10, $4,442.60.

11 Paid Vaughn and Company $2,655.80; check no. 6983, in payment of their $2,710 invoice, less discount.

14 Sold merchandise on account to Vessey Appliance, $1,900, invoice no. 6485.

Jan. 14 Received check from L. Parker, $607.60, in payment of $650 invoice, less return of $30 and less discount.

19 Bought merchandise on account from Crosby Products, $3,600; their invoice no. 7281, dated January 16; terms 2/10, n/60; FOB shipping point, freight prepaid and added to invoice, $140 (total $3,740).

21 Issued check no. 6984, $265, for advertising to Barclay Agency not recorded previously. (Miscellaneous Expense)

21 Cash sales for January 11 through January 20, $3,565.

23 Received credit memo no. 163, $96, from Crosby Products for merchandise returned.

29 Sold merchandise on account to Bryan Supply, $1,864; invoice no. 6486.

29 Received and paid invoice from Pacific Freight, check no. 6985, $78, for freight charges on merchandise purchased January 4.

31 Cash sales for January 21 through January 31, $3,987.

31 Issued check no. 6986, $45, to M. Pierce for miscellaneous expenses not recorded previously.

31 Recorded payroll entry from the payroll register: total salaries, $5,800; employees' federal income tax withheld, $812; FICA tax withheld, $443.70.

31 Recorded the payroll taxes: FICA, $443.70; state unemployment tax, $313.20; federal unemployment tax, $46.40.

31 Issued check no. 6987, $4,544.30, for salaries for the month.

31 E. Yu, the owner, withdrew $970 for personal use, check no. 6988.

Check Figure

Trial balance totals, $60,448.60

Instructions

1. Record the transactions for January, using a sales journal, page 91; a purchases journal, page 74; a cash receipts journal, page 56; a cash payments journal, page 63; a general journal, page 119. The chart of accounts is as follows:

111 Cash	411 Sales
113 Accounts Receivable	412 Sales Returns and Allowances
114 Merchandise Inventory	413 Sales Discounts
115 Supplies	
116 Prepaid Insurance	511 Purchases
121 Equipment	512 Purchases Returns and Allowances
212 Accounts Payable	
215 Salaries Payable	513 Purchases Discounts
216 Employees' Federal Income Tax Payable	514 Freight In
	521 Salary Expense
217 FICA Tax Payable	522 Payroll Tax Expense
218 State Unemployment Tax Payable	527 Rent Expense
	531 Miscellaneous Expense
219 Federal Unemployment Tax Payable	
311 E. Yu, Capital	
312 E. Yu, Drawing	

2. Post daily all entries involving customer accounts to the accounts receivable ledger.

3. Post daily all entries involving creditor accounts to the accounts payable ledger.

4. Post daily those entries involving the Other Accounts columns and the general journal to the general ledger. Write the owner's name in the Capital and Drawing accounts.
5. Add the columns of the special journals, and prove the equality of debit and credit totals on scratch paper.
6. Post the appropriate totals of the special journals to the general ledger.
7. Prepare a trial balance.
8. Prepare a schedule of accounts receivable and a schedule of accounts payable. Do the totals equal the balances of the related controlling accounts?

Instructions for General Ledger Software

1. Record the transactions in the sales journal, purchases journal, cash receipts journal, cash payments journal, and general journal.
   a. For efficiency, analyze the transactions, indicate what journal each transaction goes into, and key the entries in five groups or batches, one for each journal.
   b. Because the program uses a single-column purchases journal, add the amount of the freight to the amount of purchases.
2. Print the journals.
3. Post the amounts from the sales, purchases, cash receipts, cash payments, and general journals.
4. Print a trial balance.
5. Print a schedule of accounts receivable and compare the total with the balance of the Accounts Receivable controlling account.
6. Print a schedule of accounts payable and compare the total with the balance of the Accounts Payable controlling account.

The Computer Lab

Cash Receipts and Cash Payments Journals

Remember, an entry goes in one journal ONLY!

Since Jeep Jockeys decided to streamline accounting operations by adding purchases and sales journals, Mr. Kennedy agreed that it would be logical and efficient to add two more special journals: a cash receipts journal for all increases to cash, and a cash payments journal for all decreases to cash. That will leave only a small number of entries to go into the general journal—for instance, returns and allowances, payroll entries (except the payment of the net payroll), adjusting and closing entries, and any other entry that does not fit the definition of what goes in a particular special journal. Mr. Kennedy has brought you the summary of transactions for the month so that you can record them in one of the four new special journals and record the other entries in the general journal.

The first thing you want to do is to open your general ledger accounting software package and bring up the June 30, 20— trial balance for Jeep Jockeys.

It should look like this. The purpose here is to know you are building on the correct month.

Jeep Jockeys
Trial Balance
June 30, 20—

	Debit	Credit
Cash	31,181.09	
Accounts Receivable	17,346.81	
Prepaid Insurance	1,650.00	
Supplies	21.00	
Office Equipment	759.00	
Accumulated Depreciation, Office Equipment		11.32
Vehicles	46,000.00	
Accumulated Depreciation, Vehicles		1,250.00
Kiosk Equipment	478.69	
Accounts Payable		9,344.73
H. Kennedy, Capital		63,952.68
H. Kennedy, Drawing	750.00	
Tour Revenue		30,064.00
Sales		5,287.80
Sales Returns and Allowances	10.99	
Purchases	3,684.00	
Purchases Returns and Allowances		24.00
Freight In	232.69	
Wages Expense	6,435.00	
Rent Expense	320.00	
Advertising Expense	753.26	
Utilities Expense	87.00	
Accounting and Legal Expense	150.00	
Miscellaneous Expense	75.00	
	109,934.53	109,934.53

Purchases of Merchandise on Account for July

Date	Supplier's Name	Invoice No.	Invoice Date	Terms	Details of Purchase
July 1	Mug Shots	33761-A	July 1	2/10, n/30	12 cases logo mugs (12 mugs per case) @ $24/case plus $10.43 freight charge (Please extend amounts)
1	T-Mart	1001-C	July 1	2/10, n/30	13 cases logo T-shirts— 1 child, 6 lg., 6 x-lg. (12 shirts per case) @ $84/case plus $75.90 freight charge
2	Cost-Less	521485	July 2	n/30	5 cases disposable cameras (12 cameras per case), 35 mm, 24 shot @ $72/case plus $10.30 freight charge
3	CapCo	6-47238	July 3	2/10, n/30	8 cases logo baseball caps, (12 caps per case), adjustable @ $108/case plus $29.80 freight charge
3	TanShine	372461-4	July 3	n/30	2 cases 25 SPF suntan lotion (twelve 12-oz. bottles per case) @ $60/case plus $5.45 freight charge

Sale of Merchandise on Account for July

Date	Invoice No.	Details of Sale	Amount
July 4	9	Enchanted Village, 3 cases lotion (12 bottles per case) @ $9.99/bottle; 3 cases logo mugs (12 mugs per case) @ $7.99/mug (Hank wants you to extend the totals because he didn't have time to do it.)	
6	10	Harlton Hotel, 2 cases T-shirts—1 lg., 1 x-lg. (12 shirts per case) @ $16.99/shirt	
12	11	Morgan B and B, 2 cases disposable cameras (12 cameras per case) @ $10.99/camera	
14	12	Masters' Family Reunion, 2 cases T-shirts—1 lg., 1 x-lg. (12 shirts per case) @ $16.99/shirt; 2 cases caps (12 caps per case) @ $14.99/cap	
18	13	Roe Wedding, 2 cases disposable cameras (12 cameras per case) @ $10.99/camera; 3 cases T-shirts—1 med., 1 lg., 1 x-lg. (12 shirts per case) @ $16.99/shirt	
22	14	Robbins' Incentive Seminar, 4 cases T-shirts—2 lg., 2 x-lg. (12 shirts per case) @ $16.99/shirt	
29	15	The Rafters, 3 cases caps (12 caps per case) @ $14.99/cap	
31	16	Corlis' Anniversary, 5 cases logo mugs (12 mugs per case) @ $7.99/mug	

Other July Transactions

Date		Amount
July 1	Paid rent, Ck. No. 1023	320.00
1	Advertising Expense—July photo ad, Ck. No. 1024	410.00
2	Miscellaneous Expense—Silk desert flowers for Kiosk, Ck. No. 1025.	52.00
3	Supplies—4 cases bottled water for clients, Ck. No. 1026. (Debit Supplies—Chapter 12 explains the asset account supplies.)	42.00
5	Advertising Expense—new brochures, Ck. No. 1027.	68.00
6	Olympus Digital Camera for courtesy customer photos, with free mini tripod, on account, Rolley's Cameras.	979.00
8	Paid T-Mart on account, Ck. No. 1028.	1,836.80
17	Paid CapCo on account, Ck. No. 1029.	431.52
18	The Chamber of Commerce paid on account.	431.52
18	Made Jeep payment to Jeep Town, Ck. No. 1030.	784.00
20	Harlton Hotel paid on account.	611.64
21	H. Kennedy withdrew funds for personal use, Ck. No. 1031.	850.00
21	Morgan B and B paid on account.	120.89
22	Wilkins' Reunion paid on account.	4,351.28
23	Paid Store Depot on account, Ck. No. 1032.	478.69
24	Paid J. Graiff, CPA on account, Ck. No. 1033.	179.00
25	Mikels' Wedding paid on account.	4,671.52
25	Received partial payment on account from the Drake Car Rally.	909.76
27	Received partial payment on account from Finch's B and B.	185.00
28	Received partial payment on account from Simms' Sales Conference.	2,005.82
28	Received payment on account from Welcomer's luncheon.	958.80
29	Paid Sign Masters on account, Ck. No. 1034.	307.35
30	Paid month's wages, Ck. No. 1035. (Wages Expense)	5,728.00
30	Accounting and Legal Expense, Ck. No. 1036.	150.00
30	Tour Revenue received in cash	16,265.00

Date		Amount
July 30	Tour Revenue on account (verify total) Corlis' Anniversary 3,300.00 Roe Wedding 3,900.00 Robbins' Incentive Seminar 3,600.00 The Rafters 1,200.00	12,000.00
30	Paid TanShine on account, no discount, Ck. No. 1037.	250.90
30	Paid Cost-Less on account, no discount, Ck. No. 1038.	449.40 − return = 437.06
30	Paid Mug Shots on account, no discount, Ck. No. 1039.	571.99
30	Masters' Family Reunion returned 1 case of water-damaged T-Mart T-shirts.	203.88
31	We returned 2 defective disposable cameras to Cost-Less @ $6.00 each plus $0.34 freight.	12.34
31	Paid utilities for July, Ck. No. 1040.	93.00

Now what? Four special journals and one general journal. I'll sort the entries like laundry into the sales on account, purchases on account, cash increases, and cash decreases. In the general journal, I'll just continue where I left off and journalize those entries that don't fit into the four special journals.

After entering all transactions into the five journals, posting individual and total entries to the general ledger, and posting to Accounts Receivable and Accounts Payable accounts, prepare the following papers:

General ledger trial balance dated July 31, 20—.

Schedule of accounts receivable (its total must be equal to the balance of the Accounts Receivable account in the general ledger).

Schedule of accounts payable (its total must be equal to the balance of the Accounts Payable account in the general ledger).

General ledger

Accounts receivable ledger

Accounts payable ledger

Before a Test Check: Chapters 10–11

PART I: Completion

Complete each of the following statements by writing the appropriate word(s) in the spaces provided:

1. The normal balance of the Purchases Discounts account is on the _____ side.

2. Entries in the Accounts Payable Debit column of a cash payments journal are posted daily to the _____.

3. A _____ is the amount a customer may deduct for paying a bill within a specified period of time.

4. The form sent to the supplier of merchandise is called a(n) _____.

5. The _____ account is used to record the buying of merchandise only.

6. If the freight charges are FOB shipping point, the _____ pays the transportation charges.

7. Plans and procedures built into the accounting system to promote efficiency and prevent fraud and waste are called _____.

8. Increases in Sales Returns and Allowances are recorded on the _____ side.

9. The sales journal is used to record all _____.

10. The schedule of accounts receivable lists the balances of all the _____ accounts at the end of the month.

PART II: Matching

For each numbered item, choose the appropriate journal, and write the identifying letter.

____ 1. Paid freight bill on merchandise purchased.

____ 2. Bought office equipment for our office on account.

____ 3. Received a credit memo for merchandise we returned.

____ 4. Bought office equipment for cash.

____ 5. Sold merchandise on account.

S   Sales journal
P   Purchases journal (3 columns)
CR   Cash receipts journal
CP   Cash payments journal
J   General journal

Note: Answers to Before a Test Check begin on page A-1.

_____ 6. Journalized the closing entries.

_____ 7. Paid state sales tax to the state revenue department.

_____ 8. Bought merchandise on account.

_____ 9. Sold merchandise for cash.

_____ 10. Bought merchandise for cash.

PART III: True/False

For each question circle T if it is True or circle F if it is False.

T   F   1. The Purchases Discounts account is classified as a revenue account.

T   F   2. The normal balance of the Sales Discounts account is on the debit side.

T   F   3. Check marks in the Posting Reference column of the sales journal indicate that the amounts are not to be posted.

T   F   4. When you post directly from the purchases invoice, you eliminate the accounts payable ledger.

T   F   5. The purchases journal is used for the buying of merchandise for cash and on account.

12 Work Sheet and Adjusting Entries

Performance Objectives

After you have completed this chapter, you will be able to do the following:

1. Prepare an adjustment for supplies.

2. Prepare an adjustment for merchandise inventory under the periodic inventory system.

3. Prepare an adjustment for unearned revenue.

4. Record the adjustment data in a work sheet (including merchandise inventory, unearned revenue, supplies used, expired insurance, depreciation, and accrued wages or salaries).

5. Complete the work sheet.

6. Journalize the adjusting entries for a merchandising business under the periodic inventory system.

7. Journalize the adjusting entry for merchandise inventory under the perpetual inventory system.

We have talked about the special journals and accounts kept by a merchandising business. Now we take another step toward completing the accounting cycle by presenting the related adjustments and the work sheet. Many of the adjustments made by a service business are also made by a merchandising firm. First, let's briefly review the adjusting entries described so far. To begin, look over the following accounts. Here are the data for the adjustments, along with the related adjusting entries:

Insurance expired, $260. (The amount expired is the amount used.)

Prepaid Insurance					Insurance Expense		
	+	−				+	−
Bal.	300	Adj.	260	Adj.		260	
Bal.	40						

Additional depreciation, $280. (Add to both accounts.)

Depreciation Expense				Accumulated Depreciation		
	+	−		−	+	
Adj.	280				Bal.	1,000
					Adj.	280
					Bal.	1,280

Accrued wages (owed but not yet paid), $390. (Add to both accounts.)

Wages Expense				Wages Payable		
	+	−		−	+	
Bal.	2,600				Adj.	390
Adj.	390					
Bal.	2,990					

In this chapter, we introduce three more adjusting entries. One adjustment is for Supplies. This adjustment can be used for merchandising and manufacturing businesses. One adjustment is for merchandise inventory, which is used exclusively for a merchandising business. Another adjustment is for unearned revenue, which could apply to either a merchandising or a service business. We also discuss how to handle the specialized accounts of a merchandising business in the work sheet. Finally, we briefly describe the perpetual inventory system and the accompanying adjustment.

ADJUSTMENT FOR SUPPLIES

OBJECTIVE 1
Prepare an adjustment for supplies.

Previously, when we were talking about the buying of supplies for a service business, we debited Supplies Expense and credited Cash or Accounts Payable.

However, when a merchandising business buys supplies for cash or on credit, we must debit Supplies (an asset account) and credit Cash or Accounts Payable. So purchases of supplies all during the year are all debited to the Supplies account. But we have not taken into consideration the fact that a business continually uses up supplies in the process of carrying out its activities. For a retail concern supplies would consist of everything from paper or plastic bags to paper forms. Rather than going to the trouble of journalizing the amount of the supplies used each day, the company waits until the end of the month or fiscal period and then takes a physical count of the supplies left over. To find the amount of the supplies used, subtract the amount left over from the total amount that was available over the course of the fiscal period.

As an illustration, let's say that Joan Doe Company has a balance of $6,200 in the Supplies account as a result of buying supplies all during the fiscal period. Now, by taking a count of the goods on hand, it is determined that $1,200 of supplies are left.

Balance of Supplies account $6,200	−	Amount of supplies left $1,200	=	Amount of supplies used up and the adjusting entry amount $5,000

To record the amount of the supplies used, Joan Doe Company has to make an adjusting entry. The purpose of an adjusting entry is to bring the books up to date at the end of the accounting period.

Let's look at this in T account form. We need to take the amount of supplies used ($5,000) out of the Supplies account (credit Supplies) because we no longer have that much of the asset. Also, we need to put the amount of supplies used ($5,000) in the Supplies Expense account (debit Supplies Expense) because we have incurred this expense.

	(a)	**Supplies**			**Supplies Expense**	
		+	−		+	−
(Old)	Bal.	6,200	Adjusting 5,000	Adjusting 5,000		
(New)	Bal.	1,200				

ADJUSTMENT FOR MERCHANDISE INVENTORY USING THE PERIODIC INVENTORY SYSTEM

OBJECTIVE 2
Prepare an adjustment for merchandise inventory under the periodic inventory system.

Under the **periodic inventory system**, we do not make an entry in the Merchandise Inventory account until an actual **physical inventory** or count of the stock of goods on hand has been taken. Instead, we record the purchase of merchandise as a debit to Purchases for the amount of the cost and the sale of the merchandise as a credit to Sales for the amount of the selling price. Finally, after a physical count of merchandise has been taken, one method of adjusting inventory is to make two adjusting entries to record the dollar amount of the inventory. The first adjusting entry is to remove the beginning inventory. The second entry is to enter the ending inventory.

Consider this example. A firm has a Merchandise Inventory balance of $74,000, which represents the cost of the inventory at the beginning of the fiscal period. At the end of the fiscal period, the firm takes an actual count of the stock on hand and determines the cost of the ending inventory to be $80,000. Naturally, in any business, goods are constantly being bought, sold, and replaced. The cost of the ending inventory is larger than the cost of the beginning inventory because the firm bought more than it sold. When we adjust the Merchandise Inventory account, we place the new figure of $80,000 in the account. This method can require two steps.

Step 1 Eliminate the amount of the beginning inventory from the Merchandise Inventory account by transferring the amount into Income Summary. (Remove the beginning inventory.)

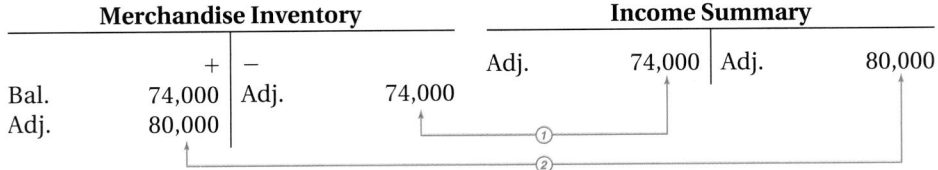

We credit Merchandise Inventory and then debit Income Summary.

Step 2 Enter the ending Merchandise Inventory, because you must record on the books the cost of the asset remaining on hand. (Enter the ending inventory.)

Let's repeat the T accounts, showing step 1 and adding step 2.

Merchandise Inventory				Income Summary	
	+	−		Adj. 74,000	Adj. 80,000
Bal. 74,000	Adj. 74,000				
Adj. 80,000					

In step 2, we debit Merchandise Inventory (recording the asset on the plus side of the account) and do the opposite to Income Summary.

The reason for adjusting the Merchandise Inventory account in these two steps is that both the beginning and the ending amounts appear as distinct figures in the Income Statement columns of a work sheet, and these columns are used as the basis for preparing the income statement.

ADJUSTMENT FOR UNEARNED REVENUE

OBJECTIVE 3
Prepare an adjustment for unearned revenue.

Now let's introduce another adjusting entry, **unearned revenue**, which is cash received in advance for goods or services to be delivered or performed later. This entry could pertain to a service business as well as to a merchandising business. Frequently, cash is received in advance for services to be performed in the future. For example, a professional sports team sells tickets in advance, a concert association sells season tickets in advance, a magazine publisher sells subscriptions in advance, and an insurance company receives premiums in advance. If the cash amounts received by each of these organizations will be earned during the present fiscal period, the amounts should be credited to revenue accounts. On the other hand, if the amounts received will *not* be earned during the present fiscal period, the amounts should be credited to unearned revenue accounts. **An unearned revenue account is classified as a liability,** because an organization is liable for (owes) the amount received in advance until it is earned.

College students pay in advance to participate in a meal plan. Until all those meals are consumed, this money represents unearned revenue for the college or university dining hall services.

To illustrate, assume that on April 1, Bell Publishing Company receives $82,000 in cash for subscriptions covering two years and records them originally as debits to Cash and credits to Unearned Subscriptions. At the end of the year, Bell finds that $30,750 of the subscriptions have been earned. Accordingly, Bell's accountant makes an adjusting entry, debiting Unearned Subscriptions and crediting Subscriptions Income. In other words, the accountant takes the earned portion out of Unearned Subscriptions and adds it to Subscriptions Income. T accounts show the situation as follows:

Cash		Unearned Subscriptions	
+	−	−	+
April 1 82,000		Dec. 31 Adj. 30,750 (9 months)	April 1 82,000 (24 months)
			Bal. 51,250

Subscriptions Income	
−	+
	Dec. 31 Adj. 30,750 (9 months)

To take another example, suppose that Dodson Plumbing Supply offers a course in plumbing repairs for home owners and apartment managers. On November 1, Dodson Plumbing receives $1,200 in fees for a three-month course. Because Dodson Plumbing's present fiscal period ends on December 31, the three months' worth of fees received in advance will not all be earned during this fiscal period. Therefore, Dodson Plumbing's accountant records the transaction as a debit to Cash of $1,200 and a credit to Unearned Course Fees of $1,200. Unearned Course Fees is a liability account, because Dodson Plumbing must complete the how-to course or refund a portion of the money it collected. **Any account beginning with the word _Unearned_ is always a liability.**

On December 31, because two months' worth of course fees have now been earned, Dodson Plumbing's accountant makes an adjusting entry to transfer $800 ($\frac{2}{3}$ of $1,200) from Unearned Course Fees to Course Fees Income. By T accounts, the situation looks like this:

Cash		Unearned Course Fees	
+	−	−	+
Nov. 1 1,200		Dec. 31 Adj. 800 (2 months)	Nov. 1 1,200 (3 months)
			Bal. 400

Course Fees Income	
−	+
	Dec. 31 Adj. 800 (2 months)

Dodson Plumbing Supply's chart of accounts is presented on the next page. The account number arrangement will be discussed in Chapter 13.

Assets (100–199)

111 Cash
112 Notes Receivable
113 Accounts Receivable
114 Merchandise Inventory
115 Supplies
116 Prepaid Insurance
121 Land
122 Building
123 Accumulated Depreciation, Building
124 Equipment
125 Accumulated Depreciation, Equipment

Liabilities (200–299)

211 Notes Payable
212 Accounts Payable
213 Wages Payable
217 Unearned Course Fees
221 Mortgage Payable

Owner's Equity (300–399)

311 L. E. Dodson, Capital
312 L. E. Dodson, Drawing
313 Income Summary

Revenue (400–499)

411 Sales
412 Sales Returns and Allowances
413 Sales Discounts
421 Course Fees Income
422 Interest Income

Cost of Goods Sold (500–599)

511 Purchases
512 Purchases Returns and Allowances
513 Purchases Discounts
514 Freight In

Expenses (600–699)

611 Wages Expense
622 Supplies Expense
623 Insurance Expense
624 Depreciation Expense, Building
625 Depreciation Expense, Equipment
626 Taxes Expense
634 Interest Expense

Before we demonstrate how to record adjustments, let's first look at the trial balance section of Dodson Plumbing Supply's work sheet (Figure 1).

DATA FOR THE ADJUSTMENTS

OBJECTIVE 4
Record the adjustment data in a work sheet (including merchandise inventory, unearned revenue, supplies used, expired insurance, depreciation, and accrued wages or salaries).

Listing the adjustment data appears to be a relatively minor task. In a business situation, however, one must take actual physical counts of the inventories and match them up with costs. One must check insurance policies to determine the amount of insurance that has expired. Finally, one must systematically write off, or depreciate, the cost of equipment and buildings.

For income tax and accounting purposes, land cannot be depreciated. Even if the building and lot were bought as one package for one price, the buyer must separate the cost of the building from the cost of the land. For real estate taxes, the county assessor appraises the building and the land separately. If there is no other qualified appraisal available, one can use the assessor's ratio or percentage as a basis for separating building cost and land cost.

Here are the adjustment data for Dodson Plumbing Supply. We will show the adjustments recorded in T accounts.

a–b. Ending merchandise inventory, $65,800. This adjustment is generally placed first.

Merchandise Inventory				Income Summary			
	+	**−**		**(a)** Adj.	67,000	**(b)** Adj.	65,800
Bal.	67,000	**(a)** Adj.	67,000				
(b) Adj.	65,800						

Dodson Plumbing Supply
Work Sheet
For Year Ended December 31, 20—

	ACCOUNT NAME	TRIAL BALANCE DEBIT	TRIAL BALANCE CREDIT	ADJUSTMENTS DEBIT	ADJUSTMENTS CREDIT
1	Cash	19 1 5 4 00			
2	Notes Receivable	4 0 0 0 00			
3	Accounts Receivable	29 4 4 6 00			
4	Merchandise Inventory	67 0 0 0 00			
5	Supplies	1 4 4 0 00			
6	Prepaid Insurance	9 6 0 00			
7	Land	12 0 0 0 00			
8	Building	130 0 0 0 00			
9	Accumulated Depreciation, Building		52 0 0 0 00		
10	Equipment	33 6 0 0 00			
11	Accumulated Depreciation, Equipment		16 4 0 0 00		
12	Notes Payable		36 4 0 0 00		
13	Accounts Payable		3 0 0 0 00		
14	Unearned Course Fees		1 2 0 0 00		
15	Mortgage Payable		8 0 0 0 00		
16	L. E. Dodson, Capital		140 5 7 4 00		
17	L. E. Dodson, Drawing	56 9 0 0 00			
18	Sales		235 1 8 0 00		
19	Sales Returns and Allowances	8 4 0 00			
20	Sales Discounts	1 8 8 0 00			
21	Interest Income		1 2 0 00		
22	Purchases	87 1 4 0 00			
23	Purchases Returns and Allowances		8 3 2 00		
24	Purchases Discounts		1 2 4 8 00		
25	Freight In	2 4 6 0 00			
26	Wages Expense	45 8 0 0 00			
27	Taxes Expense	1 9 6 0 00			
28	Interest Expense	3 7 4 00			
29		494 9 5 4 00	494 9 5 4 00		

FIGURE 1

c. Course fees earned, $800

Unearned Course Fees				Course Fees Income		
−	+			−	+	
(c) Adj. 800	Bal. 1,200				(c) Adj. 800	

d. Ending supplies inventory, $412

Supplies				Supplies Expense	
+	−			+	−
Bal. 1,440	(d) Adj. 1,028		(d) Adj. 1,028	

Dodson Plumbing Supply
Work Sheet
For Year Ended December 31, 20—

	ACCOUNT NAME	TRIAL BALANCE DEBIT	TRIAL BALANCE CREDIT	ADJUSTMENTS DEBIT	ADJUSTMENTS CREDIT
1	Cash	19 1 5 4 00			
2	Notes Receivable	4 0 0 0 00			
3	Accounts Receivable	29 4 4 6 00			
4	Merchandise Inventory	67 0 0 0 00		(b) 65 8 0 0 00	(a) 67 0 0 0 00
5	Supplies	1 4 4 0 00			(d) 1 0 2 8 00
6	Prepaid Insurance	9 6 0 00			(e) 3 2 0 00
7	Land	12 0 0 0 00			
8	Building	130 0 0 0 00			
9	Accumulated Depreciation, Building		52 0 0 0 00		(f) 4 0 0 0 00
10	Equipment	33 6 0 0 00			
11	Accumulated Depreciation, Equipment		16 4 0 0 00		(g) 4 8 0 0 00
12	Accounts Payable		3 0 0 0 00		
13	Notes Payable		36 4 0 0 00		
14	Unearned Course Fees		1 2 0 0 00	(c) 8 0 0 00	
15	Mortgage Payable		8 0 0 0 00		
16	L. E. Dodson, Capital		140 5 7 4 00		
17	L. E. Dodson, Drawing	56 9 0 0 00			
18	Sales		235 1 8 0 00		
19	Sales Returns and Allowances	8 4 0 00			
20	Sales Discounts	1 8 8 0 00			
21	Interest Income		1 2 0 00		
22	Purchases	87 1 4 0 00			
23	Purchases Returns and Allowances		8 3 2 00		
24	Purchases Discounts		1 2 4 8 00		
25	Freight In	2 4 6 0 00			
26	Wages Expense	45 8 0 0 00		(h) 1 1 2 0 00	
27	Taxes Expense	1 9 6 0 00			
28	Interest Expense	3 7 4 00			
29		494 9 5 4 00	494 9 5 4 00		
30	Income Summary			(a) 67 0 0 0 00	(b) 65 8 0 0 00
31	Course Fees Income				(c) 8 0 0 00
32	Supplies Expense			(d) 1 0 2 8 00	
33	Insurance Expense			(e) 3 2 0 00	
34	Depreciation Expense, Building			(f) 4 0 0 0 00	
35	Depreciation Expense, Equipment			(g) 4 8 0 0 00	
36	Wages Payable				(h) 1 1 2 0 00
37				144 8 6 8 00	144 8 6 8 00
38					
39					
40					
41					
42					

FIGURE 2

e. Insurance expired, $320

Prepaid Insurance		Insurance Expense	
+	−	+	−
Bal. 960	(e) Adj. 320	(e) Adj. 320	

f. Additional year's depreciation of equipment, $4,800

Accumulated Depreciation, Equipment		Depreciation Expense, Equipment	
−	+	+	−
	Bal. 16,400	(f) Adj. 4,800	
	(f) Adj. 4,800		

g. Additional year's depreciation of building, $4,000

Accumulated Depreciation, Building		Depreciation Expense, Building	
−	+	+	−
	Bal. 52,000	(g) 4,000	
	(g) 4,000		

h. Wages owed but not paid to employees at end of year, $1,120

Wages Payable		Wages Expense	
−	+	+	−
	(h) 1,120	Bal. 45,800	
		(h) 1,120	

We now record these in the Adjustments columns of the work sheet, using the same letters to identify the adjustments (see Figure 2).

COMPLETION OF THE WORK SHEET

OBJECTIVE 5
Complete the work sheet.

Previously, in introducing work sheets, we included the Adjusted Trial Balance columns as a means of verifying that the accounts were in balance after recording the adjusting entries. At this time, to reduce the number of columns in the work sheet, we will eliminate the Adjusted Trial Balance columns. The account balances after the adjusting entries will be carried directly into the Income Statement and Balance Sheet columns.

The completed work sheet looks like Figure 3 on pages 430 and 431.

Observe in particular the way we carry forward the figures for Merchandise Inventory and Income Summary. **Income Summary is the only account in which we don't combine the debit and credit figures. Instead, we carry them into the Income Statement columns in Figure 3 as two distinct figures.** As we said, the reason is that both figures appear in the income statement itself. The amount listed as Income Summary in the Income Statement Debit column is the beginning merchandise inventory. The amount listed as Income Summary in the Income Statement Credit column is the

Dodson Plumbing Supply
Work Sheet
For Year Ended December 31, 20—

	ACCOUNT NAME	TRIAL BALANCE DEBIT	TRIAL BALANCE CREDIT	
1	Cash	19 1 5 4 00		
2	Notes Receivable	4 0 0 0 00		
3	Accounts Receivable	29 4 4 6 00		
4	Merchandise Inventory	67 0 0 0 00		
5	Supplies	1 4 4 0 00		
6	Prepaid Insurance	9 6 0 00		
7	Land	12 0 0 0 00		
8	Building	130 0 0 0 00		
9	Accumulated Depreciation, Building		52 0 0 0 00	
10	Equipment	33 6 0 0 00		
11	Accumulated Depreciation, Equipment		16 4 0 0 00	
12	Accounts Payable		3 0 0 0 00	
13	Notes Payable		36 4 0 0 00	
14	Unearned Course Fees		1 2 0 0 00	
15	Mortgage Payable		8 0 0 0 00	
16	L. E. Dodson, Capital		140 5 7 4 00	
17	L. E. Dodson, Drawing	56 9 0 0 00		
18	Sales		235 1 8 0 00	
19	Sales Returns and Allowances	8 4 0 00		
20	Sales Discounts	1 8 8 0 00		
21	Interest Income		1 2 0 00	
22	Purchases	87 1 4 0 00		
23	Purchases Returns and Allowances		8 3 2 00	
24	Purchases Discounts		1 2 4 8 00	
25	Freight In	2 4 6 0 00		
26	Wages Expense	45 8 0 0 00		
27	Taxes Expense	1 9 6 0 00		
28	Interest Expense	3 7 4 00		
29		494 9 5 4 00	494 9 5 4 00	
30	Income Summary			
31	Course Fees Income			
32	Supplies Expense			
33	Insurance Expense			
34	Depreciation Expense, Building			
35	Depreciation Expense, Equipment			
36	Wages Payable			
37				
38	Net Income			
39				
40				
41				
42				

FIGURE 3

	ADJUSTMENTS		INCOME STATEMENT		BALANCE SHEET		
	DEBIT	CREDIT	DEBIT	CREDIT	DEBIT	CREDIT	
					19 1 5 4 00		1
					4 0 0 0 00		2
					29 4 4 6 00		3
	(b) 65 8 0 0 00	(a) 67 0 0 0 00			65 8 0 0 00		4
		(d) 1 0 2 8 00			4 1 2 00		5
		(e) 3 2 0 00			6 4 0 00		6
					12 0 0 0 00		7
					130 0 0 0 00		8
		(f) 4 0 0 0 00				56 0 0 0 00	9
					33 6 0 0 00		10
		(g) 4 8 0 0 00				21 2 0 0 00	11
						3 0 0 0 00	12
						36 4 0 0 00	13
	(c) 8 0 0 00					4 0 0 00	14
						8 0 0 0 00	15
						140 5 7 4 00	16
					56 9 0 0 00		17
				235 1 8 0 00			18
			8 4 0 00				19
			1 8 8 0 00				20
				1 2 0 00			21
			87 1 4 0 00				22
				8 3 2 00			23
				1 2 4 8 00			24
			2 4 6 0 00				25
	(h) 1 1 2 0 00		46 9 2 0 00				26
			1 9 6 0 00				27
			3 7 4 00				28
							29
	(a) 67 0 0 0 00	(b) 65 8 0 0 00	67 0 0 0 00	65 8 0 0 00			30
		(c) 8 0 0 00		8 0 0 00			31
	(d) 1 0 2 8 00		1 0 2 8 00				32
	(e) 3 2 0 00		3 2 0 00				33
	(f) 4 0 0 0 00		4 0 0 0 00				34
	(g) 4 8 0 0 00		4 8 0 0 00				35
		(h) 1 1 2 0 00				1 1 2 0 00	36
	144 8 6 8 00	144 8 6 8 00	218 7 2 2 00	303 9 8 0 00	351 9 5 2 00	266 6 9 4 00	37
			85 2 5 8 00			85 2 5 8 00	38
			303 9 8 0 00	303 9 8 0 00	351 9 5 2 00	351 9 5 2 00	39
							40
							41
							42

ending merchandise inventory. We will talk about this topic in greater detail in Chapter 13.

When developing the work sheet, complete one stage at a time:

1. Record the trial balance, and make sure that the total of the Debit column equals the total of the Credit column.
2. Record the adjustments in the Adjustments columns, and make sure that the totals are equal.
3. Complete the Income Statement and Balance Sheet columns by recording the adjusted balance of each account. Here are the accounts and classifications pertaining to a merchandising business that appear in these columns:

Income Statement		Balance Sheet	
Debit	**Credit**	**Debit**	**Credit**
Expenses	Revenues	Assets	Liabilities
+	+	+	+
Sales Returns and Allowances	Purchases Returns and Allowances	Drawing	Capital
+	+		+
Sales Discounts	Purchases Discounts		Accumulated Depreciation
+	+		
Purchases	Income Summary		
+			
Freight In			
+			
Income Summary			

Study the following example, noting especially the way we treat these special accounts for a merchandising business:

	Location in Work Sheet			
	Income Statement		Balance Sheet	
Account Name	**Debit**	**Credit**	**Debit**	**Credit**
Merchandise Inventory			65,800.00	
Sales		235,180.00		
Sales Returns and Allowances	840.00			
Sales Discounts	1,880.00			
Purchases	87,140.00			
Purchases Returns and Allowances		832.00		
Purchases Discounts		1,248.00		
Freight In	2,460.00			
Income Summary	67,000.00	65,800.00		

ADJUSTING ENTRIES UNDER THE PERIODIC INVENTORY SYSTEM

OBJECTIVE 6
Journalize the adjusting entries for a merchandising business under the periodic inventory system.

Figure 4 shows the way the adjusting entries look when they are taken from the Adjustments columns of the work sheet and recorded in the general journal.

FIGURE 4

GENERAL JOURNAL   PAGE ___96___

	DATE		DESCRIPTION	POST. REF.	DEBIT	CREDIT	
1	20–		Adjusting Entries				1
2	Dec.	31	Income Summary		67 0 0 0 00		2
3			Merchandise Inventory			67 0 0 0 00	3
4							4
5		31	Merchandise Inventory		65 8 0 0 00		5
6			Income Summary			65 8 0 0 00	6
7							7
8		31	Unearned Course Fees		8 0 0 00		8
9			Course Fees Income			8 0 0 00	9
10							10
11		31	Supplies Expense		1 0 2 8 00		11
12			Supplies			1 0 2 8 00	12
13							13
14		31	Insurance Expense		3 2 0 00		14
15			Prepaid Insurance			3 2 0 00	15
16							16
17		31	Depreciation Expense, Building		4 0 0 0 00		17
18			Accumulated Depreciation,				18
19			Building			4 0 0 0 00	19
20							20
21		31	Depreciation Expense,				21
22			Equipment		4 8 0 0 00		22
23			Accumulated Depreciation,				23
24			Equipment			4 8 0 0 00	24
25							25
26		31	Wages Expense		1 1 2 0 00		26
27			Wages Payable			1 1 2 0 00	27
28							28

ADJUSTMENT FOR MERCHANDISE INVENTORY UNDER THE PERPETUAL INVENTORY SYSTEM

OBJECTIVE 7
Journalize the adjusting entry for merchandise inventory under the perpetual inventory system.

Under the **perpetual inventory system**, a business continually maintains a record of each item in stock. **Under the perpetual inventory system, when merchandise is purchased, the Merchandise Inventory account (not the Purchases account) is debited for the cost of the merchandise and Accounts Payable or Cash is credited. When merchandise is sold, the Merchandise Inventory account is credited for the cost of the merchandise and the Cost of Goods Sold account is debited for the cost of the merchandise.**

Many firms use electronic devices to keep track of stock items. For example, when a sale is made at a supermarket checkout counter, as the bar code on each item is scanned, the price and stock number are recorded. The cash register is connected to a computer that updates the inventory record and records the cost of the item. So the business perpetually (always) knows how much inventory it should have on hand.

However, to verify the inventory record, a physical count should be taken from time to time. The amount shown by the physical count may be less than the recorded amount as a result of errors, shrinkage, or shoplifting. If this is the case, an adjusting entry must be made to record the amount of the loss. This entry is a debit to the Cost of Goods Sold account (an expense account) and a credit to the Merchandise Inventory account.

ADJUSTING ENTRY UNDER THE PERPETUAL INVENTORY SYSTEM

Here is a comparison of entries in T-account form under both the periodic and the perpetual inventory systems. Assume a beginning inventory of $80,000.

1. Bought merchandise on account, $50,000.

Periodic Inventory

Purchases				Accounts Payable		
+	−			−	+	
(1) 50,000					(1) 50,000	

Perpetual Inventory

Merchandise Inventory				Accounts Payable		
+	−			−	+	
Bal. 80,000					(1) 50,000	
(1) 50,000						

2. Sold merchandise for $82,000 having a cost of $61,200.

Periodic Inventory

Accounts Receivable				Sales		
+	−			−	+	
(2) 82,000					(2) 82,000	

Perpetual Inventory

Accounts Receivable				Sales		
+	−			−	+	
(2) 82,000					(2) 82,000	

Cost of Goods Sold				Merchandise Inventory		
+	−			+	−	
(2) 61,200				Bal. 80,000	(2) 61,200	
				(1) 50,000		

3. Adjusting entry for ending inventory by physical count, $68,400. The recorded balance of the perpetual inventory is $68,800 ($80,000 + $50,000 − $61,200).

Periodic Inventory

Income Summary				Merchandise Inventory		
				+	−	
(3a) Adj.	(3b) Adj.		Bal. 80,000	(3a) Adj.		
80,000	68,400		(3b) Adj.	80,000		
			68,400			

Perpetual Inventory

Cost of Goods Sold				Merchandise Inventory		
+	−			+	−	
(2) 61,200				Bal. 80,000	(2) 61,200	
(3) Adj. 400				(1) 50,000	(3) Adj. 400	

The difference of $400 ($68,800 − $68,400) is the adjustment amount under the perpetual inventory system (actual physical count versus the accounting records). The adjusting entry required to record the $400 loss is shown in Figure 5.

FIGURE 5

| | | | GENERAL JOURNAL | | | | PAGE 96 | |

	DATE		DESCRIPTION	POST. REF.	DEBIT	CREDIT	
1	20–		**Adjusting Entries**				1
2	Dec.	31	**Cost of Goods Sold**		4 0 0 00		2
3			**Merchandise Inventory**			4 0 0 00	3
4			or				4
5		31	**Merchandise Inventory**		5 0 0 00		5
6			**Cost of Goods Sold**			5 0 0 00	6

Suppose, on the other hand, that the physical count of the stock of merchandise ($65,300) were more than the recorded amount ($64,800), the adjusting entry is to debit Merchandise Inventory and credit Cost of Goods Sold (account) for the difference ($65,300 − $64,800 = $500). (See Figure 5.)

Additional adjusting entries would follow, such as those for supplies used, insurance expired, accrued wages, and other such expenses.

In the income statement, under the perpetual inventory system, the Cost of Goods Sold account is listed under one line, rather than there being a Cost of Goods Sold section.

Here is a comparison of income statements under each of the two systems.

Periodic			**Perpetual**	
Sales		$82,000	Sales	$82,000
Cost of Goods Sold:			Cost of Goods Sold	61,600
Merchandise Inventory (beginning)	$ 80,000		Gross Profit	$20,400
Purchases (net)	50,000			
Cost of Goods Available for Sale	$130,000			
Less Merchandise Inventory (ending)	68,400			
Cost of Goods Sold		61,600		
Gross Profit		$20,400		

CHAPTER REVIEW

Review of Performance Objectives

1. Prepare an adjustment for supplies.

   When supplies are bought during the year, they are recorded by debiting (increasing) Supplies. At the end of the year, an inventory is taken to determine the amount of supplies on hand. An adjusting entry is made for the amount used (total minus amount) debiting Supplies Expense and crediting Supplies.

2. Prepare an adjustment for merchandise inventory under the periodic inventory system.

The adjustment for merchandise inventory under the periodic inventory system requires two adjusting entries. In the first adjusting entry (to remove the beginning inventory), debit Income Summary and credit Merchandise Inventory. In the second adjusting entry (to enter the ending inventory), debit Merchandise Inventory and credit Income Summary.

3. Prepare an adjustment for unearned revenue.

For revenue received in advance, an adjustment is required to separate the portion that has been earned from the portion that is unearned. We assume that the amount of cash received in advance was originally recorded as unearned revenue, which is a liability. In the adjusting entry for the amount actually earned, debit the unearned revenue account (Unearned Course Fees) and credit the revenue account (Course Fees Income).

4. Record the adjustment data in a work sheet (including merchandise inventory, unearned revenue, supplies used, expired insurance, depreciation, and accrued wages or salaries).

In the Adjustments columns of the work sheet, record the following adjusting entries:

For merchandise inventory: first, debit Income Summary and credit Merchandise Inventory (to remove the beginning inventory); next, debit Merchandise Inventory and credit Income Summary (to enter the ending inventory).
For unearned revenue: debit the unearned revenue account and credit the revenue account (to record revenue earned).
For supplies used: debit Supplies Expense and credit Supplies.
For expired insurance: debit Insurance Expense and credit Prepaid Insurance.
For depreciation: debit Depreciation Expense and credit Accumulated Depreciation.
For accrued salaries or wages: debit Salaries Expense or Wages Expense and credit Salaries Payable or Wages Payable.

5. Complete the work sheet.

Carry the Income Summary account from the Adjustments columns into the Income Statement columns as two separate figures. For merchandise inventory, record the amount of the ending inventory in the Balance Sheet Debit column. For unearned revenue, record the unearned revenue account in the Balance Sheet Credit column and the revenue account in the Income Statement Credit column.

6. Journalize the adjusting entries for a merchandising business under the periodic inventory system.

Take the adjusting entries recorded in the journal directly from the Adjustments columns of the work sheet.

7. Journalize the adjusting entry for merchandise inventory under the perpetual inventory system.

Assuming that the amount of the physical count of the stock of merchandise is less than the recorded amount, the adjusting entry is a debit to Cost of Goods Sold (account) and a credit to Merchandise Inventory for the amount of the difference. On the other hand, if the physical count of the stock of merchandise is more than the recorded amount, the adjusting entry is to debit Merchandise Inventory and credit Cost of Goods Sold (accounts) for the amount of the difference.

Glossary

Periodic inventory system The system under which the buying of merchandise during the year is recorded as a debit to Purchases and a credit to Accounts Payable or Cash. At the end of the year, a physical count of the stock of goods is taken and adjusting entries are made to record the amount of the physical count. (423)

Perpetual inventory system The system under which the buying of merchandise during the year is recorded as a debit to Merchandise Inventory and a credit to Accounts Payable or Cash. When merchandise is sold, the cost of the merchandise is recorded as a debit to the Cost of Goods Sold account and a credit to Merchandise Inventory. At the end of the year, a physical count of the stock of goods is taken and an adjusting entry is made to record the difference between the amount of the count and the amount previously recorded. (433)

Physical inventory An actual count of the stock of goods on hand. (423)

Unearned revenue Revenue received in advance for goods or services to be delivered later; considered to be a liability until the revenue is earned. (424)

QUESTIONS, EXERCISES, AND PROBLEMS

Discussion Questions

1. What is a physical or periodic inventory? What does the word *periodic* mean in the term *periodic inventory*?

2. On the Income Summary line of a work sheet, $126,200 appears in the Income Statement Debit column, and $124,100 appears in the Income Statement Credit column. Which figure represents the beginning inventory?

3. Using the perpetual-inventory system, what account is debited when a business buys more merchandise?

4. On a work sheet, where will the amount of the ending merchandise inventory be recorded?

5. Explain what is meant by unearned revenue and why it is treated as a liability?

6. Why is it necessary to adjust the Merchandise Inventory account under a periodic inventory system?

7. A merchandising company shows $952 in the asset Supplies account on the preadjusted trial balance. After taking inventory of the actual supplies, they still own $627.
   a. How much was used or expired?
   b. Write the adjusting entry.

8. When a college receives one semester's dormitory rent in advance, an entry is made debiting Cash and crediting Unearned Rent. At the end of the year, a large portion of the rent has been earned. What adjusting entry would you suggest?

Exercises

P.O. 2

Journalize adjustments for merchandise inventory.

Exercise 12-1 After adjusting entries are posted, the Merchandise Inventory account appears as follows. Journalize the complete entries that support these postings. The Income Summary account is numbered 313.

ACCOUNT __Merchandise Inventory__   ACCOUNT NO. __114__

	DATE		ITEM	POST. REF.	DEBIT	CREDIT	BALANCE DEBIT	BALANCE CREDIT	
1	2003								1
2	Dec.	31	Balance	✓			96 4 0 0 00		2
3	2004								3
4	Dec.	31	Adjusting	J112		96 4 0 0 00	—	—	4
5		31	Adjusting	J112	97 1 0 0 00		97 1 0 0 00		5
6									6
7									7
8									8

P.O. 3

Journalize the adjustment for unearned revenue.

Exercise 12-2 On October 31, the Vermillion Igloos Hockey Club received $800,000 in cash in advance for season tickets for eight home games. The transaction was recorded as a debit to Cash and a credit to Unearned Admissions. By December 31, the end of the fiscal year, the team had played three home games and received an additional $450,000 cash admissions income at the gate.

a. Journalize the adjusting entry as of December 31.
b. List the title of the account and the related balance that will appear on the income statement.
c. List the title of the account and the related balance that will appear on the balance sheet.

P.O. 3

Determine the entries in an unearned revenue account.

Exercise 12-3 For the basketball federation's Unearned Season Tickets account, list the debits and credits for each amount posted to the account and briefly describe the transaction.

ACCOUNT __Unearned Season Tickets__   ACCOUNT NO. __214__

	DATE		ITEM	POST. REF.	DEBIT	CREDIT	BALANCE DEBIT	BALANCE CREDIT	
1	20–								1
2	Jan.	1	Balance	✓				10 4 0 0 00	2
3	Mar.	6		J71	10 4 0 0 00			—	3
4	Oct.	15		CR42		12 6 0 0 00		12 6 0 0 00	4
5	Nov.	1		CR43		22 1 0 0 00		34 7 0 0 00	5
6	Dec.	31	Adjusting	J99	22 6 0 0 00			12 1 0 0 00	6
7									7
8									8

P.O. 1

Determine entries in the Supplies account.

Exercise 12-4 For the Supplies ledger account, determine the debits and credits for each amount posted to the account and briefly describe each transaction. The entry of December 9 involved the return of defective goods. The purchases of December 17 involved the Beebe Company.

ACCOUNT Supplies							ACCOUNT NO. 115	
						BALANCE		
DATE	ITEM	POST. REF.	DEBIT	CREDIT		DEBIT	CREDIT	
20–								1
Jan. 1	Balance	✓				4 2 0 00		2
Apr. 6		CP42	1 6 0 00			5 8 0 00		3
May 31		CP44	9 0 00			6 7 0 00		4
Nov. 21		CP53	2 2 5 00			8 9 5 00		5
Dec. 9		CR41		4 2 00		8 5 3 00		6
17		J77	1 4 1 00			9 9 4 00		7
31	Adjusting	J78		2 2 0 00		7 7 4 00		8

P.O. 5

Place account balances in work sheet columns.

Exercise 12-5 Indicate the work sheet columns (Income Statement Debit, Income Statement Credit, Balance Sheet Debit, Balance Sheet Credit) in which the balances of the following accounts should appear:

a. F. Dexter, Drawing
b. Advertising Expense
c. Merchandise Inventory (ending)
d. Purchases Discounts
e. Unearned Fees
f. Sales Returns and Allowances
g. Accumulated Depreciation, Building
h. Income Summary
i. Fees Income
j. Prepaid Rent

P.O. 3,4

Journalize adjustments for expired insurance, unearned revenue, and depreciation.

Exercise 12-6 Journalize the required adjusting entries for the year ended December 31 for Mallory Dance Studio. Begin on journal page 42.

a. On June 1 of this year, $600 was paid for a one-year insurance policy.
b. On October 1 of this year, $160 was paid for four months of advertising.
c. As of December 31, the balance of the Unearned Membership Fees account is $12,400. Of this amount, $8,200 has now been earned.
d. Equipment purchased on April 1 of this year for $3,400 is expected to have a useful life of five years and will have a trade-in value of $400. All the other equipment has been fully depreciated. The straight-line method is used.
e. As of December 31, two days' wages of $240 per day had accrued.

P.O. 3,4

Journalize adjusting entries.

Exercise 12-7 On December 31, the end of the year, the accountant for *Fidelity Magazine* was called away suddenly because of an emergency. However, before leaving, the accountant jotted down a few notes pertaining to the adjustments. Record the necessary adjusting entries.

a. Subscriptions received in advance amounting to $136,400 were recorded as Unearned Subscriptions. At the end of the year, $90,200 has been earned.
b. Depreciation of equipment for the year is $18,600.
c. The amount of expired insurance for the year is $916.

d. The balance of Prepaid Rent is $2,800, representing four months' rent. Three months' rent has now expired.

e. Three days' salaries will be unpaid at the end of the year; total weekly (five days') salaries are $3,600.

P.O. 7

Journalize adjustment for merchandise inventory using the perpetual inventory system.

Exercise 12-8 On December 31, Bold Company took a physical count of their merchandise inventory. They operate under the perpetual inventory system. The physical count amounted to $178,400. The Merchandise Inventory account shows a balance of $180,200. Journalize the adjusting entry to Merchandise Inventory.

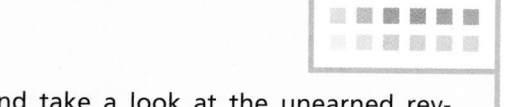

REFLECTING ON
THE WORLD WIDE WEB

Let's go back to Meredith again and take a look at the unearned revenues from advance magazine subscriptions and publications sales. Look at page 29 of Meredith's 2002 annual report found at **http://www.meredith.com/investors/AR2002/AR2002.pdf.**

1. Where would you find Meredith's unearned revenue in the financial statements, and what was the account balance as of December 31, 2002?
2. How would Meredith record the receipt of cash for these advance subscription sales?
3. How would Meredith record the current portion of unearned subscription revenues when it becomes earned?

CONSIDER AND COMMUNICATE

You have a friend who is a seamstress specializing in western ensembles. She receives cash well in advance of the required date, often in the fiscal period prior to the date of delivery of the ensemble, not only to enable her to purchase material, but to cover her labor. She always debits Cash and credits Ensemble Income. First, explain to her why this entry violates the matching principle. Second, identify the classification of Unearned Revenue. Third, explain when the Unearned Revenue account is used.

WHAT'S WRONG WITH THIS PICTURE?

What would happen if a business spent the cash it had received in advance for services it promised to perform at a later date?

CRITICAL THINKING

On November 1, an exterior painting company received $3,420 for a paint job that will not be finished for a few months. As of December 31, which is the end of the fiscal period, $1,200 worth of painting will have been completed. The bookkeeper completed the following entries prior to leaving on vacation:

	Cash		Painting Income		Unearned Painting Income
11/1 3,420		12/31 2,220	11/1 3,420		12/31 2,220

The owner wants to get a bank loan by December 1. The bank requires interim financial statements to be submitted as of December 1. How will the bookkeeper's entries affect the accuracy of the interim balance sheet and statements? What difference will the bookkeeper's methods make in the December 31 balance sheet and income statement?

A MATTER OF ETHICS

The owner of a motorcycle shop allows his two sons to take motorcycles home to try them out on different types of ground because he believes that they need to be familiar with the products they sell. Sometimes the motorcycles are not returned to the store by the time the physical count of inventory takes place. Respond to this practice.

PROBLEM SET A

P.O. 4,5

Problem 12-1A The trial balance of Swenson Company as of December 31, the end of its current fiscal year, is as follows:

Swenson Company
Trial Balance
December 31, 20—

	ACCOUNT NAME	TRIAL BALANCE DEBIT	TRIAL BALANCE CREDIT
1	Cash	9 5 6 3 92	
2	Merchandise Inventory	63 5 2 2 84	
3	Store Supplies	1 4 4 1 12	
4	Prepaid Insurance	9 6 0 00	
5	Store Equipment	37 4 8 0 00	
6	Accumulated Depreciation, Store Equipment		24 3 2 0 00
7	Accounts Payable		14 5 7 8 80
8	Sales Tax Payable		2 4 3 36
9	D. N. Swenson, Capital		55 6 3 0 00
10	D. N. Swenson, Drawing	29 4 4 0 00	
11	Sales		179 0 3 6 74
12	Sales Returns and Allowances	1 4 4 3 04	
13	Purchases	76 3 6 8 46	
14	Purchases Returns and Allowances		1 8 7 8 94
15	Purchases Discounts		1 4 9 7 90
16	Freight In	4 8 7 5 00	
17	Salary Expense	36 6 5 8 80	
18	Rent Expense	14 4 0 0 00	
19	Miscellaneous Expense	1 0 3 2 56	
20		277 1 8 5 74	277 1 8 5 74
21			

Here are the data for the adjustments.

a–b. Merchandise Inventory at December 31, $66,832.56.
c. Supplies inventory, $396.40.
d. Insurance expired, $360.
e. Salaries accrued, $563.
f. Depreciation of store equipment, $3,880.

Check Figure

Net income, $45,097.72

Instructions

Complete the work sheet after entering the account names and balances onto the work sheet.

P.O. 4,5,6

Problem 12-2A The balances of the ledger accounts of Talbot Furniture as of December 31, the end of its fiscal year, are as follows:

Cash	$ 11,592
Accounts Receivable	42,962
Merchandise Inventory	121,838
Supplies	1,570
Prepaid Insurance	1,628
Store Equipment	36,924
Accumulated Depreciation, Store Equipment	29,420
Office Equipment	9,436
Accumulated Depreciation, Office Equipment	1,720
Notes Payable	4,000
Accounts Payable	30,822
Wages Payable	—
Unearned Rent	3,200
P. Talbot, Capital	120,532
P. Talbot, Drawing	28,000
Income Summary	—
Sales	652,000
Sales Returns and Allowances	9,748
Rent Income	—
Purchases	518,374
Purchases Returns and Allowances	13,440
Purchases Discounts	7,634
Freight In	24,724
Wages Expense	55,200
Depreciation Expense, Store Equipment	—
Depreciation Expense, Office Equipment	—
Supplies Expense	—
Insurance Expense	—
Interest Expense	772

Data for the adjustments are as follows:

a–b. Merchandise Inventory at December 31, $101,676.
c. Wages accrued at December 31, $1,956.
d. Supplies inventory at December 31, $744.
e. Depreciation of store equipment, $5,868.
f. Depreciation of office equipment, $1,732.
g. Insurance expired during the year, $632.
h. Rent earned, $2,400.

Check Figure

Net income, $35,480

Instructions

1. Complete the work sheet after entering the account names and balances onto the work sheet.
2. Journalize the adjusting entries.

P.O. 4,5,6

Problem 12-3A The accounts in the ledger of Monroe Mountain Shop, with the balances as of December 31, the end of its fiscal year, are as follows:

Cash	$ 12,600
Accounts Receivable	2,040
Merchandise Inventory	120,600
Store Supplies	1,620
Prepaid Insurance	2,940
Land	18,000
Building	90,000
Accumulated Depreciation, Building	36,600
Store Equipment	56,100
Accumulated Depreciation, Store Equipment	12,600
Notes Payable	10,800
Accounts Payable	19,260
Sales Tax Payable	5,940
Salaries Payable	—
B. Monroe, Capital	171,000
B. Monroe, Drawing	54,000
Income Summary	—
Sales	468,000
Sales Returns and Allowances	8,700
Purchases	284,820
Purchases Returns and Allowances	6,900
Purchases Discounts	4,800
Freight In	18,180
Salary Expense	52,500
Advertising Expense	6,150
Depreciation Expense, Building	—
Depreciation Expense, Store Equipment	—
Store Supplies Expense	—
Insurance Expense	—
Utilities Expense	5,610
Taxes Expense	270
Miscellaneous Expense	990
Interest Expense	780

Data for the adjustments are as follows:

a–b. Merchandise Inventory at December 31, $124,800.
 c. Store supplies inventory at December 31, $540.
 d. Depreciation of building, $4,200.
 e. Depreciation of store equipment, $3,600.
 f. Salaries accrued at December 31, $1,650.
 g. Insurance expired during the year, $2,280.

Check Figure

Net income, $93,090

Instructions

1. Complete the work sheet after entering the account names and balances onto the work sheet.
2. Journalize the adjusting entries.

Instructions for General Ledger Software

1. Record the adjusting entries in the general journal.
2. Print the journal.
3. Post the general journal amounts to the general ledger.
4. Print a trial balance.
5. Print the income statement, statement of owner's equity, and balance sheet.

P.O. 4,5,6

Problem 12-4A A portion of the work sheet of Hurst Oxygen Company for the year ended December 31 is as follows:

	ACCOUNT NAME	INCOME STATEMENT DEBIT	INCOME STATEMENT CREDIT	BALANCE SHEET DEBIT	BALANCE SHEET CREDIT	
1	Cash			9 3 4 0 00		1
2	Merchandise Inventory			76 9 4 0 00		2
3	Supplies			2 5 6 00		3
4	Prepaid Insurance			2 4 0 00		4
5	Store Equipment			39 2 8 0 00		5
6	Accumulated Depreciation, Store Equipment				26 2 2 0 00	6
7	Accounts Payable				14 6 0 0 00	7
8	P. R. Hurst, Capital				68 9 4 0 00	8
9	P. R. Hurst, Drawing			27 6 0 0 00		9
10	Sales		173 4 2 0 00			10
11	Sales Returns and Allowances	1 5 2 0 00				11
12	Purchases	82 3 1 2 00				12
13	Purchases Returns and Allowances		9 4 0 00			13
14	Purchases Discounts		1 6 0 0 00			14
15	Freight In	1 9 4 8 00				15
16	Salary Expense	37 5 6 0 00				16
17	Rent Expense	14 8 0 0 00				17
18	Income Summary	65 6 8 0 00	76 9 4 0 00			18
19	Depreciation Expense, Store Equipment	4 0 4 0 00				19
20	Insurance Expense	7 6 0 00				20
21	Supplies Expense	9 4 4 00				21
22	Salaries Payable				5 6 0 00	22
23		209 5 6 4 00	252 9 0 0 00	153 6 5 6 00	110 3 2 0 00	23

Check Figure

Salaries accrued, $560

Instructions

1. Determine the entries that appeared in the Adjustments columns and present them in general journal form.
2. Determine the net income for the year.
3. What is the amount of the ending capital?

PROBLEM SET B

P.O. 4,5

Problem 12-1B The trial balance of Hakala Company as of December 31, the end of its current fiscal year, is on the next page.

Here are the data for the adjustments:

a–b. Merchandise Inventory at December 31, $65,749.80.
 c. Store supplies inventory, $404.32.
 d. Insurance expired, $736.
 e. Salaries accrued, $586.80.
 f. Depreciation of store equipment, $3,920.

Hakala Company
Trial Balance
December 31, 20—

	ACCOUNT NAME	TRIAL BALANCE		
		DEBIT	CREDIT	
1	Cash	9 1 3 6 54		
2	Merchandise Inventory	62 8 5 4 82		
3	Store Supplies	1 4 6 6 84		
4	Prepaid Insurance	1 0 2 0 00		
5	Store Equipment	37 3 4 0 00		
6	Accumulated Depreciation, Store Equipment		24 8 3 6 00	
7	Accounts Payable		14 2 8 6 96	
8	Sales Tax Payable		2 4 6 98	
9	R. P. Hakala, Capital		55 0 5 9 84	
10	R. P. Hakala, Drawing	29 0 0 0 00		
11	Sales		177 9 6 6 34	
12	Sales Returns and Allowances	1 4 9 3 84		
13	Purchases	78 8 0 0 84		
14	Purchases Returns and Allowances		1 8 5 7 82	
15	Purchases Discounts		1 5 0 3 64	
16	Freight In	2 6 3 7 00		
17	Salary Expense	36 5 6 8 86		
18	Rent Expense	14 4 0 0 00		
19	Miscellaneous Expense	1 0 3 8 84		
20		275 7 5 7 58	275 7 5 7 58	

Check Figure

Net income, $42,978.08

P.O. 4,5,6

Instructions

Complete the work sheet after entering the account names and balances onto the work sheet.

Problem 12-2B The balances of the ledger accounts of Balzimer Home Center as of June 30, the end of its fiscal year, are as follows:

Cash	$ 14,775
Accounts Receivable	51,300
Merchandise Inventory	72,900
Supplies	1,470
Prepaid Insurance	1,080
Store Equipment	26,790
Accumulated Depreciation, Store Equipment	16,200
Office Equipment	9,600
Accumulated Depreciation, Office Equipment	4,815
Notes Payable	3,600
Accounts Payable	42,900
Salaries Payable	—
Unearned Rent	2,700
F. C. Balzimer, Capital	95,340
F. C. Balzimer, Drawing	24,000
Income Summary	—
Sales	466,500
Sales Returns and Allowances	3,210
Rent Income	—
Purchases	368,010
Purchases Returns and Allowances	7,170
Purchases Discounts	2,280

Freight In	$23,490
Salary Expense	44,250
Depreciation Expense, Store Equipment	—
Depreciation Expense, Office Equipment	—
Insurance Expense	—
Supplies Expense	—
Interest Expense	630

Here are the data for the adjustments:

a–b. Merchandise Inventory at June 30, $114,600.
c. Salaries accrued at June 30, $1,440.
d. Insurance expired during the year, $900.
e. Supplies inventory at June 30, $285.
f. Depreciation of store equipment, $3,750.
g. Depreciation of office equipment, $1,950.
h. Rent earned, $2,250.

Check Figure

Net income, $71,085

Instructions

1. Complete the work sheet after entering the account names and balances onto the work sheet.
2. Journalize the adjusting entries.

P.O. 4,5,6

Problem 12-3B Here are the accounts in the ledger of Palmer's Jewel Box, with the balances as of December 31, the end of its fiscal year.

Cash	$ 11,280
Accounts Receivable	1,554
Merchandise Inventory	116,100
Store Supplies	1,284
Prepaid Insurance	2,286
Land	15,000
Building	78,000
Accumulated Depreciation, Building	29,340
Store Equipment	77,490
Accumulated Depreciation, Store Equipment	17,160
Accounts Payable	14,070
Sales Tax Payable	2,784
Salaries Payable	—
Mortgage Payable	43,860
L. Palmer, Capital	151,830
L. Palmer, Drawing	46,500
Income Summary	—
Sales	379,254
Sales Returns and Allowances	3,888
Purchases	250,768
Purchases Returns and Allowances	3,261
Purchases Discounts	4,410
Freight In	12,200
Salary Expense	23,400
Advertising Expense	1,926
Depreciation Expense, Building	—
Depreciation Expense, Store Equipment	—
Store Supplies Expense	—
Insurance Expense	—
Utilities Expense	1,158
Taxes Expense	162
Miscellaneous Expense	813
Interest Expense	2,160

Here are the data for the adjustments.

a–b. Merchandise Inventory at December 31, $113,070.
c. Insurance expired during the year, $1,254.
d. Depreciation of building, $4,200.
e. Depreciation of store equipment, $8,580.
f. Salaries accrued at December 31, $420.
g. Store supplies inventory at December 31, $318.

Check Figure

Net income, $72,000

Instructions

1. Complete the work sheet after entering the account names and balances onto the work sheet.
2. Journalize the adjusting entries.

Instructions for General Ledger Software

1. Record the adjusting entries in the general journal.
2. Print the journal.
3. Post the general journal amounts to the general ledger.
4. Print a trial balance.
5. Print the income statement, statement of owner's equity, and balance sheet.

P.O. 5,6

Problem 12-4B A portion of the work sheet of Susan's Flowers for the year ended December 31 appears below.

	ACCOUNT NAME	INCOME STATEMENT DEBIT	INCOME STATEMENT CREDIT	BALANCE SHEET DEBIT	BALANCE SHEET CREDIT	
1	Cash			7 7 3 6 00		1
2	Merchandise Inventory			74 2 9 8 00		2
3	Supplies			2 9 8 00		3
4	Prepaid Insurance			2 5 0 00		4
5	Store Equipment			37 9 6 0 00		5
6	Accumulated Depreciation, Store Equipment				29 4 4 0 00	6
7	Accounts Payable				13 7 6 0 00	7
8	S. R. Hale, Capital				75 1 4 2 00	8
9	S. R. Hale, Drawing			30 8 0 0 00		9
10	Sales		171 8 1 6 00			10
11	Sales Returns and Allowances	1 4 3 4 00				11
12	Purchases	85 9 3 4 00				12
13	Purchases Returns and Allowances		9 6 4 00			13
14	Purchases Discounts		1 6 3 6 00			14
15	Freight In	2 6 5 8 00				15
16	Salary Expense	37 8 5 2 00				16
17	Rent Expense	14 4 0 0 00				17
18	Income Summary	68 2 2 8 00	74 2 9 8 00			18
19	Depreciation Expense, Store Equipment	4 3 6 0 00				19
20	Insurance Expense	5 5 2 00				20
21	Supplies Expense	8 8 4 00				21
22	Salaries Payable				5 8 8 00	22
23		216 3 0 2 00	248 7 1 4 00	151 3 4 2 00	118 9 3 0 00	23

Check Figure

Accrued salaries, $588

Instructions

1. Determine the entries that appeared in the Adjustments columns and present them in general journal form.
2. Determine the net income for the year.
3. What is the amount of the ending capital?

The Computer Lab

Adjustments

<table>
<tr><td colspan="3" align="center">**Jeep Jockeys**
Preadjusted Trial Balance
July 31, 20—</td></tr>
<tr><td></td><td>**Debit**</td><td>**Credit**</td></tr>
<tr><td>Cash</td><td>48,349.93</td><td></td></tr>
<tr><td>Accounts Receivable</td><td>19,692.98</td><td></td></tr>
<tr><td>Prepaid Insurance</td><td>1,650.00</td><td></td></tr>
<tr><td>Supplies</td><td>63.00</td><td></td></tr>
<tr><td>Office Equipment</td><td>759.00</td><td></td></tr>
<tr><td>Accumulated Depreciation, Office Equipment</td><td></td><td>11.32</td></tr>
<tr><td>Vehicles</td><td>46,000.00</td><td></td></tr>
<tr><td>Accumulated Depreciation, Vehicles</td><td></td><td>1,250.00</td></tr>
<tr><td>Kiosk Equipment</td><td>1,457.69</td><td></td></tr>
<tr><td>Accounts Payable</td><td></td><td>7,537.88</td></tr>
<tr><td>H. Kennedy, Capital</td><td></td><td>63,952.68</td></tr>
<tr><td>H. Kennedy, Drawing</td><td>1,600.00</td><td></td></tr>
<tr><td>Tour Revenue</td><td></td><td>58,329.00</td></tr>
<tr><td>Sales</td><td></td><td>10,084.08</td></tr>
<tr><td>Sales Returns and Allowances</td><td>214.87</td><td></td></tr>
<tr><td>Purchases</td><td>6,408.00</td><td></td></tr>
<tr><td>Purchases Returns and Allowances</td><td></td><td>36.00</td></tr>
<tr><td>Freight In</td><td>364.23</td><td></td></tr>
<tr><td>Wages Expense</td><td>12,163.00</td><td></td></tr>
<tr><td>Rent Expense</td><td>640.00</td><td></td></tr>
<tr><td>Advertising Expense</td><td>1,231.26</td><td></td></tr>
<tr><td>Utilities Expense</td><td>180.00</td><td></td></tr>
<tr><td>Accounting and Legal Expense</td><td>300.00</td><td></td></tr>
<tr><td>Miscellaneous Expense</td><td>127.00</td><td></td></tr>
<tr><td></td><td>141,200.96</td><td>141,200.96</td></tr>
</table>

It has been two months (June and July) since Hank Kennedy has seen Jeep Jockeys' financial statements—it is time to prepare them. But first, let's think about whether there are any accounts that may not be accurate because an asset has been used.

> Hmm. What have we used? Looking at the preadjusted trial balance, I would say supplies, inventory, and insurance protection. We'll also have to depreciate Office Equipment, Vehicles, and Kiosk Equipment—careful record keeping will pay off.

With a little review of my accounting book, I can see that the merchandise inventory adjustment can take two steps—get rid of the old and enter the new or latest. And now that Jeep Jockey has added merchandising to its activities, I need to adjust the supplies because we have used some of them. And finally, at this time, I can see that we have had insurance protection

> And no work sheet! The joy of computers—most days anyway.

every day and used the asset Prepaid Insurance. I'd better gather some numbers in preparation for these adjustments.

First, the supplies adjustment. According to the preadjusted trial balance, we bought supplies that cost $63, but when I count what is left of the actual supplies and place a price on them, only $24 is left. That means if I subtract what is left ($24) from what we bought ($63), we have used $39 and no longer own $63 in the asset Supplies. So, I would have to reduce Supplies by $39 (a credit) and increase Supplies Expense by $39 (a debit). That wasn't so bad.

Second, Prepaid Insurance requires some calculation too. According to the preadjusted trial balance, we own $1,650, but the last time it was adjusted was on May 31 for $150. The original policy provided 12 months' coverage for $1,800. That means $1,800/12 = $150 per month. Therefore, for the months of June and July, the adjustment is $300 to reduce the asset Prepaid Insurance to reflect the coverage we used and to increase Insurance Expense to reflect the amount used or expired.

Third, the inventory adjustment. We started with zero inventory on June 1 and have purchased $6,408 in June and July. But we have reduced the inventory through sales. Step 1 is to get rid of the old by debiting Income Summary and crediting Merchandise Inventory, a new account. Since the beginning or old inventory amount is zero, there's no need to make an entry. Step 2 is to journalize the new or latest inventory. I have done an inventory count and costed it; it amounts to $3,978. So, debit Merchandise Inventory (new asset account numbered 113) for $3,978 and credit Income Summary for $3,978.

Fourth, depreciation of office equipment, vehicles, and kiosk equipment. Let's take them one at a time. The Office Equipment balance is $759. Accumulated Depreciation, Office Equipment carries a balance of $11.32, which was the amount adjusted in May. Two months are being adjusted now, so the debit to Depreciation Expense, Office Equipment will be $22.64 and the credit to the contra account Accumulated Depreciation (*not Office Equipment*) will be $22.64 for June and July. The new book value of Office Equipment is what? Cost less accumulated depreciation = _____.

The adjustment for the Vehicles account for May was $1,250. Two months are being adjusted now, so the debit to Depreciation Expense, Vehicles will be $2,500 and the credit to the contra account Accumulated Depreciation (*not Vehicles*) will be $2,500 for June and July. The new book value of Vehicles is what? Cost less accumulated depreciation = _____.

The adjustment for the Kiosk Equipment account for May was zero because we bought the items in June ($478.69 for the neon sign) and in July ($979 for the digital camera). Each must be separately calculated. Let's use the straight-line method with which you are most familiar. When we enter the information into the formula cost less salvage divided by years of service, we arrive at the amount of depreciation estimated for a year. Divide by 12 to find the amount per month. We have owned the neon sign for two months, so multiply the amount by 2.

> Remember, there are other types of depreciation methods—all of them are an estimate of the loss of usefulness that the IRS allows businesses to write off against their revenue.

$478.69 − $100 = $378.69/3 years = $126.23/12 = $10.52/month × 2 = $21.04 (salvage value)

Calculate the digital camera similarly.

$979 − $150 = $829/3 years = $276.33/12 = $23.03/month (salvage value)

There is no need for a Wages Expense/Wages Payable adjustment this month. The adjustments go into the general journal, page 8, and are posted to the general ledger.

Once the adjustments are journalized and posted, print:

General Journal, page 8
General Ledger so that you can see how some accounts have changed.
Trial Balance as of July 31.

We'll do the financial statements as our next step.

13

Financial Statements, Closing Entries, and Reversing Entries

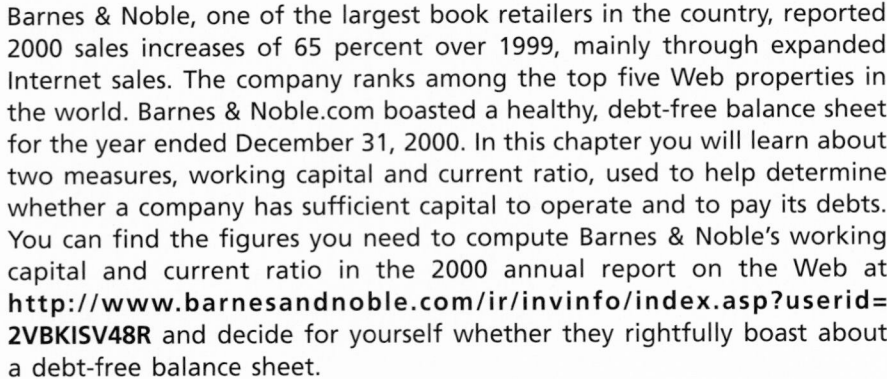

WINDOWS ON
THE WORLD WIDE WEB

Barnes & Noble, one of the largest book retailers in the country, reported 2000 sales increases of 65 percent over 1999, mainly through expanded Internet sales. The company ranks among the top five Web properties in the world. Barnes & Noble.com boasted a healthy, debt-free balance sheet for the year ended December 31, 2000. In this chapter you will learn about two measures, working capital and current ratio, used to help determine whether a company has sufficient capital to operate and to pay its debts. You can find the figures you need to compute Barnes & Noble's working capital and current ratio in the 2000 annual report on the Web at **http://www.barnesandnoble.com/ir/invinfo/index.asp?userid= 2VBKISV48R** and decide for yourself whether they rightfully boast about a debt-free balance sheet.

Performance Objectives

After you have completed this chapter, you will be able to do the following:

1. Prepare a classified income statement for a merchandising firm.

2. Prepare a classified balance sheet for any type of business.

3. Compute working capital and current ratio.

4. Journalize the closing entries for a merchandising firm.

5. Determine which adjusting entries can be reversed, and journalize the reversing entries.

This chapter again demonstrates how to prepare financial statements directly from a work sheet. We also explain the functions of closing entries and reversing entries as means of completing the accounting cycle. Finally, we look at the financial statements in their entirety, and explain their various subdivisions.

First, here is the chart of accounts for Dodson Plumbing Supply.

First, here is the chart of accounts for Dodson Plumbing Supply.

FYI

Accountants sometimes number contra accounts as subaccounts. For example, Accumulated Depreciation, Building, is 122.1, Sales Returns and Allowances is 411.1, Sales Discounts is 411.2, Purchases Returns and Allowances is 511.1, and so on.

Assets (100–199)

111 Cash
112 Notes Receivable
113 Accounts Receivable
114 Merchandise Inventory
115 Supplies
116 Prepaid Insurance
121 Land
122 Building
123 Accumulated Depreciation, Building
124 Equipment
125 Accumulated Depreciation, Equipment

Liabilities (200–299)

211 Notes Payable
212 Accounts Payable
213 Wages Payable
217 Unearned Course Fees
221 Mortgage Payable

Owner's Equity (300–399)

311 L. E. Dodson, Capital
312 L. E. Dodson, Drawing
313 Income Summary

Revenue (400–499)

411 Sales
412 Sales Returns and Allowances
413 Sales Discounts
421 Course Fees Income
422 Interest Income

Cost of Goods Sold (500–599)

511 Purchases
512 Purchases Returns and Allowances
513 Purchases Discounts
514 Freight In

Expenses (600–699)

611 Wages Expense
622 Supplies Expense
623 Insurance Expense
624 Depreciation Expense, Building
625 Depreciation Expense, Equipment
626 Taxes Expense
634 Interest Expense

THE INCOME STATEMENT

OBJECTIVE 1

Prepare a classified income statement for a merchandising firm.

As you know, the work sheet is merely a tool used by accountants to prepare the financial statements. In Figure 1, shown on page 454, we present the part of the work sheet for Dodson Plumbing Supply that includes the Income Statement columns. Of course, **each of the amounts that appear in the Income Statement columns of the work sheet will also be used in the income statement.** Notice that the amounts for the beginning and ending merchandise inventory appear separately on the Income Summary line. Figure 2 on page 455 shows the entire income statement. Pause for a while and look it over carefully; then we will break it down into its components.

The income statement follows a logical pattern that is much the same for any type of merchandising business. The ability to interpret the income statement and extract parts from it is very useful when gathering information for decisions. To realize the full value of an income statement, however, you need to know the basic format of an income statement. Let's look at the statement section by section.

Net Sales	$232,460
− Cost of Goods Sold	88,720
Gross Profit	$143,740
− Operating Expenses	59,028
Income from Operations	$ 84,712

Dodson Plumbing Supply
Work Sheet
For Year Ended December 31, 20—

	ACCOUNT NAME	TRIAL BALANCE DEBIT	TRIAL BALANCE CREDIT	ADJUSTMENTS DEBIT	ADJUSTMENTS CREDIT	INCOME STATEMENT DEBIT	INCOME STATEMENT CREDIT
1	Cash	19 1 5 4 00					
2	Notes Receivable	4 0 0 0 00					
3	Accounts Receivable	29 4 4 6 00					
4	Merchandise Inventory	67 0 0 0 00		(b) 65 8 0 0 00	(a) 67 0 0 0 00		
5	Supplies	1 4 4 0 00			(d) 1 0 2 8 00		
6	Prepaid Insurance	9 6 0 00			(e) 3 2 0 00		
7	Land	12 0 0 0 00					
8	Building	130 0 0 0 00					
9	Accumulated Depr.,						
10	Building		52 0 0 0 00		(f) 4 0 0 0 00		
11	Equipment	33 6 0 0 00					
12	Accumulated Depr.,						
13	Equipment		16 4 0 0 00		(g) 4 8 0 0 00		
14	Notes Payable		3 0 0 0 00				
15	Accounts Payable		36 4 0 0 00				
16	Unearned Course Fees		1 2 0 0 00	(c) 8 0 0 00			
17	Mortgage Payable		8 0 0 0 00				
18	L. E. Dodson, Capital		140 5 7 4 00				
19	L. E. Dodson, Drawing	56 9 0 0 00					
20	Sales		235 1 8 0 00				235 1 8 0 00
21	Sales Returns and						
22	Allowances	8 4 0 00				8 4 0 00	
23	Sales Discounts	1 8 8 0 00				1 8 8 0 00	
24	Interest Income		1 2 0 00				1 2 0 00
25	Purchases	87 1 4 0 00				87 1 4 0 00	
26	Purchases Returns						
27	and Allowances		8 3 2 00				8 3 2 00
28	Purchases Discounts		1 2 4 8 00				1 2 4 8 00
29	Freight In	2 4 6 0 00				2 4 6 0 00	
30	Wages Expense	45 8 0 0 00		(h) 1 1 2 0 00		46 9 2 0 00	
31	Taxes Expense	1 9 6 0 00				1 9 6 0 00	
32	Interest Expense	3 7 4 00				3 7 4 00	
33		494 9 5 4 00	494 9 5 4 00				
34	Income Summary			(a) 67 0 0 0 00	(b) 65 8 0 0 00	67 0 0 0 00	65 8 0 0 00
35	Course Fees Income				(c) 8 0 0 00		8 0 0 00
36	Supplies Expense			(d) 1 0 2 8 00		1 0 2 8 00	
37	Insurance Expense			(e) 3 2 0 00		3 2 0 00	
38	Depreciation Expense,						
39	Building			(f) 4 0 0 0 00		4 0 0 0 00	
40	Depreciation Expense,						
41	Equipment			(g) 4 8 0 0 00		4 8 0 0 00	
42	Wages Payable				(h) 1 1 2 0 00		
43				144 8 6 8 00	144 8 6 8 00	218 7 2 2 00	303 9 8 0 00
44	Net Income					85 2 5 8 00	
45						303 9 8 0 00	303 9 8 0 00
46							

FIGURE 1

Dodson Plumbing Supply
Income Statement
For Year Ended December 31, 20—

Revenue from Sales:			
Sales		$ 235 180 00	
Less: Sales Returns and Allowances	$ 840 00		
Sales Discounts	1 880 00	2 720 00	
Net Sales			$ 232 460 00
Cost of Goods Sold:			
Merchandise Inventory, January 1, 20—		$ 67 000 00	
Purchases	$ 87 140 00		
Less: Purchases Returns and			
Allowances $ 832.00			
Purchases Discounts 1,248.00	2 080 00		
Net Purchases	$ 85 060 00		
Add Freight In	2 460 00		
Delivered Cost of Purchases		87 520 00	
Cost of Goods Available for Sale		$ 154 520 00	
Less Merchandise Inventory, December 31, 20—		65 800 00	
Cost of Goods Sold			88 720 00
Gross Profit			$ 143 740 00
Operating Expenses:			
Wages Expense		$ 46 920 00	
Supplies Expense		1 028 00	
Insurance Expense		320 00	
Depreciation Expense, Building		400 00	
Depreciation Expense, Equipment		480 00	
Taxes Expense		1 960 00	
Total Operating Expenses			59 028 00
Income from Operations			$ 84 712 00
Other Income:			
Course Fees Income		$ 800 00	
Interest Income		120 00	
Total Other Income		$ 920 00	
Other Expenses:			
Interest Expense		374 00	546 00
Net Income			$ 85 258 00

FIGURE 2

To illustrate the concepts of **gross** and **net**, here is an example of a simple single-sale transaction.

Several years ago, Billie Reed bought an antique table at a second-hand store for $90. She decided to sell the table for $160. She advertised in the daily newspaper at a cost of $5. How much did she make as clear profit?

Sale of Table	$160
Less Cost of Table	90
Gross Profit	$ 70
Less Advertising Expense	5
Net Income or Net Profit (gain on the sale)	$ 65

Gross Profit is the profit on the sale of the table before any expenses have been deducted; in this case, it is $70. **Net Income**, or **Net Profit**, is the final or clear profit after all expenses have been deducted. In a single-sale situation such as this, we refer to the final outcome as the net profit. But for a business that has many sales and expenses, most accountants prefer the term *net income*. Regardless of which word you use, *net* refers to clear profit—after all expenses have been deducted.

Revenue from Sales

Now let's look at the Revenue from Sales section of the income statement for Dodson Plumbing Supply:

Revenue from Sales:				
Sales			$ 235 1 8 0 00	
Less: Sales Returns and Allowances	$ 8 4 0 00			
Sales Discounts	1 8 8 0 00		2 7 2 0 00	
Net Sales				$ 232 4 6 0 00

When we introduced Sales Returns and Allowances and Sales Discounts, we treated them as deductions from Sales. You can see that in the income statement, they are deducted from Sales to give us **Net Sales**. Note that we record these items in the same order in which they appear in the ledger.

REMEMBER!
Returns and Allowances (Sales or Purchases) is listed on one line, and Discounts (Sales or Purchases) is listed below.

Cost of Goods Sold

The section of the income statement that requires the greatest amount of concentration is the **Cost of Goods Sold** section, where the cost of the goods we sold is computed. Let's repeat it in its entirety:

Cost of Goods Sold:				
Merchandise Inventory, January 1, 20—			$ 67 0 0 0 00	
Purchases	$ 87 1 4 0 00			
Less: Purchases Returns and				
Allowances $ 832.00				
Purchases Discounts 1,248.00	2 0 8 0 00			
Net Purchases	$ 85 0 6 0 00			
Add Freight In	2 4 6 0 00			
Delivered Cost of Purchases			87 5 2 0 00	
Cost of Goods Available for Sale			$ 154 5 2 0 00	
Less Merchandise Inventory, December 31, 20—			65 8 0 0 00	
Cost of Goods Sold				$ 88 7 2 0 00

First, let's look closely at the Purchases section.

Purchases			$87	1	4	0	00					
Less: Purchases Returns												
and Allowances	$ 832.00											
Purchases Discounts	1,248.00		2	0	8	0	00					
Net Purchases			$85	0	6	0	00					
Add Freight In			2	4	6	0	00					
Delivered Cost of Purchases								$87	5	2	0	00

Note the parallel to the Revenue from Sales section. To arrive at **Net Purchases,** we deduct the sum of Purchases Returns and Allowances and Purchases Discounts from Purchases. To complete the Purchases section we add Freight In to Net Purchases to get **Delivered Cost of Purchases.**

Now let's look at the full Cost of Goods Sold section. You might think of Cost of Goods Sold like this:

Amount we started with (beginning inventory)	$ 67,000
+ Net amount we purchased, including freight charges	87,520
Total amount that could have been sold (available)	$154,520
− Amount left over (ending inventory)	65,800
Cost of the goods that were actually sold	$ 88,720

Here's the Cost of Goods Sold expressed in proper wording.

Merchandise Inventory, January 1, 20—	$ 67,000
+ Delivered Cost of Purchases	87,520
Cost of Goods Available for Sale	$154,520
− Merchandise Inventory, December 31, 20—	65,800
Cost of Goods Sold	$ 88,720

Operating Expenses

Operating expenses, as the name implies, are the regular expenses of doing business. We list the accounts and their respective balances in the order in which they appear in the ledger.

Many firms use subclassifications of operating expenses, such as the following:

1. **Selling Expenses** Any expenses directly connected with the selling activity, such as

   - Sales Salaries Expense
   - Sales Commissions Expense
   - Advertising Expense
   - Store Supplies Expense
   - Delivery Expense
   - Depreciation Expense, Store Equipment

2. **General Expenses** Any expenses related to the office or administration, or any expense that cannot be directly connected with a selling activity:

   - Office Salaries Expense
   - Taxes Expense

FYI

In preparing the income statement, classifying expense accounts as selling expenses or general expenses is a matter of judgment. The only reason we're not using this breakdown here is that we're trying to keep the number of accounts to a basic few.

- Depreciation Expense, Office Equipment
- Rent Expense
- Insurance Expense
- Office Supplies Expense

If the Cash Short and Over account has a debit balance (net shortage), the balance is added to and reported as Miscellaneous General Expense. Conversely, if the Cash Short and Over account has a credit balance (net overage), the balance is added to and reported as Miscellaneous Income, which is classified as Other Income.

Income from Operations

Now let's repeat the skeleton outline:

Net Sales
− Cost of Goods Sold

Gross Profit
− Operating Expenses

Income from Operations

If Operating Expenses are the regular, recurring expenses of doing business, then Income from Operations should be the regular or recurring income from normal business operations. When you compare the results of operations over a number of years, Income from Operations is the figure to use as a basis for comparison.

Other Income and Other Expenses

The Other Income classification, as the name implies, includes any revenue account other than Revenue from Sales. What we are trying to do is to isolate Sales at the top of the income statement as the major revenue account, so that the Gross Profit figure represents the profit made on the sale of merchandise *only*. Additional accounts that may appear under the heading of Other Income are Rent Income (the firm is subletting part of its premises), Interest Income (the firm holds an interest-bearing note or contract), Gain on Disposal of Plant and Equipment (the firm makes a profit on the sale of plant and equipment), and Miscellaneous Income (the firm has an overage recorded in the Cash Short and Over account).

The classification Other Expenses records various nonoperating expenses, such as Interest Expense or Loss on Disposal of Plant and Equipment.

THE STATEMENT OF OWNER'S EQUITY AND THE BALANCE SHEET

REMEMBER!
Net income appears on both the income statement and the statement of owner's equity.

Figure 3 is a partial work sheet for Dodson Plumbing Supply. Here again we find that **every figure in the Balance Sheet columns of the work sheet is used in either the statement of owner's equity or the balance sheet.**

Preparation of the financial statements follows the same order we presented before: first, the income statement; second, the statement of owner's equity; third, the balance sheet. The statement of owner's equity shows why the balance of the Capital account has changed from the beginning of the

Dodson Plumbing Supply
Work Sheet
For Year Ended December 31, 20—

#	ACCOUNT NAME	TRIAL BALANCE DEBIT	TRIAL BALANCE CREDIT	ADJUSTMENTS DEBIT	ADJUSTMENTS CREDIT	BALANCE SHEET DEBIT	BALANCE SHEET CREDIT	
1	Cash	19 1 5 4 00				19 1 5 4 00		1
2	Notes Receivable	4 0 0 0 00				4 0 0 0 00		2
3	Accounts Receiv.	29 4 4 6 00				29 4 4 6 00		3
4	Merchandise Inven.	67 0 0 0 00		(b) 65 8 0 0 00	(a) 67 0 0 0 00	65 8 0 0 00		4
5	Supplies	1 4 4 0 00			(d) 1 0 2 8 00	4 1 2 00		5
6	Prepaid Insurance	9 6 0 00			(e) 3 2 0 00	6 4 0 00		6
7	Land	12 0 0 0 00				12 0 0 0 00		7
8	Building	130 0 0 0 00				130 0 0 0 00		8
9	Accum. Depr., Build.		52 0 0 0 00		(f) 4 0 0 0 00		56 0 0 0 00	9
10	Equipment	33 6 0 0 00				33 6 0 0 00		10
11	Accum. Depr., Equip.		16 4 0 0 00		(g) 4 8 0 0 00		21 2 0 0 00	11
12	Notes Payable		3 0 0 0 00				3 0 0 0 00	12
13	Accounts Payable		36 4 0 0 00				36 4 0 0 00	13
14	Unearn. Course Fees		1 2 0 0 00	(c) 8 0 0 00			4 0 0 00	14
15	Mortgage Payable		8 0 0 0 00				8 0 0 0 00	15
16	L. E. Dodson,							16
17	Capital		140 5 7 4 00				140 5 7 4 00	17
18	L. E. Dodson, Draw.	56 9 0 0 00				56 9 0 0 00		18
19	Sales		235 1 8 0 00					19
20	Sales Returns and							20
21	Allowances	8 4 0 00						21
22	Sales Discounts	1 8 8 0 00						22
23	Interest Income		1 2 0 00					23
24	Purchases	87 1 4 0 00						24
25	Purchases Returns							25
26	and Allowances		8 3 2 00					26
27	Purchases Discounts		1 2 4 8 00					27
28	Freight In	2 4 6 0 00						28
29	Wages Expense	45 8 0 0 00		(h) 1 1 2 0 00				29
30	Taxes Expense	1 9 6 0 00						30
31	Interest Expense	3 7 4 00						31
32		494 9 5 4 00	494 9 5 4 00					32
33	Income Summary			(a) 67 0 0 0 00	(b) 65 8 0 0 00			33
34	Course Fees Income				(c) 8 0 0 00			34
35	Supplies Expense			(d) 1 0 2 8 00				35
36	Insurance Expense			(e) 3 2 0 00				36
37	Depr. Expense,							37
38	Building			(f) 4 0 0 0 00				38
39	Depr. Expense,							39
40	Equipment			(g) 4 8 0 0 00				40
41	Wages Payable				(h) 1 1 2 0 00		1 1 2 0 00	41
42				144 8 6 8 00	144 8 6 8 00	351 9 5 2 00	266 6 9 4 00	42
43	Net Income						85 2 5 8 00	43
44						351 9 5 2 00	351 9 5 2 00	44
45								45

FIGURE 3

REMEMBER!
The columns *do not* represent debit or credit columns. The columns are for making computations and listing totals.

fiscal period to the end of it. In preparing the statement of owner's equity, always look into the ledger for the owner's Capital account to find any changes, such as additional investments, made during the year.

In Figure 4 we observe the balance of L. E. Dodson, Capital, listed on the work sheet as $140,574. We also note a credit of $8,000 representing an additional investment. Therefore, the beginning balance of L. E. Dodson, Capital, was $132,574 ($140,574 − $8,000).

FIGURE 4

Dodson Plumbing Supply
Statement of Owner's Equity
For Year Ended December 31, 20—

L. E. Dodson, Capital, January 1, 20—								$	132	5	7	4	00
Additional Investment, August 26, 20—									8	0	0	0	00
Total Investment								$	140	5	7	4	00
Net Income for the Year	$	85	2	5	8	00							
Less Withdrawals for the Year		56	9	0	0	00							
Increase in Capital									28	3	5	8	00
L. E. Dodson, Capital, December 31, 20—								$	168	9	3	2	00

BALANCE SHEET CLASSIFICATIONS

OBJECTIVE 2
Prepare a classified balance sheet for any type of business.

Balance sheet classifications are generally uniform for all types of business enterprises. You are strongly urged to take the time to learn the following definitions of the classifications and the order of accounts within them. As you read, refer to Figure 5.

Current Assets

FYI
Some companies are so successful that they accumulate cash from earnings that is not needed to pay current obligations. Rather than leaving the cash in a bank account, companies may prefer to invest it in short-term government or corporate notes or bonds. These are called marketable securities. On the balance sheet, Marketable Securities is a separate account listed just below Cash.

Current Assets consist of cash and any other assets or resources that are expected to be realized in cash or to be sold or consumed during the normal operating cycle of the business (or one year, if the normal operating cycle is less than twelve months).

Accountants list current assets in the order of their convertibility into cash—in other words, their **liquidity**. (If you've got an asset such as a car or a stereo and you sell it quickly and turn it into cash, you are said to be turning it into a *liquid* state.) If the first four accounts shown under Current Assets in Figure 5 are present, they are always recorded in the same order: (1) Cash, (2) Notes Receivable, (3) Accounts Receivable, and (4) Merchandise Inventory.

Notes Receivable (current) are short-term (one year or less) promissory notes (promise-to-pay notes) held by the firm. A note is generally received from a customer as a substitute for a charge account.

Supplies and Prepaid Insurance are considered prepaid items that will be used up or will expire within the following operating cycle or year. Generally, these prepaid items are not converted into cash and that's why they appear

Dodson Plumbing Supply
Balance Sheet
December 31, 20—

Assets									
Current Assets:									
Cash				$ 19 1 5 4 00					
Notes Receivable				4 0 0 0 00					
Accounts Receivable				29 4 4 6 00					
Merchandise Inventory				65 8 0 0 00					
Supplies				4 1 2 00					
Prepaid Insurance				6 4 0 00					
Total Current Assets						$ 119 4 5 2 00			
Plant and Equipment:									
Land				$ 12 0 0 0 00					
Building	$ 130 0 0 0 00								
Less Accumulated Depreciation	56 0 0 0 00			74 0 0 0 00					
Equipment	$ 33 6 0 0 00								
Less Accumulated Depreciation	21 2 0 0 00			12 4 0 0 00					
Total Plant and Equipment						98 4 0 0 00			
Total Assets						$ 217 8 5 2 00			
Liabilities									
Current Liabilities:									
Notes Payable				$ 3 0 0 0 00					
Mortgage Payable (current portion)				2 0 0 0 00					
Accounts Payable				36 4 0 0 00					
Wages Payable				1 1 2 0 00					
Unearned Course Fees				4 0 0 00					
Total Current Liabilities						$ 42 9 2 0 00			
Long-Term Liabilities:									
Mortgage Payable						6 0 0 0 00			
Total Liabilities						$ 48 9 2 0 00			
Owner's Equity									
L. E. Dodson, Capital						168 9 3 2 00			
Total Liabilities and Owner's Equity						$ 217 8 5 2 00			

FIGURE 5

at the bottom of the Current Assets section. There is no particular reason to list Supplies before Prepaid Insurance. Prepaid Insurance could just as easily have preceded Supplies.

Plant and Equipment

Plant and Equipment are relatively long-lived assets that are held for use in the production or sale of other assets or services; some accountants refer to them as *fixed assets*. The three types of accounts that usually appear in this category are Land, Building, and Equipment (refer to Figure 5). Note that the Building and Equipment accounts are followed by their respective

REMEMBER!
Since Accumulated Depreciation is a contra account, it is deducted from the appropriate asset.

The barn, the tractor, and the land this man is working are all classified as fixed assets in the Plant and Equipment account. Only the barn and tractor, however, are subject to depreciation.

OBJECTIVE 3
Compute working capital and current ratio.

FYI
The current ratio has a weakness. It favors companies with lots of current assets. However, the current ratio does not attempt to measure the overall strength of a company.

Accumulated Depreciation accounts. We list these assets in order of their length of life, with the longest-lived asset placed first.

Current Liabilities

Current Liabilities are debts that will become due within the normal operating cycle of the business, usually within one year; they normally will be paid, when due, from current assets. List current liabilities in the order of their expected payment. Mortgage Payable is the payment one makes to reduce the principal of the mortgage in a given year. Accounts Payable are debts owed to creditors. Wages Payable and any other accrued liabilities, such as Commissions Payable and the current portion of unearned revenue accounts, usually fall at the bottom of the list of current liabilities.

Long-Term Liabilities

Long-Term Liabilities are debts that are payable over a comparatively long period, usually longer than one year. Ordinarily, Mortgage Payable is the only account in this category for a sole-proprietorship (or one-owner) type of business. One single amount in a category can be placed in the column on the extreme right.

Working Capital and Current Ratio

Both the management and the short-term creditors of a firm are vitally interested in two questions:

1. Does the firm have a sufficient amount of capital to operate?
2. Does the firm have the ability to pay its debts?

Two measures used to answer these questions are a firm's working capital and its current ratio; the necessary data are taken from a classified balance sheet.

Working capital is determined by subtracting current liabilities from current assets; thus,

Working Capital = Current Assets − Current Liabilities

The normal operating cycle for most firms is less than one year. Because current assets equal cash—or items that can be converted into cash or used up within one year—and current liabilities equal the total amount that the company must pay out within one year, working capital is appropriately named. It is the amount of capital the company has available to use or to work with. The working capital for Dodson Plumbing Supply is as follows:

Working Capital = $119,452 − $42,920 = $76,532

The **current ratio** is useful in revealing a firm's ability to pay its bills. It is determined by dividing current assets by current liabilities:

$$\text{Current Ratio} = \frac{\text{Current Assets (amount coming in within one year)}}{\text{Current Liabilities (amount going out within one year)}}$$

The current ratio for Dodson Plumbing Supply is calculated like this:

$$\text{Current Ratio} = \frac{\$119,452}{\$\ 42,920} \qquad 42,920\overline{)\ 119,452} = 2.78$$

In the case of Dodson Plumbing Supply, $2.78 in current assets is available to pay every dollar currently due on December 31.

Chart of Accounts

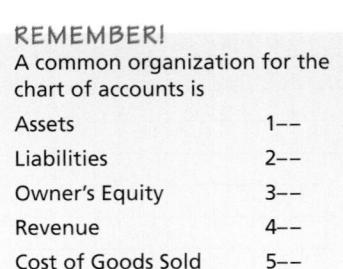

REMEMBER!
A common organization for the chart of accounts is

Assets	1--
Liabilities	2--
Owner's Equity	3--
Revenue	4--
Cost of Goods Sold	5--
Expenses	6--

When we introduced the chart of accounts and the account number arrangement, we said that the first digit represents the classification of an account. Since you are now acquainted with classified income statements and balance sheets, we can introduce the second digit. The second digit stands for the subclassification.

Assets	1--	Revenue	4--
Current Assets	11-	Revenue from Sales	41-
Plant and Equipment	12-	Other Income	42-
Liabilities	2--	Cost of Goods Sold	5--
Current Liabilities	21-	Purchases	51-
Long-Term Liabilities	22-	Expenses	6--
Owner's Equity	3--	Selling Expenses	61-
Capital	31-	General Expenses	62-
		Other Expenses	63-

The third digit indicates the placement of the account within the subclassification. For example, account number 411 represents Sales, which is the first account listed under Revenue. Account number 512 represents Purchases Returns and Allowances, which is the second account listed under Cost of Goods Sold. Account number 312 represents Drawing, which is the second account listed under Owner's Equity.

CLOSING ENTRIES

OBJECTIVE 4
Journalize the closing entries for a merchandising firm.

Now let's look at closing entries for a merchandising business. You follow the same four steps to close or zero out the revenue, expense, and Drawing accounts as you do for a service business.

At the end of a fiscal period, you close the revenue and expense accounts so that you can start the next fiscal period with zero balances. You close the Drawing account because it, too, applies to one fiscal period. Recall that these accounts are called **temporary-equity accounts**, or *nominal accounts*.

Figure 6, shown on page 464, shows the isolated Income Statement columns. After you have looked them over, let us look at the four steps of the closing procedure.

Four Steps in the Closing Procedure

These four steps should be followed when closing:

1. Close the revenue accounts and the other accounts that appear in the income statement and have credit balances (all temporary or nominal

	ACCOUNT NAME	TRIAL BALANCE DEBIT	TRIAL BALANCE CREDIT	INCOME STATEMENT DEBIT	INCOME STATEMENT CREDIT
1	Cash	19 1 5 4 00			
2	Notes Receivable	4 0 0 0 00			
3	Accounts Receivable	29 4 4 6 00			
4	Merchandise Inventory	67 0 0 0 00			
5	Supplies	1 4 4 0 00			
6	Prepaid Insurance	9 6 0 00			
7	Land	12 0 0 0 00			
8	Building	130 0 0 0 00			
9	Accumulated Depreciation, Building		52 0 0 0 00		
10	Equipment	33 6 0 0 00			
11	Accumulated Depreciation, Equipment		16 4 0 0 00		
12	Notes Payable		3 0 0 0 00		
13	Accounts Payable		36 4 0 0 00		
14	Unearned Course Fees		1 2 0 0 00		
15	Mortgage Payable		8 0 0 0 00		
16	L. E. Dodson, Capital		140 5 7 4 00		
17	L. E. Dodson, Drawing	56 9 0 0 00			
18	Sales		235 1 8 0 00		235 1 8 0 00
19	Sales Returns and Allowances	8 4 0 00		8 4 0 00	
20	Sales Discounts	1 8 8 0 00		1 8 8 0 00	
21	Interest Income		1 2 0 00		1 2 0 00
22	Purchases	87 1 4 0 00		87 1 4 0 00	
23	Purchases Returns and Allowances		8 3 2 00		8 3 2 00
24	Purchases Discounts		1 2 4 8 00		1 2 4 8 00
25	Freight In	2 4 6 0 00		2 4 6 0 00	
26	Wages Expense	45 8 0 0 00		46 9 2 0 00	
27	Taxes Expense	1 9 6 0 00		1 9 6 0 00	
28	Interest Expense	3 7 4 00		3 7 4 00	
29		494 9 5 4 00	494 9 5 4 00		
30	Income Summary			67 0 0 0 00	65 8 0 0 00
31	Course Fees Income				8 0 0 00
32	Supplies Expense			1 0 2 8 00	
33	Insurance Expense			3 2 0 00	
34	Depreciation Expense, Building			4 0 0 0 00	
35	Depreciation Expense, Equipment			4 8 0 0 00	
36	Wages Payable				
37				218 7 2 2 00	303 9 8 0 00
38	Net Income			85 2 5 8 00	
39				303 9 8 0 00	303 9 8 0 00
40					

FIGURE 6

accounts with credit balances). **(Debit the figures that are credited in the Income Statement columns of the work sheet, except the figure on the Income Summary line.)** This entry is illustrated as follows:

GENERAL JOURNAL   PAGE __97__

	DATE		DESCRIPTION	POST. REF.	DEBIT		CREDIT	
1	20–		**Closing Entries**					1
2	Dec.	31	Sales		235 1 8 0 00			2
3			Interest Income		1 2 0 00			3
4			Purchases Returns and					4
5			Allowances		8 3 2 00			5
6			Purchases Discounts		1 2 4 8 00			6
7			Course Fees Income		8 0 0 00			7
8			Income Summary				238 1 8 0 00	8

2. Close the expense accounts and the other accounts appearing in the income statement that have debit balances (all temporary or nominal accounts with debit balances). **(Credit the figures that are debited in the Income Statement columns of the work sheet, except the figure on the Income Summary line.)**

    Note that you close Purchases Discounts and Purchases Returns and Allowances in step 1 along with the revenue accounts. Note also that in step 2 you close Sales Discounts and Sales Returns and Allowances along with the expense accounts.

GENERAL JOURNAL   PAGE __97__

	DATE		DESCRIPTION	POST. REF.	DEBIT		CREDIT	
9	Dec.	31	Income Summary		151 7 2 2 00			9
10			Sales Returns and Allowances				8 4 0 00	10
11			Sales Discounts				1 8 8 0 00	11
12			Purchases				87 1 4 0 00	12
13			Freight In				2 4 6 0 00	13
14			Wages Expense				46 9 2 0 00	14
15			Taxes Expense				1 9 6 0 00	15
16			Interest Expense				3 7 4 00	16
17			Supplies Expense				1 0 2 8 00	17
18			Insurance Expense				3 2 0 00	18
19			Depreciation Expense, Build.				4 0 0 0 00	19
20			Depreciation Expense, Equip.				4 8 0 0 00	20
21								21

3. Close the Income Summary account into L. E. Dodson, Capital. **(Debit Income Summary by the amount of the net income; credit it by the amount of a net loss.)**

	GENERAL JOURNAL			PAGE 97

	DATE	DESCRIPTION	POST. REF.	DEBIT	CREDIT	
22	Dec. 31	Income Summary		85 2 5 8 00		22
23		L. E. Dodson, Capital			85 2 5 8 00	23
24						24

Here is what the T accounts look like. Note that the Income Summary account already contains adjusting entries for merchandise inventory.

Income Summary

Adjusting (Beginning Merchandise Inventory)	67,000	Adjusting (Ending Merchandise Inventory)	65,800
(Expenses and other debit balance accounts)	151,722	(Revenue and other credit balance accounts)	238,180
(Net Income)	85,258	
		Balance ——

L. E. Dodson, Capital

−	+
	Balance 140,574
	(Net Income) 85,258

Like service businesses, merchandisers such as this CD store need to prepare close entries to track net income.

4. Close the Drawing account into the Capital account.

	DATE		DESCRIPTION	POST. REF.	DEBIT	CREDIT	
25	Dec.	31	L. E. Dodson, Capital		56 9 0 0 00		25
26			L. E. Dodson, Drawing			56 9 0 0 00	26
27							27
28							28
29							29

GENERAL JOURNAL   PAGE __97__

Here is what the T accounts would look like:

L. E. Dodson, Drawing

	+	–	
Balance	56,900	Closing	56,900
Bal.		———	

L. E. Dodson, Capital

	–	+	
(Drawing)	56,900	Balance	140,574
		(Net Income)	85,258
		Bal.	168,932

REVERSING ENTRIES

Reversing entries are general journal entries that are the exact reverse of certain adjusting entries. A reversing entry enables the accountant to record routine transactions in the usual manner, *even though* an adjusting entry affecting one of the accounts involved in the transaction has intervened. We can understand this concept best by looking at an example.

Suppose there is an adjusting entry for accrued wages owed to employees at the end of the fiscal year. Assume that all the employees of a certain firm earn, altogether, $400 per day for a five-day week and that payday occurs every Friday throughout the year. When the employees get their checks at 5:00 P.M. on Friday, the checks include their wages for that day and for the preceding four days. And assume that, one year, the last day of the fiscal year happens to fall on Wednesday, December 31. A diagram of this situation would look like this:

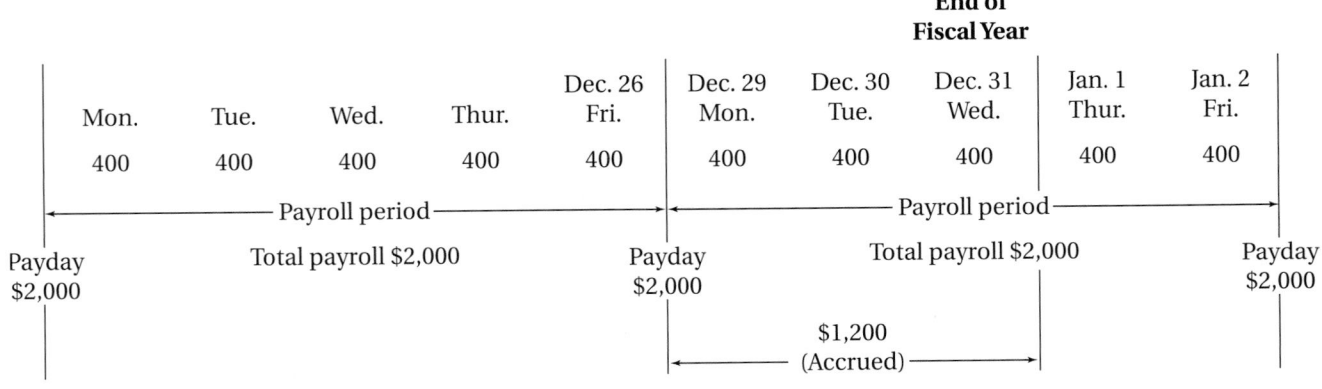

Each Friday during the year, the payroll has been debited to the Wages Expense account and credited to the Cash account. As a result, Wages Expense has a debit balance of $102,800. Here is the adjusting entry in T account form:

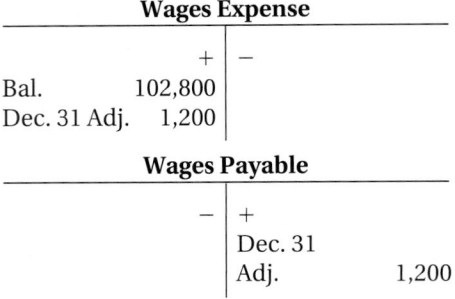

Wages Expense		
	+	−
Bal.	102,800	
Dec. 31 Adj.	1,200	

Wages Payable		
	−	+
		Dec. 31
		Adj. 1,200

Next, when all the expense accounts are closed, Wages Expense is closed by crediting it for $104,000. However, Wages Payable continues to have a credit balance of $1,200. The $2,000 payroll on January 2 must be split up by debiting Wages Payable $1,200, debiting Wages Expense $800, and crediting Cash $2,000.

The employee who records the payroll not only has to record this particular payroll differently from all other weekly payrolls for the year but also has to refer back to the adjusting entry to determine what portion of the $2,000 is debited to Wages Payable and what portion is debited to Wages Expense. In many companies, however, the employee who records the payroll does not have access to the adjusting entries.

There is a solution to this problem. The need to refer to the earlier entry and divide the debit total between the two accounts is eliminated *if a reversing entry is made on the first day of the following fiscal period.* You make an entry that is the exact reverse of the adjusting entry, as follows:

GENERAL JOURNAL   PAGE **118**

	DATE		DESCRIPTION	POST. REF.	DEBIT	CREDIT	
27							27
28	20–		Reversing Entries				28
29	Jan.	1	Wages Payable		1 2 0 0 00		29
30			Wages Expense			1 2 0 0 00	30
31							31

Now let's bring the T accounts up to date.

Wages Expense			
	+	−	
Balance	102,800	Dec. 31 Closing	104,000
Dec. 31 Adjust.	1,200		
Bal.	———	Jan. 1 Reversing	1,200

Wages Payable			
	−	+	
Jan. 1 Reversing	1,200	Dec. 31 Adjust.	1,200
		Bal.	———

The reversing entry has the effect of transferring the $1,200 liability from Wages Payable to the credit side of Wages Expense. Wages Expense will temporarily have a credit balance until the next payroll is recorded in the routine manner. In our example, this occurs on January 2 as shown below.

Wages Expense

	+	−	
Balance	102,800	Dec. 31 Closing	104,000
Dec. 31 Adjust.	1,200		
Bal.	———		
Jan. 2	2,000	Jan. 1 Reversing	1,200
Bal.	800		

Wages Payable

	−	+	
Jan. 1 Reversing	1,200	Dec. 31 Adjust.	1,200
		Bal.	———

Cash

	+	−	
		Jan. 2	2,000

There is now a *net debit balance* of $800 in Wages Expense, which is the correct amount ($400 for January 1 and $400 for January 2). To see this, look at the following ledger accounts. December 26 was the last payday of one year, and January 2 is the first payday of the next year.

GENERAL LEDGER

ACCOUNT __Wages Expense__   ACCOUNT NO. __611__

	DATE	ITEM	POST. REF.	DEBIT	CREDIT	BALANCE DEBIT	BALANCE CREDIT
11	20–						
12	Dec. 26		CP16	2 0 0 0 00		102 8 0 0 00	
13	31	Adjusting	J116	1 2 0 0 00		104 0 0 0 00	
14	31	Closing	J117		104 0 0 0 00	—	—
15	20–						
16	Jan. 1	Reversing	J118		1 2 0 0 00		1 2 0 0 00
17	2		CP17	2 0 0 0 00		8 0 0 00	

ACCOUNT __Wages Payable__   ACCOUNT NO. __213__

	DATE	ITEM	POST. REF.	DEBIT	CREDIT	BALANCE DEBIT	BALANCE CREDIT
1	20–						
2	Dec. 31	Adjusting	J116		1 2 0 0 00		1 2 0 0 00
3	20–						
4	Jan. 1	Reversing	J118	1 2 0 0 00		—	—

OBJECTIVE 5
Determine which adjusting entries can be reversed, and journalize the reversing entries.

The reversing entry for accrued salaries or wages applies to service as well as merchandising companies. You can see that a reversing entry simply switches around an adjusting entry. The question is: Which adjusting entries should be reversed? Here are two handy rules for reversing. **If an adjusting entry is to be reversed, it must meet both of the following qualifications:**

1. **The adjusting entry increases an asset or liability account.**

2. **The asset or liability account did not have a previous balance.**

With the exception of the first year of operations, Merchandise Inventory and contra accounts—such as Accumulated Depreciation—always have previous balances. Consequently, adjusting entries involving these accounts should never be reversed.

Let's apply these rules to the adjusting entries for Dodson Plumbing Supply.

(Do not reverse; Merchandise Inventory is an asset, but it was decreased. Also, it has a previous balance.)

Merchandise Inventory				Income Summary			
	+	−					
Balance	67,000	Adjust.	67,000	Adjust.	67,000		

(Do not reverse; Merchandise Inventory is an asset, but it has a previous balance.)

Merchandise Inventory				Income Summary			
	+	−					
Balance	67,000	Adjust.	67,000	Adjust.	67,000	Adjust.	65,800
Adjust.	65,800						

(Do not reverse; Unearned Course Fees is a liability, but it was decreased. Also, it has a previous balance.)

Course Fees Income				Unearned Course Fees			
	−	+			−	+	
		Adjust.	800	Adjust.	800	Balance	1,200

(Do not reverse; Supplies is an asset account, but it was decreased. Also, it has a previous balance.)

Supplies Expense				Supplies			
	+	−			+	−	
Adjust.	1,028			Balance	1,440	Adjust.	1,028

(Do not reverse; Prepaid Insurance is an asset account, but it was decreased. Also, it has a previous balance.)

Insurance Expense				Prepaid Insurance			
	+	−			+	−	
Adjust.	320			Balance	960	Adjust.	320

(Do not reverse; Accumulated Depreciation is a contra-asset, and it always has a previous balance after the first year.)

Depreciation Expense, Building				Accumulated Depreciation, Building			
	+	−			−	+	
Adjust.	4,000					Balance	52,000
						Adjust.	4,000

(Do not reverse; Accumulated Depreciation is a contra-asset, and it always has a previous balance after the first year.)

Depreciation Expense, Equipment				Accumulated Depreciation, Equipment			
	+	−			−	+	
Adjust.	4,800					Balance	16,400
						Adjust.	4,800

(Reverse; Wages Payable is a liability account. It was increased, and it had no previous balance.)

Wages Expense				Wages Payable			
	+	−			−	+	
Balance	45,800					Adjust.	1,120
Adjust.	1,120						

REMEMBER!
Reversing entries are optional.

Whenever we introduce additional adjusting entries, we will make it a point to state whether they can be reversed.

CHAPTER REVIEW

Check out ACE for
a Review Quiz at

**http://college.hmco.com/
accounting/students/**.

Review of Performance Objectives

1. Prepare a classified income statement for a merchandising firm.

   The outline of the income statement looks like this:

   Revenue from Sales
   - Gross Sales
   - − Sales Returns and Allowances
   - − Sales Discounts
   - = Net Sales

   − Cost of Goods Sold
   - Beginning Merchandise Inventory
   - + Delivered Cost of Purchases
       - Gross Purchases
       - − Purchases Returns and Allowances
       - − Purchases Discounts
       - + Freight In
       - = Delivered Cost of Purchases
   - = Cost of Goods Available for Sale
   - − Ending Merchandise Inventory
   - = Cost of Goods Sold

   = Gross Profit
   − Operating Expenses
   - Selling Expenses
   - General Expenses

   = Income from Operations
   + Other Income
   - Interest Income
   - Rent Income
   - Gain on Disposal of Plant and Equipment

   − Other Expenses
   - Interest Expense
   - Loss on Disposal of Plant and Equipment

   = Net Income

2. Prepare a classified balance sheet for any type of business.

   The outline of the balance sheet looks like this:

   Assets Current Assets (listed in the order of their convertibility into cash)

   1. Cash
   2. Notes Receivable
   3. Accounts Receivable
   4. Merchandise Inventory
   5. Prepaid items (Supplies; Prepaid Insurance)

   Plant and Equipment (listed in the order of their length of life; the asset with the longest life is placed first)

   1. Land
   2. Buildings
   3. Equipment

   Liabilities Current Liabilities (listed in the order of their urgency of payment; the most pressing obligation is placed first)

1. Accounts Payable
2. Notes Payable
3. Accrued liabilities (Wages Payable; Commissions Payable)
4. Unearned Revenue
5. Mortgage Payable or Contracts Payable (current portion)

Long-Term Liabilities (Contracts Payable; Mortgage Payable)

Owner's Equity Capital balance at end of the fiscal year

3. Compute working capital and current ratio.

These two measures help analysts determine whether a firm has enough capital to operate and whether it can pay its debts.

Working capital = Current assets − Current liabilities

$$\text{Current ratio} = \frac{\text{Current assets}}{\text{Current liabilities}}$$

4. Journalize the closing entries for a merchandising firm.

There are four steps in making closing entries for a merchandising business:

Step 1. Close all revenue accounts, Purchases Returns and Allowances, and Purchases Discounts into Income Summary (any accounts listed as credits in the work sheet Income Statement columns except Income Summary).

Step 2. Close all expense accounts, Sales Returns and Allowances, and Sales Discounts into Income Summary (any accounts listed as debits in the work sheet Income Statement columns except Income Summary).

Step 3. Close Income Summary into Capital (transfer net income or net loss into the owner's Capital account). The Income Summary balance should now be zero.

Step 4. Close Drawing into Capital.

5. Determine which adjusting entries can be reversed, and journalize the reversing entries. The use of reversing entries is optional.

Reverse the adjusting entries that increase either asset or liability accounts and that do not have previous balances. A contra-account like Accumulated Depreciation should not be reversed. Reversing entries are dated as of the first day of the next fiscal period.

Glossary

Cost of Goods Sold A section of the income statement in which the amount of the cost of the goods we sold is calculated. Terms often used to describe the same thing are *cost of merchandise sold* and *cost of sales*.

Merchandise Inventory (beginning)
Plus Delivered Cost of Purchases

Cost of Goods Available for Sale
Less Merchandise Inventory (ending)

Cost of Goods Sold

(456)

Current Assets Cash and any other assets or resources that are expected to be realized in cash or to be sold or consumed during the normal operating cycle of the business (or one year, if the normal operating cycle is less than twelve months). (460)

Current Liabilities Debts that will become due within the normal operating cycle of a business, usually within one year, and that are normally paid from current assets. (462)

Current ratio A firm's current assets divided by its current liabilities. Portrays a firm's short-term debt-paying ability. (462)

Delivered Cost of Purchases Net Purchases plus Freight In:

Net Purchases
Plus Freight In

Delivered Cost of Purchases   (457)

General Expenses Expenses incurred in the administration of a business, including office expenses and any expenses that are not completely classified as Selling Expenses or Other Expenses. (457)

Gross Profit Net Sales minus Cost of Goods Sold, or profit before deducting expenses:

Net Sales
Less Cost of Goods Sold

Gross Profit   (456)

Liquidity The ability of an asset to be quickly turned into cash, either by selling it or by putting it up as security for a loan. (460)

Long-Term Liabilities Debts payable over a comparatively long period, usually more than one year. (462)

Net Income or **Net Profit** The final figure on an income statement after all expenses have been deducted from revenues. (456)

Net Purchases Purchases minus Purchases Returns and Allowances and minus Purchases Discounts:

Purchases
Less Purchases Returns and Allowances
Less Purchases Discounts

Net Purchases   (457)

Net Sales Sales minus Sales Returns and Allowances and minus Sales Discounts:

Sales
Less Sales Returns and Allowances
Less Sales Discounts

Net Sales   (456)

Notes Receivable (current) Written promises to pay the seller/lender the amount due in a period of less than one year. (460)

Plant and Equipment Long-lived assets that are held for use in the production or sale of other assets or services; also called *fixed assets*. (461)

Reversing entries The reverse of certain adjusting entries, recorded as of the first day of the following fiscal period. The use of reversing entries is optional. (467)

Selling Expenses Expenses directly connected with the selling activity, such as salaries of sales staff, advertising expenses, and delivery expenses. (457)

Temporary-equity accounts Accounts whose balances apply to one fiscal period only, such as revenues, expenses, and the Drawing account. Temporary-equity accounts are also called *nominal accounts*. (463)

Working capital A firm's current assets less its current liabilities. The amount of capital a firm has available to use or to work with during a normal operating cycle. (462)

QUESTIONS, EXERCISES, AND PROBLEMS

Discussion Questions

1. What is the order for listing accounts in the Current Assets section of the balance sheet?
2. What is the difference between the cost of goods available for sale and the cost of goods sold?
3. What are the basic classifications found on an income statement for a merchandising business compared to a service business?
4. On a balance sheet, what is the difference between Current Liabilities and Long-Term Liabilities? Give an example of an account in each classification.
5. On an income statement, what is the difference between income from operations and net income? Which is more useful in comparing the results of operations over a number of years?
6. Explain the calculation of net sales and net purchases.
7. In the closing procedure, what happens to (a) Purchases Discounts, (b) Sales Returns and Allowances, (c) Freight In, (d) Gain on Disposal of Plant and Equipment?
8. What are the rules for recognizing whether or not an adjusting entry should be reversed?

Exercises

P.O. 1

Provide missing amounts on an income statement.

Exercise 13-1 Calculate the missing items in the following:

	Sales	Sales Returns and Allowances	Net Sales	Beginning Merchandise Inventory	Net Purchases	Cost of Goods Available for Sale	Ending Merchandise Inventory	Cost of Goods Sold	Gross Profit
a.	$248,000	$ 6,000	—	$148,000	$170,000	—	$136,000	$182,000	—
b.	304,000	—	$296,000	144,000	—	$404,000	196,000	208,000	—
c.	—	12,000	628,000	—	412,000	496,000	92,000	—	—

P.O. 1

Prepare Cost of Goods Sold section.

Exercise 13-2 Using the following information, prepare the Cost of Goods Sold section of an income statement.

Purchases Discounts	$ 9,000
Merchandise Inventory, December 31	192,000
Purchases	480,000
Merchandise Inventory, January 1	188,000
Purchases Returns and Allowances	16,000
Freight In	27,000

P.O. 1

Classify income statement accounts.

Exercise 13-3 Identify each of the following items relating to sections of an income statement as Revenue from Sales (S), Cost of Goods Sold (CGS), Selling Expenses (SE), General Expenses (GE), Other Income (OI), or Other Expense (OE).

a. Advertising Expense
b. Rent Expense
c. Purchases Discounts
d. Sales Returns and Allowances
e. Interest Income
f. Freight In
g. Depreciation Expense, Building
h. Interest Expense
i. Insurance Expense
j. Delivery Expense

P.O. 1

Prepare an income statement.

Exercise 13-4 The Income Statement columns of the June 30 (year-end) work sheet for the Baki Company are shown here. From the information given, prepare an income statement for the company. To save time and space, the expenses have been grouped together into two categories.

	ACCOUNT NAME	INCOME STATEMENT	
		DEBIT	CREDIT
21	Income Summary	27 0 0 0 00	23 0 0 0 00
22	Sales		291 0 0 0 00
23	Sales Returns and Allowances	11 1 0 0 00	
24	Sales Discounts	4 1 0 0 00	
25	Purchases	116 0 0 0 00	
26	Purchases Returns and Allowances		1 2 0 0 00
27	Purchases Discounts		1 0 0 0 00
28	Freight In	7 5 0 0 00	
29	Selling Expenses	56 0 0 0 00	
30	General Expenses	49 0 0 0 00	
31		270 7 0 0 00	316 2 0 0 00
32	Net Income	45 5 0 0 00	
		316 2 0 0 00	316 2 0 0 00

P.O. 2

Classify balance sheet items.

Exercise 13-5 Identify each of the following items relating to sections of a balance sheet dated 20X5 as Current Assets (CA), Plant and Equipment (PE), Current Liabilities (CL), Long-Term Liabilities (LTL), or Owner's Equity (OE).

a. Accounts Receivable
b. Building
c. Wages Payable
d. Prepaid Taxes
e. Mortgage Payable (current)
f. Supplies
g. Mortgage Payable (due in 3 years)
h. Unearned Fees
i. D. Mann, Capital
j. Notes Payable (due in 3 months)

P.O. 3

Determine working capital and current ratio.

Exercise 13-6 On December 31, 20—, the following selected accounts and amounts appeared in the balance sheet. Determine the amount of the working capital and the current ratio.

Building	$160,000
Prepaid Insurance	600
Merchandise Inventory	72,000
Store Equipment	14,000
Unearned Fees	700
Notes Payable	7,000
Accumulated Depreciation, Building	72,000
Accounts Payable	22,000
Land	40,000
Store Supplies	1,000
Cash	9,000
Accumulated Depreciation, Store Equipment	6,000
Notes Receivable	4,000
Mortgage Payable (current portion)	4,400
Salaries Payable	2,000
C. Ray, Capital	101,500
Mortgage Payable (due in 4 years)	85,000

P.O. 4

Journalize closing entries.

Exercise 13-7 From the following T accounts, journalize the closing entries dated December 31:

Salary Expense	H. Beal, Drawing	Purchases Returns and Allowances
+ | −	+ | −	− | +
68,000 |	54,000 |	| 7,600

Purchases	Miscellaneous Expense	Rent Expense
+ | −	+ | −	+ | −
236,800 |	13,200 |	24,000 |

Sales Returns and Allowances	Freight In	Sales
+ | −	+ | −	− | +
8,000 |	15,200 |	| 504,000

Income Summary	H. Beal, Capital	Purchases Discounts
88,000 | 104,000	− | +	− | +
	| 336,000	| 5,600

P.O. 4

From T accounts, prepare a statement of owner's equity.

Exercise 13-8 From the following information, journalize the last two closing entries, and present a statement of owner's equity for Reece Company:

T. H. Reece, Capital

−	+
	Jan. 1 Balance 440,000
	Apr. 7 16,000

Income Summary

Dec. 31 Adj.	192,000	Dec. 31 Adj.	204,000
Dec. 31 Closing	410,000	Dec. 31 Closing	490,000

T. H. Reece, Drawing

+	−
Mar. 1 32,000	
Dec. 9 37,000	

> ### REFLECTING ON
> ## THE WORLD WIDE WEB
>
> Let's analyze Barnes & Noble's working capital and current ratio for 2000. The 2000 annual report can be found at **http://www.barnesandnoble. com/ir/invinfo/index.asp?userid=2VBKISV48R**.
>
> 1. What was Barnes & Noble's working capital for 2000, and what does it say about the business?
> 2. What was Barnes & Noble's current ratio for 2000, and what does it say about the business?

CONSIDER AND COMMUNICATE

A music store sells instruments. The store also sells used instruments for people who are willing to give the store part of the sales price. The sale of used instruments amounts to about one-fourth of total sales, called commissions. On the firm's classified income statement under the Revenue heading are both New Instrument Sales and Sales Commissions. Comment on this practice.

WHAT'S WRONG WITH THIS PICTURE?

What if the freight charges on a new desk for the owner were journalized and posted to the Freight In account? Would this affect the Cost of Goods Sold section? If so, how?

CRITICAL THINKING

You are an owner/bookkeeper in a country whose economy has been nearly destroyed. Goods are scarce; in fact, you have no goods to sell at the start of each day. You go out early each morning to purchase goods and haul them back to sell. At the end of the day, you have sold everything. Prepare a Cost of Goods Sold section for a day when you purchased $400 in goods. What conclusion can you draw?

A MATTER OF ETHICS

Malissa is an accountant. Sometimes printouts of financial statements have errors and are not usable. Malissa doesn't like to waste anything, so she takes the unusable financial statements to her son's day care center to use for drawing paper. Explain why you think this is or is not unethical behavior.

PROBLEM SET A

P.O. 1,4

Problem 13-1A A partial work sheet for Pope Music Store is presented here. The merchandise inventory at the beginning of the fiscal period was $49,584. F. L. Pope, the owner, withdrew $32,000 during the year.

Pope Music Store
Work Sheet
For Year Ended December 31, 20—

	ACCOUNT NAME	INCOME STATEMENT DEBIT	INCOME STATEMENT CREDIT
21	Sales		326 5 9 2 80
22	Sales Returns and Allowances	5 2 2 9 20	
23	Sales Discounts	1 9 0 8 00	
24	Interest Income		3 2 4 98
25	Purchases	195 1 9 1 00	
26	Purchases Returns and Allowances		1 6 5 6 00
27	Freight In	14 2 6 5 00	
28	Wages Expense	39 5 2 4 00	
29	Rent Expense	9 3 6 0 00	
30	Commissions Expense	9 4 4 0 00	
31	Interest Expense	6 5 6 32	
32	Income Summary	49 5 8 4 00	43 9 7 2 00
33	Supplies Expense	6 3 7 20	
34	Insurance Expense	9 3 6 00	
35	Depreciation Expense, Equipment	3 3 4 0 00	
36	Depreciation Expense, Building	4 8 0 0 00	
37		334 8 7 0 72	372 5 4 5 78
38	Net Income	37 6 7 5 06	
39		372 5 4 5 78	372 5 4 5 78
40			
41			
42			
43			
44			
45			
46			
47			
48			
49			

Check Figure

Cost of Goods Sold, $213,412

Instructions

1. Prepare an income statement.
2. Journalize the closing entries.

P.O. 2,3

Problem 13-2A Here is the partial work sheet for Olsen Mountain Shop.

Olsen Mountain Shop
Work Sheet
For Year Ended December 31, 20—

	ACCOUNT NAME	BALANCE SHEET DEBIT	BALANCE SHEET CREDIT	
1	Cash	9 7 2 3 00		1
2	Notes Receivable	3 6 0 0 00		2
3	Accounts Receivable	42 8 7 9 60		3
4	Merchandise Inventory	56 6 9 7 00		4
5	Supplies	4 7 4 00		5
6	Prepaid Taxes	6 1 3 50		6
7	Prepaid Insurance	6 3 0 00		7
8	Land	8 4 0 0 00		8
9	Building	63 0 0 0 00		9
10	Accumulated Depreciation, Building		21 6 0 0 00	10
11	Office Equipment	5 4 2 4 00		11
12	Accumulated Depreciation, Office Equipment		4 1 7 0 00	12
13	Store Equipment	6 5 7 0 00		13
14	Accumulated Depreciation, Store Equipment		4 9 9 5 00	14
15	Delivery Equipment	5 5 6 5 00		15
16	Accumulated Depreciation, Delivery Equipment		4 3 0 5 00	16
17	Notes Payable		5 4 3 0 00	17
18	Accounts Payable		29 5 9 1 70	18
19	Mortgage Payable (current portion)		2 7 0 0 00	19
20	Mortgage Payable		55 7 1 3 00	20
21	N. Olsen, Capital		65 0 5 8 90	21
22	N. Olsen, Drawing	25 1 9 4 00		22
23	Wages Payable		1 2 7 8 00	23
24		228 7 7 0 10	194 8 4 1 60	24
25	Net Income		33 9 2 8 50	25
26		228 7 7 0 10	228 7 7 0 10	26

Check Figure

Working capital, $75,617.40

Instructions

1. Prepare a statement of owner's equity (no additional investment).
2. Prepare a balance sheet.
3. Determine the amount of the working capital.
4. Determine the current ratio (carry to two decimal places).

P.O. 4,5   **Problem 13-3A** The following partial work sheet covers the affairs of Komo and Company for the year ending June 30:

Komo and Company
Work Sheet
For Year Ended June 30, 20—

	ACCOUNT NAME	INCOME STATEMENT DEBIT	INCOME STATEMENT CREDIT	BALANCE SHEET DEBIT	BALANCE SHEET CREDIT	
1	Cash			32 3 8 4 34		1
2	Accounts Receivable			104 6 3 4 54		2
3	Merchandise Inventory			119 4 5 6 00		3
4	Supplies			1 0 3 2 00		4
5	Prepaid Insurance			1 3 2 0 00		5
6	Delivery Equipment			12 9 2 0 00		6
7	Accumulated Depreciation, Delivery Equipment				6 4 8 0 00	7
8	Store Equipment			36 5 0 0 00		8
9	Accumulated Depreciation, Store Equipment				10 3 6 0 00	9
10	Accounts Payable				67 4 3 7 34	10
11	Salaries Payable				8 5 2 00	11
12	C. P. Komo, Capital				195 9 2 1 14	12
13	C. P. Komo, Drawing			37 4 4 0 00		13
14	Income Summary	115 2 2 6 00	119 4 5 6 00			14
15	Sales		536 3 5 2 40			15
16	Purchases	393 9 3 0 00				16
17	Purchases Returns and Allowances		7 8 2 8 00			17
18	Purchases Discounts		5 7 4 6 00			18
19	Freight In	23 3 5 0 00				19
20	Salary Expense	51 4 0 0 00				20
21	Truck Expense	9 3 4 2 00				21
22	Supplies Expense	2 5 6 4 00				22
23	Insurance Expense	1 9 2 0 00				23
24	Depreciation Expense, Delivery Equipment	2 7 0 0 00				24
25	Depreciation Expense, Store Equipment	2 8 9 6 00				25
26	Miscellaneous Expense	1 4 1 8 00				26
27		604 7 4 6 00	669 3 8 2 40	345 6 8 6 88	281 0 5 0 48	27
28	Net Income	64 6 3 6 40			64 6 3 6 40	28
29		669 3 8 2 40	669 3 8 2 40	345 6 8 6 88	345 6 8 6 88	29

Check Figure

Reversing entry amount, $852

Instructions

1. Journalize the seven adjusting entries.
2. Journalize the closing entries.
3. Journalize the reversing entry.

P.O. 1,2,4,5

Problem 13-4A The following accounts appear in the ledger of The Shirer Company on January 31, the end of this fiscal year:

Cash	$ 5,400
Accounts Receivable	14,100
Merchandise Inventory	55,500
Store Supplies	690
Prepaid Insurance	1,080
Store Equipment	27,900
Accumulated Depreciation, Store Equipment	2,700
Accounts Payable	13,800
Wages Payable	—
M. R. Shirer, Capital	113,620
M. R. Shirer, Drawing	36,000
Income Summary	—
Sales	224,000
Sales Returns and Allowances	3,000
Purchases	170,000
Purchases Returns and Allowances	3,450
Purchases Discounts	2,400
Freight In	7,000
Wages Expense	27,000
Advertising Expense	3,900
Depreciation Expense, Store Equipment	—
Store Supplies Expense	—
Rent Expense	8,400
Insurance Expense	—

The data needed for adjustments on January 31 are as follows:

a–b. Merchandise inventory, January 31, $53,400
c. Store supplies inventory, January 31, $390
d. Insurance expired for the year, $615
e. Depreciation for the year, $6,395
f. Accrued wages on January 31, $1,270

Check Figure

Net loss, $130

Instructions

1. Prepare a work sheet for the fiscal year ended January 31.
2. Prepare an income statement.
3. Prepare a statement of owner's equity. No additional investments were made.
4. Prepare a balance sheet.
5. Journalize the adjusting entries.
6. Journalize the closing entries.
7. Journalize the reversing entry.

Instructions for General Ledger Software

1. Record the adjusting entries in the general journal and print a copy of the entries.
2. Post the general journal amounts to the general ledger.
3. Print an adjusted trial balance and the general ledger after adjustments.
4. Print the income statement, statement of owner's equity, and balance sheet.

5. Record the closing entries in the general journal and print a copy of the entries.
6. Post the general journal amounts to the general ledger.
7. Print a post-closing trial balance.
8. Record the reversing entry in the general journal at the beginning of the next month.

PROBLEM SET B

P.O. 1,4

Problem 13-1B A partial work sheet for The Town Shop is presented here. The merchandise inventory at the beginning of the year was $53,200. C. A. Flagel, the owner, withdrew $26,500 during the year.

The Town Shop
Work Sheet
For Year Ended December 31, 20—

	ACCOUNT NAME	INCOME STATEMENT DEBIT	INCOME STATEMENT CREDIT
21	Sales		328 0 0 0 00
22	Sales Returns and Allowances	4 4 8 0 00	
23	Sales Discounts	3 7 0 7 32	
24	Interest Income		1 8 4 0 00
25	Purchases	199 4 9 0 00	
26	Purchases Returns and Allowances		2 9 8 0 00
27	Freight In	12 7 5 0 00	
28	Wages Expense	43 2 0 0 00	
29	Rent Expense	9 6 0 0 00	
30	Commissions Expense	10 3 2 0 00	
31	Interest Expense	9 6 4 22	
32	Income Summary	53 2 0 0 00	44 3 6 0 00
33	Supplies Expense	8 3 2 46	
34	Insurance Expense	1 0 4 0 00	
35	Depreciation Expense, Equipment	3 6 0 0 00	
36	Depreciation Expense, Building	4 8 0 0 00	
37		347 9 8 4 00	377 1 8 0 00
38	Net Income	29 1 9 6 00	
39		377 1 8 0 00	377 1 8 0 00
40			
41			
42			
43			
44			
45			
46			

P.O. 2,3

Check Figure

Cost of Goods Sold, $218,100

Instructions

1. Prepare an income statement.
2. Journalize the closing entries.

Problem 13-2B Here is the partial work sheet for Westhaven Stereo.

Westhaven Stereo
Work Sheet
For Year Ended December 31, 20—

	ACCOUNT NAME	BALANCE SHEET DEBIT	BALANCE SHEET CREDIT	
1	Cash	12 9 1 5 00		1
2	Notes Receivable	6 3 0 0 00		2
3	Accounts Receivable	33 2 7 0 00		3
4	Merchandise Inventory	55 3 4 4 00		4
5	Supplies	4 2 0 00		5
6	Prepaid Taxes	6 3 0 00		6
7	Prepaid Insurance	5 4 0 00		7
8	Land	7 8 0 0 00		8
9	Building	60 0 0 0 00		9
10	Accumulated Depreciation, Building		18 9 0 0 00	10
11	Store Equipment	4 3 9 2 00		11
12	Accumulated Depreciation, Store Equipment		1 6 7 4 00	12
13	Testing Equipment	7 2 3 0 00		13
14	Accumulated Depreciation, Testing Equipment		5 4 2 4 00	14
15	Delivery Equipment	5 4 0 0 00		15
16	Accumulated Depreciation, Delivery Equipment		4 4 7 0 00	16
17	Notes Payable		4 2 1 5 00	17
18	Accounts Payable		28 1 4 0 00	18
19	Mortgage Payable (current portion)		1 8 0 0 00	19
20	Mortgage Payable		55 2 0 0 00	20
21	C. R. Gonzales, Capital		67 3 1 4 00	21
22	C. R. Gonzales, Drawing	22 4 4 0 00		22
23	Wages Payable		9 8 4 00	23
24		216 6 8 1 00	188 1 2 1 00	24
25	Net Income		28 5 6 0 00	25
26		216 6 8 1 00	216 6 8 1 00	26
27				27
28				28
29				29
30				30

Check Figure

Working capital, $74,280

Instructions

1. Prepare a statement of owner's equity (no additional investment).
2. Prepare a balance sheet.
3. Determine the amount of the working capital.
4. Determine the current ratio (carry to two decimal places).

P.O. 4,5

Problem 13-3B The following partial work sheet covers the affairs of Breski and Company for the year ended June 30:

Breski and Company
Work Sheet
For Year Ended June 30, 20—

	ACCOUNT NAME	INCOME STATEMENT		BALANCE SHEET		
		DEBIT	CREDIT	DEBIT	CREDIT	
1	Cash			28 1 9 6 61		1
2	Accounts Receivable			92 0 0 6 00		2
3	Merchandise Inventory			112 4 0 0 00		3
4	Supplies			8 3 7 39		4
5	Prepaid Insurance			1 2 2 0 00		5
6	Delivery Equipment			12 4 0 0 00		6
7	Accumulated Depreciation, Delivery Equipment				5 8 0 0 00	7
8	Store Equipment			33 4 0 0 00		8
9	Accumulated Depreciation, Store Equipment				9 6 0 0 00	9
10	Accounts Payable				60 2 0 0 00	10
11	Salaries Payable				1 2 4 0 00	11
12	L. Breski, Capital				167 8 2 0 00	12
13	L. Breski, Drawing			28 0 0 0 00		13
14	Income Summary	109 2 0 0 00	112 4 0 0 00			14
15	Sales		520 0 0 0 00			15
16	Purchases	380 0 0 0 00				16
17	Purchases Returns and Allowances		7 6 0 0 00			17
18	Purchases Discounts		4 8 0 0 00			18
19	Freight In	24 0 0 0 00				19
20	Salary Expense	48 0 0 0 00				20
21	Truck Expense	8 6 0 0 00				21
22	Supplies Expense	2 2 0 0 48				22
23	Insurance Expense	1 8 4 0 00				23
24	Depreciation Expense, Delivery Equipment	2 4 0 0 00				24
25	Depreciation Expense, Store Equipment	2 8 0 0 00				25
26	Miscellaneous Expense	1 9 5 9 52				26
27		581 0 0 0 00	644 8 0 0 00	308 4 6 0 00	244 6 6 0 00	27
28	Net Income	63 8 0 0 00			63 8 0 0 00	28
29		644 8 0 0 00	644 8 0 0 00	308 4 6 0 00	308 4 6 0 00	29
30						30
31						31
32						32

Check Figure

Reversing entry amount, $1,240

Instructions

1. Journalize the seven adjusting entries.
2. Journalize the closing entries.
3. Journalize the reversing entry.

P.O. 1,2,4,5

Problem 13-4B The following accounts appear in the ledger of Clark and Company as of June 30, the end of this fiscal year:

Cash	$ 4,349.76
Accounts Receivable	14,910.00
Merchandise Inventory	51,480.00
Store Supplies	735.52
Prepaid Insurance	975.00
Store Equipment	29,640.00
Accumulated Depreciation, Store Equipment	7,880.00
Accounts Payable	11,085.00
Wages Payable	—
D. E. Clark, Capital	102,195.00
D. E. Clark, Drawing	28,260.00
Income Summary	—
Sales	202,630.00
Sales Returns and Allowances	2,640.00
Purchases	137,050.00
Purchases Returns and Allowances	4,395.00
Purchases Discounts	2,565.28
Freight In	9,260.00
Wages Expense	33,100.00
Advertising Expense	8,150.00
Depreciation Expense, Store Equipment	—
Store Supplies Expense	—
Rent Expense	10,200.00
Insurance Expense	—

The data needed for the adjustments on June 30 are as follows:

a–b. Merchandise inventory, June 30, $48,196
c. Store supplies inventory, June 30, $269.20
d. Insurance expired for the year, $640
e. Depreciation for the year, $6,290
f. Accrued wages on June 30, $472

Check Figure

Net loss, $1,962.04

Instructions

1. Prepare a work sheet for the fiscal year ended June 30.
2. Prepare an income statement.
3. Prepare a statement of owner's equity. No additional investments were made during the year.
4. Prepare a balance sheet.
5. Journalize the adjusting entries.
6. Journalize the closing entries.
7. Journalize the reversing entry.

Instructions for General Ledger Software

1. Record the adjusting entries in the general journal and print a copy of the entries.
2. Post the general journal amounts to the general ledger.
3. Print an adjusted trial balance and the general ledger after adjustments.
4. Print the income statement, statement of owner's equity, and balance sheet.
5. Record the closing entries in the general journal and print a copy of the entries.
6. Post the general journal amounts to the general ledger.
7. Print a post-closing trial balance.
8. Record the reversing entry in the general journal at the beginning of the next month.

The Computer Lab

Closing and Financial Statements

It is now July 31, you have journalized and posted the adjustments, and Mr. Kennedy wants to compare the results of these last two months to those of May.

Here is a copy of the trial balance after adjustments—you may prepare the closing entries from this trial balance or from the general ledger. (If your software package makes them automatically, just be sure you have all your financial statements printed, and that they make sense.)

> That would mean I must print out the financial statements (income statement, statement of owner's equity, balance sheet) and back up (make a copy of) my data before recording the four closing entries. That way, if an error is found after closing, I can return to the backup data, correct the error, reprint the financials, and then close. (Note: Some general ledger packages do the closing entries automatically while still allowing you to return to prior periods.) Of course, I need to print a post-closing trial balance to see if debits and credits still equal each other and that all temporary-equity accounts have been closed.

Jeep Jockeys

Adjusted Trial Balance

July 31, 20—

	Debit	Credit
Cash	48,349.93	
Accounts Receivable	19,692.98	
Merchandise Inventory	3,978.00	
Prepaid Insurance	1,350.00	
Supplies	24.00	
Office Equipment	759.00	
Accumulated Depreciation, Office Equipment		33.96
Vehicles	46,000.00	
Accumulated Depreciation, Vehicles		3,750.00
Kiosk Equipment	1,457.69	
Accumulated Depreciation, Kiosk Equipment		44.07
Accounts Payable		7,537.88
H. Kennedy, Capital		63,952.68
H. Kennedy, Drawing	1,600.00	
Income Summary		3,978.00
Tour Revenue		58,329.00
Sales		10,084.08
Sales Returns and Allowances	214.87	
Purchases	6,408.00	
Purchases Returns and Allowances		36.00
Freight In	364.23	
Wages Expense	12,163.00	
Rent Expense	640.00	
Supplies Expense	39.00	
Advertising Expense	1,231.26	
Utilities Expense	180.00	
Accounting and Legal Expense	300.00	
Insurance Expense	300.00	
Depreciation Expense, Vehicles	2,500.00	
Depreciation Expense, Office Equipment	22.64	
Depreciation Expense, Kiosk Equipment	44.07	
Miscellaneous Expense	127.00	
	147,745.67	147,745.67

After closing is done, assemble the following printouts:

Income statement
Statement of owner's equity
Balance sheet
Journal page containing the closing entries
General ledger
Post-closing trial balance

Before a Test Check: Chapters 12–13

PART I: Completion

Complete each of the following statements by writing the appropriate word(s) in the spaces provided.

1. An actual count of a stock of goods is called a(n) _____.

2. Under the _____ system, entries to record the purchase of merchandise are recorded in the Merchandise Inventory account.

3. Unearned revenue is classified as a(n) _____.

4. Under the periodic inventory system, the first adjustment is to debit _____ for the amount of the beginning inventory.

5. Under the perpetual inventory system, after recording the sale of the goods, the accountant debits the _____ account and credits _____.

6. An increase in Rent Expense results in a(n) _____ to net income.

7. Gross Profit is calculated by subtracting _____ from Net Sales.

8. Current Assets minus Current Liabilities equals _____.

9. Gross Profit minus Total Operating Expenses equals _____.

10. Net Purchases plus _____ equals Delivered Cost of Purchases.

PART II: True/False

T	F	1. The second adjustment for Merchandise Inventory under the periodic inventory system is to debit Cost of Goods Sold and credit Merchandise Inventory.
T	F	2. Unearned Rent Income is classified as a revenue.
T	F	3. The perpetual inventory system requires that each sale of goods has two entries: one to reduce inventory and affix the cost of the goods sold and one to record the sale.
T	F	4. The periodic inventory system requires two adjusting entries: one to remove the old inventory amount and one to enter the latest inventory amount.
T	F	5. The adjustment to unearned revenue allows the correct amount of liability and revenue to be applied to each fiscal period involved.
T	F	6. Freight In is classified in the Operating Expenses section of an income statement.
T	F	7. Under the perpetual inventory system, the cost of goods sold is calculated by subtracting ending inventory from the cost of goods available for sale.
T	F	8. Reversing entries are optional, and only some adjusting entries are reversed.

Note: Answers to Before a Test Check begin on page A-1.

T   F   9. Delivery Expense is added to net purchases to arrive at delivered cost of purchases.

T   F   10. Purchases Returns and Allowances increases Income from Operations.

PART III: Application

1. Alphonse Company uses the periodic inventory system. Employees have just taken a physical count of its inventory. This ending inventory has been valued at $136,000. The company's accounting records show the Merchandise Inventory account with a debit balance of $132,000. Journalize the entries on December 31 to adjust the records for this situation.

2. Regletto Company uses the perpetual inventory system. Employees have just taken a physical count of its inventory. This ending inventory has been valued at $146,000. The company's accounting records show the Merchandise Inventory account with a debit balance of $148,000. Journalize the entry on December 31 to adjust the records for this situation.

3. On December 1, Wesley Company collected $20,000 for a remodeling job that will be completed on March 31 of the following year. Wesley Company's fiscal period ends December 31. Make the entries to record the collection of the cash and the year-end adjustment to reflect the amount of revenue earned in December.

4. Yorkland Company has total assets of $250,000, of which noncurrent assets amount to $140,000. The company also has total liabilities of $130,000, of which $80,000 are long-term liabilities. Calculate (a) working capital and (b) current ratio.

Comprehensive Review Problem

You are to record transactions completed by Fine Fabrics during the month of February of this year. This company is located in Dallas. To gain practice in completing the steps in the accounting cycle, assume that the fiscal period consists of one month.

CHART OF ACCOUNTS

Assets

111 Cash
112 Petty Cash Fund
113 Accounts Receivable
114 Merchandise Inventory
117 Supplies
118 Prepaid Insurance
122 Equipment
123 Accumulated Depreciation, Equipment

Liabilities

221 Accounts Payable
226 Employees' Income Tax Payable
227 FICA Tax Payable
228 State Unemployment Tax Payable
229 Federal Unemployment Tax Payable
230 Salaries Payable

Owner's Equity

311 J. L. Fisher, Capital
312 J. L. Fisher, Drawing
313 Income Summary

Revenue

411 Sales
412 Sales Returns and Allowances

Cost of Goods Sold

511 Purchases
512 Purchases Returns and Allowances
513 Purchases Discounts
514 Freight In

Operating Expenses

611 Salary Expense
612 Payroll Tax Expense
613 Rent Expense
614 Utilities Expense
616 Supplies Expense
617 Insurance Expense
618 Depreciation Expense, Equipment
619 Miscellaneous Expense

JOURNALS

Sales Journal, page 56
Purchases Journal, page 62
Cash Receipts Journal, page 69
Cash Payments Journal, page 75
General Journal, pages 89–92

ACCOUNTS RECEIVABLE

Hotel Bentnor
Jerome and Woods
Wilkes Decorators

ACCOUNTS PAYABLE

Byran, Inc.
Keller Textiles
Meldon Fabrics
Taylor Manufacturing Company

TRANSACTIONS

The following transactions were completed during February of this year.

Feb. 1 Reversed the adjusting entry for accrued salaries, $710.

1 Sold merchandise on account to Hotel Bentnor, $13,052.97, invoice no. 5221.

2 Issued Ck. No. 7216, $17,271.62, to Keller Textiles, in payment of its invoice no. D1739 for $17,624.10 less 2 percent discount.

5 Bought merchandise on account from Meldon Fabrics, $4,551.90; invoice no. RE275, dated February 2; terms 1/10, n/30; FOB Orlando; freight prepaid and added to the invoice, $147 (total, $4,698.90).

5 Received an electric bill and paid Regional Power, Ck. No. 7217, $121.

6 Received check from Jerome and Woods for $11,619.50 in payment of account.

7 Issued Ck. No. 7218, $9,519.84, to Meldon Fabrics, in payment of its invoice no. RE64 for $9,616 less 1 percent discount.

9 Cash sales for February 1 through February 9, $7,951.60.

12 **Recorded the payroll in the payroll register** for regular semimonthly salaries for period ended February 12. Salaries: M. B. Corson, $2,730; K. L. Vickers, $2,240. Income tax withholdings are $382.20 for Corson and $313.60 for Vickers. Assume the following tax rates and taxable earnings limits (see payroll register for beginning cumulative earnings):

- Social Security taxable earnings, $84,900, with a rate of 6.2 percent.
- Medicare taxable earnings, all earnings, with a rate of 1.45 percent.

12 Recorded the payroll entry in the general journal, crediting Salaries Payable.

Feb. 12 Issued Ck. No. 7219, $2,138.95, to M. B. Corson. Issued Ck. No. 7220, $1,755.04, to K. L. Vickers. Use two lines and debit Salaries Payable. (Verify these amounts.)

12 Recorded payroll taxes. Assume the following tax rates and taxable earnings:

- Federal unemployment taxable earnings, $7,000, with a rate of 0.8 percent.
- State unemployment taxable earnings, $7,000, with a rate of 5.4 percent. *Note:* Corson's taxable earnings for unemployment amount to $1,540 and Vickers's amount to $2,240.

12 Received a credit memo from Meldon Fabrics for defective merchandise, $542, credit memo no. 916.

14 Issued Ck. No. 7221, $2,912.44, to State Bank for monthly deposit of January employees' federal income tax withheld, $1,391.60, and FICA taxes, $1,520.84.

14 Sold merchandise on account to Jerome and Woods, $15,692.50, invoice no. 5222.

14 Issued Ck. No. 7222, $4,116.80, to Meldon Fabrics in payment of its invoice no. RE275 less the credit memo for defective merchandise and less the discount ($40.10). *Note:* Debit Accounts Payable, $4,156.90, and credit Purchases Discounts, $40.10. Verify these amounts: $4,698.90, less $147 freight, less $542 return, less 1 percent cash discount (cash discounts can't be taken on freight). Remember to add $147 freight back to compute the cash credit.

18 Bought merchandise on account from Byran, Inc., $20,488.20; invoice no. 164M, dated February 14; terms 2/10, n/30; FOB Miami; freight prepaid and added to the invoice, $1,152 (total, $21,640.20).

18 Cash sales for February 10 through February 18, $7,994.14.

19 Issued Ck. No. 7223 payable to Faster Printing for invoice forms, $327 (not previously recorded). (Debit Supplies.)

19 Received check from Wilkes Decorators for $4,920.14 in payment of account.

22 Issued Ck. No. 7224, $12,710, to Taylor Manufacturing Company, in payment of its invoice no. 9264D.

22 Sold merchandise on account to Wilkes Decorators, $16,721.42, invoice no. 5223.

24 Issued credit memo no. 214 to Wilkes Decorators, $156, for merchandise returned.

24 Bought merchandise on account from Keller Textiles, $16,448.01; invoice no. D1797, dated February 22; terms 2/10, n/30; FOB Dallas.

26 **Recorded the payroll in the payroll register** for regular semi-monthly salaries for period ended February 26. Salaries: M. B. Corson, $2,730; K. L. Vickers, $2,240. Income tax withholdings are $382.20 for Corson and $313.60 for Vickers. *Note:* See the entry of February 12 for taxable earnings limits and tax rates. See payroll register for beginning cumulative earnings.

26 Recorded the payroll entry in the general journal, crediting Salaries Payable.

26 Issued Ck. No. 7225, $2,138.95, to M. B. Corson. Issued Ck. No. 7226, $1,755.04, to K. L. Vickers. Use two lines and debit Salaries Payable.

Feb. 26 Ck. No. 7227 voided.

26 Recorded payroll taxes. *Note:* Vickers's taxable earnings for unemployment amount to $280.

27 Issued Ck. No. 7228, $994, to Greater Freight Line for transportation charge on merchandise purchased from Keller Textiles.

28 Issued Ck. No. 7229, $48.63, payable to Cash to reimburse the petty cash fund. Petty cash payments consist of Supplies, $27.16, and Miscellaneous Expense, $21.47.

28 Cash sales for February 19 through February 28, $7,685.20.

28 Issued Ck. No. 7230, $650, to Grandy Realty for monthly rent.

28 J. L. Fisher (owner) withdrew $3,000 for personal use, Ck. No. 7231.

INSTRUCTIONS

1. Journalize and post the transactions completed during February.

   a. Post the amounts in the Other Accounts columns of the special journals daily.
   b. Post the general journal daily.
   c. Post the totals of the special columns of the special journals at the end of the month.

2. Prepare a schedule of accounts receivable and a schedule of accounts payable.
3. Complete the work sheet for February.
   Data for the month-end adjustments are as follows:

   a–b. Merchandise inventory at February 28, $44,262
   c. Salaries accrued at February 28, $710
   d. Supplies inventory at February 28, $472
   e. Insurance expired during February, $40
   f. Depreciation of equipment during February, $105

4. Journalize and post the adjusting entries.
5. Prepare an income statement.
6. Prepare a statement of owner's equity. (No additional investment was made during the month.)
7. Prepare a balance sheet.
8. Journalize and post the closing entries.
9. Prepare a post-closing trial balance.

INSTRUCTIONS FOR GENERAL LEDGER SOFTWARE

1. Journalize and post the transactions completed during February.
2. Print the journals and the general ledger.
3. Print a trial balance.
4. Print a schedule of accounts receivable and a schedule of accounts payable.

5. Journalize and post the month-end adjustments:

   a–b. Merchandise inventory at February 28, $44,262
   c. Salaries accrued at February 28, $710
   d. Supplies inventory at February 28, $472
   e. Insurance expired during February, $40
   f. Depreciation of equipment during February, $105

6. Print the adjusting entries, an adjusted trial balance, and the general ledger after adjustments.
7. Print the income statement, the statement of owner's equity, and the balance sheet.
8. Journalize and post the closing entries.
9. Print the closing entries.
10. Print a post-closing trial balance.

C Inventory Methods

Performance Objectives

After you have completed this appendix, you will be able to do the following:

1. Determine the amount of the ending merchandise inventory by the weighted-average-cost method.

2. Determine the amount of the ending merchandise inventory by the first-in, first-out method.

3. Determine the amount of the ending merchandise inventory by the last-in, first-out method.

To determine the dollar amount of the ending merchandise inventory, it is necessary to take a physical count of the various items in stock and match them up with their costs. In other words, the ending inventory consists of the number of units of each type of item on hand multiplied by the cost of each unit.

If each unit were purchased at exactly the same price, the job of determining the total cost of the inventory would be simple. For example, if there are 100 units of Product A on hand, and all 100 units were bought at $15, the total cost of the ending inventory is $1,500 (100 × $15). However, over a period of time, costs of individual purchases of units may differ. Changes in costs of individual units make the different methods of inventory valuation necessary.

We will use Coe Appliances, a distributor of dishwashers, to illustrate the three methods of inventory valuation. Coe's ending inventory consists of 176 Model M43 dishwashers acquired through various purchases, as follows:

Specific Purchase	Number of Units	Cost per Unit	Total Cost
Beginning inventory	34	$270	$ 9,180
First purchase	60	282	16,920
Second purchase	256	298	76,288
Third purchase	164	312	51,168
Total units available	514		$153,556

Of the 514 units available for sale, 176 units are still on hand and 338 have been sold (514−176).

Coe Appliances may choose any one of the following three methods of recording the total cost of the 176 units in the ending inventory of dishwashers.

WEIGHTED-AVERAGE-COST METHOD

OBJECTIVE 1
Determine the amount of the ending merchandise inventory by the weighted-average-cost method.

$$\text{Average Cost per Unit} = \frac{\text{Total Cost}}{\text{Total Units Available}} = \frac{\$153,556}{514} = \$298.75 \text{ (rounded)}$$

Cost of 176 units = $298.75 × 176 units = $52,580

Cost of 338 units sold = $298.75 × 338 units = $100,976 (rounded)

FIRST-IN, FIRST-OUT METHOD

OBJECTIVE 2
Determine the amount of the ending merchandise inventory by the first-in, first-out method.

This method is based on the **assumption** that the first units of dishwashers purchased will be sold first. The costs of the units left will be those of the most recently purchased units. You may think of this as the way a grocery store sells milk. Because milk will sour, the oldest milk is moved to the front of the display shelf and is sold first. Consequently, the cartons of milk remaining on the shelf are the freshest milk.

Relating to our illustration of dishwashers:

Specific Purchase	Number of Units	Cost per Unit	Total Cost
Beginning inventory	34	$270	$ 9,180
First purchase	60	282	16,920
Second purchase	256	298	76,288
Third purchase	164	312	51,168
Total units available	514		$153,556

The cost of the 176 dishwashers on hand (most recently purchased) is as follows:

164 units (third purchase) @ $312 each = $51,168
12 units (second purchase) @ $298 each =   3,576
176 units $54,744

LAST-IN, FIRST-OUT METHOD

OBJECTIVE 3
Determine the amount of the ending merchandise inventory by the last-in, first-out method.

This method is based on the **assumption** that the last units of dishwashers purchased will be sold first. The costs of the units left over will be those of the earliest purchased units. You may think of this as the way a coal yard sells coal. When the coal yard sells coal to its customers, it takes coal off the top of the pile. Consequently, the tons of coal in the ending inventory consist of those first few tons at the bottom of the pile.

Relating to our illustration of dishwashers shown above, the cost of the 176 dishwashers on hand (earliest purchased) is as follows:

34 units (beginning inventory) @ $270 each = $ 9,180
60 units (first purchase)   @ $282 each =   16,920
82 units (second purchase)   @ $298 each =   24,436
176 units $50,536

Comparison of Three Methods		
Method	Ending Inventory (176 units)	Cost of Goods Sold (Goods Available for Sale − Ending Inventory) (338 units = 514 − 176)
Weighted-average-cost	$52,580	$100,976 ($153,556 − $52,580)
First-in, first-out	54,744	98,812 ($153,556 − $54,744)
Last-in, first-out	50,536	103,020 ($153,556 − $50,536)

Assume that the dishwashers were sold for $380 each.

	Weighted-Average-Cost	First-in, First-out	Last-in, First-out
Sales (338 units × $380 each)	$128,440	$128,440	$128,440
Cost of Goods Sold	100,976	98,812	103,020
Gross Profit	$ 27,464	$ 29,628	$ 25,420

PROBLEMS

P.O. 1
Check Figure
Cost of ending inventory, $279.24

Problem C-1 Bermingham Nursery sells bark to its customers at retail. Bermingham buys bark from a plywood mill in bulk and transports the bark in its own trucks. Information relating to the beginning inventory and purchases of bark is as follows:

Beginning inventory   1,500 cubic yards @ $0.20 per cubic yard
First purchase   2,100 cubic yards @ $0.22 per cubic yard
Second purchase   1,400 cubic yards @ $0.26 per cubic yard
Third purchase   1,000 cubic yards @ $0.27 per cubic yard

Find the cost of 1,200 cubic yards in the ending inventory by the weighted-average-cost method. Carry average cost per cubic yard to four decimals.

P.O. 2
Check Figure
Cost of ending inventory, $322

Problem C-2 Using the information presented in Problem C-1, find the cost of the ending inventory by the first-in, first-out method.

P.O. 3
Check Figure
Cost of ending inventory, $240

Problem C-3 Using the information presented in Problem C-1, find the cost of the ending inventory by the last-in, first-out method.

D Financial Statement Analysis

Performance Objectives

After you have completed this appendix, you will be able to do the following:

1. Determine gross profit percentage.

2. Determine merchandise inventory turnover.

3. Determine accounts receivable turnover.

4. Determine return on investment.

A n important function of accounting is to provide tools for interpreting the financial statements or the results of operations. This appendix presents a number of percentages and ratios that are frequently used to analyze financial statements.

GROSS PROFIT PERCENTAGE

OBJECTIVE 1
Determine gross profit percentage.

DeClerk Card Shop will serve as our example (see the comparative income statement on the next page).

For each year, net sales is the base (100 percent). All other items on the income statement can be expressed as a percentage of net sales for the particular year involved. For example, let's look at the following percentages:

$$\text{Gross Profit \% (2004)} = \frac{\text{Gross Profit for 2004}}{\text{Net Sales for 2004}} = \frac{\$150,000}{\$428,000} = 0.35 = 35\%$$

$$\text{Gross Profit \% (2003)} = \frac{\text{Gross Profit for 2003}}{\text{Net Sales for 2003}} = \frac{\$152,000}{\$400,000} = 0.38 = 38\%$$

$$\text{Sales Salary Expense \% (2004)} = \frac{\text{Sales Salary Expense for 2004}}{\text{Net Sales for 2004}}$$

$$= \frac{\$63,600}{\$428,000} = 0.1486 = 15\%$$

$$\text{Sales Salary Expense \% (2003)} = \frac{\text{Sales Salary Expense for 2003}}{\text{Net Sales for 2003}}$$

$$= \frac{\$58,000}{\$400,000} = 0.145 = 14.5\%$$

Here's how you might interpret a few of the percentages:

2004

• For every $100 in net sales, gross profit amounted to $35.
• For every $100 in net sales, sales salary expense amounted to $15.
• For every $100 in net sales, net income amounted to $4.

DeClerk Card Shop
Comparative Income Statement
For Years Ended January 31, 2004, and January 31, 2003

	2004		2003	
	AMOUNT	PERCENT	AMOUNT	PERCENT
Revenue from Sales:				
Sales	$ 453 6 0 0 00	106	$ 420 0 0 0 00	105
Less Sales Returns and Allowances	25 6 0 0 00	6	20 0 0 0 00	5
Net Sales	$ 428 0 0 0 00	100	$ 400 0 0 0 00	100
Cost of Goods Sold:				
Merchandise Inventory, February 1	$ 116 0 0 0 00	27	$ 64 0 0 0 00	16
Delivered Cost of Purchases	320 0 0 0 00	75	300 0 0 0 00	75
Cost of Goods Available for Sale	$ 436 0 0 0 00	102	$ 364 0 0 0 00	91
Less Merchandise Inventory, January 31	158 0 0 0 00	37	116 0 0 0 00	29
Cost of Goods Sold	$ 278 0 0 0 00	65	$ 248 0 0 0 00	62
Gross Profit	$ 150 0 0 0 00	35	$ 152 0 0 0 00	38
Operating Expenses:				
Sales Salary Expense	$ 63 6 0 0 00	15	$ 58 0 0 0 00	14.5
Rent Expense	24 0 0 0 00	6	24 0 0 0 00	6
Advertising Expense	21 4 0 0 00	5	16 0 0 0 00	4
Depreciation Expense, Equipment	20 0 0 0 00	5	18 0 0 0 00	4.5
Insurance Expense	2 0 0 0 00	0.5	2 0 0 0 00	0.5
Store Supplies Expense	1 0 0 0 00	—	1 0 0 0 00	—
Miscellaneous Expense	1 0 0 0 00	—	1 0 0 0 00	—
Total Operating Expenses	$ 133 0 0 0 00	31	$ 120 0 0 0 00	30
Net Income	$ 17 0 0 0 00	4	$ 32 0 0 0 00	8

2003

- For every $100 in net sales, gross profit amounted to $38.
- For every $100 in net sales, sales salary expense amounted to $14.50.
- For every $100 in net sales, net income amounted to $8.

The gross profit percentage declined from 38% in 2003 to 35% in 2004 because the Cost of Goods Sold percentage increased from 62% in 2003 to 65% in 2004.

MERCHANDISE INVENTORY TURNOVER

OBJECTIVE 2
Determine merchandise inventory turnover.

Merchandise inventory turnover is the number of times a firm's average inventory is sold during a given year.

$$\text{Merchandise Inventory Turnover} = \frac{\text{Cost of Goods Sold}}{\text{Average Merchandise Inventory}}$$

$$\text{Average Merchandise Inventory} = \frac{\text{Beginning Merchandise Inventory} + \text{Ending Merchandise Inventory}}{2}$$

	2004	**2003**
Beginning Merchandise Inventory (from the Cost of Goods Sold section of the income statement)	$116,000	$ 64,000
Ending Merchandise Inventory (from the Cost of Goods Sold section of the income statement or the balance sheet)	158,000	116,000

2004

$$\text{Average Merchandise Inventory} = \frac{\$116,000 + \$158,000}{2} = \frac{\$274,000}{2} = \underline{\underline{\$137,000}}$$

$$\text{Merchandise Inventory Turnover} = \frac{\$278,000}{\$137,000} = \underline{\underline{2.03}} \text{ times per year}$$

2003

$$\text{Average Merchandise Inventory} = \frac{\$64,000 + \$116,000}{2} = \frac{\$180,000}{2} = \underline{\underline{\$90,000}}$$

$$\text{Merchandise Inventory Turnover} = \frac{\$248,000}{\$90,000} = \underline{\underline{2.76}} \text{ times per year}$$

With each turnover of merchandise, the company makes a gross profit, so the higher the turnover, the better.

The inventory turnover deteriorated from 2.76 in 2003 to 2.03 in 2004 because the beginning inventory in 2003 of $64,000 nearly doubled to $116,000 at the end of 2003 and increased to $158,000 at the end of 2004. Over the same period net sales increased only 7% from $400,000 in 2003 to $428,000 in 2004.

ACCOUNTS RECEIVABLE TURNOVER

OBJECTIVE 3
Determine accounts receivable turnover.

Accounts receivable turnover is the number of times charge accounts are turned over (paid off) during a given year. A turnover implies a sale on account followed by the cash collection of the amount owed to us.

$$\text{Accounts Receivable Turnover} = \frac{\text{Net Sales on Account}}{\text{Average Accounts Receivable}}$$

$$\text{Average Accounts Receivable} = \frac{\text{Beginning Accounts Receivable} + \text{Ending Accounts Receivable}}{2}$$

Going back to DeClerk Card Shop, let's assume the following information for 2004 and 2003.

	2004	**2003**
Net sales on account (from the sales journal)	$330,000	$302,000
Beginning accounts receivable (from Accounts Receivable account)	39,680	37,500
Ending accounts receivable (from Accounts Receivable account)	45,840	39,680

2004

$$\text{Average Accounts Receivable} = \frac{\$39,680 + \$45,840}{2} = \frac{\$85,520}{2} = \$42,760$$

$$\text{Accounts Receivable Turnover} = \frac{\$330,000}{\$42,760} = 7.72 \text{ times per year}$$

2003

$$\text{Average Accounts Receivable} = \frac{\$37,500 + \$39,680}{2} = \frac{\$77,180}{2} = \$38,590$$

$$\text{Accounts Receivable Turnover} = \frac{\$302,000}{\$38,590} = 7.83 \text{ times per year}$$

A lower turnover rate indicates that a firm is experiencing greater difficulty in collecting charge accounts. In addition, more investment capital is tied up in accounts receivable.

The receivable turnover deteriorated slightly from 7.83 in 2003 to 7.72 in 2004, possibly because the seller granted easier credit terms or the buyers incurred cash flow problems because of a declining economy. From the end of 2003 to the end of 2004, the receivables balance increased almost 16% from $39,680 to $45,840. However, over the same period net sales increased only 7%. This provides further evidence of the company's deteriorating financial condition.

RETURN ON INVESTMENT (YIELD)

OBJECTIVE 4
Determine return on investment.

Return on investment represents the earning power of the owner's investment in the business.

$$\text{Return on Investment} = \frac{\text{Net Income for the Year}}{\text{Average Capital}}$$

$$\text{Average Capital} = \frac{\text{Beginning Capital} + \text{Ending Capital}}{2}$$

Getting back to DeClerk Card Shop, let's assume the following information for 2004 and 2003:

	2004	2003
Beginning balance of owner's Capital account	$176,920	$181,440
Ending balance of owner's Capital account	184,780	176,920

2004

$$\text{Average Capital} = \frac{\$176,920 + \$184,780}{2} = \frac{\$361,700}{2} = \$180,850$$

$$\text{Return on Investment} = \frac{\$17,000}{\$180,850} = .094 = 9.4\%$$

2003

$$\text{Average Capital} = \frac{\$181,440 + \$176,920}{2} = \frac{\$358,360}{2} = \underline{\$179,180}$$

$$\text{Return on Investment} = \frac{\$32,000}{\$179,180} = .179 = \underline{17.9\%}$$

As a result, we can state the following:

- In 2004, for an average investment of $100, the business earned $9.40.
- In 2003, for an average investment of $100, the business earned $17.90.

The return on investment deteriorated from 17.9% in 2003 to 9.4% in 2004 because net income declined 47% from $32,000 in 2003 to $17,000 in 2004.

▮ PROBLEMS

P.O. 1

Problem D-1 Ross Company's abbreviated comparative income statement for years 2004 and 2003 is as follows:

Ross Company
Comparative Income Statement
For Years Ended December 31, 2004 and December 31, 2003

	2004	2003
Net Sales	$ 487 2 0 0 00	$ 462 0 0 0 00
Cost of Goods Sold	287 4 0 0 00	277 2 0 0 00
Gross Profit	$ 199 8 0 0 00	$ 184 8 0 0 00
Total Operating Expenses	152 2 4 0 00	146 1 6 0 00
Net Income	$ 47 5 6 0 00	$ 38 6 4 0 00

Check Figure

Net income % (2003), 8.4%

Instructions

1. For the years 2004 and 2003, determine gross profit as a percentage of net sales.
2. For the years 2004 and 2003, determine net income as a percentage of net sales.

P.O. 2

Problem D-2 Ross Company's merchandise inventory figures are:

	2004	2003
Beginning merchandise inventory (January 1)	$ 88,420	$106,110
Purchases	302,190	259,510
Ending merchandise inventory (December 31)	103,210	88,420

Check Figure

Merchandise inventory turnover (2004), 3 times

Instructions

Determine the merchandise inventory turnover for the years 2004 and 2003.

P.O. 4

Problem D-3 A. L. Ross, Capital, account balances are as follows:

January 1, 2003	$375,670
January 1, 2004	493,970
December 31, 2004	526,820

Check Figure

Return on investment (2003),
8.9%

Instructions

Determine the return on investment for the years 2004 and 2003 if net income is $47,560 for 2004 and $38,640 for 2003.

The Statement of Cash Flows

Performance Objectives

After you have completed this appendix, you will be able to do the following:

1. Classify cash flows as Operating Activities, Investing Activities, and Financing Activities.

2. Prepare a statement of cash flows.

The fourth major financial statement is the statement of cash flows. This statement explains in detail how the balance of Cash has changed between the beginning and the end of the fiscal period. Some accountants refer to the statement as the "where got, where gone" statement of cash.

SECTIONS OF THE STATEMENT OF CASH FLOWS

OBJECTIVE 1
Classify cash flows as Operating Activities, Investing Activities, and Financing Activities.

The statement has three main sections: Operating Activities, Investing Activities, and Financing Activities. Cash flows are subdivided as cash inflows and cash outflows.

Operating Activities

This section covers cash received and used in carrying out the company's operations.

Cash Inflows

- Cash from selling of services or merchandise
- Cash from collection of miscellaneous income

Cash Outflows

- Payments for purchases of merchandise and supplies from suppliers
- Payments of salaries or wages
- Payments of rent, utilities, insurance
- Payment of interest to creditors

Investing Activities

This section covers cash used in or received from buying or selling of plant and equipment assets and all other noncurrent assets, such as long-term investments.

Cash Inflows

- Cash received from the sale of noncurrent assets

Cash Outflows

- Cash payments to buy noncurrent assets

Financing Activities

This section covers cash related to changes in the owner's equity accounts and long-term liabilities accounts.

Cash Inflows

- Investment of cash by the owner
- Borrowing from creditors

Cash Outflows

- Withdrawals of cash by the owner
- Repayment of loans to creditors

FINANCIAL STATEMENTS NEEDED FOR PREPARING THE STATEMENT OF CASH FLOWS

The financial statements required for preparing the statement of cash flows consist of the income statement and statement of owner's equity for the fiscal period, the balance sheet at the end of the fiscal period, and the balance sheet at the end of the previous fiscal period. Using the two balance sheets, we can prepare a comparative balance sheet for the two fiscal periods, showing the increases and decreases in the various accounts.

ILLUSTRATION OF THE STATEMENT OF CASH FLOWS

OBJECTIVE 2

Prepare a statement of cash flows.

The financial statements for Morrow Company are shown here. To save space, we present the comparative balance sheet. Based on the comparative balance sheet, the first step is to record the increases and decreases in the accounts.

Morrow Company
Income Statement
For Year Ended December 31, 2004

Revenue from Sales:			
Net Sales	$ 647 0 0 0 00		
Less Cost of Goods Sold	500 0 0 0 00		
Gross Profit		$ 147 0 0 0 00	
Operating Expenses:			
Salary Expense	$ 70 0 0 0 00		
Rent Expense	10 0 0 0 00		
Depreciation Expense, Equipment	6 0 0 0 00		
Supplies Expense	1 0 0 0 00		
Total Operating Expenses		87 0 0 0 00	
Net Income		$ 60 0 0 0 00	

Morrow Company
Statement of Owner's Equity
For Year Ended December 31, 2004

B. Morrow, Capital, January 1, 2004		$ 120 0 0 0 00
Additional Investment, March 2, 2004		10 0 0 0 00
Total Investment		$ 130 0 0 0 00
Net Income for the Year	$60 0 0 0 00	
Less Withdrawals for the Year	50 0 0 0 00	
Increase in Capital		10 0 0 0 00
B. Morrow, Capital, Dec. 31, 2004		$ 140 0 0 0 00

Morrow Company
Comparative Balance Sheet
December 31, 2004, and December 31, 2003

	2004	2003	INCREASE (DECREASE)
Assets			
Cash	$ 12 0 0 0 00	$ 7 0 0 0 00	$ 5 0 0 0 00
Accounts Receivable	70 0 0 0 00	66 0 0 0 00	4 0 0 0 00
Merchandise Inventory	120 0 0 0 00	113 0 0 0 00	7 0 0 0 00
Supplies	3 0 0 0 00	4 0 0 0 00	(1 0 0 0 00)
Equipment	$72 0 0 0 00	$60 0 0 0 00	12 0 0 0 00
Less Accumulated Deprec.	(62 0 0 0 00) 10 0 0 0 00	(56 0 0 0 00) 4 0 0 0 00	(6 0 0 0 00)
Total Assets	$ 215 0 0 0 00	$ 194 0 0 0 00	$21 0 0 0 00
Liabilities			
Accounts Payable	$71 0 0 0 00	$69 0 0 0 00	$ 2 0 0 0 00
Salaries Payable	4 0 0 0 00	5 0 0 0 00	(1 0 0 0 00)
Total Liabilities	$ 75 0 0 0 00	$ 74 0 0 0 00	$ 1 0 0 0 00
Owner's Equity			
B. Morrow, Capital	140 0 0 0 00	120 0 0 0 00	20 0 0 0 00
Total Liabilities and Owner's Equity	$ 215 0 0 0 00	$ 194 0 0 0 00	$21 0 0 0 00

Note the $5,000 increase in Cash. First let's see how this increase comes about.

- Cash flows related to operating activities involve changes in current asset and current liability accounts.
- Cash flows related to investing activities involve changes in plant and equipment (long-term asset) accounts (with the exception of Accumulated Depreciation).
- Cash flows related to financing activities involve changes in owner's equity accounts and long-term liabilities accounts.

Now let's present the statement of cash flows.

Morrow Company
Statement of Cash Flows
For Year Ended December 31, 2004

Cash Flows from (Used by) Operating Activities		
Net Income	$ 60 0 0 0 00	
Add (Deduct) Items to Convert Net Income from Accrual Basis to Cash Basis		
Depreciation Expense	6 0 0 0 00	
Increase in Accounts Receivable	(4 0 0 0 00)	
Increase in Merchandise Inventory	(7 0 0 0 00)	
Decrease in Supplies	1 0 0 0 00	
Increase in Accounts Payable	2 0 0 0 00	
Decrease in Salaries Payable	(1 0 0 0 00)	
Net Cash Flows from Operating Activities		$ 57 0 0 0 00
Cash Flows from (Used by) Investing Activities		
Purchase of Equipment	$ (12 0 0 0 00)	
Net Cash Flows Used by Investing Activities		(12 0 0 0 00)
Cash Flows from (Used by) Financing Activities		
Cash Investment by Owner	$ 10 0 0 0 00	
Cash Withdrawals by Owner	(50 0 0 0 00)	
Net Cash Flows Used by Financing Activities		(40 0 0 0 00)
Net Increase (Decrease) in Cash		$ 5 0 0 0 00

EXPLANATION OF ITEMS IN THE STATEMENT OF CASH FLOWS

Cash Flows from Operating Activities

- Net income of $60,000, from the income statement, included such items as sale of services or merchandise, miscellaneous income, and payment of expenses such as salaries or wages, utilities, and interest.
- Depreciation of $6,000 was included as an expense on the income statement, but it did not result in the payment of cash to anyone. Since depreciation expense was deducted on the income statement, we now add $6,000 back in. Depreciation expense is always an addition under Cash Flows from Operating Activities.
- Accounts Receivable increased by $4,000. Of the amount shown as Sales on the income statement, $4,000 was in the form of additional charge account balances and therefore were not cash inflows. So we deduct $4,000 from Cash Flows from Operating Activities.
- Merchandise Inventory increased by $7,000. Because the inventory increased by $7,000 during the year (more merchandise was bought than was sold), we can assume that the change resulted in a $7,000 decrease in Cash Flows from Operating Activities.
- Decrease in Supplies of $1,000 means that the company used up supplies bought in a previous fiscal period and included the entire amount of supplies used as Supplies Expense on the income statement. In other words, the $1,000 of Supplies Expense shown on the income statement did not result in a payment of cash in the current period.
- Increase in Accounts Payable of $2,000 in this case means that $2,000 of the amount listed as Purchases on the income statement (not shown

because we included Purchases in Cost of Goods Sold) did not result in the payment of cash. So we add $2,000 to Cash Flows from Operating Activities.
- Decrease in Salaries Payable of $1,000 means that the amount listed as Salary Expense on the income statement is $1,000 less than the amount of cash spent by the company. So we deduct $1,000 from Cash Flows from Operating Activities.

Cash Flows from Investing Activities

Equipment increased by $12,000. We would have to look at the journal entry to determine how much cash was involved. In this case, we assume that the purchase of equipment resulted in a payment of $12,000 cash. So we deduct $12,000 from Cash Flows from Investing Activities.

Cash Flows from Financing Activities

- The owner's Capital account increased by $10,000 as a result of an additional investment. We would have to look at the journal entry to determine how much cash was involved. In this case, we assume that the investment was in the form of cash. So we add $10,000 to Cash Flows from Financing Activities.
- The owner's Drawing account increased by $50,000. We would have to look at the journal entries to determine how much cash was involved. In this case, we assume that the withdrawals were in the form of cash. So we deduct $50,000 from Cash Flows from Financing Activities.

Here are some handy guidelines for preparing a statement of cash flows.

Add to Net Income	
If Current Assets decrease	Why? If an account like Accounts Receivable decreases, this means that we received more cash than the amount listed as Net Sales.
If Current Liabilities increase	Why? If an account like Accounts Payable increases, this means that we bought more merchandise or supplies than we paid for in cash.
Deduct from Net Income	
If Current Assets increase	Why? If an account like Prepaid Insurance increases, this means that we paid more cash for insurance than the amount listed as Insurance Expense on the income statement.
If Current Liabilities decrease	Why? If an account like Notes Payable decreases, this means that we paid out cash to pay off the note.

PROBLEMS

P.O. 1,2

Problem E-1 Metter Company has the following financial statements for 2003 and 2004. Assume that the withdrawals were in the form of cash.

Instructions

Prepare a statement of cash flows for the year ended December 31, 2004.

Metter Company
Income Statement
For Year Ended December 31, 2004

Revenue:		
Income from Services		$ 134 000 00
Expenses:		
Wages Expense	$77 000 00	
Rent Expense	8 000 00	
Depreciation Expense, Equipment	5 000 00	
Supplies Expense	2 000 00	
Total Expenses		92 000 00
Net Income		$ 42 000 00

Metter Company
Statement of Owner's Equity
For Year Ended December 31, 2004

B. N. Metter, Capital, January 1, 2004		$94 000 00
Net Income for the Year	$42 000 00	
Less Withdrawals for the Year	40 000 00	
Increase in Capital		2 000 00
B. N. Metter, Capital, December 31, 2004		$96 000 00

Metter Company
Comparative Balance Sheet
December 31, 2004, and December 31, 2003

	2004		2003		INCREASE (DECREASE)
Assets					
Cash		$ 9 000 00		$ 6 500 00	$2 500 00
Supplies		5 000 00		2 500 00	2 500 00
Equipment	$100 000 00		$98 000 00		2 000 00
Less Accumulated Depreciation	(18 000 00)	82 000 00	(13 000 00)	85 000 00	(5 000 00)
Total Assets		$96 000 00		$94 000 00	$2 000 00
Owner's Equity					
B. N. Metter, Capital		$96 000 00		$94 000 00	$2 000 00
Total Liabilities and Owner's Equity		$96 000 00		$94 000 00	$2 000 00

P.O. 1,2

Problem E-2 The financial statements for Arms and Company are presented below. Assume that the additional investment and the withdrawals were both in the form of cash.

Check Figure

Net cash flows from operating activities, $77,000

Instructions

Prepare a statement of cash flows for the year ended December 31, 2004.

Arms and Company
Income Statement
For Year Ended December 31, 2004

Revenue:		
Income from Services		$ 270 000 00
Expenses:		
Wages Expense	$ 161 000 00	
Rent Expense	18 000 00	
Depreciation Expense, Equipment	12 000 00	
Supplies Expense	4 000 00	
Insurance Expense	1 000 00	
Total Expenses		196 000 00
Net Income		$ 74 000 00

Arms and Company
Statement of Owner's Equity
For Year Ended December 31, 2004

S. T. Arms, Capital, January 1, 2004		$ 150 000 00
Additional Investment, April 1, 2004		2 000 00
Total Investment		$ 152 000 00
Net Income for the Year	$74 000 00	
Less Withdrawals for the Year	70 000 00	
Increase in Capital		4 000 00
S. T. Arms, Capital, December 31, 2004		$ 156 000 00

Arms and Company
Comparative Balance Sheet
December 31, 2004 and December 31, 2003

	2004	2003	INCREASE (DECREASE)
Assets			
Cash	$ 11 8 0 0 00	$ 2 8 0 0 00	$ 9 0 0 0 00
Accounts Receivable	32 0 0 0 00	26 0 0 0 00	6 0 0 0 00
Supplies	10 0 0 0 00	9 4 0 0 00	6 0 0 00
Prepaid Insurance	3 2 0 0 00	6 0 0 00	2 6 0 0 00
Equipment	$145 4 0 0 00	$145 4 0 0 00	——————
Less Accumulated Depreciation	(36 0 0 0 00) 109 4 0 0 00	(24 0 0 0 00) 121 4 0 0 00	(12 0 0 0 00)
Total Assets	$166 4 0 0 00	$160 2 0 0 00	$ 6 2 0 0 00
Liabilities			
Accounts Payable	$ 10 4 0 0 00	$ 10 2 0 0 00	$ 2 0 0 00
Owner's Equity			
S. T. Arms, Capital	156 0 0 0 00	150 0 0 0 00	6 0 0 0 00
Total Liabilities and			
Owner's Equity	$166 4 0 0 00	$160 2 0 0 00	$ 6 2 0 0 00

P.O. 1,2

Problem E-3 The financial statements for Torres Company are presented below. Assume that the withdrawals were in the form of cash.

Check Figure

Net cash flows used by financing activities, ($70,000)

Instructions

Prepare a statement of cash flows for the year ended December 31, 2004.

Torres Company
Income Statement
For Year Ended December 31, 2004

Net Sales	$ 942 0 0 0 00	
Less Cost of Goods Sold	753 6 0 0 00	
Gross Profit		$ 188 4 0 0 00
Operating Expenses:		
Salary Expense	$ 86 9 0 0 00	
Rent Expense	18 0 0 0 00	
Depreciation Expense, Equipment	10 0 0 0 00	
Supplies Expense	4 7 0 0 00	
Insurance Expense	2 8 0 0 00	
Total Operating Expenses		122 4 0 0 00
Net Income		$ 66 0 0 0 00

Torres Company
Statement of Owner's Equity
For Year Ended December 31, 2004

C. L. Torres, Capital, January 1, 2004			$ 196 0 0 0 00
Net Income for the Year	$ 66 0 0 0 00		
Less Withdrawals for the Year	70 0 0 0 00		
Decrease in Capital			(4 0 0 0 00)
C. L. Torres, Capital, December 31, 2004			$ 192 0 0 0 00

Torres Company
Comparative Balance Sheet
December 31, 2004 and December 31, 2003

	2004		2003		INCREASE (DECREASE)
Assets					
Cash		$ 9 4 0 0 00		$ 10 9 0 0 00	$ (1 5 0 0 00)
Accounts Receivable		56 0 0 0 00		48 6 0 0 00	7 4 0 0 00
Merchandise Inventory		104 6 0 0 00		104 4 0 0 00	2 0 0 00
Supplies		8 2 0 0 00		6 0 0 0 00	2 2 0 0 00
Prepaid Insurance		1 6 0 0 00		1 8 0 0 00	(2 0 0 00)
Equipment	$156 0 0 0 00		$156 0 0 0 00		—
Less Accumulated Depreciation	(76 4 0 0 00)	79 6 0 0 00	(66 4 0 0 00)	89 6 0 0 00	(10 0 0 0 00)
Total Assets		$259 4 0 0 00		$261 3 0 0 00	$ (1 9 0 0 00)
Liabilities					
Accounts Payable	$ 62 7 0 0 00		$ 60 4 0 0 00		$ 2 3 0 0 00
Salaries Payable	4 7 0 0 00		4 9 0 0 00		(2 0 0 00)
Total Liabilities		$ 67 4 0 0 00		$ 65 3 0 0 00	$ 2 1 0 0 00
Owner's Equity					
C. L. Torres, Capital		192 0 0 0 00		196 0 0 0 00	(4 0 0 0 00)
Total Liabilities and					
Owner's Equity		$259 4 0 0 00		$261 3 0 0 00	$ (1 9 0 0 00)

Before a Test Check Solutions

Part I: 1. d;   2. e;   3. d;   4. b;   5. e;   6. a

Part II: 1.

GENERAL JOURNAL   PAGE ___31___

	DATE		DESCRIPTION	POST. REF.	DEBIT	CREDIT	
1	20–						1
2	Dec.	1	Cash	111	10 0 0 0 00		2
3			Service Income	411		10 0 0 0 00	3
4			Sold services for cash.				4
5							5
6		4	Rent Expense	513	9 0 0 00		6
7			Cash	111		9 0 0 00	7
8			Ck. No. 2331.				8
9							9
10		11	Cash	111	1 8 6 0 00		10
11			Accounts Receivable	112		1 8 6 0 00	11
12			Cash on account from				12
13			customers, Cash Receipt				13
14			Nos. 1430-1438.				14
15							15
16		19	Accounts Receivable	112	2 1 5 0 00		16
17			Service Income	411		2 1 5 0 00	17
18			J. Lorn, Sales Inv. No. 2591.				18
19							19
20		22	Utilities Expense	512	1 9 7 00		20
21			Cash	111		1 9 7 00	21
22			Ck. No. 2332.				22
23							23
24		23	Supplies Expense	514	2 4 8 00		24
25			Accounts Payable	221		2 4 8 00	25
26			Office Works, Inv. No. 2606.				26
27							27
28		31	Wages Expense	511	1 6 6 5 00		28
29			Cash	111		1 6 6 5 00	29
30			Paid month's wages, Ck. No.				30
31			2333.				31
32							32
33		31	D. Stanfill, Drawing	312	1 0 0 0 00		33
34			Cash	111		1 0 0 0 00	34
35			Ck. No. 2334.				35

2, 3, 4.

Assets	=	Liabilities	+	Owner's Equity	+	Revenue	−	Expenses
+ −		− +		− +		− +		+ −
Debit Credit		Debit Credit		Debit Credit		Debit Credit		Debit Credit

Cash   111

+	−
Debit	Credit
Bal. 18,900	12/4 900
12/1 10,000	12/22 197
12/11 1,860	12/31 1,665
30,760	12/31 1,000
26,198	3,762

Accounts Receivable   112

+	−
Debit	Credit
Bal. 6,300	12/11 1,860
12/19 2,150	
8,450	
Bal. 6,590	

Prepaid Insurance   114

+	−
Debit	Credit
Bal. 1,230	

Equipment   124

+	−
Debit	Credit
Bal. 31,200	

Accounts Payable   221

−	+
Debit	Credit
	Bal. 6,340
	12/23 248
	Bal. 6,588

T. Shafer, Capital   311

−	+
Debit	Credit
	Bal. 49,590

D. Stanfill, Drawing   312

+	−
Debit	Credit
Bal. 11,200	
12/31 1,000	
Bal. 12,200	

Service Income   411

−	+
Debit	Credit
	Bal. 39,600
	12/1 10,000
	12/19 2,150
	Bal. 51,750

Wages Expense   511

+	−
Debit	Credit
Bal. 10,450	
12/31 1,665	
Bal. 12,115	

Utilities Expense   512

+	−
Debit	Credit
Bal. 2,760	
12/22 197	
Bal. 2,957	

Rent Expense   513

+	−
Debit	Credit
Bal. 12,620	
12/4 900	
Bal. 13,520	

Supplies Expense   514

+	−
Debit	Credit
Bal. 870	
12/23 248	
Bal. 1,118	

5.

Shafer Services
Trial Balance
December 31, 20—

ACCOUNT NAME	DEBIT	CREDIT
Cash	26 9 9 8 00	
Accounts Receivable	6 5 9 0 00	
Prepaid Insurance	1 2 3 0 00	
Equipment	31 2 0 0 00	
Accounts Payable		6 5 8 8 00
T. Shafer, Capital		49 5 9 0 00
T. Shafer, Drawing	12 2 0 0 00	
Service Income		51 7 5 0 00
Wages Expense	12 1 1 5 00	
Utilities Expense	2 9 5 7 00	
Rent Expense	13 5 2 0 00	
Supplies Expense	1 1 1 8 00	
	107 9 2 8 00	107 9 2 8 00

6.

Shafer Services
Income Statement
For Year Ended December 31, 20—

Revenue:		
Service Income		$51 7 5 0 00
Expenses:		
Wages Expense	$12 1 1 5 00	
Utilities Expense	2 9 5 7 00	
Rent Expense	13 5 2 0 00	
Total Expenses		29 7 1 0 00
Net Income		$22 0 4 0 00

7.

Shafer Services
Statement of Owner's Equity
For Year Ended December 31, 20—

T. Shafer, Capital, January 1, 20—							$49	5	9	0	00
Net Income for year	$22	0	4	0	00						
Less Withdrawals for year	12	2	0	0	00						
Increase in Capital							9	8	4	0	00
T. Shafer, Capital, December 31, 20—							$59	4	3	0	00

8.

Shafer Services
Balance Sheet
December 31, 20—

Assets										
Cash	$26	9	9	8	00					
Accounts Receivable	6	5	9	0	00					
Prepaid Insurance	1	2	3	0	00					
Equipment	31	2	0	0	00					
Total Assets						$66	0	1	8	00
Liabilities										
Accounts Payable						$6	5	8	8	00
Owner's Equity										
T. Shafer, Capital						59	4	3	0	00
Total Liabilities and Owner's Equity						$66	0	1	8	00

CHAPTERS 4–5

Part I

1. b;   2. d;   3. d;   4. a;   5. a;   6. b;   7. c;   8. c

Part II

	DATE		DESCRIPTION	POST. REF.	DEBIT	CREDIT	
	GENERAL JOURNAL					PAGE ___1___	
1	20–		**Closing Entries**				1
2							2
3	Dec.	31	Income from Services		35 9 0 0 00		3
4			Income Summary			35 9 0 0 00	4
5							5
6		31	Income Summary		20 4 0 0 00		6
7			Wages Expense			11 5 0 0 00	7
8			Rent Expense			2 4 0 0 00	8
9			Utilities Expense			1 0 0 0 00	9
10			Depreciation Expense,				10
11			Equipment			5 0 0 00	11
12			Supplies Expense			4 1 0 0 00	12
13			Miscellaneous Expense			9 0 0 00	13
14							14
15		31	Income Summary		15 5 0 0 00		15
16			K. Pitts, Capital			15 5 0 0 00	16
17							17
18		31	K. Pitts, Capital		16 4 0 0 00		18
19			K. Pitts, Drawing			16 4 0 0 00	19

Part III

1. b;   2. h;   3. m;   4. q;   5. d;   6. k;   7. u;   8. w;   9. o;   10. s;   11. e;
12. f;   13. i;   14. n;   15. a;   16. t;   17. x;   18. p;   19. y;   20. v;   21. j;   22. c;
23. r;   24. l;   25. g

CHAPTERS 7–9

Part I

1. canceled; 2. deposit in transit or late deposit; 3. endorsement; 4. payee; 5. petty cash fund.

Part II

1. $1,775 per month × 12 months = $21,300 per year
$21,300 per year ÷ 52 weeks = $409.62 per week
$409.62 per week ÷ 40 hours = $10.24 per regular hour
$10.24 per regular hour × 1.5 = $15.36 per overtime hour

Earnings for 45 hours:

Forty hours at straight time = 40 × $10.24 = $409.60
Five hours overtime = 5 × $15.36 =   76.80

Total gross pay $486.40

2.

GENERAL JOURNAL   PAGE _____

	DATE		DESCRIPTION	POST. REF.	DEBIT	CREDIT	
1	20–						1
2	June	30	Cleaning Salaries Expense		9 0 0 0 00		2
3			Office Salaries Expense		3 0 0 0 00		3
4			Employees' Federal Income Tax Payable			1 5 0 0 00	4
5			FICA Tax Payable ($12,000 × .062) + ($12,000 × .0145)			9 1 8 00	5
6			Savings Bonds Payable			5 0 0 00	6
7			Medical Insurance Payable			9 6 2 00	7
8			Salaries Payable			8 1 2 0 00	8

3.

GENERAL JOURNAL   PAGE _____

	DATE		DESCRIPTION	POST. REF.	DEBIT	CREDIT	
1	20–						1
2	Dec.	31	Payroll Tax Expense		12 4 7 7 50		2
3			FICA Tax Payable ($143,000 × .062) + ($155,000 × .0145)			11 1 1 3 50	3
4			State Unemployment Tax Payable ($22,000 × .054)			1 1 8 8 00	4
5			Federal Unemployment Tax Payable ($22,000 × .008)			1 7 6 00	5

Part III

1. T; 2. F; 3. F; 4. T; 5. F

CHAPTERS 10–11

Part I

1. credit; 2. accounts payable ledger; 3. cash discount; 4. purchase order; 5. Purchases; 6. buyer; 7. internal controls; 8. debit; 9. sales of merchandise on account; 10. charge customers.

Part II

1. CP; 2. J; 3. J; 4. CP; 5. S; 6. J; 7. CP; 8. P; 9. CR; 10. CP

Part III

1. F; 2. T; 3. F; 4. F; 5. F

CHAPTERS 12–13

Part I

1. physical inventory; 2. perpetual inventory; 3. current liability; 4. Income Summary; 5. Cost of Goods Sold, Merchandise Inventory; 6. decrease; 7. Cost of Goods Sold; 8. working capital; 9. Income from Operations; 10. Freight In.

Part II

1. F; 2. F; 3. T; 4. T; 5. T; 6. F; 7. F; 8. T; 9. F; 10. T

Part III

1.

GENERAL JOURNAL PAGE _____

	DATE		DESCRIPTION	POST. REF.	DEBIT	CREDIT	
1	20–		**Adjusting Entries**				1
2	Dec.	31	Income Summary		132 0 0 0 00		2
3			Merchandise Inventory			132 0 0 0 00	3
4							4
5		31	Merchandise Inventory		136 0 0 0 00		5
6			Income Summary			136 0 0 0 00	6

2.

GENERAL JOURNAL PAGE _____

	DATE		DESCRIPTION	POST. REF.	DEBIT	CREDIT	
1	20–		**Adjusting Entries**				1
2	Dec.	31	Cost of Goods Sold		2 0 0 0 00		2
3			Merchandise Inventory			2 0 0 0 00	3

3.

GENERAL JOURNAL   PAGE _____

	DATE		DESCRIPTION	POST. REF.	DEBIT	CREDIT	
1	20–						1
2	Dec.	1	Cash		20 0 0 0 00		2
3			Unearned Revenue			20 0 0 0 00	3
4			To record collection of cash				4
5			for a four-month job.				5
6							6
7			Adjusting Entry				7
8		31	Unearned Revenue		5 0 0 0 00		8
9			Remodeling Revenue			5 0 0 0 00	9
10			To record one month's				10
11			revenue earned.				11

4. a. $250,000 total assets − $140,000 noncurrent assets = $110,000 current assets
    $130,000 total liabilities − $80,000 long-term liabilities = $50,000 current liabilities
    $110,000 current assets − $50,000 current liabilities = $60,000 working capital

$$\frac{\$110,000 \text{ current assets}}{\$50,000 \text{ current liabilities}} = 2.2 \text{ current ratio}$$

Credits

(credits continued from p. iv)

Chapter 3
p. 75, John Elk/Stock Boston; p. 91, Barbara File/Getty Images.

Chapter 4
p. 122, Brink/The Image Works.

Chapter 5
p. 151, Jeff Greenberg/PhotoEdit, Inc.; p. 158, David Young Wolff/PhotoEdit, Inc.

Chapter 6
p. 194, R.P. Kingston/Index; p. 196, Richard Pasley/Stock Boston; p. 198, Brian Hainer/PhotoEdit, Inc.

Chapter 7
p. 226, AP/Wide World Photos; p. 236, Tony Freeman/PhotoEdit, Inc.; p. 240, Chris Salvo/Getty Images.

Chapter 8
p. 264, Bruce Forester/Getty Images; p. 265, C. Greenlar/The Image Works; p. 265, J.L. Bernice/Getty Images.

Chapter 9
p. 291, Stephen Perry/Getty Images; p. 297, B. Roland/The Image Works; p. 308, Rubberball Productions/Getty Images; p. 310, Gregg Mancuso/Stock Boston.

Chapter 10
p. 353, David Wells/The Image Works.

Chapter 11
p. 380, © AFP/Corbis; p. 385, Bill Aaron/PhotoEdit, Inc.

Chapter 12
p. 424, Bob Mahoney/The Image Works.

Chapter 13
p. 462, Joe Sohm/Stock Boston; p. 466, Bob Daemmrich/Stock Boston.

Index

The Accounting Cycle

During the accounting period

Source Document
Check, invoice, receipt, cash register tape, etc.

↓

Analyze
Transactions

↓

Journalize
Transactions

post to ↓

Ledger

At the end of the accounting period

Work sheet

Trial Balance	**Adjustments**	**Adjusted Trial Balance**	**Income Statement**	**Balance Sheet**
Assets	Prepaid expenses		Revenue	Assets
Liabilities	Depreciation		Expenses	Liabilities
Owner's Equity	Accrued expenses			Capital
Capital				Drawing
Drawing				
Revenue				
Expenses				

Income Statement
   Revenue
− Expenses
= Net Income
   (or Net Loss)

Statement of Owner's Equity
   Beginning Capital
+ Investments (if any)
+ Net Income (− Net Loss)
− Withdrawals
= Ending Capital

Balance Sheet
   Assets
= Liabilities
+ Ending Capital

Journalize
adjusting entries

post to ↓

Ledger

↓

Journalize
closing entries

post to ↓

Ledger

↓

Post-closing Trial Balance
Assets
Liabilities
Capital

End of Cycle

Normal closing entries

1. Revenue
     Income Summary
2. Income Summary
     Expense
     Expense
     Expense
3. Income Summary*
     Capital
4. Capital
     Drawing

*Assuming a net income. If there is a net loss, the entry would be:
3. Capital
*   Income Summary*